Conversing on

Gender.

A Primer for Entering Dialog

G. G. Bolich, Ph.D.

Psyche's Press

Psyche's Press

Raleigh, NC

©2007 G. G. Bolich

ISBN   978-0-6151-3836-7

This volume is affectionately dedicated to the students of my Seminar on Gender.

May we all remember . . .

> that gender matters,
> but perhaps not *too* much.

Let us celebrate diversity, be tolerant of what we do not understand, and reckon that our common humanity matters more than our differences in sex or gender.

Brief Table of Contents

Part 5: Special Topics

Detailed Table of Contents

Part 5: Special Topics

Introduction
Conversing in Context

Welcome to a dialog on one of the most important aspects of being a person. This dialog is meant to serve as an entry point into a much larger ongoing conversation. In one way or another, conversations concerning gender happen around us all the time. From casual remarks about appearance, to observations about personality and behavior presumed to be gender-based, to ponderings on weighty social issues, gender is being talked about.

Yet for all the words, many of us remain unaware of ideas on gender that might significantly change our thinking. If our thinking about gender shifts, so also may our attitudes, which in turn may motivate changes in behavior. In short, engaging more purposefully in the conversation on gender has the potential to broaden our understanding, challenge long unexamined assumptions, change our mind, alter our feelings, prompt new ways of behaving, and perhaps even become motivated to do what we can to help change the world we live in.

Such possibilities reflect the weight and seriousness of this dialog. This book is intended as a primer—a basic introduction to some of the key terms, concepts, and areas at the heart of today's conversing on gender. Both because we tend to think we know more than we actually do, and because it assists retention, there is some calculated repetition in this dialog. That includes repeating basic points and reiterating the meaning of basic words. Be patient. Once something is mastered, it doesn't hurt to hear it again. We need to digest it.

This aspect of our conversing will especially be found in discussing the relation of gender to sex—perhaps the most common point of contention in the larger conversation. This matter will be examined repeatedly, but in different connections. We cannot afford to take for granted what has proved the biggest issue affecting clarity and meaning in the conversation. Even should we early determine a position on this subject, we should engage in discussing it anew as each new topic arises. Let us resolve to give this topic our full attention.

Along the way, we will hear—albeit briefly—from many, many voices. As often as possible, those voices have been allowed to speak with their own words. The purpose of paraphrases and summaries is to allow us to move rapidly across a wide array of matters; the purpose of brief quotes is to make us pause and hear how the speaker frames a salient point. Together these features invite us to interact with many of the perceptive, challenging, often controversial figures who are participating at the table of conversation.

This dialog also employs an inclusive voice. As often as possible, the words will embrace all of us, regardless of our gender identities or roles. In other words, the pronouns 'we,' 'us,' and 'our' occur frequently. They are used purposefully at times to remind all of us that not all of us are the same. Traditionally, some gender voices have been left out of the conversation, or muted. In our dialog that tendency is contested. Men, women, transgender and third gender people are all embraced in the 'we,' 'us,' and 'our' of this dialog. An important function of an inclusive voice is to facilitate an empathetic identification with other genders. We all profit from walking awhile in others' shoes.

Finally, on a more technical note, we should consider a feature of special concern to social science students. Our conversing together will be complicated enough by the actual subject matter without other hindrances entering in. One such hindrance can be the American Psychological Association (APA) style of citation, which interrupts the flow of discussion with parenthetical notations. In a conscious decision to prevent this, our conversing will use end notes marked in the text with superscript numbers to minimize the interruption. Those desiring to track down cited materials or to follow finer points of the discussion can easily find the additional material at the end of the text.

Now, let us get started by entering our dialog with a sensible, honest question: Why does gender matter enough anyone should take a lengthy chunk of time to ponder on it and to talk about it?

Why Gender Matters

I suspect at least a partial answer is already in mind even as that question is asked. Chances are you aren't looking at this unless you already believe the subject of gender matters. I agree. The fundamental assumption of this work is that gender matters to all of us, and perhaps especially to those of us who find we do not easily fit within the gender categories sanctioned by our culture. Gender matters because in a culture like our own, where sex and gender are so central to the way we define our identities and relationships, we cannot escape the consequences of being a gendered individual in a gendered society.

In Western culture, both our personal identities and our social ones are largely shaped and constrained by gender. For men this traditionally has meant power and privilege not enjoyed by women. Moreover, only two gender options have come to be culturally sanctioned: masculinity and femininity. The reason often put forward for this state of affairs is the difference in bodies between males and females. The size and strength of the former has been used to subordinate the latter. Sex-based differentiation in social roles has promoted the development of separate and unequal expectations, which in turn craft different identities and give rise to the notion of forever separate genders, with distinctly different experiences and roles—all based ultimately in body differences.

Simply put, gender as popularly conceived is another name for body sex. People often use 'male' and 'female' to mean either anatomical sex or individual gender. To the degree there is a difference between sex and gender in this common perspective, the former is biological while the latter is personal and social. But gender is assumed to be utterly dependent on sex. Boys and men must have male bodies; girls and women must have female bodies. There are no other alternatives.

To most of us this all seems very . . . natural. We grow up believing that sex and gender as we know them are biologically determined. We seldom question that gender differences are simply meant to be, as inevitable and as regulated as any other phenomenon of nature. So our gender expectations about how boys and men, girls and women, should think, feel, and behave are casually justified by an appeal to Nature. We learn to attribute differences to a kind of biological determinism with a dose of cultural seasoning tossed in.

Thus, while we recognize how important gender is in our lives, we seldom imagine we can do much beyond either railing against the inequities of Nature or trying to change the cultural seasoning. In our society this has meant at different times either trying to formalize and strengthen a gender hierarchy, or to expose it as a cultural artifact that must be overthrown. In sum, we either try to support gender as a vertical reality, with one gender on top, or we try to craft a horizontal reality where there is gender equality.

In neither of these conditions do we normally question the presumed role of Nature in dividing the genders into two differently endowed camps. Indeed, most of us want there to be differences—not merely in bodies but also in personalities and social functioning—and we resist any suggestion such things have been artificially constructed. The sex and gender order we are born into, with our allegiance established at birth by others assigning us to one side or the other, seems to most of us beyond challenge.

Yet some very basic notions are being challenged. Gender study is among the most exciting areas of investigation into human experience these days because old assumptions are being seriously disputed. More and more people are resisting the idea that gender depends entirely and inevitably on the body's apparent sex. The growing visibility of transgender people has been instrumental in this development, as has the success of feminism in eroding masculine privilege. Today, perhaps more so than at any other time in history, we are aware of the importance gender has come to possess, and we are rethinking it.

Make no mistake. Gender matters. The consensus a society reaches as expressed in social expectations and norms for gender carry consequences for all of us. Masculine males have a stake in how feminine females are viewed and treated no less than in how they are themselves seen and treated. Not only whether we reaffirm a gender hierarchy or embrace a greater gender equality matters; so, too, does how we conceptualize the very nature of gender itself. If we cling to the conviction there are only two genders, that belief will bear fruit in how we regard ourselves and others, and conduct relationships. If we accept that multiple genders exist and range themselves along a spectrum, that view will change what we tolerate and influence what we believe society should recognize, including its social policy, laws, and regulations.

The stakes are high. Our culture's long trek into a position where gender has become so central to identity has made it so. In this situation we stand at something of a crossroads, a place of creative turmoil where what we do now will matter not only to ourselves, but to future generations. The conversation is too important for us not to involve ourselves in it.

Gender in Context

Conversing on Gender is meant to remind us that gender is a multifaceted reality dependent on context. In this volume the intent is to establish how gender is discussed in a number of basic contexts. Before we turn to these, though, a word is in order about the discussion itself. Our context as writer and reader is that of conversationalists. We hope to engage in a dialog across these pages. But this is a preparatory discussion meant to facilitate entry into the wider, ongoing conversation about gender. That wider conversation is not confined to scholars; there is a cultural debate percolating over what gender is, or ought to be. Since this conversation concerns us all, we should do our best to enter into it, and do so well-prepared. And that leads us once more to the matter of gender in context.

There are a number of important contexts in which gender must be situated and our separate discussion parts indicate some of these. First there is *scholarly history*, a body of work by various theorists and researchers that represents the construction of a language and ongoing dialog about gender. Living a gendered life, however, occurs in the context of a *gendered society*. Our public identities and our relationships are significantly shaped by gender as it is articulated, promoted, protected, and challenged by social realities. Next, consistent with the focus of our American life, there is the context of *the individually gendered life*. In our culture we are all assigned at birth a gender identity and face in our development the task of adopting that identity and fulfilling its expected roles. Yet despite all the pressures we face to conform to an assigned gender, most of struggle. In a society that seems to insist we all fit into one or the other of only two choices, many of us find our assigned gender box an uncomfortable fit—an indication that there exists a *gender spectrum*—another important context.

In trying to make sense of such matters, serious students of gender have advanced a number of different theories. These vary in their scope and focus. They also add liveliness to discussion and often provoke controversy and a reappraisal of matters we may have thought we understood. We shall encounter many theories as we go along. After orienting ourselves to these theories we may better appreciate some of the issues involved in three other very basic areas of life: sexuality, dress and religion. Though these may seem very far apart, gender is important in each. Gender informs our sexual attitudes and behaviors. Dress provides perhaps the central mechanism through which we experience and express gender. Religion provides for most people a context in which gender and many of the matters associated with it are made sensible, attached to specific values, and placed in an ethical framework that guides decisions about right and wrong.

Not all contexts relevant to gender are discussed in these pages. That cannot prove anything other than an impossible task in a world where gender infuses everything and some consciousness of its various roles permeates a great many of those things. Because this work is meant to serve as an introduction to the subject, the contexts selected are basic ones. They interact dynamically and they participate in situations, circumstances, thoughts, feelings, and behaviors not even remotely contemplated in this book. This modest volume aims only to provide an introductory aid to those wishing to get caught up on some facets of a lively, ongoing conversation, and perhaps inspire efforts to join that conversation and advance it.

Author Qualifications

This is not the first work I have written concerning gender. As this goes to press, my four volume work on gender and transgender realities, *Crossdressing in Context* nears completion. Volume 1 of that work, *The Context of Dress and Gender* has appeared already. Some of the content from those four volumes reappears here in reworked form suitable to the purpose of this book's discussion. But merely having an interest in, and writing about, a subject may not be enough to reassure readers that I am qualified to tackle the topic. It seems prudent, therefore, to briefly provide some information about my professional life.

My background includes more than 30 years working with people, primarily as a scholar and educator, but also as a counselor. I hold advanced degrees in the fields of religious studies and psychology, and my teaching and counseling have been in both areas. I have published a variety of books and articles in each field. Both psychology and religious studies have played important roles in shaping my thinking and in crafting my writings on gender. Because gender is so central to personal and social identity in our culture, my experience in psychology seems relevant. This discipline concerns itself with people's thinking, feeling, and behaving. Gender studies are often conducted by psychologists and social scientists in related fields such as anthropology and sociology. Because many people regard gender issues as important moral or religious concerns, my experience in religious studies seems relevant, too. For the most part, people contend that their spiritual or religious experience informs their moral sensibility. They derive value from religion and impute to gender a religious orientation. In fact, between these two areas, I find many of the questions and concerns about gender that I have encountered from students, clients, and others.

Let's begin with my specific qualifications to address the relation of gender and religion—one of the special focuses receiving treatment in this book. In terms of religious studies, I am seminary trained, holding a M.A. in Theology, and the Master of Divinity—or M.Div.—the degree used to prepare people for professional ministry. My first Ph.D., in Educational Leadership, also focused on religious studies, culminating in a dissertation in the area of New Testament introduction. I am trained in biblical and classical languages (Hebrew, Greek, Latin), and in both traditional and modern methods of translating and interpreting sacred texts. Beginning in 1974, I have taught courses in religious studies at undergraduate and graduate levels in a wide variety of settings, including churches and synagogues, bible school, community college, public university, private college, and seminary extension program. These courses have covered matters of ethics, ancient and modern world religions, theology, history, sacred texts, and the relation of religion to psychology. My area of particular interest and specialization has been the religious writings of the period extending from about a century or so before Christ, to the end of the second century after Christ. But in recent years I have given more and more attention to gender and sexuality as they are wrestled with in the world's religions. In addition to scholarly work, I also have been involved in ecumenical work, notably between the Christian and Jewish communities. As a counselor, many people have identified my background in religious studies as an important reason why they chose to come see me.

My second doctorate is in psychology (Ph.D.). I started working with people as a counselor in 1973, while still a college student, on a crisis line. As time passed, my interests began to turn more and more to matters of human development and human sexuality. As a counselor I gradually developed a specialization in Trauma Resolution Therapy, principally working with adult survivors of sexual abuse. Today I teach graduate students in counseling and undergraduate students in psychology about human sexuality and gender. Both as a teacher and as a therapist I have continually encountered curiosity about various gender issues, especially in recent years concerning gender alternatives to masculinity and femininity. Because of my additional background in religious studies this curiosity by my students and clients has often extended to specific matters of faith and practice as well as the more specific psychological concerns about how different gender issues play out in an individual's life and in society.

Accordingly, this work grows out of many years of interest and experience. I think my background contributes some layers of knowledge that may not be as easily accessible to other professionals whose experience is confined to only one or another of the areas relevant to a full consideration of gender. To these credentials I will add my intention of being fair-minded and honest throughout this work. I intend this work to be educational in nature. At the same time, I am aware that when educating people on controversial subjects—and much in gender studies *is* controversial—it may not be either feasible or even particularly desirable to attempt being completely above the fray and studiously neutral. In truth, I am not neutral on many topics—and I do not know anyone who is. Even scholarly works serve social and political ends, and every work—including mine—must be soberly appraised for fairness. I have every confidence that fair-minded readers who pursue the logic and evidence set down within this work will be able to accurately assess the value of this endeavor.

Chapter 1

Terminology

Introduction: Every field has its own distinctive vocabulary, used to shape a language for dialog. Talking about gender is no different. Before we can immerse ourselves in the conversation, we need to know the language. But we do not need to know all of the vocabulary and grammar at once. It will suffice to start with a few basic terms. Obviously the most important of these is the word *gender*. The most important aspect of understanding this word concerns its relationship to the word 'sex.' This topic is so large and so critical that while we shall wrestle with it here, we shall give it further consideration later (chapter 3). 'Gender' is regarded by most participants in the conversation as referring to social rather than biological characteristics, though the degree of connection between the psychosocial and the biological remains hotly debated.

Other terms are important, too. Though the words *male* and *female* are often casually employed to refer to gender, they properly refer to body sex. In the West, gender terms commonly thought to match up to body sex include *boy* and *man* (with pronouns such as *he* and *him*) to correspond to the male body, and *girl* and *woman* (with pronouns like *she* and *her*) to correspond to the female body. This division along body sex creates two distinct gender groups, with the accompanying labels differentiating members by age or maturity. Presumed personality and other behavioral characteristics belonging to these two gender groups are bunched under two broad labels: *masculinity* is thought to properly belong to boys and men, while *femininity* is reserved for girls and women.

Most of us readily recognize this neatly paired division runs headlong into the real and messy world of experience. Just as in terms of body sex there are those who are neither unambiguously male nor female, so there are those whose gender is not clearly masculine or feminine. So we have words like *intersex*, *androgynous* and *transgender*. The last of these considers the possibly of more than two genders; some thus prefer we speak about *third gender* realities. New pronouns (*s/he*, *hir*) have been coined to match this kind of gender.

Finally, there has developed a full set of subsidiary terms to name various aspects of gender experience. These include *gender assignment*, *gender identity*, and *gender roles*, among others. Such terms remind us that gender is multifaceted and complex. Understanding gender requires mastering a vocabulary that itself is undergoing change as the language of gender evolves.

The Dictionary and 'Gender'

How hard can it be to define 'gender'? Most of us will probably start from the standpoint that the definition is obvious. Yet why, then, does so much controversy surround the word? Gender today evokes not just debate, but often *hot* debate—and it occasionally rises to an international platform.

Joan Wallach Scott recounts what happened in the mid-1990s, prior to the Fourth World Conference on Women. In the United States, a number of cultural conservatives, including various members of Congress, voiced their concern that the word 'gender' was being used by some to suggest more than two genders. This was usage conservatives were convinced had serious negative implications for 'family values,' since it might be used to 'legitimize' as 'natural' gender identities and expressions (e.g., homosexuality, bisexuality, and transsexuality) they believed were 'unnatural.' The debate seemed to be over whether gender is an autonomous, natural reality, or one socially constructed and therefore subject to change. In response to the outcry, the U.N. Commission on the Status of Women established a contact group whose task was to offer for the Conference attendees a statement on the 'commonly understood' meaning of gender. However, as Scott points out, the resulting *Statement on the Commonly Understood Meaning of the Term 'Gender'* does not actually clarify what the 'ordinary, generally accepted usage' is. Scott remarks, "It was as if the meaning were self-evident, free of ambiguity and all possible misinterpretation." That it is not was soon seen at the Conference as delegates from different nations then attempted to define the term.[1] No definition won universal assent.

Perhaps the most amazing thing about this word 'gender' is that it simultaneously appears so clear and yet under scrutiny proves either ambiguous or contentious. We assume we know what it means, but a nagging uncertainty shows itself in common questions arising from the way we use the word. We often treat 'gender' as though it were a synonym for 'sex,' referring simply to a division of people into two biological categories based on their apparent reproductive organs. Is gender the same as sex? If it is, why do we bother with a different word? If it isn't, just exactly what does it refer to? In a time and place where gender—whatever it is—receives much attention, we want to be sure our confidence about its meaning is warranted, and if we find it is not, then we need to rethink the term and learn to use it more appropriately. A trip to the dictionary is not a bad way to begin.

The word 'gender' has been around a long time.[2] Our current English form traces back to the Middle English *gendre*, which in turn was derived from Old French, which was an adaptation from Latin. The root form for our modern word is the Latin noun *genus*, equivalent to the Greek word γένος (*genos*), used by Aristotle as a grammatical term,[3] and referring to origin or kind. This is a long pedigree and suggestive of the term's basic sense. The Latin noun supplied an adjectival suffix to words reflecting 'born of' and gave rise to other words such as 'genre' ('kinds' of literature, or other things). Not surprisingly, there is a verb counterpart, stemming from the Greek root meaning, 'to beget,' so that today we can actively 'gender' things—sort them into assigned kinds, or categories—though we more often use related words like 'engender' when we want to employ 'gender' as a verb.[4]

As we shall see in our foray into discoursing about gender (the noun) we shall on occasion find it convenient to use verb forms like 'gendered.' In either instance, the core sense remains a division into kinds following some logical process, such as descent. One form of descent, of course, derives from sexual procreation and results in differently appearing bodies. Based on these differently appearing bodies, *'gender' came to represent a division into kinds based on apparently distinct and mutually exclusive sexual bodies.* Thus 'masculine' was paired with 'male' and 'feminine' with 'female.' Not merely human beings, or even just animals, came to be 'gendered.' So, too, did many nonliving things. For those things where neither sex-paired gender sufficed, a third 'kind' was established: 'neuter.'

Language Problems: Usage and Limitations

The ability to gender things proves useful linguistically. In grammar, 'gender' divides words into 'kinds' sorted by assignment to 'masculine,' 'feminine,' or 'neuter.' For many things, like animals and people, this practice has intuitive appeal. Yet, while it sounds simple and clear, when it comes to actual application, this gendering of things into discrete categories does not always work as well as we might like. The problem proves to be in the nature of the pairing of gender with sex.

Chambers' Etymological English Dictionary points out in defining gender that the grammatical process creates "a distinction of words, *roughly* corresponding to sex."[5] Likewise, the *Oxford Universal Dictionary* notes the grammatical kinds correspond "*more or less* to distinctions of sex (or absence of sex)."[6] Such nuance apparently has been lost in modern Western society when gendering human beings. As Western culture devolved[7] to its present rigid division among human beings into two-and-only-two sexes, a similar phenomenon occurred with gender divisions. Rather than *roughly* corresponding to sex, gender was treated as *exactly* corresponding to sex. Hence words like male and female came to be used both for sex and for gender.[8]

If gender and sex are made synonyms, then perhaps no problem exists. But despite occasionally using the words like that, no one is seriously arguing that sex and gender are exactly the same. So the consequence of too casual a usage of the words is a situation today we might charitably call a muddled mess. Some of the dimensions of this are indicated in the following discussion from *The American Heritage Book of English Usage*:

> Traditionally, writers have used the term Gender to refer to the grammatical categories of masculine, feminine, and neuter, as in languages such as French or Spanish whose nouns and adjectives carry such distinctions. In recent years, however, more people have been using the word to refer to sex-based categories, as in phrases such as

gender gap (as in voting trends) and *politics of gender*. Anthropologists especially like to maintain a distinction between the terms Gender and *sex*, reserving *sex* for reference to the biological categories of male and female and using Gender to refer to social or cultural categories, such as different gender roles in a religious organization. According to this distinction, you would say *The effectiveness of the treatment appears to depend on the sex* (not Gender) *of the patient* but *In society, gender* (not *sex*) *roles are clearly defined*. A majority of the Usage Panel approves of this distinction, but opinions are mixed. In a sentence similar to the first one above, 51 percent choose *sex*, 31 percent choose *gender*, and 17 percent would allow both. Similarly, for the example *Sex/gender differences are more likely to be clearly defined in peasant societies*, 47 percent prefer Gender, 38 percent would use *sex*, and 15 percent would allow both words.[9]

It seems reasonable to suppose that as long as this state of affairs pertains in how the terms are used, difficulties both in conception and communication are likely to persist.

Defining Gender

While a trip to the dictionary provides some help, at least in getting a sense of the history of the word and its troubled usage today, it just starts us on our way to a useful working definition with which to ground ourselves as we enter the conversation. What do we need next?

Given the evident problems arising from blurring the lines between sex and gender, our next task should be to reestablish some clear boundaries linguistically. We can begin with the most obvious usage problem—treating male and female as equally appropriate in talking about sex or about gender. In this work, male and female are terms meant to convey sex, *not* gender. But this simple step, as important as it is, does not suffice by itself. The ties between sex and gender are too old and too well-established to be more than modestly modified. Yet modify them we must. The empirical realities of lived experience in a changing culture mandate a clarity that includes modifying the pairing of sex and gender so that the boundary between them becomes clearer.

Gender

All this is easier said than done. Two major considerations confront us right away. First, the historical association of gender with sex underscores a particular way to envision a division into 'kinds' of human beings, one that makes intuitive sense to most people, and has been supported for millennia as the most basic way to sort people—by their apparent body sex characteristics.[10] Second, it is entirely practical to ask, as many people do, 'Why *not* divide genders along the lines of sex since it appears biological, especially reproductive, differences do generate psychosocial differences?' In other words, while sex and gender should not be seen as synonymous, they should be retained in the closest proximity. The former refers to dividing people by reproductive organs into males and females (biological kinds), while the latter follows suit but extends the division along lines of psychological and social functioning that reflects natural differences among boys and girls, men and women (psychosocial kinds).[11]

Whether we end up agreeing with this logic or not, we should recognize most contemporary definitions or descriptions of gender are constructed in such a way to preserve a relation to sex but also a distinction from it. Consider the following efforts:

- ❏ "'Gender' as a term differs from 'sex' in being about socially expected characteristics rather than biology."[12]
- ❏ "*Sex* has to do with body parts, *gender* with the manner in which a person puts the assignment of *male* or *female* into practice *within societal limits.*"[13]
- ❏ "'Gender' typically refers to the social process of dividing up people and social practices along the lines of *sexed identities.*"[14]
- ❏ "I believe gender to be a combination between biology and social roles."[15]

Though there seems to be a common way to describe what gender is, definitions often differ in ways that complicate the conversation. Most prominently, this occurs by phrasings that suggest how, or how not, the boundary between sex and gender might be negotiated. For example, the first two statements in the list above establish a boundary (gender is about socially expected characteristics; sex is about biology). But in using the phrase 'rather than,' the first suggests that gender is *not* founded upon or derived from sex divisions. The second makes sex rather incidental; it is culture that matters. The third statement in the list agrees that gender involves a psychosocial process (thus distinct from sex which involves a biological process), but suggests that the boundary is negotiated 'along the lines of *sexed identities*'—suggesting a derivation of gender from sex, which here is intimated to be more than just a division by genitalia because it also incorporates a sense of identity. The last statement, aiming less at definition than at personal affirmation, wants to find a way between an 'either-or' dilemma by embracing a 'both-and' position: gender combines biology (the domain of sex) with social roles (thus acquiring a unique flavor). This kind of statement fuzzes the boundary without destroying it.

For our purposes it does not matter where the respective authors go in their reasoning. What matters is that in talking about gender the conversation can seem to endorse broad agreement on the character of a boundary line but then either blur that line or introduce ambiguity in trying to describe what kind of relation does or does not exist between sex and gender across the boundary. Some participants in the conversation want to stress the firmness of the boundary and distance sex and gender from one another. Others wish to soften the line, preferring a more permeable boundary where gender displays a dependence on sex.

However, we should *not* settle back comfortably and decide it really doesn't matter which side we take. There are important consequences logically, which have bearing on decisions and actions taken in the world of lived experience. We also have to reckon with whether one or the other position squares more responsibly with empirical facts. Perhaps the reason the conversation is so lively is not because the arguments on different sides have equal merit, or the facts are evenly divided, but because personal and social values are coloring the discourse. Maybe a position is supported less because it coincides with reason and evidence, but resonates more with what supporters *want* to be true.

Ultimately, responsible participation in the ongoing conversation requires us to become as informed as possible and to take a side. Our position here is that it is better to take a side based on reason and evidence than merely on values. The reason for this decision is that values embraced by a society too often irrationally reside in the beliefs and wishes of the majority, whose sex, race, or cultural heritage may weigh more than facts, and whose values often prove oppressive to minorities. Worse, such oppression is contrary to evidence, as when modern White males of European descent conclude that Black women are less competent than themselves (because of sex, race, and/or culture), despite empirical evidence that this belief is untrue. In such instances, which could easily be multiplied, one group preserves a position of privilege and power at the expense of others. Far better would be our resolve to align our values with facts.

While we might agree with one another (based on our own values of fairness and justice) that we want to avoid such consequences, it may remain unclear how a position on the relation between sex and gender plays a part. Let us return to the earlier logic we found many people endorse. It started with this query: 'Why not divide genders along the lines of sex since it appears biological differences generate psychosocial differences?' The problem is this: do biological differences generate psychosocial differences such that gender divisions should closely follow sex divisions? This latter question asks whether the boundary between sex and gender is very permeable and if it is unidirectional. It also tends to be paired with a generally unasked question: 'Do these apparent differences matter in such a way that they justify a hierarchical order?'

For a long time, it has proved convenient for men in power to hold on to their masculine privilege by contending that their position is according to Nature. The logic is that sex generates gender differences, which establish a natural hierarchy. Most commonly this argument suggests that body differences make it inevitable that males and females will sort out into different kinds of labor according to which they are most naturally suited. Males, for example, will do physical labors suited to their superior strength, which take them out into the world of work and communal governance; females, on the other hand, must give precedence to their natural vocation of bearing and rearing children, which makes the domestic realm—not wider society—their natural domain. This natural sorting by sex thus gave rise to differing kinds of work, which gave rise to different psychosocial identities, which we call genders.

Perhaps this is exactly the way it came about. If so, we should be able to explore the evidence. We shall do that later in our dialog, but we can state now that the argument advanced above, whatever the evidence it appeals to, appears to be convenient to a set of values that enforce what has been called *patriarchy*—dominion by men in a fatherly ('paternalistic') role. Though *gender hierarchies*—arrangement of the genders vertically so that some enjoy positions of prestige and power over others—are common and persistent, we should ask if they are also natural and inevitable. The above argument, if accepted, might compel us to think so. But it is worrisome that such a position seems to rely on beliefs founded upon values espoused and propagated by those most likely to benefit from them—an occasion giving rise to some of the theories we shall investigate in a short while (see the next chapter).

Right now we do not want to go too far astray from our initial task. All we have established so far in our effort to define gender is this:

❑ 'Gender' is a dividing of people into kinds, similar to 'sex,' and commonly following the same lines of division as sex.

❑ Yet gender and sex are not synonyms.

❑ The boundary line between sex and gender is a recognition of their different characters; the former is biological, the latter psychosocial.

❑ There are some transactions between gender and sex across this boundary, but the nature of these is debated.

Let us look at the third point again. Many who talk about the relation of sex and gender contend that *both* have biological elements, and *both* have psychosocial dimensions, even though they remain distinct. We shall investigate this matter more thoroughly later (in chapter 3). For now let us be content to grant that sex and gender are multifaceted along the lines just stated.

If we take such a stance we shall then be free to acknowledge the likelihood that transactions between them are *bidirectional*. Instead of gender being solely dependent on sex, with the line of influence from the latter to the former, both influence each other. We might laugh at the notion that gender can influence sex, since sex is rooted in biology. But lived experience shows this happens in our world. People referred to as transgendered or transsexual often modify their bodies to better fit their gender. This can include a complete change of sex genitalia. To object that this does not actually change their sex misses the point; sex almost never is about genetics. In its common usage it refers to *apparent* maleness or femaleness. Sex can be altered by changing the appearance of the body.

So let us put our thoughts together to arrive at least at a working definition of gender. Let us start by building on our reasoning to this point. We can tentatively agree that whereas sex is a term rooted in biology but mediated by personal and social beliefs, gender is a term rooted in personal and social beliefs but mediated by biology. The case for this assertion will be built later. We can also agree, because we see it in the world, that sex can be influenced by gender, even though we are more accustomed to assuming that gender is influenced by sex. The relationship is bidirectional.

Now let us add in the core sense from many centuries of usage: gender is a division into kinds. Whether that division ultimately relies on recognition of biology, or on certain cultural decisions, or both, we shall continue to grapple with. At least in contemporary popular use, gender involves differentiating sex-based groups into corresponding types with distinct psychological and social markers. For better or ill, we can start with the conception that prevails in our culture and consider its adequacy. Thus, we can work from a definition of 'gender' that posits it is, "*the set of experiential and presentational characteristics associated with and culturally arising from pairing with a particular sex.*"

This working definition establishes gender as multifaceted ('the set of . . . characteristics'), links it to sex distinctions ('pairing with a particular sex'), and places emphasis on psychosocial concerns ('experiential . . . presentational . . . culturally arising'). It also emphasizes a fluid conception of gender reflecting how we encounter it in the real world—as something personally experienced, as known through presentation, and as governed by how culture pairs personal experience and social presentation with its own notion of how each sex ought to manifest in human affairs. Since some parts of this definition have not yet been adequately discussed, we should give a moment to them.

Gender as just defined is a 'set of . . . characteristics.' The qualifiers for this set are *psychological* ('experiential') and *social* ('presentational'). It might also be argued that in some senses there exists a *biological* qualifier, too, since our experience of gender entails some manner of body awareness focused around sex, and because gender presentation is always embodied in a way either clearly displaying a particular sex or trying to avoid such a display. Psychologically, gender can refer to the presumed personal experience (including thoughts, feelings, and behaviors) expected to follow from having a certain body sex—the social demand placed on each of us. The social dimension includes the presentation of characteristics culturally approved for such a body—and that inescapably carries a psychological element as the presentation may give rise to a profound sense of congruity or a discomfiting sense of incongruity.

Though we have not been at the task long, we now do possess a definition adequate to ease us into the conversation. But we won't go far without some attention to other important words that surround talking about gender. Some of these will be familiar, even if we probably have not closely considered them before. Others are likely to be unfamiliar words, or at least ones we remain unclear about. All, however, are part of the basic vocabulary of gender.

The Basic Vocabulary of Gender

The words most commonly used as basic to conversing about gender are all tinged by the pairing of sex with gender. As long as this remains the case we will be mandated to reckon with the nature of that connection. So our remarks here will continually wrestle with what our vocabulary means for conceptualizing gender. In order, we will examine important nouns, pronouns, and adjectives.

However, even before we begin examining specific words we must caution ourselves that language *denotations* often fade before the force of *connotations*. The explicit dictionary sense of a word is frequently embedded by a context of associations that we learn and unconsciously incorporate into our understanding of the word. So even as we attempt to define it, our sense of it is shaped by a lifetime of finely wrought cultural experience and expectation.[16] Gender words not only do not escape this reality, they may offer its best examples!

Language scholar Angela Goddard and social psychologist Lindsey Mean Patterson highlight the role of socialization in how we gender language. They argue that our gendered conversation betrays our possession of "a shared system of reference about traditional roles and about what is deemed masculine or feminine."[17] This shared frame of reference can be found, they say, in vocabulary used exclusively for one sex or the other (e.g., 'hunk' for males, 'buxom' for females); vocabulary where the meaning changes according to its referent (e.g., 'well-built'), sometimes carrying positive connotations for one gender, but negative for another (e.g., an aggressive man in sport is praised, but aggressive women are never viewed positively); and vocabulary applied selectively to highlight what culture believes the most salient social aspects of being a man (e.g., 'worker'), or woman (e.g., 'mother').[18]

Our brief examinations will not be able to explore fully the rich connotations of many important terms. All we can reasonably hope for is an entry into their worlds of meaning. Our goal is to get enough of a sense of what these words are about to enable us to dialog more fruitfully. We shall begin with the basic nouns attached to gender as gender labels.

Nouns: 'Boy' and 'Girl,' 'Man' and 'Woman,' 'Sissy' and 'Tomboy'

When we gender people we divide them into kinds and attach a label naming the categories into which they have been sorted. In contemporary Western culture people are sorted into two basic kinds, ostensibly based on their sex. The two broad groups are linguistically referred to in age-differentiated ways: *boys* (masculine males) and *girls* (feminine females) in childhood; *men* (masculine males) and *women* (feminine females) in adulthood.[19] Everyone in our culture is sorted into one or the other gender group at birth or shortly thereafter, depending on apparent body sex. Males are assigned to be boys expected to grow into men, while females are assigned to be girls expected to grow into women. (We'll talk more about this assignment process later.)

Since boy and girl are terms subordinated to, and referenced to man and woman, we will focus on the terms for adult members of a gender. Both man and woman are primary gender terms rather than sex terms. However, Goddard and Patterson observe that they also can be referenced to biological differences.[20] This use of the words as secondary sex terms can be construed either as reinforcing the idea that gender properly rests on sex, or as contributing to the blurring of the line between sex and gender. Either way can add to confusion.

The words themselves are not neutral. While the ultimate origin for the word man is uncertain, its meaning is much like the Latin word *homo*, a generic descriptor of one who appears to be male. Woman is derived from two words, *man* and the prefixed *wif*, meaning 'wife.' A 'woman' is literally a 'man's wife.' This is why down through the centuries many have believed that to become a woman a girl must be married.[21] The word woman connotes subordination through dependence on a man to achieve her status. That men (not all males) are established at the top of a gender hierarchy is clear when we learn that 'girl' can be applied to "a child or young person of either sex."[22] Even 'boy,' reserved for apparent males, signifies subordinate status, as it is applied not only to immature males, but to any male of an inferior social status, such as servants. In other words, man actually functions like two different words, one a generic descriptor, but the other a marker of position and privilege.

Classics scholar Francesca Santoro L'Hoir observes that our English terms are "lackluster" compared to their Latin counterparts. Latin provides four words in place of our two. A man may be termed *homo*, or *vir*. Similarly, a woman is *mulier* or *femina*. Two of these labels are generic and roughly correspond to body sex: *homo* and *mulier*; every man is *homo* and every woman *mulier*. The other two display both the social side of gender—referring to class distinctions such that only members of the upper class may be *vir* or *femina*—and the moral side of gender, for specific virtues as well as status adhere to the genders.[23] English may not possess such a clear way to express gender in these different dimensions, but that does not mean that man and woman do not retain social and ethical dimensions as well as biological elements.

As we noted a moment ago, boy and girl are subordinate nouns. They are sometimes qualified or replaced by other terms, notably *sissy* and *tomboy*. Part of the importance of these two labels is their recognition that there is more than one way to be a boy or girl. A sissy remains a boy just as a tomboy remains a girl—each term is exclusively reserved for one gender. But each signifies, as it were, a subspecies of the kind. A sissy is a boy who is too feminine; a tomboy is a girl who is too masculine. Of course, to say either is too much like the other gender is both a subjective judgment and an acknowledgment that gender displays along a continuum—an idea we shall return to.

Gender Pronouns

The basic gender nouns are accompanied by pronouns. As we all learned early in our schooling, pronouns stand in for nouns. In English, pronouns like *he* and *she* stand in for both nouns of sex (male and female), and nouns of gender (man and woman). This functionality is convenient, but it serves to further the tacit association between sex and gender. We see this also in the limitation of pronoun alternatives. There are only three kinds in standard English: masculine pronouns, feminine pronouns and neuter pronouns. The kinds preserve the sex and gender scheme of the culture.

Two noteworthy problems emerge from this situation. First, pronouns with their gender are applied to many nongendered things. English language scholars Niels Davidsen-Nielsen and Carl Bache remind us that "pronominal gender terms are not simply a question of objective sex distinctions but often reflect the speaker's attitude toward the referent. . . ."[24] This, they observe, is especially true in the use of 'she' for objects of affection. Far from being objective, neutral terms, pronouns carry value-laden connotations in many contexts.

Second, no generally accepted pronouns exist for sex or gender types outside the two sex/two gender scheme. Thus the language inhibits conceptualizing and communicating other sex or gender kinds. If empirical reality demonstrates a 'third gender' or more actually exist, then this language poverty needs to be addressed. As it is, our limitation in pronouns constitutes a rather significant obstacle to furthering the gender conversation. If there are people who do not clearly fit the noun categories man or woman—and many identify themselves as such—then what pronoun(s) should be used?

While 'he' and 'she' won't do, 'it' is inadequate too. Author and activist Leslie Feinberg, who as a self-identified transgender person is one for whom the traditional gender pronouns don't fit, argues that to apply 'it' is to employ "an epithet meant to strip us of our humanity."[25] Feinberg, in the mid-1990s, noted that new pronouns were being experimented with in cyberspace.[26] Nearer the end of that decade, in *Trans Liberation: Beyond Pink or Blue*, Feinberg wrote:

> Some people use either *s/he* or *sie*—both pronounced "sea," like the ocean. Others use *ze* (zee). The possessive gender-neutral pronoun coming into popular usage is 'hir' (like here and now). It is easier for some people, at first, to use these pronouns in writing than in speech because we've been so conditioned all our lives to use *she* or *he*.[27]

The proposed forms respond to the deficiency of the language by adopting new, non-gendered, or perhaps multi-gendered, pronouns.

'Masculine/Masculinity' and 'Feminine/Femininity'

Similar problems plague the reigning adjectives, though not as acutely. The dominant gender adjectives are *masculine* and *feminine*. We will on various occasions refer to dominant genders, and when we do so we will mean these two. Most of us identify with one or the other. However, the term 'androgynous' has gained popularity as an alternative to the other two. We shall consider this alternative in a moment, but first we must examine more closely the standard, predominant forms.

The English adjective masculine derives from the Latin *masculus*, an adjectival form associated with the Latin *mas*, meaning male. The English feminine, also an adjective, similarly derives from Latin, specifically the words *femininus* (an adjective), which is related closely to *femina* (a noun), meaning female. Goddard and Patterson call attention to the fact that the very form of the words masculine and feminine point to ties with other things. The '-ine' in each means 'like.' Masculine and feminine, therefore, are terms suggesting qualities or attributes—being like a male, or being like a female.[28]

Of course, that doesn't prove very helpful when the way we speak of males and females is largely in terms of psychological and social characteristics—the very things presumably belonging to gender! The words we are now describing are very broad catch-alls for the characteristics presumed to distinguish the genders. Both have noun counterparts—masculinity and femininity—which have come to label the stereotyped characteristics associated with being one or the other gender. So, if masculine and feminine represent the broadest gender labels, with boy and man differentiating members of masculinity while girl and woman differentiate members of femininity, then masculinity and femininity label the set of characteristics supposed to be shown by the members of the respective groups.

We can easily see where this is headed. Boys and men are expected to exhibit masculinity; girls and women are supposed to show femininity. Of course, we know things are not really so starkly divided. In real-world parlance we accept that *both* masculinity and femininity exist to some degree in all of us. Otherwise, words like sissy and tomboy would not exist. Yet our language seems almost to resist words that suggest too much range in the genders. Those that persist tend to be cautionary in nature. We know sissy is not meant as a compliment, and tomboy reminds girls that being too masculine is only tolerated until they mature. We know qualities of both genders exist in each of us, yet few women wish to be called masculine and fewer men desire to be called feminine. In short, we pretend there is a clearer distinction than is generally warranted.

Alongside words that signify awareness of modest degrees of gender-blending, we may find efforts to distinguish kinds or types within a gender. There is a difference, for example, between 'dominant' and 'subordinate' masculinities. At any given time in a society's history a particular form of masculinity may be prized above others.[29] Thus, as people have become more aware that a homosexual male can be a very masculine man, though perhaps without being masculine in exactly the same way a heterosexual male might be, it has proven easier to see that some masculinities are culturally subordinated to others. In short, our culture may grudgingly admit there is more than one way to be masculine, but insists one way is best.

While gender may be a many splendored thing, comprised of multiple interacting factors, each varying in intensity, quality, and degree of influence for an individual, limits remain. Most of us still expect a preponderance of the dominant masculinity in most males and a preponderance of the dominant femininity in most females. Nor do we make much effort to distinguish among members of the two recognized genders, save by age. We presume most of us will conform either to the set of characteristics named by masculinity or to those of femininity.

Those who do not submit to gender expectations pose at best a puzzle, and at worst a problem in any society where only two gender kinds are sanctioned. What do we do with nonconformists?

The solution has been to simultaneously acknowledge the nonconformity but to treat it as an exception that proves the rule. In other words, anyone who exhibits nonconforming gender behavior, whether mild or severe, is still viewed as a member of the assigned gender—even if an ill-fitting, or 'deviant' member. The milder expressions of nonconformity are commonly clustered under the label 'androgynous.' *Androgyny*—a calculated label derived from Greek words blending masculinity and femininity—offers a balancing through blending of characteristics associated with both genders. The concession made by most of us to such expressions is to label such adult persons either an 'androgynous woman' (rather than a feminine one), or 'androgynous man' (rather than a masculine one).

In recent decades, it even has become popular among social scientists to use *androgynous* as a label for desirable psychological gendering wherein the individual avoids the rigidity of gender stereotyped attitudes and behaviors in favor of a sensible gender-equity of masculine and feminine traits.[30] Psychologist Sandra Bem, who more than anyone else reinvigorated the idea of androgyny with her work in the 1970s, commented in 1981 that androgyny challenges the social prescription to be *either* a woman *or* a man, and offers the possibility of embracing *both* the masculinity *and* the femininity within the self.[31]

Mostly, though, this idea amounts culturally to encouraging men to be gentler and less aggressive while applauding women who become more like men in a man's world. In either instance, the man or woman is still expected to be masculine or feminine; androgynous in our culture typically functions as a modest counterpoint to being *too* masculine or feminine. In effect, it is often functionally used as a way to redefine what is normative masculinity or femininity so as to ease the obvious stress created by trying to adhere closely to stereotype.

Less often, androgyny is seen as a 'third gender.' In this respect, the apparent male or female body is dressed to mask the sex and sever it from the paired gender. Thus androgynous dress serves to mark out a possible 'third gender' appearance. There is evidence of similar things happening in societies where a particular group is separated from the dominant genders. Historically, for example, when children were viewed as asexual beings, their dress often was androgynous; other socially inferior people, regardless of their sex, might be made to publicly appear in androgynous garb.[32]

In societies with a rigid gender hierarchy, androgyny is likely to be judged as closer to femininity. This is why in societies like our own androgynous dress is much more acceptable for girls and women.[33] Ironically, today many of the young people who are choosing to blend genders through androgynous dress (and use of makeup) are males. This probably reflects both protest against masculine stereotypes and the lessened distance between the genders—the very things desired under the promotion of an androgynous psychological profile. Nevertheless, particularly among other males, androgynous dress among men and boys commonly fetches disparaging comments.

Transgender

Transgender has become the more common term for those who not only do not fit comfortably within their assigned masculine or feminine gender kinds, but whose degree of nonconformity exceeds a culture's ability to reasonably fit them into either of the dominant genders. Some prefer the label *third gender* to transgender, but both have their limitations and the robustness of 'transgender' has led to rather widespread adoption.

In its simplest and most direct sense transgender means 'to cross,' so that 'cross-gender' and transgender both can mean to move from one gender to another. Since in our culture gender is so closely paired with anatomical sex, crossing gender is typically understood to mean presenting in a gender not paired by our culture with the person's anatomical sex. Thus, a female who presents as masculine is displaying *trans*gender.

But 'trans' is affixed to a variety of words that lend depth and coloration to the term transgender. For example, consider the word '*trans*gression.' Some people view transgender as a transgression of gender rules and boundaries; the word transgender, for them, is decidedly negative. On the other hand, consider the word '*trans*cend.' Some people view transgender as a transcending of too-narrow gender rules and boundaries; the term transgender, for them, is definitely positive. Other instances of how 'trans' might be construed—any of which can influence how one views the term—include '*trans*late' (transgender as rendering the gender associated with a different sex into a gender paired with one's own sex, as in biological males who represent a certain language of femininity through their crossdressing), '*trans*form' (transgender as reshaping gender in distinctive ways), or '*trans*ition' (transgender as moving from one gender to another while dragging one's sex along behind, as in transsexuals who live as a gender before undergoing surgery to become anatomically the sex typically paired with that gender).

There are both wider and narrower senses for the term transgender. The word itself permits a range of applications since it simply means 'cross' (or 'across') gender. Both broad and narrow uses of the term merit some exploration. But initially it should be noted that the term was first used in a narrower sense and only later became used in a wider one. Currently, both uses of the word are relatively common; exact meaning must often be inferred from the context. Either way, the essence of the idea is this: *what makes us who we are lies more between our ears (psychosocial gender), than between our legs (biological sex).*

The more common use of the term is in its broad sense. For example, Walter Bockting, among the most well-known experts on transgender, remarks that "transgender people are a diverse group of individuals who cross or transcend culturally defined categories of gender."[34] Similarly, sex therapist Richard Carroll observes, "the term 'transgendered experience' is currently used to refer to the many different ways individuals may experience a gender identity outside the simple categories of male or female."[35] So transgender can be an umbrella term, whether applied to members of various identifiable groups or used to describe different gender experiences regardless of group affiliation. The phrasing of the Gender Public Advocacy Coalition (GenderPAC), in a 1997 report, offered a description of transgendered people that fits well a broad sense of the term: "Transgendered people are people who manifest gender characteristics, behavior, or self-identification typical of or commonly associated with persons of another gender."[36]

As useful as such descriptions are, they do not actually list any groups already existing under other labels. One description of the term rectifies this situation by proposing that transgender names "the community of all self identified cross gender people whether intersex, transsexual men and women, cross dressers, drag kings and drag queens, transgenderists, androgynous, bi-gendered, third gendered or as yet unnamed gender gifted people."[37] With this list in mind, the term transgender in its wider sense may be used to embrace members of the following groups (each listed with a defining characteristic), most of whom also are commonly referred to as 'sexual minorities':

❑ *bigendered*—those who perceive themselves as both masculine and feminine;

❑ *gender impersonators*—professional impersonators of a gender different than the one assigned them at birth (typically male impersonators of females);

❑ *homosexuals*—those whose fixed erotic attraction pattern is toward members of their own sex (and thus contrary to the majority gender pattern);

❑ *intersexed*—those born with ambiguous genitalia or sexual characteristics that make simple identification as male or female impossible;

❑ *third gender people*—those who perceive themselves as belonging to neither gender pole but instead possessing a separate sense of gender;

❑ *transgender*—those who identify with a different gender than that assigned at birth, and persistently living in that identity and role, but without viewing the body sex as incorrect or seeking sex reassignment surgery;

❑ *transsexuals*—those who have a persistent sense of inhabiting the body of the wrong sex, and who typically pursue body-altering strategies including hormonal and surgical treatment; and,

❑ *transvestites*—those who dress in the clothes associated with the opposite gender, including those who do so occasionally or regularly, and whose identification with another gender is variable.[38]

The appropriateness of one or another group being placed under this large umbrella is often debated. What they often have in common is what sociologists

Patricia Gagne and Richard Tewksbury call "quests to find room to be themselves within a system that made no space for them."[39]

Transgender in the narrower sense is found on the above list. Interestingly, the word was originally intended to mean this narrow sense.[40] However, over time the broad sense has become predominant.

Secondary Gender Vocabulary

In addition to the most fundamental terms for conversing about gender, there are a number of common words that have come to be attached to the term 'gender' to derive more specialized meanings. A few of these are both recurrent enough and conceptually important to merit some coverage here.

Gender Assignment and Gender Attribution

On more than one occasion already we have mentioned that all of us are placed at birth into a gender. *Gender assignment* refers to the decision to call a newborn a boy or girl based on the *apparent* sex. The assignment is not made based on genetic testing to determine the genetic sex of the child. It is based on visual examination of the lower genitalia. This process will be looked at more closely later (chapter 3).

Gender assignment carries with it all the rights, responsibilities, and privileges (or lack thereof) attached to the gender assigned. It is accompanied by gender development, an ongoing process of being shaped to conform to our gender assignment. In the famous words of philosopher Simone de Beauvoir, "One is not born, but rather becomes, a woman."[41] The same pertains to men. This process is examined more carefully further into our dialog.

Gender attribution is a more ambiguous term. It can be used as synonymous to gender assignment. More commonly, though, it refers to ascribing a particular set of gender characteristics (masculinity or femininity) to the child *as if* those characteristics are due the child based on sex and gender assignment. Initially, gender attribution is a conscious process—a choice to regard the child according to the set of characteristics associated with the assigned gender. But this persistent attributional process soon becomes and largely remains unconscious. It surfaces in the many judgments we make when encountering others whereby we label them with gender according to cues, like dress, speech, and mannerisms.[42]

Gender Stereotyping

Gender assignment and gender attribution are accompanied by a number of important processes. One of these is stereotyping, or holding a mental composite picture of generalized, expected characteristics. *Gender stereotyping* names the process of maintaining a template of gender characteristics for masculinity and femininity that can be used and reused without much, if any, change. Stereotypes are hard to avoid because in a complex world filled with many cognitive demands they make mental work easier. Far less effort is required to put a label like 'man' or 'woman' on a person, and then fit that label to a pre-existing template of expected traits, than to focus at length on every individual in order to form a careful, nuanced appraisal of each person we encounter. Stereotyping provides a mental tool readily available to quickly and efficiently sort information, especially routine or mundane information.[43]

Gender Expectations and Gender Conformity

Gender stereotypes parallel and mirror broad, general expectations about how a boy or girl, man or woman, *should* think, feel, speak, and act. *Gender expectations* mean a child, once assigned as a boy or girl, is anticipated to exhibit the gender qualities attributed to him or her. To some degree, at least, we won't be wrong to say the child is *required* to display these gender attributes. Just as gender attribution brings a number of implied privileges, it also carries obligations. These obligations include endorsing, embracing and exhibiting qualities, summarized in stereotypes, to mark the individual as a member in good standing within the gender. Boys and men are expected to demonstrate masculinity, and in so doing accrue the privilege attending status at the top of the gender hierarchy. Likewise, girls and women enjoy certain privileges deemed suitable to their station.

Gender attributions and expectations are so pronounced they lead to subtle distortions in the ways adults perceive infants. A 1974 study underscores this point. Babies of both sexes were presented for observation. The average weight of the babies was the same and the length of the girls slightly more on average. Despite these facts, the adult observers underestimated both the weight and the size of the baby girls relative to the infant boys.[44] What they saw conformed to a cultural expectation that boys be big and strong, while girls should be small and delicate. A 1976 study offers more dramatic evidence. Young mothers were asked to interact with a 6 month-old infant named Beth. They smiled at her often, offered her dolls and viewed her as a 'sweet' child who had a 'soft cry.' Another group of young mothers were asked to interact with Adam, the same age as Beth. This child was treated and perceived quite differently. However, 'Beth' and 'Adam' were exactly the same child, dressed as either a boy or a girl.[45]

No one expects us to meet our gender expectations perfectly all of the time. As long as we do so reasonably well and most of the time we can get by. *Gender conformity* refers to the process of adhering to gender expectations. Most of us, most of the time, conform well enough to gender norms (average social expectations) to escape censure. Obviously, though, gender conformity is relative in nature. Some degree of nonconformity is permissible because it is inescapable; being an individual means none of us will ever perfectly match an idealized and generalized version of any gender. Still, the degree of nonconformity tolerated is generally contingent on maturity. The younger a person is, the greater the slack accorded in conforming to gender expectations.

After gender assignment and accompanying gender attributions comes a process of developing a *gender identity* and trying to fit into a *gender role*. Both are expected to be consistent with assignment and attributions; in other words, both are anticipated to conform to expectations. Babies assigned to be boys must become boys by endorsing and embracing the gender attributions, at least to an extent sufficient to satisfy societal demands, first placed in the interpretive hands of their parents. As gender assignment with its attributions is incorporated in the child an identity is shaped that prompts adoption by the child of the label 'boy' or 'girl' as a self-identifier. This identity is experienced and proven largely through successfully fulfilling expected patterns associated with the gender.

Gender identity and gender role are expected to complement each other and flow inevitably from gender assignment and attributions. Sexologists John Money and Anke Ehrhardt posit the intrinsic unity of gender identity and gender role by describing gender identity as the private experience of gender role, and gender role as the public expression of gender identity. [46] The problem with this formulation, which imagines identity and role as two sides of the same coin, is that it tacitly assumes an individual will perform gender role consistent with gender identity though that is manifestly not the case all too often. Gender identity and role are more separable that Money and Ehrhardt envision.

Psychologist Marjorie Hardy, in describing gender identity, explains how things sometimes happen: "*Gender identity* is the personal belief that one is either a male or a female, regardless of assigned gender. Thus, a male transsexual may have been assigned a male gender at birth, but his gender identity is female.[47]" The expectations of others, no matter how powerful, may not be enough to prevent developing an identity at odds with expectations.

In what we have put forward so far, gender identity looks like a *product* that once attained is fixed. But perhaps gender identity is really *gender self-identifying*, an ongoing process that generally reflects stability, but isn't fixed. In this broader sense of the term, gender identity continues to develop beyond self-identification as labeling and affiliating with a particular gender. Viewed this way, gender identity involves a rich and evolving series of experiences that are then translated in gender expressions.

Gender Experience and Expression

We do not know why gender identity sometimes develops contrary to assignment, attributions, and expectations. Theories abound.[48] What matters to our discussion here is that gender identity is inseparable from personal experience of gender and such experience may shape an identity at odds with expectation.

Gender experience refers to the actual, lived gendering done by each of us. Whether such gendering is construed as biologically driven or determined, or thought to be culturally crafted, or imagined as derived from and influenced by both, it remains uniquely individual. Gender experience includes how we feel about our gendered self, how we think of that gendered self, and how we incline ourselves to act based on those thoughts and feelings. This inclination, or will, may or may not always be carried out, but it persists and motivates some behavior consistent with itself. If we experience ourselves as feminine, our inclination will lead at least some of our behaviors to express that, even if social sanctions in one or more contexts otherwise inhibit such expressions.

Gender expression refers to the behaviors we enact to display gender, whether or not that display is congruent with our gender identity or according to the inclination of our gender experience.[49] It also may or may not be identical at any given moment to our gender role. Where our gender role is socially proscribed, gender expression is highly individualized and typically only somewhat fits our gender role. In sum, we can choose to express our assigned gender role regardless of our gender identity. We may also choose to express our experienced inner gender identity though it means violating our assigned gender role.

As we live our lives within society others routinely use socially sanctioned cues, such as our dress and mannerisms, to attribute to us one or another gender. In so doing the one making the attribution assumes it is consistent with gender assignment—a low risk assumption since most of us most of the time conform to gender assignment, attributions, and expectations. In our adherence to those cues we present as that gender, regardless of how well it fits our identity or experience. For many of us, gender assignment and development do fit our gender identity and experience, and comfortably guide our gender expression in such a manner that we win and keep social approval.

Conclusion

Though we have barely scratched the surface of the pertinent language employed in the conversation about gender, we have made a start. This basic vocabulary needs to be well-mastered to make best sense of what lies ahead. Now it is time to turn to the history of gender study and to prominent theories of gender.

Chapter 2

History & Theories

Introduction: Gender is a concept whose importance has grown over time. Historically, as we saw in our opening chapter, 'gender' has a long pedigree. But its emergence as a robust concept applied to human identity and behavior is fairly recent. Seeded in the latter half of the 19th century, it emerged in the latter half of the 20th century, and continues to blossom. Not surprisingly, the history of the concept is a history of the ongoing struggle to understand different influences on our humanity, including biology and the environment.

One way to understand the history of gender as a subject of inquiry is to trace its bearing in systems of thought. Our modern controversy over gender stems largely from new ways of considering it that challenge a dominant perspective called *essentialism*. This view closely ties sex and gender together, and makes the latter dependent on biology rather than culture. The seeds of challenge to this view came when some of its staunchest defenders were confronted by an immense challenge. In an effort to scientifically comprehend the sexual nature of people, society turned to medicine for help. Those professionals brought their own model to bear. That model proved inadequate. As a result, medical and mental health professionals themselves turned to other ideas, hoping to incorporate them in the medical model. One such notion was gender, fetched to help explain certain conditions (notably transsexualism), which were gaining more attention. Once this new idea was introduced, it began to change and broaden in application.

The implicit distinction between sex and gender invited a distancing of the latter from the biological nature of the former. By linking gender to nonbiological forces the way was clear to show that the obvious inequality in society was a product of culture rather than Nature. *Feminists*, in particular, capitalized on this possibility. They mounted evidence and persuasive arguments that what had been legitimized as a matter of sex was actually a discrimination based on gender. In place of essentialism they offered other theories of gender. Among the new perspectives that soon took shape, *social constructionism* would become especially influential. It deconstructs the essentialist assumptions and reveals gender as something artificial rather than natural. Another theory—*queer theory*—would also capture attention and offer a new voice for many people. Put most simply, theories divide as to whether culture or biology most determines gender.

The Problem of Gender

As we have discussed, gender is not a straightforward term. We might well ask, 'Has today's muddled mess and controversy always been the case?' The question is not a particularly easy one to answer. In one respect, gender for a long time was rather unremarkable. For most of its history the term principally referred to language items rather than to a concept important to understanding human identity and roles. When it was spoken of in connection to people it was so closely tied to sex as to be little more than a subcategory. Only recently has gender gained special importance in its own right, received much more attention, and become a subject both attached to many other ideas and controversial.

How did our present circumstance come about? To answer that query requires reviewing the history of the study of gender. But to do that requires first distinguishing between the *idea* of gender and its formal *study*. The former is obviously older than the latter. The notion that gender is something people possess, and not entirely the same as sex, has been around much longer than academic gender studies, which are relatively recent in origin. But that idea remained implicit for a long time. For many people past and present, gender just meant sorting the two sexes into men and women.

We shall begin by proposing that gender has come to be seen by many as a *problem*. Though the idea was applied in the late 20th century to solve certain dilemmas, since then it has come to be seen by many as itself the problem! Gender proves itself problematic in the difficulties people encounter in articulating exactly what it encompasses and what it means. Yet that seems trivial—a thorn in the side of academicians—when compared to real world concerns. Much more potently, gender proves a problem many wish to solve because of its consequences in individual experience and in social policy.

Why Is Gender a Problem?

The very ubiquity of gender in human experience contributes both to its significance and to it posing a problem in various respects. Psychologist Marjorie Hardy contends that a relatively small proportion of total social behavior is due to gender.[50] But we should qualify that as behavior *directly* derived from gender, and then understood in its closest connection to sex differences; the overall influence is much broader. *In contemporary Western culture gender has come to epitomize a central element in self-identity and a defining role in what one does in society and how one relates to others.*[51]

Despite that long reach, we often seem surprisingly oblivious of gender. "Although gender governs the full spectrum of human behaviors," remarks writer and transgender activist Jessica Xavier, "almost all people are wholly unconscious of it. Thus gender is also an unspoken and unwritten social contract that all people enter into without much discussion or debate."[52] If this is true at an individual level, it is no less the case at a societal level. Political scientist Sabrina Petra Ramet describes what she calls 'gender culture':

. . . society's understanding of what is possible, proper, and perverse in gender-linked behavior, and more specifically, that set of values, mores, and assumptions which establishes which behaviors are to be seen as gender-linked, with which gender or genders they are to be seen as linked, what is the society's understanding of gender in the first place, and, consequently, how many genders there are.[53]

This social-cultural 'understanding' is only partially conscious, but that makes it no less pervasive or binding on us.

That leads us to a second problem: we can't help but make gender attributions to everyone we meet—and those extend beyond what we presume to be the person's sex to assumptions about the way their personality is likely to be and how they should act. In the social contract we find thrust upon us in our culture, as writer Claudine Griggs notes, "Gender attribution is generally immediate, unconscious, and dimorphic. And it carries contiguous rules about masculine/feminine protocol, which are also immediate, unconscious and dimorphic."[54] In other words, we may not be conscious about why we draw the conclusions we do, but still we make our judgments without hesitation and uniformly as 'boy' or 'girl,' 'man' or 'woman.' It is our gender (or gendered) culture.

Of course, our attributions are often wrong—a corollary to our second problem. Sometimes we err in what we think the sex of the person must be based on their apparent gender. At other times we mistakenly conclude a person should be and act in a way their actual behavior belies. These errors can prove embarrassing, but we are most upset when a dramatic disjunction between gender and sex becomes evident. And therein seems to lie the principal problem many have with the way gender is conceived and discussed today: placed at too far a remove from sex, gender seems to open the door for almost anything in the way of self-identity and self-presentation vis-à-vis sex, including homosexuality, transvestism, and transsexualism.

But others contend a different corollary to this second problem is really the most critical issue: society is constructed along gender attributions and expectations that produce a hierarchy in which all but certain kinds of masculine men are disadvantaged. In this respect, the problem of gender lies in construing it in such a manner that identities based upon it and social rules formed around it collude to keep human affairs vastly unequal. The danger, then, is not too open a door, but too many closed doors.

From either end of the spectrum many people find gender poses a problem—and one that needs to be solved sooner rather than later. Under the first corollary described above, what some see as the personal liberation offered by gender, others view as the social liberalism of gender. While the former group champions the chance to be who they see themselves as, the latter group warns that such so-called 'freedom' is mere sexual anarchy and a sign of the ruin of culture. Under the second corollary, what some see as the natural order others experience as culturally-based oppression. While advocates of the gender hierarchy appeal to a natural division determined by biology, critics dispute that claim and produce evidence that there is nothing natural or inevitable about one gender lording it over others.

How did we ever manage to find ourselves in such a situation?

The Essentialist Heritage

Remember that the word gender refers to a division into kinds, and that applied to people this division was made based on sex—or rather, apparent sex, the perceived maleness or femaleness of a newborn. An easy presumption to make is that different bodies lead to different activities, which shape different personalities, and consequently shape different social destinies. Put bluntly, advocates of the view that gender differences are sex-based claim that male bodies *make* men. Their bodies direct them naturally to certain activities—forms of work—and over time these create a masculine mind, which inheres social roles and a special place in society. Similarly, female bodies *make* women. Their natural capacity to bear offspring and to nourish them directs them into different activities than men. As with men, the activities of women shape their personalities because they take place in different environments, entail different demands, and involve different ways of looking at things congruent with their experiences and needs. Taken together, these activities and personalities place women into a distinctive niche in the social order.

The label *essentialism* has become affixed to the above perspective, because it holds there is an *essence* to human nature. Essentialism emphasizes an inevitability in the shaping of human culture based on a natural, enduring, fixed distinctive, and transcultural difference between male and female bodies. "The essentialist view that behavioral differences are rooted in biological differences," comments psychologist Linda Gallahan, "presumes that an individual's core personality, which determines such behaviors, is separable from the individual's social and cultural contexts."[55] Separable, perhaps, but linked; biological differences undergird the formation of culture.

The label 'essentialism' itself is fairly recent. Its first application was not just descriptive, but also somewhat pejorative, made by feminist critics of what they deemed a sexist orientation. Of course, the essentialist position hardly needed any label for a long time because it reigned without significant challenge. Even those disadvantaged by it found it hard to entirely dismiss. Some feminists, for example, implicitly accept the logic of the essentialist view though they frame it differently. Thus religious scholar Mary Daly, a prominent feminist in the latter half of the 20th century, does not dispute that biology makes men and women, but argues that instead of making men superior it makes them demonically desperate to control the natural superiority of the female body through patriarchy. For Daly, the problem of gender is not its conception as rooted in biology, but that in our society it has been rooted in the wrong biology.[56]

Without doubt, whether logically necessary or not, essentialism's constant companion has been a gender hierarchy dominated by a certain kind of masculinity. Despite some questioning of this scheme it reigned without serious challenge into the mid-20th century. By that time, though, a number of forces converged to alter the conceptual landscape. Surprisingly, one of those forces came from within that bastion of masculine privilege and power, the profession of medicine. As that profession laid intellectual claim to owning the conversation on sex and sexuality, the matter of gender inevitably came under new purview.

The Role of the Medicalization of Sex

The development to our present concept of gender follows in part from a major shift in the conversation about sex and sexuality. In the latter half of the 19th century began a change now labeled *the medicalization of sex*.[57] The phrase refers to the invention of a new way of understanding and talking about human sexuality. Previous to this new way of looking at things, folk had focused on sexual *behaviors* rather than musing about the inherent dispositions and psychological states said to produce them.[58] In fact, for most of human history, sexual acts were judged mostly by practical measures: did they produce offspring? Pleasure? Social accord or discord?[59]

The motivations for a change in perspective were several. One force for change was an understandable desire to scientifically classify and categorize the particulars of human sexuality in order to facilitate study and precise discourse. In an age where psychology and psychiatry were nascent, medicine was the branch of science looked to for guidance. As medical professionals consolidated their hold in the 19th century as the authoritative voices on human sexuality, they recast its discussion consistent with a new vocabulary. Words like 'homosexual' and 'heterosexual' began to emerge. The variants of human sexual behavior were being labeled, including those society found problematic.

In one respect, this shift was both invited and sanctioned by a perceived societal need. As historian Angus McLaren recounts, "Sexology—the science of sexuality—emerged in the last decades of the nineteenth century as magistrates in European courts increasingly called upon medical experts to aid them in understanding a variety of sex crimes that were more difficult to fathom than simple rape or sodomy."[60] The rule of law required clear boundaries for judicial decisions—and such boundaries were not apparent. It became the task of modern medicine to provide those boundaries, which they did by coining labels to accompany categories into which they could place 'deviant' behaviors.

Ostensibly the new language of sexuality was scientific, especially medical, and rooted in an objective discernment of natural reality. But as McLaren points out, medical professionals solidly ensconced in the middle class proved oblivious to their social class' efforts to impose its own values on everyone else. Like others of their class they accepted certain social conventions about behavior and, especially, masculine sexuality.[61] In our terms, they accepted without much scrutiny the essentialist perspective. So in practice, the quest to accomplish an objective science blind to the subjective bias of its architects proceeded, as Robert Nye puts it, "to conflate sex, gender, and sexuality and to treat the sexual identity of individuals as biologically or 'naturally' determined."[62] The supposed triumph of science denied—and effectively hid—the cultural values that guided the all-too-human architects of the new science of sexology. But medical professionals were themselves soon to yield at least partial control to emerging disciplines with an even greater claim on the subject matter.

The establishment of psychiatric and psychological disciplines further shifted the emerging discourse on human sexuality. These professions gained a measure of scientific legitimacy by committing to the medical model. But they also uncritically accepted an essentialist perspective. Moreover, their focus was often on people brought to them—willingly or unwillingly—who were deemed to suffer from disordered sexuality. The medical model and its embedded essentialism led mental health professionals to pathologize much of the sexual behavior they were confronted by and then to seek for it a causal path, much as a doctor looks for the cause of a physical illness. Similarly, psychiatrists and psychologists often sought a physical basis for psychological disturbances, thinking, for example, that sexual abnormalities might be explained by some body deficiency.[63] The essentialist sense of biological determinism sorted everyone into categories, starting with sex. Born either male or female—save for the unfortunate few whose hermaphroditism showed Nature makes mistakes—resulting identities and behaviors were expected to reflect the 'natural' consequences of biological origin.

When things went astray, whether through intersex birth or influences that prompted deviant behavior, the medicalization of sex pointed the path to follow. First, the condition had to be properly labeled—sorted to where it belonged. Then it had to be investigated in terms of biological forces at work. If these could not be found, the medical model need not be abandoned. Instead, it merely required shifting its logic to searching out environmental factors as though they could be summed up through either a single causal pathway (a disease), or multiple causes resulting in a coherent symptom pattern (a syndrome).[64]

The medicalization of sex laid the foundation for a new way for the idea of gender to be employed. In one respect, although it required roughly a century to emerge, the new use seems in retrospect to be inevitable. The logical limitations of the medical model in attempting to explain the complexities of human experience and behavior made such a happenstance necessary. We would be fair in claiming that the new emergence of an invigorated gender concept serves in itself as an indictment of the paucity of language and logic in the medical model when applied to phenomena studiously linked to sex and sexuality.

Additionally, it points to problems arising from the uncritical acceptance of essentialism. As doctors, psychiatrists, psychologists, and sexologists tried to sort out the different displays of sex and sexuality they were confronted by the need to draw on gender. In so doing they were about to change the language of gender and open new avenues for conversation. Nothing would be the same afterwards.

The Rebirth of 'Gender'

Gender studies as a distinct discipline followed a rebirth of the idea of gender in the latter half of the 20th century. This rebirth is reflected in the development of the secondary vocabulary discussed earlier—a flowering of terminology disclosing a reconsideration and elaboration of the concept of gender. Feminist literary critic Tori Moi claims, "The English-language distinction between the words sex and gender was first developed in the 1950s and 1960s by psychiatrists and other medical personnel working with intersexed and transsexual patients."[65] Particularly in the case of the latter, there was a pronounced mismatch between the apparent body sex and the sense of what the body sex should be. The appropriation of the word 'gender' to counterbalance 'sex' allowed doctors to conveniently distinguish what the body showed (sex = biology), and what the mind protested (gender = psychology). Thus, in Moi's view, "At its inception, the distinction medicalizes 'sex' and turns 'gender' into a purely psychological category."[66]

This latter contention may overreach. In fact, Moi points out that such a division—a Cartesian mind-body split—would be deplored by the very architect of the reinvigoration of gender as a utilitarian tool: sexologist John Money.[67] He lays claim to being the first to define 'gender role' in print. In a 1955 article with colleagues, Money established gender role as, "all those things that a person says or does to disclose himself or herself as having the status of boy or man, girl or woman, respectively. It includes, but is not restricted to sexuality in the sense of eroticism."[68] Moi is correct, though, in noting that Money's formulation would not be the one to prompt a seismic shift in consciousness.

The Contribution of Robert Stoller

That honor, claims Moi, belongs to psychodynamic psychiatrist Robert Stoller. In 1963, at the 23rd International Psycho-Analytical Congress, in Stockholm, Sweden, he introduced his own notion of what he termed 'gender identity.' For Stoller, gender identity pairs with sex—knowing whether one is male or female—but has its significance in being an aspect of self-image.[69] The apparent severance of sex and gender, contends Moi, is "what fired feminists' imagination."[70] But does Stoller so completely distance sex from gender?

Although he can speak of the relation of sex and gender in such a way as to suggest a complete severance between them[71]—the very notion Money objected to so strenuously—Stoller often qualifies their relationship in a more nuanced manner. He posits that a person's core gender identity is the product of three components—the anatomy of the external genitalia, infant-parent relationships, and a biological force—and "remains unchanged throughout life."[72] The three core components he later amended to five: (1) a biologic "force"; (2) sex assignment at birth; (3) "the unending impingement of parents' attitudes, especially those of mothers, about *that* infant's sex . . .": (4) "biopsychic" phenomena

---

(e.g., early postnatal effects, imprinting, conditioning, or other forms of learning); and (5) a developing body-ego (i.e., body, especially genital, sensations).[73]

What Stoller accomplished for feminists and others was to transfer attention to the psychological sense of self that appears importantly shaped by much more than biology. A respected psychiatrist liberating gender from biological determinism was victory enough for thinkers who were looking for a better way to explain the realities obvious in the world. That it would also serve to buttress attacks on sexism was icing on the cake—the long term repercussions are still being felt. Cracks were beginning to show more visibly in the edifice of essentialism.

But Stoller was not alone in creating space between sex and gender. Others had been considering the distinction theoretically, and scientific research on sex differences offered more fuel for the utility of a gender concept relatively distanced from biological influence. Studies that showed differences between men and women that could be better attributed to nurture than to nature became part of the new articulation of gender, regardless of whether the work itself used the term.

Science and the Erosion of the Essentialist Perspective

Such early influential work included, for example, psychologist's Ralph Exline's study of person perception published in the early 1960s.[74] This work established gender-differentiated nonverbal differences in communication style: men and women vary in eye contact when conversing. This variation reflects differences in interpersonal patterns, with women exhibiting more inclusive and affectionate styles than men. While such differences might be called 'sex' differences, they fit well within the emerging sense of 'gender' differences, owing their origin at least as much to nonbiological as to biological factors.

Experiments increasingly found differences that sex differentiation could not explain. For example, a study reported in the mid-1970s, using psychologist Sandra Bem's ideas on androgyny, showed that women who could be gender-typed as androgynous conformed to an opinion endorsed by confederates less often than did either men gender-typed as masculine, or women gender-typed as feminine.[75] Gender, not sex, explained the difference. By the end of the 1970s, psychologists and other social scientists were having to seriously reckon that what most of them had been labeling sex differences might better be described as gender differences—the observed differences between men and women could better be accounted for by nonbiological factors.[76]

The essentialist perspective depended on a tight connection between sex and gender. The former gave rise to the divisions of the latter and directed their course, both in personal development and in society. If the ties binding sex and gender were weakened, the essentialist assumptions were threatened. Rather than biology determining the shape of culture, perhaps culture had true independence. If so, then the essentialist notion that biology guides activities and the forming of personality might not be the whole truth. Perhaps culture exercises as great, or greater influence on how personality forms. That, in turn, suggests that the social roles men and women are directed to are not the result of biological destiny but the product of cultural forces. In short, maybe it isn't sex that matters in making us who we are, but gender.[77]

The Feminist Challenge

Even as the medicalization of sex tried to capitalize on a new appropriation of the idea of gender, interested onlookers were contemplating the new possibilities being opened up. Prominent among these onlookers were feminists. Most of them had always found distressing the essentialist perspective, but an effective ideology to contest it had been lacking. However, by the 1960s feminism had entered into a new phase in Western societies, one that would not merely reinvigorate the movement, but find ways to appropriate gender such as to sharply change the conversation about it. The two developments are closely bonded. As political writer Varda Burstyn, puts it: "the second half of the twentieth century, with its crises of gender . . . produced another great wave of feminism. . . ."[78]

'Second Wave Feminism'

This 'second wave feminism' surfaced in the late 1960s and early 1970s.[79] The timing coincided with the emergence of gender as a reinvigorated concept. Although the movement is often thought of as the political and social struggle for equal rights, especially in employment opportunities, a principal force driving feminist thinking was the notion that inequality was a product of cultural decisions about gender rather than the inevitable result of biological, sex-based destiny. [80] Indeed, feminists could even stand traditional essentialism on its head by championing the superiority of femaleness! "As a theoretical force," writes feminist linguist Judith Baxter, "'second wave' feminism has been largely preoccupied with celebrating the notion of a universal female nature, and critiquing the influence of the 'big variable' of gender on social relations in order to promote female emancipation."[81]

What medical and social scientists began in loosening the bond between sex and gender, feminists appropriated and extended. Though the feminist agenda reached in many directions, and looked to multiple disciplines for inspiration, with reference to the importance of gender reconsidered, psychoanalysis and the social sciences proved especially important. The former from our vantage point today might seem a natural ally; psychoanalysis early welcomed women and both male and female psychoanalysts had from the beginning—starting with Freud himself—been steadily offering up thoughts on a 'feminine psychology.'[82] Yet, at the onset of the second wave, most feminists were overtly hostile to Freud and psychoanalysis.[83] This soon changed. By the mid-1970s, collections of important psychoanalytic writings on women were being offered up to feminists to facilitate the new vigor in the movement.[84] In psychoanalytic theory were found ideas that offered a way to further shape the conversation on gender.

The Psychoanalytic Contribution: Nancy Chodorow

What changed feminists' minds? One important factor was that women psychoanalysts by the 1960s-1980s had moved well past many of Freud's formulations, even as they retained some of his basic ideas. Leslie Bell explains the appeal to many feminists:

> Many second-wave feminists writing during the 1970s and 1980s turned to psychoanalytic theory because it addressed gender and sexuality, and because it seemed to account for the persistence of gender inequalities, both in individual psyches and in cultural and social institutions, despite U.S. society's political and social commitment to gender equality.[85]

Psychoanalyst Nancy Chodorow was an especially critical influence. Chodorow, with a doctorate in sociology as well as psychoanalytic training, was well-positioned to tackle dimensions of gender critical to feminist thinking. The titles of some of her major works—*The Reproduction of Mothering: Psychoanalysis and the Sociology of Gender* (1978) and *Feminism and Psychoanalytic Theory* (1989)—make clear her interests. By the time she retired from teaching in 2005, Chodorow had received many honors and was generally regarded as the most significant feminist psychoanalyst of her generation.

The Reproduction of Mothering, which we shall examine further in a later discussion, set out a cogent analysis of the differential development of girls and boys. In particular, Chodorow set out a plausible hypothesis of how girls develop into women who seek out the mothering role, and pass it on to their own daughters. The psychoanalytic theory in *The Reproduction of Mothering* offered second wave feminists a potent explanation to an enduring problem—why women keep mothering in a system that keeps them locked into adult roles defined by reproduction and relegated to an unequal status.[86]

In her 1989 *Feminism and Psychoanalytic Theory*, appearing near the end of the second wave, Chodorow continued to promote psychoanalytic theory as a rich resource for feminists. She observes of feminism that, "Its basic argument is that gender and sexuality, whatever the biology that helps to inform these, are created culturally and socially; they are not immutable givens. Therefore, feminism demands a theory of how we become sexed and gendered."[87] She argues that Freud gave us such a theory, one that answers the feminist desire to change the social organization and psychology of sex and gender.

By the time *Feminism and Psychoanalytic Theory* appeared, Chodorow could distinguish three feminist psychoanalytic approaches: object-relations, interpersonal, and Lacanian. Chodorow offers her own work as an example of the first approach, which emphasizes early relationships. Boys and girls experience different parenting and accordingly form differing selves with distinct experiences of gender and gender identity.[88] The interpersonal (or 'Neo-Freudian') approach is similar to the object-relations one, but emphasizes cultural learning in the development of gender qualities, with feminine qualities attributed to cultural prescription and suppression.[89] Both of these approaches separate gender personality from gender identity.[90] The Lacanian approach, named after French psychoanalyst Jacques Lacan, criticizes the other approaches as too narrow. Lacanians offer a more extreme view of the role of the unconscious and symbolic. According to this approach, language and culture are determinant of the subjectivity both men and women develop—and both genders are trapped and wounded by a sexually unequal world.[91]

As the second wave ebbed, Chodorow's recognition that "we need to talk" reflected both the divisions in and between psychoanalysts and feminists, and the continuing elusive search for an adequate feminist theory. But while the creative developments among feminists attracted to psychoanalysis was transpiring, other currents were also at play.

Feminist Science: Sandra Bem & Ann Oakley

In addition to the language and thought appropriated from women psychoanalysts, the theory and research undergirding second wave feminism owed no small measure to the work of feminist social scientists. These women, in anthropology, sociology, psychology, history and other disciplines, added important contributions, especially with reference to gender and sex.[92] Collectively, this work further eroded confidence that essentialism was as objective and factually-based as commonly believed.

In psychology, Sandra Bem would emerge as among the best-known names laboring to clarify conceptually the role of gender. In addition to her academic work, Bem offered a very public presentation of a feminist life, modeling the possibilities of an egalitarian marriage.[93] Through most of the 1970s, Bem was at Stanford University, where she conducted novel research into gender, most importantly articulating the place of androgyny and developing an instrument—the Bem Sex Role Inventory (BSRI)—that would achieve prominence as a research tool.[94] As we heard in the first discussion, 'androgyny' describes a psychological blending of characteristics attributed to masculinity and femininity.

Bem argued in contradistinction to the prevailing cultural notion that psychological health in the modern world required androgyny rather than strong endorsement of a gender stereotype. In itself, this idea was favorable to feminism. But Bem went on to point out that the dominant cultural view, which overvalued masculinity and undervalued femininity, was decidedly unhealthy. To test her hypothesis that psychologically healthy individuals would score high in both masculine and feminine psychological traits, Bem devised an inventory that had separate scales for masculinity and femininity. [95] The BSRI, in numerous studies, confirmed Bem's hypothesis—and drove another stake into what some feminists were calling the vampirism of essentialism.[96]

While Bem was investigating the consequences of gender in individual lives, British sociologist and feminist Ann Oakley was looking at large groups of people. In the 1970s, she applied the distinction between sex and gender to the study of women in capitalist societies. She argued, as had Simone de Beauvoir before her, that being a woman is not predicated merely on biological sex. Oakley agrees it is a fact that every person born is a 'sexed' individual. But, she argues, the making of men and women is a socialized task. Gender is learned, she contends, and the teachers are parents and others who instruct children. This 'gender socialization' occurs via manipulation (selective rewarding or discouraging of gender-typed behavior), canalization (channeling children's interest toward gender-approved objects and activities), and verbalization (language labeling to reinforce gender identity). However, the process is culturally variant; masculinity and femininity are variously construed and constructed around the world.[97] The essentialist assumption that sex reliably directs gender in transcultural paths is thus sharply challenged.

The Multidisciplinary/Interdisciplinary Nature of Feminist Work

Second wave feminism drew energy from multiple fountains. An abiding characteristic of its feminist scholarship has been a multidisciplinary and interdisciplinary nature. This trait was evident early in the second wave, for example, in the work of anthropologist Gayle Rubin. Her groundbreaking 1975 essay, "The Traffic of Women," draws upon sources as diverse as Marxism, Levi-Strauss, and a Lacanian reading of psychoanalysis—all oriented around the role trafficking of women has played in human history.[98] As Rubin recounts, the confluence of her readings while a student at the University of Michigan, prompted by the need to write a paper for a course, produced the seeds of the essay.[99]

Rubin was not the only woman in academia looking for help from multiple sources. The lens of gender facilitated the organization not only of ideas from many varying disciplines, but also ultimately of a new way to engage in study: Women's Studies.[100] The formal academic study of gender that emerged in the late 1960s, write sociologist Jane Pilcher and Women's Studies scholar Imelda Whelehan, was birthed in the 'second wave of feminism.'[101] The conversation on gender now worked a transformation on higher education as women's voices insisted on being heard among the masculine chorus.

Women's Studies, Men's Studies, and Gender Studies

The second wave feminist movement had its academic counterpart in Women's Studies. The success of this development was not without controversy and sparked a countermovement, which also inspired efforts for a counterpart in formal Men's Studies. But the Men's Movement, smaller and perhaps less diverse than the Women's Movement, also had less impact, if only because men largely remained in power despite the gains of feminists. Because men were already at the top of the gender hierarchy, the movement aroused some suspicion whether it presented itself as supportive of feminism or opposed to it. And there were at least three branches to the movement, one embracing the feminist indictment of masculine privilege, another choosing to celebrate masculinity, and a third embracing masculinity within a specific conservative religious sensibility.[102]

Eventually, the academic study of both men and women came increasingly to be embraced under a single generic label: Gender Studies. Political scholar Chris Beasley, with an attention to the issue of power in conversing about gender, points out this shift to a supposed neutral position is seen by some as a covert operation to deflect attention from the continuing subordinate role of women in the gender hierarchy. Others respond that even under this designation there is often more attention given to women than to men. Yet others worry that the development excludes other gender realities and thus reinforces an inadequate cultural system. In short, notes Beasley, many folk are not satisfied with the label 'Gender Studies.'[103]

'Third Wave Feminism' and Gender

Ironically, the very success of second wave feminism in establishing Women's Studies contributed to a new group of feminists critical of their forebears. Pilcher and Whelehan describe 'third wave feminism,' which emerged at the end of the 20th century and beginning of the 21st century, in this manner:

> Third wave feminists seem to largely be women who have grown up massively influenced by feminism, possibly with feminist mothers and relations, and accustomed to the existence of women's studies courses as the norm as well as academic interrogations of race and class.[104]

This new generation of feminists may still attend to gender, but it no longer has preeminence—even as an identity marker. As third wave feminist Carol Sorisio puts it, "Perceiving gender as the primary identity marker led many scholars to ignore race, class, and cultural differences that are not incidental but absolutely essential to feminism."[105] When gender is examined it reflects the shift in the gender conversation advanced by second wave feminism.

English scholar Sara Mills characterizes the feminist linguistics of 'third wave feminism' as concerned with developing an "anti-essentialist analysis of gender and language, whilst being keenly aware of the force of institutional and societal pressures on women and their resistances to those pressures."[106] One consequence of this, she continues, has been a focus on the 'performative' nature of gendered identity. This focus invites us to return to our investigation of challenges to essentialism.

Social Constructionism

Let us for a moment reprise a basic point: views of human nature roughly divide into two along the answer to the question whether our nature is *essential*, a given of Nature, or *existential*, something constructed. Similarly, views of gender tend to either see it as something fixed and autonomous, or as something flexible and dependent. Sometimes these groups are labeled, respectively, as 'essentialists' and 'social constructionists.' The former view is the older, and perhaps remains the most popular among the masses. The latter has been more accepted among social scientists, particularly those who specialize in the study of gender and who are more aware than most people of the limitations and social consequences of the essentialist position.[107]

The *social constructionist* approach to gender most immediately dates to the period since the early 1970s, when it offered feminists an alternative to psycho-analytic ideas, but the theory itself has deeper roots. Sociologist Liam O'Dowd, in tracing the origin and development of today's social constructionism, notes it has antecedents in earlier work such as the theories of sociologists Emile Durkheim and Max Weber, and the philosophy of Karl Marx. Even more pertinent is the influence of the phenomenological approach of such American social scientists as William I. Thomas, George Herbert Meade, and Erving Goffmann. Post-structuralists like Michel Foucault, so influential in rethinking human sexuality, also have played a role.[108] Suiting these diverse roots, contemporary social constructionism is best conceived as, in the words of Mary and Kenneth Gergen, "an unfolding dialogue among participants who vary considerably in their logics, values, and visions."[109]

Despite their differences, though, they adhere to several common core convictions and a general sense of what they mean by 'gender' is not hard to obtain. Sociologist Stevi Jackson, a leading proponent of social constructionism, together with Sue Scott, succinctly states the conception of gender according to this approach:

> Gender as we define it denotes a hierarchical division between women and men embedded in both social institutions and social practices. Gender is thus a social structural phenomenon but is also produced, negotiated and sustained at the level of everyday interaction. . . . Gender thus encompasses the social division and cultural distinction between women and men as well as the characteristics commonly associated with femininity and masculinity.[110]

With reference to the conversation on gender, social constructionism has come to play a major role, both in its critique of essentialism and in putting forward an alternative. Let us highlight a view of the key ideas with respect to gender as viewed differently by these competing approaches:

❑ Essentialists posit an *independent reality* for gender; social constructionists view it as a *culturally conditioned, socially modified contingent set of ideas that guide behavior.*

❑ Essentialists locate human gender in an *innate biological reality*: sex. Social constructionists dispute an innate sense of gender and contend *even sex itself is a social construction.*

❑ Essentialists view gender as *separable from and prior to the influence of culture*, where social constructionists argue *it cannot be abstracted* from its wider context of social relations, which also include such matters as race, class divisions, and sexuality.

❑ Where essentialists favor evidence that purports to show *universals* for men and women across cultures or linked uniformly to one or the other gender, social constructionists favor evidence that purports to show *variations* among cultures or among members of the same gender.

Social constructionism supports the feminist critique of essentialism. But it is not only feminists who embrace it. Many social scientists, whether men or women, feminists or not, see in it a more rational and factual articulation of gender. In successfully conceptualizing gender as something built and conducted within a complex set of social relations, it seems increasingly less plausible to imagine gender as something we simply *have* as an inalienable possession. The dynamic flexibility of the personal actor within a particular social matrix highlights the manifold possibilities for gender. Those possibilities are taken in new directions by another approach: queer theory.

Queer Theory

The first thing most of us are struck by is the name. 'Queer' is a term associated with a history of pejorative use against homosexuals.[111] Beasley attributes the formal introduction of the term into theoretical discussion with its use by Teresa de Lauretis in the then young journal *differences* in 1991.[112] Although this is generally accepted as marking the first labeling of the theory, the use of the term as a deliberate, proud, and rebellious identity marker had been occurring at least since the mid-1980s.[113] As Beasley aptly notes, the use of the term has not met with universal favor, even by some who otherwise concur with the theoretical ideas. Queer theory is an unabashedly in-your-face approach to gender.

GenderPAC[114] founder Riki Wilchins acknowledges the activist nature of queer theory in stating, "Queer theory is at heart about politics—things like power and identity, language, and difference."[115] But it is about politics in a decidedly distinctive way—as historian David Halperin puts it, "Queer is by definition *whatever* is at odds with the normal, the legitimate, the dominant."[116] Despite this expansiveness in principle, in practice the term and the emphasis has been with respect to sexuality and gender. To be 'queer' is to engage a political identity defending identities marginalized by society: gays, lesbians, transgender people, and others.

While 'queer' today is sometimes used even in academic materials to refer strictly to people with a homosexual orientation, in our dialog we will use it in its larger sense, with application to those whose sex, sexuality, and/or gender put them in a non-normative group—what are commonly called 'sexual minorities.' As for 'queer theory,' we shall accept its dynamic and flexible character, and not attempt a further definition.

We can, however, note some salient characteristics. Queer theory is heavily indebted to the thinking of Michel Foucault about sexuality.[117] Foucault regards the conversation about sexuality as intimately connected to the power structures of modern societies. Sciences of sexuality control the language of our discourse about sex, sexuality, and gender. Having made these things objects of study, these sciences create categories, norms, and expectations—all of which are internalized by people. These resulting 'identities' are not natural—though they may feel that way to those who have thoroughly internalized them—but are constructed and controlling. Not only normative identities, such as 'heterosexual' or 'masculine' and 'feminine' are constructed by social powers, but so also are non-normative identities like 'homosexual' or 'transgender.' As such, these identities can be deconstructed, their controlling power challenged and broken. Queer theory intends to do exactly that. It aims to take the 'essence' out of all 'identities' and resist the controlling social powers so insistent on making us embrace one or another identity.

Foucault concerns himself primarily with sexualities. Since our dialog is about gender, we must turn to a theorist who advances that part of the conversation. One such individual is Judith Butler, a philosopher indebted to Foucault who has gained renown for her ideas about gender.

Judith Butler and Gender 'Performativity'

While acknowledging her connection and contributions to queer theory, the label is not primary to Butler's own identification; her first allegiance is to feminism. Nevertheless, her ideas about gender arguably are the most influential of any of the theorists of any of the approaches considered in this discussion. We must accordingly take time to become acquainted with her most distinctive idea: *performativity*.

Like many recent writers on gender, Butler opposes essentialism and starts from a critique of its assumptions. She argues that we got off on the wrong foot when we made the decision that gender *is*—in other words, that gender exists as a real and fixed attribute. In fact, she contends, in the way our Western culture has come to embrace it gender fits into the middle of a linkage between biology and desire. Biological, dimorphic sex permits only two sex outcomes: male and female. These in turn generate only two possible genders: masculine and feminine. With only two possibilities, desire is 'naturally' the attraction of one for its opposite. This whole conception, says Butler, is wrongheaded. [118]

Butler poses some questions we may find hard to answer—if for no other reason than because we have never thought of them before. She asks:

> Is there 'a' gender which persons are said *to have*, or is it an essential attribute that a person is said *to be*, as implied in the question 'What gender are you?'? . . . If gender is constructed, could it be constructed differently, or does its constructedness imply some form of social determinism, foreclosing the possibility of agency and transformation? Does 'construction' suggest that certain laws generate gender differences along universal axes of sexual difference? How and where does the construction of gender take place? . . . When the rele-

vant 'culture' that 'constructs' gender is understood in terms of such a law or set of laws, then it seems that gender is as determined and fixed as it was under the biology-is-destiny formulation. In such a case, not biology, but culture, becomes destiny. [119]

In fact, Butler contends, gender is *not* fixed and no matter how much contemporary culture might picture it as an essential and natural attribute, it is actually socially constructed and can change. Instead of gender-as-destiny, Butler describes gender-as-performative. Better put, gender is something we *do* rather than something we *have*. It is 'performative' in that *it makes what it names*, rather than being the result of a fixed identity. Gender is constructed relation; it unfolds in real relationships in specific contexts. Rather than being fixed, gender is fluid. 'Masculine' and 'feminine' are not fixed poles.

But if this is the case, why do so many of us feel strongly that our gender *is* fixed? Butler has an answer. She argues that "the performance of gender creates the illusion of prior substantiality—a core gendered self."[120] For most of us, performativity of gender seems seamlessly constant and fixed. We thus conclude that we *are* rather than we *do* and ignore evidence to the contrary (i.e., all the small instances where we perform in ways stereotypically associated with a gender different than the one we identify with).

Because gender is socially constructed, we all play roles. Gender performativity and performance are inevitable, but the part we play is not. Biology is *not* destiny. Most of us occupy a conventional masculine or feminine role; some of us do not. Once we understand that gender is performative art rather than predestined, perhaps our individual identities can have the freedom to find the expression most suitable for them.

Or can we? Butler cautions us against viewing the matter purely as one of individual choice and invention. "Performativity," she says, "is a matter of reiterating or repeating the norms by which one is constituted; it is not a radical fabrication of a gendered self."[121] Society presents us with gender scripts, which read well bring social approval, though within whatever box is reserved for the gender group we belong to, *and* provided that group fits our natal assignment. We can choose to reject the script and attempt to write our own, but social scripts are normative—they set a standard against which all other choices and constructions are judged. Though gender may be a masquerade, we switch from our assigned mask at our own risk. Nowhere is that risk greater than when we dare to depart in public fashion from the identity and role expected of us—a risk looked at more closely in later chapters.

Conclusion

In this brief and general survey our story has moved from a perhaps naïve assumption that gender follows natural and inevitably from sex, to a contention that its socially constructed, to a more rebellious declaration that whether biologically constructed or socially constructed, any identity is something we do rather than have. Quite clearly, the conversation on gender has undergone numerous twists and turns, especially since the late 1960s. Essentialism, once virtually unquestioned, has experienced sharp attack in the last few decades. Second wave feminists capitalized on cracks in the theory, perhaps especially those visible as a consequence of the medicalization of sex. Their critique was aided in some cases by the appropriation of ideas from psychoanalysis. It was bolstered, too, by social science research. The success experienced in introducing Women's Studies, Men's Studies, and Gender Studies into formal academic curricula helped spread ideas and further them. Alternative theoretical approaches like social constructionism and queer theory added new flavor—and controversy—to the conversation.

Always, it seems, at the center of debate remains the issue with which we entered this dialog: the question of the relation of sex and gender. We must now give that matter our full attention.

Chapter 3

Sex & Gender

Introduction: We began this dialog by considering some of the vocabulary of the language used in conversing about gender. We must begin here by reminding ourselves that sex and gender are terms that in casual conversation tend to be used interchangeably. We will do well to be more careful.

Sex properly refers to the typing of the body based on anatomical presentation as presumably related to reproductive function. Thus, whatever the genetic code, if a body at birth looks like it will eventually provide semen it is sex-typed male; otherwise it is sex-typed female. Judging the difference in bodies is not always easy, but it is always *phallocentric*—determining, typically by length and appearance, whether the phallus is a penis or a clitoris.

Our culture recognizes only two sexes. Thus those born with an apparent mix of male and female characteristics, or ambiguous genitalia, pose a problem. Once called hermaphrodites, such individuals are now termed *intersexed*. The cultural insistence on pairing two sexes with two genders means that intersex individuals are assigned to one or another sex and its paired gender. The default option historically has been female-and-girl. While this assignment sometimes works out, sometimes it doesn't—and the latter cases show vividly the problem of too narrow a sex and gender scheme.

Male bodies are expected to produce masculine boys and men; female bodies are expected to produce feminine girls and women. The key word is 'expected': once assigned a gender we are raised with the *expectation* of conformity in personal experience and social presentation to what is believed to be appropriate for the experiences and characteristics of a particular sex. Most of the time this arrangement works out. When it doesn't, problems abound for the individual. Today societies like our own are facing increased pressure to be more realistic about the actual variety in gender experience and expression found in the world.

Despite our culture positing a binary system pairing anatomical sex with gender in a predictable fashion, nature produces astounding *variation* in sex, gender, and the ways they interact. Though both sex and gender separately raise issues, the larger problem lies with the modern construction of gender. The contemporary Western view has created more problems than it has solved by insisting on only two genders. We need a more robust view.

A Difference That Makes a Difference

In the mid-1990s, gender scholar Gerda Siann opened her book, *Gender, Sex and Sexuality: Contemporary Psychological Perspectives*, by offering a candid, if rather chilling observation: "It has taken psychologists a long time to realize the importance of drawing a distinction between sex and gender, and even longer to pay sufficient attention to the significance of drawing this distinction."[122]

We began our dialog by attending to some of the basic vocabulary attending the contemporary conversation on gender. We made some reference to the word sex, mostly to make the point it is not identical with gender, but left until now a more sustained examination. It may seem tiresome to keep coming back to the distinction between sex and gender. Yet, as Siann pointed out, even our scientists have been slow to see why it matters at all, let alone matters so much. In that light, we need to be absolutely sure we get why the distinction matters— and, of course, its actual dimensions. This is a topic we will revisit often.

Let's start by returning a moment to where most of us were when we entered this dialog—not having thought too much about the nature of gender, casually interchanging the vocabulary of sex and gender, and assuming that whatever difference there might be is not that pronounced because sex predicts and dictates gender. Yet we soon found that neither the idea of sex, nor that of gender, is as straightforward as we had supposed, or might desire. Hopefully, a positive sense of uneasiness set in, and even now persists, as we wonder about this matter. We will be doing well if we are asking questions like these:

- ❑ Is our society's ease with how it understands sex and gender merited?
- ❑ Does our society really comprehend either in a way that warrants what seems to happen—raising our beliefs to the position of universal truth?
- ❑ Are the modern assumptions of *only* two sexes and *only* two genders empirically established, or a socially limited and inadequate construction?
- ❑ Is gender itself a modern social construct, or is it an accurate and adequate label for an objective, essential reality?

These questions matter immensely in a culture where gender is so central to the sense of self and functions so critically in structuring and guiding social relations. While these things affect all of us, they especially impact those of us who do not fit within the two options our culture sanctions. We have a moral obligation to ask if the judgments that come so easy within the framework we were raised with are warranted. Does it arrogate to itself an authority unwarranted by the facts? Many important questions occupy contemporary scholars and they must also busy our minds if we are to be honest with our subject matter.

'Sex'

What is sex? The subject is one endlessly fascinating for most of us. We use the word often and in a variety of contexts. We probably feel quite confident in our use, believing we know what it means. Nevertheless, because the term is important and because people use it in different ways, we need to take a moment to define it. But before we do, let's be clear about what sex is *not*. Sex is *not* the same as gender. Sex is *not* the same as sexuality. In this dialog it does not refer to sexual activities, though that is a common, popular use of the word.[123] Although most of us are often sloppy in our use of language, we need here to clear some space and see our terms precisely.

Defining 'Sex'

For our dialog the term sex will be used in a manner conforming to general academic usage. We may or may not conclude that the usual and customary understanding of sex needs changing. But even if we decide it does, such change will lack relevance without first understanding what it has been changed from. Since the purpose of our dialog is to comprehend gender, we will not reoccupy ourselves with making a change in the usual and customary sense of sex as used by social scientists. What we will do is adopt a utilitarian definition reflecting as best we can what science knows at this point and how that is actually used. In those twin respects, sex refers to *anatomical presentations presumably related to reproductive capacity*. [124] This definition roots itself in biology ('anatomy,' 'reproductive capacity'), but as it is importantly modified by environmental factors, such as the influence of culture on observers' judgments ('presentations,' 'presumably related').[125]

Secondary Vocabulary

Two allied terms are 'sexuality' and 'sexology.' Both terms are much broader than the word sex. Both also involve personal and social dimensions as well as biological ones. For our dialog, *sexuality* refers to "attitudes, beliefs and behaviors organized around and with respect to sex." We should have no objection if the clause "and gender" is added at the end because attitudes, belief, and behaviors organized around and with respect to gender are commonly considered alongside those about sex. *Sexology* is the study of these matters. A sexologist may belong to a discipline such as psychiatry or psychology, sociology or anthropology, or some other academic discipline, but focuses that discipline on researching and understanding sexuality.

Genetic Sex

We may say that *sex begins with biology*, though it does not end there. At a fundamental level sex is a matter of genetic coding. The karyotype[126] for a generic male is 46, XY; for a generic female it is 46, XX. The genetic coding guides the eventual anatomical display, but in itself does not ensure for sexual organs that all 46, XX females will look anatomically alike and all 46, XY males will present anatomically the same. Between genotype (genetic potential) and phenotype (realized presentation) are many intervening variables. For example, SRY (sex-determining region Y) is a specific gene on the Y chromosome that triggers critical events leading to the sex characteristics associated with being male. Later, there are specific hormonal influences that further shape ongoing development. However, despite all this rich biological background, when we talk about the sex of people we are not typically referring to their karyotype or prenatal sex development, but to their anatomical presentation at birth, and specifically those anatomical parts associated with reproduction.

Apparent Sex

We each have a body that displays certain physical characteristics associated with reproduction. These include body parts such as the breasts, penis, testes, clitoris, labia, vagina, and ovaries—some of which clearly are not directly related to reproduction. Those body parts visible for inspection in the newborn—the genitals—such as the penis or labia, are conventionally relied upon in making an assignment of sex that, contrary to logic, is relied on throughout life in social situations calling for identification. It matters little whether the observed anatomical parts accurately represent reproductive ability; they serve to separate individuals. In our culture only two such camps—male and female—are recognized and socially sanctioned. Thus, all newborns are assigned one or the other sex status on the assumption of a particular future reproductive role, whether they will ever play that role or not. From birth forward, genital anatomy is used as the basis of sex assignment and sexual expectations.

Superficially, at least, the arrangement seems to make sense and to work. Certain body parts seem generally mutually exclusive. Someone who appears to have a penis and testes is presumed not to have ovaries; someone with a clitoris and labia is presumed not to possess testes. Where unexpected mixing of genital features occurs the presumption is that a 'mistake' is present which calls for medical intervention to 'correct.' A common standard has been visible inspection of the penis or clitoris, with length determining sex assignment. Once a determination has been made medical interventions such as surgery are used to adjust genital appearance for better conformity to the cultural expectations. As a general rule, ambiguous cases are assigned to the sex status female.

A Critique of 'Sex'

With a moment's reflection on these matters we might find it remarkable how easily we accept the idea of two mutually exclusive sexes. The cultural conception of sex depends on premises that seem rather dubious. Especially critical to sustaining this scheme are the following notions:
- ❏ Sex is about reproductive biology.
- ❏ The essential and central purpose of sexuality is reproduction.

❑ Only two anatomical sex representations are natural.

Each needs further examination.

Even the little we have considered thus far should indicate that sex is about more than just reproductive biology. Although the sexual body provides a foundation, upon that foundation is constructed an elaborate set of *beliefs* about that body. One such belief in our culture, fundamental to the others, is that only two kinds of sexual bodies are possible. We see all bodies as if they represent 46, XX or 46, XY karyotypes. Of course, throughout human history what people have had available to rely on in coding babies with respect to reproductive anatomy was visible inspection. The understanding of human genetics is still in its infancy. The contemporary realization that genetic differences might really matter in a way calling into questions such a neat and simple division as historically practiced is only slowly gaining hold.

For practical purposes we tend to ignore the importance of atypical karyotypes such those with extra X chromosomes associated with maleness (e.g. XXY, XXXY, or XXXXY), or those X chromosome differences associated with femaleness (e.g. X, XXX, XXXX, or XXXXX)—except to the degree these differences result in anatomically different presentations and impact reproductive ability. A male whose karyotype features more than a single X is still grouped along with generic XY males because the genital presentation, though generally judged 'underdeveloped' is still more like an XY person than an XX one. Though typically sterile, these males still *appear* reproductively capable—and that is enough for sorting purposes.

What emerges, then, is that *presentation* matters preeminently. Although the rubric used is that the genitalia appear capable of reproductive functioning, what truly matters is that the genitalia serve to place the individual into one or another of two camps. Thus biology matters, but the eye of the perceiver of that biology matters more. The reason sex-based differences are important lies not in intrinsic biological differentiation, real as it may be, but in the uses put to such differences. As philosopher Moira Gatens observes, "the male body and the female body have quite different social value and significance"[127]— valuations that both underscore the priority placed on anatomical presentations and that then shape gender expectations to keep people in their respective places at their respective poles.

As it presently exists in our culture, the justification for this binary system where only two sexes are recognized depends on the belief that what matters most about sex is reproduction and reproduction requires two different contributions (sperm and ovum). Since only two contributions are needed, and since each contribution comes from a person whose body is different and accommodates the meeting of sperm and egg, any further category for sex is superfluous. What presumably matters is only that one sex desires the other so that they sexually join. Therefore, only male (contributor of sperm via testes and penis) and female (contributor of ovum via ovaries and vagina)—and heterosexuality (the 'natural' desire between male and female)—are needed.[128]

Again, at first blush this premise seems entirely plausible. The human species depends on the sexual contributions of sperm and ovum to share genetic material and create new members. We do not reproduce asexually. Although technology allows for fertilization outside the context of sexual intercourse, it remains true that one person contributes sperm and another an egg, and that these parties look anatomically different. Without reproduction the species ends.

However, as English sociologist and sexologist Myra Hird points out, nonlinear biology shows us how ridiculously narrow our conception of reproduction can be even from a biological standpoint. As Hird observes, "the *vast* majority of cells in human bodies are intersex . . . . *Most* of the reproduction that we undertake in our lifetimes has nothing to do with 'sex.'" In fact, as she lists them, reproduction can occur by recombination of DNA strands, merging, meiosis, or mitosis. "Moreover," she says, "there is no linear relationship between sexual dimorphism and sexual reproduction." After all, in a number of species males can become pregnant, or the animals can be both sexes either simultaneously or sequentially.[129]

We need also to recognize that most sexual behaviors and activity prove nonreproductive in nature. Indeed, as biologist Joan Roughgarden observes, if we are to judge the success of sexual intercourse as a reproductive mechanism, its high failure rate (more than 100 couplings per conception) would compel us to see it as remarkably inefficient.[130] But then, many of us don't want conception. In fact, many of us go to some lengths to prevent it. Some of us intentionally avoid reproduction our entire lives—without foregoing sexual activity.

Inarguably, sexual activity is widely regarded as a pleasurable and meaningful activity in its own right. It is almost certainly pursued in solitary masturbation more often than in pair couplings. When intercourse does occur it often is for nonreproductive reasons, such as relationship building or the shared pleasure of genital contact.[131] Logically, in terms of actual sexual practice and the motivations involved, it is implausible to claim reproduction as either essential or central—which calls into doubt, too, the notion that only heterosexual desire is 'normal.' Reproduction may be required for human species propagation, but it is a small part of sex.

We need to put the matter the other way around: sex is essential and central to reproduction. From a logical standpoint there is no necessity to posit reproduction as a justification for assigning human beings to one or the other of two sexes. Not only is reproduction neither essential nor central to sex, the supposed pairing of anatomical presentation to reproductive capacity is spurious. Some of us look capable of reproduction but aren't; some of us look dubious in reproductive ability but prove capable. Any way it is examined the idea that reproduction should be seen as key to sex determination proves flawed and inadequate.

This recognition leads us to reconsider the third proposition. In a system where reproduction is inaccurately made central, it is of no surprise that anything that raises doubt about reproductive ability should be seen as 'unnatural,' or 'defective.' Logically, though, it is not only unnecessary that all of us be able to reproduce, it is not even in our species' best interest that all of us who can should actually do so. In short, reproduction matters more at a species level than at an individual level. Moreover, because species survival depends on variability—Nature's way of hedging the odds in a world where environments change—it is logically natural for many variations to occur that prove nonreproductive. These are neither 'unnatural' nor 'mistakes.' That is why we are better off speaking of 'generic' and 'atypical' or 'different' presentations than the current value-laden choices 'natural' and 'defective,' or 'normal' and 'abnormal.'

Sex and Intersex

Our rigidly binary system is challenged both by reason and by evidence. Clearly there are individuals born whose genital presentation makes easy placement as male or female impossible. Once called hermaphrodites, sometimes referred to as *androgynes* (or androgynous in its pre-1970s use), those of us with such a presentation are now termed intersexed. Unfortunately, that term retains the notion of two sexes with some folk in-between. Our allegiance to binary thinking has meant any of us in-between must be moved one direction or the other. Since sex coding starts at birth, none of us gets a choice in the matter. Others make the decision.

Phallocentric Perspective

In our culture this is done at birth and is one of the prerogatives of the medical profession. The presiding medical official makes this life-defining judgment based principally on a single visual cue: the presence or absence of a penis.[132] This phallocentric perspective itself reflects a gendered view of the priority of the sexes. A large phallus (penis) is better than a small phallus (clitoris). Unless a phallus is clearly large enough to qualify as a penis, the bearer must be assigned status as a female. Size matters. A child with a penis is labeled male and comes under the immediate weight of social gender expectations that he be perceived and act as masculine. Absent any obvious penis the designation is female, with the expectation of perceptions and actions corresponding to a feminine gender identity and role.

But what seems easy enough to do at birth with a naked neonate becomes problematic later. We do not rely on the nude presentation of genitalia to tell us the sex of a person. Instead, we rely on gender. That, in turn, relies on physical cues as diverse as size, shape, and absence or presence of physical features like hair on the face or visible breasts. Still, our judgments are based on cues that only are partially about anatomy. Our cues also include behavioral expectations (such as manner of dress) for each gender stemming from culture. In fact, we can often be quite crass in how we utilize such cues, especially when we make physical ones primary. Consider, for example, the not-so-long-ago practice Anne Fausto-Sterling reminds us about: "Until 1968 female Olympic competitors were often asked to parade naked in front of a board of examiners. Breasts and a vagina were all one needed to certify one's femininity." [133]

This might seem charmingly naïve if it weren't so patently offensive. As Fausto-Sterling accurately points out:

> Our bodies are too complex to provide clear-cut answers about sexual difference. The more we look for a simple physical basis for 'sex,' the more it becomes clear that 'sex' is not a pure physical category. What bodily signals and functions we define as male or female come already entangled in our ideas about gender. [134]

A striking illustration of this is provided by what happens to intersex neonates (babies formerly termed true- or pseudo- 'hermaphrodites'), As Alice Dreger, a scholar in medical humanities and medical ethics, documents, genital ambiguity has been viewed as a social danger for a long time. Any uncertainty in sexual designation has been imagined to produce all sorts of disorder—not merely in the individual, but for the society. Hence, an immense pressure is exerted to define each individual according to a 'one body—one sex' rule, where the only allowable options are male or female. Science, like the culture at large, finds it difficult to tolerate challenges to this rule.[135]

Like most people, physicians who work with intersex infants generally resist ambiguity. Instead, adhering to the cultural insistence on two distinct sexes, they make observations and decisions meant to reinforce a black-and-white schema where the empirical reality is gray. Dreger observes how the births of such infants are typically treated as an emergency, with strict protocols calling for a sex-determination within 48 hours. If this means invasive surgery (e.g., clitorectomy), then so be it. The rationale is that prompt action prevents later confusion over the individual's sexual and gender identity. [136]

Sex Assignment Guidelines

Psychiatrist Susan Bradley and colleagues, writing in *Pediatrics*, summarize the guidelines for sex and gender assignment as including three important considerations:

- ❑ Sex appearance of normality, with the best prognosis for sexual functioning including reproduction should be balanced with an assignment carrying the best hope for stable gender identity.
- ❑ Any decision on sex reassignment is better made sooner than later, and certainly by age 2 years old.
- ❑ Parental and professional ambiguity as well as uncertainty over the decision should be minimized.[137]

The guidelines reflect the cultural judgment that sex determines gender. In our culture, such a complex of concerns surrounding ambiguity of sex is most easily resolved by assignment of gender to match the *most apparent* sex, with a presumption as to what appears male as the basic yardstick. The determination is then later buttressed with medical modifications and hormonal supplements to heighten the apparent match, together with any other support needed.

Psychologist Suzanne Kessler, in her book *Lessons from the Intersexed*, concurs that cultural factors weigh heavily. She charges that medical teams working on such cases follow "standard practices for managing intersexuality, which rely ultimately on cultural understandings of gender." [138]

In fact, Kessler notes:

> [P]hysicians who handle cases of intersexed infants consider several factors besides biological ones in determining, assigning, and announcing the gender of a particular infant. Indeed, biological factors are often preempted in physicians' deliberations by such cultural factors as the 'correct' length of the penis and capacity of the vagina. . . .

Moreover, in the face of apparently incontrovertible evidence—infants born with some combination of female and male reproductive and sexual features—physicians hold an incorrigible belief that female and male are the only 'natural' options. [139]

If even professionals find it hard to rise beyond cultural conventions, how can we reasonably hope the rest of us will do so? Moreover, we ought to pause and ask ourselves what purpose is served by the official and legal sex identification made at birth. Attorney Martine Rothblatt, Vice-Chair of the Bioethics Subcommittee of the International Bar Association, argues that the immediate categorization at birth of an individual as either male or female constitutes a form of sexual segregation that should raise the specter of apartheid. Her contention is that such legal categorization, the basis of binary gender assignments, is as wrong as the legal division into races. [140] All our ordinary practice does is confirm an erroneous, limiting, and ultimately harmful view of sex and gender.

Fortunately, the above situation shows signs of changing. Intersex people have been vigorous in giving voice to their concerns about such practices. Slowly, the medical community has begun to listen. What do intersex people want? The Intersex Initiative says:

> We are working to replace the current model of intersex treatment based on concealment with a patient-centered alternative. We are not saying that intersex babies are better off left alone; we want there to be social and psychological support for both the parents and intersex children so that they can deal with social difficulties resulting from being different than others. In the long-term, we hope to remove those social barriers through education and raising awareness. [141]

The Intersex Initiative, observing that sexual anatomy does not determine gender identity, advocates that while a child be assigned a gender based on a 'best prediction' of eventual gender identity, that irreversible surgeries be avoided and that the child, when old enough, be permitted gender self-determination. [142] Not all intersex people feel comfortable being included under the gender umbrella of transgender, but like other realities described as transgender, intersex forces us to rethink what we often presume to know. The success of intersex individuals in persuading many medical professionals to rethink their practices is an encouraging sign for all of us.

Let us be honest with the evidence: we do not have to accept a limited, inadequate and inaccurate scheme regarding sex. The ancients wisely espoused the notion that *Natura non facit salut* ('Nature makes no leaps'). Our own senses confirm that in myriad ways: we range in gradations of height, hair and eye color, and so forth. None of suggests that all people have to be one of only two heights or two hair colors. Even with eye color, where we commonly group people as blue-eyed or brown-eyed, we still easily recognize gradations so that a range of color is apparent to us. Why should Nature depart from this practice in matters of sex?

The objection might be raised that eye color and reproductive ability are hardly on a par since the latter is essential to species survival. Perhaps Nature constrains and simplifies matters in the interest of reproduction. Appealing as the idea is, reproduction is a far messier matter in reality. Many individuals are infertile, a substantial percentage of conceptions never come to term, and more than 1-in-2,000 live births are visibly intersex. Either Nature is highly inefficient in maintaining a binary system, or the idea of gradations has more merit than commonly granted. The better question is not why 'abnormalities' occur, but what purposes might be served by gradations along the sex continuum, including those grades where infertility results.

While this subject merits a lengthier treatment, we shall have to content ourselves with what we have: grounds for reasonable suspicion at least, if not also sufficient warrant for rejecting the present cultural myopia about sex. A strict binary system of sex designation does not well fit human experience. Because a rigid insistence on it has important personal and social consequences for members of our culture—and those in other cultures subject to our imposition of it on them—we should consider ourselves ethically bound to rethink this matter. We are in desperate need of a better conceptual scheme and more robust vocabulary.

Reconsidering Gender

Unfortunately, because gender is pinned to sex, problems with the latter mean difficulties for the former. The first and perhaps most common difficulty arises from making the terms sex and gender synonyms. As we noted earlier, this most frequently occurs with the use of the words male and female to refer both to sex and to gender. We can accept some relationship exists between sex and gender, but we must be careful not to blur the lines separating them lest we confuse ourselves. By keeping their boundaries in view we may be able to see each distinctly and better formulate how they relate to one another.

In a very real sense, as we have discussed briefly before, defining gender depends on conceiving its difference from and relation to sex. Let us remind ourselves that while gender represents a sorting into kinds, and that sorting ostensibly is based on sex, neither sex nor gender are purely matters of biology. *Whereas sex is a term principally rooted in biology but mediated by personal and social beliefs, gender is a term principally rooted in personal and social beliefs but mediated by biology.* There is a difference in emphasis, but both sex and gender incorporate body and mind, biological and socio-psychological dimensions. More and more, scientists are concurring on this idea while debating how it works itself out.

In our culture, because there are conceived two opposing sexes there are conceived two opposing genders. The oppositional quality we posit them lends to the impression that the pairing of a certain sex with a particular gender is fixed and invariable. If not, the quality of opposition is undermined.[143] Of course, in reality we know things are not so starkly divided and rigidly paired.

In real-world parlance we accept that *both* masculinity and femininity exist to some degree in all of us. Moreover, as we remarked earlier, we may even further distinguish kinds or types within a gender. There is a difference, for example, between dominant and subordinate masculinities; at any given time in a society's history a particular form of masculinity may be prized above others.[144] We also generally have a sense that gender in any of us is comprised of multiple interacting factors, with individual variations in intensity, quality, and degree of influence. In short, with a little reflection we see that gender is not a simple matter for anybody.

A Critique of 'Gender'

Although our culture recognizes two genders, they are hardly equal. The genders exist in a hierarchy with masculinity occupying the superior position.[145] So *androcentric* (man-centered) is Western culture that masculinity is really the only gender that matters; femininity exists as that which masculinity is not—a logic that obviates the need for other gender alternatives.[146] Sex historian Vern Bullough puts the matter neatly when he writes, "Femininity . . . has been a catchall category for all those characteristics males have not claimed as their own."[147]

Our critique of gender must start from awareness of this disparity. When we see that femininity is construed as non-masculinity it becomes easier to recognize that much more than body sex is at work in constructing gender. Biologist Anne Fausto-Sterling remarks that, "labeling someone a man or a woman is a social decision."[148] She points out that scientific knowledge may be appealed to but *belief* is what proves determinative. Specifically, it is our beliefs about gender that lead us to identify a person as a boy, girl, man, or woman. We *believe* that being in the body of one sex should and does generate a certain kind of experience different from that for bodies of the opposite sex—a 'men are from Mars and women are from Venus' approach. We further *believe* that these presumed differences produce presentational differences. Boys act differently from girls; men act differently from women. Moreover, we believe they *must* act differently because of the sex of their bodies. Anatomical genitalia are thus accorded the power to determine gender experience and guide gender presentation.

Such beliefs generate consequences. Though gender is viewed as arising predictably from sex differences, it nevertheless must be proved. In this respect it is different from sex and carries a weightier load. As Vern and Bonnie Bullough cogently point out, "Gender . . . is an achieved status rather than an ascribed biological characteristic and is based on tasks performed and the significance of clothing as well as anatomical and other factors." [149] The presumed sex-based gender experience must be concretely demonstrated. It is not enough to have the body of a male—you must act like a man. The way a man (or woman) acts is itself prescribed, always along the lines believed 'natural' for a particular sexed body. In its presentational aspect gender relies on a number of cues—representational symbols (e.g., clothes) and behaviors. Cues are used both to guide and manifest our sense of our own gender and to interpret someone else's gender.

We typically possess great confidence in our ability to use gender cues to accurately determine anatomical sex. As Freud observed in the early 1930s, "When you meet a human being, the first distinction you make is 'male or female'? and you are accustomed to make the distinction with unhesitating certainty." [150] Sex is inferred from gender, which itself is based on presentation, for which we presume a corresponding internal experience. These are a *lot* of inferences based on questionable assumptions.

Let's be clear what the two critical assumptions are:

❑ Gender arises naturally and predictably from sex.

❑ Because there are only two sexes there can only be two genders.

The first assumption posits that biological differences in sexual anatomy underlie differences in experience, which in turn underlie differences in presentation. Much effort has been invested over the years to explore to what extent body differences matter in terms of such things as personality, moral reasoning, cognitive ability, and a wide variety of behaviors. In sum, the evidence shows real but generally modest differences exist between two groups differentiated as male and female. Whether and to what extent those differences are actually meaningful remains disputed. Moreover, though some differences can be seen between groups, an individual in either group may on one or more characteristics score more like members of the other group. Further, the observed differences may be attributable to environmental factors rather than biological ones. For instance, the often cited finding that males as a group do better in math must be qualified both by the fact that many female individuals outperform many male persons, and the group differences may be explained by the way females are raised and treated according to a gender belief that they *should* do more poorly.

Perhaps gender differences arise not from sex-based body differences but from other causes, such as the beliefs Fausto-Sterling referred to. If gender differences are applied to sex differences rather than flowing from them, they can scarcely be termed 'natural.' Instead they are artificial—constructions made by human beings. If so they need not prove any less 'predictable.' The fact that most females turn out to be feminine and most males turn out to be masculine can be seen as the predictable result of an efficient social system begun at birth, operating at multiple levels, strongly reinforced, and almost universally endorsed by its participants.[151]

Thomas Eckes and Hanns Trautner, in their effort to forge an integrative framework for a developmental social psychology of gender, posit three generally shared assumptions among models concerned with the nature of social influences and how men and women relate to social contexts:

❑ Social influence results from *multiple factors*, including cognitive ones (e.g., self-concept), interpersonal orientation (i.e., self- or other-oriented), group memberships, and cultural forces (e.g., ideologies).

❑ Social influence is *heterogeneous*, arising from *multiple sources*, including interpersonal, group, and cultural environments.

❑ Gender is *multidimensional*, with various dimensions and their facets interrelated in multiple ways, some tightly knit together and others only loosely connected, and varying by individual, across time and according to context.[152]

In sum, studying gender is no easier for the scholar than for the individual who must sort out all the information, much of it conflicting, and somehow still function in the world.

Some pertinent questions we should ask are: If sex is powerful enough to create gender in a predictable fashion, then why does society apply such strenuous effort to ensure the result? If Nature makes only two sexes and each has a gender, then why not relax and let Nature run its course?

The fact that we don't trust to Nature suggests that gender really doesn't follow inevitably from sex. Freud's judgment is sound: "what constitutes masculinity or femininity is an unknown characteristic which anatomy cannot lay hold of."[153] Society finds so many nonstereotypical gender presentations that it must enact a plethora of safeguards to try to constrain gender expression (and presumably gender experience) into a range of tolerable options opposite one another at two poles.

The binary system again proves dubious. Yet, for argument's sake, let us accept the premise there are only two sexes, male and female. Why must there then only be two genders? If gender does not arise naturally and predictably from sex, then what constrains us to two genders? Consider a different pairing: sex with eye color. Let us accept there are only two sexes and only two eye colors. We are able to have blue-eyed males, blue-eyed females, brown-eyed males, and brown-eyed females. A 2 x 2 matrix yields four logical alternatives. Why don't we look at gender similarly?

The failure of the first premise about gender should deflate the power of the second. Even if we accept there are only two sexes and two genders we still have four possibilities: masculine males, feminine males, masculine females, and feminine females. We could as logically categorize these as four separate genders as we do two genders with acceptable and undesirable poles. But we don't.

Freud nearly a century ago told us, "make yourselves familiar with the idea that the proportion in which masculine and feminine are mixed in an individual is subject to considerable fluctuations."[154] That such 'fluctuations' actually exist is reflected in the terminology we use in everyday talk: feminine males are 'sissies' and masculine females are 'tomboys' or 'butch.' The terms may be used disparagingly or approvingly, but they *are* used; the distinctions in gender reality are noted.[155] However, they are bent to the service of the binary system. Rather than contemplate more than two genders, people regard feminine males and masculine females as deficient gender variations, with the former more seriously deficient because masculinity is prized more than femininity.

Modern Gender as Historical Artifact

Perhaps it is time we begin acknowledging that the received wisdom on sex and gender is not all that wise. Maybe our modern sense of gender makes an interesting historical artifact but a troubling contemporary belief. Just as we have had to let go other bits of received 'knowledge,' we may need to let go of thinking about gender in ways that neither squares with the facts nor serves a useful purpose.

If the notion that gender is related to sex as the flower is to the bulb forms a simple but incorrect idea, perhaps it would be useful to discern the soil in which it was nourished. Where did we go wrong in knitting gender so closely to anatomy? Since we have seen that culture employs socialization to carry forward this idea from one generation to the next, we must look back in time to see the cultural roots.

Thomas Laqueur argues that the notion that the body determines gender differences, with a dichotomy of opposites in anatomy and psychology, is essentially a post-Enlightenment way of thinking about the matter.[156] It is neither inevitable nor eternal—despite having become our culture's perspective, with all the advantages, limitations, and problems that may entail. On the other hand, an essentialist perspective is argued by anthropologist Helen Fisher, who writes, "gender differences came across the centuries, out of our distant past when ancestral men and women began to pair and raise their young as 'husband' and 'wife.'" [157] In her estimation, biological differences in spatial and verbal ability predispose males and females to success in different tasks. Coupled with the female's reproductive capacities, these physical differences engender gender-specific variations in aptitude, preference, and personality traits. Fisher concludes, "Other variations between the sexes could have a biological foundation and may also have evolved during our long nomadic past."[158]

Of course, we have heard this argument before. A central flaw in the logic is easy to overlook. Let's not contest that differences exist—we'll accept, for example, her argument that as a group men exhibit better spatial skills while as a group women exhibit better verbal skills. But why must we assume these spring from intrinsic biological differences? The brain is programmed by experience, and millennia of socialization into specific gender-based roles can as logically account for these general differences as the role of biology. In fact, if biological predisposition was the better explanation, we should expect universal expression of all those gender-specific traits and preferences that essentialists suggest exist. But this is not the actual case.

Gender Differences?

Let's look at the evidence, remembering that if divisions in labor and gender roles are based on biology, they should be universal. Cultural variations would suggest the contrary idea, that social forces are determinative, however they might have arisen. Here are a few of the more commonly named differences between the genders:

- ❑ Women raise children at home; men do work in the wider society.
- ❑ Men do heavy work because of their strength; women's weakness keeps them close to home.
- ❑ Men get food; women prepare it.

The first item on the list is the big one for most people. There is no disputing that females are the ones who bear young. Further, they are able to provide nourishment to newborns from their bodies through breast milk. So it would seem 'natural' that they would be the primary caregivers who raise the young. In today's world, across cultures, women occupy the role of primary nurturer. At the same time, in increasing numbers, they are part of the labor force. It seems regardless of their involvement outside the home, women are expected as mothers to remain the predominant nurturing force within the home. But whether this stems from biological predisposition or millennia of socialization is impossible to answer with certainty. There is nothing intrinsically compelling women to assume a greater burden in nurturing young or caring for others— and feminists rightly point out that the suggestion there is an intrinsic compulsion is a hallmark of patriarchal oppression.

Logically, men could take the larger role, and individually some do. In fact, psychologist Shawn Meghan Burn, who holds an essentialist position, nevertheless concedes that observational research documents fathers in numerous cultures in affectionate, nurturing relationships.[159] Similarly a report by psychologists Patrice Engle and Cynthia Breaux, looking at fatherhood in developing nations, summarizes data on differences in time spent with children between mothers and fathers by remarking, "Although such gender differences in time allocation to child care are common, it is important to note that fathers *are* spending time in child care—in some cases, substantial time."[160] Thus, in spite of the gender role pressure to devote the majority of their energy and time to work outside the home, fathers remain a nurturing force within the home.[161]

Moreover, even the finding that mothers spend the most time nurturing must be qualified. That contention holds for treatment of infants, but weakens seriously as children age. Anthropologists Joel Arnoff and William Crano, in a multicultural study of 186 societies across six broad geographic regions, found that between 9 months of age and about age 5, *no* society confined most child-care to the mother. In fact, in nearly a third (32%), the children spent most of their time *apart* from their mothers.[162] Stereotypes that posit a rigid division of gender roles such that men don't nurture while women don't work outside the home are obviously outdated at best.

Next on our list is the contention that the superior strength of the male means they undertake heavy labor unsuited to women. Does this idea hold up? It might if we only think of a narrow range of activities (e.g., mining) requiring certain kinds of strength (breaking down rocks). But how much strength is needed to carry water, firewood, or other loads?—tasks more often undertaken by women in societies.[163] How many men can carry 70% of their body weight?—a feat accomplished by women in some societies.[164] No mandate from Nature compels females to attend more to domestic affairs and males to master the outside world. In fact, women often do heavy work outside the home; they just tend either not to get paid for it, or paid as much.

The third contention listed above reminds us of the familiar saying, 'Men bring home the bacon; women cook it.' We may think that activities like hunting, fishing, animal husbandry, food gathering, and agriculture are masculine work. Let's start with that last item in the list: agricultural tasks like planting are seen as belonging to both males and females in 73 societies; this labor, though, is exclusively male in 31 societies and exclusively female in 37 others![165] How about gathering food items, like nuts, berries and fruit? This activity is one usually or always done by women in 78 societies, while usually or always done by men in just 15 societies. Even those supposed bastions of masculine work—hunting and fishing—are not universally the provenance of men: in a handful of societies fishing is usually or always done by women, and in at least one society the same is true of hunting![166]

As well we should remember how the division of labor can be modified, as when American involvement in World War II opened the door for women to take jobs previously held by men—and female involvement in the workforce since then has continued to erode sex-linked distinctions and gender role expectations. [167] So, while we might be tempted to see familiar divisions of labor as 'natural,' derived from the differences in sexual bodies, that conclusion must be modified by the observation that cultural variability in what is seen as appropriate sex-linked labor is just as pronounced.

Gender associated identities and roles *became* sex-linked as a seemingly inarguable justification for cultural practices. In successfully implanting the logic that Nature divided the sexes into genders with separate identities and roles, the way was set for inculcating that logic from one generation to the next. Such reasoning gave rise to socially sanctioned divisions of labor associated with separate statuses as man and woman—and generally (though not universally) kept men in charge. Indeed, as we learned earlier, the very word 'woman' owes its existence to gender-ordered thinking: a woman is a 'man's wife.' And the argument that female reproductive capacity equals a mandate to nurture most benefits men in terms of social status and power.[168]

We live in a world that neither is nor has to be identical to the past. Modern gender designations, language, and divisions in our society reflect an outdated sensibility. Our retention of the convictions that the only genders are masculine and feminine, and that each must exist in certain predetermined roles, are relics—artifacts better displayed in a museum than in civil society. Women today are much more and other than 'man's wife.' Sex-linked divisions of labor prove increasingly irrelevant as both sexes fight wars, wash dishes, cook meals, and conduct business deals. The only real utility in preserving archaic forms resides in their continued buttressing of a gender order hierarchical in nature, with masculine males (especially White ones) at the top. Contemporary retention of a bipolar scheme of sex and gender, with the former generating the latter, really serves well only the narrow interests of a few.

The Relation Between Sex and Gender

Reprising the Current Prevailing Scheme

What, then, is the true relation between sex and gender? In modern Western culture both the connection and the distinction between them have come to be heavily relied upon. On the one hand, as we have seen, we may assume sex and gender are paired in a straightforward and limited manner. Most of us prior to entering a serious conversation on the subject rather naively assume there are only two biological sexes (male and female), as well as only two genders (masculine and feminine), and that nature reliably pairs them in one way (male with masculine; female with feminine), with gender subordinate to sex, and both subservient to desire.[169] Any mixing of the sex and gender, such as a male presenting as feminine, is a deviant construction—unnatural and disordered.

In this scheme, sexual anatomy provides the foundation for social expectations about gender. If one is born anatomically male, then masculinity is expected; if born female, a feminine gender is assigned. In our culture this is so familiar we may believe it always has been the way the matter has been understood. Within this cultural framework, deviation from the pairing of anatomical sex with gender presentation is viewed as exactly that: *deviation*, with negative connotations affecting social status and regard of psychological health.

Yet while we yoke sex and gender together, we still insist on a distinction between them. Despite the critique offered earlier, for most of us sex continues to be reserved for physical matters of anatomy and physiology (as though they are all that enters in). Gender, correspondingly, encompasses the much broader psychosocial elements related to how sexual anatomy and physiology enter into human affairs. Or, as sexuality educator Lisa Maurer puts it, "*Sex* has to do with body parts, *gender* with the manner in which a person puts the assignment of *male* or *female* into practice *within societal limits*."[170] This all may continue to feel very straightforward, though we have shown how it is not.

Basic Premises

We should be able to see better now why so much space has been spent discussing two surprisingly complex terms. Unfortunately, our effort principally has elaborated and critiqued the view that currently handicaps us rather than setting forth a positive alternative. We shall do so very briefly in a sequence of steps. First, at this point in our dialog we shall enunciate a few basic premises. Then we shall return to the contemporary situation to further investigate some issues related to gender and society (chapters 4-6), and gender and the individual (chapters 7-9). That will help prepare us for closer attention to the specific genders as such (chapters 10-12). As we do so we shall attempt to move past present limitations to envision broader possibilities. Specifically, this will result in suggesting how we might speak more realistically about gender. This will be followed by focusing briefly on why such attention matters in the 'real world,' by looking at three specific topic areas (chapters 13-15).

We have defined sex and gender. Though they can be conceived in better terms than they presently are, the definitions we have posited must suffice for now. Sex refers to 'anatomical presentations presumably related to reproductive capacity,' while gender refers to 'the set of experiential and presentational characteristics associated with and culturally arising from pairing with a particular sex.' Accompanying these definitions are the following premises, each based on logical deductions:

- ❑ Because anatomical presentations presumably related to reproductive capacity vary, it is reasonable to suggest that sexes vary beyond two in number.
- ❑ Because the sets of experiential and presentational characteristics associated with and arising from a particular sex vary, it is reasonable to suggest that genders vary beyond two in number.
- ❑ Because neither sex nor gender is solely dependent on either biology or culture, both can exhibit variability that includes relative independence from each other.

Granting the plausibility of these three premises the relation between sex and gender can be reconsidered. Based on the characteristics set out in the premises, the following statements present the basic framework for a proposed modified scheme of sex and gender:

- ❑ Biology *cannot* be ignored or devalued; a biological component to both sex and gender is inescapable and links them.
- ❑ Culture *cannot* be ignored or devalued; culture shapes the perception, valuation, and application of sex and gender within both social and personal spheres.
- ❑ Variability *cannot* be ignored or devalued; natural variations in sex and gender place the individual at the nexus of their relationship.

Simply put, *sex and gender are biologically primed, socially constructed, and individually mediated.*

By now it should be clear there is a need for conceptual clarity and agreement on how terms so key to human relationships are understood and applied. But for these things to happen we must spread wider more accurate information to dispute and eventually overcome the naïve—and erroneous—assumptions so many of us hold. Most of us think the way we do about sex and gender because we accept with little question the common and received knowledge of our culture, especially about our bodies, no matter whether this be accurate or not. We rely on consensus ('Everyone thinks so.') even though we know how often consensus can be wrong (e.g., the world is not flat). It requires no little effort for us to open ourselves to new information when the old assumptions are so comfortable to wear. Normally, only when the old assumptions cause discomfort at a personal level, whether because we ourselves do not fit well within them or because holding the assumptions hurts our relationships with others, do we start questioning.

Let us resolve not to let the stakes become high and tinged with passion before we challenge ourselves to better thinking. What can we discover by looking for better ways of understanding gender? The answer lies in further investigation. We must advance our dialog in societal and individual matters of gender.

First, as we have seen, we find plenty of evidence available to challenge commonly held assumptions. That evidence immediately and persistently challenges the notion of a one-to-one connection between sex and gender. Second, we discover that less rigid ways of understanding gender facilitate more realistic ways of looking at human experience; many people do not fit in dichotomous categories as masculine or feminine. Third, we discover that greater accuracy and more realistic perceptions encourage more humane consideration of our fellow human beings. By not insisting that every round peg fit into a square hole we are able to appreciate the round peg for its own value and contributions. Those who more comfortably fit somewhere between male and female, masculine and feminine, are more likely to be accorded respect and viewed as valuable when the stigma of not fitting limited categories is removed. In sum, better ways of understanding gender advantage us all.

Of course, all this is easier said than done. Yet we must make the effort if we are to do justice to the human experience. Clearly, we need to look more closely at the problem of gender as understood in our Western culture if we are to accurately comprehend the place transgender—and crossdressing—occupies. And rest assured, gender does pose problems in our culture.

Chapter 4

Gender Socialization

Introduction: Thus far in our dialog we have discovered good grounds for doubting the commonly held belief that two genders rise naturally from two sexes. Yet if we find it difficult to relinquish our prior beliefs, we should not be surprised. That difficulty provides strong testimony to the power of *socialization*. Each and every one of us is introduced at birth into a pre-existing social framework. Somehow we must master its construction and find our place within it if we are to prosper. Since gender provides much of the basic architecture of our society, gender socialization is necessary to facilitate social existence.

Although all of us experience *gender socialization* (or 'gender typing'), it remains one of those basic, pervasive forces in life we seldom examine. When we do think about it, it proves rather puzzling. Despite the naturalness of how it feels due to our long experience with it, we are right to wonder if the way we experience it is how it *must* be. Why does gender socialization take the form it does? More than one theory has arisen trying to explain it.

Gender socialization is aided by the very convenient, if also dubious, asset of *stereotypes*. The value of a stereotype lies in its utility as a mental shortcut. Instead of having to take time to assess every person we meet based on observed individual characteristics, we can assume certain traits, dispositions, and so forth. Gender stereotypes provide boxes into which we can fit strangers and casual acquaintances. These boxes not only provide generalized information, but guide our behavior—because we tend to follow the stereotype into which we ourselves fit. Unfortunately, we all pay a price for our reliance on stereotypes, and some us pay a heavy one because we cannot conform and make ourselves fit in the box.

The boxes stereotypes create are really just one construction—a narrow one of highly generalized notions—around which are other possible constructions of gender. These possibilities are constrained by gender expectations, which both express and support gender *norms*: standards created by typical behavior that function authoritatively as generally informal rules about gender. Stray too far from the stereotyped center and the boundary of the gender is crossed. That means norm violations, which are followed by the label of the violator as 'abnormal.' In a binary gender system, third gender and transgender people are typically regarded as 'abnormal' rather than as merely 'atypical,' and *stigmatized*.

The Concept of Socialization

In the ongoing conversation on gender no one disputes that society plays a part. How large a part, and what its nature is, remains a matter of debate. In figuring out answers the concept of socialization becomes prominent because our ideas about gender and the rules by which we are gendered within our society are carried out through socialization. The acquisition and demonstration of gender identity, role, and traits associated with both is also known as 'gender typing,' but we will use 'gender socialization' because it continues to highlight for us a pivotal question—the role of the environment.

Goal: Gendered; Mechanism: Socialization

Let's consider two basic ideas here at the outset:
- ❑ First, each of us must become *gendered* within our society.
- ❑ Second, *socialization* is the principal mechanism of our gendering.

We are born beings with sex. But gender is something acquired. Remember our definition of gender: 'the set of experiential and presentational characteristics associated with and culturally arising from pairing with a particular sex.' Although we are assigned a gender at birth, we must grow into it. We must be 'gendered'—made into a gendered being. Through experience we either earn the gender we were assigned or achieve a different gender. Either way, we are in constant contact with the attributions based on our gender assignment and under the force of the social processes meant to make us the gender we were assigned.

Gender socialization is the ongoing process starting from gender assignment that aims to construct our gender identity and gender role. This process entails utilization of fundamental social institutions and structures, such as the family, religion, education, and the state, all of which promote, support, and defend the cultural ideas about how each gender should look, talk, and act, as well as think, feel, and *be*. Socialization, as the word suggests, guides our socializations with others, informing us as to what is expected of us in how we should experience ourselves and how we ought to perceive others. Socialization provides boundaries for self-formation and rules for interaction with others. It begins at birth, largely accomplishes its work in childhood, and remains a force the rest of life.

The Power of Gender Socialization

How great a force does gender socialization exert? Consider this: most of us want our children to be seen and known as members of the gender group they were assigned to at birth. By the time we become parents, we have learned through our own experience and observation both that the rewards for gender conformity are significant and the punishments for gender nonconformity often severe. We want our own children to 'fit in.' We hope for them to reap the rewards from identification with the gender they were assigned. If they find such an assignment easy to bear, the identity one they are secure within, and the role a comfortable fit, then much about life in the particular society will go more smoothly. So typically we cooperate fully with the other socializing forces, adding our parenting practices to help ensure the child grows up in accord with his or her gender assignment—and believing our efforts make a real difference.

But many of us also have been bothered by what we have seen and experienced as accompanying 'fitting in.' We disagree with gender inequalities accompanying the gender hierarchy, conclude that gender stereotypes limit rather than liberate, and determine that at least some modest effort to ameliorate gender pressures on our children is a good thing. So we may not brace ourselves to overthrow what we see as a faulty system, but we at least resolve to resist its more egregious aspects. We decide we will raise our children less according to stereotypes and more 'gender neutral,' where the benefits of the positive attributes associated with each gender might be known and embraced by our children. We also hope that those labeled different are not branded bad.

We find these tasks easier decided than done. Gender socialization is so potent that even after we recognize the less desirable features of its operation and decide to modify it, we find ourselves largely undone by it. Sociologist and gender scholar Sharon Hays writes:

> The reality and power of gender socialization . . . is indisputable. In my study this is evident not only in how mothers consider themselves primarily responsible for mothering and how deep that sense of responsibility runs, but also in the awareness of many mothers that, no matter how hard they may try to avoid it, they tend to treat their male and female children differently.[171]

Remember what we discussed earlier, when introducing the notion of gender attributions? They are so pronounced they lead to subtle distortions in the ways we see babies. Numerous studies have shown that when adults are led to believe a child is a certain gender, they perceive that child's physical and psychological characteristics according to the gender norms—or often the stereotypes—for that gender. Thus, even if the child's actual sex is at variance with what is proclaimed to be the gender, the child will be seen and treated as though a member of that proclaimed gender, and the sex will be assumed to be the sex culturally paired with that gender. Development psychologist Carole Beale summarizes the matter well when she comments, "Even though these initial inferences have a very high probability of being wrong, they reassure the viewer who is faced with an unfamiliar small baby."[172] Apparently, even a wrong judgment is better than ambiguity or uncertainty over someone else's gender.

Or is it? Our insistence on gender socialization to produce conformity to our gender assignment comes at a price. Marjorie Hardy points to the substantial impact that gender socialization has on psychological characteristics in both children and adults. She sees socialization that reinforces gender role conformity to gender stereotypes as linked to phenomena like the higher reported incidence of depression in females, who are gender socialized in such a manner that learned helplessness is more likely than for males. She also thinks such socialization is implicated in the varying performance in school between boys and girls. But they are not the only ones handicapped by a process that enforces gender conformity. Gender socialization supporting masculine aggression is a factor in a number of social problems that lead to referrals for intervention. [173]

Hardy notes that social forces continue to exert pressure toward gender role conformity despite evidence that gender nonconformity characteristics may be psychologically and physically healthier. She remarks, "Perhaps it is not conformity to a particular gender role that is healthier but rather society's encouragement and acceptance of flexibility that engenders positive characteristics in its members." [174] If so, this is welcome news to those of us whose best fit is with traits and behaviors not in step with typical, expected, or stereotyped gender role characteristics.

Gender Socialization Across Development

For all the importance and power of gender socialization, it can still be a rather elusive subject. As the authors of one sociology textbook put it, documenting the way children are gender socialized "is much like trying to document the ways in which people learn how to talk or use proper sentence structure. This socialization is such a continuous and ever-present experience that examples are both obvious and subtle."[175] At other times in our dialog we will have occasion to examine various aspects of gender socialization in development, but we can start with some general observations here.

Among the principal channels for gender socialization are:

- ❑ *Parenting*—which offers gender role models, actively shapes the child's physical environment, and reinforces social rules and expectations both verbally and behaviorally.
- ❑ *Reciprocal parent-child interactions*—at the same time parents are exercising socialization practices, children are influencing the process through their characteristics and responses.
- ❑ *Peers*—other children, including siblings, playmates, and older kids, extend the kind of work done by parents, though typically in less subtle and more stereotyped ways.
- ❑ *School*—gender segregation characterizes early education and persists, as teachers' differential expectations and treatment clarify for children their gender roles.
- ❑ *Religion*—church, synagogue, mosque and temple all generally support conservative social values to uphold social order, which in terms of gender typically means support of traditional conventions.
- ❑ *Media*—whether through literature, television, films, magazines, or advertisements, socially sanctioned gender conformity rules, stereotypes are promoted, and deviations are censored through laughter or other expressions of derision.

While most of the attention on these is with reference to gender socialization in childhood, we would do well to remember these channels of socialization are operative throughout life.

Parenting

We have already mentioned how parents follow cultural expectations about gender. In at least one respect, this starts before birth. Tacitly recognizing the gender hierarchy, most parents when asked express a preference for having a boy.[176] In fact, the *preference for a child of a specific gender* may guide some behavior even when the sex of the child is not paired with that gender. Thus, some parents dress and treat their child as a member of a gender different from the one assigned them based on their apparent sex.[177] This might be hypothesized a contributing factor in some instances of crossdressing and transgender identity.[178]

Parents also *model gender*—they present for the observation of their children a gender identity and role that may be imitated. One famous theory about how this transpires is offered in Sigmund Freud's often misunderstood idea of the Oedipus Complex. He hypothesized that in the Oedipus Complex (roughly transpiring between about ages 4½ to 6, then again rearing its specter in adolescence) a child must renounce desire for the parent of the opposite sex and affiliate with the parent of the same sex. [179] This is implicitly a form of cognitive identification, an element prominent in many later conceptions, such as the work of Lawrence Kohlberg.[180] Social cognitive theory, developed by Albert Bandura and others, also makes cognition key and explicitly develops the place held by modeling—which we shall learn more of when we consider this theory for gender socialization a bit further on.[181] Of special concern in our society is how this plays out in single-parent families compared to those where both parents are present. As might be expected, it appears that being raised in a single-parent home does make a difference, both for personal and for idealized gender roles, though in both settings contemporary adolescents endorse androgynous models over gender stereotypes.[182]

Parents also *structure home environments*. Research indicates that children's early environments typically are gender-differentiated. For example, one study investigated the home environments of 120 girls and boys in three equal groups of 40 children at three different ages: 5, 13, and 25 months (infancy into toddlerhood). The environments for both boys and girls were filled with toys, clothes, and colors endorsed by the culture as appropriate for the gender. Thus, girls were surrounded with dolls and jewelry, and wore multicolored clothes and pink; boys' toys were sports and work related, and their clothes more often red, white or blue.[183] Because of their own socialization experiences much of what parents do remains partly unconscious to themselves. Yet parents typically will acknowledge some awareness of their efforts to sculpt their children's gender, and generally possess confidence their efforts will bear fruit.

Reciprocal Parent-Child Interactions

Not surprisingly, then, parents start gender socializing right away. What may be surprising is that it isn't long into life before their children are actively involved in the process, too. In a short while we will examine reciprocal models of gender socialization, but some preliminary comments are needed now. First, we should notice this dynamic, interactive process begins very soon in life. Sociologist Emily Kane remarks that, "Parents begin gendering their children from their very first awareness of those children, whether in pregnancy or while waiting adoption. Children themselves become active participants in this gendering process by the time they are conscious of the social relevance of gender, typically before the age of two."[184] Sociologist Spencer Cahill's study of preschool children reveals how even at this tender age they "fashion themselves into gendered persons."[185]

This reciprocal process says, if nothing else, that kids are adept at figuring out that whatever else this gender stuff is, it certainly matters to the grownups. If it is that important to mom and dad, it must become important to the child. So very quickly most children try to conform to expectations and mirror the attributes assumed for them. This situation makes it all the more remarkable that so many children *fail*. Try as best they might, some kids simply do not fit the gender box everyone, including themselves, is trying to squeeze them into. The strong ones stop trying, and insist on being who they are, whatever gendered self that produces. They pay a price, often heavy, but not so heavy as those who cannot find the support or strength to forge a public self who mirrors the internal experience. Instead these individuals survive by inhabiting the shell of a false self, a gender presentation at odds with internal experience.

No one should fault the child who chooses such a course, for it is not an easy one either. The forces of socialization raised against a child are so formidable that truly blessed are those who find it satisfying to cooperate fully. Those who struggle to conform also exercise an influence on their environment, particularly their parents. Nonconforming girls are treated more gently, with less concern—a situation reflecting the lower status of femininity, a greater acceptance of tomboys in the culture, and a general tendency to be less controlling and less punitive with girls than with boys. Gender nonconforming boys meet stiffer resistance; like girls their situation reflects cultural concerns—masculinity is a higher status with stricter demands, sissies are not accepted at any age, and parents in general tend to be more demanding and less patient with boys. It is telling that a boy is more than six times as likely to be referred to a mental health professional for gender nonconforming behavior.[186]

Peers

Peer influence is a major force in development—at least one scholar has contended it is an influence greater than parents.[187] Across the life span, peers play an important role in our learning what it means to be masculine or feminine.[188] For much of that time, beginning early in childhood, we are in same-gender peer groups. The resulting *homosociality*, or socialization among same-gendered members,[189] serves to accentuate gender stereotypes.[190]

Gender segregation—the process of separating individuals into groups based on gender—occurs virtually as soon as children beginning socializing with one another. From preschool until adolescence, same-gender peer groups predominate. In fact, psychologist Eleanor Maccoby, a developmental specialist, terms children's self-assortment into same-gender social groups "the most robust manifestation of gender during childhood."[191] She notes that voluntary gender segregation begins as early as age 3, and that between ages 4-12 this process continues to the degree that children typically end up spending most of their free play time in same-gender groups. *Group size* may affect gender characteristics (e.g., the observed greater competitiveness of boys, or the collaborative efforts of girls). Same-gender groups tend to be small, usually consisting of 2-3 members, and rarely more than 5-6 members, with boys more likely to cluster in larger groups. In part this may be because boys more often engage in organized group games and sports.[192]

Children who do not conform readily or well to gender stereotypes suffer at the hands of their peers. This is especially true for 'sissies'—boys displaying feminine characteristics. As we shall discuss later, the construction of masculinity in our culture seems to incorporate both *gynephobia* (a fear of women) and *homophobia* (a fear of gay men). In childhood, peers rigorously enforce gender expectations, often employing negative behaviors such as we will detail in considering school experiences next. In adolescence, peers can prove dangerous. Shannon Wyss, in recounting the stories of transgender youth, remarks that because of their peers' hatred—one mirroring adult prejudices—teens publicly expressing their transgender identity often find themselves in unsafe situations. Many lose their friends, face ongoing harassment, and discover that teachers and school staff refuse to intervene, sometimes even suggesting the ill treatment transgender youth experience has been brought on by themselves.[193]

School

Gender segregation has already started before preschool, but this first experience of schooling accentuates it. Some research also suggests that children rapidly form a kind of *subculture for each gender*—a set of common knowledge and interests, as well as shared expectations, that differentiate the genders from each other.[194] In this respect, school provides an environment that continues, accentuates, and perhaps accelerates the effect of peers. All of this takes places within our culture's scheme of only two genders, rendering life at school potentially difficult for tomboys and sissies, but even rougher for transgender children.

Not only gender segregation, but *differential beliefs and expectations by teachers* at school further gender socialization. Teachers often endorse gender stereotypes, treating girls and boys not only differently, but in accord with a gender hierarchy that prizes masculinity.[195] Boys receive more attention, both for successes and for misbehavior. Girls are steered toward more passive and subordinate roles. Even in the selection of elementary readers children first use in school gender stereotypes and socially prescribed gender role expectations dispropor-tionately focus on masculinity. Studies in the 1970s showed dramatic discrepan-cies between exposure to masculine versus feminine gender models. One study found that boys outnumbered girls in the stories and pictures children were ex-posed to by a ratio of 11-to-1 (and 95-to-1 if animals with gender identities were included)[196]; another study found that characters in a sample of elementary school reading books were 70% White males.[197]

Have things changed much? Consider the point just made, concerning over-representation of masculine images. A large-scale analysis of materials be-tween 1900-1984 found the imbalance varied in a curvilinear fashion, with more egalitarian representation early in the century and late in it—unless one figured in only adult or animal characters, in which case masculine images became more prominent over time.[198] In 1992, after reviewing more than 100 published stud-ies over a decade's time, the American Association of University Women (AAUW) concluded that teachers still paid less attention to girls, they were in-creasingly being subjected to sexual harassment, and books students used still either ignored girls and women or stereotyped them.[199] The problems persist, and gender bias against both girls *and boys* affects children negatively.[200]

Children and youth whose gender identity does not fit conventional mascu-linity or femininity particularly find school a challenging environment. A study of School Climate conducted in the fall of 1999 by the Gay, Lesbian, and Straight Education Network (GLSEN) revealed more than 90% of these stu-dents had been subject to homophobic remarks, most often from other stu-dents (94.4% of those reporting such remarks), but frequently enough from faculty and staff, too (36.6%). GLSEN's survey for 2001 had an even wider reach and again found that school experience was marked by exposure to ho-mophobic or transphobic behavior. Nearly all of them (94%) heard homopho-bic comments (e.g., 'You're so gay'), or labels (e.g., 'Faggot,' 'Dyke'), often or frequently, and nearly a quarter (23.6%) heard such remarks from faculty or school staff.[201]

Religion

Near the end of our dialog we will focus on religion in relation to gender, so right now let us be content with a few remarks in regard to gender socializa-tion. Interestingly, despite its status as a major and fundamental social institu-tion, relatively little attention has been paid to its role in this respect. For exam-ple, in his groundbreaking work on faith development, minister and theologian James Fowler left aside the issue of gender differences and offered no attention to the role religion or faith play in gender development.[202] Yet sociologists Howard Francis Taylor and Margaret Andersen aptly observe, "Religion is an often overlooked but significant source of gender socialization."[203]

How could religion not be? Societies typically look to their dominant reli-gious traditions to offer the values and ideals that guide moral decision-making. In turn, religion is expected to conserve, support, and pass on those values and ideals as translated in the society, including other social institutions. If religion believes society is moving away from its religious roots, it protests. But the essential character of religion is to stitch society together in a value-centered community.[204] In Western culture and Western societies, gender is a central construct filled with value; it would be remarkable to think religion does *not* lend its efforts to gender socialization.

A primary task of religion in gender socialization is to lend its authority to the sanction of cultural conceptions of gender. The Western religious traditions that most shape American society—Christianity, Judaism, and Islam—are all *patriarchal* in character. They prize masculinity and subordinate femininity. This gender scheme is not merely supported by churches, temples, synagogues, and mosques in their own hierarchies, but also articulated and defended through religious dogmas, and promulgated through gender segregation at virtually every level of religious life and practice. All of these things often proceed with the confidence of truth revealed from on high.

On the other hand, Taylor and Andersen remind us that religion as a social institution is not impervious to the effects of other social forces. The prominent role given to *personal interpretation* among American religious people has meant a religious pluralism that defies seeing religion monolithically on gender or anything else. In general, the most conservative members of a religion endorse the two-sex, two-gender scheme and embrace the gender hierarchy that keeps men at the top. But even among conservatives there has been a gradual move toward more egalitarian conceptions of gender relations. Such shifts are accompanied by theological justifications for the new position as truer to the religion's values and teachings.[205]

As we shall discuss later, religion has a long and complex relationship with gender issues, including transgender and third gender realities. All we shall note now is that religions around the world often have been active in gender socialization that differentiates certain children into socially sanctioned gender identities and roles that are neither boy nor girl. In fact, in many cultures those who are 'between genders,' or cross genders, are regarded as uniquely placed to assist society and to mediate between mortals and divine figures.[206]

Media

Like the other channels of gender socialization we have discussed, the media exercises significant influence. If anything, given the omnipresence of technology and media images, this influence continues to grow. Communications and media scholar Linda Holtzman calls entertainment media "a central source of gender socialization," and elucidates some of the various gender stereotypes promoted through television and film portrayals: women are all about appearance, romance, and relationships, while men are career-driven.[207]

These stereotypes are unavoidable. Media investigators Donald Roberts and Ulla Foehr, with colleagues, published research in 2004 finding that "many young people report in excess of 10 hours daily of media exposure, amounts that may be difficult to take seriously unless one considers the frequency of media multitasking."[208] Even after adjusting to arrive at the most accurate figures possible from their accumulation of data, the researchers determined that kids ages 2-7 are exposed to more than 4 hours of media messages every day, while youth ages 8-18 are exposed to almost twice that (7½ hours a day).[209]

As in other respects, children soon follow cultural norms. Roberts and colleagues found, for example, that reading preferences were gender-differentiated, followed gender stereotypes, and were much the same as they had been when reported three decades earlier.[210] They likewise found that gender, along with age, were the two demographic variables consistently related to television program choices, with boys and girls again endorsing stereotypes (e.g., sports for boys, romance for girls).[211]

The media representation of those who do not identify as either masculine men or feminine women has always been far more limited, and generally negative. Most often, portrayals have been played for laughs—a more or less gentle way of reinforcing gender conformity. In recent years, mirroring the greater acceptance, or at least tolerance, for transgender people, media portrayals have been more serious and sympathetic. However, as with other genders, depictions of transgender remain mostly superficial and stereotypic.[212]

Now that we have briefly considered the role of socialization, its power, and some of its principal channels in society, we must dig deeper to try to uncover its interior logic. That leads us to the realm of theory. A number of different models for gender socialization have been proposed—too many for us to consider them all in an introductory discussion—but certain ones, reflecting major theoretical approaches, have garnered special attention in the last few decades. We shall look at three of the most prominent models.

A Psychoanalytic Model

Psychoanalytic theory has generated many models pertinent to considering gender socialization. A moment ago we mentioned Freud's idea of the Oedipus Complex. That notion in particular has inspired vast amounts of discussion, ranging from endorsement to vigorous objections. Among psychoanalytic models since Freud, one in particular has proven highly influential. Earlier in our dialog, we saw that one woman psychoanalyst captured the imagination of second wave feminists by providing an innovative updating of Freudian theory that supported a distancing of gender from sex. Nancy Chodorow especially succeeded in presenting a picture of gender development that made sense to many women.

The Reproduction of Mothering

Chodorow's 1978 book *The Reproduction of Mothering*, perhaps more than any other work, established the psychoanalytic 'object relations' perspective as a force on the American scene. Simultaneously, it fired the imagination of feminists. In this landmark volume, Chodorow locates the essence of gender socialization within the family. The differential treatment provided by parents to their sons and daughters often has drawn comment, but Chodorow wanted to explain why it exists. In her view, the heart of the matter lies in mothering, and more specifically, in how it is reproduced across generations in a particular way.

She begins by posing the problem of the *context for mothering*—is it biology, or role-training? The conventional wisdom held that sexual biology predisposed women to child-bearing and nurturing roles. But Chodorow caps her critique of this position by declaring, "The biological argument for women's mothering is based on facts that derive, not from our biological knowledge, but from our definition of the natural situation as this grows out of our participation in certain social arrangements."[213] Mothering, she argues, is *not* an inevitable byproduct of female sexual biology (i.e., childbearing and lactation capacities).

If biology is not the principal context, then perhaps a global socialization offers the answer. This solution, too, Chodorow eschews. Despite the universality of women occupying the predominant role in mothering, it is neither biologically determined nor universally the same across societies. "Women's mothering," she writes, "is not an unchanging transcultural universal."[214] What context, then, explains this aspect of human experience so used to illustrate the separate spheres of men and women and to justify the exclusion of women from so much that is open to men?

Chodorow proposes a third alternative, one that locates mothering at the nexus of the personal and social. *Mothering*, she contends, *is reproduced from generation to generation as a consequence of family patterns*. Though being a woman is less valued than being a man in the broader reach of society and culture, within the family she is greatly valued by the children. A mother has a different relationship with her sons and daughters, which leads to different experiences for boys and girls and to different personality structures.[215] Daughters serve as extensions of self for the mother, and as special objects for emotional intimacy. This complicates the developmental processes of separation and individuation for girls. Given this backdrop, when heterosexual connections with men prove relationally unfulfilling, women turn to mothering to meet their needs—and the mothering cycle is carried into the next generation.[216]

In *The Reproduction of Mothering*, Chodorow's psychoanalytic theory offered second wave feminists a potent explanation to an enduring problem—why women keep mothering in a system that keeps them locked into adult roles defined by reproduction and relegated to an unequal status.[217] In her 1989 *Feminism and Psychoanalytic Theory*, appearing near the end of the second wave, Chodorow continued to promote psychoanalytic theory as a rich resource for feminists. She observes of feminism that, "Its basic argument is that gender and sexuality, whatever the biology that helps to inform these, are created culturally and socially; they are not immutable givens. Therefore, feminism demands a theory of how we become sexed and gendered."[218] She argues that Freud gave us such a theory, one that answers the feminist desire to change the social organization and psychology of sex and gender. Whether or not Chodorow's own furthering of Freud's theory is adopted, psychoanalytic theory has continued to inspire and guide models of gender socialization.

A Social Cognitive Model

Social cognitive theory is best associated with psychologist Albert Bandura. Although the foundational appearance of the theory is marked by the publication of his book, *Social Foundations of Thought and Action: A Social Cognitive Theory*, in the mid-1980s, it stems from work he had been pursuing since the early 1960s. Bandura's work prioritizes cognitive operations. What makes it distinctive is the manner in which cognition is brought to bear on social experiences and then guides behavior in a complex network of interacting factors, all conducted across the lifespan. Among the best known of his concepts are modeling (also referred to as 'vicarious learning'), self-efficacy, and reciprocal determinism. By the close of the 20th century Bandura was recognized as among the most prominent and influential of all psychologists.

Psychologist Kay Bussey, with Bandura, set forth an articulation of how this theory understands gender development and differentiation. While the model recognizes that some gender differences have a biological foundation, it believes culture better explains most of the stereotypic attributes and roles associated with gender. In light of previous theoretical approaches, social cognitive theory aims to integrate psychological and sociostructural determinants. "In this perspective," they write, "gender conceptions and role behavior are the products of a broad network of social influences operating both familially and in the many societal systems encountered in everyday life." [219]

Triadic Reciprocal Causation

Bussey and Bandura call their model one of 'triadic reciprocal causation.' The triadic elements are:

- ❑ *personal factors*—affective, biological, and cognitive events, which include "gender-linked conceptions, behavioral and judgmental standards, and self-regulatory influences";
- ❑ *behavior patterns*—"activity patterns tending to be linked to gender"; and,
- ❑ *environmental events*—"the broad network of social influences that are encountered in everyday life." [220]

These all interact bi-directionally; they exert reciprocal causal force on each other, and do so without a fixed pattern.

In fact, other factors influence the strength of each triadic element. For example, egalitarian social systems permit personal factors to exert greater force, while more rigid, hierarchical systems limit personal factor influence. Bidirectional causation does *not* mean equal strength for the factors. The actual influence exerted can wax or wane over time as any number of factors play their part. Among those multiple other factors are affective, motivational, and environmental factors, which have importance alongside cognitive factors. Moreover, the environments in which factors interact are themselves variable, including those imposed, those selected, and those actively constructed through 'generative efforts.'[221]

Acquisition of Gender Conceptions and Competencies

"Gendered roles and conduct," write Bussey and Bandura, "involve intricate competencies, interests, and value orientations." The manner by which gender roles and conduct are acquired is developmental in character. That development is promoted by three major modes of influence: modeling, enactive experience, and direct tuition. Parents, peers, significant others, and the media convey much gender-linked information through *modeling* gender roles and conduct. It emerges early in development as an important force and facilitates faster learning than enactive experience, which is a more deliberative process. *Enactive experience* is a cognitive process in which we deduce how our actions are linked to gender by seeing their outcomes. Because society sanctions conforming gender behavior, we can evaluate how well we are conforming by the reaction of others (an important outcome of our behavior). Finally, *direct tuition* conveys expectations about gender roles and conduct, offering information we use to guide our behavior. The reliance on verbal conveyance of information requires a sufficient development of language skills, but does offer the advantage of providing general, or abstracted ideas that add generic significance to the specific models and experiences gained through the other two modes.[222]

Regulators of Gendered Conduct and Role Behavior

In addition to the acquisition of gender conceptions and competencies, social cognitive theory also addresses the regulators of gendered conduct and role behavior. Primary factors include self-regulatory mechanisms and self-efficacy beliefs. *Self-regulatory mechanisms* may be rooted in either social sanctions or self sanctions. When it comes to gender, most outcomes are socially proscribed. Bussey and Bandura observe, "They include socially based consequences such as approval, praise, and reward for activities traditionally linked to the same gender, and disapproval or even punishment for those linked to the other gender." As we evaluate outcomes, we both learn about social gender norms and the sanctions imposed against violators, and this information serves to provide incentives and disincentives for further action. Thus, an early developmental reliance in social sanctions for gender regulation gradually gives way to self-regulation. Through self-regulatory mechanisms we aim gender conduct that brings feelings of satisfaction and self-worth, while avoiding those that would prompt self-censure. [223]

Self efficacy beliefs also assist in regulation by providing motivation based on beliefs about what we are capable of attaining by our own acts. Self-efficacy is enhanced through success, especially after perseverance through obstacles, which builds self-efficacy resilience. It is also strengthened by social modeling. Seeing others like ourselves succeed through perseverance raises our belief in our own capabilities. Social persuasion helps too. When others, like parents, appraise us positively and offer us situations and activities conducive to success, our self-efficacy grows. To a certain extent we do this to ourselves as well, as when we make inferences about our capabilities based on our physical and emotional states at the time. Finally, we can modify self-efficacy by reducing negative states like stress, depression, misperceptions of our physical states, and poor physical condition. As we feel better, we are more likely to believe we can do better.[224]

Gender Development and Functioning

Based on the preceding ideas, social cognitive theory advances its own conception of gender development and functioning. Bussey and Bandura contest the claim that gender identity, attainment of gender constancy, or knowledge of gender stereotypes accurately predict gender-linked behavior. Rather, they argue that long before we are able to label ourselves, or others by gender, we already are aware of gender differences and act in gender-differentiated ways. *Gender understanding precedes gender self-identity*. In myriad ways parents and others are sending messages about gender—and from infancy on these messages are being received and acted upon. As cognitive capacities expand, children acquire gender role knowledge and perform *gender labeling*, categorizing themselves as boy or girl. But valuation of gender categories and even of one's own gender identity is influenced by *social valuation*; both boys and girls value masculinity because our culture values it so highly. This provides incentive to girls more than to boys to master knowledge of a gender different than their own. Nevertheless, both boys and girls typically self-regulate themselves in gender conforming ways.[225]

As children mature they move beyond mere gender categorizing to a more sophisticated *learning of gender roles*. This is cognitively demanding work, but labor aided by exemplars in the environment, which is constantly expanding as the child grows older. The more readily and persistently *gender models* show a trait or behavior to be gender-linked, the more quickly and surely it becomes incorporated into a conception of that gender role. *Parents* play a substantial role in facilitating mastery of gender roles, though they do it differently in their interactions with sons and daughters. They talk to them differently, hold varying expectations, and disapprove differently of cross-gender behaviors. *Peers* also become another agency for gender development. They provide modeling, but they also offer sanctions or disapproval of certain conduct, and serve as comparative references. Gender segregation likely increases peer influence. Other models readily available for learning gender roles come through the *media*, which especially reinforces gender stereotypes. Across much of childhood, *educational practices experienced in school* also shape gendered attributes. Boys receive more attention and interaction, including more praise for academic success and more censure for academic failings and misbehavior. All of these factors not only assist in learning gender roles, but affect self-efficacy.[226]

Social cognitive theory reminds us that gender development is life long. As we enter into the work force, we learn more directly and forcefully how *occupations are gender-differentiated*. Bussey and Bandura remark, "The gendered practices of familial, educational, peer, and media subsystems are essentially replicated in organizational structures and practices." Gender segregation is pervasive. Self-efficacy is impacted, with women suffering from the hierarchical nature of gender in our society. Even those women with high self-efficacy may be negatively impacted as they experience the frustration of a social system that prevents them from the full realization or expression of their capabilities.[227]

Reciprocal Models

When we were talking about the role of parenting in gender socialization, we mentioned that children also participate actively in their own socialization. Whereas older models generally viewed the influencing process as proceeding in one direction (unidirectional), from parents to children, some more recent models are bidirectional.[228] We shall group these as 'reciprocal models' because the different models all agree that there is mutual influencing transpiring between parents and children.[229] In these models, "Gender socialization is viewed as a dynamic process in which parents and children continually influence one another across the course of children's development."[230]

Reciprocal models aim to avoid the extremes of either attributing all gender development to biology or to culture. Instead, socialization is seen as a social construction responsive to differential biological characteristics. So parents may be guided by their culture's beliefs about gender, but biological predispositions in their children may also exert influence. In this manner these models believe they explain both how societies can vary in gender socialization and why gendered differences still reliably show up even when children are treated the same as much as possible.

The reciprocal models can be further differentiated along a basic line of the nature of the influence exercised by the children. Following the distinction set out by psychologist Eva Pomerantz and colleagues,[231] these are:

❑ *Interactional models* focus on how children are affected by parenting because of their characteristics.

❑ *Transactional models* focus on how parents act toward their children under the influence of their children's characteristics.

Both kinds of models detail reciprocal influencing, but interactional models draw special attention to the effect of influence on the *children*, while transactional models draw more attention to the effect of influence on the *parents*. The models differ in where emphasis is placed in the reciprocal interaction.

Interactional Models

Perhaps the name most associated with an interactional theory is Terrence Thornberry, a behavioral scientist with expertise on juvenile delinquency. He articulated his interactional theory in the late 1980s. Although his model has explicit reference to understanding adolescent development of delinquency, it exhibits key traits for any such perspective. First, it focuses on *social control,* a process in which parents play a key role, whether through behavioral control of their children, or by psychological control. Second, it highlights the place of *attachment* to parents as a critical factor interacting with other key variables. Third, the interactive process is *developmental,* occurring across time with varying saliency of different factors at different developmental periods.[232] These points coincide, for instance, in conflicts between parents and children in early adolescence. In fact, some research suggests that reciprocal parent-child associations are most evident under conditions of adolescent negativity.[233]

These basic ideas have been extended to understanding gender socialization. An interactional model of gender socialization emphasizes how children differentially respond to parenting based on gender differences. Girls exhibit less need of social control. They also show greater conformity to social conventions that reward parental attachment, which typically promotes such conventionality. Finally, girls exhibit these characteristics from early in development on. Perhaps the most notable insight of interactional theory lies in drawing our attention to the fact that parental socialization practices may have different effects for children because of characteristics within the child rather than because of the effectiveness of the parental practice. The difference in how children respond may lie within the child, not what the parent does. While significant variability may exist from child to child even within a family, some of the difference in response may be a result of gender, such we just mentioned.

Transactional Models

Transactional models of gender socialization focus on the interaction between parents and children as guided by the gender-differentiated characteristics of the children, but with an emphasis on how *parents* are affected. Pomerantz and colleagues argue, "Regardless of the origins of the sex differences in children's characteristics, over time, parents may respond to these differences in interactions with their children. Thus, one reason that parents may treat boys and girls differently is because they are reacting to girls and boys' distinct characteristics."[234] They list six factors influencing the effects of parents' treatment: children's ability, children's sensitivity, children's motivation, relevant types of parenting practices, congruency of sex of child and parent, and children's normative development. In ability, sensitivity, and motivation, girls exhibit more responsiveness to gender socialization. One aspect of this may be a difference in status between genders; the lower status for femininity may prompt girls to be more responsive to the socialization guided by their mothers. The effects of gender differences in the different areas, however, may be limited to certain types of parental practices. Also, the effects of differential parental practice may be most keenly felt in certain periods of development, such as early adolescence.[235]

They point to three differences as perhaps particularly important. First, the more advanced cognitive attainment of girls early in development may result, at least in part, from differences in activity levels between boys and girls; the greater activity of the former lead to difficulties in concentrating and may prompt parents to adopt a more structured approach to interacting with them. Second, girls from early in development seem more responsive to parental socialization, thus eliciting less need for parents to be heavy-handed in their socialization practices with them, and prompting gentler disciplinary practices. Finally, from as early as age two, children exhibit preferences for gender-stereotyped activities, with boys engaging in more active play; these preferences may encourage parents to provide such gender-stereotyped activities.[236]

While we may agree with the basic point that gender socialization is bidirectional, with reciprocal influencing central, we need not accept all the points set forward by such models. For example, positing that biological differences underlie gender differences prompting differential responses from parents is possible but hardly certain. Pomerantz and colleagues themselves point out that the size of presumed sex differences is quite small; separating out the effects of culture from biology proves notoriously difficult. Moreover, as we must constantly remember, within-gender variance (i.e., differences among boys and differences among girls) is greater than between-gender variance (i.e., differences between boys and girls as groups). Pomerantz and colleagues also observe there is significant variability in how parents respond because of such factors as the parents' endorsement of gender stereotypes or sensitivity to the individual characteristics of their children apart from gender stereotypes.[237]

Gender Stereotyping

Early in our dialog we introduced as part of the vocabulary of conversing on gender the notion of *gender stereotypes*—relatively stable sets of idealized characteristics for each gender, employed as a convenient template to guide expectations and perceptions of others. Thus far in this discussion we have mentioned stereotypes repeatedly. Although there may be a number of reasons why considering gender stereotyping matters, one reason alone justifies careful attention to the topic: where gender role performance does not match gender stereotypes—popular, sometimes rigid, notions of what belongs to masculinity and femininity—then there is a tendency to see the behavior as a 'problem.' But let's begin with asking how such stereotypes come to be.

Hypotheses on the Origin of Gender Stereotyping

Psychologists Alice Eagly and V. J. Steffen suggest the motivation for gender stereotyping lies in the *social aggregation of males into roles different than those as-*

signed to females. In this scenario, gender stereotypes ultimately arise from the decision to separate people based on the apparent sex of their bodies. Having done so, long habituation into these different roles presumably has cultivated different habits of thought, feeling, and action. Thus men (masculine males) and women (feminine females) form gender-differentiated personality traits.[238]

The idea that stereotypes attach to personality traits as well as behaviors based on sex is common, but not very persuasive when examined closely. The famous anthropologist Margaret Mead once famously remarked that personality traits labeled masculine or feminine generally are "as lightly linked to sex as are the clothing, the manners and the form of headdress that a society at a given time assigns to either sex."[239] So, if biology doesn't suffice, what generates these stereotypes?

Psychologists Curt Hoffman and Nancy Hurst argue that gender stereotypes do not stem from real sex differences in personality; they flow from our *rationalizations* rather than from valid perceptions. We generate stereotypes to explain why men and women sort into different roles—and our rationalizing includes the notion that gender personality differences make one gender better suited to certain roles than the other. It is not fact derived from observation that creates our belief in gender-based personality differences, but our need to explain the obvious separation into masculine and feminine roles.[240]

Whichever the case may prove to be, gender stereotypes posit concrete, stable differences in temperament and traits. Overall, in our culture the stereotype for masculinity envisions competence, including a degree of rationality capable of imposing order on chaos, of seeing clearly where things appear murky, and of narrowing a bewildering array of possibilities to the one best choice that furthers power and progress. Masculinity, in sum, is about control—of feelings, thoughts and behavior; of the personal and the social. To be a masculine male is to be in control, a situation dependent on being in position above and in front of others. Femininity, to put it bluntly, is stereotyped as not being masculine. To be feminine, then, is to be less competent, less rational (or more emotional), less orderly, more capricious (whimsical), and so forth. 'She' isn't what 'he' is.[241]

Gender Stereotyping Across the Lifespan

Gender stereotypes are learned early in our development. Parents stereotype their own children, perceiving even their toddlers as conformists to gender expectations about identity and role that will bind them to masculinity or femininity in adulthood.[242] In daycare, caregivers continue gender socialization of children, reinforcing gender stereotypes.[243] And children learn the stereotypes well. In fact, in children gender stereotypes appear to become stronger (more rigid) with age.[244] Clearly, children get how important gender differentiation is and how useful stereotypes are.

Gender stereotypes continue to surround us and influence us as adults. Women and girls are expected to be caregivers, more focused on relationships such as marriage and parenthood, more emotional, more oriented to appearance, less rational, and less competent or reliable in the workplace. The workplace, in particular, is an obvious arena where gender stereotypes exercise influence.[245] But such stereotypes are omnipresent. The media is replete with them.[246] They are present even in the daily comics we laugh at over breakfast.[247]

The Dangers of Gender Stereotyping

We may laugh at gender stereotypes, but their force is subtle and pervasive. All of us are influenced by them, and at least potentially can be victimized by them. Or, we may victimize others. Gender stereotyping most of the time is relatively harmless; if it weren't the costs would long ago have outweighed the benefits and discouraged the practice. But that does not mean no costs exist, or that no harm ever occurs. The dangers of gender stereotyping include:

❑ endorsing gender judgments we know to be exaggerated and unhealthy;

❑ attributing gender characteristics to individuals even in the face of contrary evidence; and,

❑ insisting on gender stereotypes as normative to such an extent that punishment of noncompliant individuals is viewed as just.

Psychologists Neil Macrae, Alan Milne, and Galen Bodenhausen remark that research demonstrates "an increased reliance on stereotypes when social perception occurs under taxing or resource-depleting conditions."[248] One such condition occurs when we are caught off-guard in a social situation by an encounter with someone whose gender presentation appears to us at variance with what we assume it should be. A male in a skirt is a good example. Our reflexive gender stereotyping of strangers is suddenly thrown a wrench. We experience *cognitive dissonance*—an uncomfortable sensation accompanying the coexistence of things that don't fit together. Social psychologist Leon Festinger says, "The existence of dissonance, being psychologically uncomfortable, will motivate the person to try to reduce the dissonance and achieve consonance." [249] Interestingly, though, we typically respond not by questioning the stereotype, but by becoming more inflexible in its application. Thus we use the stereotype—what we expect—as a standard for forming a judgment. The male in a skirt is a gender nonconformist—and that is bad!

Our judgment is usually reinforced by application of other stereotypes, such as 'all males in feminine dress are gay.' Our reliance on stereotypes and how we resolve cognitive dissonance can lead us to *stigmatize* others. Sociologist Erving Goffman describes the cost paid by those we stigmatize. This cost begins with a very basic price we make them pay by our judgment that their stigma makes them somehow not quite human. "On this assumption," Goffman writes, "we exercise varieties of discrimination, through which we effectively, if often unthinkingly, reduce his life chances." [250]

When we introduced the idea of androgyny, we remarked that possessing the positive characteristics of *both* genders appears healthier than endorsing only the characteristics of one gender. In other words, escaping the box of a gender stereotype is a good thing. When we endorse gender judgments by blindly, uniformly, and inflexibly applying gender stereotypes to everyone we meet, we unwittingly contribute to the pressures we all feel about gender compliance. And *that* is *not* a good thing.

Conclusion

Gender socialization, regardless of whether it stems from or incorporates biological factors, remains a primary force of culture. It shapes and directs gender development along certain lines approved by society. Basic and pervasive forces in society—institutions like church and school—join the personal modeling and influence of parents and peers. Media seeps in everywhere. And though we may find various ways to explain *why* and *how* gender socialization occurs, one fact remains startlingly clear: we all live subject to its powerful forces every day of our lives. Its effects reach even to our relationships—to which we now must turn.

Chapter 5

Gender Relations

Introduction: Gender socialization is profoundly reflected in gender relations. Because these relations are arranged vertically rather than horizontally, they emphasize *power*. In fact, gender itself is a *privilege*; it is not extended to all and it is not extended equally. Men and women are accorded gender in our culture; transgender and third gender people typically are not viewed as having gender in the same way or on an equal footing. Instead they are generally perceived as misguided souls whose abnormality and disorder lie in not accepting their 'natural' gender. These may seem remarkable contentions, and we certainly need to examine them closely. If gender privilege actually exists, it helps explain why the genders are arranged as they are.

One consequence of arranging genders vertically, so that one has higher status and more power, is an incentive to competition and *conflict*. Gender is very political. Those who have power are typically reluctant to share it, at least equally. Those who don't have it, want it. As a result there is frequent friction as one group tries to preserve its privilege while others seek a more equitable share. One gender is especially privileged: masculinity. The cry, 'It's a man's world!' is not an empty one. *Masculine privilege* extends to boys over girls, and men over women. Women have employed various strategies, with different degrees of success, to try to level the playing field. Today, many transgender and third gender people are trying to use the same or similar strategies. In gender politics, every gender strives for recognition and a share in power.

Gender relations are enacted principally in two spheres: the public world of *work* (the labor force), and the private world of the *family*. Whether within the confines of the home or in the broader reach of society, relations between the genders concern power—who has it, how it is legitimized, and how it is wielded. Gender relations may be more vertical, as in the *gender hierarchy* that has predominated in Western societies for a long time, or more horizontal, as in efforts to achieve egalitarian marriages. In the public sphere, gender relations are typified by a pronounced division of labor based on gender. The result has not been 'separate but equal,' but instead 'separate and unequal.' *Patriarchy* has dominated. The same has held true in the family. To account for gender relations being as they are, both in public and private spheres, a number of theories have been proposed. We need to examine some of the most prominent.

The Politics of Gender

If we have had any lingering doubts about why we should concern ourselves with gender, they should be ended as we dialog about gender relations. Discussions of gender are not made merely to keep academicians employed. Convictions about gender carry strong consequences socially. Gender is political because gender is used to divide and control the populace, to govern its interactions, and to establish values and policies that help structure our sense of who we are. These things require *power* and gender politics, like any politics, very much concerns struggles over power—who has it, who wants it, and how it is used. Gender politics affect us both in terms of our private sense of self and in regard to our relations with others.

While our focus in this chapter is on relations with others, a word about the private gendered self is also in order, because it raises a fundamental issue: gender privilege.

Gender Privilege

This idea of *gender privilege*—the grant of gender as an enfranchisement—requires some careful contemplation. Let's start by hearing another voice. Gender activist Kate Bornstein refers to having a clear and socially accepted gender as a 'privilege.' Bornstein comments: "When you have a gender, or when you are perceived as having a gender, you don't get laughed at in the street. You don't get beat up. You know which public bathroom to use, and when you use it, people don't stare at you or worse. You know which form to fill out. You know what clothes to wear."[251] What does Bornstein mean?

Consider this: most of us have a clear sense of our gender within the two genders scheme of our culture. Those among us who easily embrace our assigned gender identity and practice our expected gender role have little sense of gender as a privilege. Instead, it feels like an entitlement of nature. The difference between an entitlement and a privilege is that the former, as the word suggests, is a right bestowed by title, while the latter is a special grant not extended to all.

When gender comes easy to us, we enjoy the rights associated with the gender title we hold: boy or girl, man or woman. If we see everyone else as belonging to either masculinity or femininity, and assume an equal degree of comfort of fit with the title, then we feel no need to question the rightness of this entitlement. In Bornstein's terms, our sense of entitlement makes it easy for us to answer on a form which gender is ours of the two choices, which of the two bathrooms we can use, and which clothing department to shop in. It may never occur to us that not everyone finds this so easy.

Only those of us who do not enjoy this ease of gender identity, for whom the practice of what is expected in a gender role feels like hypocrisy, readily grasp that gender acceptance is *not* a right. Gender is a privilege because it is not extended to those whose experience and expression of it wanders too far from cultural norms of masculinity and femininity. Only those who conform are granted the special benefits and powers of having a gender, such as a ready and unquestioned acceptance by most others, and a right to appear dressed and acting in certain ways.

Those of us who do not conform to our society's dichotomous scheme of gender lose gender privilege and risk alienation, marginalization, and victimization. So, gender privilege is basic to the politics of gender. Much like citizenship, a clearly defined and recognized gender identity carries with it a sense of membership and attendant rights. Without such a clear identity we are left a stranger in a strange land. If politics is how we govern ourselves, then gender is as political as it comes because in a myriad of ways it shapes and defines who we are allowed to be, just as laws grant rights and impose boundaries. If we break a gender boundary we are viewed a law-breaker—and punished.

There is another side to gender privilege in gender politics. Privilege also means distinctions, separations, and advantages. Privilege cannot exist without inequality; somebody has to be refused the special status and power that somebody else gets. Women in our culture generally have some sense of this. In a culture structured such that one gender (masculine) enjoys special privilege, the matter of what gender is—or is *not*—genuinely matters. This is why women have labored so long and diligently to change their perceived status. In recent decades the awareness of gender inequality has become more acute—and the controversies and debates more pointed.[252]

But none of us can afford to ignore the political consequences of our society's decisions about gender because those decisions affect structures and processes that affect *all* of us. In practical effect, privilege sorts out the genders into a hierarchy—and each of us has a place in that hierarchy. But not only is it possible that not all genders may be recognized ('naturalized citizens' versus 'aliens'), even among those that are recognized, not all are equal. In organizing our life with one another vertically we place ourselves in a position where we are either pulling at those above us or pushing against those below us as we seek either to secure our status or improve it. In either instance we are engaged in competition and conflict as we struggle for power.

Gender Conflict

We all have heard of the 'war between the sexes.' Chris Beasley, in his examination of gender and power, remarks, "The gendering process frequently involves creating hierarchies between the divisions it enacts. One or more categories of sexed identity are privileged or devalued."[253] In modern Western culture, in societies like our own, the gendering process yields a division into two kinds—a binary gender system—and carries this out, as Beasley says, "to the point of this division even being construed as oppositional."[254]

Why wouldn't it be oppositional? Those who have want to keep, those who have not want to have—it is an implacable truth in many things, and not least with respect to gender. The rewards of status at the top mean greater power, both through influence and through control of resources and institutions that create and distribute them. In our culture, with its recognition of just two genders, the opposition is between men and women. In a patriarchal society, men not merely enjoy top status, they wield it in the lordly fashion of a father over children. Women rather sensibly perceive patriarchy as demeaning and resist. As we have seen, in recent decades, especially in the West, women have made strides in bridging the distance in the gender hierarchy.

Among the obstacles women have had to overcome is a history of efforts by men to justify their superior status. The subordination of women has often been legitimized by religious appeals or so-called arguments from Nature. Among the latter has been the claim by some scientists that men's natural endowments of mind and body confer an advantage. Our societal status quo since the late 19th century, for example, has been bolstered by the authority of science through medical men, who linked a multitude of things to sex and gender differences, and inculcated as a 'scientific' mindset the inferiority of women. Yet this situation was itself only the latest in a long line of insults and injuries.

For a considerable time in Western culture women were not merely seen as subordinate to men, but as 'belonging' to them. Daughters 'belonged' to their fathers, were 'given' in marriage, and became thereby the sole property of their husbands. Keeping girls sheltered from sexual experience prior to marriage safeguarded their value to a future husband—when they became 'women.' Despite the fact that such ideas persist in various guises, movements like feminism have sharply challenged this construction and brought about serious erosion to it.

Gayle Rubin & 'The Traffic of Women'

Anthropologist Gayle Rubin, briefly introduced before (chapter 2), helped energize the second wave of feminism with her provocative analysis of how women historically (and presently) are caught up in what she terms a 'political economy of sex.' [255] In a landmark essay entitled "The Traffic of Women," Rubin traces and explores how men make women a commodity. She begins with the unfulfilled promise by Marxist analysis to adequately explain the economic situation of women. In so doing she posits a 'preliminary definition' of what she terms a 'sex/gender system': "the set of arrangements by which a society transforms biological sexuality into products of human activity, and in which these transformed sexual needs are satisfied."[256]

Rubin then turns to Levis-Strauss and Freud for help in fleshing out this definition and applying it to a long history of activity where men use women in the political economy of sex. From Claude Levi-Strauss' writing on kinship (*The Elementary Structures of Kinship*, 1969), she focuses on how the 'gift' of a woman has been used to cement bonds between men, and forge a 'taboo' on any but heterosexual relationships. Rubin locates the origin of gender in this taboo: "The division of labor by sex can therefore be seen as a 'taboo': a taboo against the sameness of men and women, a taboo dividing the sexes into two mutually exclusive categories, a taboo which exacerbates the biological differences between the sexes and thereby *creates* gender."[257] She means that the psychological sense men and women carry of their differences from each other is formed from the forced division of the sexes that marks culture, and not from any biological necessity.

From Freud, in an extended examination of the Oedipus complex, she draws an explanation for how developmental processes interact with kinship demands in culture to divide the sexes, psychologically incorporate kinship taboos, and foster the sexual desire mandated by compulsory heterosexuality. In sum, she argues that cultural forces, guided by what we are terming masculine privilege, have instilled powerful and fundamental forces that guide development in every new generation, pushing children to accept gendered differences that retain a separation between them with men on top and women used to serve masculine desires.

But despite the damning evidence accrued for the damaging nature of the sex/gender system, Rubin does *not* advocate its removal. Rather, she contests its present form, arguing that the system itself is not immutably oppressive. But because the present system "will not wither away in the absence of opposition," she gives a call to action: "The sex/gender system must be reorganized through political action."[258] And that is what many feminists then, and now, have labored to accomplish.

Challenging the Gender Status Quo: Feminists & Dress

Still, the more things change the more they remain the same. Despite the fact some of the more visible manifestations of gender inequality have been curbed, similar dynamics remain in most matters. Consider this statement made in the United States not all that long ago:

> Today, male-female relationships are more likely to involve a different economic arrangement, one in which the male protects and supports the female in return for exclusive sexual rights and domestic obligations. Unrestricted female sexual independence would destroy this traditional bargain and all the institutions that it fosters. Thus a fundamental change in gender relationships would ensue, involving a diminution of the power traditionally exercised by males. Support for traditional sexual morality, then, operates to support traditional gender roles.[259]

Participants in the Women's Movement of the 1960s, alongside many other Americans, challenged both the gender and sexual status quo represented by the situation just described. The point in women championing their sexual liberation often was less about sexuality *per se* and more about the inequities between men and women that showed up in sexual behavior and attitudes. Of course, those same inequities between genders existed in many domains; but matters of sexuality, because they were so closely tied to gender, made people especially uneasy. One way some women expressed their new claim on liberation was to burn their bras. This action was a symbolic exclamation point on a battlefront existing between men and women for a very long time: *dress.*

We shall devote special attention to the relation of dress and gender later, but it is appropriate to discuss it briefly here in connection with gender politics. Dress may seem an unlikely field for conflict, but perhaps the principal way gender is expressed is through dress presentation.[260] Gender-differentiation in dress persists in visibly segregating the genders; styles of dress facilitate or inhibit range of activity and thus can be used to control what the wearer does. Feminine dress is far more limiting than masculine dress, and designed to symbolically present imagined qualities of femininity. If women wanted to wage war against sexist ideals, dress was a logical arena to target.

Women, even before the feminists of the 19th century, understood that statements in dress can pose commentary on gender. When feminists adopted, then adapted, masculine styles of dress they expressed a claim on masculine prerogatives held by males. The early feminists paid a price, enduring alienation, censure, and victimization. They were branded transgressors in dress—'crossdressers'—and 'mentally disordered' for upsetting what many believed was the natural and ordained order of male/masculine over female/feminine.[261] But by the end of the 20th century, they had succeeded in winning the right to wear pretty much whatever they desired, and the very notion of a crossdressing woman had become foreign to most people.

Unfortunately, that victory was robbed of some of its value by becoming largely separated from issues of even greater substance to feminists, such as equal pay for equal work. As we shall soon hear from Sylvia Walby, the patriarchy may excel in shifting the grounds of conflict such that apparent triumphs soon appear mostly Pyrrhic. Women won the right to wear clothes long associated with men, like pants, but the gender hierarchy status quo succeeded in keeping dress gender-differentiated with distinctly feminine styles for pants, shirts, and any other article appropriated from men.

Opponents to change in the gender hierarchy certainly grasped the importance of dress in the 19th and 20th centuries—and the battle over dress rules at school, in the workplace, and in other public arenas still persists.[262] Gender-differentiated dress remains instrumental in the flow and regulation of power in gender politics. However, in the 21st century the scene of battle has shifted from between men and women to between dominant genders (masculinity and femininity) and marginalized genders (third gender and transgender).

Challenging the Gender Status Quo: Crossdressers

In the complex contest among genders are those of us whose gender affiliation joins neither masculine men nor feminine women. Transgender and third gender individuals are prone today to be plagued by the same labels and censure that early feminists faced. Because the dress appearance may not match the gender assigned based on apparent sex, many transgender and third gender individuals are called crossdressers. *Crossdressing* is a remarkable phenomenon reminding us the power conflicts in gender politics are not confined to men and women; the conflict is not merely between masculinity and femininity.

Those of us claiming a third gender, or who dare to defy the separation of the genders by crossing from one to the other (*trans*gender), also become embroiled in conflict. However, historically, the power of such individuals among us, typically separated even from one another, has been much less than that held by women. If any among us is perceived as a crossdresser by the others of us who have gender privilege—we men and women with an easy sense and acceptance of our assigned gender—the consequence is being stripped of the status and power we would otherwise have. Those of us labeled crossdressers are punished as nonconformists to our 'real' gender rather than granted any legitimacy as a different gender.

Although *all* statistically unlikely variations in sexual behavior or gender identification challenge the status quo, crossdressing seems to pose a particularly thorny problem for it.[263] That problem can only be understood in light of an insistence on two-and-only-two genders. Appearances that violate the social scheme for gender cannot be ignored, but they also cannot be sanctioned as genuine displays of a different gender from man or woman. As we discussed a moment ago, women succeeded in winning the right to a wider range of dress by accepting an ongoing, albeit modified, gender-differentiation in dress. In that respect, talking about crossdressing women has become *passé* and the real issue is those judged to be men masquerading as women.

Of course, if we think about it, not everyone designated 'woman' in the days when women were still called crossdressers wore that gender label easily. For some assigned femininity crossdressing was an expression of a different gender, whether masculinity or something else. The same remains true for those designated as men who dress like women. However, the latter have received far less tolerance. In the prevailing scheme of things, when perceived 'men' crossdress they are judged as doing the unthinkable—voluntarily lowering their social status.[264] Patriarchy remains in full force, for only within a patriarchal system of just two genders, where males are valued above females and accorded higher social status, can such a judgment carry any practical force.

The Nongendered

We have come full circle. To insist on being other than a man or a woman, or to claim to be a man when the body's apparent sex is female, or a woman when the genitalia suggests maleness, is to abandon the gender citizenship awarded at birth. Such of us who risk that move are made expatriate and exiled. The ones censured the most are those perceived to have fallen the furthest— apparent males who seem to have given up masculinity—an unthinkable fall from grace. But all 'third gender' and 'transgender' people are relegated to the bottom of the gender hierarchy. Those among us called transgender or third gender people are socially *gender-neutered*—functionally treated as without legitimate gender for as long as there remains persistent nonconformity to the gender status quo. Gender-neutering means becoming nongendered in the same way that losing citizenship makes someone an alien in their own country.

We might think that women, long accustomed to similar issues, would be sympathetic to the oppression suffered by the nongendered, and to some extent that is true. Women are more tolerant than men toward transgendered and third gender people. But it is a relative thing. In the push and pull competition in the hierarchy, women are not much more willing than men to share the status and power they have. So it should not be surprising to hear feminists who complain about transgender folk appropriating some of their tactics and who resist pleas for support.[265] We all have a stake in gender politics, whether we identify ourselves as men, women, or 'other.'

Gender Relations in Society

Gender roles are enacted in two major spheres: public life, especially the world of work, and the family. Let us begin with the former. In the contest among genders men continue to hold the advantage. Women have made strides, but remain in an inferior position. Transgender and third gender people have also made modest gains, but mostly succeed either by remaining invisible within socially sanctioned identities and roles not truly their own or by proving able to capitalize on one or another of the few tolerated outlets in their own identity, such as entertainment or the sex trade.

Most attention remains on the struggle between men and women because they are the most visible genders and the largest. *Gender inequality* continues to exist and is much studied. Obviously, as with other matters we are conversing about, gender relations in society-at-large cannot be more than briefly introduced here. To do so let us continue our approach of attending to significant voices in the contemporary conversation on gender.

Sylvia Walby & Gender Inequality

Among the foremost researchers and theorists on this matter today is English sociologist Sylvia Walby, who specializes in what she terms "the tension between general social theory and specific forms of inequality, especially gender."[266] Walby has been a leading voice since the late 1980s. Her work offers some indication of how the conversation on gender in terms of social relations has progressed over the last few decades.

To understand much of Walby's work we must grasp the idea of *patriarchy*. The word 'patriarch' is very old, and refers to the head of a family, clan, tribe, or similar social unit. The extension of that idea to broader social systems, such as a society, is what 'patriarchy' refers to and has been used since the early 17th century. The term, though, became popular among feminists in the early 20th century, and especially prominent among second wave feminists.[267] In its use by feminists it is not applied to a particular social system but used broadly to refer to masculine domination pervasive in many societies and at multiple levels.

Walby, through the 1980s-1990s, worked carefully through the existing literature and theories on patriarchy and shaped her own distinctive position.

In 1986, Walby published *Patriarchy at Work*. This book examines gender segregation in the English labor force across more than a century's span. Along the way Walby critiques the existing theories of gender inequality, separating them into different kinds and arguing that none are adequate by themselves. Her own integration of existing ideas highlights her contention that patriarchy still best explains the gender inequalities she describes. According to Walby, *patriarchy's twin strategies* are to exclude women from paid labor, and to keep their work in jobs of lower social status than the jobs of men. The mechanisms of patriarchy are carried out in certain critical social structures: "The key sets of patriarchal relations are to be found in domestic work, paid work, the state, male violence and sexuality; while other practices in civil society have a limited significance." The theoretical effect of this book was to restore 'patriarchy' as a relevant and important sociological concept.[268]

Walby's 1990 book *Theorizing Patriarchy* has come to be regarded as a classic in the field. In it she both reviews major theoretical positions (e.g., Marxism, feminism, post-structuralism, and dual systems theory), and issues important to women (e.g., paid work, household production, culture, sexuality, and violence). Her concern, of course, is to understand patriarchy. She contends that it is not less important now than before in history and that it remains a potent force systematically structuring gender inequalities. Once more, six particular social structures circumscribe it through the exploitative practices shown in them: the home, the labor force, the state, cultural institutions, sexuality, and masculine coercion, especially violence.[269]

Walby also discerns two distinct forms: private patriarchy and public patriarchy. *Private patriarchy*, predominant in pre-industrial society where the male head of the house exerted great control, operates by excluding women from power, whether economic or political. It operates within a smaller sphere, where individual men lord over particular women. The narrow reach of control by men was mirrored in the narrow window women had to view or participate in public life. As capitalistic pressures in industrialism, coupled with social movements like early feminism, eroded that form of power the patriarchy shifted. *Public patriarchy* begrudgingly grants women certain rights (e.g., suffrage, better education, and the right to work), but keeps them subordinated through gender segregation in the labor force. Walby contends that patriarchy remains a formidable force precisely because it proves so adaptive. As women mount successful challenges here and there, patriarchy shifts the grounds of the gender conversation so that new dilemmas emerge.[270]

Walby's 1997 sequel, *Gender Transformations*, indicates that while women have succeeded in improving both their education and their opportunities in the labor force, new inequities have emerged. For example, she points out that a division by age has joined traditional divisions among women based on class and ethnicity. With the 20th century winding to a close, Walby identifies three important factors behind the change in women's employment opportunities:

reduced discrimination consequent to changes in laws and policies since the 1970s; increased education among young women; and, the declining significance of domestic activities for some women, especially among the young. However, while women were increasing their participation in the labor force, it remained arguable whether gender inequality was actually being reduced. She notes that some critics argue that issues like violence, and inequality in sexuality and culture are more important to women. Walby herself contends that *constrained choices* frame women's reality. "Women make choices, but not under conditions of their making. Women choose the best option that they can see, rationally, though usually with imperfect knowledge, but only within the range of options open to them." In sum, despite the gains women as a group have made, actual changes in opportunity remain highly variable among subgroups of women.[271]

In the early 21st century, Walby now participates in *gender mainstreaming*, which she describes as "a project to make visible the implications of gender in both social theory and social policy."[272] Elsewhere she describes it in this way:

> It is both a new form of gendered political and policy practice and a new gendered strategy for theory development. As a practice, gender mainstreaming is a process to promote gender equality. . . . As a form of theory, gender mainstreaming is a process of revision of key concepts to grasp more adequately a world that is gender, rather than the establishment of a separatist gender theory.[273]

We have been dialoging on the politics of gender, and gender mainstreaming is part of that. Walby calls it "inevitably and essentially a contested process."[274] This is because the quest for gender equality competes with the traditional norms and goals of the mainstream. For example, the mainstream economically prizes competition, but competitiveness among businesses means inequalities such as favoring employment of women in part-time and low paying jobs. This social prioritizing can be disputed, but that may entail negotiation and compromise where outright policy or legislative change is unlikely. Similarly, theoretical approaches in gender mainstreaming may emphasize one or another approach, each with a different goal: to transform the mainstream into something new through melding feminist ideals with traditional masculine ways; to embed, integrate, or assimilate gender equality into the mainstream without challenging existing policies; or to set an agenda for change that prioritizes gender equality and targets policy change. Put more simply, the end envisioned may focus on changes in feminist strategies, changes in mainstream thinking, or both.[275]

A key issue in gender mainstreaming—as it has been for some time among feminists—is how best to conceive what constitutes *gender equality*. Is it achieved when men and women are treated the same, with equal opportunity and equal treatment? Or is it important to retain a sense of difference between genders to accomplish true equality? If the latter is the goal, how can it be attained without once more falling into the confining box set by essentialism, where outcomes are justified by nature and culture's role is vastly diminished? Perhaps the best answer is to transform the whole matter into some broader conception of gender, but what might that entail? Can all three strategies—based on sameness, recognition of differences, and transformation—be simultaneously pursued? The answers to such questions inform the practice pursued in gender mainstreaming.[276]

Walby is quick to remind us, too, that gender mainstreaming occurs in a context of many different kinds of social inequality. Legally, complaints of discrimination can be brought on the grounds of gender, ethnicity, disability, faith, sexual orientation, and age.[277] This reality poses a challenge to gender mainstreaming, because attentiveness to this larger context of inequalities risks potential rewards that might be gained by sustaining focus on gender inequalities. Conversely, the rewards of uniting separate constituencies might be immense for furthering gender equality. Paralleling the practical dilemma is a theoretical one: understanding how the various forms of inequality intersect.[278]

Although gender mainstreaming participates in gender politics, Walby observes that sometimes it is represented as though primarily a technical process offered by experts to improve the efficiency of existing policies. In fact, she says, gender mainstreaming sits midstream in the debate between whether governance is best done by experts or by democracy. Of course, the two can be thought of as entwined rather than polar opposites. Perhaps there is a duality of expertise and participatory democracy that proves complementary rather than contradictory. In any instance, the issues involved invite renewed reflection on the nature of a democratic society and the place of gender. At a practical level one aspect of this remains the representation of women in elected positions. But it also entails their participation in movements and other parts of civil society, such as academia.[279]

The Division of Labor by Gender (Occupational Gender Segregation)

Much of Walby's work entails an examination of *gender segregation* in the public labor force. We met this idea of gender segregation earlier, while talking about gender socialization, but it is most often used in connection with labor. Sociologist Alison MacEwen Scott describes it as "the fact that women tend to work in jobs and occupations that are dominated by women and men in ones that are dominated by men." She further notes such segregation "is strongly related to inequalities in pay, career prospects, and employment protection."[280]

Economist Joyce Jacobsen tells us that at the end of the 20th century, *blue-collar* occupations (e.g., production jobs, electricians and carpenters, construction workers) remained mostly masculine. Women dominated in so-called *pink-collar* occupations (e.g., clerical positions and service positions such as cooks, kitchen workers and house servants). Among the professions (e.g., law, medicine, economics), women gained in terms of percentage representation, but segregation often took another form—disproportionate representation in the lower ranks. Similarly, while women held over one-third of managerial positions overall, they seldom reached the upper levels, a phenomenon dubbed 'the glass ceiling.'[281] In sum, Jacobsen reports, "Studies of occupations that have shown recent rises in percentage of females have concluded that these rises in female participation may be accompanied by increased intra-occupational segregation and by job *de-skilling*.[282]" The latter refers to making jobs more routine with less responsibility.

Our society is not alone in this practice of gender segregation in labor. A study published in the mid-1960s, surveying practices in 224 societies around the world, found many labors are strongly gender segregated. Not surprisingly, making war proved overwhelmingly a masculine activity; childrearing a feminine one. Hunting was an exclusively masculine activity in 166 societies, but an exclusively feminine one in none. On the other hand, cooking was an exclusively feminine labor in 158 societies, but an exclusively masculine one in only 5 societies.[283] Such divisions of labor become entrenched in gender expectations and role performance. Moreover they fuel essentialist claims that gender-divided labor is based on body differences.

However, we already have discussed this matter (chapter 3) and discovered that supposed sex-based gender segregation in labor is hardly universal for almost any kind of work we can name. Its relative character suggests culture, rather than biology, is the most prominent force. In fact, gender segregation appears to be *more* pronounced in wealthy industrial nations.[284] Alternatives to the essentialist position abound. Four common explanations are:

❑ *Patriarchy*—masculine privilege began in the family and extended into the public workforce.

❑ *Economic rational choice*—gender segregation is driven by vested self-interest.

❑ *Preference*—gender segregation is at least partly the result of varying choices made by women.

❑ *Multiple factors*—disparate strands weave gender segregation.[285]

Some theorists point to *patriarchy* as the principal culprit. Women's policy researcher Heidi Hartmann, in an influential 1976 article, bluntly asserts:

> It is my contention that the roots of women's present social status lie in this sex-ordered division of labor. It is my belief that not only must the hierarchical nature of the division of labor between the sexes be eliminated, but the very division of labor between the sexes itself must be eliminated is women are to attain equal social status with men and if women and men are to attain the full development of their human potentials.[286]

Similarly to Walby, Hartmann argues that it was in the family that men first formed a hierarchy as they controlled the work of women and children. What they learned there was extended into the public sphere. Rivka Polatnick, examining why men don't rear children, adds that gender segregation in labor carries over into the family, where it supports the gender hierarchy there. Because childrearing is labor intensive, and designated for women, their opportunities in the work force are limited. Since, as she argues, "occupational achievement is probably the major source of social status in American society," men's greater involvement translates both into higher social status and greater income—the keys to power not only in the world, but within the home. This, Polatnick says, is why men "ignore, discourage, or actively resist" reform proposals (e.g., flexible hours and childcare centers) that would make women's participation in the work force easier.[287]

Another approach, *economic rational choice*, makes a relatively simple argument: people act in their own self-interest in job choices. These rational choices are based on *human capital*—the work skills and experience an individual possesses. In capitalist economies the marketplace provides a plethora of job opportunities, but these require differing skills and experience, and so any given individual's options are constrained by the occupational openings available in accord with his or her own human capital. Thus, the explanation for the varying places men and women, as groups, hold in the workforce is a function of the rational choices individuals make based on their human capital.

It's easy to see how this is translated to the dominant genders. Because women orient themselves to the domestic realm their human capital compared to men is more limited, thus restricting their options, and creating occupational gender segregation. Much as we found with patriarchy theory, this perspective advantages men. Sociologist Sharon Hays points out that, "Many scholars have also argued that capitalists are well served by women's commitment to child rearing."[288] They use this commitment, Hays continues, to argue that since a woman's *primary* responsibility is in the home caring for children, they are at most occupying a *secondary* earning role—and hence can be paid lower wages. The rational choice argument concludes, in the words of other scholars, that, "The rational choice, therefore, is for the person with more human capital, the man, to be the principal earner, while the woman takes primary responsibility for domestic work."[289]

A third explanation, *preference theory*, stems from the work of sociologist Catherine Hakim.[290] In some respects a refinement of rational choice theory, preference theory distinguishes among three basic ways women relate to family and work. At either pole, constituting about 20% each of all women, are *work-centered women* and *home-centered women*. The former are career-oriented; the latter family-oriented. Work-centered women tend to be single and/or childless. Home-centered women are more likely to be married with children. Hakim says occupational gender segregation is low for work-centered women, who compete capably in the workforce with men, but they are more likely to face discrimination in the workplace. Home-centered women, to the extent they participate in the labor force, typically prefer flexible work that may be either part-time or temporary.[291]

But a third group, the largest, Hakim styles as *adaptive women*. Situated between the poles, these women (about 60% of all women) choose both work and family. They may work because they want to, or because they feel they have to, or simply because they drifted into a job, but work they do. Lacking the ambition of the work-centered women, these women are more accepting of occupational work typically seen as feminine. Moreover, these women—and indeed those in the other two groups—may experience changes in their preferences over time.[292]

The previous three approaches, while all enjoying advocates, have been criticized on various grounds, including being too simplistic. Most current accounts stress *multiple factors* at work in perpetuating gender segregation. Dana Dun and colleagues' examination of "how systems of gender inequality arise and maintain themselves, and why they vary in level" highlights five clusters of structural variables: ideological, family, sex ratio, economic, and political.[293] MacEwan Scott points to employment structures such as those that divide work into 'full-time' and 'part-time,' and 'tradition' in practices that accompany cultural beliefs about gender.[294] Sociologist Carolyn Vogler offers that *sexist attitudes* play an underappreciated role. She defines sexist attitudes as those that "are based on or endorse a belief in the legitimacy of inequality," and finds that sexist attitudes, which occur more in men but exist in both men and women, relate to segregation and help explain its persistence.[295] In sum, gender segregation in occupations and labor practices is a complex phenomenon with deep roots, amenable to some changes but highly resistant to significant alteration.

Gender Relations in the Family

Gender relations in the public sphere have a counterpart in the private sphere. As we have heard, some accounts for why gender relations exist as they do in the public sphere start with the premise that what is learned and modeled in the home becomes mirrored, extended, and elaborated in the wider world. No less than in society at large, gender relations in the family are political, traditionally hierarchical, and complex.

Talcott Parsons & Structural Functionalism

Much of the 20th century's Western understanding of gender relations was rooted in a sociological approach that by the 1950s was preeminently represented by sociologist Talcott Parson's *structural functionalism*. That theory sets out what many today regard as the 'traditional' view of gender roles. The essence of the theory is in the name: society is constituted of institutions and structures, and these are functional when they remain separate so each may contribute its part to the whole. The argument applied to gender is first, that society is served best by preserving distance between the public and private spheres, and second, that men and women contribute to social well-being by maintaining separate gender roles, each in their respective sphere.

In these separate spheres men and women take different, but complementary roles. The masculine role is breadwinner; the feminine role is homemaker. He brings home the bacon; she cooks it. Put more broadly, the man's role is *instrumental* in that it is goal-oriented, helpful, and pragmatic in securing for the private sphere the raw goods the family needs through activity in the public sphere. The woman's role is *expressive* in that it applies these goods in the care of the family while managing and integrating it. Though these gender roles are complementary for the good of society that does not mean they are necessarily equal. In the division of labor between the genders what matters is that any inequalities that occur reflect a *natural* inequality, such as men naturally being suited to heavy labor by virtue of their superior physical strength. If we focus too much on equity issues we may lose sight of more important ones, such as the interdependence of masculine and feminine roles for the betterment of the whole society. What jeopardizes public well-being is not men and women having different roles, for that is natural; what risks society is men and women stepping across the gender boundary into inappropriate roles.[296]

This model is hierarchical and preserves masculine privilege. It was articulated in the 1940s-1950s, and reigned until the 1970s. As we might expect, given the increased social awareness and change we saw associated with feminism in the late 1960s and forward, by the 1980s structural functionalism was no longer regarded as credible by most sociologists—nor by an increasing number of the rest of us who find such a division of gender roles neither equitable nor functional.

Randall Collins & Conflict Theory

Among the more prominent alternatives to structural functionalism is *conflict theory*, articulated prominently by sociologist Randall Collins, beginning in the early 1970s. Collins traces the roots of his model back through Max Weber and Karl Marx, to Thomas Hobbes, and all the way to Machiavelli's *The Prince*. These writers, in their own ways, each depicted the human lot as a struggle guided by self-interest within a framework where coercion lies at the heart of social order. As sociable beings, we live together, but uneasily so. Competition vies with cooperation, and conflict proves inevitable when one group uses coercion against another group that resists being dominated. Social interactions along these lines produce stratification, especially in economic structures.[297]

We have just spent some time contemplating stratification in occupational gender segregation. Its parallel in the family is what Collins terms *sexual stratification*—a hierarchical arrangement along male-female lines. "The basic feature of sexual stratification," Collins writes, "is the institution of sexual property, the relatively permanent claim to exclusive sexual rights over a particular person."[298] He uses the notion of 'property' intentionally. Speaking in economic terms, he argues that stratification in the family exists because of an unequal distribution of resources for sexual domination.

Collins views gender inequalities as a consequence of conflict between the genders for access to and control of scarce resources. Men are the dominant group, originally because their superior physical strength gave them coercive power, but later also by means of their control of the economy, politics, and the military. Men retain their dominance only by keeping women subordinate and inferior in status.[299]

When Collins turns his attention to these matters, he does so with an appreciative eye to feminist theorists—and some of them reach similar conclusions. For example, sociologist Rae Lesser Blumberg, in her *gender stratification theory*, offers an analysis congenial to conflict theory. She argues that the key for women is their degree of economic control. To the extent they exercise economic power, they can successfully resist masculine coercion and the forms of oppression they otherwise experience in relationships both society-wide (e.g., politics), and personal (e.g., marriage and family). When women hold economic power, they gain more control of their own lives, including control of their own reproductive capacities, sexuality, and roles within the home and wider society. Working against women is a stratified society where gender inequalities are 'nested' in the family, which itself is 'nested' in the inequalities of expanding social circles of community.[300]

Conflict theory starts from the premise that families are a smaller mirror of the political structures and conflicts of society at large. Collins believes that economic and political variables in a society provide accurate prediction of how families will look and explain that society's gender stratification.[301] For example, he describes how *private households in a market economy* will look:

> Men remain heads of household and control its property; they monopolize all desirable occupations in state and economy as well. Women become at least potentially free to negotiate their own sexual relationships, but since their main resource is their sexuality, the emerging free marriage market is organized around male trades of economic and status resources for possession of a woman.[302]

In response to the inequalities of the system, what is a woman to do? Collins observes, "The most favorable female strategy, in a situation where men control the economic world, is to maximize her bargaining power by appearing both as attractive and as inaccessible as possible."[303] Two consequences of this strategy are the development of the *ideal of femininity* and the promotion of an *ideal of romantic love*. The former facilitates the latter by cultivating an image of the desirable woman. "The romantic love ideal," says Collins, "is thus a key weapon in the attempt of women to raise their subordinate position by taking advantage of a free market structure."[304] Its success creates male deference during courtship and controls male aggressiveness in marriage.

Remember that Collins thinks that economic and political variables have predictive power for how we can expect families to look. The *family in an affluent market economy* will look different than the one described a moment ago. In this situation women have more education and greater economic opportunity. The increases in their resources means greater bargaining power vis-à-vis men. Increased power means *bargaining* becomes more likely and more important—and that leads us to another important idea about how families operate.

Families depend on social interactions, of which marital bargaining is one aspect. Collins views *social communication* as a key variable. Interactions, too, tend to be vertical in nature. As he puts it in one essay, "At home, the relations of husbands and housewives (as well as of parents and children) can be analyzed using the class criterion of order givers and order takers. . . ."[305] The *giving and taking of orders* is a basic kind of social interaction; the person with more power and superior status—typically the man—occupies the primary role of order giver. This kind of interaction is crucial to social development; families provide all of us an environment in which we first learn the way things are. The world is a place where giving and taking orders is fundamental to our behavior. In the wider world this kind of social interaction is central to work. But it starts at home, and thus the family prepares us for entry into the world of work.

Another basic interaction is *ritualistic*. We rely on established ritual interactions (e.g., social greetings) everyday. Collins enumerates four kinds of ritual interactions—those organized around danger, celebration, deference, and punishment. Deference ritual interactions, for example, are relied on heavily to convert what otherwise might be raw coercion into a subtler use of power. These interaction rituals become another resource to be used in social control—a way both of cementing bonds between members in a group and a coercive tool to control the behavior of others. Families employ both orders and ritual interactions, and use them to manage conflict when it happens.[306]

In and through social interactions we both discover our social reality and gain access to the social realities of others. We exercise influence, try to avoid being dominated, and engage in coercion if it furthers our own status. So there enters an inevitable competition, and stratification, as we try to maximize our own social self and status, even if that comes at the expense of others. After all, resources are scarce—not merely economic ones, but emotional ones too—and control of production, whether of goods, services, labor, or emotions, is essential to thriving and realizing personal goals. Of course, though we try to focus on where we excel, situations arise where our personal status (or our sense of it) is less than we like. Though we might prefer to withdraw from such situations and encounters rather than engage in conflict with others who have an advantage over us, that action is not always possible. So conflict happens, and its roots are the differential resources and unequal power among those pursuing the resources.[307]

Let's consider another essential connection between families and economics. The family is more than a consumer unit; families are about property rights—those conveyed through inheritance, of course, but also economic property rights and sexual property rights. In terms of the latter, for instance, modern marriage (including cohabitation) expresses sexual possession rights through mutual emotional possession. This matter of the control of emotional production—a key social resource—links us once more back to social interactions. So, whether in respect to giving and taking orders, or controlling the production and use of resources, the family functions as an economic system and certainly looks like a political one as well. In both public and private spheres men dominate and a gender hierarchy persists. Our experience of the family perpetuates that hierarchy and its inequities.

In societies like our own, where economic success is closely associated with social status, wealthy families confer on their members increased social status. Collins views women, both inside and outside the home, as heavily involved in labor related to culture-production and status-production. "Once the basic physical necessities and creature comforts become widely available," Collins remarks, "most people invest their surplus money and time in cultural goods."[308] Housewives, for example, today spend less time producing domestic necessities, and more time acquiring cultural objects to enhance the home—and the family's status. In many important respects, then, families may have a vested interest in maintaining the gender scheme that supports the economy within which they function.

John Scanzoni & Exchange Theory

This rather darker vision of gender relations and the family was inevitably counterbalanced by more optimistic appraisals. At roughly the same time conflict theory was being developed by Collins, an interest in equity and in a more egalitarian model of gender roles and relations was also being shaped within sociology. John Scanzoni witnessed at the beginning of the 1970s a reinvigoration of the sociology of the family. The time was right for his work, which drew not only on his own research, but on findings from a range of academic disciplines. Like other voices we have heard, Scanzoni recognizes the important role played by gender politics within the family.

"I utilized a conceptual model in which a dynamic version of exchange theory became indistinguishable from conflict theory," Scanzoni recalls. "Moving beyond mere reciprocity per se, the model postulated that bargaining and negotiation were now mandatory to manage the inevitable struggles between husband and wife."[309] His 1972 book *Sexual Bargaining: Power Politics in the American Marriage* posits that the behavior in interactions between men and women is governed by *reward seeking*. "The central theme of the book," Scanzoni writes, "is that of reward seeking between males and females, which in turn generates social exchanges between them, which in turn generate conflicts and changes."[310]

Scanzoni argues that conflict itself is neutral. It can have either positive or destructive consequences. Conflict is an inevitable result of the fact that men and women are competing interest groups. But it is an unequal competition because of the greater power men possess. Scanzoni argues that society sets the conditions under which a woman can challenge masculine privilege—and such challenges mean conflict.[311]

Within society, over time, four *social statuses* have prevailed for women: as the property of her husband, as his complement (a friend to him), as his junior partner, or as an equal partner.[312] Scanzoni contends that increasingly the conditions of modern society are such that more and more women are moving toward status as an equal partner. "The alteration of role relationships," he says, "has been a consequence of the increasing unwillingness of wives to remain at the property end of the continuum and their determination to move toward the partnership end."[313]

Of course, women's unwillingness alone would mean little without an increase in their own power, and—"Power rests on resources."[314] For example, in later works Scanzoni closely examines how an increase in social status and power affects women's decisions. Greater access to education and to employment opportunities means many younger women make different choices than women with less education and opportunity, often favoring their own self-actualization over pleasing a husband, having children and raising them. These contemporary women have different marriages than those found among traditional women.[315]

Scanzoni recognizes the divergent socialization boys and girls experience on their way to adulthood, but he also sees that movements like feminism, together with other changes in society, have increased women's position in relation to men. Still, families vary. Gender roles within the family may exhibit different points along a spectrum ranging from a so-called 'traditional' view to a 'modern' view. In the traditional family, masculinity as played out in husband and father roles dominates; the interests of children comes next, and the interests of the feminine roles of wife and mother last. In contrast, modern families are characterized by greater role flexibility.[316]

Let's consider how this affects women. *Traditional women* still desire a significant degree of gender role differentiation. They continue to endorse a division between home (feminine sphere) and work (masculine sphere), and to believe behavioral differences in gender roles are justified on the basis of sex differences between males and females. *Modern women*, on the other hand, prefer low differentiation of gender roles and a minimum of gender typing. Changes in society in the early 1970s led Scanzoni to predict more young women would exhibit the characteristics of modern women—and his research confirms that hypothesis.[317]

Scanzoni finds a correlation between a woman internalizing less conventional gender role expectations and her having fewer children, which in turn facilitates greater involvement in the labor force. In addition, embracing a modern gender role perspective necessitates her maintaining "vigorous and effective negotiation" with her life partner.[318] Such dynamics point Scanzoni to a need for greater attention to the power struggles within a modern American family.

Modern women's greater power affects role relationships in marriage. In marriages, *reciprocity*—a give-and-take dynamic process intended to be mutually rewarding—is crucial. The reciprocity between husband and wife in modern marriages reflects the different gender role expectations resulting from their gender socialization plus the greater power of modern women. Scanzoni comments, "Husbands and wives each have certain duties to perform for their spouses, and each has certain rights they expect to have fulfilled by them." Reciprocity brings benefits to each party, but the persistence of reciprocity is also a matter of moral obligation felt by the spouses.[319]

Scanzoni observes that in marriage both partners continually seek rewards from one another. To attain these rewards they *bargain* and *negotiate*. This is where *power*—the ability to impose one's will—matters. The greater power of modern women in marriage (based on their resources) enhances their ability to negotiate or bargain a favorable reward. This shows up especially in marital decision-making. In modern marriages decision-making is not as it is in the traditional family, where the man as provider and head of household exercises disproportionate power. Scanzoni finds that *marital decision-making* in modern marriages is influenced by three factors:

- ❑ differences in each partner's access to economic resources;
- ❑ gender role preferences; and,
- ❑ gender distinctions in negotiating styles.[320]

We already have discussed the differences in access to economic resources. We also considered gender role preferences with regard to the degree of gender role differentiation desired. But we need to note now *gender distinctions in negotiating styles*. Scanzoni claims that, "Men tend to be 'goal-oriented,' women, 'reactive.'"[321] The difference as he conceives it is this: a goal-oriented approach focuses on the behaviors of the other party conducive to resolving the conflict, while ignoring nonproductive behaviors. A reactive style does not sort out the productive from the nonproductive inputs received from the other. Thus, women tend to be less effective bargainers. Scanzoni suspects this difference may reflect men's greater exposure to decision-making in the public sphere.[322]

When reciprocity does not produce expected outcomes, so that a perceived imbalance occurs in the benefits experienced, then conflict erupts. *Conflict*, simply put, arises from the perception of excessive demands.[323] Although it may be unpleasant, it does not have to produce negative consequences. "If it is brought into the open," Scanzoni says, "bargained over, and resolved so that the result is satisfactory to both partners, their relationship reverts back to one based on ongoing reciprocities, and therefore solidarity and stability."[324]

Scanzoni follows the work of psychiatrist John Speigel in identifying the following kinds of conflict management: coercion, coaxing, evaluating, masking, postponement, role reversal, joking, referral to a third party, exploration, compromise, and consolidation.[325] However, he realizes, "Some conflicts in marriage are resolved; in other cases, the issues are never fully cleared up in a way satisfactory to both partners."[326]

Scanzoni sees the possibility in modern marriage for a truly egalitarian relationship, arguing that, "a tiny but growing minority could be described in terms of *role interchangeability*."[327] In such marriages, the wife's commitment to working outside the home becomes as strong as her husband's, while his commitment to children and domestic chores becomes as strong as hers. To what extent such marriages might come to be typical was uncertain when Scanzoni wrote *Sexual Bargaining* in the early 1970s; it remains uncertain today. As he wrote then, "The future of marriage is indeed an unsettled matter."[328]

Conclusion

While many interesting and important qualities color gender relations, clearly gender politics are a central characteristic. The reigning gender hierarchy fosters competition and conflict. The various ways in which we negotiate these tensions may include coercion or cooperation, conflict or negotiation. But comprehending the role of power remains essential to grasping the nature of gender relations—at least in Western societies. But what of gender in other cultures? Is it the same in different societies around the world? That is the question we must next address.

Chapter 6

Gender Across Cultures

Introduction: *Cross-cultural* and *multicultural studies* of gender are still in their infancy. The questioning within Western culture about our conception of gender has helped spark more interest in how other cultures understand it. But such study is complicated by a number of factors. For example, comparisons of practices in different societies are limited if we don't account for variances in cultural conceptions of gender, the relatively greater or lesser place gender holds, and so forth. Also, we must constantly struggle to overcome a bias that relegates other ideas to a subordinate position because of unconscious or conscious ideas we hold about our cultural superiority in belief and practice. Alongside that danger is another: imputing our understanding to practices that at least superficially look like our own. Studying gender across cultures is *not* easy.

A common form of cross-cultural study has been to *compare practices* across societies. While this has some value, we must remember that what looks like the same, or similar idea or practice still exists in a different cultural framework. Ignorance of cultural context, or relegating it to relative unimportance, can lead to misapprehension. This has often been the case in the past and remains a danger in the present.

One way to ease ourselves deeper into the matter is to start close to home. We live in a society that embraces the Western culture associated with the classical Greek and Roman world. That culture has dominated world affairs for so long that its members easily presume its natural and inevitable right to rule cultural ideals and conventions. Yet we tend to forget that our culture is not like a monolith, forever the same, but like a living tree, forever developing. Our current ideas and practices may have continuity with the past without being exactly the same.

Studying how our own culture has changed may help prepare us for examining other cultures. Perhaps it will also teach us that the first, the most fundamental, and probably the most important matter to learn about gender across cultures is that it is *not* uniformly the same everywhere. Although impossible to cover in any depth, we must at least expose ourselves enough to other ideas and practices to experience more profoundly how culturally rich and varied the experience and expression of gender actually is. So we will look generally at different cultures and pause for closer looks at one or two societies.

Cross-Cultural Comparisons

Archaeologist Roberta Gilchrist makes an interesting comment early in her book *Gender and Archaeology*. She writes, "Whether gender, social cognition, or sexuality are dependent fully on biology or culture is no longer the issue. The interesting questions now are how biological and/or cognitive difference is interpreted culturally, how this varies between societies, and how the mind and body may evolve in response to cultural definitions of gender."[329] Such interesting questions are what we wish to consider in this part of our dialog.

Let us begin by talking about *cross-cultural comparisons*. As we mentioned in introducing this material, cross-cultural studies are important though fraught with difficulties. We shall momentarily turn to looking at how gender itself might be variously conceived around the world, but first we will engage in a time-honored practice: selecting behaviors and seeing how they compare around the globe.

Any number of activities might serve as an entry point, but our prior discussions have prepared us for one set of activities in particular—those related to work. In our Western culture, obsessed as we are with money and power, a continuing preoccupation in talking about gender has been about how it relates to economics and politics. We Westerners have carried this interest over to how we examine gender in societies around the world. In fact, this appears to be the single subject related to gender to receive the most attention. It covers the division of labor by gender, the impact of sex ratios, and the role of women.

George Murdock & the Division of Labor By Gender

Earlier in our dialog we briefly examined the matter of how the kinds of labor done by men and women seem to be divided by gender. In fact, in 1958, anthropologist Dwight Heath said of this matter, "The sexual division of labor is a universal phenomenon in culture which makes for differential economic productivity by the sexes."[330] When we spoke of it before, it was in light of the essentialist claim that this tendency is cross-cultural and speaks to a division based on biology: differently sexed bodies are intended for different labor. At that time we also brought forth the counter claim that the alleged evidence used to support an essentialist position does not fare well under close scrutiny. Mindful of the cautions we raised when starting this particular aspect of our dialog, we would do well to heed the words of another anthropologist, Melville Herskovits, who more than half a century ago warned, "The specific forms taken by sex division of labor must be referred to the historical development of the particular body of traditions by which a particular people order their lives."[331]

Now we return to this topic, again briefly, to review some of the tendencies and differences found across societies, but with Herskovits' words in view. Though activities may engage the same behavioral repertoire, they derive their significance and meaning from the values placed on them, and interpretation of them, in a specific cultural context. Here we are examining only the activity.

An early and still often cited work useful to our endeavor is that done by anthropologist and ethnographer George Murdock in the 1930s.[332] In 1937, he originated the Cross-Cultural Survey on behalf of the Institute of Human Relations at Yale. That same year he published an important piece on the division of labor in societies around the world. It included a sample of 224 societies and some of the results are as follows:[333]

Table 6.1 Gendered Division of Labor Cross-Culturally

Activity	Number of Societies Where the Activity Is Exclusively Masculine	Number of Societies Where the Activity Is Done By Both Men & Women	Number of Societies Where the Activity Is Exclusively Feminine
Hunting	166	13	0
Trapping or Catching Small Animals	128	18	2
Weapon Making	121	1	0
Work in Wood/Bark	113	15	1
Lumber work	104	8	6
Cooking	5	38	158
Water Carrying	7	12	119
Grinding Grain	2	22	114
Clothing Manufacture/Repair	12	20	95
Fuel Gathering	22	30	89

These ten activities are selected to illustrate how some are commonly regarded as masculine in most cultures and others are commonly regarded as feminine in most cultures. But *none* of these activities are *always* the exclusive provenance of one gender. Even the oft-cited example of making war as an exclusively masculine activity knows exceptions ranging from the stories of the ancient Amazons to the modern day military exploits of women.

This little list, remember, is a very partial one. The activities selected are the *most* gender segregated. Many other activities are not so imbalanced. For example, agriculture—soil preparation and planting—belongs to both genders in 76 of the societies Murdock sampled, and is exclusively masculine or exclusively feminine in about equal numbers in other cultures (M: 31; F: 37). The crop tending and harvesting aspects of agriculture are likewise an activity belonging to both genders in most of the sampled societies (89), although it is exclusively masculine in some (N=10 societies), and exclusively feminine in others (N=44). Although various scholars have drawn broad conclusions about which activities tend to be more or less masculine or feminine across cultures, the operative term is *tend*.

Scott South & Women in the Work Force

Another aspect of gender and economics concerns the population balance between men and women, referred to as the *sex ratio*. Not surprisingly, sex ratios impact the role of women—but perhaps not in the ways we might suspect. Sociologist Scott South, in examining a cross-national study of 111 societies, hypothesized that the influence of imbalanced sex ratios will be contingent on women's economic power. Where there exists a *high sex ratio*—an undersupply of women—there is pressure on them to marry early and bear children. This means they will experience less schooling and more compliance to masculine expectations. However, South found that women's economic power exercises a significant modifying effect. The greater the participation by women in the labor force, the greater also is their power vis-à-vis men. Consistent with the prediction we heard made by John Scanzoni, South discovered that with their greater economic involvement women are less likely to conform to traditional masculine expectations for them, such as earning less education, getting married earlier, and focusing on having and raising children.[334]

In another study, South and colleague Katherine Trent analyzed data from a sample of 117 countries. They also were interested in seeing the effect of societal-level sex ratios on women's status and roles. The results they determined confirmed the study we just discussed. Interestingly, they found that the effect of sex ratio on women's roles is actually greater in developed countries than in developing ones. In societies like our own, where women have more economic power, they also exercise greater control over their own lives.[335]

Gwen Moore, Gene Shackman & Gender Inequality in Authority

As we have discussed, gender seems related to both economic and political power. Some research looks at both aspects together. For example, sociologist Gwen Moore and then graduate student Gene Shackman utilized a United Nations database for 110 nations to examine gender inequality in authority. They were specifically interested in seeing the impact of economic, social and cultural variables on the attainment of women to elected positions and their representation in administrative/managerial occupations. Of course, as we might suspect, masculine dominance in leadership roles predominates across cultures. Whether in so-called 'developed' or 'developing' nations, despite the increase in women's participation in the labor force, they remain concentrated in low-paying, low-status positions. "Yet," the researchers remark, "women are not uniformly underrepresented in such positions; gender inequality in authority does vary from nation to nation."[336]

Curiously, that inequality varies in ways that indicate neither higher educational attainment by women, nor greater participation in the work force *necessarily* result in lessening the imbalance in positions of authority. They found the factors involved in women gaining authority positions are different for high occupational authority than for high political authority. In the case of the former, more education made for better odds of women's representation in administrative occupations. On the other hand, such educational attainment had no discernible impact on the proportion of representation by women in elected positions. What did make a difference there was higher rates of women's labor force participation. In sum, gender inequality across nations should not be seen as a unitary phenomenon easily explained by any one particular factor.[337]

Gender Western Style

If studying gender through cross-cultural comparative studies yields complex and frustrating results, perhaps we might fare better by narrowing our attention to smaller sets of societies, or to particular cultures. Maybe we can still see how gender differs, but get a clearer picture of individual variations, by focusing on one culture and then another. If so, we may do well to start closest to home by looking at Western culture. But we want to avoid merely reiterating what we have discussed about the contemporary West.

Our modern ideas of sex, gender, and related notions are neither universal nor timeless. Indeed, we can characterize our culture's views as narrow when compared to conceptions found elsewhere in the world and in other ages. For example, the rigid dichotomy between the sexes—and the limitation of their number—is not a universal view. It isn't even the uniform view of Western tradition. We err if we assume that our present way of understanding things—even matters so seemingly basic and natural as sex and gender—always have been the same.

When we turn our eyes on the past, we naturally see through the lens of our present understanding. Though this process is inevitable, and not inherently bad, it complicates things. Judith Ochshorn, who examines ancient societies for data on gender roles, wonders how we can ever be confident we are doing anything more than "imposing our own familiar assumptions and stereotypes about gender on another time and place."[338] If all we do is superimpose our ideas on ancient cultures, all we will see is an imperfect reflection of ourselves. To comprehend past perspectives on their own terms is a daunting task. It requires we do our best to be conscious of what is largely unconscious about our modern view, then suspend our judgment in the interest of listening to the past rather than putting our own words on ancient writers' lips. Though we can do this only imperfectly, we cannot profit from their experience if we do otherwise.

Western culture owes much to the classical world. Contemporary classicists are aware of the ongoing gender conversation and both they, and other participants in the dialog, are talking about gender in the ancient Western world. We don't have time to visit at length such discussion, which is available elsewhere,[339] but we can get a brief idea how lively and important the discourse is.

Let us begin by hearkening back to the age of Plato in the 4th century B.C.E.[340] Consider, for example, the thought on the *origins of sex and gender* put forth by Aristophanes in Plato's *Symposium*. Aristophanes argues that original human nature differed from that seen now:

> [T]he original human nature was not like the present, but different. In the first place, the sexes were originally three in number, not two as they are now; there was man, woman, and the union of the two, having a name corresponding to this double nature; this once had a real existence, but is now lost, and the name only is preserved as a term of reproach.[341]

Though Aristophanes admits that now only two sexes seem apparent, he elucidates a number of characteristics flowing from this original reality into the world still known, including matters often placed today under the umbrella of 'third gender.' Aristophanes' speech elaborates the rather fantastic nature of these primordial beings, explains how sex and sexual attraction as we know it came to be, and also ventures that what we moderns call 'sexual orientation' is explained by the changes that have taken place since the original human beings. Thus, 'homosexuality' stems from those who have a nature from the original Androgynous ('male-female') humans.[342]

In Plato's *Timaeus* a different notion is played with: the first generation of people was exclusively masculine. *Gender differentiation* was based on sex and occurred when those of the original generation of men who proved themselves cowardly and immoral were reincarnated as women. With this division entered in a differentiation in desire so that the genders would interact and intercourse would occur. Indeed they are driven to relate to one another by the compulsion of their sex organs: "in men the nature of the genital organs is disobedient and self-willed, like a creature that is deaf to reason, and it attempts to dominate all because of its frenzied lusts." A parallel imperative exists in women: if the womb "remains without fruit long beyond the due season, it is vexed and takes it ill"—a condition long termed 'hysteria,' a woman's disease caused by a wandering uterus.[343]

We would be mistaken to focus on this idea of hysteria and laugh at the ancient thinking, for it continues to influence us today. Women are still widely regarded as more susceptible to emotional distress and mental illness, and still commonly seen as 'needing' to have children. Men remain viewed as subject to the lust of their loins and yet morally superior to women. And, like Aristophanes, we today are wondering again about the nature of both sex and gender.

There are other legacies. The patriarchal character of the classical world shows up in a familiar *division of labor*. Plato's star pupil, Aristotle (tutor to Alexander the Great), declares, "Men and women have different parts to play in managing the household: his to win, hers to preserve."[344] Similarly, Xenophon divides the world at the door to the family home: women have all the work indoors and men the outdoor activities. Further, he recounts the example of Ischomachus, who took a wife so young that she was like a blank slate he could write upon to make her a suitable administrator of the household.[345] The idea seems little different from our modern witty advice to, 'Marry her young and bring her up right.'

Of course, most of what we know about *women* in the ancient West comes from the writings of men—hardly an unbiased source. Women's studies scholar Helen King, in the mid-1990s, observed that our study of ancient women increasingly has devoted itself to the creation of a concept of 'woman' in antiquity. King offers a number of ideas about how women were regarded by men:

- ❏ Their reproductive capacities are central; their primary role is to bear (legitimate) children.
- ❏ They are inferior to men in both physical and moral strength.
- ❏ They differ from one another in social status and/or sexual availability.
- ❏ Their appearance and character matter more than their deeds.
- ❏ Their weakness and wildness means they need a guardian.
- ❏ When they work outside the home (a characteristic of lower-class women), it is in heavily gender-segregated occupations (e.g., midwife, wet-nurse, craftswomen).

Despite these ideas, the lived reality of ancient women may have been rather different—a notion being pursued in contemporary scholarship.[346]

Indeed, examples abound of strong-willed, independent women who left their mark on the ancient world in politics and art as well as in kitchen and bedroom. Many were educated—at least if fortunate enough to be born in the upper classes. And while a writer like the 2nd century Roman Juvenal in his sixth satire could inveigh against women, romantic poets pined for them, lauded them, advised them, and wrote bitterly of broken hearts by them. In short, the relations between men and women in the ancient West reveal every bit as much the complexity, wonder, and uncertainty we talk about in our own time.

We might wonder, given that what we have just examined belongs to a time largely before the impress of Christianity, whether things were different in Late Antiquity (3rd-6th centuries), when Christianity began to prevail in the West. Classics scholar Gillian Clark tackles these and other questions in her research into women of this period. She notes that the Christian pastor was in a different position from the secular philosopher; the latter's audience was almost entirely men while the former faced many women. Consequently, Christian scholarship faced a stronger imperative to consider gender relations and roles. Yet Clark warns that, "it is misleading to ask whether Christianity, as such, made people think differently about women or treat them differently. Christian teaching could either reinforce or subvert traditional beliefs about women—and it could use the traditional beliefs to construct Christian teaching." This ambiguity means, suggests Clark, that while we may be shocked by the general Christian disparagement of femaleness, we can still acknowledge that Christianity enlarged the possibilities for women.[347]

Finally, we might note that the ancient West also could be intrigued, as we are, by the possibilities of *other sexes and genders*. We already heard an indication of this in Aristophanes' remarks, but speculation about the varieties of human experience in regard to sex and gender can be found persistently through this time. Eunuchs and hermaphrodites, male and female crossdressers, and others who did not fit a convenient binary system were all known to exist and received varying explanations.

Eunuchs occupied a unique and often privileged place in many ancient societies, both East and West. Their infertility made them a logical choice for sensitive positions, such as service among the women of a ruler's harem. At the same time, such roles could place them outside marital relationships. Jewish law, for example, forbids marriage to a eunuch.[348] Many eunuchs were intersex individuals—eunuchs 'made by nature.' Others were eunuchs 'made by man,' sometimes voluntarily, often by the choice of another. However they arrived at this state, it was generally viewed as placing them in a border state between sexes.

Of course, eunuchs were not the only denizens of this space between masculine men and feminine women. Papyrologist Dominic Montserrat, in considering gender in the world of the Roman Empire, remarks that the Roman patriarchy constructed its notions of sex and gender in accordance with a priority on procreative ability. Eunuchs, lacking this power, thus existed outside the conventional gender categories; they were 'third gender' people. But they were not the only ones. Montserrat numbers among other 'third gender' members of society genetic intersexed people, medically castrated men (e.g., the Galli), and celibates such as Rome's Vestal Virgins.[349] There were also hermaphrodites.

Hermaphrodites—our contemporary 'intersex' people—were well-known and often remarked upon in the ancient West.[350] In the classical world, hermaphroditic figures are common in art. French philosopher Luc Brisson, in his study of androgyny and hermaphroditism in Graeco-Roman antiquity, observes that before the Roman Republic hermaphrodites were seen as monstrous grotesqueries, yet by the time of the Roman Empire had come to be seen "as an agreeable fluke of nature."[351] Among Jews, rabbinical scholars spoke of hermaphrodites (the Talmudic term is *androginos*) often, distinguishing kinds and sorting out their place, roles, and limitations under the Torah. In terms of marriage, hermaphrodites were like men; they could marry a woman, but not be married by a man.[352]

The name itself reflects the mythology of a divine root—a notion of the connection of other genders to divine realities that we shall speak of at length later on (chapter 15). In this instance, hermaphrodites are tied to the Greek deity Aphrodite (Roman Venus). Though ostensibly female, Aphrodite is depicted in various places as 'androgynous' in the basic sense of that combined word:

both 'male' and 'female' traits joined in the manner of a hermaphrodite. For example, the Roman writer Lucian says she has "two natures and double beauty."[353] Macrobius in his *Saturnalia* reports that in Cyprus was a bearded statue of the goddess in female clothing, but with male attributes, "so that it would seem that the deity is both male and female."[354] The deity in this form is known as *Venus Barbata* ('Bearded Venus'). By the name *Venus Castina*, she is also the patron deity of men who have feminine souls caught in male bodies.[355] Philoshorus, in his *Atthis*, reports that men offered sacrifice to the moon—associated with Venus/Aphrodite—dressed as women, and women dressed as men, because the moon was thought to be both male and female.[356] Though famous in connection to other matters of beauty, love and desire, the connections with androgyny and hermaphroditism also run deep. Our very term 'hermaphrodite' conjoins her name with that of Hermes, by whom she had a child named Hermaphroditus. Thus, in many ways Aphrodite—the so-called 'goddess of love'—may be called the patron deity of the intersexed.

Crossdressing—perhaps the preeminent marker of transgender and third gender presence—was not unusual in the Greek and Roman classical world. Even a deity might appear in the guise and garb of the opposite sex. Among mere mortals it occurred among heroes (e.g., Achilles, Hercules), powerful rulers (e.g., Caligula, Nero), and ordinary folk (e. g., the 1st century Roman philosopher Seneca mentioned in passing "a man changed into the likeness of a woman"[357]). Among the Greeks crossdressing was found in religious events (ceremonies and festivals), and was depicted in art forms.[358] The Roman world witnessed crossdressing with relatively wide social toleration.[359] In human affairs, crossdressing might be motivated by any number of things, including entertainment, puberty rituals, marriage rites, religious roles or practices, and gender identity expression.

Contributions from the Middle Ages

The age of antiquity gave way to the Middle Ages, a period we especially associate with the dominance of the Christian Church. But the medieval period in Europe was hardly the monolithic testament to social stagnation that many contemporary folk imagine. This expanse of history (from the late 5th century to the Renaissance) witnessed many changes, social and technological, intellectual and artistic. Both sex and gender were matters of interest, and examined through a variety of approaches and in manifold connections.[360] The expectations placed on boys and girls, men and women, were not invariably the same across all periods and places of the Middle Ages. Yet as a general rule we can certainly claim that throughout the medieval world there were individuals who found that their socially prescribed gender identities and role expectations were personally inadequate. These folk—'transgendered' in our use of the term—found various ways in which to experience and express their own sense of gender or to challenge existing conventions.

The nature of those gender conventions has been reexamined in our time. One conclusion we should note immediately is the idea that in the Middle Ages *gender fluidity* was accepted. Medievalists Robert Clark and Claire Sponsler, re-flecting on what the theater of the Middle Ages says about the times, write that "the supposed massive deployment of a stable two-gender system is something of a modern fiction."[361] Similarly, historian Joan Cadden argues that while Me-dieval Europe may have maintained a binary system of the human sexes, the gender continuum was anything but static. Instead, both a range of body physi-ognomies and gender behaviors were acknowledged—and viewed as relatively more susceptible to change than folk of a later time would come to regard them.

Medieval writers tried to explain what they observed, drawing variously on Christian scripture, philosophy (especially Plato and Aristotle), historical ac-counts, and medical speculation. Certainly these efforts were guided by a desire to justify and maintain a gender order that preserved pride of place for mascu-line males. Women were often described in unflattering terms: as descendents of Eve, who caused Adam to sin, they are weak-willed, lusty deceivers ever prone to get men in trouble. In the early Middle Ages, writes historian Michel Rouche, "Women were thought to be property of the cosmos, of the infernal and nocturnal powers, since their menstrual cycle, like the moon's, was twenty-eight days."[362] Marriages were arranged, a girl's virginity beforehand highly treasured, and her life both before and in marriage was designed to tame her so that she should fit her designated place. As Rouche remarks, "Woman, blamed as the source of the destructive folly of love, had to be wrested from the cos-mos, or at any rate from the world of wickedness, and made safe for the dignity of marriage and tender motherhood, the basis of society."[363]

Kathleen Bishop also reminds us that Medieval Europe remained a world dominated by men. "From the masculine point of view," she writes, "women's 'true nature' covertly confirms the male agenda of its own innate superiority and consequent license, supported by religious, philosophical, and literary author-ity."[364] Bishop quotes the medieval author Albertus Magnus, who in his *Quaes-tiones de animalibus*, remarks, "there is no woman who would not naturally want to shed the definition of femininity and put on masculinity."[365] The question naturally rises: could she? Is gender inevitably pinned to sexual anatomy, and is the latter immutable?

One of the more prominent Catholic philosophers of the 12th century, the Scholastic theologian William of Conches (c. 1080-c. 1154), is illustrative of how reasoning out these matters proceeded. Attracted to Platonic rationalism, Wil-liam seems to have been interested particularly in psychological matters, an in-terest filtered through his creative interpretation of Plato's *Timaeus* (which we discussed at the start of this portion of our dialog). In William's gloss of *Timaeus* 42, he reworks the Platonic notion of reincarnation to make his own statement about gendered souls and *gender transformations*:

> For it is not to be believed that the same soul is first in a
> man and then afterwards crosses over into a woman and later
> into brute animals down to the level of worms, as they main-
> tain a certain Pythagoras once assumed. Neither should it be

thought that the soul itself contains anything pertaining to either sex within it, but rather this transformation is held to be according to behaviors. Therefore, so long as the soul acts manfully, it is considered to be a man. But when it becomes soft through various pleasures, while still remaining something of reason about it, then it is understood to be a woman. . . .

And this is the penalty for wretched souls in this life: "and they shall be relegated," that is to say reduced, "to the weakness of a woman's nature." He did not say "to the nature of women," but rather "to the weakness of a woman's nature" to show that this transformation was being accomplished not in essence but rather in resemblance of manners.[366]

Because William locates such a transformation after fifteen years of age, it becomes a 'second birth' that modern scholar James Cain believes William associates with the age of puberty. In Cain's understanding, William of Conches has placed gender assignment at puberty and likened it to transubstantiation—there is no physical change but the invisible, underlying gender essence has been significantly altered. Any difference between pre- and post-puberty gender is manifest in gender-associated behavior, such as mannerisms, gestures, or general comportment. In Cain's view, this Neo-Platonic model allows for gender change from what was assigned at birth through sheer persistence of habit; a person can become the gender they imitate.[367]

This openness to gender fluidity seems rather widespread and corresponds to a similar openness about the sexed body, with both reflecting more a sense of *continuum* than category. Historian James Blythe remarks, "Medieval medical and scientific views of sex and gender were complex and not fully determinate, resisting binary categorization and making possible various combinations of masculine and feminine traits."[368] With regard to gender, for example, Blythe refers to the mid-14th century medical professor Jacopo da Flori at the University of Sienna, who formulated three indices of gender: complexion, disposition, and physique. Any individual can be gender-mixed along these indices; for example, feminine on one, masculine on another, and even indeterminate with regard to the third.[369]

The sexual body likewise could be conceived outside a binary system. As Cary Nederman and Jacqui True document, in 12th century Europe the intersexed ('hermaphrodites'), though subject to opinions ranging from condemnation as unnatural grotesqueries to acceptance as a natural variation, could at least be viewed medically as a distinct 'third sex.'[370]

This judgment was echoed in Church circles. For example, in the late 12th century Peter Cantor notes that:

Diego church allows a hermaphrodite—that is, someone with the organs of both sexes, capable of either active or passive functions—to use the organ by which (s)he is most aroused or the one to which (s)he is most susceptible. If (s)he is more active, (s)he may wed as a man, but if (s)he is more passive, (s)he may marry as a woman.[371]

This ecclesiastical stance is echoed by Portius Azo (late 12th-early 13th century), Italian canon jurist, who in his *Summa Codices et Institutionum* distinguished the hermaphrodite as a third sex alongside male and female.[372]

In sum, people of the Middle Ages explored in a variety of ways not only the potential for gender change, but also the gender possibilities lying between masculine men and feminine women. These other possibilities covered phenomena we today label as intersex (hermaphroditic) people, transvestism, and homosexuality.[373] Rather like our own age, medieval folk struggled with the construction of gender, often finding a disjunction between tolerated but imagined possibilities and resistance to actual transgender expressions. But they could not ignore these realities in their midst.

Changing Conceptions Since the Medieval Period

As we might expect, we can find evidence of both continuity and discontinuity with the Medieval period. These can be found in ideas about both sex and gender. For example, the intersexed (hermaphrodites) continued for a long period to be accorded recognition as a distinct sex with gender options more liberal than generally seen in modern times.[374]

Ideas about gender also continued to be debated between the end of the Middle Ages and the triumph of the medicalization of sex in the 19th –20th centuries. The notions that circulated were often more fluid than our own, which under the impress of modern medicine's way of categorizing and thinking has yielded a static dualistic system with an inflexible pairing of sex and gender. Observations about transgender realities like crossdressing abounded during this period, appearing in academic discourses, religious musings, popular literature, journalistic accounts, legal treatises, theater, and even ballads. As the world continued to shrink through increased ease of travel people around the world became more aware of each other and Westerners continued their fascination with cultural differences, though generally interpreting 'different' as 'inferior.'

Cultural openness to the fluidity of sex and gender could also generate anxiety over how each was shaped. For example, a common belief in early modern Europe was that a pregnant woman's experiences, and even her imagination, could shape the features of her unborn child. Gender violations, such as violations in gendered dress, could bring misfortune. Renaissance literature scholar Kate Chedgzoy refers to a 1560 broadsheet entitled *The True Description of a Child with Ruffles*, in which a child is born with ruffs because the mother had worn them in violation of her proper place. The description of this child, says Chedgzoy, "constitutes a dire warning to women whose dress is inappropriate either to their gender or their position in the socio-economic hierarchy."[375]

Among the changing ideas rooted in the Middle Ages but extending and being developed after them concerns *childhood*. In a highly influential work, French historian Philippe Ariès argues that 'childhood', in our sense of the term, did not exist in the ancient or Medieval worlds of the West. Instead, in a major transformation extending from the late Middle Ages through the 19th century, childhood emerged first among portions of the upper class, extended throughout the upper classes, and slowly enveloped the lower classes as well. Childhood as we envision it, though, may be linked to the development in the 17th century when the child began to be dressed not as a miniature adult, but as a different entity. In Ariès' words, the child came to possess "an outfit reserved for his own age group, which set him apart from adults."[376] The differentiation of children as *sui generis* and not miniature adults meant that 'boy' and 'girl' took on new meaning. And though boys had greater status than girls, they remained able to be dressed similarly to girls (appearing in unbifurcated clothes like dresses well into the 20th century) because they remained in an inferior status to men.[377]

In considering our own Western culture, we clearly can trace the lineage of many of our ideas back through time. Just as clearly, a growing appreciation of difference between our thinking and that of our forebears becomes more evident with close investigation. If we have freed ourselves through this brief examination of our own culture from assuming that our current way of looking at things is 'the way it has always been,' and instead realize notions experience change within the dynamic flux of culture, then perhaps we are ready to look beyond our cultural borders.

Gender Eastern Style

The East embraces many diverse societies, and we are going to resist trying to make any generalities to link all of them together. The sheer plurality of societies and the diversity among the major world religions that inform or influence so much of culture make it impossible to speak confidently of universal truths about the East.

Nevertheless, there are some broad tendencies we can note, especially among the dominant ideologies. Societies in what we call the East tend to:

❑ emphasize unity over multiplicity, including community over individuality (thus defining personal identity in terms of groups);

❑ mistrust the perceptual world, thus treating it more flexibly; and,

❑ promote deference and respect within hierarchical relations.

These tendencies are at variance with Western culture's glorification of the individual, emphasis on autonomy and self-actualization, and an independence that often defies authority. In different ways, we can see these tendencies in two prominent Eastern lands, China and India.

Gender Logic in India

How might the tendencies of Eastern thinking show themselves in gender conversation? First, let us consider India. There the *relation of unity to multiplicity*, and the primacy of the former, is found in an ancient belief that all of us start out male in the womb and that it is the work of malevolent spirits that succeed in making some fetuses female.[378] Thus an original unity—a divinely intended perfection—becomes dualistic. Moreover, in Indian thinking as found in Hinduism, an ultimate, universal Reality (*Brahmin*) can be joined by means of realization of the ultimate, universal Self (*Atman*)—a process of release to freedom (*moksha*).

But that means penetrating the illusions that keep us seeing multiplicity. Our senses lead us to focus on particularities and thereby can lead us astray. *If we mistrust the perceptual world, we can treat it more flexibly.* Sex and gender are illusory multiplicities. They deceive us, confining us to a world of illusions through a cycle of birth-death-rebirth (*samsara*), if we regard them as truly substantial and over-value them. Gender divisions may be convenient, but because they are secondary and subordinate to ultimate unity, they may also be treated flexibly. As Devdutt Pattanaik expresses it, "Masculinity and femininity are reduced to ephemeral robes of body and mind that ensheath the sexless, genderless soul."[379]

In Indian thinking, *gender crossings*—transgender realities—help expose the illusion of a binary sex and gender conception. Potentially, at least, transgender offers assistance in breaking free of sex and gender limitations in order to realize true Self. Put in other words, the masculine maleness and feminine femaleness the social world talks so much about are subordinate to the androgynous nature of reality that transcends sex and gender appearances. It is *atman* in the human breast that matters, not the genitalia or the gendered roles society imposes. Because the 'true soul' is androgynous (or perhaps more accurately *trans-* or, 'beyond gender'), the apparent gender of the mortal form is an appearance that may be manipulated. And it is, by deities and demigods, as well as by human beings.[380]

Indian languages accordingly recognize the possibility of gender beyond the dichotomy of masculine and feminine. The Sanskrit *napunsaka* and the Urdu *namard* are terms used to cover members of various groups that our term transgender is often applied to: homosexuals, transvestites, transsexuals—all kinds of cross-dressers.[381] Today, colloquial terms are used for female same-sex relationships (*sakhi*) and for those among boys (*masti*).[382] Effeminate (uncastrated) males with a homosexual orientation, who crossdress and take the passive, receptive role in sexual interactions are known locally as *Jankhas* or *Zenanas*,[383] or *Kothis*. Both in secular and in religious spheres a spectrum of gender displays itself in distinctive and culturally sanctioned ways, and in a richly diverse vocabulary.

Flexibility in gender does not mean chaos; a *gender order* exists in Indian society. Indeed, traditional Indian society is stratified in more than one manner. The caste system also lends to individuals a distinctive stamp of group affiliation that constrains individual identity and expression. Gender, too, is hierarchical. Boys are so prized over girls that today modern birth technology is utilized to try to ensure the birth of a boy and to abort female fetuses; this strong gender preference can create marital difficulties.[384] The authors of one text on world religions neatly sum up the place of women in the family as follows: "India mainly honored women for giving birth and serving their husbands."[385] And yet, plenty of instances can be put forward to show that women in some situations enjoyed better status—another sign of the instinct to be flexible in light of the illusory divisions that keep us from union with the divine.

Gender Logic in China

What kind of gender logic in China utilizes the tendencies we have identified? There, as in India, was an ancient recognition that *an essential unity inheres the multiplicities we perceive.* Gender scholar Allerd Stikker thinks that in China, the key to comprehending the mystery of Nature was found in procreation—a process that divides living things into male and female, and that became the basis for the central Chinese concept of *yin* (femaleness) and *yang* (maleness). [386] Whether we concur with Stikker or not, we must acknowledge the importance of the *yin/yang* duality. But, just as the familiar symbol for this duality depicts, this is a complementary duality, where each aspect needs the other. The activity of *yang* depends on the receptivity of *yin* no less than the yielding character of *yin* needs the strength of *yang.* Both are subordinate to the *Tao* ('Way').

Both Taoism and Confucianism, China's great historic religions, exhibit a *subordination of the perceptual world* in service of more profound realities. In Taoism this is more profound. There is recognition that *Tao*, which cannot be named, cannot be made either. Like the uncarved block that potentially can be anything, and yet is nothing but unfashioned, the *Tao* transcends our perceptions and the divisions such perceptions form. This extends to sex and gender. The *Tao Te Ching*, Taoism's central sacred text, extols, "Know the male, maintain the female, become the channel of the world."[387] Like the Tao, we are both *yin* and *yang*; being a man or woman means that one or the other predominates, but the other is never excluded. This lends a greater egalitarianism in Taoist thought and practice, as witnessed for example in Taoist religious orders. Livia Kohn observes, "Medieval Daoist sources make no distinction between male and female ranks, accomplishments, status, or even clothing."[388]

Given the profoundly social nature of Confucianism, we might be surprised to learn that there, too, the perceptual world is acknowledged as something that can be manipulated. For example, Confucian logic mandates a social artifice in how the emperor's wife is perceived and addressed: the wife of the ruler referred to herself as 'Little Boy.' Chinese scholar Arthur Waley, notes that the phrase *Hsiao T'ung* ("Little Boy") refers to a page boy and is exclusively masculine. Waley remarks that "the sovereign's wife may not be referred to (either by himself or anyone else) by any term that is feminine in implication and must in referring to herself use a term that is definitely masculine."[389] In short, the inflexibility of social relations mandates a flexibility in gender designation precisely in order to protect the social order.

How far would a Confucian permit gender flexibility to proceed though? We get no definitive answers, but we can make a logical argument from the Confucian masters themselves. They put much stock in appearance, understood both as how one looks (e.g., proper dress), and acts (proper conduct). The

Xunzi of Confucian scholar Xun Kuang (c. 310-220 B.C.E.) remarks that it is not uncommon to encounter young men who "wear striking clothing with female adornment and exhibit the blood, breath, and bearing of a young girl."[390] In the spirit of Mencius, these males *are* feminine in gender, if not female in sex. Such individuals could be regarded in more than one way in Confucian China. Chinese thinking saw the person as an organic whole, yet was dualistic in respect to distinguishing between higher internal qualities (*hun* and *shen*) and lower, body-based ones (*po*). The former matters more than the latter. In this respect, it might be argued that the feminine soul of a physical male takes priority over the body; gender means more than sex. Logically, the feminine male acting like a woman is behaving congruent to the soul.[391]

In regard to social order, Chinese society promotes *deference and respect within hierarchical relations*. How did this arrangement come to be? In Chinese scholarship, a debate has been ongoing as to whether or not ancient China was a matriarchy.[392] Those who maintain such a view account for the advent of a gender hierarchy privileging masculinity as a result of the triumph of Confucianism. Certainly the weight of the Confucian tradition has been considerable, especially in its emphasis on hierarchical and ordered social relations. Those who reject the idea of an original matriarchy point to a long tradition of masculine dominance. Stikkel, for example, observes that while there has long been an identification of the female with creation, the primacy of the male, on earth and in heaven, can be traced back at least to the emergence of the Yellow Emperor, legendary ancestor to the Chinese people.[393]

In Confucianism, the *gender order* is hierarchical with men on top. Women are bound to three obediences: to husband, to his parents, and to her own parents. Yet this only exemplifies the central value of filial piety that makes social relationships vertical. Despite the verticality, reciprocity should characterize relationships. The subordinate owes obedience to the superior, but the superior is honor-bound to exercise care toward the subordinate. *Jen* ('virtuous humanity') is the goal in relating to each other; indeed the Chinese character for *jen* combines the symbols for 'two' and 'person'—signifying *jen* as the essence of relationship.[394] The individual is meant for relationship—in the family of origin, the marital family, and the national family.

East Meets West: China & India

Both China and India have felt the power of the West. Though each has resisted it, both in their own ways have accommodated it. China, never conquered and occupied by Western people, nevertheless embraced a philosophy Western in origin—Communism—and in many ways shows the influence of Western culture. One way is in Chinese response to Western categories of sex, gender, and sexuality. Though acknowledging the claim of the Western medicalization of sex on conceptions of these matters, China officially proclaims its own people free of any of the conditions that are stigmatized in the West, such as transsexualism. India, once a prize of the British Empire, shows the heritage of that dominion in its continuing effort to find ways to talk about gender that honors its own rich indigenous tradition and still fit in a world culturally dominated by the West.[395]

The Impact of the West: The Case of Thailand

The impact of Western culture on Eastern societies has been immense. We will profit from a closer examination of a particular society, one chosen because it has long fascinated Westerners in regard to sex and gender. The modern nation of Thailand was formerly known as Siam (before 1939). Rule of the land—at least nominally—has rested in the Chakkri Dynasty since 1782, and the kingdom can trace itself to roots in the late 11th century. Unusual for the region of Southeast Asia, the land has remained independent for most of its history, despite the influence and dominion of colonial powers. However, both the impact of European colonialism in the region, as well as imperial Japan's occupation of the country during World War II, have impacted Thailand's culture.

In Thailand, three distinct gendered groups historically have been recognized: masculine (*chai*), feminine (*ying*), and what we term transgendered (*thang ying thang chai*—'both feminine and masculine'; or, *ying pra-phayt song*—'women of the second kind'; or *kathoey*—variously understood, depending on context, as 'hermaphrodite,' 'transvestite,' 'transsexual,' or 'transgender').[396] Both Eastern and Western influences from other societies have shaped gender expression in modern Thailand, especially in reference to gender outside masculinity and femininity. We may best see Western impact by studying how our notions of how the genders should be and appear can change the traditional gender practices, and perhaps also identities, in another society.

Peter Jackson, a Research Fellow in Asian and Pacific History at the Australian National University, is perhaps the best-known contemporary student of Thailand's transgender community and offers us a way into that society's experience. He remarks that Thailand, in the latter decades of the 20th century, witnessed a proliferation of new gender and sexual identities and cultures. Following the lead of Foucault's *History of Sexuality* and Judith Butler's idea of 'performative gender,' Jackson advances a case that the emergence of these new expressions flows from the Thai state's efforts to 'civilize' gender display in response to the imperial powers of the last two centuries.

Historically in Siam, transgender behaviors like crossdressing occasioned little remark. Yet by the 1960s Thai medical and mental health professionals had come to follow the West's lead in pathologizing transgender realities. The long transition to this state of affairs, Jackson proposes, was inspired by the kingdom's desire to escape Western characterizations as a barbarous land by initiating changes to earn the West's recognition as a 'civilized' nation.[397]

Jackson notes that Western observers numbered among their criticisms a complaint about the perceived similarity of appearance between Siamese men and women. This perception rested largely on the fact that there was no differentiation in clothing fashions (all wearing the unisex *jong-kraben*) or hairstyles. To

19th century foreign visitors, with their hair cut short like men's, Siamese women looked too masculine, especially when wearing *pha chongkaben*, a traditional garment somewhat resembling baggy trousers. Worse, in Western eyes, were those who crossed Western gender lines in dress and action, like the female royal guards of the king's harem outfitted in what seemed like masculine garb, or male actors portraying women onstage. The similarity in gendered appearance of Thai men and women continued to occasion comment through the 20th century until at least the post-World War II period.[398]

The Siamese government did not ignore Western criticism. Jackson says they responded with selective strategic efforts to use legal and institutional forms of power to make the populace 'civilized' in Western eyes. But, he argues, their aim was not the reforming of private sexuality but "refashioning the public gendering of their bodies."[399] Laws were passed, and enforced, to ensure that all Thai people were covered properly and that male and female could be easily distinguished.[400] This meant men wore shirts and trousers, while women wore blouses and skirts; traditional unbifurcated unisex garb was officially set aside.[401] By the mid-1960s an effective Westernization of dress fashion was entrenched.[402]

Today's Thai people experience the effects of a prolonged period of conscientious effort to change traditional sexual and gender identities and cultures. Jackson states frankly that, "Patterns of personal identity have been altered as a result of the Thai gender revolution."[403] He demonstrates the pervasiveness and significance of these changes, reflected not only in dress, but in linguistic changes, social roles, and a variety of other ways. Only in this context can the *kathoey* of today be understood. Jackson observes that, "the modern *kathoey* has emerged *together with* gay identities as one aspect of the broader gender revolution."[404]

In sum, the power of the West induced Siam/Thailand to accede to foreign conceptions. Pressure affected every gender in the country. Men and women were increasingly shaped to appear like Western men and women; changes in gender practices and roles also moved their identities closer to how we think they should be. Those whose gender experience and expression did not fit into Western categories were remade so they would fit—though that meant pathologizing them. The *kathoey* (or *katoey*, or *kathooi*), for example, traditionally represent a third gendered group, in distinction to masculine and feminine. Contemporary scholar Rosalind Morris renders the meaning of this term as "feminized maleness."[405] But that understanding better fits the modern Thai transgendered expression as strongly influenced by the West. Kittiwut Jod Taywaditep and colleagues trace a progressive change in meaning for the term. Originally referring to someone of indeterminate sex (a hermaphrodite), it came to refer to homosexual men, until the Western term 'gay' supplanted it. Now, they say, it refers to males demonstrating feminine social behaviors and as such is widely viewed by Thai gay men as a derogatory term.[406] Western categories have prevailed, at least in those parts of the country, such as major cities, where East meets West is most likely. In rural areas, traditional ideas and greater acceptance still hold some sway.

Gender in the Islamic World

Islam is a much discussed and even more misunderstood religion. Most of us know little about the religion and perhaps even less about the people and societies that embrace it. What we think we know about its ideas on gender often resolves down to a sense that it oppresses and mistreats women—at least by the standards of the Christian West. We generally remain ignorant of the holy writings of Islam that, like other religions, often extol virtues that elude most of their adherents. Also like other religions, a continuous strand of religious sentiment that honors other genders, including femininity, but perhaps not limited to just two genders, tempers the evident dominance of masculinity.

We may note in passing one instance of this greater liberality of thought than what most of us know of Islamic practice. Ibn al-'Arabî, author of the *Fusûs al-hikam* and the *Tarjumân al-ashwâq*, is among the Islamic writers who have proclaimed it permissible to refer to Allah—who, after all, transcends gender—as either *huwa* (masculine, 'He') or *hiya* (feminine, 'She'). Both masculine and feminine (e.g., 'wise,' 'merciful') qualities belong to Allah. Particularly in Sufism, Islam's mystical tradition, Allah is depicted as feminine (cf. Jalal al-Din Rumi's *Masnavi*, I.2437), the Beloved One (the *ma'shûq*), and even the Divine Mother (cf. *Masnavi*, V.701).[407]

Such reminders as we have just heard matter. We find it easy in the West to listen selectively to those parts of the conversation on gender that appeal to our own sensibilities. Certainly modern Muslim societies hold ideas and engage in practices that are unseemly to other Western minds. But they find the same sense of unpleasantness in regards to us, and the inability of both sides to engage in productive dialog keeps much of the world in turmoil. Gender in Islam is a subject of more subtlety and complexity than what television sound bites disclose. Islam is not a monolithic structure producing uniform Muslim societies. No less than Christianity, it is a vibrant, living religion that exercises influence to greater and lesser degrees, and in various ways, in numerous societies.

Dominant Genders: Masculinity & Femininity in Islam

Unfortunately, a veil no less impenetrable than that shrouding a Muslim woman's face largely covers the subject of gender in Islam for most of us. Women's studies in religion scholar Leila Ahmed, at Harvard Divinity School, tells us our learning about gender in the Islamic world, and our knowledge about Muslim women, remains in its infancy. Nevertheless, her own study of the matter shows that modern Islamic thought and practice relies heavily on early Muslim societies to form and guide its discourse on gender and on women. Those early societies had themselves relied on pre-existing cultural ideas and practices. The adoption of the veil for women, for instance, occurred at a time when its use was already prominent in the Christian Middle East and Mediterranean world. However, she also points to the impact of colonialism of shaping Islam's view of gender. Indeed, multiple forces outside and within have helped shape the discourse on gender and on women in Islam.[408]

With respect to contemporary Islam, anthropologist Mary Elaine Hegland claims that several changes in the Middle East have led to emerging dramatic Islamic gender transformations. These include changes in women's awareness through better schooling and more participation in the labor force, and the resurgence of fundamentalism ('Islamism'), with its religious spotlight on the role of women. These two forces have collided. Islamism has encountered resistance from secularist feminists from Islamic backgrounds, many of whom have been forced to flee their homelands. But they are not the only women who resist. Hegland also points to the quiet resistance of devout Muslim women in countries like Iran, women who embrace Islam but not the State's more radicalized version of it. The resulting tension, Hegland observes, puts Islamic states in a bind:

> These governments may find themselves torn between needing women as resources to maintain patriarchal family and social structure and to demonstrate religiosity and Islamic identity vis-à-vis other Islamic nations and the West on the one hand, and needing women's participation in education and work and defensively wishing to show Islam promotes women's rights and opportunities on the other.

Ironically, Hegland notes, Islamists have appropriated aspects of feminism in their efforts to defend Muslim practices against feminist critiques. But as they espouse respect for women and the advantages of Islam, the Islamists leave themselves open to demands that such words be put into actual practice. [409]

Within Muslim countries, the teachings of masculine clerics, especially in poorer nations, often constitute the primary and authoritative source of information on matters such as sexuality and gender. Throughout the Islamic world, gender-differentiated dress is a strong instrument to enforce the distance between the genders. The strong gender segregation, alongside a preeminence of masculine interests and beliefs, fosters an ignorance of women. For example, a study in Pakistan reported in 2000, involving 188 young (18-30) men who were generally of the middle class, found a high prevalence of misconceptions about female sexuality, including some 40% who endorsed the notion that women found sex less enjoyable than men, and 42% who were ignorant of the ability of females to achieve orgasm.[410] Moreover, women when raped are also likely to be accused of adultery and to be accordingly punished.

The theoretical robustness and fluidity in how gender can be conceived in Islam is overshadowed by the common reality of a relatively rigid patriarchalism. In actual practice, Islamic societies support a gender dualism favoring masculine privilege. Men define the family, which they also govern. Men are the public face of Islam throughout most of the world. Women in leadership in Muslim societies are rare, and most women in public wear the veil—a potent symbol not merely of their segregation from men, but of a masculine expectation that they preserve a secondary place in public silence. Practices like female circumcision, which blunt experiences of sexual pleasure, are intended to tame a wantonness in women and, coupled with their manner of dress and separation from men, to curb their presence as a distraction and temptation to men.

Other Genders in the Islamic World

Yet Islam's commitment to a dual gender system does not tell the whole story. Within Islamic culture gender statuses other than merely masculine and feminine can be recognized. Southeast Asian scholar Yik Koon Teh contends that Islam recognizes four distinct gender groups: men, women, intersexed ('hermaphrodites,' *khunsa*), and what we might call the transgendered ('transsexuals,' *mukhannis* and 'transvestites,' *mukhannas*). The last group is often discouraged from acting feminine through crossdressing, use of makeup, or seeking to enhance a feminine form through taking hormones or surgery.[411] Like women in many Muslim societies, less dominant genders often find life under Islam challenging.

Islamic holy writings describe biological males who do not fit into the category of masculine men. From *ahadith* (cf. *hadith* (sing.): a narration of a saying or act of the Prophet) in *Sunan Abu-Dawid* we hear that such men, called *mukhannathun* (sing., *mukhannath*), dress as women,[412] and have a lack of sexual interest,[413] and/or ability (e.g., to sustain an erection).[414] Various descriptions of them occur throughout Islamic literature. Often the meaning makes it evident that the individual is intersexed. But not always. There were also men-who-imitated women, sometimes referred to as 'effeminate men,' and also known as *mukhannathun*, and some women who 'assume the manner of men,' known as *mutarajjulat*.[415]

Because some males occupied a place between masculine men and feminine women, they might be utilized as go-betweens for the dominant genders. In a strictly gender segregated society such individuals served an important function, including helping arrange marital unions. We know such a person could even be found in the Prophet Mohamed's own household, among his wives.[416] But their existence also posed a potentially thorny social problem: what if someone posed as a *mukhannath* to gain illicit entry into the world of women? That seems a plausible explanation for why the Prophet "cursed those men who are in the similitude (assume the manners) of women and those women who are in the similitude (assume the manners) of men."[417]

Islam today is divided into two major traditions (Sunni and Shiite), with the former larger and generally more liberal in their teachings. Transgendered people are not all treated alike. *Intersexed individuals*, for example, are permitted to undergo surgical body alteration in order to unambiguously present as male or female. Egypt, long a leader among the Islamic nations of the region, is among the most progressive in some respects with reference to the treatment of transgendered people. SRS has happened for a small number of people since at least the late 1980s. In 1988, Grand Mufti Mohamed Sayed Tantawi, citing *hadith*, issued a religious edict *(fatwa)* in a letter to the Doctors' General Syndicate authorizing SRS in the case of a patient deemed a hermaphrodite.[418]

On the other hand, *transsexuals* face a harder time: behaviors like crossdressing, using hormones for body alterations, or seeking sex reassignment surgery (SRS) typically are not sanctioned, especially among Sunnis.[419] However, in an unprecedented court decision, a Kuwaiti court legally recognized the female identity of a male-to-female, postoperative transsexual. In so doing they were following a *fatwa* (edict) issued by Sunni Islam's highest legal institution, Al-Azhar, which permits gender changes through sex reassignment surgery when medically substantiated.[420] Shiite Iran has been kinder to transsexuals because the late Ayatollah Ruhollah Khomeini was persuaded by a transsexual compatriot to issue a *fatwa* supporting a sex change. [421] The authorization granted one individual has become by extension a grant to other similar individuals. SRS can proceed with the permission of the government. While it is still common for individuals seeking SRS to obtain it outside the country, many cases are known to have occurred within Iran. One physician, Dr. Mir-djalali, conducted more than 300 over a decade span.[422] However, as *New York Times* correspondent Nazila Fathi observes in a 2004 article, growing tolerance among clerics and doctors does not equal acceptance among the general populace, where prejudice remains strong.[423]

In today's far-flung Islamic world, modern *mukhannathun* are found in various groups. Some of India's *hijra*, though rooted in Hinduism, have adopted Islam and can point to ties with Islam's Sufi tradition and to a history of benevolence under Islamic rule. In Indonesia, the *Waria* (feminine men) and *Banci* (intersexed) are often Muslims.[424] In the Middle East, in Bahrain, there are the *Kaneeth* (*Xanith*, or *Khanith*), regarded as specially gendered, and the *Benaty*, who are apparently generally tolerated, being mostly ignored, though they are occasionally seen in public.[425] In Oman, the *Xanith* are transgendered males. Norwegian social anthropologist Unni Wikan, whose fieldwork was among the Arabs of Oman's city of Sohar on the northeastern coast, concluded in the mid-1970s that these distinctive folk constitute perhaps 2% of the adult males of Sohar.[426] News accounts inform us that there are transvestites found in Islamic societies, though they run the risk of criminal prosecution and severe punishment (e.g., flogging) if discovered.[427] Yet, in Egyptian film[428] or the burlesque theater of Iran, where feminine roles in *Tazieh* (morality plays) are performed by males,[429] crossdressing occurs in public venues for entertainment.

Thus, as elsewhere in the world, ambivalence and conflict are associated with transgender realities. Competition and conflict—the interplay of power and status—are central to gender in the Islamic world no less than in the Christian world. Indeed, as we found true for Eastern societies, the impact of European and American cultural thinking has exerted pressure on Muslim societies. Perhaps nowhere is that more evident than in Turkey.

The Impact of the West: The Case of Turkey

Modern Turkey is notable as another land where East meets West, and Islamic traditions coexist with many Western values. Turkish culture traditionally has been androcentric. Indeed, even in contemporary times parents there—by a 86% to 14% margin—strongly prefer male to female children. Division of labor falls along gender lines; a man who does 'woman's work' (e.g., domestic or child-rearing activities) is seen as shameful. Stereotypes about personality differences between men and women are widely embraced. Women are commonly viewed as more childlike, emotional and dependent, while men are regarded as stronger and more active. Nevertheless, over time such stereotypes may be weakening, at least among the young adults attending universities. A study reported in 2005 found evidence for more endorsement of traits like 'independent,' 'assertive,' and 'self-sufficient' for both men and women.[430] Much like in Europe and the United States, where greater gender equality has meant women becoming more like men, a similar process may be occurring in Turkey.

Nevertheless, the influence of Western cultural values remains tempered by Islamic sensibilities. For example, the critically praised movie *Brokeback Mountain*, about two homosexual men's complicated relationship, was restricted by the Culture Ministry to an adult audience, and a Ministry official expressed the view the film violated public morals. The nation's Radio and Television Higher Board stopped a show called *He's a Lady Now* from being aired. The reality-based program would have shown men competing with one another to look and act like women.[431]

Turkey has a well-known transgendered population that includes homosexuals, transsexuals, and transvestites. Members identifying themselves with one or another group typically describe themselves by particular labels and distinguish themselves from members of other groups. Transsexuals, for example, may refer to themselves as *Lubinya* (a coded term that is part of unique vocabulary derived from several languages). But members of the general population rarely make such distinctions and commonly view all transgender and third gender people alike, using the label *travesty* ('crossdresser'). [432]

Transsexuals, became highly visible in urban Turkey in the late 1990s. Many gained notice through their participation in entertainment or the sex trade. *Middle East Report* correspondent Deniz Kandiyoti notes that media attention has been widespread and included mediums as diverse as cartoons, magazine articles, televised interviews, and book materials. Kandiyoti also observes that this attention has drawn complaint from the homosexual community, which is far greater in numbers.[433]

Turkey's desire to fit within the European union, coupled with its ties to the Islamic world, make it fertile soil for the ongoing conversation on gender. It may well prove to be one of the pivotal societies for how this worldwide dialog eventually resolves itself into something that both tradition and modernity can tolerate, and that Christian Europe and Muslim Middle East can abide. On the other hand, the conflicting pressures could so threaten the society that it pulls away from any synthesis and forcibly embraces one or another alternative among the competing gender ideologies.

Gender in Africa

When we turn our attention to Africa, we need again remind ourselves that African traditions relating to our Euro-American conceptions of gender and sexuality will be inevitably distorted if we insist solely on relying on our own categories to understand them. While our ways of looking at things may make sense to us, and offer some utility, we must resist thinking of them as the only—or necessarily the best—ways of comprehending. In this matter we want, as much as we can, to draw upon the work of native scholars as well as culturally sensitive nonnative scholars (principally ethnologists and anthropologists). This determination seems all the more desirable in light of the reality that our imposition of our culture's values and views on Africa have done more than cloud our conceptions of their past. There is evidence that they are harming modern African peoples.

The sheer diversity of African tribal societies make it impossible to adequately discuss their conceptions of gender in the time allotted us.[434] All we can do here is note a few ideas organized around one key theme: *the indigenous people creatively maintain some variance from imposed European and Islamic norms.* Though influenced both by *colonization* and *conversion,* the relative degree of influence of each alongside a creative maintenance of cultural traditions makes for great diversity. Africa's modern tribal societies operate within and across national borders and show signs of both continuity and discontinuity with indigenous traditions.

Sociologist David Greenberg offers for kinship-structured societies like those common to Africa a taxonomy of sexual identity. Greenberg, whose research interest focuses on same-sex relations, suggests three general categories for kinship-structured societies:

❑ *transgenerational*—where the relationship is defined by age, with the younger partner taking a passive role associated with femininity;

❑ *transgenderal*—where the relationship finds both gender roles enacted though the parties both belong to the same sex; and,

❑ *egalitarian*—where the relationship is not defined by age or gender role differences but reciprocity.[435]

While these categories hardly exhaust the lived realities in Africa, they provide some utility in understanding some of the variation found among tribal societies.[436]

But rather than offer supposed generalities that inevitably break down under scrutiny, let us consider a few particular African realities that show some variance from Western ideas and practices. In this manner we can highlight the following points, that apply to one or more African tribal societies:

❑ gender may not be closely tied to sex anatomy;

- ❑ gender fluidity may be strongly influenced by indigenous religious ideas;
- ❑ families may be organized on a basis other than gender;
- ❑ social roles may be structured on a basis other than gender though this can have gender-related consequences; and,
- ❑ gender divisions can be into more than two categories and seen as happening at various developmental points (rather than at birth).

Let us briefly examine each of these notions.

In our culture, most people see gender closely tied to sexual anatomy. However, *some African people distance gender from sex*. African scholar and shaman Malidoma Somé says that, "at least among the Dagara people, gender has very little to do with anatomy. It is purely energetic. In that context, one who is physically male can vibrate female energy, and vice versa. That is where the real gender is." Somé also says that gender is not used as a line to divide people. As for anatomical differences, these are used to guide the nature of the contribution made by each person in the service of the entire tribe.[437] This situation by no means pertains everywhere on the continent, but it should suffice to remind us that gender need not be seen exactly as our culture views it.

The fluidity of gender in some contexts reflects the power of indigenous religious beliefs. For example, anthropologist Brian MacDermot encountered an individual among the Nuer people of Ethiopia who not only appeared in feminine dress, and acted feminine, but was actually regarded as having become a woman. No physical change of sex had transpired, yet this person was free to occupy a feminine identity and role, even to the extent that marriage to a man was permissible. MacDermot was informed that the prophet of Deng had consulted the spirits and then had declared the change in this individual's status, which the people accepted.[438] Here transpired an outcome more certain and favorable than many individuals who actually undergo sexual reassignment surgery and legal identity change experience in our own culture (which so commonly arrogantly perceives itself as more enlightened).

In Euro-American culture, the family is structured along gender lines with reliable pairings of sex (male, female) to gender (masculine, feminine) to family role (husband/father, wife/mother). This structuring of the family is no more natural or inevitable than, for example, the structure found in the families of the Yoruba in Nigeria. African scholar Oyeronke Oyewumi tells us Yoruba *families are constructed not primarily along gender lines, but by relative age* (cf. Greenberg's 'trans-generational' category). This arrangement is unlike the Western 'nuclear family.' Indeed, Oyewumi writes, "the nuclear family remains an alien form in Africa despite its promotion by both the colonial and neocolonial state, international (un)derdevelopment agencies, feminist organizations, contemporary non-governmental organizations (NGOs) among others."[439] In Yoruban families, says Oyewumi, the power centers are *not* along gender lines. Indeed, Yoruban words defy our culture's gender conventions. The word *omo* refers to offspring independent of gender. The word *oko*, translated in English as 'husband,' can encompass either a man or woman, and even the term *Iyawo*, rendered in English as 'wife,' and typically referring to women can sometimes be applied to men (e.g., devotees of the Orisa, called '*Iyawo Orisa*'). [440]

Oyewumi's comments point to the fact that *social roles which in the Euro-American cultural tradition are strictly gendered, such as 'husband' and 'wife,' need not be so in African societies.* This reality is illustrated by the 'male wives,' 'female husbands,' and 'male daughters' of Africa.[441] These, however, only name a few of the best known variations found among African peoples.

A number of tribal peoples traditionally have permitted same-sex marriages where one person occupies the gendered role of 'husband' and the other the role of 'wife.' Among such arrangements are unions between men and 'male wives,' or *boy wives*. Such 'boy wives' (*ndonga-techi-la*) are known among the Azande of the Central African Republic and Sudan. In this same-sex arrangement, the younger male in the same-sex relationship is the 'wife' while the older male is referred to as the 'husband.' As in a male-female marriage, the 'husband' contracts with the family of the 'wife.' Some men have both male wives and female ones. Traditionally, the boy-wife, unlike any female wife, might accompany the warrior husband when the latter is campaigning. The boy-wife dresses and is adorned like a woman, and tends his husband's possessions. The boy-wife, once into manhood as a warrior, is released to take on a boy-wife of his own, if he desires.[442] Other tribal societies also have known 'boy-wives,' such as the Nuba of Sudan, the Thonga of Mozambique and South Africa, the Pongo people of South Africa (who call them *tinkonkana*), and the Siwan of Egypt.

Just as there are 'male wives,' there are 'female husbands.' *Female husbands* (aka *gynegamie*[443]) are found across much of the continent, including nations in East Africa, West Africa and Southern Africa. Tribal societies include the Gikuyu and Nandi[444] of Kenya, the Ibo and Dahomey peoples of Nigeria, the Dinke and Nuer[445] peoples of Sudan, and the Lovedu, Venda and Zulu peoples of South Africa. A few dozen African societies have been documented for this practice.[446] This practice may occur when women attain enough wealth and power to take for themselves wives of their own. These women in the masculine matrimonial role become 'female husbands' (*nwanyi kwu ami*, 'a woman with balls'[447]). Their children are treated with the rights of patrilineal descent.[448]

African scholar Ifi Amadiune documents the phenomenon of so-called *male daughters* as well as female husbands among the Ibo of Nigeria. As in some other societies where patrilineage determines inheritance rights, where an Ibo man has no son to inherit, he may designate a daughter to occupy the role of a son for these rights—a 'male daughter' (*nhayikwa*). She is placed into this position by ritual and gains access to masculine privileges. These include, in addition to continuing the line of descent, authority and possession of property associated with the position.[449] This kind of social role that bends gender as understood by the West has become rarer as native traditional ideas and practices bow before the imperial pressure exerted by the West, first through European colonization but continuing by virtue of economic dominance.

In terms of *gender divisions*, some African groups, like the Pokot of Kenya, adhere to a relatively rigid binary system of masculinity and femininity—a scheme familiar to Europeans and Americans. Others, such as the Amhara of Ethiopia, the Igbo of Nigeria, or the Otoro of the Sudan, allow room for intermediate, mixed, or 'third gender' expressions. African societies vary, too, in when they see individuals becoming gendered. For instance, while the Igbo of Nigeria appear to assign gender around age 5, the Mbuti of Congo seem to find no need to do so before puberty.[450] The Dogon of Mali, in West Africa, offer yet another way of regarding gender and gender distinctions. They conceive the perfect human being as androgynous. In the male, the foreskin of the penis represents his femininity. Once removed, so also is his femininity and the fully male person is thus driven to seek a female as his mate, thus producing human community.[451]

Amidst this complex and varied gender context, African tribal cultures have a long history of *transgendered realities* and accompanying transgender behaviors like crossdressing. Some, like the Fanti people of Ghana, include cross-gender roles for both males and females.[452] The response to transgendered realities varies among different groups. Some have a history of little tolerance. Others have historically been quite tolerant. Some permit more flexibility of gender expression only at one end of the sex spectrum, male or female. Others allow some gender flexibility for all sexes. In a number of instances, as we have mentioned, there are examples of Greenberg's 'transgenderal' category in the phenomena often dubbed 'male wives' and 'female husbands'—examples of same-sex relationships with dual gender roles.

African languages reflect the diversity through a number of terms for the transgendered, some descriptive and others more value-laden. Among the former, for example, is *wor sitabane*, a phrase in the Sesotho language of South Africa that identifies some individuals as "having both penis and vagina." Among the more value-laden words is *wobo*, used among the Maale people of Ethiopia, and meaning "crooked." Because the Maale have other words for transgendered people (e.g., *ashtime*), the use of *wobo* is pejorative. Changes in language reflect developments in culture, and in that respect the influence of the West has been immense.

The Impact of the West: The Case of the Mawri

The impact of colonization, and the cultural pressures exerted by major religions, is undeniable and commonly remarked upon both by African scholars and others.[453] For example, sociocultural anthropologist Adeline Masquelier documents the struggle of modern Mawri youth in Niger, a struggle in no small measure reflecting the impact of colonial cultures and two major religions (Christianity and Islam) on a traditional society. Modern values and pressures daily interact with traditional ones. In a culture where bridewealth (a conveyance to the prospective bride's family to form a bridal contract) is key to forming marriage alliances, this interaction between tradition and modernity causes difficulties for many youth. Full maturity and adult social status is marked by assumption of primary obligations like marriage. But marriage requires transference of bridewealth to the woman's family. In modern society, Masquelier observes, many young men face twin obstacles: dwindling economic opportunities and inflated prices. These youth, unable to pay bridewealth, are confined to social immaturity longer than would likely have been the case in previous generations. As a result, there is a 'crisis of masculinity': young men are remaining longer in the domain defined by femininity—within the house. Men, who for example perform any cooking task beyond the acceptably masculine task of grilling meat, are seen as effeminate and subject to ridicule. In short, Mawri males unable to marry cannot create a socially accepted masculinity and are thus culturally feminized.[454] The modern pressures exerted by Western culture and religion have negatively interacted with indigenous traditions to harm people.

Conclusion

The remarks in this part of our dialog barely scratch the surface. But they should suffice to demonstrate that while we can generally find aspects of gender around the world reminiscent of our own ideas and practices, we must not naively assume a complete identification between them. Every experience and expression of gender occurs in a particular social matrix; every culture modifies gender in some way. The modern dominance of the West, and the consequent cultural pressure exerted on the rest of the world, has impacted gender everywhere. Whether or better or worse is a debate we must leave to another day.

Chapter 7

Gender Development

Introduction: Whether gender is thought of as biologically based or predominantly a cultural product, our sense of it changes across the lifespan. In other words, there is a *developmental dimension* to gender. As we move our focus to gender in the life of the individual, we want to begin with this dimension. It forms a foundation for our later, closer attention to gender identity and gender roles.

One key aspect of development related to our conversation on gender is *differentiation*. Whatever else it is, gender development differentiates us into one or another gender. From that point forward a series of differences, internal and external, mark gender development. Some of these we have discussed earlier: gender assignment, gender expectations, and gender socialization. Now we need to focus on the individual marker events that constitute mental mileposts as we attain a sense of gender and how it applies to our own person. These include our learning to label gender and eventually to see it as a stable rather than fluid property of persons.

Yet before we can proceed very far with such matters we must consider a question that takes us back to our old dilemma—should we be talking about 'gender development' or 'sexual development'? If gender is merely a derivative of sex, then perhaps gender development is but one aspect of sexual development. On the other hand, if sexual development is confined to discussion of biological maturation related to reproduction, plus changes in sexual awareness, attitudes, and behaviors, then gender development refers to something distinctly different. But what exactly?

If we distinguish gender development from sexual development as an entity in its own right, what are we involved in describing? The answer entails acknowledging the primary weight of cultural values and beliefs. In this respect, gender development is quite separable from sexual development because it does not depend on sexual maturation nor even principally on the sexed body. Instead, it follows from cultural decisions about how many genders are possible, how large a role gender plays in human affairs, and when we enter into gender. To keep our dialog manageable, since this is just a primer for further conversing, we shall restrain our inquiry to our own culture, and specifically our own society. That means a focus on the psychological development of the individual.

Development & Differences

Each and every one of us experiences development. We know that it means change, and we hope it means positive change in the sense of growth. But there may be a dimension to development we don't often consider. Social worker and psychotherapist Peter Wilson writes, "Development . . . involves the discovery of mind and body, which is fundamentally concerned with the emergence of differences."[455] This idea that development consists of varying processes of *differentiation* should resonate with our understanding of the fundamental nature of gender—a differentiation of human beings into various kinds.

This differentiation starts even before birth because each of us enters the world in a specific cultural context. Every culture has its own way of viewing gender, including how many gender possibilities there are and when we become a gendered person. In our society, parents wait expectantly for a child about whom they already have well-formed expectations. These include that the child's sex will be unambiguous, that *gender assignment* will coordinate with that sex into one or the other of either boy or girl, and that the new baby will immediately conform with cultural ideas about how girls and boys look and act. So when we show up, naked and squalling, virtually the first act of every adult present is to look between the legs to see if a penis is present. Immediately following this determination an assignment is made into one or the other dominant gender camp: masculinity or femininity.

From birth on a sequence of further differentiations occur. Each marks differences, some of them ascribed, some produced, and others observed. The earliest, the *gender expectations* that accompany gender assignment, are so strong they lead us to distorted perceptions as we see the baby not as he or she is, but as we believe he or she must be. In turn, expectations generate *gender socialization* (or gender typing), a process intending well-regulated differences between girls and boys that adhere roughly to cultural stereotypes. Because children are generally eager to please, they typically behave in *gender conforming* ways that others observe and reinforce. Those children who struggle in this respect are marked by others as different in a socially undesirable way, frequently labeled as mentally disordered (e.g., Gender Identity Disorder), and either marginalized or coerced to conform as best they can.

The kinds of differentiation we have just mentioned we have talked about before. Now we must add other differentiations, principally those that transpire within the child's mind. Development is marked by differences in the ages at which children regularly attain specific notions about gender in general, and about themselves as gendered persons. These kinds of differences will constitute our focus in the remainder of this particular discussion. However, our conceptualization of these developmental markers relies in part on a familiar dividing point, one we have time and again been confronted by: should we see gender development with all its differentiation as something fundamentally determined by biology—thus an aspect of sexual development—or as constituted principally by social processes embedded in cultural currents?

Gender Development, or Sexual Development?

Let's begin our musings on this question by asking a different one: How big a deal should we make of gender development anyway? After all, psychologist Marjorie Hardy claims that, strictly speaking, a relatively small proportion (5-10%) of total social behavior is due to gender (though many of us seem rather anxious about whether a person's behavior is gender appropriate or gender nonconforming).[456] Perhaps we would do better to think of gender development as a subset of *sexual development*, or perhaps of *psychosexual development*.

The latter styling may remind us of that most famous of pioneering theorists in this arena, Sigmund Freud. We shall turn to his ideas presently, but for now let us stay to the notion that perhaps gender development is just a subset of psychosexual development, which thus conceived assumes a biological foundation to both sex and gender, and coordinates the two as parallel processes. As the body sexually matures, the mind develops a sense of gender. In this respect, *gender* typing becomes the acquisition of *sex*-roles. In other words, gender is reduced to an experience of identity related to the sexed body and to the adoption of roles presumed congruent—or at least expected—for that particular sex.

This way of looking at things was more common a few decades ago. For example, when social psychologist Carol Tavris and colleague Carole Wade published their book *The Longest War* at the height of second wave feminism, they subtitled it 'Sex Differences in Perspective.' Gender received scant attention, and was clearly subordinated to sex, being the psychological counterpart and product to the biological foundation.[457] This perspective can still be found. For example, in the mid-1990s psychologist Toni Cavanaugh Johnson subordinated gender role and gender object development under sexual development, regarding these as forming one of the seven lines of sexual development in children.[458]

In the new millennium, with our even more pronounced focus on gender, we tend to distance gender development from sexual development and to speak of things formerly placed under sexual development now under gender development. The most notable instance, of course, is the preference to speak of gender roles rather than sex roles—a discussion we shall leave to the next part of our dialog (chapter 8). This separation is noticeable in contemporary publications. For example, the 2003 volume edited by John Bancroft entitled *Sexual Development in Childhood* offers scant reference to gender and does not cover the elements now commonly grouped under gender development.[459]

The argument for this separation entails a few key points we have touched on in other connections. First, gender and sex are not the same, so using them interchangeably prompts confusion. Second, sexual development consistent with the name devotes itself to the maturation of the body relevant to sexual and reproductive functioning. That means those psychological aspects involved in sexual attitudes and behaviors, but not necessarily gender identity and role. Thus, third, gender development sticks to the psychosocial processes involved in gaining an awareness of gender in general, attaining a personal sense of gender, and mastering the demands of a gender role. While sex and gender need not ignore each other—and certainly can't in our culture—their relative independence from one another is stressed. Put most bluntly, gender is not just about sex and sexuality. It merits separate consideration.

That idea returns us the question we asked a moment ago: how big a deal should we make of gender development? Even if we can justify separating it out from under sexual development, how much attention does it merit? One of the key notions we have considered in our conversation is that *gender in our society has become central to conceptions of the self and relationships*. If this is the case, then the study of gender development is very important, no matter how much of specific behavior can be exactly pinned to it. In this light, gender influences to a greater or lesser degree much more behavior than is found in what we explicitly call gender behavior. By virtue of its critical role in forming our sense of self and guiding our expectations and performance in relationships, gender is very important. That means understanding its development is instrumental to understanding our development as a person, especially as a social being.

Psychodynamic Theories of Gender Development

So where can we turn to get a broad sense of gender development? We certainly can and should look at empirical studies. But these both are guided by hypotheses and help form theories. Theories systematize findings as well as generate testable hypotheses to guide further research. So a convenient way to get at a basic grasp of gender development is to consider some of the more prominent theories on the subject. Of these, the first generally referred to is that of the psychodynamic tradition, especially by its founder, the psychoanalyst Sigmund Freud.

Before we turn to Freud we should first get a sense of psychodynamic explanations in general. They set forth the notion that *relationships within the family determine gender*. But that doesn't mean they all agree on how exactly that comes about. Freud, for instance, heavily depended on sexual biology as the foundation upon which gender is built through interactions with both parents. Social psychologist Erich Fromm also shows interest in the role of both parents. He has interest in contrasting broadly different social structures—patricentric versus matricentric—depending on whether paternal or maternal love predominates. Many psychodynamic theorists, like Nancy Chodorow, whom we have heard from earlier (chapter 4), pay great attention to the role of culture and socialization, and emphasize the role of the mother. Indeed, gender communication scholar Julia Wood captures the essence of most explanations after Freud in this remark: "Psychodynamic theory explains the development of masculine or feminine identity as the result of different kinds of relationships that typically exist between mothers and children of each sex."[460]

So we should not expect that Freud represents the only word from this large and diverse camp of thinkers. However, he does represent the first word and in important ways remains the primary word. His basic ideas continue to offer an essential framework for psychodynamic theorizing. Moreover, his notion of the Oedipus Complex remains perhaps the single most controversial idea ever set forth about gender development.

Sigmund Freud & Psychosexual Development

Freud's *psychosexual theory of development* is, properly speaking, one that belongs to the group we spoke about a moment ago—a theory that subordinates gender development to sexual development. Trained as a neurologist, Freud brought a predisposition to coordinate psychological phenomena with biological underpinnings. But it was his actual observations in a clinical setting that led him to describe a psychology characterized by the power of the unconscious, sexual energy, and developmental processes. Freud's 'talking cure,' his therapeutic technique formally known as 'free association,' dictates that a client speak uncensored whatever comes to mind. Freud found that when his patients proceeded in this manner they talked about their past. He discovered through this process a framework for reconstructing their childhood. What especially struck him was that this developmental framework was structured around sexual energy. When his patients talked about childhood, they also talked about sexuality.

He identified five psychosexual *stages*. These are discreet developmental periods marked by decisive turning points that separate each from the next, with each determined by the concentration of bodily energy at particular places. The first of these, during infancy, he termed the *oral stage* because the body's energy centers around the mouth. The infant's suckling at the mother's breast constitutes the child's first sexual experience, which is not sexual in any adult sense, but by its sensual character paves the way for later sexual experiences. The *anal stage* follows during toddlerhood. The body's energy focus has moved to the region of the anus—an understandable response to social pressures to master bowel control (toilet training). The anus is also a source of pleasure, both in the sensation of holding on to the body's waste, and then also in its expulsion. In early childhood the *phallic stage* finds a shift of the body's energy to the genital region between the legs. The 'phallus' labels the boy's penis and the girl's clitoris. In this stage, sensual pleasure centers here and accompanies the Oedipus Complex, to which we shall turn in a moment. As the child enters the school years, the *latency stage* ensues. As the name suggests, the body's sexual energy goes underground, subordinating itself to the psychosocial tasks these years present for mastery. However, sexual energy does not go away; child sex exploration and sex play are common. Finally, with puberty the child becomes a youth in the *genital stage*, where sexual energy again focuses in the genitals. Now, however, while it remains dominant for the young man in his penis, for the young woman it shifts from the clitoris to the vagina. This change, Freud believes, prepares each gender for forming mature sexual relationships characterized by penis-vaginal intercourse.[461]

Sexual development is clear in this sketch, but what of gender? In his famous *Three Essays on the Theory of Sexuality*, Freud added a footnote in 1915 to point out that the terms masculine and feminine are used in at least three different ways—which is why he called these words "among the most confused that occur in science." In one use, they refer to activity and passivity; masculinity is active and femininity passive. Another use is biological, relating masculine to the sexual reproductive function of producing sperm and feminine to the sexual reproductive function of producing ova (eggs). A third meaning is sociological, stems from observation of actual people, and leads to the conclusion that pure masculinity or femininity are not to be found in anyone, either physically or psychologically.[462] What Freud sets out to do in his writings is clear up some of the confusion even while acknowledging that gender is extraordinarily complex.

To get at Freud's conception of gender we must start with his conviction that all of us are *psychologically bisexual*. In a lecture on femininity offered late in his life, Freud starts with the observation that the sexual characteristics we depend on to distinguish male and female are certain with respect to reproduction—males produce sperm and females ova. But other body characteristics, though displaying the influence of sex, vary considerably. In fact, he remarks, each sex reflects indications of the opposite sex. This points to bisexuality, "as though an individual is not a man or a woman but always both—merely a certain amount more the one than the other." This suggests to Freud that, "the proportion in which masculine and feminine are mixed in an individual is subject to quite considerable fluctuations." For Freud this means anatomical science is insufficient for describing masculinity and femininity, so it is left to psychological science to attempt the task. Like anatomy, psychology starts with a presumption of bisexuality: "Thus we speak of a person, whether male or female, as behaving in a masculine way in one connection and a feminine way in another."[463]

Freud rejects the easy suggestion that masculinity and femininity differ in that the former is active (like the sperm), and the latter passive (like the ovum). He considers, though, that femininity psychologically may prefer *passive aims* and perhaps even passive behavior, because of either her reproductive role or social customs that force women into passive situations. Yet such a possibility remains just a possibility, because "the riddle of femininity" is not so easily solved.[464]

Freud proclaims that psychoanalysis does not aim to describe what a woman is, but asks how she comes into being. In other words, psychoanalysis focuses on *gender as the outcome of sexual development*. As far as gender is concerned, the first decisive events take place in the phallic stage. At its start, little boys and little girls are much more alike than different—so much so that he dramatically pronounces, "the little girl is a little man." What he means by that is that the girl is as aggressive and active as the boy and, sexually, does with her clitoris what the boy does with his penis, which is derive great pleasure from it.[465]

The *Oedipus Complex* (which we briefly touched on when discussing gender socialization) is Freud's most controversial idea. As we discussed before, he hypothesized that roughly between about ages 4½ to 6 a child must renounce desire for the parent of the opposite sex and affiliate with the parent of the same sex.[466] This task is more difficult for girls than for boys because girls must change their primary erotogenic zone (i.e., the place in the body where sexual pleasure is centered). For boys, the penis remains the primary source of pleasure; for girls the clitoris must give way to the vagina. In her experience of the Oedipus Complex the little girl both discovers that she lacks a penis and that so does her mother. The disappointment that follows awareness of her difference from the boy (who takes such evident pride and pleasure in his penis and who, in Freud's day, enjoyed many more privileges than a girl), leads to feelings of loss and envy. The disappointment is also connected to the mother, who is now the object of the child's hostility because she is blamed for the little girl's loss of the penis. In Freud's view, it is inconceivable to a young girl that anything so remarkable as a penis should have been denied her, so it must have been taken from her—what Freud calls the *castration complex*.[467]

How the girl resolves this situation determines which of three possible lines of development she will follow. Resolved satisfactorily, she will experience normal development. Otherwise she may become sexually inhibited and neurotic, or form a masculinity complex, which in extreme cases may lead to female homosexuality. For Freud, the castration complex is accompanied by the girl's desire for a penis, or *penis envy*. In normal development, this penis envy paves the way for femininity, which results when the disappointed girl turns from her mother to her father. This makes of her mother a rival for the father's attention, which is at the core of the Oedipus Complex. Unlike little boys, the Oedipus Complex for girls tends to last longer and be less completely resolved, a situation hindering development of the super-ego.[468]

Femininity for Freud is developmentally achieved when the girl subordinates her more aggressive and active aims. Penis envy, Freud thinks, carries psychological consequences. A feminine woman has a more constrained libido than a man, which is why sexual 'frigidity' is encountered in women. Feminine women also tend to narcissism and vanity, which lead to a greater desire to be loved than to love—and which shows an effort to psychologically compensate for early childhood's sense of sexual inferiority to the boy. This is also why women are more susceptible to shame. The complications of the Oedipus Complex also leaves her, in Freud's estimation, with a less developed sense of justice, weaker social interests, and less ability to sublimate their instincts into productive activities. By about age 30, he observes, women seem psychologically set to the point of rigidity, as though the difficulty of achieving femininity had exhausted future possibilities for personal development.[469]

Penis envy and normal femininity mean consequences in *love choices* by a woman, too. Desiring the penis, she transfers primacy of erotic satisfaction to the vagina, which will accommodate the penis of a male partner. She thus prepares herself psychologically for her gendered social role as wife. Her choice of a man may be the narcissistic ideal of the man she had wished as a young child to become. If she is still wrestling with the Oedipus Complex her choice may be a man like her father. In the latter case, sometimes during the marriage the woman begins to relate to her husband with the unconscious and unresolved hostility left over from her relationship with her mother. Thus, second marriages may turn out better than first ones. The complicated relation of the woman to her mother may also show itself in a change after the birth of her first child, which may revive an identification with her own mother. If the child is a son, the woman can transfer her own suppressed ambition to him—another remnant of penis envy. Finally, her marriage is secured when she succeeds "in making her husband her child as well and in acting as a mother to him."[470]

'Neo-Freudian' Ideas: Karen Horney & Erich Fromm

The psychodynamic perspective articulated by Freud has inspired much comment over the years—including within the psychodynamic tradition itself. For example, so-called 'Neo-Freudians' Karen Horney and Erich Fromm in their own ways took issue with some of Freud's key ideas. Horney accepted the reality of the Oedipus Complex, but questioned its universality and objected to the emphasis on penis envy in Freud's contemplation of the development of femininity. She argued instead that masculinity is as likely to entail *womb envy*— an inability to create life naturally that spurs them to make things and then glorify those things over the woman's ability to give birth—as women are to have penis envy.[471]

Fromm drew inspiration from the work of anthropologist Johann Jakob Bachofen, who reconstructed the history of civilization based on changing pre-eminence of gender. In the earliest phase was *hetaerism*, a loose social organization without law and order, without marriage, and based entirely on the natural productiveness of woman. This gave way to *matriarchy*, a dominance of the feminine positively grounded in values of equality, universality, and unconditional affirmation of life, but negatively constrained by a lack of rationality and progress, and bondage to blood and soil. The phase we are now in, *patriarchy*, is relatively recent. The positive character of masculine dominance is seen in rationality, law, science, spiritual development—the things we associate with 'civilization.' Its negative aspects include its hierarchical nature with the resulting inequality, oppression, and inhumanity. But what especially strikes Fromm as Bachofen's relevance to psychology is his analysis of *the difference between motherly and fatherly love*, which may produce either a *patricentric* or *matricentric* person or society. Fromm puts things together this way:

> Summing up, we can say that the patricentric individual—and society—is characterized by a complex of traits in which the following are predominant: a strict superego, guilt feelings, docile love for paternal authority, desire and pleasure at dominating weaker people, acceptance of suffering as a punishment for one's own guilt, and a damaged capacity for happiness. The matricentric complex, by contrast, is characterized by a feeling of optimistic trust in mother's unconditional love, far fewer guilt feelings, a far weaker superego, and a greater capacity for pleasure and happiness. Along with these traits there also develops the ideal of motherly compassion and love for the weak and others in need of help.[472]

As this little bit of eavesdropping indicates, psychodynamic theory has hardly stood still. We might also have mentioned the work of Melanie Klein, inspiration for the Object Relations approach that eventually became dominant in Britain and the United States, or other branches of this robust tradition. But while Freud and the psychodynamic approach continues to be influential, it is not alone.

Learning Theories of Gender Development

Psychodynamic theories do not disregard the importance of learning in gender development, but they relegate it to a subordinate position behind the intrapsychic and largely unconscious forces at work in parent-child relationships. On the other hand, a number of theories put *cognition* at the forefront, even if they also think family relationships are very important. Some of the theorists who prioritize cognitive processes actually have their roots in psychodynamic thinking. Others are indebted to behavioral ideas about learning.

Walter Mischel & Social Learning/Albert Bandura & Social Cognitive Theory

Psychologist Walter Mischel is best known as a personality theorist,[473] but it is his thinking on gender development that interests us here. He draws on a different approach from psychodynamic theory to explain gender development. One important difference is that Mischel moves the focus away from the individual to the environment. Another key difference is that he does not embrace a stage concept of development. For him, the learning of gender proceeds the same way we learn anything else.

The formal beginning of the *social learning theory* he employs is best set at the 1941 publication of *Social Learning and Imitation* by psychologist Neal Miller and his colleague, sociologist John Dollard.[474] But social learning theory is part of a tradition in psychology called Behaviorism, which centers on how learning occurs. On one hand, through classical conditioning, behavior is learned in response to the pairing of certain stimuli (a neutral stimulus matched with a stimulus that elicits a response can eventually produce the same effect, as when Pavlov's dogs learned to salivate to a ringing tone). On the other hand, behavior is also shaped by what comes after it, through Skinner's operant conditioning, where consequences operate on behavior to make it more or less likely to occur again. So in social learning theory there is an emphasis on the role played in development both by *environmental stimuli* and by *rewards and punishments*.

As the name of the theory highlights, Mischel views the development of gender as *social*. The environmental stimuli, as well as the rewards and punishments, come from people. We learn gender in the same way we learn most things—from watching, listening to, and interacting with others. Unlike traditional Behaviorism, which disdained cognition as something that could not be seen, social learning theory believes cognitive processes can be reasonably deduced from behavior. A key idea in this respect it that some learning is 'vicarious'—it transpires from *observation*. Observations produce inferences—an indication of cognition that becomes more sophisticated over time. As Mischel put it, a man doesn't need to wear a dress in public to figure out how it will be received by others.

Children not only observe others, they *imitate role models*. But not all possible role models are equal; choosing the wrong model to imitate leads to feedback telling the child the imitation is inappropriate, while choosing the right model brings praise. In either case, the child's *behavior precedes cognition*—the child learns through the consequences of his or her action, as shown in the social feedback from others. Thus environmental determinants shape the path of gender development through selective reinforcements (rewards) of desired behavior and incentives to discontinue a behavior (negative reinforcers and punishments). [475]

Another elaboration of this theoretical approach has taken place under Albert Bandura's *social cognitive theory*. Inasmuch as we discussed this when we talked about gender socialization (chapter 4), we shall only briefly reprise its essence. This view regards gender conceptions and role behavior as the products of a broad network of social influences found not only in the family, but in many other common social systems. Gender development occurs the conveyance of gender-linked information through the *modeling* of gender by parents, siblings, and peers, among others. It is an interactive cognitive process. Even as information comes from the environment, the child engages in *self-regulation* of gender expressive behaviors. Developmentally, gender understanding precedes gender labeling, which is an early step in learning gender roles. Such learning is life-long. [476]

Lawrence Kohlberg & Cognitive Developmental Theory

In the same year, 1966, and in the same publication, another psychologist offered an alternative view to that put forward by Mischel. Lawrence Kohlberg's *cognitive-developmental theory*, in his own words, "starts directly with neither biology nor culture, but with cognition."[477] But while his theory resembles social learning theory in the prominence of cognition, Kohlberg gives special pride of place to the growth of cognitive abilities in the person. What this means is a change in focus from the social environment back to the individual. Kohlberg's theory makes of each of us active agents in our own development as we seek to achieve a cognitive consistency that produces stable categories we can depend upon to guide us. A line can be traced from Kohlberg back through the developmental psychologist Jean Piaget to psychodynamic thinking. Also, in a manner reminiscent of psychodynamic theory, Kohlberg envisions developmental change as hierarchical, progressive and universal. But Kohlberg went to some length to differentiate his theory from both psychodynamic and social learning theories.[478]

One reflection of Kohlberg's interest in the individual is his utilization of the idea of *gender identity*—self-categorization as a boy or girl. He believes that by 3 years of age a child has acquired a solid gender identity foundation. With this identity the child selectively reinforces his or her gender by initiating gender-conforming behaviors. In short, says Kohlberg, boys endorse their gender identity by reasoning, "I am a boy, therefore I want to do boy things, therefore the opportunity to do boy things (and to gain approval for doing them) is rewarding."[479] So children very early on are active agents in their own gender development.

But development still proceeds in an orderly, sequential series of steps, or *stages*, which in each case correspond to general cognitive developmental processes and stages as conceived by Piaget. For Kohlberg, the sequence in cognitive gender development marches through the following stages:

❑ gender labeling;
❑ attainment of a sense gender stability; and
❑ acquisition of a sense of gender permanence.

These three steps help to continue to build gender identity.

Young children, Kohlberg believes, are characterized (and limited) by the cognitive traits Piaget had identified—egocentricity, cognitive inflexibility, concreteness, and body-orientation. Children by age 3 engage in *gender labeling*—identifying gender in themselves and others—long before they grasp its essential character. Thus a small child may insist that gender has changed because appearance has changed, through alterations in hair or clothes, for instance. Children learn that boys and girls look different, but fix upon that difference in concrete, inflexible ways attached to the body. Any body that looks like what a girl looks like must be a girl.

As children become more aware of body differences, they begin to associate gender characteristics with these differences. This is also accompanied and reinforced by more acute observations at home and in the world of gender differentiated tasks and behaviors. So children learn to associate in a rather rigid fashion what fits each gender and, within any given society, collectively share this developmental pattern in obvious and consistent ways. These changes typify *gender stability*—the cognitive attainment of the realization that gender means certain things consistently across time. So boys become men, not women, and girls become women, not men. This attainment generally happens by age 5 years.

However, while gender stability brings with it a sense to the child that her or his gender stays the same across time, it does not automatically bring the conviction that it *cannot* change. In other words, though they know boys become men and girls become women, they still believe that given the right conditions a boy can become a girl, or a girl become a boy. Changing appearance and behavior can still make someone a different gender. They have not yet reached a sense of *gender consistency*—the constancy of gender across circumstances—that undergirds the final critical development in their gender cognition.

Of special interest to Kohlberg is what happens in the child between ages 5-7 years old. It is during this time that a child's cognitive capacities allow him or her to realize that gender is a fixed quality across both time and situations. This sense of *gender permanence*—the realization that one's gender is fixed and invariable—is first applied to the self, then generalized to others. Gender permanence is of paramount importance to all that follows. Kohlberg believes a "child's gender identity can provide a stable organizer of the child's psychosexual attitudes only when he is categorically certain of its unchangeability."[480]

The developing gender identity is also reinforced by rigorous adherence to the *gender stereotypes* the child is still mastering. As children's cognitive capabilities advance in later years they become both more flexible and more complex in their comprehension of gender. They begin to grasp the role social relationships play, see that gender role behaviors are more varied, and gradually loosen their hold on gender stereotypes.

Although his contribution to an understanding of gender development has been sizable, Kohlberg's greatest fame rests in the application of his theory to *moral development*. He conceptualizes several stages embedded in three levels:

❏ Pre-conventional level
  ○ Stage 0: egocentric judgment
  ○ Stage 1: heteronomous moral ('punishment and obedience') orientation
  ○ Stage 2: instrumental relativist ('self-interest') orientation
❏ Conventional level
  ○ Stage 3: interpersonal concordance ('good boy/nice girl') orientation
  ○ Stage 4: authority and social order maintaining ('law and order') orientation
❏ Post-conventional level
  ○ Stage 5: social contract and individual rights orientation
  ○ Stage 6: universal ethical principles orientation

As may be evident, the stages are known by various designations.[481] Also, Kohlberg speculated on a seventh stage, an *ontological orientation*, characterized by an individual's efforts to resolve moral dilemmas marked by their complexity and the presence of conflicting claims and rights.[482]

Consideration of these ideas to our discussion of gender development is appropriate because Kohlberg finds gender differences in moral reasoning. Before we examine those, let's briefly review each level and stage. Just as Piaget had specified a central term ('operations'), and then divided development into pre-operational, concrete operational, and formal operational stages,[483] Kohlberg identifies the term 'conventional' as his theoretical pivot. *Conventional* refers to the moral reasoning typical found in and sanctioned by society. Thus moral development has as its referent the comparison of individual moral reasoning with that characterizing society.

The *pre-conventional level* of moral reasoning typifies young children and roughly corresponds to Piaget's early cognitive stages of development. Kohlberg offers a 'stage 0' to reinforce the idea that there is a pre-moral stage, or an amoral period where the child's cognitive egocentrism and immaturity make speaking of moral reasoning impractical.[484] The first stage of moral reasoning displays a *heteronomous moral orientation*. 'Heteronomy' (others' rules) is preconventional because the child simply accepts that adults set the rules and these must be obeyed or punishment will follow; no internalization to make these rules one's own has yet taken place. The second stage, an *instrumental relativist orientation* (or 'instrumental exchange orientation'), reflects a more sophisticated level of self-interest. The child now recognizes both that there are different views of right and wrong, and that there is a need for reciprocity—a sense that fairness entails each party involved getting something. Moral decisions are guided by self-interest and while fairness matters, getting what one wants while avoiding punishment matters too.[485]

As children enter the later school years (junior high and high school) they move into the *conventional level*. Kohlberg's third stage of *interpersonal concordance orientation* (or 'mutual interpersonal relations orientation') is fully conscious of the expectations of others—especially peers—and desirous of meeting those expectations. This 'good boy/nice girl' style of moral reasoning sees moral decisions as those approved by others, that is, by society in general. Acts are judged by intentions (e.g., 'She meant well'). Morality is not absolute, but relative. The fourth stage, an *authority and social order maintaining orientation* (or 'social system and conscience orientation'), extends the scope of moral purview beyond friends and family to the wider world. Moral decisions preserve the social fabric. Law and order must be upheld.[486]

Things like civil disobedience cannot be entertained by conventional moral thinking. In the *post-conventional level*, which Kohlberg believes most of us never reach, is characterized by a wider cognitive reach and greater cognitive flexibility. Stage five, a *social contract and individual rights orientation*, sees rules as tools rather than as inflexible clubs. The person recognizes that his or her own society is but one among many and that perhaps there may be basic moral ideas that should be a part of any human society. In this stage morality is a social contract willingly entered into in order to—and for so long as—basic individual rights are upheld within a democratic process making possible changes in social rules. Finally, in a sixth stage that Kohlberg admits has little empirical support but still retains theoretical validation, there is a *universal ethical principles orientation*. In this rarest of stages, moral reasoning transcends individual perspective and imaginatively takes the perspective of everyone affected. It reasons on the level of principle, not rule or law, and seeks a universal application. Kohlberg argues that these higher stages of moral development are objectively more desirable; stage 6 thus offers the most adequate moral judgments.[487] However, higher levels are also more cognitively advanced and therefore more difficult to comprehend.[488]

Kohlberg's research finds *gender differences in moral reasoning*. His theory, though, is built on research presenting moral dilemma vignettes to boys and young men in order to assess the nature of their moral reasoning. Critics contend the structuring of his theory around conventional moral reasoning in a masculine-dominated society carries consequences when applied to girls and women. Just as Piaget found a divergence in moral reasoning between boys and girls showing up as they grew older, so does Kohlberg. In a 1969 report coauthored with Richard Kramer, Kohlberg observes that while both young men and women are likely to be at the conventional level, young women are more likely to be at stage three and young men at stage four. His theory appears to privilege a masculine conception of *justice* that makes the way girls and women often make moral decisions be judged less mature. [489]

Carol Gilligan's Response to Kohlberg

Carol Gilligan, once a student under Kohlberg, took strong exception to the notion that girls and women should be found less mature in their moral reasoning. In her famous response, *In a Different Voice*, she links Kohlberg's research to that of Piaget and Freud, who also depreciate women's sense of justice. Gilligan notes that despite Kohlberg's claim of universality for his theory, the actual research base centered on a longitudinal tracking of 84 *males*. When applied to women, Kohlberg's theory finds their moral reasoning typically exemplifies stage three, an interpersonal concordance orientation. In this stage, moral reasoning involves interpersonal considerations and moral goodness equates with helping and pleasing others. Gilligan writes:

> This conception of goodness is considered by Kohlberg and Kramer (1969) to be functional in the lives of mature women insofar as their lives take place in the home. Kohlberg and Kramer imply that only if women enter the traditional arena of male activity will they recognize the inadequacy of this moral perspective and progress like men toward higher stages where relationships are subordinated to rules (stage four) and rules to universal principles of justice (stages five and six). [490]

Gilligan accepts that women reason along these lines. What she rejects is any conclusion that such reasoning is lower than or inferior to that done by men. She views Freud, Piaget, and Kohlberg as having derived their theories from study focused on boys and men; a different result obtains if we begin with the study of girls and women. If we trace their development, Gilligan contends, we find the chief moral issues derive from conflicting *responsibilities* (women) rather than from competing *rights* (men).[491]

The problem for Gilligan lies in the exclusion of women's voices when theory is being constructed. Worse, what voice they do have has been shaped by masculine demands in a masculine-dominated society. Women are defined by the place they hold in man's life cycle—nurturer, caretaker, helpmate. "But," Gilligan remarks, "while women have thus taken care of men, men have, in their theories of psychological development, as in their economic arrangements, tended to assume or devalue that care."[492]

Gilligan's aim, as the title of her book makes plain, is to give the different voice of women a chance to be heard. She thinks women bring to the life cycle a different point of view; they order human experience in terms of different priorities. The result is a difference in women's conceptions of self and morality.[493] In her view, women's development is centered around the continuing importance of attachment in life. While theories like Kohlberg's privilege masculine pursuits of separation, individuation, autonomy, and rights, the feminine pursuits of attachment, nurturance, and care need acknowledgment, too.[494]

"In their portrayal of relationships," Gilligan says, "women replace the bias of men toward separation with a representation of the interdependence of self and other, both in love and in work."[495] In short, feminine moral reasoning has a *care* orientation. But that orientation itself shows movement and growth. Girls develop from a sense that care should be taken to not hurt others to a woman's mature sensibility that care should extend to the self as well as to others. This transition facilitates an understanding that their view of relationships is a source of moral strength.[496] Gilligan believes that "in the different voice of women lies the truth of an ethic of care, the tie between relationship and responsibility, and the origins of aggression in the failure of connection."[497]

Gilligan concludes her book with a differentiation of her conception from Kohlberg's theory that has become famous: "While an ethic of justice proceeds from the premise of equality—that everyone should be treated the same—an ethic of care rests on the premise of nonviolence—that no one should be hurt."[498] Put most simply, Kohlberg prizes a masculine *justice* orientation while Gilligan champions a feminine *care* orientation.

Both Kohlberg and Gilligan have been subjected to some criticism for their conceptions. Kohlberg's stages turn out to be more flexible than he tended to regard them. Gilligan's sweeping division between the kinds of moral reasoning by the genders appears unsubstantiated. Research in the 1980s-1990s, and beyond, has found that *both* men *and* women can display a care orientation or a justice orientation. Presently, researchers are skeptical that any presumed gender differences in moral reasoning are significant.[499]

Sandra Bem & Gender Schema Theory

Psychologist Sandra Bem, whom we discussed earlier in connection with her ideas and research on androgyny, also has proposed a theory about gender development. Her *gender schema theory* was first set forward in the early 1980s, when Bem announced it as a fourth theory of sex typing (alongside the psychoanalytic, social learning, and cognitive-developmental theories). She has issues with each of the previous theoretical approaches. She faults psychodynamic theory as difficult to empirically verify and as too easily promoting an 'anatomy is destiny' view of gender development. While she has more in common with the other learning approaches, both also have weaknesses. Bem faults social learning theory both for making individuals relatively passive recipients of what the environment provides and for underestimating the effects of age. She critiques cognitive developmental theory for never asking why 'sex' should be any more central to the self than some other characteristic, such as race. Even should it prove the case that sex and gender are central in our society, these may not be central to the self in other cultures.[500]

In the 1981 article that introduced her ideas, Bem proposes that these deficiencies can be corrected. Acknowledging the indebtedness of her own theory to previous learning theories, Bem asks what it is that children are learning. "Clearly," she says, "the child is learning content-specific information, the particular behaviors and attributes that are to be linked with sex." But this is not all that is being learned. The child is also mastering a vast network of sex-related associations. This second kind of learning—the acquisition of an evolving *gender schema* by which to process content-specific information—is at the heart of her theory. [501]

Obviously the word *schema* is crucial. "A schema," Bem explains, "is a cognitive structure, a network of associations that organizes and guides an individual's perceptions." It guides gender development by anticipating and selecting for assimilation information from the environment relevant to the schema. In simpler terms, the gender schema helps a child select and organize information about sex and gender in a useful way. It filters a vast array of stimuli to pick what is needed, then places it into a pre-existing mental structure. Even the self-concept gets fit within this schema. Children learn gender by appropriating what their society links to their gender and applying that to themselves.[502]

The gender schema doesn't just select and organize content-specific information related to *attributes* or dimensions (e.g., 'boys are strong, girls are weak'), but also to these attributes' *applicability*. Bem offers the example that we rarely think of girls in terms of strength or of boys in terms of nurturance; different attributes are salient for different genders. Thus a child not only learns which attributes to apply to the self, but also how much an attribute measures. Of all the possibilities open to a human being at birth, we each learn a subset, and the ones we learn via the gender schema shape us as 'boy,' 'girl,' 'man,' 'woman.' We learn, as Bem puts it, that *through sex and gender we differ from one another not only in degree, but also in kind.*[503]

Gender development in this manner carries *value consequences*. The gender schema becomes what Bem terms a "proscriptive guide." It tells us not merely who we are in our society's view, but who we *should* be. As we internalize this message we become self-motivated to regulate ourselves to conform. Of course, that conformity has a reciprocal effect in simultaneously strengthening a personal affiliation with one's gender and endorsing the cultural myths of gender. In so doing we privilege gender itself, so that gender schema theory becomes a theory of the process of dividing us into two separate classes—masculine males and feminine females—irrespective of the actual attributes themselves. In short, it does not matter how strong a woman might be or how nurturing a man might be. What matters is that men and women define themselves and act as members of their gender class, and whatever their actual strength or nurturing might be will be interpreted along the lines of what that is supposed to be like for that gender.[504]

Bem posits that the processes of gender socialization are learned. But *why* is such learning so important? Her answer is that gender-based schematic processing is culturally insisted upon as mattering in virtually every aspect of being human. Sex determines gender and gender makes a difference in seemingly every-thing—from the clothes we wear, to the toys we play with, to the jobs open to us as adults, to the behaviors we display in relating to each other. Society thus teaches not only what becomes our gender schema, but the lesson that this schema matters because the difference between men and women is extensive and intensive across the various aspects of human life.[505]

By 1981, Bem had concluded that this theory offered a step beyond her ear-lier ideas of androgyny. From a feminist standpoint, she admits, androgyny still preserves masculinity and femininity as independent realities. Androgyny simply cannot prompt our serious examination of how gender both organizes the per-ceptions of the individual and the social world around us. Gender schema the-ory, on the other hand, offers rich possibilities of gender consciousness raising by helping us see not only how weighty and pervasive gender distinctions are, but how gratuitous is the emphasis on gender distinction itself.[506] As she put it in 1983, "From the perspective of gender schema theory, then, gender has come to have cognitive primacy over many other social categories because the culture has made it so." [507]

Bem thus recognizes in gender schema theory a way forward in challenging our cultural allegiance to a gender scheme and dichotomizing way of reasoning that is unwise, unnecessary, and undesirable. If gender notions are learned, that means they are not inevitable, nor are they immutable—a lesson she says social learning theory made plain.[508] A critical implication of this conclusion is that children can be raised *gender-aschematic*. This requires parental efforts to under-mine the dominant ideology in society before it can undermine their own. Rather than ignoring gender—which merely gives culture a free hand—parents who want to liberate their children from society's gender schema process must undertake two strategies. First, they must divorce their children's learning of sex differences from the culture's imputation of what that means—the 'sex-linked associative network' that is the gender schema. In essence, *children need to learn sex differences as tied to biology not to culture*. Second, parents can offer their own 'subversive' schemata as an alternative to the cultural gender schema. For ex-ample, children can be taught to focus on *individual differences*. The differences within members of a group typically exceed those between different groups and so generalizations that 'boys are like this and girls are like that' can be chal-lenged by showing exceptions to reinforce how varied people actually are. As the child matures, an idea of *cultural relativism* can be added: people hold differ-ent beliefs and our family's beliefs are these. Finally, a *sexism* schema can be added when the child is old enough to understand that while people may differ in their beliefs, some beliefs are immoral; sexism is not merely different, but wrong. The development of this schema aids the child in distinguishing right from wrong and taking an active stance against sexism.[509]

No matter how hypothesized, all theories agree there are a number of dif-ferent processes involved in development, to which we must now turn our at-tention more fully.

Developmental Processes

In light of what we have learned, gender development appears to comprise a number of both interacting processes and products. These include:

- ❑ gender identity—the personal process of self-identification with a gender;
- ❑ gender socialization (gender typing)—the social process that facilitates development of gender identity and mastery of social expectations for the assigned gender role;
- ❑ gender awareness—the evolving individual recognition of gender differences;
- ❑ gender labeling—the individual process of applying gender labels;
- ❑ gender stabilizing—the individual attainment of a recognition that gender persists across time;
- ❑ attaining gender constancy—the individual recognition that gender is persistent across situations and circumstances;
- ❑ reaching gender permanence—the individual accomplishment of applying gender stability and gender constancy to the self and then to others so that gender is regarded as fixed and abiding across life; and,
- ❑ gender role performance—an individual expression of gender in ways that either relatively conform or do not conform to gender expectations based on gender assignment.

While we have met with all of these things before, some brief review specifically tied to gender development is in order.

Gender Identity

The next major topic in our ongoing dialog will be about gender identity. But here we need to focus on its role in gender development. Preceding an individual's gender identity is an *imputed gender identity* that results from *gender assignment* at birth. Long before we have any sense of our own gendered being, others have attributed one to us, persistently perceived us according to it, and embraced *gender expectations* about our behavior and personality. Thus the process of gender identity—and it is a lifelong process—begins no later than with gender assignment at birth, and may well have started before birth with parental hopes and wishes.

A personal forming of gender identity is an ongoing work. Though we may eventually attain what we regard as a stable gender identity and think of it as a product—a finished process—that is inaccurate. New experiences, altered expressions, changing information, and a host of other influences demand we continue to process our sense of gendered identity quite frequently. We may not be conscious of this processing, but that makes it no less real or important. Our lives are filled with challenging opportunities to reassess what it means to us to be or have or hold or play the gender identity we embrace.

Personal gender identity, in the narrow sense of self-identifying with a particular gender, starts after infancy. In a 1975 report, developmental researcher Spencer Thompson noted that much before age 3, children do far better at gender labeling stereotyped figures than at gender identifying themselves. But by age 3 a majority of kids show an awareness of which gender label applies to their own person.[510] Of course, this leaves unresolved the issue of whether what they are identifying genuinely reflects their own internal experience of a gender or merely constitutes a recognition of their gender assignment. Nevertheless, it has become common to say that attainment of gender identity in this rudimentary sense is usually accomplished by about 3 years of age.

Gender identity may also be considered in a broader sense, as *an ongoing experiencing of gender as a core aspect of self*. In this sense, gender identity is *gender self-identifying*, an evolving process that transcends recognition of gender assignment. Through experience the child forges a unique sense of gendered self. This sense may conform to gender assignment and expectations set at birth and reinforced through socialization, but it does not have to do so. Some children possess a gender identity that defies conventional expectations—a matter we shall return to later.

In our culture, gender identity is a priority so it constitutes a primary task of childhood and a focus of parent-child interaction. The process utilizes numerous elements, but dress is central; children depend on gender-differentiated dress to help them master gender assignments and the concomitant values, attitudes, and roles.[511] Both boys and girls experience pressures to conform to their assigned gender identity. However, these pressures are more rigid and restrictive for boys because of their higher status in the gender hierarchy.[512]

Gender Socialization

Earlier (chapter 4), we gave substantial attention to gender socialization, including its role in development. It begins before birth, continues throughout life, and utilizes numerous social modalities, such as parents, peers, and social institutions (e.g., school, religion, media). *Gender socialization aims at creating and maintaining a gender identity and gender role consistent with that assigned by the agents of society (e.g., parents and medical authorities) at birth.* That purpose guides the role of gender socialization throughout development.

Gender Awareness

Whether by biological hard-wiring, or through early learning, infants rapidly prove able to distinguish between masculine and feminine presences. Between 3-4 months old, babies first show an ability to match their mother's voice with her face, and father's voice with his face.[513] Other research has found a more general ability appearing in the second half of the child's first year, but only with regard to matching feminine voices to stereotypical women's faces.[514] By 7 months of age, babies can distinguish masculine from feminine voices in general—and mere differences in pitch do not fully explain this behavior.[515] By 9 months of age they are able to differentiate in general between faces of men and women.[516] In this preverbal period the psychological significance of such awareness remains hidden to us, but the behaviors indicate early mastery of rudimentary gender distinctions. It seems plausible to suggest that the ongoing process of socialization is active in this growing gender awareness, which continues to evolve through subsequent processes.

Gender Labeling

Even with all the pressure to conformity provided by significant others and the culture at large, small children require some time to master gender. Now *gender labeling* becomes a cognitive task in the child's process of socialization. Having been color-coded themselves at birth, clothes early on become an important signifier to children of gender. In fact, throughout childhood dress functions as a primary criterion used to differentiate boys from girls.[517] But during the first two years of life gender labeling is just beginning, though it gains speed rapidly as infants turn into toddlers. Thompson noted that at 2 years old, about three-quarters (76%) of children he observed could accurately label stereotypical artistic representations of gender. This increased to more than four-of-five (83%) of children able to do so by age 2½, and to 90% of 3 year olds.[518]

While children generally are adept at knowing and adhering to gender labels and some gender standards by ages 3-4, the pace at which they develop this facility is individually varied. A longitudinal study reported in 1989 found that *early acquisition of gender labels* by a child was more likely to lead to early adoption of some sex-typed behaviors. The rapidity with which they mastered this social task correlated to the nature of the emotional reaction by their caregivers. Early gender-labeling children had parents who gave more attention—positive and negative—when their children played with gender-typed toys. This wasn't a matter of instruction from parents to children about the toys, it was the emotional response of the parents, which the child picked up on. Their parents' affective weight on gender may signal to these children the importance of gender, making them more likely to apply efforts to master what seems so important to mom and dad.[519]

Gender Stability & Gender Constancy

Not long after gender labeling leads to a basic gender identity comes another developmental milestone. *Gender stability*—the grasp that gender identity and role should be stable over time—is reached generally by age 4, although the many children and adults with transgender characteristics indicates this concept requires some modification from the way it is generally presented as an expected and universal norm. Embracing this idea—that boys will grow up to be men and girls to be women—children realize the stakes are raised in gender role behavior, including dress. Most have not yet firmly grasped a connection between anatomical sex differences and social gender differences. Gender stability depends instead on highly visible characteristics like hair length and clothes.

In this sense, children's notion of gender remains fluid for a time. They may believe that what one wears can change a boy into a girl, or a girl into a boy. Thus it is crucial to dress and act like a boy if one wants to grow up to be a man. *Gender constancy*—the cultural notion that gender will not change because it rests upon biological sex—is a gradually developed social construction. By the time a child is 6-7 years old this idea is generally well-established. Kids subject each other to rigid gender standards and punish nonconformity. According to Bem, they also develop gender schemas—ways of thinking about information associated with gender, such as gender stereotypes and gender 'appropriate' behavior.[520]

As noted a moment ago, *gender-differentiated dress* plays a significant role in gender development. Awareness of gender distinctions in dress doubtless precedes understanding of these differences. Development of awareness, endorsement, and expressed preferences along stereotyped expectations for dress may vary from individual to individual, but research suggests such matters are generally attained before a child starts school. A study reported in 1990 by developmental researchers Carol Lynn Martin and Jane Little found that a quarter of the 61 children (ages 3-5) tested attained a stereotyped knowledge about gendered clothing at age three, that more than half (54.5%) had done so at age four, and about three quarters (73.7%) at age five. As they put it, children need "only a rudimentary understanding of gender for preferences and knowledge to be influenced."[521] Given the pervasiveness of concern over sex and gender in our culture it might be said they are part of the very air children breathe.

Gender Permanence

Gender stability and gender constancy provide the foundation for *gender permanence*—the realization that one's gender is fixed and invariable. This conviction is first applied to the self, then generalized to others. It becomes an achieved product of developmental cognitive processes generally around ages 6-7. In Kohlberg's eyes, this achievement is important for gender identity. In a culture like our own, where gender is seen as fixed and immutable, gender permanence is of great significance. Of course, this focus would seem to limit Kohlberg's theory since, as we have discussed (chapter 6), not every culture regards gender in such a fashion that gender permanence has such salience.

Gender Role Performance

Our portrayal of the processes and products of gender development has boxed everything between gender identity and gender role. In our culture, the process that begins with attributing a gender identity is expected to culminate in a stable personal gender identity that is then played out within an ongoing process of gender role performance. In fact, we would not be remiss to say that our society cares more about *role performance* than it does *identity*. While we culturally prize identity, we are generally content to infer it from behavior and impute it whenever a situation is uncertain. In other words, identity is both subordinated to role performance and interpreted in light of it.

Gender role performance, like gender identity, is actually imputed to us before we actually begin it. Babies are perceived as fitting the role attached to their assigned identity. As children grow up they generally do their best to conform to expectations, to cooperate with gender socialization, and to finally and fully fit a gender role. Those who do not, or cannot, experience conflict. Though the society interprets this conflict as centered in the individual (e.g., gender identity disorder), the individual is as likely to see the conflict as centered in an intolerant society. But these are matters left to later in our conversation. We shall soon be giving special attention to the matter of gender roles, but first we need to spend more time discussing gender identity.

Chapter 8

Gender Identity

Introduction: Throughout our dialog we have talked about gender identity. We have considered a basic sense of what it means, and we have looked at its role in gender development. We also have witnessed the crucial role the concept played historically in reinvigorating the conversation on gender. In several respects we have found good reason to regard this idea as critically important.

As has consistently been the case, *the relation between sex and gender* once more must be reconsidered. Is gender identity just a more contemporary way to speak about what was previously called sex identity? The question invites us to ponder how this construct has arisen. One possibility is that gender identity is merely sex identity under a different name. Or perhaps it is a subset of sexual identity. Or, in the prevailing way it is used today, gender identity merits standing apart from sex identity and sexual identity as an independent construct.

Next we need to revisit the issue of development. Previously, we looked at the role of gender identity in gender development. Here we must examine the *development of gender identity* itself. As with so many gender terms, we must reckon with the possibility that this one is used in a narrow and a broad sense. If taken narrowly, then we can say gender identity is the developmental product that happens when gender labeling extends to the self. In a broader sense, gender identity is an ongoing process we might better term 'gender identifying.'

Gender identity is often correlated, whether correctly or incorrectly, with other matters. One such thing is *sexual orientation*, a person's relatively fixed erotic attraction pattern. Our culture expects masculine men to be erotically attracted to feminine women—what we call heterosexuality. Both same-sex attraction patterns (homosexuality), and erotic attraction to both sexes (bisexuality), pose problems for the dominant cultural scheme.

Finally, gender identity is also matched with the occasional occurrence of a specific mental disorder. *Gender identity disorder* is a very controversial designation that assumes that a mismatch between a person's actual experience of gender and the social assignment of gender signifies pathology in the person. That, however, is only one possibility. The distress some transgender people experience may be over trying to live in a gender rigid and intolerant society.

Identifying 'Identity'

Interestingly, as common as discussion about gender identity is, much of it proceeds without any attention to exactly what 'identity' means. Of course, whenever gender identity is defined, that definition includes 'identity' and modifies it in reference to 'gender.' But we might profit from taking a moment to distance ourselves from the compound label and consider 'identity' by itself.

Our word *identity* has come to mean a quality of individual self-awareness as a particular person or self who remains relatively constant across time and situations. The English word shows up in the late 16th century, being derived from French, which in turn owed itself to a late Latin form of an earlier Latin root, *idem*, meaning 'same.' This remains the heart of the matter: identity is a persistence of self as known to the self and shown to others.

The distinction just made is of relevance to gender identity. Our gender identity is our own persistent sense of, and identification with, a gender. But that identity as known to the self may not be the same as shown to others. We often hedge or hide some or all of our identity from others. This is a natural protective measure, a way of firming boundaries to guard the self. More complete disclosure of identity comes with increased trust.

Identity gains its persistent sense not from a sudden, once-for-all decision, but from a gradual accumulation and interpretation of *experience*. As we experience gender for ourselves, both in social interactions and in more private ways, we come to a realization of a particular gendered self. As we talk about gender identity, we need to keep in mind that it is built, sustained, and perhaps modified by experience. In light of this ongoing nature of identity, we are not wrong to speak of *gender identifying* alongside gender identity. To some degree we are always affirming or questioning this persistent sense of our gendered self.

Gender Identity or Sex Identity?

But perhaps we are applying the wrong label to best capture this identity.

We have found that the use of the word sex predominated conversation for a long time, only to be largely supplanted by the term gender in recent years. But is this shift indicative of a genuine change in understanding, or merely a concession to the conviction that the cultural environment matters at least as much as biology? The issue once again has to do with *the relation between sex and gender*. If gender is predicated on sex—in other words, is fundamentally shaped and constrained by biology—than gender identity can be viewed as a subset of sex, or even of sex identity. If, on the other hand, sex and gender are largely separable spheres, and gender belongs less to biology and more to psychology, than gender identity should be carefully distinguished from sex identity. In that case, they are distinct entities.

The matter is further complicated by the need to distinguish between sex and sexual. Are we dealing with *sex* identity or *sexual* identity? We won't be surprised to find that usage of terms has been inconsistent (or, if we prefer, 'evolving'). Of the two words, sexual is more comprehensive. It can include sex as the simple biological classification into male, female, or intersex, plus embrace a wide range of ideas about attitudes and behaviors associated in one way or another with sex. On the other hand, though sex identity can be limited to mere biological division along reproduction function, it doesn't have to be. It can be broadened to include psychological and social elements.

Since one of our primary aims in this dialog is to reach clearer and more consistent use of important terms, we could attempt that with these two 'identities.' Unfortunately, the act of defining either predisposes us to a particular conclusion. For better or worse, at least for the moment we must allow a certain murkiness to prevail. So we will wrestle with differentiating them as we go along.

Gender Identity as an Aspect of Sex Identity

Let us examine the case each way. If we start with the notion that today's gender identity is merely yesterday's sex identity in new clothes, we can offer the definition of *sex identity* put forward by social scientists Daniel Miller and Guy Swanson in 1960: "the total pattern of sex-linked characteristics that mark a person as masculine or feminine, both to himself or herself and to others."[522] That could pass for many contemporary definitions of gender identity. In this manner, gender identity is less subsumed under sex identity than it is made synonymous. In its broader conception, sex identity remains a comprehensive self-construct that recognizes the fundamental role played by sex among biologically distinct kinds of human beings.

This way of using the term is not all that old, even if it has largely passed from prominence. Nathaniel MacConaghy contends that the concept of sex identity derives from consideration of transsexualism and the reality of sex reassignment surgery.[523] That would place it largely in the 20th century. Linda Nicholson believes that, "This concept of sex identity as a sharply differentiated male and female self rooted in a deeply differentiated body was dominant in most industrialized countries at the time of the emergence of second-wave feminism."[524] As we learned earlier, the reinvigoration of the conversation on gender came when the word sex was severed from 'identity' in order to effect a more pronounced distance between biology (sex) and psychology (gender).

Gender Identity as an Aspect of Sexual Identity

If gender identity in terms of sex identity results in talking about the same thing using different words, then what happens if we consider gender identity in terms of sexual identity? Once more we are confronted by usage that complicates things for us. The term can be used either narrowly, or more comprehensively. Right now we are interested in the more comprehensive use.

Researchers John DeCecco and Michael Shively, noted for their study of human homosexuality, have been important participants in the discussion of what they call *sexual identity* as more broadly conceived. They note that discourse over this matter has been most prominent in European and American medical, psychiatric, and social science fields since the middle of the 19th century.[525]

Shively & DeCecco set forward a framework of sexual identity embracing four elements:

- ❑ biological sex;
- ❑ gender identity;
- ❑ social sex-role; and,
- ❑ sexual orientation.

Their aim is to set out a continuum for sexual orientation rather than a dichotomous view, and to locate it within a context of identity. [526]

In this view of sexual identity, *biological sex* refers to the physical characteristics associated with being male or female. *Gender identity* is used in the narrow sense of a person's self-identification as male or female. Although we have been discussing masculinity and femininity in reference to gender identity, Shively and DeCecco include these as aspects of the individual's *social sex-role*, which refers to the characteristics culturally associated with each sex. This articulation of the social sex-role thus incorporates most of what many people mean when they refer to gender identity. *Sexual orientation* refers to the person's pattern of sexual arousal when it is exclusively with reference to members of the opposite sex (heterosexuality), with reference to members of the same sex (homosexuality), or with reference to members of either sex (bisexuality). In their conception, it includes both physical and affectional individual preferences.[527]

More recently, clinician Walter Bockting, who specializes in working with transgender (especially transsexual) people, follows the work of Shively and DeCecco. Bockting also portrays gender identity as one of four distinct components of sexual identity. He substitutes 'natal' sex for 'biological' sex, and retains the designations of social sex role, and sexual orientation.[528] Bockting retains this way of looking at things because he finds it helpful in distinguishing certain clinical issues in working with his clients.[529] However, this manner of conceptualizing things is not currently prominent.

Gender Identity as a Separate, Independent Category

What is prominent in today's conversation is treating *gender identity as a separate, independent category*. The success of gender identity in attaining this status has meant a restriction of the ideas of sex identity and sexual identity. We might even say that these ideas have been subordinated somewhat analogously to the way gender was for a long while. For the majority of those who talk about gender today, gender identity is the most robust concept and both sex identity and sexual identity are more narrowly defined.

An example of this development can be found in the effort toward a 'sociological psychology' attempted by Andrew Weigert, Joyce Smith Teitge, and Dennis Teitge. They distinguish these three terms like this: *sex identity* is restricted to the realm of biology where it divides human beings into male or female. The other two identities are viewed as social constructions. *Gender identity* differentiates people into a dichotomous scheme based on sex identity; it refers to "internalized sociocultural meanings and expectations that accompany the normal sense of maleness or femaleness taken for granted in society." Finally, *sexual identity* refers to differentiation into kinds of sexual interaction (e.g., homosexual or heterosexual) where one's social and/or personal identity is understood with reference to such interactions with a particular gender.[530]

Similarly, philosopher and gender scholar Jacquelyn Zita also distinguishes three kinds of identity. The first, sex identity, she defines in a way familiar to us: "Sex identity is considered a physical category where bodies are sorted into clearly identifiable kinds, female and male, on the basis of biological criteria." The separation between sex identity and gender identity is clear in her definition of gender identity: "Gender identity is a behavioral and psychological category in which individuals are considered to fit or misfit expected behaviors, functions, and personal attributes associated with one sex or the other, as in femininity and masculinity." To these she adds a third identity. "Socioerotic identity is a behavioral and psychological category in which individuals are differentiated from one another on the basis of erotic desire for and/or sexual acts with the same or 'opposite' sex. This is also referred to as sexual preference or sexual orientation identity." [531]

One advantage of this kind of separation is that sex identity, at least, remains relatively straightforward and reasonably easy to establish. As Zita puts it, "Sex identity is understood to have clear biological criteria, measurable and countable in kind and number."[532] By this she means that appeal can be made to biological elements from sexual chromosomes to the proportion of various hormones in the body to the genital appearance alongside other secondary sex characteristics. Gender identity, though, still poses problems for many of us.

Zita uses the situation of a 'male lesbian' to provoke our thinking about how many of us actually think of gender and sex in relation to one another. She tells the story of a biological male who for years passed successfully as a lesbian. This person was accepted and trusted within the lesbian community. But when it was discovered the individual had male genitals, rejection was swift and severe. Zita asks whether anatomy alone justifies such a response. She wonders if even with sex reassignment surgery the person would have been welcomed. For her, the crux of the matter comes with a conflict between what she terms 'self-intending' and 'other-extending' attributions. Normally what a person intends—their self-attribution of sex and gender—matches what others extend as an attribution of those things. But, as in the case of the male lesbian, sometimes self-intending attributions conflict with other-extending ones.[533]

The implicit indictment is this: while we often espouse a generosity toward the *possibility* of gender identities outside the dominant masculine and feminine paradigm, the *actuality* of such identities often evokes a less generous behavioral response. Our contemporary vision of gender identity as an independent category presupposes that some real individuals will not have such an identity paired with their biological sex. It imagines a spectrum that does not merely the test the boundaries of masculinity and femininity, but punctures them repeatedly with manifestations of gender identity incapable of neat categorization in the ways we once felt comfortable using.

For our ongoing dialog we will consider that *gender identity is an internalized self-construction arising from experience interacting with cultural conceptions and expectations about gender, especially as these relate to the gender assigned the individual.* The value of this formulation is that while it recognizes each of us must wrestle with the weight of culture brought to bear on us through gender assignment and its accompanying socialization pressure, it does not insist that our experience result in a self-construction that must be labeled within the cultural gender scheme. Our experience is what it is. We may find accepted social gender labels more or less fitting. In gender self-identifying we engage in a lifelong process of building, testing, and revising a core aspect of self. The result at any given moment can be called a gender identity, the fruit of experience forged in the context of culture. That forging, or development, must now be our next concern.

Gender Identity Development

How does gender identity come into being? Is it a product or a process? If it is a process, how long does it continue? We already have raised such questions in talking about how to define gender identity (chapter 1), and discussing its role in development (chapter 7). But we need to take time here to look at this matter more closely.

The Development of Gender Identity in the Narrow Sense

Our position is going to be that gender identity can be understood in both a narrow and a broad sense, and that both are developmental in nature. In the *narrow sense of gender identity* it is the simple self-labeling of gender. The process that yields this product includes the following elements:

- ❑ gender assignment;
- ❑ gender socialization;
- ❑ gender awareness; and,
- ❑ gender labeling.

We talked about these not long ago, so we can content ourselves here to coordinating them with respect to gender identity. *Gender assignment* occurs at or shortly after birth. It extends an identity onto the child that expresses the beliefs, values, hopes, and expectations of the parents and culture. This attributed identity stands in for a gendered self-identity even after the child begins to form a conscious gender identity. The assumed identity posited by others is an aspect of *gender socialization*, which marshals all the forces of culture to shape a conformity by the child in self-perception, social affiliation, and behavior to the assigned gender. The expectation is that parents, siblings, peers, and social institutions (e.g., religion, school, media), will assist in teaching the child the assigned gender and this teaching will result in gender identity as a learned product. That learning shows itself in cognitive processes. *Gender awareness* in the preverbal period demonstrates an infant's early mastering of gender categories. This contributes to gender identity by establishing the culturally prescribed division into gender kinds that the child must place the self into. *Gender labeling* follows awareness as the child names ('labels') things and people as belonging to one or another gender category. When the child can attach a label to the self, gender identity is said to have been attained. This usually occurs by about 3 years old.

The Development of Gender Identity in the Broad Sense

A *broad sense of gender identity* posits both that the narrow sense constitutes only one phase of an ongoing process of gender self-identifying, and that even in this first phase there are other elements transpiring that are usually overlooked. The reason these are not typically considered is that they are difficult to establish empirically, especially in the preverbal period, but also in the immature child. So hypothetical constructs set out in this regard must be viewed rather more skeptically. At the same time, they cannot be ignored in light of the observable outcomes in actually witnessed gender identities.

So let us attempt to set out the elements of a broad sense of gender identity, or *the process of gender self-identifying*:

❏ Phase I: attaining gender identity (narrow sense).
❏ Phase II: gender identity *testing*—confirming or disconfirming through personal experience the product of phase one. It includes:
   o gender stabilizing—learning that gender persists across time;
   o attaining gender constancy—learning that gender persists across situations;
   o reaching gender permanence—applying gender stability and gender constancy to the self and to others; and,
   o measuring personal experience of gender against the culturally expected label for 'goodness-of-fit.'
❏ Phase III: gender identity *stabilizing*—the attainment of a reasonably secure gender identity with some continuing reassessment. The elements of this phase may include:
   o achieving a goodness-of-fit that persistently stabilizes the gender self-identifying across situations and for a period of time;
   o cognitive dissonance when elements of gender experience and expression no longer fit as well;
   o gender identity flux, and perhaps crisis, as competing elements vie to determine the next reasonably stable gender identity; and
   o recycling of the phase, to a greater or less degree, throughout life.

Phase I, *attaining gender identity (narrow sense)*, we have already discussed. But we must add a comment or two. First, the child at age 3 can label the gendered self as 'boy' or 'girl,' but this really doesn't tell us much about the internal identity experience. After all, what other gender labels are there? The cultural juggernaut of gender socialization admits no other possibilities and lends its full weight to confirming a label consistent with gender assignment. Thus, second, all we can be confident about is that the child has accurately learned the label applied by others.

Phase II, *gender identity testing*, tests the label—the *presumed* gender identity. Typically, gender stability is mastered by age 4. Gender constancy proves a little more elusive. Despite having labeled the self as 'boy' or 'girl,' children between 3-6 view gender as fluid; change one's appearance and the gender changes, too. But by about 6-7 years old most kids have swallowed the cultural lesson that gender is fixed and immutable, both across time and across situations. Shortly thereafter this conclusion is pasted to the gendered self. But the child of 7 still has no other referents for gender identity save 'boy' or 'girl.'

This does not mean children don't search for alternatives. Children are regularly measuring their personal experience of gender against the culturally expected label for 'goodness-of-fit.' How well does the label that has been applied to the gendered self—'boy' or 'girl'—actually fit the self's experience in light of gender expectations and stereotypes? What is a child to do when the label does not wear well?

Consider, for example, the case of elementary school-aged Jodie, who after remarking that all the girls in her class "act all stupid and girlie," declared this judgment did not apply to her "cos I'm not a girl, I'm a tomboy." She succeeded in persuading two male classmates to identify her as a boy—a reasonable judgment because 'tomboy' clearly isn't 'girl' and in a two gender scheme that only leaves 'boy.' The researcher in this study concluded Jodie appeared to be operating at the boundary line between masculinity and femininity—again, a justifiable interpretation where no other gender alternatives are allowed recognition.[534] But we can as easily imagine that Jodie was experiencing a gender identity that neither 'girl' nor 'boy' really labeled; the closest label available that fit her experience was 'tomboy.'

What Jodie may be doing is actively *measuring the 'goodness-of-fit'* between her labeled gender identity and her actual gender experience. She may be acting like a scientist. Psychologist George Kelly's personal construct theory may have some relevance to us in this respect.[535] Kelly views people as rational beings who rely on constructs to construe the environment and anticipate future events. We expect our way of looking at things to make sense and fit internally. So constructs are as valuable as their usefulness for prediction and producing meaning. A child's evolving constructs start few in number and highly dependent on others, especially one's parents. As the child grows, *role-playing* becomes a way to try on and test hypotheses about being a person. Such activity yields for most kids a highly predictable set of outcomes associated with gender conformity as opposed to gender nonconformity. But constructs are highly individual, subjected to continuous testing by experience, and modifiable. They also realize the power of personal choice so that while most children have construct systems that place high priority on *sociality*—predicting the responses and behaviors of others—to guide our behavior, some prioritize another construct. In making an *elaborative choice*, a child selects an alternative aligned with a particular construct because it appears promising to further develop one's construct system. Such choices can consolidate previous gains or seek future ones. Importantly for our consideration, such choices can test, refute, or promote a particular gender identity.

Sooner or later, given the primacy of gender to our culture's conception of self and relationships, a reasonably stable gender identity is achieved. Phase III, *gender identity stabilizing*, begins with and follows from this attainment. It starts with achieving a *goodness-of-fit that persistently secures the gender self-identifying across situations and for a period of time.* The gendered self reaches and maintains, at least for a while, a gender identity that works. It permits a congruence of self-labeling with inner experience and finds outlets, private or public, for expressing that gender. But continuing life experience in an environment where gender expectations change with time and situations may introduce challenges to this security. There may develop *cognitive dissonance* when elements of gender experience and expression no longer fit. What worked before no longer works. The new demands of a different developmental level or interpersonal situation heightens the stakes even as the feasibility of the existing gender identity is called into question. This new instability in the gender self-identifying prompts a degree of *gender identity flux*—a renewed time of testing gender identity in search of a new goodness-of-fit. This flux might persist for a long time if the person is able to tolerate the insecurity of the gender identity, or proves unable to achieve a new stability, or has little incentive to resolve the situation because the price paid for the flux is inconsequential. Perhaps more often, though, flux climaxes in *gender identity crisis*, as competing elements internally vie to determine the next reasonably stable gender identity. Resolution returns the self to a reasonably secure gender identity; there follows recycling of the phase, to a greater or less degree, throughout life.

These ideas hardly exhaust the possibilities, and have only been sketched out above. Other theories, seeking to account for nonconforming gender identities, have been proposed. We may profit from considering a couple of these.

Richard Docter & Self-theory

The study of nonconforming gender identities exerts pressure to account for their existence by broadening our way of thinking. Not enough serious theorizing has yet transpired in this respect, but there has been some. Psychologist Richard Docter, building on data obtained over a five year span from 110 self-identified heterosexual crossdressing men ('transvestites'), and some of their spouses, offers a 'self-theory' focusing on the 'self-system.' Put simply, for Docter there is a "master self" that serves to maintain and coordinate a variety of "self-systems." These subsystems interact in a reciprocal fashion with the master self, influencing and being influenced. These self-systems do, however, display some autonomy. Among them, the *gender identity self-system* is prominent. It holds the person's own highly individual self-perception and experience of masculinity and femininity. It can exercise profound influence over the entire self.

But this self-system does not suddenly appear full-blown; it emerges over time.[536]

Docter's theory integrates ideas from a number of places. He acknowledges a debt to ideas offered by other theorists on the self.[537] He embraces cognitive-behavioral theory especially for the notion of 'sexual scripts'—highly individualistic cognitive formations developed over time that become stable in adulthood—that include what one learns about gender.[538] And he adopts a sense of development that he calls "a multistage, progressive phenomena."[539] The result is a five-stage theory to explain the development of male transvestism.

While Docter's theory aims to explain a particular phenomenon—male transvestites—his ideas may hold some promise for wider application. In particular, his third and fourth stages merit further comment here because they point to an ongoing process of gender self-identifying in adulthood. Docter thinks that in stage 3, around late adolescence (about age 18), cross-gender behavior (e.g., crossdressing) becomes more frequent and complete. Accompanying it is a developing cross-gender identity. At the same time, there is cognitive dissonance because the individual is aware his behavior and identity are culturally taboo. This stage may persist over many years. In stage 4 a resolution of the cognitive dissonance occurs. This may happen in the 30s or 40s and takes one or the other of two paths: successful integration of the cross-gender identity into the entire self-system, or a splitting-off of the cross-gender identity. This second path poses a threat to the primary self and may lead in some cases to the final stage, the rise to primary position of the cross-gender self.[540]

In the mid-1990s, a team of Dutch researchers used self-theory to guide their developmental study of nearly 200 male transvestites and transsexuals. In these individuals they discovered a feminine gender identity was already forming in early childhood. They hypothesized that all people possess a masculine and a feminine gender identity subsystem, but that these subsystems vary in strength. Moreover, the expression of a subsystem may be "conditional"—only expressed if certain conditions are met—or "unconditional." When these ideas are joined, two continua emerge, one for the masculine gender identity subsystem and the other for the feminine. Each can range from "strong and unconditionally expressed" to "weak and unexpressed." The subsystems can coexist but cannot be simultaneously expressed, which may generate conflict between them. In this theoretical framework, both 'normal' females and male-to-female (MtF) transsexuals can be said to express a strong and unconditionally expressed femininity combined with a weak and unexpressed masculinity. Transvestites, on the other hand, occupy an in-between position on the continua, with both masculine and feminine subsystems conditionally expressed. Simply put, sometimes they express masculine and at other times feminine, with the latter arising only when certain conditions exist.[541]

At the end of the 1990s, Scandanavian researchers Sam Larsson and Maj-Briht Bergström-Walan also theorized that crossdressing men may be best understood utilizing 'self-theory,' but as modified by 'multiplicity of mind' perspectives. These ways of looking at things seem to fit well with research findings that male transvestites experience through crossdressing a 'feminine self'—a sub-identity in the self-system. This sense of the 'feminine self' is different from the sense of 'male self' experienced when not crossdressed. The existence of sub-identities consciously experienced is the premise of 'multiplicity of mind' theory. Thus transvestism can be explained as a unique form of multiplicity of mind in which both a male identity and a female sub-identity hold places in the self-system.[542]

While these ideas broadly support the idea that gender identity development continues past early childhood, acting in important ways at adolescence and through adulthood, they are conceptually limited by continued allegiance to a two gender scheme. The effort to understand gender nonconforming men in this framework keeps them within a dichotomous framework. While many so-called transgender individuals adopt 'masculine' and 'feminine' as ways to describe themselves, that may reflect more the poverty of our terminology and the power of the culture than the reality of their gender identities.

Richard Ekins, Dave King, & A Sociology of Transgendered Bodies

Transgender researcher Richard Ekins and sociologist Dave King offer a different approach, but one that also accepts that gender identity development is not finished early in life. In 1999, in formulating a nascent 'sociology of transgendered bodies,' they typified 'transgendering processes' as falling into one or another of four modes: 'migrating', 'oscillating', 'erasing', and 'transcending';[543] a slightly later formulation substituted the label 'negating' for 'erasing.'[544] Each of these modes derives its character from its relation to the male/female binary divide—what they call the principal social determinant for transgendering processes. Transgendering behavior—which we may plausibly imagine expressing an internal set of experiences constituting the gender identity—must in our culture shape itself with reference to this great sex/gender divide into male men and female women.

In *migrating*, as the term suggests, the transgendering mode is a permanent change from one side of the male/female divide to the other. On the other hand, *oscillating* refers to movement back and forth across the divide. *Negating* takes an alternative path by seeking to undo the divide through its elimination, thus becoming 'gender-less.' The final mode, *transcending*, stands in contrast to negating by attempting to go beyond the divide to a sense of being 'gender-full.'[545] It seems highly implausible to conclude such variation in behavior accompanies an invariant gender identity formed once and forever in childhood. These variations in transgendering, we may suppose, accompany an ongoing gender self-identifying that effects in time one or another resolution satisfactory to a greater or lesser degree to the person.

While this approach also reckons with our culture's dichotomous gender scheme, it does so in a way more robust than self-theory. Ekins and King recognize that transgender people caught in this particular cultural web must navigate it in forming gender identities. But there are multiple ways to do so—and hence the possibility of different gender identities accompanies an ongoing gender identity development process.

Gender Identity and Sexual Orientation

Another matter now presents itself. As we noticed at the beginning of this discussion, gender identity is often talked about in connection with *sexual orientation*—a person's relatively fixed erotic attraction pattern. To understand how this could be the case, we need to see *the role played by atypical gender identities in the broad social discourse on gender.* Communication studies scholar John Sloop, in examining the conversation on sex and gender in recent decades, observes that much of the talk has swirled around instances of gender nonconformity (or, 'gender trouble'), raising questions about prevailing gender norms. But, he contends, rather than actually producing substantive reassessments of cultural assumptions, "such cases were more often positioned within the larger body of public argument as aberrations in nature's plan and hence worked to reify dominant assumptions about human bodies and sexual desire." The result was predictable: a two gender scheme was mostly underscored and reemphasized.[546]

In other words, rather than be prompted by empirical reality to change our mental scheme, we have distorted our perceptions. We force what we see into our preexisting notions. This is not unexpected; we typically try to assimilate new information into old understandings rather than accommodate it with a new understanding. Generally we have to be substantially confronted by how poorly the new information fits the old scheme before we engage in the effort to create a new, better way to see things. The social default position has been to try to wedge atypical gender identities and expressions into our culturally dichotomous gender scheme. That is how a link was forged with sexual orientation.

Two Logic Chains

This connection has long roots. The presumed link is already present in John Money's introduction of the term gender identity in 1955. In his view, "It includes, but is not restricted to sexuality in the sense of eroticism."[547] But we can trace the essence of the supposed connection even further back, to a longer standing belief that socially approved gender identities (masculinity and femininity) are matched with socially approved sexual orientation (heterosexuality), while socially disapproved gender identities (all other gender alternatives) are matched with socially disapproved sexual orientation (homosexuality). In short, *atypical gender identities are assumed paired with homosexuality.*

This suspect logic is a product of the medicalization of sex (see chapter 2), which yields *heteronormativity*—the belief that heterosexuality is the only normal sexual orientation and that any other sexual orientation is thereby abnormal. Heteronormativity sets expectations for sexual desire and standards for sexual interactions. In its most extreme form it reiterates the belief that sexuality must be judged by its procreative function so that any form of sexual behavior not clearly related to and leading to the possibility of conception (e.g., masturbation, anal sex, oral sex) is *perverse*.[548] A consequence of heteronormativity is *heterosexism*—bias, prejudice, and discrimination shown by heterosexuals toward homosexuals.[549] Heterosexism logically derives from the expected moral response to perversion—disgust. In sum, people who are heterosexist justify it on moral grounds as a normal, natural reaction to that which is disgusting and thus should be strongly opposed.

When we put this all together with other ideas previously associated with the medicalization of sex, and add the vocabulary of contemporary cultural discourse, we have a string of associations that if put into words might sound like this: "There are two sexes that yield two gender identities in a straightforward, natural manner: masculine males and feminine females. These people have a natural sexual desire for one another, expressed in heterosexuality. This desire is part of romantic love, which yields the pair bonding of marriage. Such marriage results in sexual intercourse, which sooner or later leads to reproduction, which creates a natural family. Anything else is not merely *abnormal* but also *unnatural*, and thus threatens social order and must be opposed."

Atypical gender identities are caught early in this chain of associations. Since any of us with such an identity are outside the 'normal' and 'natural' chain, we must be linked in another chain that is 'abnormal' and 'unnatural'—another example of the dichotomous thinking we are so accustomed to! This presumed other chain might be described in this heterosexist way: "Those people who suffer from a mismatch between their sex and gender find their sexual desire disordered as well. A man who thinks he is a woman who desires sex with other men is obviously a homosexual, just as a woman who thinks she is a man and wants to have sex with other women is a homosexual. Such desire cannot lead to a natural union called marriage and thus cannot be associated with a normal, natural family." By this or similar thinking, many among us justify opposition to homosexual marriage and adoption by gay or lesbian couples.

Atypical Gender Identities and Homosexuality

But let us keep our focus here on gender identity, particularly *atypical gender identities*—any gender identity that does not meet the society's standards of heteronormativity. Social scientists Patricia Gagne, Richard Tewksbury and Deanna McGaughey observe of such people that, "It is those who are publicly perceived as 'not women/not men' who pose the greatest challenge to the binary system."[550] Our question is, How does this system respond? The answer that makes perhaps the best sense in light of all we have learned to this point is this: the society embracing this binary system tries to *control* deviations from heteronormativity. It does so in a variety of ways, including:

❑ distorting perceptions of reality to fit the system; and,
❑ enforcing gender norms.

Both use social power in different ways.

Distorting perceptions of reality to fit the system occurs principally in *limiting the possibilities of discourse.* If we have no ways to talk about gender except through a vocabulary built around masculinity and femininity, how can we even think about other gender possibilities? Rather than let them be what they are, we must see them in ways that allow us to talk about them. That requires us to restrict ourselves to the labels, terms, and concepts utilized by the binary system.

This distortion process does not work just within those of us who fit rather comfortably within the binary gender system. It also works within those of us who do not fit. Gagne and colleagues note it is interesting, but not surprising, that most who are labeled transgender adhere to the traditional concepts of sex and gender, because like everyone else they have a limited range of identities available to them.[551] To make even partial sense of their gender identity, those with atypical identities reach for whatever label comes closest to saying what they experience, even if all the available labels are constructions of the binary system they don't fit. Words like 'third gender' are very rare because the binary system disallows them. So folk who might find that choice appealing instead are far more likely to fall back on 'androgynous' or 'transgender.'

Society exercises power in *enforcing gender norms* on all of us. If we have atypical gender identity we are not excused from the norms; they are brought to bear coercively. We already have talked about heteronormative logic and heterosexism. These conveniently group all nonconforming gender people, whether that nonconformity is in gender identity or sexual orientation, together as one. There is an implicit assumption of *comorbidity*—if a person is disordered in one way, they are probably disordered in other ways. Hence, anyone with an atypical gender identity probably is homosexual, and homosexuals have an atypical gender identity. As Gagne and colleagues put it, "Falling in 'between' the gender binary will often result in assumptions of homosexuality, as in the case of the feminine man or the masculine woman."[552]

This cognitive distortion—a distortion because empirically one can possess an atypical gender identity and be heterosexual, or be homosexual and possess a typical gender identity—serves the coercive power of norm enforcement. After all, heterosexual people with atypical gender identities don't want to be seen as homosexual any more than homosexual people with typical gender identities want to be viewed as having an atypical gender identity. Heteronormativity thus effectively divides and conquers, putting marginalized groups against one another and thereby enlisting them in supporting the very norms that oppress them.

A real, and justified fear of violence faces both minorities. Anyone with an atypical gender identity must face the possibility of *homophobia*—an irrational fear of someone because of their sexual orientation. Anyone with a homosexual orientation must face the possibility of *transphobia*—an irrational fear of someone because of their atypical gender identity. Fear motivates conformity to gender norms.

All of this is not to deny that some overlap does occur. There are individuals with atypical gender identity who also have a homosexual orientation. But it isn't all of them. The exaggeration of the few into a presumption that it includes all serves heteronormativity, but not the facts. Unfortunately, another complicating factor is that heteronormativity enforces a certain kind of sexual behavior by labeling *any* same-sex sexual interaction as making a person homosexual. Thus an individual who experiments with same-sex behavior runs the double risk of being perceived as both homosexual and possessing an atypical gender identity.

In fact, as sexologist Holly Devor correctly points out, it has been people with atypical gender identities who engage in same-sex activity that has helped foster the chain between two groups. She argues that because transgendered people around the world have been the most visible in engaging in same-sex activity they have become emblematic of homosexuality to many. Thus thrust together in the public mind, she thinks lesbian, gay, bisexual and transgender (LGBT) people should work together for their common good.[553] This seems eminently pragmatic. At the same time, we would be remiss if we didn't point out that calling the same-sex behavior of people with atypical gender identity 'homosexual' is only possible in the binary gender system.

The *sexual orientation labels (heterosexual/homosexual/bisexual) privilege sex over gender*. Both heterosexuality and homosexuality are defined in the context of body sex, and bisexual blatantly proclaims a dualism. Given what we have learned about human sexuality, this seems indefensible. The primary sexual organ is the brain, not the genitals. If gender is given primacy an entirely different picture emerges. A transsexual who started life as a male, undergoes sex reassignment surgery, and sexually desires men is *not* homosexual if gender matters most. Such a person sees the self as feminine, has adjusted the body to the apparent sex of being female, and thus—to use the words we are stuck with in the binary system—is heterosexual, if that term is understood to mean the desire of a woman for a man. When such instances are termed homosexual the speaker is denying not only the legitimacy of the gender and sex change, but even the possibility that there can be anything that really matters except the body's sex. Such logic is reductionistic: 'anatomy is destiny.' The logic may appeal to many of us, but we have to ignore facts to embrace it.

Finally, the connection between gender identity and sexual orientation also shows up in talking about a presumed 'gender identity disorder' (GID). We shall turn to that idea in a moment, but we can mention now that through successive editions of the diagnostic model that dominates our society's mental health thinking, this link has been preserved since 1980. Back then the clinician was to specify the subtype of the disorder by the object choice of any strong sexual feelings (heterosexual or homosexual); if there were no strong feelings the coding was 'asexual' subtype, and if it could not be determined the subtype label was 'unspecified.'[554] Presently, the clinician is to specify, for sexually mature individuals, whether the "sexual attraction" is to males, to females, to both, or to neither. The choice of phrasing—'sexual attraction' rather than 'orientation'—is sensible since using descriptors like 'homosexual' and 'heterosexual' would be confusing to many. But exactly why this matters enough to be a specifier is not elaborated although the matter is briefly alluded to in discussing the course of the condition. In fact, the 'Specifiers' discussion of the model now in effect notes that males diagnosed with GID "include substantial proportions with all four specifiers," while almost all females prove to be sexually attracted to females. [555]

Gender Identity Disorder (GID)

If gender identity is understood in terms of being a subset of sexual identity, then *gender identity disorder* (GID) means an internal mismatch between gender identity and natal sex that reflects psychological disorder. GID is most famously associated with *transsexualism*—the persistent conviction that the body's sex is wrong. The notion that transsexualism is a mental disorder is the prevailing wisdom—highly controversial and seriously challenged—found in our contemporary mental health system. At present, the dominant classification system for psychological disorders used by mental health professionals in our society is the American Psychiatric Association's (APA) *Diagnostic and Statistical Manual of Mental Disorders, 4th edition, Text Revision* (DSM-IV-TR), published in 2000. This volume's manner of classifying mental disorders is designed to be compatible to the *International Classification for Diseases* (ICD) system.

The first appearance of transsexualism in the DSM model occurred in DSM-III in 1980. It was listed as one of three possible diagnoses under Gender Identity Disorder, part of a larger group called 'Psychosexual Disorders,' which also included eight 'paraphilias'—conditions previously referred to as 'sexual deviations.'[556] In the revision of this edition, DSM-III-R (1987), the Gender Identity Disorder group saw one diagnostic label changed, a fourth possible diagnosis added, and was moved under the heading 'Disorders Usually First Evidenced in Infancy, Childhood, or Adolescence.'[557] The fourth edition, DSM-IV, appeared in 1994. Once more GID was shifted, this time to a place under the heading 'Sexual and Gender Identity Disorders.' The four diagnoses were reduced to two, with yet another modification in diagnostic label.[558] In the text revision of 2000, DSM-IV-TR, the diagnostic and classification material remains the same although some comments have been added.[559]

Classification labels and diagnostic criteria have changed over the decades. In the present model, the hallmark criterion states that there is "a strong and persistent cross-gender identification (not merely a desire for any perceived cultural advantages of being the other sex)." Next on the list is this: "Persistent discomfort with his or her sex or sense of inappropriateness in the gender role of that sex." [560] Together, these make plain the notion that the perceived disorder is one of gender identity—which is why we need to discuss it here.

A key concept in the DSM model is that this 'discomfort' produces clinically noteworthy personal distress, which warrants a diagnosis of pathology. In such situations reference is made to *gender dysphoria*. The word 'dysphoria' is derived from Greek by putting two parts—*dys* ('ill') + *phoria* ('possession')—together. When coupled with the word 'gender' this phrase means an 'ill-holding' or 'ill-bearing' of the gender assigned. A felt sense of unease with the gender assigned at birth is termed by professionals 'gender dysphoria.' It has become an important and controversial label.

The term and its meaning owe much to one particular psychologist, Ray Blanchard, a controversial figure especially among transgender people, who believe he misunderstands the nature of their distress. He characterizes gender dysphoria as "the sense of awkwardness or discomfort in the *anatomically congruent* gender role" (emphasis added).[561] By itself this need not occasion automatic concern because it can still be construed as discomfort with the assigned gender role, with that assignment based on the culture's assumption that gender should be congruent with sexual anatomy. But within the medical community this pairing of gender and sex is routinely understood as natural; what then becomes unnatural is unease with this pairing.

Researchers Nancy Bartlett, Paul Vasey, and William Bukowski conducted a study to test the empirical evidence in children diagnosed with GID against DSM-IV's definitional criteria for a mental disorder. They reviewed the literature on GID in children toward the end of seeing whether research findings supported an association between symptoms and one or another of four DSM criteria for a mental disorder: present distress; present disability; a significantly increased risk of suffering death, pain, disability, or an important loss of freedom; or dysfunction in the individual (rather than merely being socially disapproved behavior). They concluded that both because of problems with DSM's definitional criteria and a lack of supportive evidence that the existing form of the diagnostic category for GID in children should not be retained.[562]

With specific regard to the second criterion, concerning gender dysphoria, Bartlett, Vasey, and Bukowski point out that the DSM inappropriately confuses sex and gender, equating discomfort with one with discomfort with the other, and assigning equal significance to symptoms associated with one or the other (e.g., considering one's genitals disgusting has the same diagnostic weight as avoiding certain types of play). Together with other flaws they find in the DSM reasoning, the problems raise questions about how to regard the relation of a child's 'distress' to GID—is it caused by the gender identity disturbance, or associated with it more indirectly, such as via social ostracism?[563]

It is easy to see how a medical professional, steeped in the medicalization of sex, might be predisposed to give the body priority and see the problem in the mind. This focus on the individual as the source of the problem may appear quite short-sighted to other professionals. Sexologist Holly Devor, for example, observes that so-called 'gender dysphoria' might apply just as well to individuals who experience discomfort with their gender status because of social or political reasons. Furthermore, gender role dysphoria among women may to at least some extent be viewed as both inevitable, given their experience within patriarchal societies, and *healthy*.[564] Limiting the concept to psychological unease is hardly inevitable or self-evidently obvious.

Nevertheless, the psychiatric establishment's boundaries for the idea have prevailed in mental health diagnosis, no matter how ill-advised, or at least debatable. Thus, among mental health professionals the distress often observed in individuals is commonly assumed to be a matter of *gender identity* rather than *cultural intolerance*. Given this presumption the question then becomes whether it is appropriate to support efforts to bring the body's apparent sex into conformity with the person's gender identity, or to seek to change that sense of gender identity to match the body's sex. Mental health professionals have been divided on this issue, but many have resigned themselves to the finding that therapy aimed at changing the sense of gender yields poorer results than changing the apparent body sex.

But let's return to the other possibility. Some professionals, like Devor, wonder if the DSM scheme doesn't miss a more salient point—that the distress observed stems from social intolerance within a rigid and unrealistic gender scheme. Psychiatrist Justin Richardson, who works with sexual minorities, critiques the DSM model by pointing out that the GID diagnosis for children makes assumptions about gender-appropriate behavior based on our own culture. The model fails to distinguish a rationale for determining the line between 'atypical' and 'pathological' gender behavior even as culture itself steadily broadens the boundaries of socially tolerated behavior. Who decides, then, what constitutes gender behavior that needs professional intervention?[565] Perhaps a better answer is to address and work to change our cultural conception of gender.

In the meanwhile, we might at least own up to the role cultural ideas have in shaping supposedly objective science. Some societies already have. Europe is far ahead of the United States in rethinking the appropriateness of diagnoses of variant gender identities as 'disorders.' For example, in December, 2002, the British Lord Chancellor's Office, in a Government Policy paper declared its conclusion that transsexualism is *not* mental illness.[566] Whether the DSM model shall follow suit is uncertain. No less an authority than Robert Spitzer, the architect behind the modern DSM system, at the 2003 American Psychiatric Association's annual meeting expressed his opinion that GID might be rethought in a future edition.[567] This is more than a matter of passing interest; it carries significance within the mental health community and beyond.

Not only mental health professionals, but all of us must remember that our ideas *mean* something. There are practical consequences that flow from the decisions mental health professionals make. They impact real people. They affect self-image, relationships, and social functioning. They either contribute to reinforcing irrational cultural notions or they challenge them. At present, the weight of the above arguments suggests that mental health professionals, both in the DSM model and through its application, may all too often be violating the preeminent precept of ethical practice: first, *do no harm.*

Though we are never far from it, we again are faced directly with the *moral dimension* involved in judging gender identities. Nowhere is this more poignant than in regard to protecting those who cannot protect themselves—children. Therapists Susan Langer and James Martin, writing with reference to the diagnosis of GID in children, have called for reappraisal of retaining it as a diagnostic category in the DSM. Their critique not only points out the conceptual and psychometric problems that have persistently plagued this category, but also raises ethical concerns. Because our notions of atypical gender are socially constructed, and such constructions vary across time as a result of various factors, locating one conception at a single point in time and within a particular cultural context is more than illogical; it is unethical. Behavior that deviates from the norm by being statistically infrequent is not thereby automatically disordered. To deem such behavior mentally disordered to justify trying to change a child's attitudes, behaviors and even identity is, in the authors' view, ethically repellant. Gender atypicality need not—and should not—be regarded as pathology.[568]

In this respect, we shall close this particular discussion with a comment from the noted biologist Joan Roughgarden:

> In any culture, people do what they must to realize that identity. The realization of identity goes far beyond gender; after all, many volunteer to die for their country, their religion, or some other cause that gives them their identity. Do we list patriotic heroes who give their lives for their country in the *Diagnostic and Statistical Manual of Mental Disorders (DSM)* as people afflicted with a life-threatening mental disease? Perhaps we should, and at the same time remove transgendered people from the *DSM*, because soldiers are dangerous, whereas transgendered people are not.[569]

Chapter 9

Gender Roles

Introduction: Thus far in our dialog we have made little explicit reference to *gender differences*. Mostly this avoidance stems from a realization that differences within the members of a gender group are far greater than the differences between separate groups. But from a cultural perspective, the supposed differences between the genders are precisely the focus in constructing distinct *gender roles*. Societies tend to be relatively more tolerant of variations in personal, internalized gender identity than of public expressions that violate norms for gender role behavior. So, regardless of our gender identity, most of us spend a great deal of time in life learning, mastering, and playing the gender role assigned us.

Or is it a *sex role*? Some participants in the conversation prefer we root our performances in a sense that they are biologically derived and constrained. Those who adhere to this sense sometimes emphasize biology to a point it sounds like 'anatomy is destiny,' but others view the matter as more complex and subtle. They acknowledge, for instance, that sex itself has a social side and is somewhat culturally constructed. This *essentialist* position today has its most forceful champions in *evolutionary psychology*.

Presently, however, it is more common to find participants in the conversation speaking about gender roles like *social constructionists*, who view them as flexible constructions maintained within societies. Many feminists regard the work of today's essentialists as a major step backward—another bolstering of masculine privilege in new scientific dress. These folk continue to point out that essentialist views have trouble accounting for cultural variations and the impact of social values even on science itself. In the impasse between evolutionary psychology and social constructionism a third alternative—*social role theory*—has offered itself as a viable option for furthering the conversation.

All participants in the conversation continue to be interested in differences, whether termed sex differences or gender differences. How real are they? How substantial? Today, scholars find differences in *development*. Boys and girls seem to grow up in different cultures. Adult relations might also be seen as cross-cultural. The way men and women *talk* appears that different. Perhaps they also differ in various internal *traits*, such as aggression or competitiveness. Certainly their *social roles* traditionally have been different—and unequal.

Roles and Role-Playing

Gender roles are one of the most commonly discussed aspects of gender. Yet despite the importance almost universally ascribed to them, and the widespread dialog about them, the very term itself remains surprisingly murky. Consider, for example, the entry on "Gender" in *The Blackwell Encyclopedia of Social Science*. In remarking on gender roles the article says, "The term 'gender roles' is sometimes used to represent gender stereotypes or gender differences. More specifically, however, it refers to the socially assigned roles traditionally associated with each sex."[570]

Stereotypes, differences, and socially assigned roles—all distinct, and all important. As we mentioned in entering this discussion, nowhere is more focus put on *gender differences* than when using the term gender roles. We might even say that the concept of differences is the key that links together the various elements in the many ways gender roles are talked about. Stereotypes exist as emphatic and sharply drawn boxes meant to provide contrast—in other words, to demonstrate compellingly the differences between genders. We will consider them more completely in our next discussion (chapter 10). When differences are themselves the ostensible focus, they are debated as to their ultimate origin and nature: *biological*, deriving from bodies with different sexes, or *environmental*, constructed from culture and displaying different values. It is the old Nature-Nurture debate. When socially assigned roles take center stage, the discussion typically revolves around profound differences in social status, power, and tasks. So we will do well to remember that no matter how we talk about gender roles, differences are at the heart of the matter.

We need, though, some way to justify narrowing our own focus in this introductory discussion. Perhaps the most sensible approach is to return to our task when we first started talking about gender—trying to get at the root meaning of the vocabulary. What are 'roles'? The English word's origin is instructive. A 'role' first stood for the written part of a character in a play. Roles do several things. The role separates the private identity of the actor from the public role of the character on stage. In this respect it is clearly a contrivance—a knowing construction that relies on both the actor and the audience to acknowledge the fictive nature of the portrayal. No two roles are exactly the same so the characters can be told apart and occupy different places within the play. Finally, the roles are symbols of reality offstage. As such they can be intended to be close to reality offstage, or can reverse it, or can modify it in any number of ways. Gender portrayals on stage, especially through vehicles like crossdressing, have long been useful to investigate, play with, and comment upon gender as it exists offstage.[571] So the concept of role when applied to gender is robust.

The originally limited use of the term came to be used in the broader figurative sense of the part played by anyone in society—a social role. There are many possible social roles but perhaps the most fundamental corresponds to the basic division of human beings by sex and/or gender. Since divisions self-evidently differentiate, social roles—whether based on gender or on sex—rely on broadly agreed upon distinctions. The set of distinctions used to create separate categories constitute the elements of the social role. In each case these categories bear labels. In a gender dichotomous culture only two boxes, or categories, are officially sanctioned: masculinity and femininity. Everything else is seen as a variant and defined in terms of the characteristics within these two boxes. We can thus imagine gender role as *a socially scripted part to be played by masculinity or femininity*. From the moment of birth we are thrust on stage and expected to play our assigned part.

This socially scripted essence in roles is why we are smart to sever them from identities. Certainly, we might so thoroughly embrace our roles that these become our identity. But that is by no means guaranteed. Perhaps it is not even wise. The parts we play—even the major and continuing roles—remain just 'parts,' partial aspects of self and social enactments that may be performed without a strong degree of inner allegiance. We put roles on and we can take them off—a quality that makes them significantly different from identities, which are much more resistant to change.

Yet, when watching any drama we soon become accustomed to a certain stability on the part of the actors. They inhabit a role in such a manner that while the role evolves it remains clear that it is continuous with the past. Role reversals only serve to further reinforce the sense of the original role, and we expect the actor to eventually revert to type. In this stability and continuity *we infer that the role we witness reflects an underlying identity*. We assume that roles are public disclosures of an underlying identity; the inner reality we presume to be the same as what the outer show mirrors. This is why we sometimes have difficulty when we meet an actor famous for a long-running role on stage or film. We see the character played, not the person behind the role. The same can be true for gender roles and gender identities. The match made between them may be only in the eye of the beholder.

In thinking about roles in this way it seems obvious they are *constructions*. But simply making that observation doesn't preclude debate on what materials construct them—biological, or environmental, or both. Perhaps the construction unfolds naturally, following predetermined sex influences, so that the resulting role is a matter of sex differences. Perhaps the construction is built instead by contrived social manipulations that reflect more the imagination of those in power than any natural necessity.

Social cognitive psychologists Kay Bussey and Albert Bandura, for example, argue that, "It is not naturally foreordained that the same behavior enacted by females should produce different outcomes than when enacted by males."[572] Yet that happens. Perhaps it does so because social filters bend what we see to fit our expectations for different gender roles. Such filters aren't hard to find; they fill our everyday conversation. Thus, a man who suddenly loses consciousness is said to 'pass out,' while a woman who does so is said to 'faint.' A man who speaks out forcefully on a topic might be called 'assertive' while a woman who does the same is termed 'aggressive.' Our language is filled with words differentially applied to men and women despite the fact that the actual behavior is the same. *Behaviors are construed through the lens of gender roles.*

Gender Roles, or Sex Roles?

Or perhaps we should say through the lens of 'sex roles.'

By this point in our dialog we should not be surprised to find once again a confusion over whether we should be speaking of 'sex roles' or 'gender roles.' Nor should we be at all surprised anymore to hear that terminology in this regard is inconsistent and often confused. Virtually any combination imaginable between sex and gender in regard to other concepts such as 'development,' 'identity,' or 'roles' seems to have happened at least once. Let's consider a single example to demonstrate our ongoing difficulty in clarifying the conversation.

Lee Combrinck-Graham and Lawrence Kerns show the too often frustrating fluidity in how terminology can be used. In speaking of families with young children, they contrast *gender* identity with *sex-role* behavior, seeing the former as fixed and the latter as plastic. Then they say that the issue of gender is a prominent concern because "families are organized around basic assumptions about male and female sex-role differences and the inequalities that are built into them."[573] What makes this usage especially problematic is that most participants in the conversation see gender as more amenable to change (i.e., 'plastic') because of its connection to culture, and sex as more fixed because of its connection to biology. Thus anything attached to sex would normally be expected to prove resistant to change because of its underlying biological character. But in this case, 'sex roles' is less attached to biology and more to stereotypes presumably based on biology. Multiple this example many times and it is easy to see why so many wanting to follow the conversation become confused.

Leaving aside especially unusual uses of the vocabulary before us, let us try again to clarify muddy waters. As we did before, in speaking of sex identity or gender identity, we will look at the case on both sides. Our goal is to try to apply a consistency in logic to matters, even while having to admit that logical consistency is not always obvious when reading scholarly literature. But rather than wring our hands in despair, or even worse, conclude that the conversation is a waste of our time because it isn't always clear or consistent, we must resolve to wade in and offer our own efforts to helping the conversation forward.

Eleanor Maccoby—Sex Roles, Not Gender Roles

The first possibility, and the one longer established, is to speak of 'sex roles.'[574] In this perspective, it is perfectly all right to talk about gender roles as long as the term is understood as a synonym for sex roles or at least as subordinated and constrained by them. Perhaps the most prominent advocate of this position within psychology over the last four decades is developmental psychologist Eleanor Maccoby. She has been a major contributor to the conversation on gender. A feminist, she rose to prominence during the second wave of feminism (see chapter 2). Maccoby has been consistent over the years in her use of terminology.

In her view, 'sex' is a more accurate terminus than 'gender' for both the concepts of identity and role. In her most famous work, *The Psychology of Sex Differences* (coauthored with Carol Nagy Jacklin), the following point is made:

> An individual's sex is obviously both a biological and social fact. If biological sex turns out to be linked with psychological functioning, the study of this linkage should help to deepen our understanding of a more basic matter: the way in which biological "predispositions" interact with the impact of social experience to shape the psychological makeup of the person.[575]

In her view, something vital is lost by severing gender from sex and relegating the latter to biology.

Because Maccoby views sex as both biological and social, there is no need to distinguish gender from it. A person thus has a 'sex identity,' and 'sex differences' underlie 'sex roles.' When she uses the term sex role she means by it a sociological definition—a set of expectations held by others toward the occupant of the role position.[576] For her, it is all right to refer to gender roles as long as it is understood as a synonym for sex roles. Thus she feels free to write, for example, "Gender is ubiquitous as a social category. All known languages include terms to distinguish boys from girls and men from women. All known societies differentiate to some degree the roles that are assigned to the two sexes."[577]

To speak of sex roles reminds us that some differences in the gender behavior expected of people may be rooted in biology. Indeed, Maccoby insists that some cultural expectations are universal and that some of them clearly stem from "the different biological roles of the two sexes in reproduction." But she is equally insistent in not making of this fact more than is warranted. She is quick to remind us that within-gender variability exceeds differences between-genders. And she is convinced that what may be the most important fact is that individuals may vary greatly from one situation to another with regard to the degree of how gender-linked it is.[578]

Still, when push comes to shove, Maccoby adopts a moderate essentialist position. Over the years her research has come more and more to focus upon the power of peer groups in sex typing (what we have been calling 'gender socialization'). She finds the most significant differences between boys and girls due to their sex-segregated groups from early childhood (age 3) onward. In her view, this tendency toward early and pronounced sex-segregation is rooted in evolution—the machinery of biological difference.[579] She minimizes the multitude of cultural differences by regarding such things as mere variations on a theme.[580]

The use of sex roles lends itself to an essentialist position. The term highlights the presumed role played by sex, and whether sex is construed in its biological or its social sense, it still links social role behavior to differences in reproductive anatomy. In other words, even if sex is said to include socially constructed ideas and expectations, these are presumed to arise from a body-based difference. Ultimately, the biological dimension trumps the cultural because it determines its character. In this way of looking at things, body-based differences most noticeable in reproductive function create social notions that produce the role expectations.

Gender Roles, Not Sex Roles

Presently, however, there is a strong preference for the use of *gender* roles rather than *sex* roles. The reasoning behind this preference is well-expressed by Bernadette Brooten, a Christian Studies scholar whose usage reflects the widespread adoption of this logic beyond the social sciences: "I prefer the term 'gender roles,' which designates socially constructed male and female roles. I use 'sex' in the sense of physical difference. Thus, 'sex differences' are physical, while 'gender differences' are cultural, and 'gender roles" are based upon culturally constructed gender differences."[581] This division is clear and simple.

As we have discussed throughout our dialog, *social constructionists* argue that the environment is more important than biology in making gender. They hold that even the determination of sex has a cultural component; we see what we want to see (e.g., *either* a male *or* a female), and what we want to see is set by culture. They also contend that *separating sex from gender* is necessary in order to accomplish several important things. First, it clarifies each. Sex is primarily about biology, tinged by culture; gender is primarily about culture, tinged by biology. Second, it undercuts essentialist claims that biology determines social roles, i.e., that sex differences determine gender roles. This historically has been used both to explain and justify inequalities between men and women. Instead, gender should be regarded as having independence from biology because culture is what crafts the shapes into which biology is poured. Third, it highlights the primacy of gender over sex. Gender is not merely relatively independent, it is also relatively more important, in that it is the cultural values, decisions, and expectations of gender that determine how girls and boys, women and men—and gendered others—are regarded (or not regarded) within a society. If we are to sum up the situation in a manner a social constructionist might put it, we could do worse than how gender scholar Paula Nicolson puts it:

> Gender is central to the ways in which social and emotional life is organized among human beings, so that the study of gender brings insights into complex issues that transcend the study of sex differences. Gender is biological, social and psychological. Gender is dynamic in the way roles and relationships are played out. Gendered behaviours vary cross-culturally. Gender . . . is political as well. Gender underlies social organization in all cultures. . . and thus gender lies at the heart of *power*.[582]

Social constructionism agrees with essentialism that gender is about differences. But it disagrees that these differences are rooted in something essential, like sex-differences. They point out that careful search over several decades of research has failed to yield much evidence of sex-differences in human psychology, and when such differences are found they typically are not all that pronounced or significant. Moreover, often apparent differences when looked at more closely can be explained as artifacts of the research method used or due to the interpretive slant of the researcher.

That brings us to a central contention: *gender is constructed by the human tools of discourse and relationship.* Yes, sex differentiates bodies. So what? It is *culture*, not biology, that determines what that differentiating *means*. If the meaning ascertained favors masculine men, then that reflects their social power rather than any biological favoritism or anatomical destiny. *Language* becomes a powerful way of establishing the cultural perspective, lending over time a sense of it as so unquestioned as to appear natural. Thus essentialism gains its appeal not from hard scientific fact, but from a cultural paradigm whose language limits what can be investigated, how it can be seen, and how it must be interpreted.[583]

Gender roles are truly *artificial scripts*, claim social constructionists. They are writ not by Nature but by Nurture. We raise our children to conform to stereotypes that fit what our culture desires. Even if we try to resist our culture, as in trying to be parents who raise gender egalitarian children, we fight a losing battle because social structures (e.g., family, religion, education, media, politics) align against us. Even more frightening, the power of culture is so pervasive that we may unconsciously undermine our own efforts by holding attitudes and engaging in behaviors contrary to our own expressed goals.

Gender roles serve social power. As we have talked about before, gender relations are marked by power struggles. Those who have power have little incentive to share it. Those with less power devise strategies (e.g., limiting sexual access until a more equitable distribution of resources occurs) to equalize power; no recourse to evolutionary biology is required to make sense of these things. Rather, the all-too-human strivings of politics and economics explain adequately the social construction of the gender roles we see today.

If social constructionists are right, then essentialist views are not merely factually incorrect but morally objectionable. Essentialists advocate a line of thinking that only supports the status quo and dresses it up in apparently respectable scientific dress. But not everyone thinks social constructionists are right. In fact, essentialism is mounting a comeback.

Evolutionary Psychology

In recent years, another set of champions of the essentialist view have become more prominent—evolutionary psychologists. As the name proclaims, *evolutionary psychology*, as a coherent theoretical perspective, aims to explain psychological subject matter in terms of evolution. Because evolution is rooted in natural selection, and focuses on body-based sex differences, critics complain it amounts to simply a sophisticated effort to justify the social inequities we observe in the name of inherited predispositions. In short, it is accused of being an updated form of the 'anatomy is destiny' logic. In recent years, evolutionary psychology has mounted a serious alternative to social constructionist views of gender. This development has particularly exercised concern among many feminists who see in evolutionary psychology a convenient science for telling people what men want them to hear.

What especially irks some critics of evolutionary psychology is the apparent smugness with which they hold their position. Psychologist Linda Gannon points out, for example, that while evolutionary psychologists readily acknowledge the role of ideology and politics in shaping and supporting scientific paradigms in general, in practice they deny this influence on their own paradigm.[584] And many worry that, disclaimers by evolutionary psychologists like David Buss aside, the idea of *evolutionary lag time*—the slow pace of evolution that means we in the present remain constrained by adaptations shaped in a far different environment—amounts to an appeal to accept traditional gender inequities as something we cannot at present fully surmount. It smacks of 'we can't help but be the way we are because of our evolutionary heritage.' So as we turn our attention to evolutionary psychology perhaps our first need is to discover how its advocates respond to such complaints.

Common Misunderstandings & Responses

Buss, perhaps the best-known evolutionary psychologist, replies that there are five common misunderstandings of evolutionary theory and these are what prompt common criticisms of the position. One misunderstanding is that evolutionary theory teaches that human behavior is genetically determined. Rather, Buss says, evolutionary psychology holds to an interactionist perspective: evolved adaptations need environmental inputs to trigger their development and activation. Second, people often think evolutionary theory purports that human behavior can't be changed. Buss replies that knowing how we evolved gives us the possibility to change if we want to. Third, some people believe evolutionary theory relies on improbable computational abilities to explain complex behaviors, whereas it actually holds that adaptations can and are executed without conscious reliance on complex computations. Fourth, critics often charge that evolutionary theory regards present human adaptations as optimal, where the actual view is that the adaptations we find reflect a selection of mechanisms where benefits outweigh costs. But this process is a very long and slow one. "The lag in time," writes Buss, "between the environment that fashioned our mechanisms (the hunter-gatherer past that created much of our selective environment) and today's environment means that our existing evolved mechanisms are not optimally designed for the current environment." Finally, some people misunderstand evolutionary theory as implying a conscious motivation by people to maximize their gene reproduction. Buss counters that our motives and goals are products of the process of genetic reproduction rather than the process itself. In short, while people may not consciously plan how to maximize their own genetic reproduction, they remain guided by that process nonetheless.[585]

In their turn, many advocates of evolutionary psychology have been sharply critical of nonessentialist positions. For example, English psychologist Anne Campbell, in her *A Mind of Her Own: The Evolutionary Psychology of Women*, suggests that a desirable political goal—social equality between the genders—has infected academic theorizing and produced bad science. She argues that as women's studies became steeped in a politically-driven rejection of essentialism, they unwisely committed both to social constructionism and to extreme environmentalism. "Neither road," she complains, "has taken us very far towards an accurate understanding of why men and women differ."[586]

For Campbell, who considers herself a 'broad sense' feminist,[587] hard science dismantles what most feminists want to believe. She contends that research published at the beginning of the 1990s, examining some 172 studies from around the world, refutes the notion that gender socialization by parents largely determines later observed gender differences. She writes:

> Considering them all together, the evidence for differential treatment was virtually nil. Parents did not differ in the amount of interaction with the child, with the warmth they showed, their tendency to encourage either dependency or achievement, their restrictiveness, their use of discipline, their tendency to reason with the child or the amount of aggression that they tolerated.[588]

In fact, she argues, "if parents' behavior towards their children was being guided by their desire for them to conform to traditional gender stereotypes then we would expect to find that the most sex-typed adults have the most sex-typed children."[589] But we don't actually observe anything so neat and simple.

Sexual Selection & Parental Investment

So what do we see when we look at sex roles through the lens of evolutionary psychology? The general thrust of the essentialist position is simple enough to describe, and we already have talked about it. Biological differences between the sexes influence cultural decisions about the respective roles of each sex, and these roles construct distinctive personality characteristics suitable to the sex role. Evolutionary psychology places this logic in a particular framework. *Evolution* is about biological adaptations over time to increase fitness to particular environments. The increase in fitness promotes higher survival rates and greater success in reproduction. Since reproduction is key to evolution, *sexual selection*—a subset of natural selection that focuses on evolution through mating advantage—becomes critical to understanding human behavior. Moreover, *parental investment*—the idea that the sex most invested in offspring will be the choosier in selecting a mate—is also predicted to be crucial in human behavior. Put together, these ideas mean that gender behavior will be the way it is because males and females have different stakes in reproduction and use different strategies in acquiring sexual partners.

The most famous proposal for the sex-based difference in sexual selection comes from biologist Robert Trivers. He argues that males and females vary markedly in parental investment. Males experience comparatively little cost in time or energy in producing sperm, and freed from having to carry a child they are inclined to have sex as often as they can. This puts them into competition with one another and promotes the development of aggressiveness. Females, on the other hand, have a limited supply of ova, are fertile a limited time each month, and once pregnant must share at great personal cost and risk their body resources to carry any child conceived. Because her parental investment is so high, she will be more selective in whom she has sex with.[590] Thus reproductive differences drive behavioral ones.

But let's be a bit more specific. Buss explains how men and women evolve certain mate preferences in response to specific adaptive problems. Women, because of their great cost in reproduction, have the adaptive problems of securing a mate able and willing to invest his resources, capable of protecting his family, able to parent well, and personally compatible so that he will stick around for the long term. So her evolved mate preferences will include a desire for a man with social status and resources, who is ambitious and hard-working, with enough size, strength and athleticism to provide and protect. Such men are likely to be a little older, so a woman tends to prefer a slightly older man. She also wants him to be dependable and committed, to like kids, have emotional stability coupled with generosity and kindness, and share her own values. In fact, compatible personalities are desirable because being friends will mean a greater likelihood he will stay in the relationship.[591]

Men, continues Buss, have different adaptive problems and evolved preferences because of their less investment in parenting. He points out that the first puzzle is why men would want to marry at all given that it would seem in their best interest to have sex as often as they can with as many women as they can. But the adaptive problem they face is women who won't provide access to their bodies unless men show a willingness for commitment—and faking it won't get far in the long run. So men had to evolve reliable ways of demonstrating commitment or risk getting virtually shut out of the mating market. There were advantages to commitment, too. Such men are more likely to get a desirable woman, can enjoy more confidence that her children are also his, help ensure his own children survive, and even increase their later reproductive success, which furthers his own genetic reproduction. Another principal adaptive problem for a man is ascertaining that the woman gaining this commitment will be able to bear his children. So men evolve preferences associated with signs of *female reproductive value*—a calculation of how many children she is likely able to bear—and fertility, which is actual reproductive performance. Such preferences include youth (or slightly older women if the male is still adolescent), and beauty (defined as signs of health and reproductive value). A 'beautiful woman' is one both physically desirable and behaviorally pleasing, with the attributes making up each of these defined by what they seem to say about her ability to bear children. One consistent preference across cultures, for example, is a man's preference for women with a waist-to-hip ratio between 0.67-0.80—an accurate indicator or female reproductive status.[592] As philosopher of science David Buller quips, "males prefer nubility, while females prefer nobility."[593]

The Maternal Dominance Hypothesis

The *maternal dominance hypothesis* presents another way an evolutionary psychologist might argue that sex differences are instrumental both in behavior differences and outcomes. Medical psychologist Valerie Grant notes this hypothesis rose from research showing that women more dominant than other women in personality are more likely to conceive males. She observes that both this personality dominance and greater likelihood of bearing males appear tied to above average serum testosterone. Elevated levels of this hormone, in turn, appear tied to environmental factors both psychological and physical in nature. Chronic stress, for instance, elevates serum testosterone levels. This might be highly adaptive since the response to chronic stress both strengthens the woman to withstand it and, in a broader social context, a greater proportion of males to females in the next generation may protect against excess population growth in a time of environmental stress.[594]

This hypothesis, as Grant articulates it, might explain how biology and the environment interact to produce different outcomes, but what about behavioral differences? How does this presumed adaptive advantage show that biological difference leads to behavioral difference? Grant answers by arguing that, "Behaviourally, at least in humans and rats, it seems likely that maternal testosterone underpins small, but important qualitative differences in maternal-neonate interactions according to the sex of the infant/offspring."[595] She points to research that mothers of girls are more responsive to their child, while mothers of boys stimulate them more. In sum, then, it seems that sex-based biological differences not merely *between* the sexes but also *within* a sex carry important behavioral differences. Of such differences are sex roles made.

Sex-Segregated Labor

Of course, what we have talked about to this point has seemed to leave aside one of the major issues of gender: the segregated labor of the genders. What might an evolutionary psychology position on this matter be like? Sociologist and anthropologist Tim Megarry has an answer. He offers that contemporary research shows that while females are different from males, they are not biologically inferior. Moreover, such research suggests that in our distant past— if contemporary hunter-gather and forager societies are an indicator—women were not only economically important, but frequently superior. However, such societies also show "a highly distinctive division of labour based on sex that is marked by genderized specializations for female gathering and male hunting."[596] The importance of these findings for Megarry is that they support "a case for human evolution in the context of a sexual division of labor, though not one of gender inequality."[597] Biological and social forces combined to build and sustain social organization revolving around sex-segregated labor.

Evolution and Culture

In fact, one could argue, as biologist Edward Wilson did in the mid-1970s with two major works, *Sociobiology: The New Synthesis* (1975) and *On Human Nature* (1978), that culture itself arose from biological evolution, which persists in shaping it and providing its boundaries. In Wilson's view, evolutionary biology undergirds everything human, right down to human nature itself. In *On Human Nature* he purports that the facts of evolutionary biology do not support elitism or racism, but rather champion the value of diversity and tolerance. Against his critics he asserts the compatibility of his theory with a broad humanism[598] Wilson calls his view *sociobiology*, and its heir has been evolutionary psychology—but how much an heir is debatable.

Many contemporary evolutionary psychologists have distanced themselves from sociobiology, which garnered storms of controversy for quite some time. In fact, today it is not uncommon to find sociobiology and evolutionary psychology discussed as two separate theoretical orientations. For some evolutionary psychologists, talking as widely as culture itself goes beyond what hard science can demonstrate. Most evolutionary psychologists prefer to content themselves with more limited horizons of study. Yet, with respect to human gender, it can be fairly argued that evolutionary psychology has set out a theory of the *origins of gender*—an effort at tacking down the distal causes of human psychology.

Social Role Theory

This effort to find the *distal causes* of human gender is precisely what interests social psychologist Alice Eagly, a friendly critic of evolutionary psychology and a chief architect of one of it most prominent theoretical alternatives.[599] The opening line of one important article, coauthored with her frequent collaborator Wendy Wood, signals their interest: "What causes sex differences in human behavior?" This query's answer has proved elusive. The reason, according to Eagly, is that, "The task of explaining the origins of sex differences challenges scientists because theories of origins involve multiple levels of analysis in which proximal causes are embedded within more distal causes."[600]

However, before considering the origin of sex differences, we must first be persuaded there really are such differences. In the mid-1980s, Eagly took stock of where psychologists seemed to be on this question. It had seemed that by the mid-1970s, just a decade earlier, they had resolved the matter in favor of sex differences being so few and so generally minor that it might even be better to talk about 'sex similarities' instead. Yet the general public persisted in believing differences existed—and mattered. This led psychologists to focus more on the power of stereotypes, while still regarding the differences they posited as illusory. By 1987, when Eagly set out her *social role theory*, she thought it time to give more credence to what most people were perceiving, at least with regard to social behaviors.[601]

In order to get at sex differences in social behavior Eagly adapts social role theory and theories of social influence. In her new framework for studying social behavior, she writes, "the overall emphasis of this analysis is on the person as a recipient of social pressures, albeit a person who actively collaborates in creating and reacting to these pressures."[602] She recognizes from the start her work places itself outside social constructionism. Her analysis proceeds like this:

> [T]o account for differences in the behavior of social groups, it is necessary to determine what the members of each group possess in common. Once it is realized that they share a certain position within a social structure, the social pressures that group members experience begin to become evident and emerge as the most likely source of their distinctive social behaviors.[603]

As a result, she contends that differences in the social positions of males and females expose them to systematically different role expectations. Thus it is *social roles*—not biology, early socialization, or anything else—that explain sex differences in social behavior. However, she cautions against inferring from her use of terms like 'sex,' 'sex differences,' and 'gender' that she is promoting any particular cause of the differences.[604]

By the time the century closed out, a very different environment had emerged. It was once more fashionable to speak of either sex or gender differences, and two rival alternatives had forcefully emerged, both offering the cause for differences that Eagly had avoided. The rivals were the essentialism of evolutionary psychology and social constructionism, both of which we have discussed. As the 1990s ended, Eagly and Wood characterized the essence of each as follows: evolutionary psychology implicates evolved psychological dispositions as the ultimate cause of differences, while social constructionism implicates social structure. The causal chain in evolutionary psychology starts with an adaptive problem, which prompts sex-specific evolved mechanisms derived through natural selection. The sex-specific evolution yields different psychologies and thus the tendency to occupy different social roles. The causal chain in social constructionism starts with an existing social structure, which places men and women into different social roles, to which they adjust by developing psychological (gender) differences.[605]

Put in the simplest fashion, in order to highlight the differences, to explain the origin of differences the chains look like this:

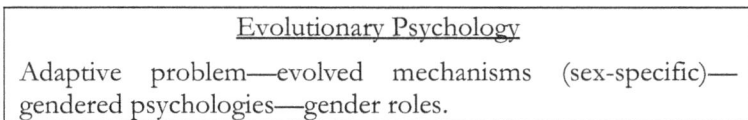

Evolutionary Psychology
Adaptive problem—evolved mechanisms (sex-specific)—gendered psychologies—gender roles.

> ## Social Constructionism
>
> Existing social structure—sex-segregation into different social (gender) roles—gender differences in psychology.

The chains agree that *the starting point is a response to the environment*. The key differences are twofold: the *mechanism of response* to the environment (evolutionary biology vs. social forces), and *the relative relation between gender psychologies* (what we might term 'gender identities') and *gender roles*. With regard to the latter, evolutionary psychology posits that biology forms identity, which yields social roles. Social constructionism counters that social structure forms roles, which yield identities. The former position is essentialist because it contends our body sex is the given that forms the core from which our identity (our 'psychology') unfolds and then, as an offshoot of the differences in identity, the genders sort themselves naturally into different roles. The latter position disagrees that there is anything 'natural' about this process. It argues that social structures favoring men led to an exercise of power whereby unequal roles were crafted to separate the sexes. The necessity of fitting within the role assigned then elicited the psychological adjustments that produced distinctly masculine and feminine identities. It wasn't natural, necessary or inevitable that gender roles be unequal or that gendered identities be so different.

Eagly believes there is a way between these two alternatives. She and Wood consider the possibility that these approaches may differ in their causal focus, with social constructionists appealing to proximal, contemporaneous causes while evolutionary psychologists invoke more distal ones. But they do not find these theoretical approaches to be fundamentally different in this manner; the approaches differ, instead, in the primacy they give to different psychological causes—role expectations versus evolved dispositions. Moreover, they do not regard the approaches as inherently incompatible. [606] However, they do find both approaches, as *origin* theories, to be flawed. In particular, more of their attention is given to evolutionary psychologists, with whom they share the belief that some evolved genetic influences are important to human behavior. Yet, in their view, "social change emerges, not from individuals' tendencies to maximize their inclusive fitness, but instead from their efforts to maximize their personal benefits and minimize their personal costs in their social and ecological settings."[607]

In a major article published in 2002, Eagly and Wood propose a *biosocial model* to explain the origins of sex differences. The *bio* aspect of the model is the physical difference between the sexes, especially in terms of reproduction. The *social* aspect refers to the distribution of men and women into different social roles in any given society. The model presumes these aspects *interact*. In a nutshell, "sex differences in social behavior arise from the distribution of men and women into social roles within a society."[608]

This model pictures interaction between biological and environment factors, as well as between proximate and distal causes. If we try to depict the causal chain set out by the biosocial model, it might link together this way:

> ### Biosocial Model
>
> Sex differences (physical attributes and especially reproductive differences) + contextual factors (social, economic, technological)—social roles—psychological sex differences (gender roles)—social behavior.

Two key features merit noting. First, the model blends elements from both social constructionism and evolutionary psychology, but posits it is their interaction that makes them the first link in the chain. Second, the key mediating link between the start of the chain and gender roles is *social roles*—which are viewed as neutral in the sense that the roles women and men might fill are neither mutually exclusive nor tied to the 'instrumental' and 'expressive' content expected in structural functionalism (see chapter 5).

Let's trace this chain. Wood and Eagly maintain that, "Physical sex differences, in interaction with social and ecological conditions, influence the roles held by men and women because certain activities are more efficiently accomplished by one sex."[609] However it came about, human males typically exhibit larger size than females. They generally are faster and possess greater upper body strength. Females, on the other hand, are biologically equipped for childbearing and nursing infants. These sex differences are presumed to predispose the sexes to different social roles, especially because a woman's reproductive functions can conflict with the demands of certain social functions. "Our biosocial perspective," write Wood and Eagly, "anticipates that women's reproductive activities interfere with the performance of nonreproductive tasks to the extent that these other tasks require time-consuming, intensive skill development and labor by specialized workers."[610]

The *form* of social roles follows the *function* of the role players. Roles change responsively as the domestic and nondomestic tasks typically performed by men and women alter. Domestic roles are associated with women because women are the ones who most often fulfill domestic functions; men are more associated with working outside the home because they more typically undertake such functions. As men and women are sorted into distinct social roles, gender roles are formed. The purpose of such roles is to facilitate development of psychological characteristics to equip men and women for the social roles their sex typically fill. Thus, over time, "the characteristics that are required to carry out sex-typical tasks become stereotypic of women and men."[611]

Wood and Eagly anticipate much variability• among sex-typed activities. This variability arises from 'biologically specialized individuals' navigating their society in ways intended to maximize rewards to themselves while minimizing costs. The ways open to them pose relative constraints on their behavior. Theo-

187

retically, either sex might emerge with the superior social status, or with egalitarian social status, depending on the value placed by the society on the tasks typically performed by members of that sex. [612]

The reality is that while some egalitarian societies seem to exist, in industrialized societies *patriarchy* is prominent. Wood and Eagly see patriarchy as an outcome that fits biological specialization and the activities that garner status in a society. But they are not prescribing patriarchy; they are describing it as a predictable outcome given the presence of certain variables. In societies where economic contributions are highly valued, and men contribute more than women, men accrue more status and power. The society even may structure itself so that women are treated as commodities. In *patrilocal* societies, women move to their husband's kin group at marriage, which strengthens ties between men while weakening those between a woman and her own kin. Inheritance lines in such societies are *patrilineal*—through the father's line. This adds incentive to men to try to control women's sexuality so as to ensure certainty of their paternity. "Patriarchy," Wood and Eagly conclude, "thus emerged in large part from the difficulties women experienced in efficiently combining their reproductive activities with skilled tasks of production, which maximally contributed to power and status in more complex societies."[613]

The biosocial model views the interactive processes as reciprocal—bidirectional in nature. Biology stays in play through hormonal changes. Social aspects are variable across both cultures and time. For example, in a post-industrial society women find more economic participation because the labor involved does not favor male bodies. Coupled with that, birth control offers women greater ability to regulate their reproductive capacities. Thus social roles change as women more typically become associated with various tasks. This means changes in gender roles, too.

The question then becomes, do differences persist?

Role Differences

Perhaps nothing in the conversation on gender gets talked about more than the various differences alleged to exist between genders. Essentialists see these differences are naturally arising from sex-based differentiation; social constructionists see nothing natural or inevitable about them and view their development as products of culture. A social role theory, or biosocial model, approach takes a position between. But all perspectives agree there *are* differences. It is time we look at some of these.

First, we should recall what Eagly said about psychological research calling into question the reality of so-called sex differences. The exhaustive review of the research recounted in the mid-1970s by Eleanor Maccoby and Carol Nagy Jacklin had concluded sex differences do exist, but that much of what people believe about such differences is myth. For example, they found that the belief that girls are more 'social' than boys is a myth, as is the notion that girls are more 'suggestible' than boys. So, too, are beliefs that boys are more 'analytic' or that they do better at tasks requiring higher-level cognitive processing.[614]

On the other hand, they did substantiate four famous differences. Girls as a group tend to have greater verbal ability. Boys as a group tend to excel in visual-spatial ability. Boys also tend to do better in mathematical ability. They also exhibit more aggressiveness.[615]

Remaining as open questions at the time of their review were supposed differences in girls possessing more tactile sensitivity, showing more fear, timidity, and anxiety, being more compliant, or being more nurturing. Likewise still in doubt were supposed differences in boys being more active, more competitive, or more dominant.[616]

Maccoby and Jacklin recognized that their conclusions retained some tentativeness for a number of reasons. Nothing has changed in that regard. We still face difficulties in interpreting research results because of thorny problems in how the study is conceived, conducted, and interpreted. All the various ways in which terms are used further complicates matters. Despite the manifold obstacles, though, the endeavor is worthy and it continues.

In this introductory dialog we probably will do best if we avoid getting caught up too deeply in this research. Instead, let us just dip a toe in the water and test the temperature. Let's begin with an area highlighted by social constructionists.

Language Differences

As pointed out by social constructionists, culture follows from language. A significant aspect of gender difference is the role of language, which we can examine in two ways:

❑ Language sets the framework in which gender is described; and
❑ Language is carried out differently in the conversational styles that accompany gender roles.

With regard to the first of these points, we have already discussed at some length a number of the issues. Our dependence on a dichotomous sex and gender scheme derives in no small measure from the paucity of our vocabulary. We can only talk with the words we are given, and with respect to sex and gender these are limited. Efforts to expand the vocabulary are meritorious, but plagued by the constraints of a system that bends everything to fit it. Thus efforts to describe other genders than masculinity and femininity tend to get bogged down by the masculine-feminine polarity. Indeed, we need look no further than our pronouns to see how great a linguistic mountain must be climbed to reach beyond our current horizons.

Earlier in this discussion we also mentioned the problem of how we differentiate many words not by meaning but by *association with a specific gender*. We do this with words referring to physical differences, psychological traits, social roles, and behaviors. In terms of *physical characteristics*, different areas of the body are typically called attention to in the ways we speak. Women's breasts and hips are commonly referenced; men's shoulders get attention. Only women can be 'busty.' Both men and women might be 'ballsy,' but the word means different things for each gender. When it comes to *psychological traits*, women are much more likely to be termed 'receptive,' 'gullible,' or 'yielding,' to say nothing of being more often viewed as 'childlike,' and 'emotional.' Men, on the other hand, are more likely to called 'forceful,' or 'bull-headed.' We could probably multiple examples all day long. In regard to *social roles*, men's greater role in public life can be glimpsed in expressions like 'man in the street.' The greater likelihood of men being in positions of leadership is seen in words like 'chairman.' The greater involvement of men in the labor force is recognized in a word like 'manpower.' Many specific jobs also carry gender tags, like 'policeman' or 'fireman.' Of course, the most notorious examples include dedicated words like 'mother' (men not apply) and 'father' (women not welcome). With regard to *behavior*, we already noted that men 'pass out' where women 'faint.' Women can be 'shrill' but men apparently never are. It seems easy for a woman to be 'hysterical' while men seem prone to be 'belligerent' or 'bellicose.' A 'loud' man is less likely to be seen as obnoxious than a loud woman. So, while any word can be applied to either gender, in actual practice there are strong tendencies to associate many words with one or the other.[617]

Some words combine different aspects. For example, we often talk about men as 'broad-shouldered," but rarely refer to women that way. The term is not just used to distinguish an anatomical difference, but to metaphorically refer to a presumed masculine ability to bear many more things than a woman does, or to be more responsible. Women are more likely to called 'wallflowers'—a term combining behavior with a presumed underlying trait. Or we characterize men as 'strong' and women as 'weak'—and we aren't just referencing upper body strength. This use of language reinforces stereotypes and maintains the existing gender hierarchy.

The second facet of language listed above is different in character. It proposes that differing socialization for the genders prompts some distinctive gender features in development, including how the genders communicate. Linguist Deborah Tannen, who specializes on gender differences in communication, says bluntly, "Male-female conversation is cross-cultural communication."[618] Tannen explains what she means:

> Culture is simply a network of habits and patterns gleaned from past experience, and women and men have different past experiences. From the time they're born, they're treated differently, talked to differently, and talk differently as a result. Boys and girls grow up in different worlds, even if they grow up in the same house. And as adults they travel in different worlds, reinforcing patterns established in childhood.[619]

Just as Eastern and Western cultures can be distinguished from one another by varying values, so can men and women. In Western culture, where independence is prized, this value shows up in patterns of conversing. But, as we have discussed, our society also privileges masculinity, which both bestows greater autonomy and bequeaths an expectation of greater independence. Not surprisingly, men's conversation reflects this situation. Tannen suggests that masculine independence displays in a distancing from *metamessages* (a level of talk that comments on relationships) in favor of *information*, the kind of communication exchange practical in the workplace. Women, on the other hand, typically attend to metamessages and use conversation for social *involvement*.[620]

Tannen regards the question, 'Who talks more?' as dependent on context. Given men's traditionally greater involvement and investment in work, they tend to talk more in public. Women feel more comfortable in 'private' speaking. Tannen tries to capture this difference by referring to two distinct kinds of talk. Women rely mostly on *rapport-talk*--speaking that aims to establish personal connections and negotiate relationships. Establishing similarities and matching experiences—elements of relationship building—are the priorities. Men excel at *report-talk*—the kind of speaking that aims at drawing attention while exhibiting knowledge and skill. This kind of talking fits masculine goals of maintaining independence, conducting negotiations, and establishing status.[621]

Other differences in conversational style or in the use of language could be pointed out, but this material should suffice to substantiate two basic and related points. First, we all use gendered language; we have no other choice. But we do have some say in how or whether we use that gendered language, either to challenge or to perpetuate prevailing social values and/or stereotypes. Second, not only the vocabulary we rely on is gendered, but so also is our very style of talking. Conversational styles both reflect differences—and perpetuate their consequences. To the extent that these differences are valued, to that extent the genders will be discouraged from adopting another conversational style. But an attendant consequence will be a difference that also separates and complicates relationships between the genders. This separation makes communication more difficult whether in the home or outside it. In sum, maintaining language differences like those we have discussed carry a high price.

Trait Differences

What about differences believed to reside inside the person's character or personality? A host of alleged differences in *personality traits* have been put forward over the years—too many to cover in this brief dialog. But we can look at a few, emphasizing the more noted and ones presently discussed. We won't resolve here either how significant these differences are, or what ultimately causes them. But we will try to see how the debate between social constructionists and evolutionary psychologists impinges on each.[622]

Perhaps the most often cited example of a sex-based difference is *aggression*. There seems no doubt that men are more aggressive, and their aggression is more violent in character. An evolutionary psychologist like Buss can argue that male aggression is a complex, context-dependent response to one or more adaptive problems. In fact, he names six problems aggression might have evolved to address: as a way to co-opt the resources of others, as a defense against attack, as a manner to inflict costs on same-sex rivals, as a method for negotiating status and power, as an incentive to rivals to avoid their own shows of aggression, and as a threat meant to deter long-term mates from sexual infidelity.[623] A social constructionist might point out that the hierarchical nature of society has men on top and that masculine privilege is protected by male aggression. The man's typically greater size and strength make the threat of aggression frightening to women and functions to suppress behavior challenging the gender hierarchy. As far as aggression being most often practiced against members of the same sex, this also may reflect long-held culturally sanctioned beliefs and values with regard to power and politics. An evolutionary biological view is not needed to explain such behavior.

A long-held belief has been that men are more *competitive* than women. No one denies that both genders are competitive to some degree, but many argue that there is a degree of difference. Evolutionary psychologists think this difference is sex-based and rooted in evolutionary biology. They usually describe competition in terms of sexual selection and note the role of rivalry, especially as linked to aggression.[624] Psychologist Robert Deaner, on the other hand, points to competitive running as an example of a more general difference in competitiveness. He notes that among elite runners, "two to four times as many males as females run fast relative to sex-specific world-class standards." He also finds this to be true among non-elite runners, at least among the top performers. He is not saying men are faster, but that relative to running standards for each gender, men are proportionately more likely to run closer to the standard because they train more competitively. He views this as reflecting an evolved disposition.[625] However, Deaner himself notes that among the mass of 'ordinary' runners such a difference does not show itself, and he admits other possible explanations may pertain. For example, a social constructionist might point out that few social incentives exist to elicit more competitiveness among women in a system that offers them few opportunities or rewards. Additionally, as opportunities and rewards have slowly developed, women's competitiveness appears to have demonstrably increased, as any observer of women's sports might attest.

Evolutionary psychologists commonly put forward *jealousy* as a sex-based difference. The gist of the idea is this: human females and males differ in the kinds of situations in which they show greater jealousy as a result of evolutionary pressures stemming from different adaptive problems. For women the problem is the need to ensure *paternal investment*—how can they keep men invested in parenting? For men the problem is *paternal uncertainty*—how do they know their mate's child is also their own? These different problems elicit greater jealousy by each sex under specific conditions. Women prove more jealous in response to *emotional* infidelity; men are more jealous in response to *sexual* infidelity. This is not to suggest each sex does not also experience jealousy in the opposite condition; either sex can respond with jealousy to either emotional or sexual infidelity. But whether in hypothetical or actual situations, the sexes differ in degree of response according to what cues their jealousy.[626] Critics point to other research finding little, if any, difference in frequency or magnitude of jealousy, but the response of evolutionary psychologists like Buss is that this finding comes from too broad an analysis of the problem.[627] From a social constructionist perspective, then, there are two issues: are there real and significant differences between men and women when it comes to jealousy, and if there are, then is a biologically-based explanation the best one? Perhaps women are more cued to jealousy by emotional infidelity because they are acculturated to give primacy to emotional closeness over sexual contact. On the other hand, men may be culturally conditioned to prize sexual conquest and thus are more sensitive to the threat of sexual infidelity.

Debates over differences in particular internal characteristics should not get in the way of seeing a broader point: masculinity and femininity are associated with different personality dispositions and/or traits. We have seen various explanations exist for this, ranging from the idea that such differences are illusory and reflect observer bias and the power of stereotypes, to theories that accept such differences as real, and account for them largely in terms of evolutionary biology or social constructions. Far less debatable are the easily observed differences in social roles, with their accompanying differences in social status and power.

Social Role Differences

Because we have devoted time already to looking at differences between men and women in terms of gender socialization and gender relations, we can keep this part of our present discussion tightly targeted. The so-called 'traditional' family divides the masculine and feminine roles into separate domains of predominant interest and influence: the home belongs to the woman in her social roles as housewife and mother. The outside world belongs to the man in his social role as provider. The man's role as father often tends to become subordinate and largely as the gatekeeper to and symbol of the world beyond the home.

The social role of *wife* highlights several important things. First, the word itself originally stood as a general gender marker. Like the gender term 'woman' it came to have its meaning in reference to man, and as a subordinate term: 'a man's wife.' It could also be used in connection with work of lower social status, woman's work such as a 'fishwife' or a 'midwife.' It remains common to find it in the compound 'housewife.'

Housewife is a culturally feminine role conditioned by three qualities: sex, marital status, and domain. A housewife must be female (males in a comparable role are termed 'househusbands,' a position of inferior status and power). She must be a man's wife; her place is his home. The designation—unique to English—sets the modern woman apart from her forebears who might have done similar tasks. In traditional societies the woman's work within the home could be valued differently because it wasn't reduced, as today's housewife is, to a status lower than even a hired housekeeper, who at least is paid for the labor. It is not that the activities involved in maintaining a domicile are demeaned, but the role is denigrated because it exists as unpaid labor in a society where status is associated with wage-earning.[628] Although our own society has moved modestly in the direction of more egalitarianism, research continues to show that women are expected to do more of the tasks associated with the role of housewife even when they work outside the home.[629]

The social role of *mother* is about more than reproductive function. 'Mother' is a term used as more than a simple marker of 'the female who bore this child.' As a social role, mother involves a coordinated set of tasks and functions broadly captured by the term 'nurturing.' As a housewife is a 'home-keeper,' so a mother is a 'child-keeper.' As a housewife takes care of a home, so a mother takes care of a family. While the ostensible primary referent of the caretaking, or nurturing, is a child or children, there often has been the suggestion that this mothering extends to the husband as well.

The masculine role of *father* is relatively less about nurturing and relatively more about preparing children for the outside world. As a nurturer, the father's role typically has been in a support capacity to the mother. In the so-called 'traditional' father role, the chief functions are those of a custodian—someone charged with keeping others safe and guiding their direction. Fathers do this by being the primary disciplinarian, the model of the morality needed to prosper in the world outside the home, and the gatekeeper to that world. With changes in our society a 'new' father role is emerging. It emphasizes more personal involvement in childrearing, with an expectation of greater competence in it.[630]

Both in the past and presently, the principal social role occupied by men is that of *provider*. In many societies, like our own, this social role carries more status and power than the other roles mentioned here. This increases the likelihood that men will devote proportionately more time and energy into it. It carries other consequences as well. Within the family the provider role continues to carry status and power, which the man can use to rule the household. For example, as Rivka Polatnick points out, the social authority men derive from providing extends into parenting, where men hold on to a right to make the final decision on any matter.[631]

Clearly, masculine social roles within the family are privileged compared to feminine ones, despite the relatively greater attention the latter receive. Just as in the wider role, where social roles are gendered disproportionately in favor of men in the spheres of work, politics, and most other public roles, a clear gender hierarchy is evident. *A gender hierarchy preserves differences for purposes of status and power.* We have documented in our ongoing dialog this reality in numerous ways, but here we have come to the heart of it. A hierarchy depends on differences to exist, though this necessary condition is not sufficient by itself. The *differences must also be valued differently.* Ultimately, the gender role differences we observe are not merely a matter of differences, but a matter of how those differences are judged.

So, in an increasingly vigorous debate, essentialists and the other camps trade criticisms and make appeals to varying bodies of research. Everything from the hypotheses, to research methodologies, to inferences and interpretations of the data are scrutinized and critiqued. Nicolson sums up the impasse existing between feminists and evolutionary psychologists as the 20th century closed: feminist psychologists regarded evolutionary psychologists as reductionistic, dependent on crude models extrapolating from animal behavior to human beings, ideologically conservative, and politically dangerous in supporting a view that might undermine hard-won victories in the battle for gender equality. In turn, evolutionary psychologists viewed their feminist colleagues as biased, unscientific, and so committed to ideology they would rather suppress evidence than gain knowledge.[632]

Most of us, most of the time, remain oblivious to this lively, often contentious conversation. Those of us who see the stakes want to take part. Some of us choose sides, while others of us seek common ground. We *should* want to take part, because the conversation *matters*. Regardless of our scientific theory and methodology, all science is a human endeavor fraught with limitations, replete with values, and generally blind to its cultural convictions. This makes it no less valuable, but should caution us. In conversing we need science—still our most reliable human avenue to dependable knowledge—but we need it retained within a context recognizing both the value of other ways of knowing and sensitive to the scientist's blind spots. It does no dishonor to science to recognize its limits and limitations, which should only spur us on to be better scientists.

Chapter 10

Conforming Genders

Introduction: Every culture has its own way of thinking about, speaking of, and valuing gender. Cultural ideals for gender give rise to *gender stereotypes*. Although we have discussed gender stereotypes and stereotyping at various points throughout our dialog, we have not yet actually specified much the specific qualities in the stereotypes of different genders. In this discussion we will open with a brief review of stereotypes and offer what seem to be the quality sets most of us in our society hold as stereotypes of masculinity and femininity.

In this discussion we will confine ourselves to just masculinity and femininity. These are the dominant genders in our society and culture. Here we will call them *conforming genders*, meaning they fit with the bipolar, dichotomous thinking our culture embraces. The fit of any given individual with either of these conforming genders is a relative one. Some of us fit more tightly and comfortably than others of us do. But all we have to do is fit well enough to be recognized as a member of that gender. In fact, fitting too exactly with the gender stereotype, which though used by all is still seen by most adults for what it is—an artificial and exaggerated portrait—lends itself to being judged as fake and laughable. On the other side, being too loose a fit carries risks, too. So we all face the pressure of finding the right degree of fit so we can wear our gender comfortably without undue attention being called to it.

Obviously, such a task takes time and effort. Both are supplied in the long developmental path we all take in life. We already have looked at *gender development* in a variety of ways. Once more in this discussion we will consider it again, this time in the form of how *gender constructs of masculinity and femininity* affect us. For each conforming gender this has two dimensions: what the construct is, which is the broad representation in our mind of the gender, and how that construct guides the construction of that gender in individuals' lives.

But gender constructs play out in groups as well as individuals. Belonging to a gender constitutes membership in one of the most fundamental and salient of social groups we can belong to. Conforming gender groups have marked their own identities in social movements. The *Men's Movement* and the *Women's Movement* each have contributed efforts to further the conversation on gender. These broad social movements have sparked academic interest in *gender studies*, one product of which is this very dialog we are participating in today.

Gender Stereotypes

To understand *conforming genders*—those that are expected and accepted within a culture's gender scheme—requires a sense of what they are conforming to, which are cultural expectations and standards for masculinity and femininity. *Gender stereotypes*—mental composite pictures of generalized, expected characteristics—anchor these standards. The expectations are both as to the way people are and to the way they should be, as viewed from a hypothesized norm set held by most people in a society. *Gender stereotyping*, in turn, names the process of maintaining any template of gender characteristics for masculinity and femininity so that it can be used and reused without much, if any, change. Stereotypes, as idealized and thus exaggerated sets, do not reflect reality. Virtually all of us, after even a little reflection, recognize both that stereotypes are artificial and illusory, and that actually attaining one is probably not a good idea. So while we can say that stereotypes anchor cultural standards, they do so in a peculiar fashion.

On the one hand, there are *descriptive stereotypes*—normative sets that express a social consensus on the way men and women typically are. On the other hand, there are *prescriptive stereotypes*—normative expectations of desired gender identities and roles, a hypothesized standard of how a man or woman should be.[633] *Gender stereotypes use both descriptive and prescriptive idealized qualities to guide gender within definable boundaries.* They are not exactly the same as the cultural standards for gender, which are more flexible and adaptive. Rather, gender stereotypes reflect the imagined center of each aspect of the cultural standards and thus provide convenient compass points for people to navigate their perceptions, expectations, and behavior by.

A number of different conceptual frameworks have guided the development of instruments to research gender stereotypes. One employs a gender division we have discussed before (chapter 5): *instrumental* (masculine) and *expressive* (feminine). Instrumentality is task-oriented, and references masculine traits such as active, self-confident, independent, competitive, ambitious, and decisive—all traits especially associated with work. Expressiveness is emotion-oriented, and references feminine traits like gentle, warm, understanding, helpful to others, affectionate, tender, and sensitive to others' needs—all traits especially associated with home, family, and relationships. This way of establishing a framework to investigate gender has been used often—and criticized often. [634] Another conceptual scheme has proven perhaps more influential.

David Bakan—Agency and Communion

Psychologist David Bakan, in the mid-1960s, formulated a conception that has remained popular in studying gender stereotypes. In his book *The Duality of Human Existence*—a work exploring both psychology and religion—Bakan proposes there are two fundamental principles governing human existence. One is *agency*—the existence of an organism as an individual. Agency manifests in *agentic* characteristics, which Bakan conceived as masculine in nature. The other principle is *communion*—the relational participation of the individual in some larger organism, such as a social group. Communion manifests in *communal* characteristics, which Bakan viewed as feminine in nature.[635] Agency, Bakan thinks, manifests in isolation, alienation, and aloneness as self-protection, self-assertion, and self-expansion are pursued. Communion seeks contact, openness, and union. The former aims at mastery, the latter at cooperation.[636] Both principles exist in every person. Bakan declares:

> The moral imperative is to try to mitigate agency with communion. The moral imperative to which I subscribe was magnificently expressed by Hillel many years ago: "If I am not for myself, who will be for me? But if I am only for myself, what am I?" The first speaks of agency, the second, of communion, both together, the integration of the two.[637]

The notion of agentic (masculine) and communal (feminine) traits has been utilized in gender stereotype research rather often.

Examples of Research into Gender Stereotypes

Research done by anthropologists Evalyn Jacobson Michaelson and Leigh Aaland in the mid-1970s, tested Bakan's concepts as guides in interviews intended to assess the degree to which interviewees admired traits they identified as feminine in women and masculine in men. They asked 60 persons (half faculty and half graduate students, all at UCLA) to define 'masculine' and 'feminine,' and then describe both a man and a woman they admired, explaining why. The researchers then coded the responses using Bakan's concepts, together with the idea of androgyny and the possibility of a rejection of gender stereotypes by the respondent. Their results offer three conclusions: first, "People are more likely to *define* masculinity as agency and femininity as communion than they are to *admire* pure agency in men or pure communion in women." Second, the higher a person's level of education, the less likely they are to find a clear dichotomy between the genders, and the more likely they are to approve similar behavior patterns for both genders. Finally, they found education is a more potent predictor than a person's sex; education seems the greater force in shaping gender beliefs.[638] These findings seem to have stood the test of time.

Many studies have employed Bakan's concepts. For example, experimental research published in 2006—forty years after Bakan introduced his ideas—tests social role theory (or 'role congruity theory') using agentic and communal traits in labor roles. Thus, agentic roles are business competition roles while communal roles are caretaking ones. The researchers also desire to see how descriptive and prescriptive stereotypes are at work when people are asked about their beliefs concerning the gendered division of labor across a century span (1950-2050). With regard to three experiments, they find in general that participants project a pattern of accommodation to changing roles rather than resistance to change. This means a projected openness and acceptance both of women in competitive contexts and of a greater display of stereotyped masculine traits by them as their future social roles expand. At the same time, participants do not expect men's characteristics will change much because their roles are believed to remain relatively stable and invariant.[639]

In a longitudinal study also published in 2006, another team of researchers offers the results from a twenty-year analysis of selected influences on gender-linked personality traits in women. They test, among other matters, the hypothesis that societal demands for labor exert a substantial influence on how feminine personality unfolds. They acknowledge the assumption "that work roles promote traits thought to be more characteristic of men than women, whereas family roles foster traits thought to be more characteristic of women than men." Focusing on socially desirable characteristics, they examine age-related changes in gender-linked traits in 758 mothers, assessed four times between 1983-2003. They specifically wish to consider the influence of social role experiences and birth cohort (baby boomer [born between 1945-1958] or pre-baby boomer) membership. The researchers focus on positive agentic (e.g., autonomy) and communal (e.g., generativity, warmth, relatedness) traits with regard to personality development.[640]

Their results find that participation in the labor force does exert influence. Women working either full-time or part-time show higher masculinity than nonworking women. Family roles also exert influence: marital support is associated with more femininity compared to that found among unmarried women. Family and work roles interact in that working women with high marital support endorse more feminine-linked traits than working women with less support. Other results indicate an increase in positive feminine-linked traits *and* positive masculine-linked traits. Interestingly, though, those women already higher in femininity increase in femininity with age at a more rapid rate than women higher in masculinity—resulting in what they label "an increasingly extreme sex-congruent orientation." Finally, birth cohort also matters, at least to a modest extent. Baby boomer women seem to experience greater changes with age in relation to reduced marital conflict and increased support; these accompany both higher agentic and higher communal traits in baby boomer women than in pre-baby boomers.[641]

Of course, other ways of organizing the content of gender stereotypes has been used—too many for our introductory discussion. We should note, before moving on, that *meta-analysis of the research* reveals some provocative findings. Sociologists Lloyd Lueptow, Lori Garovich-Szabo, and Margaret Lueptow reviewed a half-century of literature on the subject and trends found in analyzing more than two-dozen studies conducted between 1974-1997. They note that while extensive social change transpired over this period—which reduced both sex-typed role assignments and attitudes—there has *not* been a corresponding change in sex typing. In fact, as they summarize the research literature, "With few exceptions, this research has shown that there has been stability in sex typing of women and men from at least the 1950s to the late 1990s, and even an increase in sex typing, especially regarding the stereotypes and self-concepts focusing upon the personality traits of women." Similarly, their trend study covering 1974-1997 yields a succinct judgment: "Thus, the findings of this study with regard to *gender stereotypes* are very clear: *they are not decreasing, if anything they are intensifying.*"[642]

This conclusion may not surprise us if we consider the possibility that the very social changes our society has experienced are a significant factor in the intensification of gender stereotypes. The consequences of change, however desirable and positive, are uncertainty and some anxiety. A reflexive response could be intensification of stereotypes as both men and women try to make sense of who they are as gendered beings in the new landscape. In Piagetian terms, they may be both trying to assimilate change and accommodate it as they seek to make cognitive sense of it.

In trying to look at meta-analysis of our subject we are distancing ourselves from specific dimensions of the gender stereotypes. We may find it profitable to back even further away from the trees in order to get a still clearer look at the forest. After all, we would find it impossible to neatly and exactly specify all the contents of gender stereotypes for the conforming genders. But perhaps we can paint in broad strokes some of the familiar features. For example, in a review of 10 studies conducted between 1957-1980, Lueptow found the following traits were the most frequently appearing for each gender:

❑ Masculinity: dominant, aggressive, competitive, independent, ambitious, self-confident, adventurous, decisive.

❑ Femininity: affectionate, submissive, emotional, sympathetic, talkative, and gentle.[643]

Probably the broadest stroke of all resides in a simple idea: *what men are, women are not*. French philosopher Simone de Beauvior, in her landmark work *The Second Sex*, put it most starkly: "He is the Subject . . . she is the Other."[644] Thus, stereotypes typically begin with masculinity, depicting an idealized vision of a man, and then generating *antonyms* for women. Thus, if a man is strong, a woman is weak; if he is rational, she must be emotional.[645]

Let's look an example of how this questionable 'logic' plays out. In a basic text on human sexuality, psychologist Robert Crooks and clinical social worker Karla Baur offer five stereotypes with specific reference to sexuality, which are adapted here to a modest extent to set them in a wider framework:

❑ Men are oversexed; women are undersexed.

❑ Men are initiators; women are recipients.

❑ Men are 'sexperts'; women are sexually naïve.

❑ Men are movers; women are controllers.

❑ Men are strong and unemotional; women are nurturing and supportive.[646]

If we drop the 'sexed' part from the first stereotype we find a broad set of stereotypical ideas: men are often pictured as 'more' of most things than women: more loud, more forceful, more competent, and so forth. The second stereotype follows a very old notion, one usually set out as 'men are active, women are passive.' Another variant of this is 'men are givers, women are receivers.' In sum, men take the lead and women follow. The third also can be generalized. Men are stereotypically viewed as more knowledgeable, better informed, and more expert in most things—hence the frequent joke that men never will stop to ask for directions. The fourth stereotype, with regard to sexual activity, refers to men acting as though women are a challenge to be conquered while women act as though their job is to restrain male lust. But the same dynamics hold across many stereotypical ideas about how men and women relate: he is pictured as charging ahead while she tries to pull him back. We might even see this as a reflection of that basic stereotype that he is drawn to plunge into the wider world, while she tries to keep him tied to hearth and home. That thought then leads us to the last stereotype listed. In sexual behavior, in the crassest terms, this is the picture that he is interested in the mechanics—the specific sex acts, as though they are athletic feats to be performed and show his prowess, matters of competence rather than passion. For her, though, the picture is of someone little interested in mere matters of the flesh when matters of the heart are what matter. Likewise, in other matters, the man becomes stereotyped as unencumbered by emotions, a rational being able to make complex judgments—including moral ones—with a skill the woman lacks because she is weakened by sentimentality. But, then, her role is to be supportive of her big, strong man as he ventures out to slay the dragons of the world while she keeps the castle warm and tends the children.

Of course, when we hear such drivel said in such an exaggerated fashion we are more likely to recognize it as not merely overdrawn, but unrealistic. Many of us may also conclude such a picture, when attempted to be made real, is undesirable. Yet to a greater or lesser extent such stereotypes have been a part of all our lives. A number of instruments have been created to assess the kinds of beliefs that contribute to the gender stereotypes.

Research Instruments

Historically, the M-F Test developed in the 1930s by Lewis Terman and Catherine Miles looms large. In 1936 they published *Sex and Personality*, the first systematic analysis in personality psychology of masculinity and femininity.[647] As the name of the instrument implies, they regard the genders as opposite poles on a continuum. Gender is measured through seven subsets to yield an aggregate score (ranging from a possible –200 to +200), or as a profile of scores for each subset. The -/+ range reflects the poles: feminine responses are scored negatively and masculine ones positively. Psychologist Peter Hegarty, in his review of this test and the BSRI (see below), observes that Terman and Miles "cast persons who embodied both masculinity and femininity as social problems. . . ." In fact, as Hegarty points out, the very purpose of the test, as originally conceived, is to detect and comprehend persons not conforming to one or the other pole. The gender stereotypes on which the test are built—like so many subsequent instruments—are upon the responses of a mostly White, relatively affluent, and well-educated population.[648]

One of the most widely employed ways the content of gender stereotypes has been explored is through adjectives. In this regard, the *Adjective Check List* (ACL) has been a frequently employed tool. This 300 item list of adjectives used in daily living was developed in the mid-1960s by Harrison Gough and Alfred Heilbrun, Jr. as a versatile tool with a wide range of applications.[649] One such application has been to identify gender stereotypes, including across societies. For example, university students in more than two dozen countries ranging across the world were asked whether each item (or its translated equivalent) was more frequently associated with men, women, or neither. A score noted as M% ('male frequency') was computed for each item by dividing the male frequency by the sum of both male and female frequencies, then multiplying by 100 to eliminate decimals and create a scale ranging to 100. In this fashion the 300 items could be ranged from those most associated with masculinity (masculine stereotype = high M% of 67 or higher) to those most associated with femininity (feminine stereotype = low M% of 33 or lower); neutral gender items were scores in the middle (between 34-66). The results were then analyzed by different theoretical models, each of which found the masculine stereotype stronger than the feminine one.[650]

Sandra Bem's research instrument, the *Bem Sex Role Inventory* (BSRI), which we have touched upon before and will look at more closely in our next discussion, is perhaps the most well-known tool using stereotypes to roughly measure self-identification with presumed gender traits. The items selected to represent masculinity include traits such as analytical, aggressive, competitive, ambitious, and dominant—qualities popularly believed to better fit men than women, regardless of whether they are thus empirically substantiated, as we discussed earlier (chapter 9). In a like manner, items selected to represent femininity included traits like yielding, tender, gentle, gullible, and childlike. This instrument differentiates people into groups based on their endorsement, or self-identification with masculine and/or feminine positive stereotypical traits.

Other commonly employed tools include the Attitudes toward Women Scale (AWS) and Personal Attributes Questionnaire (PAQ), both developed by Janet Spence and Robert Helmreich.[651] As the first of these suggests, some instruments are targeted to a specific gender. For example, in respect to femininity a well-known instrument is the Gough Femininity Scale (GFS). Tools used with regard to masculinity include the Attitudes Toward Masculinity Transcendence Scale (ATMTS), Brannon Masculinity Scale (BMS), Gender Role Conflict Scale (GRCS), Index of Homophobia (IHP), Liberal Feminist Attitude and ideology Scale (LFAIS), Macho Scale (MS), Masculine Gender Role Stress Scale (MGRS), Sex Role Egalitarianism Scale, Form BB (SRES-BB), and Sociosexual Orientation Inventory (SOI).[652] Finally, some tools are part of larger instruments, such as the Masculinity-Femininity Scale of the Strong Interest Inventory (SII), or the Masculinity-Femininity Scale of the Minnesota Multiphasic

Personality Inventory (MMPI), or the F/M Scale of the California Psychological Inventory (CPI). Of the making of tests there is no end!

Unequal Genders

In a moment we shall look at the content of stereotypes for each conforming gender. But we must pause a moment to reckon with a sobering possibility: *even in stereotypes the genders are not equal.* Masculinity emerges as the more socially valued gender. Evidence for this conclusion comes from at least three researchable ideas. First, the masculine construct creates a more rigid gender construction among its members, a sign that the gender is more carefully protected by pressure to conformity. Second, the masculinity stereotype is more heavily endorsed and fits more tightly with how we perceive human personality. For example, young girls are far more likely to be drawn to masculine role models than young boys are to feminine role models; both genders quickly comprehend that being masculine is more socially desirable. Third, masculinity appears to set the standard for understanding femininity in a way that does not seem true in reverse. One of the tasks girls face is digesting the social reality that the more desirable gendered way to be and act is tantalizingly out of reach. Boys have no comparable incentives to want to be like women.

Research evidence suggests that *masculinity is more rigid than femininity.* All of us are subject to strong socialization pressures to conform to our assigned gender. But girls and women enjoy greater gender role flexibility because the stakes are not as high; any fall from grace is not as far as that risked by nonconforming boys and men. Adherence to rigid gender roles may result in psychological distress—a state called *gender role conflict.* Research by psychologist Jim O'Neil and colleagues into gender role conflict began in the 1970s with hypotheses later tested through an instrument known as the Gender Role Conflict Scale (GRCS). Results from it suggest four underlying factors: first, success, power, and competition (SPC); second, restrictive emotionality (RE); third, restricted sexual and affectionate behavior between men (RABBM); and fourth, conflict between work and family relations (CBWFR).[653] Gender role conflict can result in distress and is negatively related to mental health.[654] While women, too, are subject to gender role conflict, the present state of research suggests a greater risk for men.[655]

The stereotype of masculinity appears to be more heavily endorsed and to fit more tightly with how we perceive human personality. This seems true not only in our own society, with its gender hierarchy, but in many others as well. Researchers reported at the end of the 20th century having analyzed cross-cultural gender stereotype data previously collected from 25 countries. Using the Five Factor (OCEAN) Model of personality, when results were averaged across nations the researchers found the pancultural masculine stereotype was higher than the pancultural feminine stereotype on four of the five factors (Openness, Conscientiousness, Extraversion, and Emotional Stability [Neuroticism]). Only in Agreeableness was the pancultural feminine stereotype higher. The researchers observe that the results suggest the masculine stereotype is apparently more positive, which has implications for gender socialization during development.[656] There are important consequences for establishing one gender—in this case masculinity—as the standard for understanding human beings, as we have seen for example in the less research pursued in areas such as women's health.

Finally, *masculinity seems to set the boundaries for femininity*, which can be characterized as 'that which masculinity is not.' If masculinity is normative, then everything else must be conceptualized in reference to it. One gender serves as 'canon,' the authoritative rule used to measure all other genders. This privileged position fuels the protests of feminists in depicting masculinity as the standard against which women are measured as 'Other.'[657] Sociologist Robert Connell, who has specialized in the study of masculinity, conceptualizes the gender as an array of masculinities, at the head of which stands the privileged White heterosexual man of economic wealth and social status. He frames masculinity as an *hegemony*—a dominant force ruling gender. Femininities—the array of the feminine gender—share in common subordination to masculinities.[658]

Masculinity: Construct & Construction

What is this gender that shows such dominance? At least since the 1980s, and largely motivated by the sting of feminist critiques, a variety of efforts have been made to understand masculinity. At one level, the gender can be understood in terms of the stereotypes that anchor it. This level is one we all find ourselves familiar with, a level at which differentiating one conforming gender from another is done by comparison on traits varying significantly in their association with each gender. We already have examined one example of this, and all too many examples may come readily to mind.

At another level, masculinity may be comprehended in both broader and deeper terms, in relation to the many dimensions we have been dialoging about. At this level masculinity is discussed in terms of its essential logic, or fundamental essence, or actual functioning. The stereotypes then become inviting signposts to ask directions toward a more nuanced and realistic appraisal of the gender. At either level, masculinity is a *construct*—an abstract summary of some regularity in nature related to or connected with concrete, observable entities or events.[659]

The Masculinity Construct

So what is the construct 'masculinity'?

John Stoltenberg, who roots himself in radical feminism, declares that masculinity is an *ethical construction*, built by choices and acts.[660] The logic of ethics is to justify our values—to explain why it is right and good to find something meaningful and important in what we do. In a culture prone to view gender as something that unfolds as naturally as a flower in a field, this notion of gender as something constructed to reflect values may seem odd. Yet imagine the difference it might make if all of us believed that our building of boys and men carries moral weight.

If boys and men are largely what we have made them, then what have we wrought? Let us start at the first level described a moment ago. The *masculinity stereotype* offers one way to examine the construct. This stereotype has been studied extensively in our own society and across societies, and in a wide array of specific connections. For example, the cross-cultural research of psychologists John Williams and Deborah West, using the ACL and Five Factor model of personality, found that men were especially associated with adjectives like adventurous and forceful (M% = 93), strong (92), coarse and tough (91). Women were markedly associated with adjectives like affectionate (10), emotional (12), superstitious (13), and sensitive, attractive, and sexy (14).[661] In either instance, it is clear that the *gender stereotypes include both decidedly positive and negative characteristics.*

Since the success of the second wave of feminism, in particular, much publicity has attended the negative features of the masculinity stereotype. But more than that, many features most men took pride in were called into question as positive traits. For instance, being strong would appear to be desirable, both physically and psychologically. But feminists were quick to point out that stereotypical strength in men translated all too often into rigidity—an unbending belief they can do anything and bear anything, even as it kills them—accompanied by a disparagement of women as weak in body and mind alike. From the point of view of women, who needs that kind of strength?

Robert Connell—Masculinities & Hegemonic Masculinity

The questions feminists raised were pointed and stuck like sharp barbs. They provoked a flurry of responses from men, who aimed to get beneath and behind the stereotypes to uncover a deeper appreciation of masculinity. Those efforts lead us to the second level of considering gender, a level where theorizing and serious research about masculinity predominates. At this level one name stands out: Australian sociologist Robert Connell, who admits his work in this area began as a response to feminism.[662]

His 1995 book *Masculinities* has proved arguably the most important work for redirecting thinking about masculinity. Connell operates within a broadly feminist framework and shares with them a wide-reaching grasp of ideas from various disciplines and sources. In *Masculinities* he begins with Freud's telling observation that gender terms like masculine and feminine are among the most confused in science. For Connell this situation is understandable because of "the character of gender itself, historically changing and politically fraught."[663] He tracks the gender discourse on 'masculinity' through multiple avenues, examining theoretical alternatives, historical and political factors, and lived experiences of men seeking to grapple with what it means to be a man. As he says elsewhere, "My rather complicated definition of masculinity arose from a strong sense of the multileveled and multidimensional character of gender. . . ."[664]

One of his most influential ideas is that masculinity is actually *masculinities*—multiple ways to be masculine, with some occupying a subordinate status. A decade before *Masculinities* appeared, Connell, with colleagues Tim Corrigan and John Lee, offered ideas toward what they termed a 'new sociology of masculinity.' In their outline of a social analysis of masculinity, they argue that any starting point for comprehending masculinity that evades a simply biologistic or subjective orientation must root itself in the *social relations* that constitute the gender order. Taking their cue from Gayle Rubin's analysis (see chapter 5), they argue that the sex/gender system she describes is constructed in history and thus subject to change. In its internal differentiation, this system has most often found focus given to two aspects of its organization: the division of labor and the structure of power. They add the structure of 'cathexis'—"the social organization of sexuality and attraction." And they remark that the central feature of this structure in the modern world of capitalist societies is patriarchy.[665]

However, the world is not a uniform place. While the relations between genders may be depicted in broad ways, there are plenty of exceptions. In a key passage these men write:

> The overall relation between men and women, further, is not a confrontation between homogenous, undifferentiated blocs. . . . We would suggest, in fact, that the fissuring of the categories of "men" and "women" is one of the most central facts about patriarchal power and the way it works. In the case of men, the crucial division is between hegemonic masculinity and various subordinated masculinities.[666]

Hegemonic masculinity—the dominance of one form of masculinity—has become the idea most associated with Connell. The notion depends on multiple masculinities, with one in a superior position. In the mid-1980s, he and his colleagues conceived of masculinities differentiated not merely by power relations, but also by their interplay with the division of labor and with patterns of emotional attachment—all of which results in masculinity being psychological *and* institutional (meaning, an aspect of collective practice by men). This means that individual men can have a gender identity and affiliation with other men that is both masculine and subordinate to another masculine identity and group. The most ready instance that comes to mind is homosexual men—a *subordinated masculinity* characterized by lower social status and power. These subordinated masculinities may be either stable (as in the case of the gay man), or transient (e.g., the ritualized homosexuality found in some cultures where younger men gain their manhood under the guardianship of older men).[667]

Hegemonic masculinity involves the power to impose a particular definition of masculinity on other men. The men who hold the highest status and exercise the most social influence are able to use their positions of power and wealth to justify their own sense of what a man is—and to perpetuate the social relationships that generate their dominance. While only a few men actually occupy this highest niche in the gender hierarchy, very large numbers of men are complicit in sustaining the system even though it keeps them in a subordinate position. They do so because their position is still privileged over that of women. They benefit from a hegemonic masculinity that has as a central feature a successful strategy for keeping women subordinate.[668]

Corrigan, Connell and Lee assert that hegemony always refers to the historical reality of power won and then held. They point to three central features. First, hegemony means *persuasion*. In this respect, control of mass media offers a pervasive avenue for disseminating ideas about gender. Second, hegemony supports gender segregation in the work force—*the division of labor into 'men's' and 'women's' work* that reinforces and perpetuates gender divisions and definitions. Third, hegemony employs *the State* to negotiate and enforce its sense of gender. This is seen, for example, in efforts to keep homosexuals out of schools as teachers and to erode civil protections extending to all people.[669]

In the decades since this seminal piece, prominently through *Masculinities* but also via other books and articles, Connell has continued to extend his thinking on masculinities and masculine hegemony. In 1987, he published *Gender and Power*, a work examining existing theories while building his own. A significant aspect of this book is his critique of sex role theories, which he accuses of reducing gender in a dichotomous fashion both simplistic and naïve in its underestimation of social inequality and power dynamics. A chief failing in this regard is sex role theory's apparent inability to grasp the significance of power relations within a gender, not merely between genders. He views the *relations* between men and women as notably marked by three things: the division of labor, the division of power, and the division of affective attachments and social norms (what he terms 'cathexis'). The first two of these had been noted before; the third is his own contribution. It refers to emotional and sexual attachments between individuals that are gendered with different values, expectations, and activities for men and women. Each kind of relation corresponds to a *gender regime*—a specific social structure—respectively, the labor market (labor), the State (power), and the family (cathexis).[670]

At the beginning of the current century, Connell offered his thoughts on *The Men and the Boys*. He notes how over the years since the mid-1970s questions about men and boys, as well as about gender in general, had moved out of the narrower arena of academic discourse and become part of a wider public conversation. "How we understand men and gender," he writes, "what we believe about masculinity, what we know (or think we know) about the development of boys, may have large effects—for good or ill—in therapy, education, health services, violence prevention, policing, and social services."[671] But to understand these things requires a larger perspective than often given them. So Connell attempts to look at boys and men in a global perspective, continuing an analysis that argues that traditional conceptions of gender and gender roles keep boys and men at risk no less than they injure girls and women.

One aspect of this book is the addition by Connell of a fourth gender relation and corresponding gender regime. He acknowledges the structure of *symbolism* as a gender relation and points to the process of *communication* as an increasingly recognized vital element in social processes. "The symbolic structures called into play in communication—grammatical and syntactic rules, visual and sound vocabularies etc.—are important sites of gender practice," he writes. Our gender dichotomy is reinforced by 'symbolic oppositions' between the genders. The gender hierarchy is sustained by practices both subtle and obvious, such as subordinating women by referring to them by titles that define them by marriage—a practice rarely if ever done with men. In symbolic relations communication is conducted along gendered lines in many ways, including dress, makeup, gestures, tone of voice, and other everyday things.[672]

Of course, Connell's voice is scarcely the only one speaking to what masculinity is. But his voice has been central to the recent conversation on this gender. Some scholars are attempting to refine or extend his work.[673] Even Connell himself, in response to critics both friendly and unfriendly, has reexamined his thinking. He agrees that the concept of hegemonic masculinity should be reshaped. He suggests retaining the heart of the idea, writing, "The fundamental feature of the concept remains the combination of the plurality of masculinities and the hierarchy of masculinities." He also believes two decades of research has found support for the idea that the hierarchy of masculinities is a pattern of hegemony rather than a matter of simple domination by force. Likewise, he finds supported the suggestion that hegemonic masculinity need not be the commonest pattern in everyday gender experience of boys and men. Fourth, he believes the research has fully supported the claim that hegemonic masculinities are historical creations—products of specific times and places—and so amenable to change. Connell does desire discarding two ideas: his early, over simplified model of the social relations surrounding hegemonic masculinities, and the view of hegemonic masculinity as an assemblage of traits. Finally, he proposes that four main areas need more research and theoretical reformulation: the nature of the gender hierarchy, the 'geography' of masculine configurations (i.e., a more global perspective that includes attention to the significance of transnational arenas for constructing masculinity), the process of social embodiment (i.e., the particular ways of representing and using men's bodies), and the dynamics of masculinities (i.e., their internal complexities).[674]

The Construction of Masculinity

While debates about the nature of the construct persist, the reality of masculinization also continues. The construct 'masculinity' leads to the construction of masculinity. It begins with gender assignment. A child, now labeled 'boy,' enters a group whose membership is as much demand as it is gift. Through the long developmental trek of childhood and adolescence, gender socialization exerts both push and pull to bring about at least an apparent conformity that allows the individual to retain his membership in good standing. For most assigned to be boys this process occurs with such regularity as to be predictable and seems like an inevitable product to Nature. Others struggle more, but still manage to stay within bounds of masculinity. Yet, easy or hard, all boys and men are *made*.

The making of a man proceeds in varying ways in different cultures. Some societies have rituals that mark the transition into manhood. In our society, boys face an inherent ambiguity in status. Though attributed a degree of masculinity and socialized to someday become men, they spend early formative years clustered with girls and women. In effect, they are segregated from men. The dominant influence is a woman and the primary sphere is the home—the domain traditionally allocated to femininity. At the same time, boys are encouraged to separate themselves from the femininity they are surrounded by, to resist the attractions of homemaking and caretaking, to segregate themselves in same-sex groups away from girls, and to imitate a gender model to which they often have much less direct exposure. Complicating things further, the very effort to adhere to same-sex peer groups carries the risk and pressure of too close an emotional affiliation with its attendant charges of being homosexual. Homophobia forces the boy to keep an emotional distance and restrict physical contact to rough play and sports. In short, virtually every significant process in the making of a Western man is geared to producing a relatively isolated individual. Autonomy is purchased at the price of emotional alienation.

Since we already at some length have investigated gender development and gender socialization in general, we may now concentrate on the processes we have just mentioned. In this regard, perhaps apt metaphors for the process in our society are pressure-cooker and mold. Certainly social forces set a mold into which the unshaped person is poured. Just as certainly, pressure is maintained to set that mold and to ensure that the qualities of the assigned gender are internalized—cooked thoroughly in and out. If these metaphors strike us as negative in tone, perhaps we may find correspondence in the process itself. In this light we might note three characteristics of the construction of masculinity:

- ❏ It tends to be prohibitive in its prescriptions.
- ❏ It tends to make demands more than offer opportunities.
- ❏ It tends to rely on negation of others for self-definition.

The construction of masculinity in our society tends to be prohibitive in its prescriptions. Developmental psychologist Ruth Hartley long ago noted that prescriptions of desired behavior for boys more often comes in the form of what he ought *not* to do than in encouragement of what he should do.[675] Research has consistently found that boys are more liable than girls to draw attention for negative behavior and are more likely to be punished.

Masculinity also tends to make demands more than offer opportunities. Both boys and girls experience pressures to conform to their assigned gender identity. However, these pressures are more rigid and restrictive for boys because of their higher status in the gender hierarchy.[676] More than three decades ago Hartley wrote, "Demands that boys conform to social notions of what is manly come much earlier and are enforced with much more vigor than similar attitudes with respect to girls."[677] If anything, these pressures have intensified. The advances by girls and women, ironically, may increase masculine stress because they both invite gender reappraisal and because they elicit a tightening of masculine boundaries even as a renewed sense of the gender is sought. Rather than be offered freedom to explore a variety of ways to be a gendered person, boys are strongly censored for feminine behaviors. In short, they are offered a narrow path along a steep incline to achieve a satisfactory gender.

Hypergender

As just implied, the climb also seems to be built by trampling on others. *The construction of masculinity tends to rely on negation of others for self-definition.* This aspect is most noticeable among those who have been termed *hypergender*—persons who exhibit very strict adherence to their gender stereotype.[678] Hypergender individuals may be either masculine or feminine—and tend to seek each other out. Hypergender men especially emphasize the desirability of being tough. They tend toward intolerance for less gender conforming individuals, and especially toward nonconforming genders (e.g., transgender people). Some research also shows greater intolerance toward the mentally ill.[679]

But while hygender men may be the most remarkable examples of masculine negation of others, there appears plenty of evidence for broader, more pervasive manifestations. The most obvious recipients of this negation are girls and women. The masculine assertion of social dominance is practiced early and often. Psychologist Carole Beal writes, "Researchers have found that even 4 year-old boys act 'as if they own the classroom,' claiming access to toys and play areas, as well as to the teacher's attention."[680] Adult men may be more generally subtle, but the tendency still shows itself even in such common things as women deferring in a group to let a man speak first, and men being far more likely to interrupt women than the reverse.

Homophobia

There are few worse epithets a boy can hear than to be called a 'sissy.' The label not only threatens his gender, but also his sexuality, for it is associated both with girls (in being a feminine boy), and with nonnormative boys (in being homosexual). A boy must not merely be masculine, but heterosexually so. Thus to guard his own masculine identity is to denigrate other gender identities to at least some extent. Where a girl has some latitude in desiring and displaying masculinity, a boy has none in the opposite direction.

A significant complicating factor for boys is the role *homophobia* plays in the construction of a masculinity based on heterosexuality. The irrational character of this process is summarized by health researcher David Plummer's remark: "Prior to consolidating adult sexual identity, homophobic rhetoric is used frequently and with meaning, even when there is little or no concept of what a homosexual is and a definitive target in the peer group is lacking."[681] The character of homophobia, says Plummer, is different in childhood than in adulthood. Instead of zeroing on rigid sexual identities, it focuses on the appearances and behaviors that are unpopular and transgress a boy's peer group expectations—a process that potentially makes any boy a target.[682]

If nothing else, the constant implicit recognition that at any time one might become labeled as a member of a stigmatized group fosters an inordinate, hyper-attentiveness to any cues signaling the danger of such a judgment. There is relative safety in the harbor of vocal homophobia. If a boy visibly demonstrates he is against homosexuals—whatever that means—he safeguards against the possibility of being labeled one. The other course, steering shy of feminine company and behavioral displays (e.g., crying), is also necessary, but more hazardous. No boy can so completely avoid the feminine as to protect against homophobia unless he strongly practices homophobia.[683]

David Plummer's study of the role homophobia plays in the construction of a Western sense of masculinity provides evidence of how crossdressing is linked to homosexuality; to cross the gender line in dress is correlated with also crossing out of heterosexuality.[684] Just as the construction of masculinity in our culture depends in part on homophobia, it may depend also on transphobia; both homosexuality and crossdressing challenge stereotyped notions of masculinity and, by inference, maleness.[685]

Masculine Privilege

Throughout our dialog we have noted how gender in our society is vertical rather than horizontal in arrangement. In a *gender hierarchy* the genders are not equal. The gender hierarchy in Western culture clearly has favored masculinity. The result of this favored position is conveniently summarized as *masculine privilege*. This privilege means the masculine gender enjoys greater status and wields more power than any other.

But it has not gone unchallenged. Feminist challenges have elicited a wide range of responses from men, including very defensive ones. Masculine privilege in the face of pressure from a more expansive, 'liberated' femininity has responded in the mainstream with even greater rigidity that often traps males into narrow and static expectations in many areas, including dress.[686] The fewer avenues offered for men for experience and expression of gender carries consequences, such as in the often remarked upon emotional constriction seen in men.[687] Though masculine privilege continues, its cost seems greater than ever.

We may glance a moment at one visible sign of the pressure men face to preserve a distinct masculinity. For men, safeguarding masculine privilege generates the 'Golden Rule' of dress, that men must at all costs not appear feminine. This simple rule stands at an intersection of identity, social roles, and sexuality. For example, if women are viewed as wantonly sexual beings (or objects), then men's own sexuality must be either downplayed or depicted in strikingly different ways. The latter course results in masculine dress fashions like the codpiece, which emphasize virility through attention to the genitals. Less crudely but no less effectively the modern business suit symbolizes virility by signifying competence, success, and status. The wearer is publicly declared as someone with resources—the very thing available females are likely to desire. At the same time, while demonstrating virility such dress presents a restrained and orderly sexuality. Unlike the wildness of women, men are portrayed as procreative producers for whom all good things must come as an order of course. Men can possess women because they first have possessed their own virile sexuality. However men define their masculinity, it must be *apparent*—and that is why dress anchors appearance. Other behaviors then complete a gender ensemble that declares a man's masculinity.

Many of us are bothered by the gender divide and gender stratification. We see how a gender hierarchy inherently disadvantages girls and women—and harms everyone. Boys and men also are trapped within their gender status and because of masculine privilege find themselves confined within narrow but weighty expectations. Ways of easing the pressure may be sought through minimizing or eliminating the gender divide. Or, if the gender divide is preserved, perhaps a 'new masculinity' might be made—an improved version of man.

Some among us believe this is exactly what has transpired in recent decades. Chastened by the criticism of women, many men have sought to shed the old masculinity constrained by egregious stereotypical traits like dominance and toughness to embrace a kinder, gentler version of manhood. Psychologist Herb Goldberg is one man who thinks real progress has been made in this regard. In the late 1980s he argued that the new masculinity "is a movement away from the defensive, rigid, insatiable conditioning that perhaps was once functional for men but now only serves to press them relentlessly into narrow, rigid patterns of behavior that produce their psychological or inner death in the service of a pursuit of an externalized fulfillment and satisfaction that can *never* happen."[688]

Indeed, from the 1970s on any number of examples might be advanced to argue that men are reclaiming masculinity. But, like women, they do not all agree on what masculinity should look like. Despite the wide variance in individual beliefs and practices, some collective action has seemed cohesive enough and sustained long enough to give rise to the sense of a men's movement.

The Men's Movement

However it is appraised, the masculine responses to feminism and to the Women's Movement resulted in a number of broad enough events to warrant being dubbed 'the Men's Movement.' The Men's Movement, like the Women's Movement, was not a uniform or unified one. Unlike the Women's Movement, no aspect of the Men's Movement to date appears to have prompted the same kind of large scale attention or significant changes that can be said to have altered our social landscape.[689]

History of the Men's Movement

At least three major branches of the Men's Movement can be traced. Each enjoyed at least a moment in the sun before being relatively eclipsed in the public consciousness by another branch. In chronological order of their prominence, the three branches are:

- ❑ *The pro-feminist men's movement*—a largely uncoordinated movement of men sympathetic to at least some of the criticisms and claims being made by second wave feminists.
- ❑ *The 'mythopoetic' men's movement*—another generally uncoordinated movement embracing a variety of forms, though associated in the public's mind most with Robert Bly.
- ❑ *The religious men's movement*—a coordinated, organized effort to bring men together based on certain religious values.

These branches gained notable public attention in the successive decades of the 1970s, 1980s, and 1990s.

The first branch—*the pro-feminist men's movement*—came to prominence during the heyday of second wave feminism, in the 1970s. This aspect of the Men's Movement is also known as *Men's Liberation*. It displayed in different forms. On the one hand, there were the 'consciousness-raising' men's groups that appeared in the 1970s and acknowledged the effects on their members of masculine privilege, including their potential to be oppressors of women. On the other hand, there were activist groups that took their support of feminist ideas further. For instance, in 1973 the Berkeley Men's Center issued a manifesto in which they declared:

> We no longer want to strain and compete to live up to an impossible oppressive masculine image—strong, silent, cool, handsome, unemotional, successful, master of women, leader of men, wealthy, brilliant, athletic, and 'heavy.' We no longer want to feel the need to perform sexually, socially, or in any way live up to an imposed male role, from a traditional American society or a 'counterculture.'[690]

This wing of the men's movement also had its counterpart in academia with the development of Men's Studies.

Men's Liberation peaked in the mid-1970s. Perhaps the most salient moment came in 1974 when government and legal scholar Warren Farrell, now prominent for more than three decades in both women's and men's organizations, published *The Liberated Man*. This work presents a pro-feminist treatise acknowledging the costs accrued by both men and women by the demands of existing sex/gender roles. In his book's three parts he sought to define and move beyond the existing sense of masculinity, adopt women's liberation as men's liberation, and promote both men's consciousness-raising and joint consciousness-raising.[691] In the decades since, Farrell has continued to write popular books on gender issues, focusing on men's issues.[692]

As for Men's Liberation itself, it persists in a rather limited fashion. Gender scholar Chris Beasley observes that a small 'network' of pro-feminist men's organizations and groups still exist. But he is right in characterizing this aspect of the Men's Movement as always more psychological than political in nature. The men involved here principally offer support and consciousness-raising rather than direct political action or sweeping social change programs. Beasley also points out that these men maintain some contact with other aspects of the Men's Movement,[693] to which we now must turn.

A rather different branch of the Men's Movement—*the 'Mythopoetic' Men's Movement*—also originated in the mid-1970s, but really took flight only in the late 1980s and early 1990s. This wing, writes historian Bruce Shulman, "by far the biggest and most important, . . . was the mythopoetic men's movement—the motley assemblage of drum-beating retreats, New Age-style group therapy, men's health magazines and cosmetics, poetry readings, and celebrations of primal masculinity."[694] Its singular soul and inspirational leader was the poet Robert Bly. He wrote books[695] and organized events championing a masculine sensibility that rejected both the macho image of men like John Wayne and the 'sensitive' man image becoming popular in figures like Robert Alda. Instead, Bly and others in this wing appealed to the masculine figures of myth, men like King Arthur. Bly's best known work, *Iron John*, is constructed around one such figure, drawn from the Grimm Brothers' fairy tale of the same name. The book—and the Men's Movement—received a boost from his 1990 appearance on a television special hosted by Bill Moyers.[696]

A final wing of the Men's Movement—*the Religious Men's Movement*—was later in developing but has become probably the largest in number of participants. Its most notable manifestation, the 'Promise Keepers', burst into the national consciousness of Americans in the 1990s. Born in the Spring of 1990, the new organization was co-founded by college football coach Bill McCartney and Dave Wardell, a leader with the organization Fellowship of Christian Athletes (FCA). This conservative, largely evangelical movement, centered itself in the theme of discipling Christian men. Among the 'seven promises' made by Promise Keepers is a commitment to "building strong marriages and families through love, protection and biblical values."[697] Their concern to return to a biblical model of gender relations is interpreted as meaning re-establishing the man's authority as the head of his wife and family.

The National Organization of Women opposes the Promise Keepers. To them, this organization looks like one more wing of patriarchy. They point to remarks by Promise Keepers like Tony Evans, who declared, "The demise of our community and culture is the fault of sissified men who have been overly influenced by women." Or, this from cofounder Bill McCartney: "You do know, don't you, that we're raising our children at a time when it's an effeminate society. It's not the proper climate."[698] Beasley seems accurate in characterizing Promise Keepers as promoting a reassertion of the old masculinity where masculine privilege meant an unquestioned primacy of men in the family and the community.[699]

A Muslim counterpart to the Christian movement is Louis Farrakhan's led Nation of Islam. The organization itself stretches back to the first third of the 20th century, but has been reinvigorated by Minister Farrakhan's often controversial leadership. With respect to the Men's Movement, while the Nation of

Islam addresses both men and women, a special place is held for men. This was most dramatically visible in the 'Million Man March' in 1995, which brought a new level of awareness to this movement. To the gathered throng Minister Farrakhan proclaimed, "We must accept the responsibility that God has put upon us, not only to be good husbands and fathers and builders of our community, but God is now calling upon the despised and the rejected to become the cornerstone and the builders of a new world."[700] One consequence of the success of this event was a significant boost in voter enrollment among African-Americans.

All aspects of the Men's Movement share in common a recognition of the need to strengthen masculinity in some respect. As we noted earlier, the cogent challenge mounted by feminists prompted reappraisal. Yet after several decades, many men find themselves thinking that women have gained far more while men are increasingly losing power—and self-identity. Thus masculinity continues in a relative state of flux. The uncertainty and creative tension can be glimpsed at home and in the workplace—arenas we have discussed at various points in our ongoing dialog. But we need look no further than contemporary trends in dress (an aspect of Connell's fourth gender relation, the symbolic structure) to see it played out before our eyes in increasingly public ways.

Men Responding to the Success of Women

Women once used changes in dress behavior to challenge inadequate social conventions; some men are doing so now. Women capitalized on the status men enjoyed by copying their dress and thus borrowing some of the privilege and power associated with the wearers of masculine apparel. Some men are re-acting to the success and perceived power of contemporary women by utilizing a similar strategy. In the past, some women in appropriating elements of dress considered masculine lived with the charge of crossdressing; others denied it, claiming their dress was appropriate to their gender despite the wider public perception. Today some men—regardless of their motivation for dressing as they do—are likewise living with the charge of crossdressing, while others are vigorously denying it and contending their apparel is appropriately masculine regardless of what many might believe. Are we seeing a historical parallel?

Today's masculinity—much like yesterday's femininity—certainly appears to be heavily stereotypically framed, both in how it is construed in terms of personality traits and in regard to appearance traits.[701] Masculine privilege in the face of pressure from a more expansive, 'liberated' femininity has responded in the mainstream with even greater rigidity that often traps males into narrow and static expectations in many areas, including dress.[702] The fewer avenues offered for males for experience and expression may carry consequences in the often remarked upon emotional constriction seen in men.[703]

Not all men acquiesce. The so-called *metrosexual phenomenon* represents an interesting, one-step-removed-from-the-mainstream, response. But though it tests the narrow limits of conventional masculine appearance, metrosexual fashion remains identifiably masculine, though leaning away from stereotypical masculinity. Inspired by the influence of gay men, metrosexual dress attempts to find middle ground between the social sensibilities of homosexuals and the homophobia integral to conventional masculinity. Or, as it was put in *Advertising & Society Review*, "what used to be referred to as the gay sensibility has kind of diffused into a more mainstream masculinity."[704]

In this light, another, more radical manifestation of rebellion against the tyranny of masculine demands may be *crossdressing*. Apart from any gender relief it may provide—what some dismissively label a 'retreat into femininity'—male crossdressing may less pejoratively be conceived as a legitimate desire to increase opportunities for self-experience and expression through dress. In so doing they are following a path first forged, with great success, by women.[705] The fashion industry periodically attempts to inject unbifurcated apparel like skirts and dress for men, but to date the men who appear in public so dressed still tend to be those whose social status (i.e., the rich and powerful), or social identity (e.g., entertainers) allow them to flaunt conventionality.[706]

Why are women today more often seen as 'winning' the gender wars? All our evidence to this point suggests that simply isn't so. We need to now give this other conforming gender our attention. We need to grapple with femininity.

Femininity: Construct & Construction

To men, women have always been the great mystery. "What do women want?" has been the cry of many men, including pioneers in gender theorizing like Sigmund Freud (see chapter 7). Yet men were instrumental in early theories of gender, including ideas about what femininity is and how it develops in the individual. Moreover, the mystery of womanhood may be no less profound for women, as a remark at the end of a paper by renowned psychoanalyst Clara Thompson attests: "The basic nature of woman is still unknown."[707] However true that may be, we are not excused from investigating the matter. Our course shall be to offer a parallel treatment to what we just did with masculinity. That means looking first at the femininity construct, then investigating how femininity is constructed.

The Femininity Construct

Masculinity, we heard earlier, is stereotyped to mean 'agency,' individual competence with a degree of rationality capable of imposing order on chaos, of seeing clearly where things appear murky, and of narrowing a bewildering array of possibilities to the one best choice that furthers power and progress. Masculinity, in sum, is about control—of feelings, thoughts and behavior; of the personal and the social. To be a masculine male is to be in control, a situation dependent on being in position above and in front of others. So masculinity becomes about competition and strength—of mind and body, and most of all of a will that suppresses the seductive undertow of emotion that can undermine all a man's labor.

216

"Women's corresponding socially-ascribed image," write Joanna Brewis, Mark Hampton, and Stephen Linstead, "is of being comfortable in disturbing the masculine sense of certainty, raising questions, and opening things up."[708] *Femininity is culturally constructed as antithesis to masculinity.* Where masculinity must be narrow, femininity can be broad; masculinity follows an ordered course, femininity can be spontaneous and flexible; masculinity champions competition, femininity embraces nurturing cooperation. Girls and women do not have to chain creativity to the service of production. They are free to express emotions rather than constrict them.

But what has just been said sounds more positive than many descriptions of femininity. Remember, we prize masculinity to a degree where stereotypical masculine traits become identified as the 'most' human or the 'best' a person can be. Consider, instead, the following picture of women—one much more common as a depiction of stereotypes:

> Women are thought to be followers rather than leaders. Women are thought to be more sympathetic, sensitive, compassionate, and concerned about others. They are portrayed as more inclined toward artistic and aesthetic activities. They are assumed to be less inclined toward mathematics, science, and even intellectuality. Women are often thought to be more moral, more religious, or, in some cultures, "purer" than men.[709]

Yes, these statements are all generalizations—the very stuff of stereotypes. That is precisely the point. Masculinity and femininity are both idealized constructs that few, if any, real individuals ever realize fully. Yet many of us, much of the time, aspire to the ideal, judge ourselves and others by the stereotypes as though they constitute a natural law, and suffer the consequences for our failures to be perfectly masculine or feminine. If these pressures from one vantage point seem less severe for femininity, they are no less real or potent. Moreover, regardless of the pressures exerted by the stereotype of femininity, the multitude of other pressures attending a subordinate position in the gender hierarchy make the lot of femininity in many ways more stressful than what boys and men face. Masculine privilege protects them from what girls and women face daily, a systemic inequality in status and power that plays itself out in myriad ways.

Clara Thompson—A Psychoanalytic Perspective on Women

So much for the first level of analysis, that of stereotypes. Let us proceed to the second level, that of theory. Even as the medicalization of sex contributed stimulus to rethinking gender, psychoanalysis—born about the same time—offered a new beginning to a consideration of femininity. In our discussions so far we have heard from psychoanalytic thinkers, notably Sigmund Freud and Nancy Chodorow. Given this theoretical tradition's rich contributions to the gender conversation, we owe it more time to hear from another noted woman psychoanalyst on the construct of femininity. Clara Thompson, an American, was a leading voice in psychoanalysis for decades. Though she died in 1958, we may be surprised to hear how contemporaneous some of her words remain.

As a psychodynamic thinker, Thompson acknowledges a debt to Freud, of whom she says there is no one who has as yet presented anything comparable in detail or specificity, and whose work has stimulated most of the significant things said about femininity even if said in contradiction to his thought. Indeed, she herself is not hesitant to say that although she believes many of his observations to be empirically correct, she thinks it a basic fallacy to regard a woman as essentially a castrated male.[710]

Similarly, she rejects Freud's understanding of penis envy. "In brief," she says, "it has been shown that cultural factors can explain the tendency of women to feel inferior about their sex and their consequent tendency to envy men. . . ."[711] She observes that envy is one characteristic of a competitive culture—and women and men are in a competition of the nature of a minority group to a dominant one. It isn't neurotic, Thompson contends, to find a real basis for envy in woman when a patriarchal society has restricted her opportunities, and limited her development and independence. Women internalize this.[712]

Gender segregation is a fact of life for women. Thompson points out that, "in some form, the greater proportion of a woman's waking life is spent with her own sex." Indeed, even when the genders are together, the conversation is apt to be separate: the men talk business or politics, the women talk about children and domestic matters. Unlike men, though, women find it easier to offer open demonstrations of affection to members of their own gender group. Still, she notes this ability becoming more restricted even among women, especially in 'sophisticated' groups.[713]

Consistent with many contemporary analyses, Thompson finds a woman's involvement, or lack thereof, in the labor force to be a major factor in her self-appraisal. During the early 1940s, as the nation went to war, new opportunities for women expanded in that regard. Thompson recognizes that women in the United States enjoy a unique situation, freer to live their lives than is true for women in any other patriarchal country in the world. But she does not think that they have ceased to be an underprivileged group because they remain discriminated against in many situations without regard for their needs or ability.[714]

"Our problem with women today," she explains, "is not simply that they are caught in a patriarchal culture, but that they are living in a culture in which the positive gains for them are failing." To understand this requires a historical context. Women, she reminds us, had for centuries been viewed as the property of a particular man. As long as the compensations for her status were adequate—a full emotional life around husband and children, economic security, and a chance to express her capacities in managing a home—for so long could she adjust herself and be relatively content, even if she was also relatively enslaved. But a changing world had brought a devaluing of things a traditional housewife could find definition in. The traditional role for a woman was being progressively narrowed and so also opportunities for development within it.

"Increasingly," Thompson concludes, "the woman finds herself without an occupation and with an unsatisfactory emotional life."[715]

What is a woman to do? Thompson suggests there are three types of reaction to the situation just described. First, a woman may marry and try to live according to the old pattern. These women are unemployed and often discontented. Second, they may choose work and remain unmarried. Some of them make work central in their lives and achieve "economic freedom without emotional freedom." Others in this group combine love and work, but remain single and prioritize work. The third type of response is found in the group of women who, in modern terms, try to have it all—marriage, family, and career. The success of this path may hinge on how the marriage handles her involvement in the work force. And that is complicated by the reality that her work will likely be for lower pay even if the responsibilities are the equal of a man's.[716]

Thompson rejects the conclusion that a woman's situation is inevitable because of her biology. She acknowledges that the problems a woman faces are different from those of a man, and that reproductive biology plays a part. But she is insistent that the cultural attitude toward women is *not* driven by biological necessity. She is particularly unhappy with Freud's suggestion that a woman embraces her ability to reproduce as a compensation for her lack of a penis. "Surely," she wryly comments, "only a man could have thought of it in terms of compensation or consolation."[717]

Yet the long-accepted idea that a woman's inferior position in society is due to a biologic fact poses a problem for women because this notion has been a part of their life training. Moreover, men are resistant to giving up the idea because it obviously advantages them. Not only enculturation of this idea, but the fact of her economic dependence on man has hindered women. Accompanying these matters are other fundamental matters, such as perpetuating the belief that the woman is sexually passive and masochistic, limiting her opportunities for intellectual development, and discouraging her personal initiative. Out of this situation, concludes Thompson, come several personality traits supposed to be typical of femininity: greater narcissism, a greater need to be loved, greater rigidity of personality, weaker superegos, passivity, and masochism.[718]

A more realistic appraisal, though, she argues to be the cultural pressures on women. Despite economic gains many women remain relatively dependent on men. She remains more restricted than a man in what is allowed her in the way of pursuing romantic and sexual relationships. The charge that her conscience and convictions are less than a man's, to the extent that it is true at all, has mostly to do with living in a culture where her security depends on winning the approval of those who hold power—men. And for the idea that a woman's personality is more rigid, Thompson can find no evidence save for the connection of it to the idea that a woman must marry while she has the bloom of youth or her opportunity for success in life is lost—all of which point only to the truth that a woman who lacks opportunity and is forced into economic dependency may very well develop a narrowed outlook on life and corresponding rigidity. In sum, accepting the feminine role—embracing the femininity of the culture she finds herself in—"may not be an affirmative attitude at all but an expression of submission and resignation."[719]

Thompson recognizes that a woman's refusal to be feminine as her culture prescribes may be an effort to assert her *independence as a person*. She points to the reality that women have not enjoyed a long-established tradition of independence. She is, in fact, educated in two directions at once: to succeed in the way a man does (the world of work), and to succeed in ways men rarely consider (the world of family relationships). She must be a woman, but to succeed as a person she must be like a man, without being too much like one. In this historically new context, woman has not yet found her place in the social order. No wonder, then, "she is in conflict as to what and who she is." Thus the remark we heard earlier: the basic nature of woman remains unknown.[720]

Remember, all these things Thompson spoke about *before* the Women's Liberation Movement of the 1960s. We might give ourselves pause, though, to wonder how substantially things have changed for women. From an historical standpoint, not much time has accrued for women to incorporate a rich sense of gender apart from a traditional subordination. The struggle goes on not only in society, but also in every woman's individual life.

The Construction of Femininity

Perhaps the first thing we should note in speaking about the construction of femininity in the individual is the shaping of a *subordinated gender*. This can hardly be overstated and constitutes the most likely reason so many women have a reluctance to embrace the term 'feminine.' Femininity, as a symbol, stands for that which is weak or which must be restrained and controlled because of its wanton emotionality. If woman is 'the Other,' her entire gender identity and accompanying role must be construed in terms of relationship to 'the Subject'—man in his masculinity—to whom her relation is subordinate. In essence, then, we can think of femininity, as historically passed on from one generation of girls to the next, as conditioned by *dependent relationship to men.*

For a considerable time in Western culture females were not merely seen as subordinate to males, but as 'belonging' to them. Daughters 'belonged' to their fathers, were 'given' in marriage, and became thereby the sole property of their husbands. Keeping girls sheltered from sexual experience prior to marriage safeguarded their value to a future husband—and a girl only became a woman when she entered into the role of wife. Despite the fact that such ideas persist in various guises, movements like feminism have sharply challenged this construction and brought about serious erosion to it.

Still, the more things change the more they remain the same. Despite the fact some of the crasser manifestations of gender inequality have been curbed, similar dynamics apparently remain:

> Today, male-female relationships are more likely to involve a different economic arrangement, one in which the male protects and supports the female in return for exclusive sexual rights and domestic

obligations. Unrestricted female sexual independence would destroy this traditional bargain and all the institutions that it fosters. Thus a fundamental change in gender relationships would ensue, involving a diminution of the power traditionally exercised by males. Support for traditional sexual morality, then, operates to support traditional gender roles.[721]

We are living in a time when change in this arrangement continues. Men and women with their different agendas are engaged in a contest where more than reproductive strategy is in play. Those who have held power—mostly white heterosexual males—are often reluctant to share it, let alone relinquish it. Women dissatisfied with the preexisting arrangement, because it is unfavorable to them in ways that often produce violence alongside deprivation, continue to seek greater equalization of power. The resulting stress fuzzes the gender line used to keep one group above another, and that blurring of the line not only makes it less clear, but also renders it more permeable.

A highly visible way of confronting the status quo by blurring the gender lines has long been by changing the manner of one's dress. When feminists adopted, then adapted masculine styles of dress they expressed a claim on masculine prerogatives held by males. The early feminists paid a price, enduring alienation, censure, and victimization. They were branded transgressors in dress—'crossdressers'—and 'mentally disordered' for upsetting what many believed was the natural and ordained order of male/masculine over female/feminine. Clothes were an important part of the battle because of their position in the expressive and experiencing system we rely on so heavily. Opponents certainly understood this and the battle over dress rules at school, in the workplace, and in other public arenas still persists.[722]

Obviously, though, gender inequality has proven stubbornly resistant to substantive and enduring change. A mere change of dress has never been enough—a reason early feminists shifted attention away from challenging society's dress rules to obtaining the right to vote. At the personal level, in individual experience and family relations, constructing femininity as something more than 'Other' also remains challenging. Even the most well-intentioned of women find it difficult to escape society's gender pressures, whether in their own life experience, or in how they parent. For example, with regard to the latter, psychologists Susan Gelman, Marianne Taylor, and Simone Nguyen found that even with mothers who express egalitarian gender beliefs, their actual conversations with their children are filled with essentialist content endorsing gender stereotypes.[723]

Despite the difficulties—or better, because of them—many of us work unceasingly to change this culture with its ideals and practices perpetuating inequalities in gender and otherwise. Those of us who do so place ourselves in ah historical stream that often is characterized as producing significant waves of movement. The construction of femininity is, in part, conducted in conjunction with changes fought for, and incompletely accomplished by feminists and the Women's Movement.

The Women's Movement & Feminism

Without doubt, at this historical moment, it is clear that the Women's Movement and feminism have had both a broader and deeper impact than the Men's Movement can claim. Though it often happens that these two things—feminism and the Women's Movement—are treated as though they are one, they are not. The former, exactly as the name suggests, is a collective action sweeping across social scenes and interested in political and other social changes. The latter shares similar interests but has come in its broadest sense to refer to anyone—man, woman or otherwise—who believes, on the one hand, that woman have been and are subjugated to a subordinate social status because of their sex and/or gender, and, on the other hand, finds this objectionable and needing change.[724]

The Women's Movement

Historically, the Women's Movement surfaced in the United States in the mid-19th century. During July 19-20, 1848, in Seneca, New York, a women's rights convention gathered some 300 women and men (of whom there were at least 40) together. Among the most well-known of the attendees were Elizabeth Cady Stanton, Lucretia Mott, and Frederick Douglas. At this convention a Declaration of Sentiments and a Declaration of Resolutions, based on the Declaration of Independence were signed by 68 women and 32 men. The centerpiece of this effort was the proposal to permit women to vote.[725]

Other features associated with the early Women's Movement, like the right of women to control their own property and the right to obtain custody of their children in the event of divorce, receive less attention in light of the long struggle to gain the franchise to vote. That finally happened with suffrage in the 1920s.

The Women's Liberation Movement of the 1960s-70s offers the most dramatic example of the Women's Movement to date. An early event of significance was President Kennedy's establishment, in 1961, of the Commission on the Status of Women (PCSW). Significant changes were occurring in American society, and some of these were being felt in legislation passed at the Federal level. In 1963, the PCSW published recommendations for equal opportunity in employment. The next year, Title VII of the Civil Rights Act made it illegal to discriminate against women in hiring and promotion practices. The Equal Employment Opportunity Commission (EEOC) was established in 1965 to enforce the law. However, in September of that year, by a 3-2 vote among its commissioners, the EEOC decided to permit sex-segregated job advertising—a signal to many that the commission was unwilling to fulfill its charter. Resulting frustration over the government's lack of effort was palpable at the Third National Conference of Commissions on the Status of Women, held at the end of June, 1966. Writer Betty Friedan, author of the best-selling *The Feminine Mystique* (1963), was among the attendees at the conference and wrote the acronym

NOW on a napkin as participants considered alternative strategies. The basic shape of a plan soon took shape and prompted the formal founding of the National Organization of Women (NOW). The Statement of Purpose read, in part, "The purpose of NOW is to take action to bring women into full participation in the mainstream of American society now, exercising all the privileges and responsibilities thereof in truly equal partnership with men." NOW is presently the largest organization of feminist activists in the United States. [726]

NOW was not alone. Other formal organizations such as the Federally Employed Women (FEW), in 1968, and the National Woman's Political Caucus (NWPC), in 1971, were taking shape, too. So were grass roots efforts in various cities. Political scientist Jo Freeman, in a well-known account of the movement published in 1971, relates that initially there was little ideology in the movement; there was plenty of strong feeling though.[727] That feeling suffuses some of the documents of the time—and elicited some of the strong responses, both for and against the movement.

The strong voice found by participants of the Women's Liberation Movement is exemplified by the words of Robin Morgan, who wrote in 1970, "It seems obvious that a genuine revolution must be led by, *made* by those who have been most oppressed: black, brown, and white *women*—with men relating to that the best they can." But masculine relating, in her estimation, did *not* include parallel 'men's liberation groups.' Morgan railed against the 'great lie' that men also are oppressed by sexism. She pointed out that oppression is what the members of one group to do members of another group because of some characteristic the latter group shares that is seen as 'threatening.' She punctuated her argument with the strongest language possible: "The oppressors are indeed *fucked up* by being masters (racism hurts whites, sexual stereotypes are harmful to men) but those masters are not *oppressed*."[728]

Coincident with the rise of second wave feminism, the Women's Movement was visible and effective. Involvement by women in politics increased and women over the next few decades made some progress in attaining positions previously reserved for men only (e.g., Supreme Court; Secretary of State). As sociologists William Kornblum and Joseph Julian note, effects can be seen also in changes in social attitudes. They recount how about 75% of Americans in the 1930s frowned on women working if there was a man to provide for them; by the time the second wave of feminism's full force had been felt, the end of the 1970s, only about a quarter of Americans still had this attitude (and the percentage has continued to decline). Similarly, in the Eisenhower administration of the later 1950s, some 80% of Americans agreed that any woman who voluntarily remained unmarried "must be 'sick,' 'neurotic,' or 'immoral.'"[729] While many of us believe the task of liberating women is unfinished, the real gains of the Women's Movement should not be gainsaid.

Feminism

It is impossible to speak of the Women's Movement without talking about feminists. 'Feminism' is, in the words of Roger Lancaster and Micaela Di Leanardo, "the critical examination of gender relations from the position of protest against women's unequal status."[730] The history of feminism is punctuated by highs and lows of activity by groups of people united in the pursuit of feminist ideas. "The apparent rise and fall of feminism over time," write Jane Pilcher and Imelda Whelehan, "has led to the 'wave' analogy; the peaks and troughs of the feminist movement are characterized as following the motion of tidal water, with its ongoing cycle of gradual swelling, eventual cresting and final subsiding."[731] To this point, three such 'waves' have been identified.

First Wave Feminism

Political scientist Vicky Randall observes that individual women have throughout history advanced what we can identify as 'feminist' ideas. However, she points out, an actual substantial *movement*, one embodying scores of people, did not appear on the scene until the mid-19th century. Randall locates the impetus in the American antislavery movement of the 1830s as women "drew inferences for their own situation."[732]

The so-called 'first wave of feminism' is variously dated in its origin to the late 18th century (Mary Wollstonecraft's *A Vindication of the Rights of Women* in 1792), or the mid-19th century (the 1848 Women's Rights Convention in Seneca, New York), or later (e.g., the late 19th century).[733] The first wave was preoccupied with efforts to secure basic rights such as the right to vote, to enter the work force, and to own property after becoming married. This push for political and social equality had run its course by the end of the first third of the 20th century.[734]

Second Wave Feminism

The 'second wave' of feminism emerged in the late 1960s-early 1970s. It had pretty much run its course by the end of the 1980s. In an earlier discussion (chapter 2) we covered the pivotal role played by second wave feminists in reinvigorating the conversation on gender. Second wave feminists might hold either an essentialist position or, more commonly, a social constructionist one. Either way they were committed to redressing the social inequalities women experienced. As we have seen, they not only emboldened and supported women, they challenged and chastised men. The resulting effects continue to be felt today.

Third Wave Feminism

'Third wave feminism' began in the mid-1990s, in part as a critique of the second wave. Some feminists worried over lost momentum, others proposed a re-invention of feminism, and some women suggested that the term 'post-feminism' be adopted as recognition that the era of feminism had passed.[735] In their setting out a 'third wave agenda,' feminists Leslie Haywood and Jennifer Drake write that many of them, like themselves, "grew up with equity feminism, got gender feminism in college, along with poststructuralism, and are now hard at work on a feminism that strategically combines elements of these feminisms, along with black feminism, women-of-color feminism, working-class feminism, pro-sex feminism, and so on."[736]

While third wave feminism is still recent enough to defy the kind of analysis afforded by time to previous waves, Julia Wood believes it possible to identify four features characteristic of the wave, as well as a fifth feature embraced by some third wave feminists:

- ❑ They remake feminist solidarity so as to incorporate differences among women.
- ❑ They are committed to alliances with other groups, including men, who share their opposition to various kinds of oppression.
- ❑ They seek to build on previous theoretical and structural gains by integrating these into everyday life.
- ❑ They practice personal politics, believing power displays itself and can be resisted in concrete, local situations and in particular moments.
- ❑ Some also feel free to embrace aspects of traditional 'girl culture,' such as found in popular culture.[737]

We remain too close historically to third wave feminism to know how it will end standing in relation to previous waves.

Women's Studies

One consequence of second wave feminism, which helped prepare the ground for the next wave, was the birth of *Women's Studies*—the formal incorporation into academia of the study of women as a subject in its own right. Deborah Felder's chronicle, *A Century of Women*, explains the mechanism of change. "Women's Studies courses first appeared in the last half of the 1960s," Felder observes, "when women faculty, who had entered the professorate in greater numbers than ever before, began to create new courses to redress this imbalance."[738] The first Women's Studies Program was inaugurated in the Fall term of 1970 at San Diego State College. The West Coast led the charge; other early programs were at Portland State University in Oregon, the University of Washington, and at another California institution, Sacramento State University. By 1974, Felder records, nearly 40 such programs could be found, and by the end of the decade that number had expanded more than tenfold.[739] By the end of the 20th century the Women's Studies movement had become a global phenomenon, with manifestations in North America, Europe, Australia, Asia, and the Middle East.[740]

Conclusion

Of the conforming genders two facts emerge as perhaps of particular salience. First, femininity, though not as popular a term perhaps as it once was, labels a gender whose members have made such remarkable strides that some men believe we now live in a woman's world. Second, we still live in a man's world. Despite all the change that we might point to in favor of progress for women in reaching social equality, the gender hierarchy remains intact and men remain in the superior position. The conflict between masculinity and femininity seems unabated. Moreover, both conforming genders are now facing unprecedented pressure from the nonconforming genders, to which we must next turn.

Chapter 11

Nonconforming Genders

Introduction: Not all of us find conformity to our assigned gender possible. Though a variety of reasons have been hypothesized for this reality, we will do well first to simply acknowledge this *is* a reality. Those who are unable or unwilling to enact masculinity or femininity in socially prescribed ways are *gender nonconformists* with respect to our culture's gender system. On the other hand, the gender they experience, which they may or may not actually display, might be termed a *nonconforming gender*. This label does not mean this gender is any less real or salient than culturally accepted femininity or masculinity. It simply means that the gender does not fit within socially expected or generally accepted gender notions. The cultural gender scheme has trouble with gender nonconformity and in two gender societies like our own reinterprets variant, atypical, nonconforming genders as *deviations* of the expected, accepted, conforming genders.

If we are to discuss nonconforming genders we need appropriate vocabulary. Unfortunately, that is harder to come by because our culture is so resistant to other gender possibilities. One logical candidate is *androgyny*. After all, the word has a long history and in recent decades has been proposed as a way to challenge the rigidity of the gender binary scheme. However, the way in which this has developed has produced a concept dependent on the binary scheme. The end result is that we may speak of an androgynous woman or an androgynous man, but we don't speak of *androgynes*—distinct members of a separate gender group.

Another possibility is to refer to people as *transgender*. Such individuals are gender nonconformists, but do they belong to a nonconforming gender? Those people who self-identify as transgender are unlikely to think so. Like everyone else in this culture, transgender folk have been raised to think in binary sex and gender terms. They generally regard themselves as affiliating with a conforming gender—just not the one they were assigned to. So, like androgyny, transgender is limited by its being defined in terms of the conforming genders.

One other possibility is to speak of a *'third gender.'* The label itself seeks to step outside the two-and-only-two gender paradigm. Some cultures acknowledge a third gender—or more. Ours does not. Yet even so, there are persons in our culture who self-identify as 'third gender.' Such individuals truly belong to a nonconforming gender.

Gender Nonconformity & Nonconforming Genders

By now we should be quite clear on what we mean by 'conforming genders' and 'nonconforming genders.' *Conforming genders* fit the expected and accepted gender categories in a society. Ours is a binary gender system so only masculinity and femininity are conforming genders. *Nonconforming genders* do not meet a culture's expectations for gender reality and are so not accepted but are redefined in terms of the conforming genders. Thus, in a certain sense, we have to say that nonconforming genders do not exist! They are denied, not only legitimacy, but also even real existence. Instead, they are recast as deviations from the norm. In our society this means anything expressed by gender nonconformists is interpreted as deviance with respect to their 'real' gender—the conforming gender to which they were assigned at birth.

So now we must reckon with two notions. On the one hand, we can speculate that there really are no nonconforming genders, just *gender nonconformists*—people who, for whatever perverse reason, have deviated from their expected and acceptable gender path. Their nonconformity often isn't even in terms of distorting masculinity or femininity, but with adopting the wrong one. In other words, someone assigned to be a man who identifies as feminine may very expertly display stereotypical feminine traits and appear as a woman. But this individual is still viewed as a gender nonconformist because a violation has occurred of the sex-gender pairing normative in our culture. Born with an apparently male body, such a person must forever be 'he' and assume masculinity. In this sense, there can't be any nonconforming genders, just gender nonconformists.

On the other hand, we can speculate there may be other genders. They are by definition nonconforming if no place is made for them in the social gender system. In fact, they may be forthrightly despised, barely tolerated, regarded indifferently, or warmly embraced—but they are at least tacitly recognized as actually existing. Of course, the mere denial of the possibility that other genders than masculinity and femininity exist does not mean the case is closed. What it does mean is that such genders are excluded from the conversation in such a way that their conforming members are doomed to be seen as gender nonconformists to the prevailing gender scheme. The irony might be delicious if the price paid was not so high. *One can be a conforming member of a nonconforming gender, but so long as that gender's existence is denied its members can only be regarded as gender nonconformists.* In our society that means being marginalized, or worse.

In this discussion we are going to attempt talking about what our society makes very difficult to speak about—nonconforming genders. Whether that is even truly possible is an open question. Ana Mariella Bacigalupo, an anthropologist who has focused on the Mapuche people indigenous to Southern Chile, points out that not only words like androgynous and transgender draw upon Western gender binarism, but so too does the term 'third gender.' They all can reinforce our culture's idea that sex and gender are naturally paired such that gender, like sex, becomes an attribute regarded as fixed. In Bacigalupo's eyes, this denies the culturally variable and context-specific nature of the realities Westerners term 'transgender.'[741]

Another big obstacle we will face throughout is that because our culture only recognizes two genders anyone who might be a conforming member of a third gender is automatically cast as a gender nonconformist—a very undesirable status. This valence may make it difficult to keep an open mind. We are culturally predisposed to consider everyone by our two genders standard. So folk who in some other culture might be accorded status as belonging to a real gender are in our society seen as pretenders who have rebelled against their proper place. In short, we are likely throughout this discussion to struggle with whether such people are simply gender nonconformists or belong to a legitimate gender alternative.

We must also consider that whatever inclination we adopt—toward seeing folk as nonconformists or as belonging to another gender—that there may be exceptions that defy us. Even if there are other genders, certainly there are some who are best described as gender nonconformists. Likewise, even if we believe most everyone we encounter who doesn't fit our binary gender scheme is a gender nonconformist, we should retain the hypothetical possibility some people somewhere may actually not be so easily dismissed. With these cautions in mind, let us examine the rather limited range of possibilities our own culture allows in exploring this matter.

Androgyny

Androgyny may or may not be a nonconforming gender. Our waffling on the matter results from the various ways androgyny can be conceived. Our present general usage is not identical with past usage, and variant senses remain. Remember, the word itself combines Greek words for man and woman. In itself this suggests any person identifying with the word must be understood in conjunction with the two conforming genders. But exactly how such a person stands vis-à-vis the conforming genders is an open question, at least theoretically.

If we regard androgyny as gender experience and expression that steers a clear middle course between the conforming genders, then it warrants consideration as a legitimate 'third gender.' On the other hand, if we regard androgyny as the blending and endorsement of conforming gender characteristics, then it still holds a kind of middle ground, but either relatively more within femininity or within masculinity. In other words, an androgynous man is still a *man* and an androgynous woman remains a *woman*. 'Androgynous' in this manner is merely a qualifying adjective that reflects a person pushing a particular gender boundary but still residing safely inside that boundary. In sum, we may need to distinguish between androgyny that produces an *androgyne*—a distinctly third gender person—and an androgynous man or woman who remains recognizably within a conforming gender.

Sandra Bem & the Bem Sex Role Inventory

Let us begin with this latter possibility, which is the overwhelming way the word 'androgyny' is used in contemporary conversation on gender. Psychologist Sandra Bem's work on androgyny, briefly introduced earlier in our dialog (chapters 1-2), needs a closer look now. Bem, remember, believes androgyny challenges the social prescription to be *either* a woman *or* a man, and offers the possibility of embracing *both* the masculinity *and* the femininity within the self.[742] Her argument is that the psychologically healthiest people embrace the positive traits associated with both genders. The question she faced in the 1970s was how to test the hypothesis that there are individuals who are androgynous in the manner she conceived.

In the mid-1970s, Bem introduced the *Bem Sex Role Inventory*, an instrument important not only for empirically studying gender, but conceptually important for weakening the notion of a rigidly dualistic two gender scheme.[743] Bem derived the items included on the BSRI by starting with a large list of personality traits, some of which were socially desirable, some socially undesirable, and some neutral in social desirability—but all of which might be attributed to either men or women. These were then tested on people to determine the desirability of each trait for both conforming genders. This narrowed a list of hundreds of items to only those found significantly more desirable for one conforming gender than for the other. Then judges were used to narrow the remaining candidates to the final list of included items. Judges of both sexes were used, in equal proportions, and both genders had to agree on the item fitting into one of three categories: masculine, feminine, or 'neutral.'

The BSRI finally derived contains 60 items, of which 20 name socially desirable stereotypical masculine characteristics, 20 feminine ones, and the remaining 20 qualities non-gender specific. Individuals are asked to rate themselves on each item, using a seven point Likert scale (1 = Never, or almost never true; 7 = Always, or almost always true). Scoring sorts individuals into one or another of four groups:[744]

- ❑ *Masculine*—high on endorsing masculine items, low on endorsing feminine items.
- ❑ *Feminine*—high on endorsing feminine items, low on endorsing masculine items.
- ❑ *Androgynous*—high on endorsing both masculine and feminine items.
- ❑ *Undifferentiated*—low on endorsing both masculine and feminine items.

The BSRI has stood the test of time fairly well, receiving support in numerous studies for its reliability and, though less well-attested, its validity.[745] In recent years a number of studies have sought to discover how well the BSRI functions in other cultural contexts.[746] Under the influence of Western culture, the BSRI seems to differentiate similarly among people in many societies outside the West.

The BSRI functions within a binary scheme—a reality that ultimately led to some dissatisfaction on Bem's part, since her desire has been to weaken rather than to strengthen the prevailing gender scheme in our society. The instrument's interest in androgyny, coupled with traditional interest in and familiarity with the conforming genders, has left the fourth possibility relatively undeveloped. Very little attention has been given to the 'undifferentiated,' the low scorers on both masculinity and femininity. The fact that 'undifferentiated' individuals do not perceive themselves as either masculine or feminine opens up the possibility they perceive themselves in a 'third gender' way, or possibly apart from gender at all. Unfortunately, little interest seems to exist in these individuals.

Androgynes

The very unfamiliarity of the term 'androgyne' should probably alert us to its very small place in the contemporary conversation on gender. Prior to the 1970s the occasional encounter with this term was in the context of the sexed body. Religious scholar Wendy Doniger O'Flaherty points out that an androgyne in ancient times was, literally, "a creature simultaneously male and female in physical form."[747] Thus, historically at least, an androgyne was a hermaphrodite, whom today we refer to as intersexed. The term androgyne had nothing at all to do with gender in the modern sense.

O'Flaherty also observes that the androgyne, as standing outside the binary system, could be evaluated either positively or negatively. In some societies, she says, androgynes occupy a positive social role. In others they are despised as an undesired blurring of the accepted cultural categories. But either way they are forced into a binary code. One is made either to be seen as an ill-formed man or as an ill-formed woman—and the former are typically viewed more positively. Moreover, in the ancient world the label androgyne could be applied loosely, to cover not only 'true' and 'false' hermaphrodites, but eunuchs, transvestites, and folk who today we call transsexual.[748] Perhaps, then, it is just as well the term has fallen into disuse—we hardly need to add to the current confusion!

Yet, in our modern conversation, if we consider androgyny as a possible third gender, a distinct gender apart from the conforming genders, then members of this gender logically might be termed *androgynes*—persons in some manner combining characteristics associated with men and women but who identify as neither a man, nor a woman. In this sense, an androgyne is not an androgynous man, not an androgynous woman, and not an individual who has a cross-gender identity (i.e., a male identifying as a woman or a female identifying as a man). Whether this sense of the word could be separated from old associations, and whether it could also stand apart from the last few decades' use of androgynous in the sense used by Bem and others, seems unlikely. So we must turn elsewhere for 'third gender' possibilities.

Transgender

By far the most popular vocabulary choice today for alternative, nonconforming gender experiences and expressions is 'transgender.' Although we introduced the term in our opening discussion, we need to spend more time with it now. In so doing we must keep in mind how bound to our existing binary gender system this word is. Inevitably, this carries consequences.

The Meaning of 'Transgender'

Perhaps the first step in that regard is to consider a little history. Virginia Prince, a crossdressing male active in promoting understanding and support for crossdressers, claims to have coined the terms 'transgenderism' and 'transgenderist' to refer to people who live full time as members of the opposite sex but without intending sexual reassignment.[749] This would place 'transgender' people between 'transvestites' on one side and 'transsexuals' on the other.

But the power of the word soon outstripped this narrow application. This power derives from both parts of the word. The 'gender' stem in 'transgender' firmly locates this as a psychosocial matter. It is not giving primacy to sex, but to gender. The 'trans' prefix affords multiple metaphorical applications. 'Trans' is generally interpreted in the sense of 'to cross,' so that 'transgender' means 'to cross from one gender (i.e., the assigned gender) to the other (i.e., the desired gender).' Obviously, this way of understanding keeps transgender firmly locked into a binary scheme—a solution satisfying to almost all nontransgender people (to whom it affords a justification to see transgender as deviant), and to most transgender people, too (because they want to belong in the conforming genders).

Despite the general interpretation—today having attained the status of a core meaning—there are other ways to understand the 'trans' part of the word. Some use it in the sense of 'against' as in the word 'transgression.' For them, transgender means to go against conforming gender. Those who do not identify as transgender who use the term in this way are especially likely to see transgender people as willfully perverse rebels. Transgender people who view the term in this sense are more likely to understand it as a desire and experience of gender that just doesn't fit at all with the prevailing scheme. In this regard they may accept the label transgender but treat it more-or-less as a synonym for 'third gender.'

Another possibility is to see the 'trans' as 'over' as in the word 'transcend.' In this use, transgender means a positive embracing of a gender beyond the way most of its members engage. This may be visible in males whose femininity exceeds that of most female women. Or it might play out in a gender sense that simply denies that conventional gender ways are adequate to express the individual's own gender experience.

The possibilities are numerous—as we recounted in our very first discussion when we introduced the term (chapter 1). No wonder, then, that so many people have accepted it for one use or another. Today it has become an umbrella term gathering beneath its cover members of many diverse groups—crossdressers, transsexuals, homosexuals, and the intersexed, among others. Of course, that has caused not a little difficulty since members of these various groups generally do not desire to be associated with groups other than their own. But it certainly suits those whose interest is in preserving the dominant gender scheme because it allows lumping all of them as gender nonconformists.

The Role of Crossdressing

For our introductory dialog we can adopt a more modest, intermediate position between an extremely narrow or overly broad sense. By far the largest constituency to adopt the term 'transgender' is people others regard as *crossdressers*. Neither homosexuals nor the intersexed are likely to adopt 'transgender' as a label, despite it sometimes being applied to them. They like to point out that neither body sex nor sexual orientation is causally related to gender identity. Intersexed people more often than not accept without difficulty their assigned gender. Most homosexual males identify as men; most homosexual females identify as women. Cross-gender—*trans*gender—identity is not a regular feature of many people who are sometimes grouped as 'transgender.'

Crossdressers themselves are a mixed population and not all of them accept, or warrant, the label 'transgender.' Nevertheless, *crossdressing*—appearing in dress associated with members of a different gender than the one assigned to the person—is a hallmark cultural sign of transgender reality. Crossdressing is a visible expression of an internal cross-gender experience. It provides the most convenient manner of displaying a disavowal of one's assigned gender and affiliation with a different gender. In our binary gender culture, crossdressers almost always accept the two gender scheme and use crossdressing as a way to express the 'opposite' gender.

Stereotype and Reality: Research on Transgender Males

Frequently in our dialog we have needed to confront the power of stereotypes. We have learned that stereotypes can forge links that serve as chains to bind people. One set of links places gender identity alongside sexual orientation. A male who identifies as a woman is seen as homosexual if erotic attraction is toward men; sex (male-to-male) trumps gender (woman-to-man). But this is hardly as far as it goes when *stereotyping transgender people*.

An easy presumption—because our culture makes sex and gender so central to identity and relationships—is that anything we see as a 'disturbance' in either sex or, especially, gender must reverberate throughout the individual. In short, a person who does not conform to the assigned gender must be so deeply disturbed that a pervasive disorder characterizes the whole of the person. Thus many of us tacitly assume a crossdresser is severely disturbed across the personality. Such an assumption helps us justify to ourselves our distancing from the person. We are simply being safe.

Actual evidence disconfirms such nonsense. Transgender people prove to be much more similar than dissimilar to everyone else. Because of our society's stake in a masculine-dominated gender hierarchy, transgender males have garnered most of the concern and attention. The research we will now consider principally examines the population of males who variously self-identify as transgender, transvestite, or transsexual—the three 'T's making up most of those normally identified as transgender. (We should assume the subjects involved in the studies we discuss are biological males unless otherwise noted.)

First, let us consider some basic matters of life experience, such as the families transgender people grow up in, their educational attainment, and their employment. We will begin with *family*. A study of 110 crossdressing males, reported by psychologist Richard Docter in 1988, showed that four-fifths (80%) came from intact families.[750] But that in itself says nothing about the nature of the child's relationship to his parents, an important matter since some speculate that cross-gender identity in males results from family dysfunction, specifically in relation to father and mother. One very common idea has been that cross-dressing boys develop in homes where there is a dominant mother and absent father. Yet self-reports from most crossdressing males do not seem to support this hypothesis. A 1972 survey conducted by psychologist Peter Bentler with Virginia Prince reported that about half (51%) of their subjects identified their father as the dominant parent. Moreover, nearly three-quarters (72%) affirmed that their father had been a good masculine image for them.[751] A survey study conducted by Docter and Prince a generation later, patterned on the 1972 survey, found similar numbers: a little more than three-quarters (76%) reared by both parents through age 18 and a like number (76%) reporting their father had provided a good masculine image.[752] Another study, involving over 200 males (65 transvestites, 33 male-to-female (MtF) transsexuals, 57 homosexuals, and 61 men whose sexual orientation remained unidentified), also found no support for this idea. Specifically, the hypothesis was tested that transvestites and transsexuals would be more likely to have grown up in a family headed by a female (an idea also often held to be true for homosexuals). This hypothesis was refuted by the data collected. Indeed, for all three groups—transvestites, transsexuals, and homosexuals—absent fathers were no more common than in the general population.[753] As well, most transgender adults do not recall their childhoods as unhappy.[754] The overall picture, as a team of researchers concluded in their 1997 study, is one of a "more or less normal childhood."[755]

Educational attainment shows, if anything, greater success by transgender people. An early large scale study, based on data from the 1960s when far fewer people attended college, found more than a third (37%) with a bachelor's degree or better.[756] Subsequent studies have also found strong results in this respect. A 1997 study found nearly two-thirds (65%) with a bachelor's degree or better,[757] and a 2001 study reported almost three-fourths (73%) with such attainment.[758] In one study asking about their educational experience more than a third (35%) of transvestites reported having been "excellent" students, and only 11% said they had been "poor" students. The numbers for transsexuals were a bit worse: 30% "excellent," but 21% "poor."[759]

Occupational social status—one useful way to look at employment success— also shows transgender people in general doing well, presuming they successfully keep their transgender identity hidden. Male crossdressers are represented in a range of occupations, some lower and others higher in social status. Prince and Bentler's 1972 report showed that one out of six (17%) were either president of a company or business owners.[760] A 1983 comparative study found that nearly two-thirds (64%) of transvestites ranked above the national median in occupational prestige. They were also well above the undifferentiated group they were compared to (64% to 48% above the national median). The authors of this study noted these males were heavily represented in the mainstream white-collar world, including occupations such as engineering, sales, teaching, and accounting. [761] Similar findings pertained in later studies reported in 1988 and 1997, though in the latter with relatively more representation in technical and professional groups and relatively less in unskilled positions.[762]

Next, we may turn to *psychological testing*. Transgender people have been subjected to mental testing covering everything from intelligence to personality traits to mental disorders to gender identity. In this respect, studies mostly date from the 1970s onward. In the mid-1970s, researcher and theoretician Peter Bentler sought to articulate a rough and preliminary list of 32 factors involved in the development of a feminine sex role in males. He was interested in a typology useful with three groups: homosexuals, transsexuals, and transvestites. Some of his factors indicate developed personality traits. All three conditions, he felt, show an emphasis on independence, with an absence of same-sex affiliative behavior. Transsexualism and transvestism he associated with training in impulse control, harm avoidance, and behavioral inhibition. For transvestism alone he also found an emphasis on intellectual success.[763]

Some psychological testing has used so-called *projective personality tests*. The most famous of these tests is the Rorschach Ink Blot test. All of these tests share in common the conviction that ambiguous stimuli can elicit the projection of basic personality traits without the conscious intention of the subject. One early study, conducted by Peter Bentler, Richard Sherman and Charles 'Virginia' Prince, was reported in 1970. In it, 25 male crossdressers not in therapy were administered the Holtzman Ink Blot Test. This projective test consists of a set of 45 inkblots presented the individual, with only one response per card permitted. The results obtained were then compared to norms for the general population. Crossdressers tended to respond more to the form of the inkblots than to their color or shading, a response style associated with relative rigidity of personality. Although crossdressers exhibited some greater preoccupation with the body, and elevated levels of anxiety and hostility, overall they did not differ significantly from the general population. The researchers concluded that "the scores for transvestites seem to indicate generally organized and intellectually adequate thought processes."[764]

In a 1982 study with a group of transsexual subjects the Rorschach itself was used. The Rorschach employs a series of 10 bilaterally symmetrical inkblots, on 5"-by-9" cards, presented in order. The subject is asked to describe fully what is seen in each. In this study, 20 transsexuals (10 male-to-female (MtF) and 10 female-to-male (FtM)) were administered the Rorschach both before and after sexual reassignment surgery. The results of these tests were compared to norms drawn from subjects in the general population. There was "a lack of obvious difference from norms for the general population."[765]

Most academic psychologists find self-report, or 'objective' personality tests to be more valid instruments. One early study, in 1965, using the Maudsley Personality Inventory's Extraversion Scale, found a group of 19 transvestite males to be somewhat more introverted and somewhat more anxious than the general adult male population[766]—perhaps understandable in a society that encourages them to stay 'in the closet,' but the sample size is too small to infer much. Another early study, reported in 1969, was much larger. It involved 181 adult male crossdressers, 1,029 norm subjects, and 62 control subjects. The crossdressers were not clients in clinical treatment. The research examined variables on the Personality Research Form (PRF), Form BB, an instrument used to measure normal personality traits. A total of 22 traits are assessed through the 440 items of the test. The results showed crossdressers as "clearly more controlled in their impulses" as signified by tendencies such as relatively greater risk avoidance of bodily harm, concern to maintain neat and organized personal surroundings, preference for routine over new and different experiences, more deliberate rather than spontaneous acts, and a reluctance to express feelings and wishes. In addition, with respect to interpersonal orientation, transgender subjects tested as relatively more withdrawn socially, introverted, displaying a preference not to be the center of attention, less involved in nurturing behaviors, less concerned for approval from others, less likely to seek or enjoy dominant social roles, more averse to arguments and conflict, and relatively more self-reliant and autonomous.[767]

Some studies are mixed, combining, for example, ability testing with personality testing. Transsexuals awaiting sex reassignment surgery (SRS) were subjects in a 1981 study using two kinds of tests. The 22 persons were administered both a standard mental ability test and a comprehensive personality test. For the former, the Wechsler Adult Intelligence Scale (WAIS)—the most widely used measure of adult intelligence—was employed. It has both vocabulary and performance tests. For the latter, the Minnesota Multiphasic Personality Inventory (MMPI) was used. It consists of more than 500 statements to which the respondent must answer 'true,' 'false,' or 'cannot say.' A total of 10 clinical scales are reported, which provide a measure of any psychopathology. Results on the WAIS were mixed: subjects scored congruent to their genetic sex except on a measure of conceptual styles, where scores were congruent instead with their gender identity. The MMPI found no major psychopathology process involved in the subjects.[768]

Studies often differ in size. George Brown and associates reported a study in 1996 with much larger numbers than the one we just reviewed. This research involved 188 subjects classified in one or another of three conditions: 83 transvestites (44% of the subjects); 44 transsexuals (23%); and, 61 transgendered (33%; a group equivalent to what other researchers term the 'marginal transvestites'). They were further differentiated by whether they had received treatment or not into four groups: 'no treatment' (81 subjects; 43%), 'treated for psychological problems' (49 subjects; 26%), 'treated for transvestism' (41 subjects; 22%), and, 'treated for gender change' (17 subjects; 9%). The study examined these subjects both with reference to personality characteristics and for sexual functioning. Personality traits were measured by Costa and McRae's NEO Personality Inventory (NEO-PI). This instrument is a 181 item questionnaire based on the five-factor model of personality. Sexual functioning was assessed using the Derogatis Sexual Functioning Inventory (DSFI). It employs 255 items to measure 10 dimensions. With regard to personality characteristics, the researchers concluded that the personality profile of the sample did not deviate substantially from the NEO-PI normative sample of community-dwelling men. Specifically, crossdressers scored in the normal range on all personality dimensions of the NEO-PI except one. For the 'O' ('Openness') dimension, crossdressers were in the high range for Fantasy, Feelings, and Values scales. The researchers reached a similar conclusion about sexual functioning. The DSFI results found that crossdressers did not deviate dramatically from so-called 'normal' male heterosexual subjects. A modest difference was found in one respect. As a group, crossdressers' scores were lower in the area of the DSFI that indicates they are more likely to endorse a poorer body image. [769]

Interestingly, in the little research done comparing transgender males when crossdressed as compared to when dressed congruent to their gender assignment, results support the healthiness of dressing congruent to their personal sense of gender. In a limited study involving 13 crossdressing males, reported by Chris Gosselin and Sybil B. Eysenck, subjects were administered the Eysenck Personality Inventory (EPI) both while crossdressed and when not crossdressed. Results showed that the subjects, while crossdressed, scored significantly *lower* on the Neuroticism scale. They also scored lower on Psychoticism but higher on Extraversion.[770] In other words, these folk demonstrated less anxiety and were more at ease and outgoing when crossdressed.[771]

As we might expect, the one area where transgender males do show a significant difference from their male counterparts in the general population is in gender identity. In 1982, sociologist John Talamini reported on a study using the BSRI. In the research reported by Talamini, matched groups of heterosexual males who don't crossdress and those who do scored differently. The crossdressing males scored significantly higher in androgyny.[772] Perhaps the endorsing of a more feminine gender identity and/or role leads to greater androgyny among these men. Talamini himself feels that "cross-dressing is somehow bound up with the universal personal drive toward androgyny."[773]

In 2001, Richard Docter and James Fleming explored transgender identity through 26 items of their 70-item questionnaire administered to 516 adult males (ages 19-78), 88% of whom were identified as transvestites who periodically crossdressed fully as women and 12% identified as transsexual. The 26 items had content such as "I wish I had been born a woman," "I do not enjoy functioning as a man," and "My true gender is feminine." All 26 items had some endorsement with factor loads ranging from .48 ("I daydream of being a woman at least 10 times per day") to .92 ("I would choose to live as a woman"). There was overlap between the two groups on this scale, with the mean score for transsexuals (20.9) somewhat higher than for transvestites (12.2).[774]

We could multiply examples, but the overall picture that emerges is clear enough. If we try to back away from specific studies to garner an overview, the following features emerge:

❑ Psychological testing shows that *transgender people are more like members of the general population than they are unlike them.*

❑ In the few ways that transgender people as a group are different from general population norms, the differences are generally not *statistically* significant (i.e., the findings are judged to not be the products of chance), and even less likely to be *clinically* significant (i.e., the findings do not suggest psychopathology).

❑ In addition to personality features, *transgender individuals are also more like than unlike the general population in sexual functioning.* In fact, one team of researchers characterized the situation as being that crossdressers are virtually indistinguishable from noncrossdressers in both personality and sexual functioning.[775]

❑ One area where transgender males display a consistent difference from others is in *greater feminine gender affiliation.* Yet, not all crossdressers show the same level of difference; transvestite and transsexual groups can be distinguished from homosexuals and from one another.

As with any other group, there are some differences between those crossdressers who are 'distressed' and seek treatment, and those who do not seek treatment. Thus, the subjects of any study should be noted when interpreting the results. In sum, while some differences can be found between crossdressers and the general population, these generally seem not to rise to a level of either statistical or clinical significance. When clinically significant differences are found, not surprisingly they are with crossdressing subjects in treatment.

However, we should not conclude that transgender people are either more likely to seek professional mental health professionals—or to need to. Most crossdressers never seek counseling, either for their crossdressing or anything else. In this respect, apparently, they are like the population at large. As the 1994 entry in the *Encyclopedia of Psychology* sums this matter up, "Concerning their psychological makeup, transvestites as a group are no more neurotic or psychotic than matched control groups. . . ."[776] However, because of our culture's view that such behavior constitutes gender nonconformity—not a desired status—crossdressing can complicate relationships and it can prompt self-questioning. Often, though, when transgender people are in counseling their concern is not about their gender identity but about the consequences of social intolerance that they experience.[777]

To conclude, transgender therapist and columnist Gianna Israel offers us a succinct summary of what we have been examining:

> Transgender individuals can come from any racial, economic, or religious background. They work in many types of fields; there are transgender physicians, teachers, insurance underwriters and auto mechanics. Finally, most transgender persons have families, and a large proportion have children. This knowledge should be passed on to other family members and relatives who are misinformed or who are afraid of catching 'transgender germs.'[778]

Despite these facts, being transgender in a two gender society where gender matters is not an easy task.

Being Transgender in a Non-transgender Society

Stereotypes hurt. They can, in fact, kill. Because some of us rely uncritically on feelings generated by learned stereotypes, we may find ourselves engaging in verbal and other behavior harmful to those of us who are transgender. Being a transgender person in a culture that prizes gender and expects conformity to our birth assigned gender is not easy.

While many of us may believe that transgender people "choose" their "lifestyle," the facts cast doubt on that assertion. Much as has been argued with respect to homosexuality, it is difficult to envision why someone would voluntarily adopt a condition with so many possible negative consequences. In the case of transgender reality, the use of the word 'choice' seems problematic in light of how early and persistent transgender identity often is. If we accept crossdressing as a sign of transgender identity, it certainly appears early in life. Research finds that crossdressing typically begins in childhood and is well established by the end of adolescence. This is probably the most well-attested fact associated with transgender experience developmentally.[779]

Often childhood is complicated by cross-gender behavior that makes them different from peers. They may feel isolated, confused, conflicted by self-doubt and guilt. Yet though being a transgender person may result in extra social pressures, virtually all learn to cope despite the obstacles. In truth, as researcher Richard Schott reminds us, we cannot even generalize in assuming all transgender children struggle with their transgender identity or with behaviors like crossdressing. As he says, some take things in stride and adjust more easily than others. [780]

This is not to minimize the social obstacles, though. A study reported in 1981 by Neil Buhrich and Trina Beaumont of 222 adult male crossdressers in

America (N=126) and Australia (N=86) found that nearly one-quarter (24%) overall had been called "sissy" during childhood.[781] Given the pejorative associations with the term, we might expect this labeling correlated to some degree with peer difficulties such as ostracism or being bullied. Researcher Shannon Wyss, in recounting the stories of transgender youth, remarks that because of their peers' hatred—one mirroring adult prejudices—teens publicly expressing their transgender identity often find themselves in unsafe situations. Many lose their friends, face ongoing harassment, and discover that teachers and school staff refuse to intervene, sometimes even suggesting the ill treatment transgender youth experience has been brought on by themselves. In such environments survival rather than learning becomes the priority. As a consequence, Wyss notes, transgender youth are at special risk for self-destructive behaviors.[782]

In fact, school often proves a hazardous place—making the success of transgender people in this regard all the more remarkable. A study of School Climate conducted in the fall of 1999 by the Gay, Lesbian, and Straight Education Network (GLSEN) returned responses from 496 lesbian, gay, bisexual and transgender students in 32 states. Survey results reveal more than 90% of these students were subject to homophobic remarks, most often from other students (94.4% of those reporting such remarks), but frequently enough from faculty and staff, too (36.6%). Nearly two-thirds (61%) experienced verbal harassment, almost half (46.5%) sexual harassment, and more than a quarter (27.6%) physical harassment, including physical assault. No wonder, then, 41.7% report not feeling safe at school.[783] The *SIECUS Report* covering this study notes that, "transgender kids probably suffer even more harassment and discrimination than lesbian, gay, or bisexual students."[784] GLSEN's survey for 2001 has an even wider reach: 904 LGBT youth from 48 states and the District of Columbia. Of these, 4.3% self-identify as transgender or other gender identity; 95.7% regard themselves as identifying at one of the two gender poles. Yet regardless of gender identity, transgender, homosexual, and bisexual youth tend to be lumped together in the eyes of others. Their school experience is marked by exposure to homophobic or transphobic behavior. Nearly all of them (94%) hear homophobic comments (e.g., 'You're so gay'), or labels (e.g., 'Faggot,' 'Dyke'), often or frequently, and nearly a quarter (23.6%) hear such remarks from faculty or school staff.[785]

Clearly, *transphobia*—an irrational and largely unconscious fear or anxiety over those who are transgender—poses a danger similar to homophobia, which often accompanies it. Transgender males are especially subject to it. Gregory Herek's claim that "prejudice against men who display feminine behavior is nearly as common as prejudice against homosexuality in our society"[786] is hard to dispute. Yet actions inspired by transphobia are less likely to be reported or to gain our attention and sympathy. Even more than homosexuals, transgender individuals are marginalized, rejected, and subject to violence.

Crimes committed against transgendered people *because* they are transgendered are no different in their nature than like crimes committed against homosexuals because they are homosexual, or racial groups because of their race, or Muslims because of their religion. These crimes are hate crimes.[787] To date, though, federal legislation on hate crimes only recognizes crimes motivated by race, religion, national origin or color. So, from a federal legal standpoint, crimes against transgendered people motivated by the fact the victim is transgendered, are not hate crimes, though logically and morally they clearly are. The lack of recognition of such crimes as hate crimes has carried with it at least two very unfortunate consequences: there has been little incentive to collect data substantiating the extent of the problem, and there remain no specific legal provisions at the federal level to protect potential victims or to punish perpetrators motivated by their hate of transgendered people.

A study published in 1997 by the Gender Public Advocacy Coalition (GenderPAC)[788] finds a serious incidence of violence against transgendered people. The study utilizes a questionnaire designed to assess transgendered people's lifetime experiences with violence. The questionnaire was not randomly distributed—infeasible given the nature of the target population—but distributed through events, volunteers, and the internet. In a 12 month period, 402 cases were collected from respondents. The data yielded from these cases found that well over half (59.5%) reported having been a victim of harassment or violence. Other highlights of the study include:

❑ *Verbal abuse* was the most common adverse act; over half (56%) of the cases involved such an incident just within the previous year.

❑ *Assault*, either with a weapon (10%) or without one (19%) had occurred at least once in nearly a third (29.6%) of cases.

❑ *Being followed or stalked* had occurred at least once in nearly a quarter (23%) of the cases.

❑ *Robbery* was involved in about 1-in-7 (14%) of the cases.

❑ *Rape* or *attempted rape* had happened in about 1-in-8 (13%) of the cases.[789]

A 1999 online survey of more than a thousand male crossdressers discovered that a substantial minority either had personally experienced public harassment or knew someone who had. Specifically, more than 1-in-10 (13%) had been confronted either by law enforcement or security while crossdressed, about 1-in-6 (16%) had been either verbally abused or physically assaulted while crossdressed in public, and 1-in-4 (25%) personally knew someone who had been either verbally abused or physically assaulted while crossdressed in public.[790] Similarly, a 1992 study of transsexuals in London found that more than half (52%) of the male-to-female (MtF) transsexuals had been physically assaulted.[791]

Are There Any Encouraging Signs?

In light of these numbers and all we have learned, it may seem absurd to ask if things are showing any signs of changing for the better. Yet there are some positive indicators—though not always unmixed. Some recent evidence suggests that the American public may be becoming more tolerant of the trans-gender community—or at least more willing to protect their basic human and civil rights. Some legislative changes aimed at ensuring the transgendered the same rights and protections (*not* more) as other citizens have occurred.[792] In various states around the country (e.g., California, Florida, New York, and Texas), inclusionary safe schools legislation has been introduced.[793] These trends offer one indication of trends in attitudinal shifts.

Public attitudes have been probed by survey and interview research, too. A national poll commissioned by the Human Rights Commission, conducted with 800 randomly selected registered voters and 6 focus groups, and reported at the end of the Summer of 2002, revealed the following: more than three-quarters (77%) of the respondents think transgendered children should be permitted to attend public schools; more than two-thirds (70%) are familiar with the term 'transgender'—a sign of increased awareness and more than two-thirds (68%) also support hate-crime laws inclusive of protection for transgendered people. However, awareness and concern do not equal knowledge. For instance, almost two-thirds (61%) agree to the need for legal protection from discrimination for members of the transgendered community, but more than half (57%) incor-rectly assume that present laws already protect transgendered people from being fired because of their transgender status. And stereotypes persist in harmful ways: only half (50%) agree that a transgendered adult should be allowed to hold a job teaching in a high school.[794] Moreover, more than half (60%) do not agree that a transgendered adult should be allowed to hold a job teaching in an elementary school, serve as a scout master, or work in day care.[795]

What was most worrisome for the transgendered community was that some of the positive impression people reflected in the survey might have been the result of a misapprehension of what it means to be transgendered. When pro-vided a description of a "transgender person,"[796] the percent of those who re-garded transgendered people *unfavorably* rose by nearly a third, and rose by more than a quarter among those who regard transgenderism as "morally wrong."[797] In this light, then, we may well wonder how much progress of substance is be-ing made.

Transgender people are receiving more and more serious attention. Unfor-tunately, most of that attention remains as a deviation from the norm—as gen-der nonconformists, rather than as conformists to a nonconforming gender. To the extent that transgender people continue to endorse the binary system and identify their gender experience and expression in its terms, this is likely to con-tinue. We might speculate, however, that at least some of those who identify as transgender do so only because they cannot find anything that fits better. They may form a kind of compromise gender identification reflecting the cultural poverty in conception and vocabulary. Given better alternatives we might well wonder how many would endorse a third gender alternative.

'Third Gender'

The idea of 'third gender' broadly conceives any and all genders beyond the dominant two gender scheme. In other words, 'third' here can mean 'three or more.' Some societies appear to recognize definite gender alternatives to masculinity and femininity. They have gender words for adults other than 'woman' or 'man.' Our own culture lacks this same sensibility, choosing to label nonconforming genders as *trans*gender (crossing the conforming genders' boundaries) rather than *third* gender (a legitimate, independent gender with its own boundaries). Therefore, to make sense of this idea we need to do two things. First, we can briefly look at examples of other societies whose gender schemes are broader and more flexible than our own. Then we can consider those of us in our own culture who self-identify as 'third gender.'

Third Genders

Examples of other genders are not hard to find around the world. But they are hard for those of us raised in a strict binary gender system to think of as truly distinct genders. Instead we tend to rework them to fit our accustomed ways of thinking. Lacking adequate gender vocabulary we are reduced to speaking of them using binary gender language. While our own cultural limitations produce this sorry situation, we can resist these limitations both by adopting the language labels used in other societies and by trying to conceive of new gender possibilities. Unfortunately, we remain hampered by our paucity in language and, because of our culture's powerful influence abroad, by the fact that our binary logic has crept into other culture's thinking. As a result, even in other cultures the way in which third genders are talked about today has changed from the way they once were spoken about. Today Western terms—and biases—are strongly influential in most parts of the world.

Perhaps the best known examples of supposed 'third gender' groups are found in the East. The Indian subcontinent is especially noted in this regard. Indian languages recognize the possibility of gender beyond the dichotomy of 'man' and 'woman.' The Sanskrit *napunsaka* and the Urdu *namard* are terms used to cover members of various groups that our term 'transgender' is often applied to: homosexuals, transvestites, transsexuals—all kinds of crossdressers.[798] Today, colloquial terms are used for female same-sex relationships (*sakhi*) and for those among boys (*masti*).[799] Effeminate (uncastrated) males with a homosexual orientation, who crossdress and take the passive, receptive role in sexual interactions, are known locally as *Jankhas* or *Zenanas*,[800] or *Kothis*.

Kothis

The term *Kothis* is used locally as a self-identifier in India, Bangladesh, and parts of Pakistan; regional equivalents include the *Metis* of Nepal and *Zenanas* of Pakistan. *Kothis* are 'feminized males' who do not regard themselves as members of a masculine gender, but as 'not males.'[801] They demonstrate culturally feminine characteristics, often in a highly performed manner in public in order to attract sexual partners. They accept the female (passive) role when engaging in sex with men. However, *Kothis* are sometimes married, and occasionally have sex with other *Kothis* (though this is kept secret and denied).[802]

The *Kothis* reality stands as an exemplar of the construction of gender consonant with cultural rules for sexual interaction. The male-dominated societies of South Asia facilitate environments where males are free to congregate, show public displays of affection, and engage in sex. But what we in the West style homosexuality—same-sex interactions between like-gendered people—is frowned upon. Same-sex sexual behavior between so-called 'real men' (*Giryas* or *Pathi*) and 'not-men' (*Kothis*) is acceptable because they occur between differently-gendered people. The 'real men' occupy the active, penetrating role; the 'not men' a passive, receptive role like that also expected of women.[803]

However, we should be wary of concluding that *Kothis* as a gender status is merely contrived to fit sexual desire. These males are noticeably effeminate in behavior before and apart from sexual activity. Those who go into the sex trade are often pressed into it by economic necessity or thrust into it as unwilling victims of sexual abuse. To reduce the gendered nature of the *Kothis* to a cultural convenience for sex simply would be wrong.

Hijras

Even better known are the *Hijras* of northern India and Pakistan. The *Hijras* are culturally regarded as neither 'male' nor 'female,' neither 'man' nor 'woman'—but a 'third' sex *and* gender. Tramsgendered *hijra*, living together in communities (*hijra gharanas*) include ritual categories for those preparing for castration (*akwa*) and those castrated (*nirwaan*).[804] The *nirwaan* ceremony confers status as irrevocably a 'real' *Hijra*.[805] But while some voluntarily become eunuchs (as an act of religious devotion), and some may be sexually ambiguous by nature (true or pseudo-hermaphrodites), many *hijras* are neither. They do not easily fit any Western categories, though Western scholars have likened them, variously, to homosexual or heterosexual crossdressers, or to transsexuals. The Indian National AIDS Control Organization (NACO), influenced by Western categorization, specifies four subgroups: transvestite, transsexual, hermaphrodites, and drag queens/*Satia Kothi*.[806] We do best, though, to leave them as themselves—a distinct and unique group. They are included among crossdressers only because from a Western standpoint they are biological males who appear in the dress and gender role paired with biological females.

Found principally in India's larger cities, like Bombay and Delhi, the number of *Hijras* have not been kept by official census data and estimates range widely; anthropologist Laurent reports unofficial estimates from a half million to 5 million.[807] They belong to a distinct community, with its own order, rules, and customs. Adolescents leave their birth families to join a new household—one of seven lineages preserved by the *Hijras*—organized in communes where at least five *chelas* ('disciples') are led by a *guru* ('spiritual master'). In this new family they take a feminine name, refer to one another by feminine pronouns, put on feminine clothing, and adopt feminine mannerisms. They receive training in *Hijra* traditions and activities such as the ritual performances by which they will earn income. They may have sex with males, typically assuming a passive-receptive role in anal intercourse. Their sexual activity may be motivated by personal desire or as an act of prostitution.

Their place, historically, has been within Hinduism where they are especially associated with the female deity Bahuchara Mata,[808] who has a temple in Gujarat. The *Hijras* served as eunuchs in the royal courts of Muslim rulers and thus gained influence with many adherents of Islam too. Indeed, the influence may have been reciprocal, as *Hijras* follow certain practices more in keeping with Islamic tradition than Hindu, such as burying their dead rather than cremating them—and some *Hijras* have become Muslim.[809] Even today many Muslims, like many Hindus, believe that the *Hijras* mediate a divine ability to bless or curse; refusing them money or gifts is thought by some to bring bad luck. However, British colonialism marked a severe downturn in *Hijra* fortunes. They increasingly became an ostracized group.[810]

While within their community they have both place and identity, in the larger society *Hijras* remain marginalized. Siddharth Narrain remarks, "Hijras in India have virtually no safe spaces, not even in their families, where they are protected from prejudice and abuse." Narrain observes that some *Hijras* have become politically active to redress their lot in society. In Bangalore, they joined with local *Kothis* and other sexual minorities to form an organization named Vividha, with a charter calling for legal reforms (e.g., equal housing and employment rights), repeal of laws such as Section 377 of the Indian Penal Code (which makes even voluntary same-sex sexual behavior illegal), and recognition of *Hijras* as women.[811]

Far more in the past than presently, they fulfilled a social function within society by serving as mediums for the feminine divine. Today they retain a place in society but largely without the social status once enjoyed. They still are sometimes employed at wedding or birth ceremonies to provide entertainment through ritual song and dance. Their sexually suggestive routines constitute a bawdy fertility ritual meant to bless the couple but often today is viewed as rude and offensive. Still, because many common folk worry that not paying the *Hijras* will bring ill fortune, they are commonly given gifts of food, clothing, or money.

Similarly, *Hijras* often show up at religious festivals. However, they have occasioned controversy and censure in some circles for sometimes involving themselves in public activities whether invited or not, and insisting on remuneration, with rude displays (e.g., not wearing underwear and lifting their skirts to expose themselves) if payment is refused. Accordingly, some have characterized them in unflattering terms as 'bitchy," 'bad-tempered,' and 'demanding.'[812] Today they may be thought of as much for their begging and prostitution as for the historical role they have occupied in India's folk spirituality. Still they persist, India's most noted and durable transgender population.[813]

Acault

As the *Hijras* illustrate, transgender is often associated with religion and spirituality. Another, perhaps better example comes from Burma (Myanmar). An important indigenous religious influence is belief in 37 spirit deities (*Nat*), whose powers can enact good or ill among the people. Transgender folk—*Acault* ('spirit-possessed one'), or *Nat Kadaw* ('spirit wife')[814]—play an important role in relation to these spirits. Some are male shamans (*kadaw*) who crossdress as they enact the role of a female *Nat*—and who may experience temporary spirit possession.[815] A female *Nat* named Manguedon sometimes takes possession of a biological male and changes the individual into someone regarded by others as no longer a masculine male, but as an *Acault*—neither male nor female (but more like a female than a male). This typically occurs at an early age, though such spirit possession can happen at other times. Ceremonially wedded to Manguedon, who bestows femininity upon them, the *Acault* stand between the sexes and genders. Their crossdressing reflects this change in status. Given their origin, it is no surprise the *Acault* are connected to spiritual roles, serving as shamans, seers, or in similar roles.[816]

Because the *Acault* have become a kind of variant of female sex and feminine gender, those who have sex with *Acault* are viewed as engaged in heterosexual behavior—an important factor in a society that finds homosexual activity objectionable. As for the *Acault* themselves, a team of Western researchers who presented three cases studies in a report in the early 1990s, found both masculine and feminine gender identities. They concluded individual *Acault* might be categorized by one or another Western labels, including transvestite and transsexual; Westerners would be prone to also see them as homosexual.[817] This discrepancy between Western and native perceptions occurs often around the world, and the situation of the *Acault* when separated from cultural, especially religious, considerations leads to misunderstanding. Sociologist Stephen Murray notes that because Manguedon is thought to be jealous of any contact by the *Acault* with females the *Acaults'* exclusively same-sex sexual behavior should be regarded as a consequence of the religious proscription against contact with women[818]—an eminently sensible conclusion.

Bissu

The many island societies of the Pacific offer a number of people who might be considered representatives of a third gender. On the island of Sulawesi, part of Indonesia, are the *Bissu*. The *Bissu* are viewed as possessing the attributes of both males and females; they are perceived as both sexes and both genders. The Bugis believe such people may be marked from birth. Sometime ambiguous genitalia at birth indicate the child will one day become *Bissu*. However, they are often unremarkably male (or female) anatomically; those who become *Bissu* are presumed to be a different sex/gender on the inside. By adolescence a child who demonstrates an affinity for the spiritual world may be apprenticed to an adult *Bissu* and began a long process of training and testing.[819]

Bissu present as a conscious mix of male and female. For instance, they may carry a knife like a man would, but wear flowers in their hair as a woman might. Their transcendence of the gender divide is paralleled by their transcendence of the ordinary mortal realm. Regarded as both partly human and partly spirit, they occupy an important role in indigenous spiritual traditions as a priestly people who mediate between this world and the heavens. Through elaborate rituals the *Bissu* contact the realm of spirits (*dewati*), allow a divine spirit to inhabit them for a time, and provide a blessing. These blessings cover a wide range of important events in the lives of the Bugis, including domestic matters (e.g., consecrating marriages), agricultural ones (e.g., blessing both plantings and harvests), and other religious events.[820]

Xanith

If we turn to the Middle East we can find examples like the *Kaneeth* (*Zanith*, or *Khanith*) of Bahrain, regarded as specially gendered, or the *Xanith* of Oman, a Muslim nation sitting at the edge of Arabia. The *Xanith* are 'third gender' males. Norwegian social anthropologist Unni Wikan, whose fieldwork was among the Arabs of Oman's city of Sohar on the northeastern coast, concluded in the mid-1970s that these distinctive folk constitute perhaps 2% of the adult males of Sohar.[821] Although considered by law as male, *Xanith* speak of themselves as women. However, they are not permitted to dress as women; such behavior is a crime. Instead, *Xanith* speak in a falsetto voice and present in distinctive dress that lies intermediate to the appearance of men and women. For example, while men and *Xanith* both wear ankle-length tunics, those of the *Xanith* are cinched at the waist like a woman's dress. Where a man wears white and a woman wears bright colors in patterned cloth, the *Xanith* wear unpatterned colors. Men keep their hair short, women wear theirs long, and the *Xanith* have hair whose length is in-between men and women styles.

The *Xanith* occupy a distinctive role in Sohar. Unlike other males, they are free to move among women, who may show their face to them. However, if they marry a woman they then lose this privilege and are treated like other males. *Xanith* sing at weddings, and perform other social tasks, but are perhaps best known for their involvement as prostitutes.[822] Both the Euro-American terms of 'transvestite' and 'transsexual' have been applied to the *Xanith*, though they may also be considered an example of a third gender.

Kitesha

The continent of Africa affords many possible examples. One of these is the *Kitesha* among the Basongye (Mbala) people of Central Africa. The term *Kitesha* (pl. *bitesha*) is unfortunately a derogatory term. These individuals appear to be representative of a 'third gender' in which the person performs gender that is neither typically masculine nor typically feminine but distinctive. More is known about the male *Kitesha* than the female, so the remarks that follow relate to the male *Kitesha*. Such a person dresses in a manner that incorporates feminine dress without being fully like that of a woman (e.g., they might wear a woman's skirt, but not otherwise be garbed in a feminine manner). They also engage in behavior unconventional for males, such as baring their chest or exposing their genitals. Others may view them as wanting to avoid work; when they do undertake tasks these are those associated with women, such as gathering firewood (and even this is seen by some as being selected simply because it is the easiest work). In terms of sexual relationships, the male *Kitesha* might establish a relationship with a female *Kitesha*. Or, the *Kitesha* might have sexual relations with either males or females who are not themselves *Bitesha*.[823]

Machi Weye

The world of Latin America also knows people often called transgender by Americans but who may perhaps qualify as a third gender. Among these are the *Machi* of the indigenous Mapuche people of Southern Chile. These are anatomical males who historically, remarks anthropologist Ana Mariella Bacigalupo, "were culturally defined as possessing co-gendered status."[824] This meant such males could become either masculine or feminine, or both.[825] This ability opened up important avenues to function as mediators in this world and between this world and the realm of spirits. Like women, they could open themselves to possession by spirits.[826] Persons who performed this and other shamanistic functions are called *Machi*.

Most *Machi* are female; male shamans (*Machi Weye*[827]) are transgendered people. Bacigalupo has studied the *Machi Weye* extensively, both in terms of their historical presentation and perception, and in the modern world. Bacigalupo comments that the Spanish newcomers forged a complex relationship with the *Machi Weye*, one characterized both by fear and concern over their appearance and spiritual practices, but also respect for their healing abilities and role in peace councils. The appearance of one *Machi Weye* was described as 'like Lucifer': he wore his hair long and straight, and wore an allegedly feminine garment (a *puno*[828]) in place of pants. Their atypical gender presentation was commonly construed as signifying a *puto*, or sodomite who engaged in devil worship.[829]

Misunderstood by the Spaniards who colonized the area, they remain misunderstood by other Chileans today. Not dissimilar to indigenous people in other countries, the Mapuche are a minority population relatively separated from other Chileans. The *Machi*, honored among the Mapuche, do not enjoy the same esteem from others. The *Machi Weye* are even further separated from the majority population and if their dual status as Mapuche and *Machi* were not enough, their transgender characteristics further complicate their reception within the larger society. Bacigalupo cites a case in which "a *machi* who identifies as a woman but has a male body was jailed without trial under a false accusation of homicide and was described as a 'strange sexual deviant,' and a 'dangerous uncivilized indian' because she challenged Chilean gender and social norms."[830]

Bacigalupo presents a study of a modern *Mache Weye* named Marta. Born male, Marta became feminine through a complex of developments, experiences, and behaviors that encompass past and present, traditional spirituality and modern life. These acts include such obvious gender markers as a change in dress, adopting feminine clothing and feminine manner. Marta's shamanic status represents a spiritual transformation accompanied and marked by a change in gender status and performance, including crossdressing.[831]

Virgjinesha ('Sworn Virgins')

Europe, too, has its candidates for consideration as a third gender. Among these are the *Virgjinesha* ('sworn virgins') of Albania. These are genetic females who by their manner of dress as males signal a male gender identity, assume a male gender role, are accorded status as males, but remain celibate. This unusual situation is found principally in northern Albania among families who adhere to the *Kanun*, a code governing gender and marital relations. As a part of this code, gender is clearly marked by dress. But unlike many societies, where biological sex governs perception of gender regardless of dress, under *Kanun* one's gender is as one presents it. A female may become male by swearing a vow, so long as certain conditions are met. One such is that the girl's family has no sons to inherit, thus threatening the loss of the family's wealth (because all wealth is transmitted from generation to generation through the males). Since a sworn virgin is treated as male—right down to being referred to as 'he'—this provides a male heir.[832] In this social setting there is no shame in so-called 'crossdressing'; the sworn virgin is an honored part of society.

Fa'afafine

The United States is not stranger to third gender possibilities among the indigenous people it embraces. We will leave aside here the case of the so-called *berdaches*—a European term of pejorative content that nevertheless has stuck as a label for transgender Indian people. (A modern alternative to this label—also not without its problems—is to term such folk 'two-souled' people.) Instead we will return for a moment to the world of Pacific Ocean nations and visit American Samoa, part of the Polynesian culture.

Polynesia embraces a number of distinct islands and societies, including Fiji, Hawaii, Samoa (both American Samoa and, some 60 miles to its west, Independent Samoa), Tahiti (part of French Polynesia), and Tonga, among others. Among the Polynesian people can be found a distinctive group of males, who occupy a place in society analogous to a 'third sex' or 'third gender.' Anthropologist Jeannette Marie Mageo interprets this phenomenon as reflecting an historical instability in male-paired gender identity, one paralleled by a similar instability in female-paired gender identity, where it gave rise to experiences of spirit possession rather than crossdressing. Because Polynesians conceive gender in terms of social role rather than as a stable, inner trait, the expression of atypical gender in Polynesian culture is reflected in adoption of feminine dress and work roles.[833]

Transgendered or third gender islanders have been well known in the modern West at least since reports of them from British sailors in the 18th century. In French Polynesia they bear the name *Mahu* or *Rae Rae*; in Samoa they are called *Fa'afafine*; in Tonga they are known as *Fakaletei* (or, sometimes, *Tangata Fakafefine*, 'a man acting like a woman').[834] In this part of our discussion, primary reference is to the *Fa'afafine* unless otherwise noted.

The *Fa'afafine* ('in the manner of a woman,' or 'like a lady') are genetic males raised as females. Traditionally, this family choice was neither arbitrary nor governed by sexual considerations. As sociologist Johanna Schmidt observes, Samoan culture, centered in villages, largely views gender in terms of what one contributes through labor; if a person fills a woman's roles, then that person can be identified as feminine. *Fa'afafine* do women's work (e.g., washing, cleaning, cooking).[835] The selection by a family of a boy to be *Fa'afafine* may have transpired because the family decided it had enough sons but not enough daughters.[836] A male child thus chosen to fill a traditional female role was dressed as a girl and accorded a feminine gender role. Such an individual might, as an adult, eschew marriage and remain at home to care for aging parents.[837]

Today, under the influence of Western culture, some males self-select this status. As Schmidt notes, Western emphasis on individuality has shifted the Samoan conception of gender and led to a greater reliance on appearance and bodily expression rather than the labor role. When *Fa'afafine* leave their families and villages they simultaneously leave the primary markers used to identify their gender; new ones, emphasizing gender-specific Western forms of appearance and behavior, may now be adopted. This has resulted in two distinct kind of *Fa'afafine*—the traditional and socially approved 'womanly' *Fa'afafine* of the villages and the tolerated but often criticized, modernized 'wild' *Fa'afafine* of the cities (and other lands).[838]

Some *Fa'afafine* continue to occupy the role because their parents placed them in it, often because their cross-gender behavior as a child led to parental recognition of them as transgendered. Though their numbers are not large, most villages know of a few and they hold an accepted place in the community.[839] However, despite the long tradition of acceptance of the *Fa'afafine*, not all such children in Samoa receive warm support or approval from their parents, perhaps because of the encroachment of modern Western ideas about transgenderism. Still, research reported by psychologists Nancy Bartlett and P. L. Vasey in 2004 of 20 adult *Fa'afafine* found that all warmly remembered their childhood participation in female-typical behaviors, regardless of parental approval or resistance. Their study notes that—by Western psychiatric standards—the degree of gender dysphoria reported by the *Fa'afafine* did not differ significantly whether their parents opposed their transgender behavior or not, but where any difference was detected it correlated with parental opposition.[840]

These examples, drawn from around the world, are the tip of an iceberg. If even one represents a genuine alternative to a binary gender scheme, then we should pause and seriously rethink gender. But we have yet to look at the possibility that some third gender people walk among us in the mainstream of American life in the United States.

Third Gender People in the U.S.

Both in non-Western societies and in the West there persist people who experience themselves as not existing at the gender poles. We have sampled some of these experiences, but now we need to look closer to home. Even in the United States there are people who self-identify as 'third gender.' Little study has been done on such folk, though in a cultural framework that implicitly denies the very idea this must almost certainly be the case. What modest research there is merits special attention and given the controversy over the notion needs to be broached here in our consideration of fundamental terms.

Clinician Ingrid Sell is one professional who has taken self-identified people at their word and sought to understand their life experience. In a study published in 2004, she reports on 30 male and female individuals, ages 29-77. Among her findings concerning their developmental experience are the following:

- ❑ Awareness of being differently gendered occurred very early for most (90%) of them, typically by age 5.
- ❑ Female third gender people experienced less pressure to conform to their assigned gender during childhood.
- ❑ In adulthood, social pressures to gender conform varied according to gender presentation—those who could more easily 'pass' as a member of their assigned gender experienced less pressure.
- ❑ Coping with gender pressures and ostracism was met in different ways: self-imposed isolation, taking on leadership roles, projecting a 'don't mess with me' appearance, engaging in creative arts, excelling in school, and using substances.[841]

Sell wisely regards her data in a context larger than Western culture. She notes how American third gender people have life experiences and characteristics parallel to third gender folk elsewhere in the world. In many places such individuals, precisely because they are situated between the gender poles, are seen as a valuable resource for their insights and abilities to mediate. Such mediation often extends not only to working with the dominant gender groups (i.e., bridging men and women), but also other groups and often between this ordinary world and a sacred world beyond.

In this latter regard, third gender people often gain legitimacy in their sacred roles by exhibiting a greater sensitivity to spiritual matters. Sell found among her subjects both that they were very likely to have been called upon to mediate between men and women (77%), and that they were especially likely to have experienced a transcendent spiritual event and/or exhibit paranormal-type abilities (93%). Further consistent with such people's experiences elsewhere in the world, these American third gender people were likely to be healers (43% work in health and helping professions), and to be highly creative and artistic (47% were writers, musicians, or performers; an additional 10% were in other very creative fields). She remarks, "Perhaps, as non-Western cultures recognize, there is indeed an element of spirit or 'calling' involved in our being men, women, or mediators between."[842]

As is true for many persons labeled 'transgender,' the participants in Sell's study showed some ambivalence toward the designation. From our discussion above, we can readily see why—'transgender' is a term with wide possibilities of meaning and application, which means it also carries easy potential for misunderstanding. There is no easy solution to the dilemma posed by our current muddled situation. Time will tell what position on the word will prevail.

Conclusion

We need to find ways past the obstacles placed by our current Western limitations in conceiving of gender and conversing on it. This is desirable because more and more evidence demonstrates our present conventions are not merely inadequate, but actually harmful. The world as we *experience* it should trump the world as we *wish* it when it comes to scientific description. Forcing the gender experiences and expressions of many people into a lump classification as gender nonconformists may be logical and work for the existing scheme, but it penalizes people on extremely shaky logical and evidential grounds.

Imagine how different things might play out in the social arena if we succeeded in envisioning gender in ways more resonant with the experiences and expressions of *all* people. Imagine what might happen if we could overcome our cultural arrogance and admit the possibility other cultural conceptions, characterized by greater breadth and fluidity, might come close to lived truth than the rigid scheme we rely upon. We would do well to imagine such things and work toward their realization. As we have learned in our ongoing dialog, there are high stakes in conversing on gender. It is a conversation that matters. All of us are paying a terrible price for our willingness to remain confined by ideas, vocabulary, and practices that only serve some at the expense of all.

Chapter 12

A Gender Spectrum

Introduction: Most of us do not fit so well within our assigned gender that we consistently exhibit the stereotypical signs of that gender. At the same time, though, most of us accept that we are either masculine or feminine, and that so is everyone else. But some of us fit so poorly what others expect of us that neither of the predominant gender labels seem appropriate. In such instances, what are we to do?

In recent decades, partly as a result of our shrinking world and partly as a result of the shifting conversation on gender, Western societies have become increasingly aware of people who claim to belong either to a different gender than the one they were assigned at birth, or to a different gender outside the confines of masculinity and femininity. As a result, there has been more talk about transgender people and discussion about a possible third gender—or more.

Two critical contributing factors to this situation were the widening of the constructs sex and gender, as well as a growing distance between them. In the widening of gender a particular notion helped illustrate the empirical distance between sex and gender by demonstrating that in real life men and women do not always exhibit either stereotypical masculinity or femininity. In fact, healthy people tend to weakly conform to gender stereotypes and instead exhibit a mixing, or blending, of gender characteristics. This truth is embraced in the term androgyny, as persuasively set forward in the 1970s by psychologist Sandra Bem.

But while the notion of androgyny weakened the strict pairing of sex and gender, it was the visible reality of people whose sense of gender was a complete mismatch with their body sex that forced closer examination of the ties between sex and gender. Further, multicultural studies demonstrated numerous instances of genders outside the parameters of conventional Western masculinity and femininity. Scholars began seeking ways to more accurately describe the gender realities of our world.

What we have in this discussion is a brief exploration of *possibilities*. How else might we conceive of genders? Can we escape a binary system with discrete categories at poles and find a more robust spectrum? Let's find out.[843]

Is There a Gender 'Spectrum'?

In our era, the medicalization of sex and gender into dichotomous poles, with nothing between them, and exact pairings of male/masculine, female/feminine, means that any gender presentation not conforming closely to the socially expected norm will be labeled negatively. A feminine female is rewarded with the label 'lady.' A relatively gender nonconforming female is less approvingly called a 'tomboy.' Similarly, a masculine male might be referred to as a 'real man.' But a relatively gender nonconforming male may be disapprovingly labeled a 'sissy.' Those whose nonconformity in gender identity and role is more pronounced are branded 'gender dysphoric'—a pathology reflecting such deviance from the norm of the pole that is considered 'disordered.' Of course, only a disturbed few inhabit this narrow region—and no one ever truly escapes either their anatomical sex or their assigned gender. To even try proves the absurdity of the proposition and thus warrants the negative judgment.

In our culture we are all in one box. Gender is bipolar, but one-dimensional. The situation might be pictured like this:

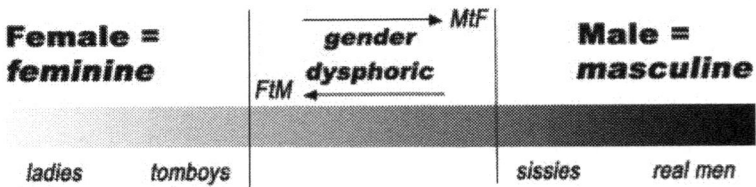

In this picture there is no room for the intersexed or a 'third gender.' Transgendered people are not genuinely trans*gendered*, because only two genders exist; they are *trans*gressors, inappropriately crossing gender lines that society insists remain clear and strong boundaries.

But the sheer persistence of a continuing group of well-adjusted, high functioning people in every generation and pretty much every place shows that this picture, whatever its simple appeal, does not work well. It neither fits the facts of experience nor succeeds in constraining human expression. Just as the indisputable reality of the intersexed has forced a more nuanced appraisal of sex, so those called transgendered (a clearly inadequate term) beckon us to a more realistic appraisal of gender. We need a new picture and a new vocabulary.

Unfortunately we continue to lack in our culture any clear and accepted parallel in gender discussions to the concept of the intersexed with respect to sex. Unlike other cultures that acknowledge a 'third gender,' ours maintains the ridiculously rigid dichotomy portrayed above. Until we can even admit to the possibility of something other than merely masculine or feminine, we can scarcely imagine what the evidence best supports—a continuum where alternative gendered realities coexist alongside those recognized as masculine and feminine. Our conceptualizations of gender continue to lag behind those of sex in this regard.

There are alternative schemes available, if we look for them. For example, Norwegian scholar Per Schioldborg proposed in 1983 that gender be ranged along *two* continua rather than one; masculinity comprises one dimension, femininity another, and intersecting at right angles they create four quadrants:

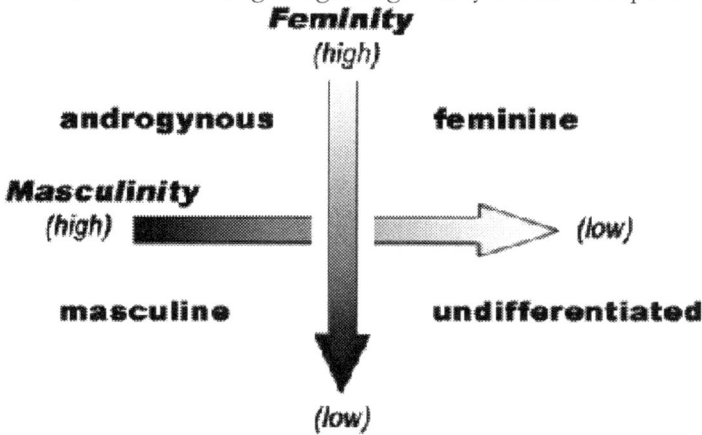

Those high in both masculinity and femininity are androgynous; those low in both are undifferentiated. One who is masculine ranks high in the masculinity dimension and low in femininity, and one who is feminine ranks high in femininity and low in masculinity.[844]

To adopt a scheme wherein gender is presented along a continuum will be advantageous over a rigid, bipolar dichotomy only when a rigid and simplistic binding of sex to gender is severed. Otherwise we end with a variant of what we have now: males are either 'masculine' or 'effeminate' ('sissies'), and females are 'feminine' or 'tomboys.' Once anatomical sex is better separated from gender genuine 'other gender' recognitions are possible.

What might such a continuum look like? Evan Eyler and Kathryn Wright propose a nine point gender scale they devised for clinical work with genetic females, which is summarized here:

- ❑ Female always identifying as a girl or woman.
- ❑ Female with maleness; at times has identified more as a boy or man.
- ❑ Genderblended (predominantly female), with identification as both woman and man, but more as woman.
- ❑ Othergendered; neither woman nor man, but of another gender.
- ❑ Ungendered; neither woman nor man nor any other gender.
- ❑ Bigendered; a combination of man and woman, where either might predominate at times.
- ❑ Genderblended (predominantly male), with identification as both woman and man, but more as man.
- ❑ Male with femaleness; at times has identified more as a girl or woman.

❏ Male always identifying as a boy or man.[845]

This scale retains recognition of the pairing of sex and gender but in a more flexible way.

In my own view, the conceptual underpinning of a continuum suggests fluidity. Boundaries between points on the continuum are artificial constructs, which in their extremes yield the stereotypes of masculine and feminine found at the poles. (We can retain masculine and feminine at the poles—indeed it is difficult to imagine a continuum so divorced from our present way of seeing things that other poles could be envisioned.) Between these poles other gendered realities exist. In the lived world of experience all gendered realities are fluid rather than static; our experience and expression of our gendered selves varies over time and across contexts. Yet within our own individuality the range of these changes is rarely extreme. Moreover, we all can find others whose ranges are similar to our own while being different from the rest. Thus, classifying points along the continuum as distinct gender categories merely represents an abstracted picture of experiential and expressive ranges of gendered reality.

Consider the following as one possible depiction of a gender continuum:

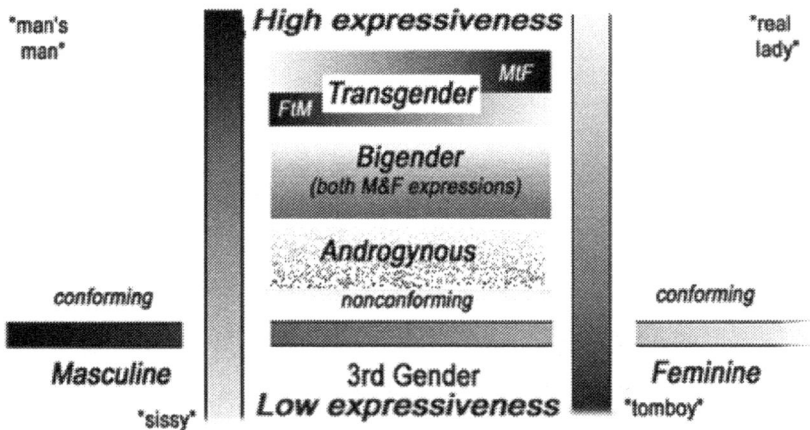

The continuum is ranged along two axes. One axis is gender expressiveness, the degree to which an individual presents gender. Some folk express masculinity in a very strong way (high expressiveness), while others do so more weakly (low expressiveness). The second axis is conformity/nonconformity. Some people strongly conform to social expectations about gender identity and role, while others do so more weakly. Some are nonconformists to assigned gender identity and role, either weakly and partially, or strongly and completely.

An individual might, for example, strongly express femininity and also highly conform to the social expectations for femininity—a 'real lady.' The masculine counterpart would be styled a 'man's man.' Another person might strongly express femininity but be less conforming, such as a 'tomboy' who engages in rough and tumble play while simultaneously wearing makeup and unambiguously embracing her gender identity. Someone who weakly expresses the assigned masculine gender role and does not conform to gender role expectations might be called a 'sissy' even though he retains a discernible masculine gender identity. A range of gender expressiveness and conformity is possible for those who still self-identify at the poles of masculinity and femininity.

The continuum, though, reflects the reality of a 'third gender'—a cluster of other possible gendered realities distinguishable from the poles. For simplicity this cluster has been represented by just three terms: transgender, bigender, and androgynous. The androgynous person is viewed here differently from Schioldborg's scheme. In this continuum the androgynous are seen as weakly expressing gender as well as being nonconforming in a relatively mild fashion. The transgendered individual, by contrast, strongly expresses gender and gender nonconformity. Such a person may regard the 'trans' as referring to transcending the gender dichotomy, transgressing it, or merely crossing from one pole to the other at will. The bigendered person exists between the androgynous and transgendered, as well as between masculine and feminine. This individual expresses both masculinity and femininity, either weakly or more strongly, but does not conform to social expectations for either masculine or feminine. This nonconformity, too, may be greater or lesser but always accompanies a sense of being neither masculine nor feminine, or more often of being both. Because current ways of talking about gender in our culture do not use the term 'bigender,' this group is tacitly included in my use of the term 'transgender' in this work.

A Multiaxial, Multidimensional Model of Gender

An even more robust picture is possible, and this next alternative represents a model put forward as better than those considered above. Gender is dependent on sex, but not as its destiny. Rather, gender *interprets* sex, and it does so in ways that may more or less reflect strong personal identification with one's sexual body (experience), more or less show strong communication of one's sexual body (expressiveness), and more or less fits expectations about one's sexual body (conformity).

Consider the following image:

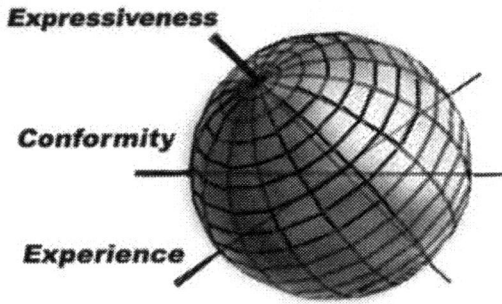

3 Gender Axes

The three axes (conformity, experience and expressiveness) are embedded in multidimensional space. Each axis has three dimensions: physical, social, and personal. In this gender universe there are also degrees (high to moderate to low) in the axes. As the axes, dimensions, and levels interact a rich matrix of gendered realities emerge.[846] For our purposes it will be enough to sketch out some of these after first elucidating further on the axes and dimensions. These remarks are all preliminary and suggestive in nature. The most important impression to gain is that gender truly is multiaxial and multidimensional, capable of division into many gender states or statuses beyond masculine and feminine, which themselves need not be viewed at polar ends.

The Three Axes

The notion of *gender conformity* is simple and practical. The axis of conformity recognizes that gender is assessed partly in terms of conformity to at least three dimensions. One is physicality. Assignment of the label 'masculine' is easier when the apparent physical body looks sexually male. Depictions of a masculine male are far more likely to show a bodybuilder than a short, slender, long-haired and beardless male. Likewise, conformity has a social dimension. Others hold expectations based on their beliefs about how a boy or girl, man or woman, should experience and express the assigned gender. In particular, more conforming gender expressions are recognized and rewarded over less conforming ones. Finally, a personal dimension mediates the others. An individual's own beliefs and expectations—whether highly, moderately, or lowly conforming to social standards—exerts a modifying influence. All three dimensions display degrees of intensity and interact. Thus any given individual may strongly, moderately, or weakly conform to the physical standard, social standard, or self standard existing for the assigned gender and/or the selected gender the person experiences and expresses.

Gender experience refers to the internal feelings and thoughts, as well as the enacted behaviors, in relation to both one's assigned gender identity and role, and one's assumed gender identity and role. Gender experience it what it means to be a gendered self as both subject and object. There is a physical dimension to this experience that entails both the perception and use of the sexual body. But this is especially the feelings, thoughts and behaviors accompanying the embodiment of the sexual body in gendered apparel, with ornamentation, hairstyle and so forth included. An individual's gender experience of the physical dimension may be strong, moderate, or weak. One may be little moved by the sexual body or attach great significance to gendered clothing; the range of possible experience is inexhaustible. There is likewise a social dimension to gender experience, a process and collection of feelings, thoughts and behaviors organized around interaction with others, or at least an awareness and accounting of others. This, too, may be strong, moderate or weak in degree. Finally, there is a personal dimension to experience; the variations in experience are as unique and many as there are individuals. But these also have degrees as individuals do not all have the same intensity or depth of felt experience, vary in their consciousness of gender, and act with more or less reserve.

Gender expressiveness refers to the display of gender, regardless of actual experience. In other words, an individual can express a gender, or degree of gender, relatively apart from any lived-in sense of it. Anyone can fake any gender experience. But anyone can also present the gender they do experience in a variety of ways and degrees. The physical dimension of gender expressiveness involves the ways an individual presents the sexual body, clothed or unclothed, so as to communicate a gender experience, whether actual, imagined, or pretended. Obviously, this may be done to a higher or lower degree. For example, not everyone who does drag does so in the same manner, to the same degree, or to reflect the same internal gender experience. Similar dynamics inform the social dimension. Gender expressed is not the same as gender experienced. Many individuals conform to social standards in their gender expressiveness despite their relative lack of gender experience for the gender being displayed. Some use gender expressiveness to glory in a rich experience of that gender. Once more variability in motivation and behavior is immense. Finally, gender expressiveness has a personal dimension. Regardless of expectations accompanying the sexual body and social standards, each person makes choices that shape how, when, to what extent, and what gender is expressed.

The above remarks, sketchy as they are, should suffice to show that the axes are each multidimensional. They are also multidimensional in the ways they interact with one another. When degrees are added in the result is a richly complex system of signification that better reflects gender reality as lived. This shall become more apparent as we turn next to the three dimensions.

The Three Dimensions

The *physical dimension* includes both the sexual body and the manner in which its appearance is constructed through things like clothing. The sexual body is never completely nude; even without clothes or makeup perceptions add layers of meaning to the biological entity. The physical dimension of gender includes both the symbolic body and the agentic body. As Erica Reischer and Kathyrn Koo summarize these, the symbolic body is "a conduit of social meaning," whereas the agentic body is "an active participant or agent in the social world."[847] The physical dimension of gender involves the ways our sexual bodies are produced, presented, and perceived as they transmit information to self and others, *and* as they exert influence on self and others. As Reischer and Koo put it, "the ideal gendered body does not merely remain in the realm of the symbolic; its power lies in its ability to directly influence behavior within the social sphere."[848]

The *social dimension* of gender refers to the matrix of relations, expectations, behaviors and so forth that give gender its widest context. Gender is always connected to some degree to the sexual body, impossible to divorce from the presentation of that body by means of dress, and inescapably personal. Yet the social dimension defines the essence of gender in ways the other dimensions cannot. It both places and connects every personal gendered body with every other one, if through no other means than the weight of shared beliefs and expectations, however derived and no matter whether reasonable or irrational. Both conscious and unconscious, the social dimension imposes the values, morality, and judgment of others. But because of how it is constructed, the social dimension evolves. It has fluidity and flexibility; it can change.

The *personal dimension* of gender refers to the individual contribution made to gender experience, expression, and conformity. Intertwined and incapable of being divorced from the other dimensions it enjoys a reciprocal interaction with them. An individual's gender is not merely the result of a sexual body, however dressed, or a social assignment, however enforced. It is always also personal, constructed in a unique configuration by personal motivations, attitudes, desires, and acts. No matter the utility of designating gender categories, the individual dimension inevitably renders them constructs unequal to life.

Gender Categories Along a Continuum

All of the above axes, dimensions and degrees contribute to reconceptualizing gender. We need not be terminologically confined to 'masculine' and 'feminine.' Moreover, 'masculine' and 'feminine' need not be conceived as poles at opposite ends; there may be gender statuses more extremely associated with the characteristics we have discussed. Even if we grudgingly accept division into two sexual body camps ('male' for bodies apparently like 46, XY; 'female' for bodies apparently like 46, XX), we can identify distinct gender statuses or states. Consider a few of the possibilities set out in the accompanying table; they are by no means all of the possibilities.

Table 12.1 Genders

Name (Sex assignment)	Brief Description
Gynaikine (F)	From Greek 'like a woman'; a 'lady's lady.' An individual whose sexual body represents cultural ideals of femaleness, and who embraces this body with high physicality. She possesses an exceptional experience of femaleness, strong conformity to stereotypical gender ideas associated with a female body, and exaggerated expressiveness; these axes are strongly endorsed personally though viewed socially as extreme.
Theline (F)	From the Greek 'one who suckles,' an individual whose sexual body presentation and gender traits emphasize in stereotypical fashion the attributes of 'woman-as-mother.' Her experience, expressiveness and conformity all stress those things associated with a female's role of bearing and nurturing children. Though socially approved, this approval is modified by a perception that the individual's identity and roles are more limited than is true for other people having female-type bodies.
Feminine (F)	A generic gender; the default label for those whose anatomical presentation appears female and whose experience, expression, and conformity fall within the social norms to win high approval as a woman who knows and keeps her gendered place.
Masimiline (F)	From Latin *mas* + *similes*, 'mannish'; an individual whose sexual body is labeled female but whose physical presentation emphasizes traits more associated with a male body. This person weakly expresses personal and social traits culturally associated with a female body, and weakly conforms to accompanying gender standards for such a sexual body. Personal experience of gender may be high, moderate, or low.
Andreiazine (F; FtM transsexual)	From the Greek for 'a manly spirit'; an individual whose sexual body is labeled female but whose expressiveness of cultural traits is much more like that expected for those whose bodies are labeled male. Nonconformity to cultural standards for gender traits associated with a female body is moderate to high. Personal experience of female sexual body may range from acceptance to discomfort or rejection (including sex change). Social disapproval is moderate to high, perhaps prompting this individual to be highly selective in expressiveness of gender,

	depending on context.
Neutroine *(or Anthropine)* (F or M)	From Latin *neutron*, 'towards neither side,' this gender lies midway. It is weakly associated with a sexual body, whether because of intersex condition or simply an unendorsed physical dimension. Conformity to cultural standards to either maleness or femaleness is weak, as is expressiveness of either in gender traits. The individual presents in a way where anatomical sex is not immediately apparent, or seems not to matter at all.
Gynnisine *(or gynanarine)* (M; MtF transsexual)	From Greek 'woman-man'; an individual whose sexual body is labeled male but whose expressiveness of cultural traits is much more like that expected for those whose bodies are labeled female. Nonconformity to cultural standards for gender traits associated with the male body is moderate to high. Personal experience of male sexual body may range from acceptance to discomfort or rejection (including sex change). Social disapproval is moderate to high, perhaps prompting this individual to be highly selective in expressiveness of gender, depending on context.
Muliebrine (M)	From Latin *muliebris*, 'womanish,' or 'effeminate'; an individual whose sexual body is labeled male but whose physical presentation emphasizes traits more associated with a female body. This person weakly expresses personal and social traits culturally associated with a male body, and weakly conforms to accompanying gender standards for such a sexual body. Personal experience of gender may be high, moderate, or low. Social approval tends to be lower than for gender states or statuses more conforming to cultural standards associated with a male body.
Masculine (M)	A generic gender; the default label for those whose anatomical presentation appears male and whose experience, expression, and conformity fall within the social norms to win high approval as a man who knows and keeps his gendered place.
Andrikine (M)	From Greek for 'manly'; a 'man's man.' An individual whose sexual body represents cultural ideals of maleness, and who embraces this body with high physicality. He possesses an exceptional experience of maleness, strong conformity to stereotypical gender ideas associated with a male body, and exaggerated expressiveness; these axes are strongly endorsed personally though

	viewed socially as extreme.
Viriline (M)	From Latin *vir*, 'a heroic man'; a 'stud.' An individual whose sexual body represents cultural ideals of male sexuality and aggressiveness, and who embraces this body with high physicality. He possesses an exceptional experience of maleness, strong conformity to stereotypical gender ideas associated with the male body as a sexual and physical instrument, and exaggerated expressiveness; these axes are strongly endorsed personally though viewed socially as extreme.

Each of these gender statuses, or states, can be operationally defined, empirically observed and tested, and described with discrete boundaries. In short, they meet the criteria for categories and thus have as much validity as 'masculine' and 'feminine.' As is, the two genders our culture endorses are conceptually overly broad, embracing gender presentations of great diversity, some with characteristics overlapping the other gender, and of increasingly less utilitarian value. If, for example, social science can continue to multiply categories of mental disorders using the logic of distinguishable traits and relatively clear boundaries, there is no reason not to apply the same logic to gender realities. In both cases the categories are artificial constructions intended to help us better sort out experiential realities. Lord knows we need some clarification for the existing muddle created by confining discussion to two genders!

The point in multiplying genders must not be to make them ends-in-themselves. The advantage of adding new gender labels, where each gender status is demarcated from the others, is to show their conceptual equality. 'Masculine' and 'feminine' not only are not the only valid gender terms, they are not qualitatively superior to other designations or statuses. One may even question their presumed numerical superiority once a continuum with enough distinct points is identified. If we are going to insist on gender labels—and there is no sign this fact is going to change any time soon—then we might as well have enough of them both to reflect gendered life as it is lived and diminish the power presently held by one privileged gender (masculinity) over another gender (feminine).[849]

Concluding Comment on Gender Models

Now, if we move away from theoretical language we can put the matter like this: people tend to cluster in recognizable gender patterns. There are those who clearly present as feminine most of the time, and whose experience and expression of femininity does not vary greatly across time or contexts. Likewise, there are those who clearly present as masculine most of the time, and whose experience and expression of masculinity does not vary greatly across time or contexts. These folk may well be the majority among us, just as unambiguously anatomically male or female persons are more common than intersexed individuals. Yet there are also those who do not fit at or even near these generic gender labels. Among such people other recognizable gender patterns may be discerned. Indeed they have been in distinguishing so-called 'third gender' groups in various cultures around the world. However, as we have seen, there is no logical reason to confine ourselves to either two or three genders—we can create as many labels as there are identifiably distinct patterns to name.

All of this modeling depends on overcoming the simplistic pairing between sex and gender, where the former invariably and predictably yields particular forms of the latter. At this point in time, evidence suggests a different conclusion: any sex can indwell any gendered reality. Hopefully we may soon come at least far enough in our thinking that we can weaken the monopoly held by a scheme limited to two sex labels and two gender labels. Perhaps even if we cling to the notion of just two basic camps we can better describe the range in each, naming gender statuses subordinate to gender states (e.g., naming 'viriline' as a status of the gender state 'masculine'). Though this seems less desirable than a thorough overhaul of our present gender scheme, at least it would be more nuanced.

Even granting legitimacy to new genders a significant linguistic challenge remains. So wed are we to dichotomous thinking that we would still need either new words to accompany terms like 'man' and 'woman,' or we would have to make those words label a range of distinct genders that share in common bodies that are more male-like or more female-like. If we become more culturally accepting of sexual bodies with mixed genital features, then perhaps we can add a third general term, like 'androgyn,' to stand alongside 'man' and 'woman.' Then, at least, there would be three camps, all body-based, but permitting a range of associated gender statuses or states.

We would still face, too, the issue of pronouns. One solution is merely to retain the present pronouns but use the one that best fits the *presentation* rather than presumed sexual body. Thus an anatomical male who lives within the gendered experience and expression of femininity should be referred to by the pronoun 'she.' The term 'transsexual' might still be appropriate if the person is transitioning in body appearance, but the term 'transgender' would not be appropriate for such a label depends on our current dichotomous system—as does '*cross*dressing'. Our own use of these terms in this book is an unwelcome concession to the limitations of current dialog.[850] Let's be clear: either anatomical males or females can be feminine; either sex can be masculine—and the same claim holds for intersexed people. Once we add new gender labels our ability to see people as they are grows, and so must our language.

Unfortunately, we are clearly not yet to this perspective as a culture. Until we can create an acceptable vocabulary to match our escape from our current dichotomous thinking we must struggle to find ways to adequately express the reality of gender for crossdressers using the limited terms already in place. But that should not hinder us from questioning and dialoging. Change happens.

So we return to a question we began with. If our thinking about gender changes, is it for better or worse? We are only being fair if we query whether our society's present view is the result of a better understanding of the biology of human sexuality, coupled with more clarity about social gender roles, or the reflection of cultural pressure to uphold a paradigm that has an inadequate scientific basis. If the latter is the case, it is fair to ask *why?*

Chapter 13

Gender & Sexuality

Introduction: An earlier discussion (chapter 3) considered the relation of gender to anatomical sex. But what about gender's relation to sexuality? This is a broader question, and a multifaceted one. As interesting as it may be, our primary pursuit of this question will not be organized along who (subject) does what (aim) to whom (object)—a common approach in survey and interview research into *individual sexuality*. On the other hand, we don't wish to ignore this interest. What we will focus upon is probing *differences along gender lines in both sexual attitudes and behaviors*.

When we discuss *masculine sexuality*, we continue to struggle with *stereotypes*. The traditional model familiar in our culture for many generations now is a *phallocentric* one, where a man's sexuality is prized above a woman's. A more *egalitarian* model has been advanced in recent decades with a concerted effort to combat the sexual scripts and myths of the older model.

Women, too, struggle with the expectations generated by the past. They are presented *multiple, conflicting scripts*, with perhaps only one common theme—that a woman's sexuality does not matter as much as a man's. Against this theme and the many myths surrounding it has been a push to *liberate women's sexuality*. The goals of such liberation include empowering women to an equal status in sexual interactions and reclaiming possession of their own sexual bodies.

Not only the conforming genders, but nonconforming genders also struggle with stereotypes. In the case of those who are often called *sexual minorities*, two matters seem to be objects of fascination for the general public. One, *sexual orientation*, is a subject we discussed earlier (chapter 8). The supposed link between nonconforming gender and nonconforming sexuality is often accompanied by another one: *cross-dressing*. Especially crossdressing by biological males is commonly, if erroneously, associated with both atypical gender and atypical sexuality. Crossdressers are often seen by others as *fetishists* and linked with other forms of sexual deviance, especially *sadomasochism* and *bondage*.

But we cannot really ignore sexual orientation if we are discussing sexuality and gender. So we must return to the subject, this time focusing on *homosexuality* and *heterosexism*. The persistent link between these continues to plague ordinary people in their conversing on gender. No other area of the discourse seems so fraught with problems in nonproductive, misleading, and even hurtful speech.

Gender Group Beliefs About Sexuality

More than one way exists to talk about the relationship between gender and sexuality. We will discuss a select few of these, beginning with an approach that receives much media attention—considering if men and women vary significantly in their attitudes about, and practice of, sexual behaviors. But if we content ourselves just to trod ground most of us are already likely to be familiar with, we will have wasted an opportunity to examine other important matters. At least as important are beliefs we hold about fundamental features of sexuality such as sexual power and the abiding question of whether presumed differences in masculine and feminine sexuality are natural or culturally constructed. Some wrestling with these basic features will prepare us to then examine more closely specific matters of sexuality for both conforming and nonconforming genders.

Differences Between Women and Men in Sexual Attitudes and Behaviors

The most common way gender is spoken about in relation to sexuality is through a *comparison/contrast model*: How are men and women alike or different in their sexual attitudes and practices? This kind of research is voluminous and often confusing because so many matters can be asked about in so many different ways. Identifying truly dependable results has proved elusive because methodologies and vocabularies in studies vary so widely. For example, the simple word 'sex' can be used to mean just intercourse or any sexual behavior. So, if we ask someone how often they have had 'sex' with a partner in the last month, and don't clarify what we mean by the term, respondents may interpret the word in widely different ways. The results then are meaningless because they aren't comparable. Similarly, if we ask people how many sexual partners they have had in their life, without clarifying what constitutes a sexual partner, respondents' answers once more will be impossible to compare because we don't know what they consider constitutes a sexual partner. Similar problems exist in many other matters.

Still, such research is an honored tradition in this country extending back at least since the famous studies by Alfred Kinsey and his colleagues in the 1940s-1950s. The 1948 volume on men, for instance, found that the average American man experienced an orgasm between 1-4 times weekly, with a gradual decline after age 30. The 1953 volume on women reported that about 10% of American women had never had an orgasm during sexual interactions with their husbands. Both volumes found differences in attitudes and behaviors between college-educated men and women and those with less education. More education was correlated with more liberal attitudes and more adventuresome behavior.[851] There has been no lack of survey and interview research since.

One interesting report that appeared during second wave feminism was a 1974 survey undertaken by social science writer Morton Hunt of more than 2,000 readers of *Playboy* magazine. Though this audience may not be a representative cross-section of America, the results were suggestive of a liberalizing trend among both men and women. For example, there was greater acceptance of oral sex and more time reported spent in foreplay.[852] These kinds of trends have been found repeatedly in recent decades. But our interest here is not in sexuality in its own right, but for how it sheds light on gender. So we must turn to a focus on differences reported by women and men (nonconforming genders are generally shunted into a conforming gender category).

The first matter to note about such differences is that they are more alleged than confirmed. As psychologist and sex therapist Michele Burnette puts it, "scientific research on men and women suggest that they are far more similar than different."[853] *Men and women do not typically differ significantly in either sexual attitudes or practices.* Perhaps the key word here is 'significantly.' Studies consistently find men reporting greater involvement in many sexual practices and their attitudes often appear more liberal. However, the *size of the differences is modest* in almost all instances. They also appear to be shrinking.

Let's begin with *differences in attitudes about sexual practices.* One attitudinal difference is most often pointed to as significant, which we can partly get at it by examining responses to two common assertions:

❏ "Premarital sex is always wrong": women are much more likely to frown upon premarital sex than are men.

❏ "Extramarital sex is always wrong": women are somewhat more likely to regard extramarital sex as always wrong than are men.

Clustering these two attitudes together, and with other research in mind on things like the so-called 'one-night stand,' we can draw the conclusion that a difference exists between the genders in their approval or tolerance of *casual sex*—sexual activity occurring outside a commitment to enduring relationship. This seems to be the one dependable difference in attitude found between the conforming genders, though even it may be lessening.

If we probe each of these a little more deeply we find differences in the way research studies obtain results, but results that nevertheless appear to point to similar differences. In asking about *sexual behavior before marriage,* a 1970 study sponsored by the Kinsey Institute found nearly half (45.5%) of men agreed with the statement the 'premarital sex is always wrong', *if* the qualifier 'without love' was added; closer to two-thirds (61.5%) of the women agreed—a 16% gender difference.[854] A study in the mid-1980s found significant differences between women and men in regard to sexual permissiveness. Men were generally in agreement with the statements, "I do not need to be committed to a person to have sex with him/her" and "Casual sex is acceptable." Women disagreed with both.[855] The *Janus Report* of the early 1990s approached the subject differently, asking 'how important is it to have sexual experience before marriage?' for each gender. With regard to men, both genders endorsed the attitude that it was important or very important (56% of men; 52% of women). With regard to women, both genders were again in agreement—but somewhat in the opposite direction (46% in each gender group thought it important or very important).[856] In this matter of premarital sexual experience the infamous *double standard* clearly appears to be applied to the genders. While men are encouraged to become sexually experienced before marriage, women are expected to remain chaste and to enter marriage sexually naïve virgins. Although this attitude ostensibly has relaxed in recent decades,[857] it still seems very much in place. Young people, in particular, often contrast 'good girls' from 'sluts'—with boys wanting sex with the latter, but only taking the former home to meet their parents!

Both conforming genders disapprove of extramarital sex, although men not so much as women. In the 1970 Kinsey study 83.5% of men and 90.3% of women agreed it was either always wrong (M: 66.5%; F: 78.4%), or almost always wrong (M: 17%; F: 11.9%).[858] Once again, the *Janus Report* approaches the topic somewhat differently, asking respondents whether extramarital affairs seriously affect marriages. Among men, 74% agreed or strongly agreed that they do, while 83% of women agreed or strongly agreed.[859] Beneath the numbers, though, may be other significant factors. Robert Michaels and colleagues found that the picture alters if people are clustered into different broad attitudinal groups (traditional, relational, and recreational). In this case, 98% of 'conservative traditional' people regard extramarital sex as always wrong, while just 32% of 'libertarian recreational' people do. However, more than three-quarters (76.7%) of all respondents thought it always wrong. Differences between men and women were found here, too, since men more often than women identify themselves in one or the other of the groups with more liberal attitudes.[860] All of these 'facts,' though, we may wish to balance against the observation of survey research expert Tom Smith, who remarks, "There are probably more scientifically worthless 'facts' on extramarital relations than any other facet of human behavior."[861]

Next, let us consider *differences in sexual practices*. Again we may draw upon well-known studies. These suggest that men typically engage in many sexual behaviors more often than do women, with perhaps the most significant disparity in practice involving masturbation. However, as we noted with attitudes, the gap between men and women in the practice of sexual behaviors seems to be shrinking. For our purposes here, we can content ourselves with using one outstanding example of well-received scholarly research, the work done by social scientists Robert Michael and colleagues. They include gender differences in the practice of various sexual behaviors, with more men reporting having engaged in the behavior at least once in their lifetime than women for each of these:

- ❑ masturbation (in the last 12 months)—60% men; 40% women.
- ❑ masturbation once a week or more—25% men; 10% women.
- ❑ anal sex—26% men; 20% women.
- ❑ oral sex (giving)—77% men; 68% women.
- ❑ oral sex (receiving)—79% men; 73% women.
- ❑ more than one sexual partner in the last 12 months—23% men; 12% women.[862]

To the above we might add two other findings often used to fuel the common belief that men are oversexed: more than half (54%) of men report thinking about sex every day, whereas less than one-in-five (19%) women do.[863] Men are much more likely to initiate sexual activity; one study in the mid-1990s found 60% of men reporting they always or almost always start things, compared to just 22% of women making that assertion.[864] Of course, all of these results can be questioned and sometimes are.

Of course, it is probably more common to interpret these differences as both larger than they are and more meaningful than they are. As we have noted before, *within-group differences are typically as great if not greater than between-group differences*. As heard a moment ago, education has an effect on attitudes and practices alike. For example, Michael and associates found that men with at least some college education were more likely both to give and receive oral sex than men with less than a high school education. In fact the size of the differences (81%-59% for giving oral sex; 84%-61% for receiving it) were *larger* than the overall differences between men and women for each (22% among men, but 9% difference between men and women for giving oral sex; 23% among men, but 6% difference between men and women for receiving oral sex).[865]

We might also point to *physiological comparisons of the sexual response*. Burnette points to studies conducted in the 1970s indicating that women are just as sexually arousable as men are. Moreover—in direct contrast to a common myth—women, like men, are more aroused by sexually explicit materials than they are by romantic content. Further, heterosexual men and women are similar in certain preferences for arousing material: both groups are more aroused by group sex than sexual activity between individuals.[866]

Although this portion of our discussion is likely to feel truncated and inadequate, because this kind of information is so readily available and threatens to sidetrack us from other significant matters, we must move on. Before we do we must note one danger in this kind of research: it is easy to frame questions in a manner that solicits responses that do little more than tell the researcher what he or she desires to hear. Even where researchers are scrupulously careful to ask questions in as scientific a manner as possible, two other factors may creep in.

First, people have a tendency to answer in ways they believe will be socially appropriate and approved. For this and many other reasons they may over-report or under-report their actual practices and exaggerate or understate their actual beliefs. Coupled with our previously mentioned problem of how vocabulary is used and interpreted this constitutes a constant threat to validity. Second, science itself is colored by culture. Our cultural beliefs about sexuality guide the way we think about the subject, including what we think to ask about and how we choose to ask about it.

Put together, there are many reasons to wonder whether research such as we have been discussing does little more than endorse such cultural stereotypical ideas as 'men are more sexual than women,' not because they actually are, but because our culture says they are and our research and responses conform to that belief despite our best intentions. Finally, even if the facts prove trustworthy and confirm a particular belief, such as the one just named, that in no way explains *why* the facts are as they are. They might be that way more because of biology or more because of culture—but we should not assume we know why. Most often people assume an essentialist explanation, which we have seen is highly debatable.

Differences Between Men and Women in Beliefs About Gender and Sexuality

As fascinating as differences between men and women in sexual attitudes and practices may be, they do not get at something at least as important—fundamental beliefs about gender and sexuality. Are women and men different in this respect? Sociologists Emily Kane and Mimi Schippers investigate this question. While there are many pertinent subjects that might be probed in this regard, Kane and Schippers choose three of fundamental importance: beliefs about sexual drives, about sexual power, and about compulsory heterosexuality. The first of these issues matters because the prevailing belief that men have stronger sexual drives may elicit particular ways people interpret gender inequality. The second matters because men and women today appear to have a variety of views on which gender has more power in sexual matters. Finally, the last issue matters because it has emerged as a central feature in the construction of gender inequality (and is a matter we shall look at more closely later in our discussion).[867]

Kane and Schippers utilize information collected via a probability sample of 453 American adults. This sample shows the following similarities and differences:

❑ Both men and women believe men have stronger sexual drives, but men are more likely to see these as natural in origin.

❑ Women and men strongly disagree on who has greater sexual power; each gender tends to see the other as possessing more power, with few regarding power as equal. They also strongly disagree as to the source (origin) of this difference.

❑ Both conforming genders agree they experience pressure toward heterosexuality. But they disagree in their beliefs about homosexuality, with women being significantly more accepting.

About 70% of the respondents see men's *sexual drives* as stronger than women's. Both men (69.5%) and women (74.8%) endorse this belief. But they differ in how they explain this difference. More than half (58.2%) of men attribute this stronger drive to Nature, while women are evenly split on whether this is due to Nature (50.8%) or to culture (49.2%).[868]

With reference to *sexual power* there are significant differences in belief between men and women. Women are much likelier to view men as holding the greater power (61.3% of women; 38.3% of men). On the other hand, men are more than twice as likely to see women as having the greater power (21.2% of women; 47% of men). Small minorities of women (17.5%) and men (14.8%) regard power as equal. While both genders tend to agree that sexual power differences are social in origin, they disagree in how strongly this shared belief is endorsed. About three-quarters (74.3%) of women hold this view compared to somewhat more than half (55.7%) of men. Put another way, just as with sexual drives, men (44.3%) are much more likely than women (25.7%) to see sexual power as natural in origin. Not surprisingly, the gender groups also disagree on which gender benefits most from the perceived differences in power, whether the power of each gender is too great, and who is harmed by the difference. In each case, members of a gender group are prone to see the other gender as benefiting more and having too much power, while seeing their own group as more harmed.[869]

Compulsory heterosexuality—the sense one *must* be heterosexual—is something both women and men believe they experience pressure toward. In fact, the percent in both groups who believe they experience such pressure is the same— 82%. Moreover, they are very similar in perception of how great the pressure is, with more than twice as many in each group viewing that there is a great deal of pressure. Both groups also agree in explaining this pressure as a mix of natural and social causes, though women are somewhat more likely to endorse this belief. However, when it comes to *acceptance of homosexuality*, beliefs are significantly different. More than half of men believe homosexuality endangers the family (52.5%), is detrimental to society (61.4%), and view homosexuality as unacceptable (67.3%). Women are more tolerant, though only relatively so; nearly half (49.6%) believe homosexuality is detrimental to society and more than half (58.2%) disagree that it is acceptable.[870]

Kane and Schippers draw some inferences we should attend to carefully. First, the generally endorsed belief that men have a stronger sexual drive and that this drive is natural may be potentially important because beliefs about sexual drives have played a role in justifying men's sexual aggression and also in depicting women as generally passive. Second, the difference in beliefs over sexual power may pose a significant obstacle, especially for men, in seeing gender inequalities in general and recognizing sexual coercion in particular. Third, it is troubling that while most men and women believe there is pressure to conform to heterosexuality, there is also a strong element of belief that such pressure is normal and that homosexuality is not acceptable. These beliefs tend not to be closely examined. The researchers remark, "This lack of criticism and the prevalence of naturalizing beliefs about heterosexuality may provide further ideological justification for gender inequality. . . ."[871]

Differences in beliefs are presumed to elicit differences in behavior. For example, we might consider how particular beliefs about sexuality shape the way women and men talk to each other in heterosexual interactions, especially when the partners are sexually inexperienced. This was precisely the interest of researchers June Crawford, Susan Kippox, and Catherine Waldby. They analyzed memories and accounts of early sexual encounters as shared by men and women in same-gender group discussions. They found many episodes recounted where shared meanings were either completely, or almost completely absent (which they term 'intersubjectivity lacking'). Such episodes, they believe, reflect what has been termed the *'male sex drive' discourse*—the cultural belief that men have a strong, largely uncontrollable sex drive. In this style of discourse women are reduced to the status of objects and any attempt at sexual negotiation becomes unintelligible. The male sex drive discourse is evident in certain familiar social scenarios: a woman being 'picked up'—typically like a commodity—and passed from one man (or occasionally from another woman) to another man; a woman feeling 'pressure' from a man's behavior, where he acts as though she has an obligation to reciprocate sexually (as in return for taking her on a date); and, a man 'doing what comes naturally'—where 'nature takes its course' and he proceeds sexually, assuming he has the woman's consent.[872]

Not all episodes are bereft of negotiations, of course. In some interactions women are accorded more respect than as a mere object, but a woman's voice is still typically reduced to a whisper or silenced by anxiety, uncertainty, or inexperience. In such episodes some communication may occur, though there are missed opportunities for more. The researchers term these encounters examples of *incomplete intersubjectivity*—episodes of partial communication and lost chances for negotiation between the sexual partners. In some episodes the partners do experience shared meanings. These seem to occur within what has been termed the *permissive discourse*—where the needs and behaviors of both parties are assumed equally important. However, these kinds of episodes appear to be less frequent. "One reason why such encounters appear to be the exception," they speculate, "is that men seem to feel an obligation for commitment if they relate to their female partner as a person." In sum, for relatively sexually inexperienced individuals, the beliefs couples are likely to share most likely derive from dominant cultural notions about how such interactions proceed.[873] This increases the likelihood that stereotypical patterns disadvantageous to women will occur.

If our very way of talking about one another and about our sexual interactions is so troubled, why would we imagine other aspects of gender and sexuality would be less problematic? But to keep our focus in this introductory dialog, let us stay at the level we have just been exploring. Let us consider how *cultural scripts about gender and sexuality* influence us. In fact, in a very real sense we can talk about both masculine and feminine sexuality as scripted, providing us roles to play, stereotypical characters to develop, and dialogs to speak.

Masculinity & Sexuality

Consider first masculine sexuality. It is only fitting we keep starting with masculinity because we must confront the primacy this conforming gender has among the genders. Masculinity and sexuality sometimes are so closely identified with one another that each is defined by the other. In other words, some of us view men primarily in terms of their sexuality. Likewise, some of us see sexuality as mostly about what men want and try to get. Either way, few of us think about how heavily scripted male sexuality is. We are trained for our parts from such an early age it all seems perfectly . . . natural.

Phallocentric Model of Sexuality

What we need to remember is that many things acquire the feeling of naturalness simply because they are so commonly practiced and routinely endorsed that we never consider what their origin is or whether they might be other than we experience them. Masculine sexuality traditionally has been phallocentric. A *phallocentric model of sexuality* privileges the phallus—the penis and the clitoris as a penis-like organ. It promotes the belief that what is most important for sexuality is what is between the legs—specifically between the man's legs. The primacy of the penis is assumed; the clitoris is invariably described as an inferior, 'penis-like' organ in the female. Masculine sexuality is guaranteed by possession of the penis. Correspondingly, feminine sexuality is subordinated by the lack of one.[874] Many of us grew up with this model as the theatrical set within which the playing out of our gendered sexuality would occur.

This model tends to see the man's role as active, aggressive, competitive, and conquest-oriented. It assumes women will be passive, reluctantly receptive, and restraining of male aggression. Physical pleasure rather than psychological intimacy is prioritized. In short, the phallocentric model emphasizes that it is what lies between the legs, not between the ears, that matters most in sexuality. For those of us raised with this model all of these, while perhaps brutally put, ring more or less true. But in the last few decades this model has seen sharp opposition. Many among us believe this particular play has had enough of a run.

Bernie Zilbergeld & Masculine Sexuality

This might never have happened if not for the impact of feminism. To their credit, some men listened—and agreed that things are wrong and they need to change. Sex therapist Bernie Zilbergeld's books on male sexuality, published between the late 1970s and late 1990s, frequently surface in discussions of masculine sexuality as it has been reappraised. Psychologist and men's studies scholar Gary Brooks credits Zilbergeld with being "one of the first to harshly criticize the phallocentric model of male sexuality."[875] Zilbergeld offers a positive and optimistic appraisal of changes in masculine sexuality.

Zilbergeld's 1978 volume, *Masculine Sexuality: A Guide to Sexual Fulfillment*, indicts cultural conceptions of what men's sexuality *ought* to be as the source of most masculine problems in sexuality. In this book and his later work, he argues that *cultural sexual scripts* provide unrealistic parts for men to play, parts that lead them to feeling frustrated and unfulfilled. These scripts are encapsulated in common *myths* many of us may unwittingly accept because they are so often promoted as 'facts,' such as:

❑ *Size matters*—'the bigger, the better'; a focus on the size of the penis (usually length, sometimes girth) is accompanied by exaggerated images in media such as pornography, leading many men to feel inadequate.

❑ *Readiness matters*—'a real man is always ready for sexual action.' In fact, observes Zilbergeld, about a third of the men he sees express the feeling that sometimes sexual performance is a burden they'd like to set aside for the moment.

❑ *Leadership matters*—'the man is in charge'; men often want a partner to initiate and guide sexual interaction but may feel strong pressure to be the one who takes the lead from start to finish. A corollary of this myth is the 'sexpert' stereotype discussed earlier (chapter 10).

❑ *Progress matters*—'it's not just getting to second base that counts, one needs to get all the way to home plate'; once sexual interaction starts, men may feel cultural pressure to 'go all the way' or be judged a sexual failure. This myth makes everything other than intercourse just 'foreplay'—a brief stop on the way to the goal.

❑ *Performance matters*—'it's all about the climax'; orgasm is the product that an achievement-oriented, task-oriented approach extols, even at the price of intimacy and emotional satisfaction.

These scripts, and other myths, limit men rather than liberate them.

Myths need to be challenged; scripts need to be rewritten. Assessment of where one is at sexually forms a starting point. Goal identification offers a way forward by establishing a path for change. Zilbergeld urges that men pursue positive change oriented around two conditions: knowledge and decisions about what one can do on one's own (e.g., abstinence and masturbation), and the same with regard to sexual partners. In the latter respect, Zilbergeld gives much attention to the *relational context for sexual interactions*. This includes matters such as learning what a partner desires (e.g., shared contact, gentleness), actually talking about sexual matters, and coping with the boredom that may accompany long-term relationships.[876]

In the 1990s, Zilbergeld updated his work to reflect changes that had occurred in society. "Throughout the book," he writes, "I offer the elements of a new model of sex, one that emphasizes pleasure, closeness, and self- and partner-enhancement rather than performance and scoring." His desire, in part, is to do for men what the second wave of feminism and Women's Liberation helped do for women—increase their awareness and redirect it. In fact, the success of new awareness of and by women has consequences for men. Zilbergeld notes that social change in relations between the genders in recent decades has increased concern among men to please their partners. In fact, he argues that media blasting of masculine insensitivity to the needs of women has helped 'feminize' sexuality, promoting sensitivity in men even to the point where more are seeking professional help to better learn how to sexually please women. But, as he points out, adult men need such help because their development as boys has been largely ignored, facilitating the gender socialization that leads them to adopt restrictive and harmful myths. [877]

Of course, Zilbergeld's has not been the only voice among men seeking to raise self-awareness and chart a better path for masculine sexuality. Unfortunately, while some individuals have made personal progress, social stereotypes remain firmly in place. Men, as a gender group, still have a long way to go if masculine sexuality is to prove less oppressive.

Femininity & Sexuality

We may fairly ask if the situation is any better for women. After all, we may imagine that women have made the greater strides in recent decades with respect to achieving sexual liberation and greater self-possession of their own sexuality. However, even women as self-aware and activist as feminists have been deeply divided over what a woman's sexuality should look like. In 1984, Gayle Rubin observed two strains of thinking among feminists on the matter. One trend criticizes the cultural restrictions of women's sexual behavior and the high social costs incurred by women who choose to be sexually active. Feminists who think in this manner call for a sexual liberation of women as equally efficacious as that enjoyed by men. Another tendency, though, has been for some feminists to regard such efforts at sexual liberation as playing into men's hands and further extending their sexual privilege. So this group takes a conservative, anti-sexual discourse (at least in respect to heterosexual activity).[878] We may well wonder if things are much different among women today.

Without doubt modern women face a complicated situation. Like men, women often are limited by socially-derived sexual scripts. The *traditional model of feminine sexuality*, no less than the traditional masculine model, sets a script for women to follow. In fact, this script by its nature probably poses more difficulties for women in their gender-subordinated position than what men face—and probably is better thought of as a master script with several competing, sometimes contradictory subscripts in its messages.

Lonnie Barbach & Feminine Sexuality

Sex therapist Lonnie Barbach offers us entrance into this subject. She has written a number of books exploring women's sexuality from a practical standpoint. In one of them, she observes, "Until recently, it really was not known exactly what women experienced sexually. Most of what was believed came from writings by men about women's experiences."[879] The content of these writings often prompt feelings of abnormality or inadequacy in women. Though voices like Barbach's are now offering a different perspective, the old messages from men remain potent forces for most women.

Barbach exposes some of the *cultural role scripts* established within a masculine-dominated framework that plague women and affect their sexuality. For example, there is the 'Puritanical/Victorian' script, especially prevalent before 1940, that neither permits educating women about sexuality nor expects them to want to know about it. There are many other scripts: 'sex is good/bad' (i.e., good in marriage, bad outside it); 'don't touch down there' (the genitals are not regions to be explored); 'sex is for men' (women are here sexually to please men); 'men should know' (if a man really loves her, he'll know what she wants);

'women can't talk' (sexuality is not something nice girls discuss); 'romance and candlelight' (women need romance); 'sex equals intercourse' (the be-all and end-all of sexual activity is intercourse with orgasm); 'dependent and helpless' (a woman needs a man); 'nurturers' (others should always come first); 'one right way' (orgasm should be vaginal rather than clitoral); 'lesbian' (women are given scripts for being female, but not for being lesbians); and, 'let's be modern' (anything goes for sexually liberated women).[880]

If we try to put some of these scripts together, and juxtapose them with what we talked about for men, the myths of the cultural *feminine sexual script* include notions like these:

❑ *Being sexual doesn't matter*—'don't touch down there!' 'romance and candlelight' and 'nurturers' offer strong scripts. Girls are often discouraged from curiosity about, and exploration of their genitals. As a result, adult anxiety over them is common. Instead of thinking about being sexual, says the script, a woman should think about romance and putting her man's (sexual) needs first. In sum, her own sexuality is inconsequential.

❑ *What a woman wants sexually doesn't matter*—'women are passive and naïve'; this myth suggests women don't even know enough about sex (naiveté) to know what they want. They need a sexpert (man) to teach them, while they 'lie there and enjoy it.'

❑ *Sexual satisfaction doesn't matter*—'sex is for men'; what women want, says this script, is love—they exchange sex for love. A woman's own pleasure should be in pleasing her man, and if that means 'let's be modern,' then she ought to remember, 'boys will be boys' and 'he can't help it' if his pleasure comes at the cost of her own.

In sum, what sexuality is for a man—the active pursuit of a woman like some big game hunter—is not at all what it is for a woman—a passive waiting for true love to sweep her off her feet by a man who will take her as his own. But these scripts are not oppositional—they are *complementary* in a dominant-submissive master script that relatively advantages men.

Barbach advocates women actively take charge of their own sexuality. She pictures this as a journey in which the first step is some observation and risk taking. Along the way communication and change prove important features. In the new sexual script a woman can write she can overcome obstacles— problems sex therapists like Barbach commonly encounter, such as a lack of orgasm. But women, she contends, cannot only become orgasmic, they can expand their orgasmic potential. In a similar fashion, other sexual problems (e.g., low sexual desire, relationship difficulties) can be successfully addressed. Although her focus is on providing practical help rather than theory, Barbach is not atheortetical. Her work depends on a woman's willingness to become more sexually self-aware, challenge old and hurtful sexual scripts, and strive assertively for a healthier sexuality in which her needs and desires matter, and are so treated. In sum, Barbach advocates an alternative model to feminine sexuality.

That alternative is an *egalitarian model*—the same alternative we have noted is also offered to men. In this model the old scripts are torn up and burned; the new script has women as active agents asserting their own desires, owning their bodies, and teaching men what they want. This is not role reversal, where women seize the place formerly held by men. Rather, it is an effort to balance sexual power. Equalizing sexual power requires both men and women to change their scripts. Whether in a heterosexual or homosexual relationship, the relationship will either be relatively equal, or unequal. The egalitarian model strives for equality by fostering for both partners an openness and flexibility to express and meet sexual needs in each.

But are women today succeeding any more than contemporary men in overcoming the scripts they have inherited and that remain culturally supported? Perhaps one way to get at this question is to measure 'intraindividual' (within the individual) aspects of sexuality in young women—such personal attributes as self-perceptions and self-cognitions about key factors. This is the goal in work done by psychologists Sharon Horne and Melanie J. Zimmer-Gembeck. They developed the Female Sexual Subjectivity Inventory (FSSI), a 20 item instrument representing three core elements and five factors assessing sexual body-esteem, sexual desire and pleasure, and sexual self-reflection. Put together, such elements are part of *sexual subjectivity*—the pleasurable sense of being attractive and desirable, entitled to sexual pleasure, and able to critically reflect on the sexual self and sexual experiences. The instrument shows good psychometric properties and reliably differentiates adolescents and emerging adults on the factors tested.[881]

Horne and Zimmer-Gembeck find that girls with higher FSSI scores also are higher in sexual consciousness. Put another way, young women with *higher sexual subjectivity* are more aware of internal aspects of their sexuality (e.g., sexual feelings, motivations, desires, tendencies, preferences), more confident in their use of condoms, more resistant to sexual double standards, and display more voice in close relationships. The authors see such findings as supportive of the notion that "for girls to possess sexual subjectivity, they must be both aware of and resilient to social forces against sexual subjectivity in girls." Not surprisingly, higher sexual subjectivity correlates with less sexual anxiety, which in turn helps predict more positive sexual well-being.[882]

Interestingly, among the women studied in establishing the FSSI, Horne and Zimmer-Gembeck find significant differences between heterosexual and non-heterosexual young women on all elements save sexual body-esteem. Non-heterosexual girls score show a higher sense of entitlement to sexual pleasure from themselves and their partners. They also show more self-efficacy in achieving sexual pleasure. Finally, they are more likely to reflect more on the sexual aspects of their life experience. It may be, the researchers speculate, that being a sexual minority may make sexuality a more salient aspect during this developmental period and elicit more focus on sexual self-discovery and definition.[883]

Perhaps more women are making progress in staking out for themselves a feminine sexuality equal to masculine sexuality. Or perhaps—and more likely—the case is the same as among men: some individuals are bucking a system that remains firmly in place. As we saw in examining sexual attitudes, these seem resistant to change in core beliefs such as the difference in sex drive. As long as most people endorse stereotypes and culturally constructed beliefs that keep the existing gender hierarchy intact, little of substance will change.

Other Genders & Sexuality

When we turn to considering nonconforming genders our approach must be a little different at this introductory level. That is because nonconforming genders tend not to be talked about in the same way or concerning the same matters as the conforming genders are. In an earlier discussion (chapter 8), we briefly considered the matter of nonconforming gender identities in relation to *sexual orientation*. We recognized then that often a link is made such that anyone who has a nonconforming gender identity is believed must also have a nonconforming sexual orientation. We also recognized such an association is logically unsound and does not reflect reality. Nevertheless, that link is only one among many forged by many of us in joining together nonconforming genders with nonconforming aspects of sexuality.

Most of the attention given to nonconforming genders in terms of sexuality (other than in respect to sexual orientation) is focused around *crossdressing*—utilizing the dress appearance associated with members of another gender.[884] Because dress is gendered (see chapter 14), and because a primary way of signaling nonconforming gender is through crossdressing, and because nonconforming gender is associated with nonconforming sexuality, crossdressing is commonly linked to sexual deviance. This is famously notable in the notion of transvestic fetishism—crossdressing for sexual arousal and relief. But crossdressing is also sometimes linked to other deviant forms of sexual behavior. Let us begin with fetishism.

Crossdressing & Fetishism

The term 'fetish' (spelled in more than one manner) comes from outside medicine and psychiatry, deriving from the language of anthropology and religion. A *fetish* is a charm, an object associated with enchantment. Already by the end of the 18th century it was being applied among French physicians to a certain kind of sexual 'perversion.' The idea of fetishism gained prominence especially through the influence of psychoanalysis. Sigmund Freud (1856-1939) adopted the term in his small 1905 book, *Three Essays on the Theory of Sexuality*. This proved a landmark work. In it, he sets forth basic ideas about fetishism that guided later psychoanalysts, and through them a broader reach of physicians and psychiatrists.

Freud gives some attention to what he calls 'sexual aberrations,' activities that don't conform to either the 'normal aim' or 'normal object' in sexual behavior. For Freud, and others of his era, the 'normal sexual object'—the person toward whom sexual behavior is aimed—is a member of the opposite sex and the 'normal sexual aim' is intercourse. Anything different (i.e., deviating) is deviant—a 'perversion.'[885] For example, kissing, oral sex, or other sexual activities commonly part of sexual interactions, are all perversions if they detract from or substitute for the act of intercourse with a member of the opposite sex. Among the perversions, Freud considered cases he considered "quite specially remarkable—those in which the normal sexual object is replaced by another which bears some relation to it, but is entirely unsuited to serve the normal sexual aim."[886]

What he is referring to is the *sexual fetish*—an object that has some symbolic connection with sexuality. Freud regarded it possible for such a fetish to be part of the human body (e.g., hair or feet), or an inanimate object (e.g., hosiery or high heels). Today most discussions of fetishism drop the former element and only refer to inanimate objects. For Freud—and probably most modern sexologists—the presence of a sexual fetish is neither unusual nor worrisome unless it becomes such a powerful enchantment that it can substitute for the other person. Thus, a man aroused by a woman in high heels is one thing, but a man who doesn't need the woman as long as he has the high heels is something else.

Why does sexual fetishism occur? Why is it almost exclusively a masculine matter? For Freud the answer lies in development. The child, through accidental circumstances, attaches to an object as a penis-substitute in order to overcome anxiety about castration—a feature of the Oedipus Complex we discussed earlier (chapter 7). This fear is aroused by awareness that some others (girls and/or women) do not have a penis, which is the source of so much pride and pleasure for himself. The sexual fetish offers a symbolic way of denying the absence of the penis in others, and thus removes the potential threat of his own castration.

We may well wonder what this has to do with gender. In this regard, two things must be discussed. First, as we mentioned a moment ago, there has been a chain forged of supposed links between nonconforming gender and nonconforming sexuality, with crossdressing (a sign of nonconforming gender) matched with sexual fetishism (a sign of nonconforming sexuality). Second, it has been proposed that Freud's thinking on the sexual fetish opens up the possibility that gender can be constructed without reliance on gender roles.

Donovan Miyasaki & Fetishism

Let's start with that latter idea. Philosopher Donovan Miyasaki believes Freud's analysis opens the possibility of *nonpathological fetishism*, in which the fetishist successfully evades the construction of gender in terms of sexual roles. In Miyasaki's reading, one of the remarkable aspects of fetishism is that the fetishist actually gets the objective facts right: unlike the 'normal' boy who believes in the castration of the female to explain her loss of the penis, the fetishist disavows this misperception, which allows him to then disavow the threat of his own castration by his father. In Miyasaki's interpretation, the fetishist has not believed the woman retains a penis, but rather that she possesses a phallus—and this allows the fetishist to attribute sexual subjectivity to her.[887]

As Miyasaki points out, the 'normal' boy's belief in the castration of the female produces a deprecating view of femininity—after all, a woman is one who has lost what makes a man a man! Not so the fetishist. "Unlike other sexual subjects," Miyasaki remarks, "the fetishist has, in accordance with reality, attributed sexual wholeness and subjectivity to the sexual other generally and women specifically."[888] In essence, the fetishist's belief in his mother's retention of a phallus deconstructs the normal view of gender and clears the way for a different perception of sexual roles, one in which the feminine is not equated with passivity and masculinity with sexual domination.[889]

Accordingly, for Miyasaki two advantages are implicit in Freudian fetishism. First, the customary feminine role of 'being-for-domination' is overcome. Second, any attachment between sexual role and gender is severed. Thus the fetishist need not dominate the sexual object; he can derive pleasure in desire as such, and enjoy the object while it retains its independence. These ideas should give us pause in considering fetishism. The abundantly negative connotations attaching to it by virtue of its being assigned a mental disorder may obscure a complex reality. As Freud noted, some fetishistic element is habitually present in human sexuality. And as Miyasaki demonstrates, nonpathological fetishism actually represents some advantages in overcoming a rigid, patriarchal gender order in sexual roles. Before we start casting stones, we ought to be looking at our own glass walls.

Transvestic Fetishism

Now let us return our attention to the supposed pathology of *transvestic fetishism*. We can legitimately ask two questions: Is crossdressing a fetishistic activity? If it is, is it necessarily a bad thing? With regard to both questions, scholars are divided. Some argue that it is fetishistic whenever sexual arousal accompanies it—and a few believe that always occurs in crossdressing whether the crossdresser admits it or not. Others argue that crossdressing is misunderstood by viewing it as a form of fetishism. They point to the much different and more complex psychological situation that seems to accompany crossdressing as compared to simple fetishism. To this some respond that crossdressing is merely the most elaborate form of fetishism, but that at its heart the fetishistic process is what makes the behavior so compelling to the individual.

In terms of the second question, modern Western mental health, as represented in the prevailing diagnostic model, regards crossdressing as a mental disorder only if certain criteria are met: the individual in question must be male, heterosexual, and have had for at least six months "recurrent, intense sexually arousing fantasies, sexual urges, or behaviors involving crossdressing," and these must either be significantly distressing to the individual or cause impairment in some important area of functioning, such as at work or in social relations.[890] The criteria are interesting. Despite evidence that some gay men, lesbians, and heterosexual women also crossdress for erotic pleasure, when they do so it is not—by definition—disordered behavior. Moreover, *homeovestism*, sexual arousal from dressing in the clothes of one's assigned gender, is also not regarded as pathological. The focus on heterosexual males—the pinnacle of the gender hierarchy—implies a cultural safekeeping of masculinity by making pathological any behavior that deviates from the conformist standard. Nonconforming males and all females—lower on the hierarchy—don't matter enough to warrant special pressures to enforce gender (and sexual) conformity. Like we learned with Gender Identity Disorder, this diagnosis is fraught with problems and is controversial, with some mental health experts arguing that it needs to be discarded as both unscientific and culturally biased.[891]

In sum, the easily made causal link between crossdressing and sexual disorder we may be prone to make is, at best, suspicious. We are justified in regarding it, at least in most aspects and instances, as one consequence of our cultural commitment to a bipolar gender scheme. We leave little room for nonconforming genders to express themselves, and then when they do so, we label it pathological. Calling crossdressing disordered *behavior* serves as a covert way of labeling nonconforming gender *identities* as pathological.

Crossdressing and Other Sexual Deviance

One hypothesized connection has been between crossdressing and sadomasochistic behavior, especially bondage. Both sadism (deriving sexual pleasure from inflicting pain) and masochism (deriving sexual pleasure from receiving pain) are included among the paraphilias listed under sexual disorders in the American Psychiatric Association's diagnostic and classification system.[892] Another proposed link is between crossdressing and fetishism that is not transvestic fetishism. Like other categories among the paraphilias, there are some who advocate removal of some or all of these categories. Be that as it may, the research into a link between these behaviors and crossdressing has been mixed.

A large-scale self-report study of crossdressing men found behaviors like *sadism and masochism*, in the words of the researchers, "a trivial component."[893] But other studies, of varying sizes, have found an incidence of such behaviors—or at least attraction to them—greater than that found in the general population.[894] Similarly, at least one study has reported a significant correlation between crossdressing and *fetishes* such as rubber or leather.[895] A large, self-admittedly unscientific, online survey reported significant interest in and experimentation with *bondage*.[896] Unfortunately, complicating interpretation of the research is that convenience samples are almost invariably relied upon because representative samples are unavailable. That means we don't know to what degree, if any, the results obtained can be generalized to all crossdressing men, let alone also crossdressing women and children. Nor do such studies always differentiate among the gender identities espoused by those crossdressing, which can range from conforming genders (masculinity or femininity) to nonconforming genders (e.g., transgender, transsexual, or 'third gender').[897]

Crossdressers & Noncrossdressers

In general, except with regard to gender identity, most research confirms that nonconforming gender individuals are like gender conforming ones. For example, as we discussed before, in research using the Five Factor (OCEAN) Model of personality, no substantial differences were found between male crossdressers and other males, though crossdressers did score higher than normal for Fantasy, Feelings, and Values scales of the O ('Openness') dimension.[898] Similarly, the Derogatis Sexual Functioning Inventory (DSFI), which employs 255 items to measure 10 dimensions, found just one modest difference from so-called heterosexual 'normals'—a greater tendency to endorse a poor body image.[899] Even that changes, though, for transsexuals after undergoing sex reassignment surgery; they report an increase in body satisfaction as measured by the Body Image Scale (BI-I).[900] These kind of findings extend to the likelihood of crossdressers experiencing a mental disorder. As the article on transvestism for the *Encyclopedia of Psychology* put it in the mid-1990s, "Concerning their psychological makeup, transvestites as a group are no more neurotic or psychotic than matched control groups. . . ."[901]

Heterosexuality, Heterosexism & Homosexuality

Few matters seem to so fascinate many Americans as does *sexual orientation*. Although we have discussed this before, it seems essential to return to the subject because it serves as a conversational lynchpin when considering gender and sexuality with respect to both conforming and nonconforming genders. Put most simply, many of us erroneously regard sexual orientation as the hallmark difference between conforming and nonconforming genders. As mentioned before, we may be prone to think that anyone whose gender does not conform must have a nonconforming sexual orientation—or vice versa, that a nonconforming sexual orientation is always paired with a nonconforming gender. So let us look again at this matter, but this time with specific reference to the relation of homosexuality to heterosexuality.

When it comes to a *homosexual sexual orientation* we might fairly say, 'Never have so many been bothered so much by the bearing of so few.' Despite the widely known and often repeated estimate of 10% of the population having a homosexual orientation, the most methodologically stringent research consistently finds much lower percentages. These more reliable and current studies typically find about 2-3% of sexually active men and 1-2% of sexually active women identify as having a homosexual *orientation*. In terms of same-sex sexual *behavior*, the percentages are a little larger, though still modest. About 5% of men report having had a same-sex partner at least once since age 18.[902] The numbers for women are similar, but perhaps slightly less. However, orientation—a relatively fixed erotic pattern of attraction—is not identical with behavior; one can engage in either same-sex or opposite-sex sexual behavior regardless of orientation.

Male homosexuality appears to consistently have bothered most people more than female homosexuality. This reflects both masculine privilege in the gender hierarchy and how masculinity is constructed. Homosexual men remain a subordinated masculinity. But female homosexuality—*lesbianism*—also has been negatively perceived, except for when men pursue pornography. Sociologist Karin Martin, in reviewing the medical literature on homosexuality between 1900-1950, discerns two distinct periods, each with a distinctive emphasis. In the first, 1903-1925, lesbianism was not merely branded deviant, but also employed as a reason to resist women's quest for equality and suffrage. "In this case," Martin writes, "the claim of deviant gender behavior is used to sanction (undiscussed) sexual behavior, all of which is then used to resist challenges to the gender hierarchy by women." In the latter period, 1934-1942, the focus was on male homosexuality, probably as part of the effort to resist and oppress the new sexual communities then forming in urban areas.[903]

We might argue that in our present time neither gay men nor lesbian women face the problems they once did. We might point to progress in laws and policies combating discrimination based on sexual orientation. Yet we need not deny the real gains made in society to point out that sexual minorities remain in a precarious position, dependent in many things on the good will of a majority whose attitudes persist in being largely negative. Instances of outright hostility and violence still occur, but if we argue they have become less, we cannot yet argue it is because the majority of us accept homosexuality. Rather, it is because most of us detest violence and crude behavior more than we detest homosexuality—which all evidence suggests remains the attitude of most Americans.

Why does bias toward individuals with a non-heterosexual sexual orientation persist? Why are attitudes so resistant to change even in the face of veritable mountains of evidence indicating the only significant difference between someone with a heterosexual sexual orientation and someone with a non-heterosexual orientation is that *one* difference? To answer such questions we must critically examine not just homosexuality and bisexuality, but heterosexuality as well. When we do so we may discover some uncomfortable truths.

Christine Overall & Heterosexuality as a Cultural Institution

Let us start by acknowledging that most of us who are heterosexual are uncomfortable with homosexuality. Signs of the ways in which so many of us are bothered by sexually nonconforming sexual orientations abound. Consider, for instance, the one-sidedness of our thinking and speaking. Social philosopher and feminist scholar Christine Overall points out some of the *oddities of discourse on homosexuality*:

Historically, for example, there has been a tendency to investigate the causes of forms of non-heterosexuality, but not of heterosexuality; to consider whether non-heterosexuality, but not heterosexuality, can be spread through a sort of contagion effect; to ask whether non-heterosexuality is unnatural, but not to contemplate whether heterosexuality in any sense could be.[904]

Further, she notes that most of us assume our children will be heterosexual, assume the people we meet are heterosexual, and assume that *real* sexuality is *hetero*sexuality. Why is our thinking and speaking so unidirectional?

Overall points our attention where it needs to go—to *heterosexuality as a cultural institution* rather than as merely a matter of individual sexuality. She means by this designation the sense of heterosexuality as a systematized set of social standards, customs, and expected practices. These both regulate and restrict relationships, whether romantic or sexual. The institution—as the name states—incorporates both women and men, though their experience of it varies. The institution 'speaks' differently to each gender.[905]

Overall adopts a social constructionist perspective to consider the manner in which women are addressed by the institution of heterosexuality and how they experience it. Logically, this means that no sexual orientation—including heterosexuality—is natural, or innate, or an 'essence.' *All sexual orientations are socially constructed.* The notion of 'bisexuality' has no more claim on being 'natural' than any other; it simply points out the obvious fact that all of us are capable of sexual interactions with members of either sex. Despite this reality, enormous social pressure is exerted on all of us to be heterosexual.[906]

This pressure is the institution of heterosexuality in action. Overall wonders why anything so supposedly innate must be so constantly impressed upon us as necessary to behaviorally master. She indicates the overwhelming variety of advice and instruction we all receive on 'how' to be heterosexual, whether in dating or marriage, or simply as a way to be among others in society. Throughout life we are subjected to intense socialization to be heterosexual. For women this means a particular—*heterosexual*—way to be a woman. That, of course, is where the rub is: *the heterosexual way of being a woman is constructed in a manner favorable to men, but not to women.* As an institution, heterosexuality promotes a femininity unequal in power or status to the masculinity it is supposed to desire. Historically, men benefit by heterosexual desire on the part of women by obtaining easy sexual access to them, and a way to pass on both their genes and their goods in a social framework (the family) that bears their name and their leadership. The benefits men receive are matched by the costs women accrue. They face a system that perpetuates violence, degradation and exploitation against them through heterosexual practices ranging from rape to prostitution to many forms of sexual assault. Further, by allying women to men it separates them from one another, effectively decreasing even further their social powers politically and otherwise.[907]

Put in this way, why would any woman want to participate? Overall points out that the institution rewards women who comply. *Heterosexual privilege*— validation of her 'legitimate' femininity and accompanying sanction by men— offers women the better of two poor choices. By allying with and desiring men she is saved from the worse fate reserved for non-heterosexual women. This privilege bears with it the price of *heterosexism*—censure of any deviations from heterosexuality. To be accepted by the powerful in society—heterosexual men and heterosexual women—a woman must be one of them, conforming to their standards. Otherwise there will be censure, marginalization, and a host of practical consequences ranging from consequences for employment to loss of affection from significant others, to threats and acts of violence. The label 'lesbian' is a dangerous one to bear. Yet there is a price, too, experienced by women who conform. They may well feel the pain of forced conformity to heterosexual standards.[908]

So what is a woman to do? If she is in a double bind, damned if she is homosexual and damned if she is heterosexual, what other possibility is there? For Overall the way out lies in the very constructed nature of sexual orientation. If we truly grasp that orientation is made by culture, not nature, we can use that awareness for liberation. A feminist, aware of the power of patriarchy, can choose whether and how she will be heterosexual or homosexual. A woman who thus chooses to be heterosexual does so with an awareness that already has begun to distance her from heterosexuality as an institution. Her heterosexuality as a personal choice has leverage to not conform to the heterosexual institution. She can, for instance, distinguish between her sexual attraction and passion, on the one hand, and dependence, need, fear, and insecurity on the other hand. She has, in short, the possibility of *coming out as a self-aware heterosexual*—someone who chooses heterosexuality without also choosing the heterosexual institution. She need not be dominated by the expectations of the patriarchy or trapped within heterosexism. As a consequence, she may become free to also differentiate individual men from 'manhood'—the coercive gender dominant in the gender hierarchy, the architects of patriarchy. In the end, to choose heterosexuality is an act of faith, both in oneself and in the man one chooses to be with.[909]

Heterosexism

Overall's distinction between heterosexuality and the heterosexual institution is a useful one. It reminds us that individuality is lived out in relation to social structures, which while they exert constant pressure on us, need not necessarily define us. We can attain awareness and at least some degree of independence. Regardless, though, of whether we agree with Overall's argument, we should be able to concur with her that heterosexism poses a problem—one most of us remain oblivious to.

The essence of heterosexism is a danger inherent to all power, if we concur with the oft-repeated maxim that 'power corrupts and absolute power corrupts absolutely.' By placing the unanswerable power of natural necessity in heterosexuality, making it Nature's intention and default, non-heterosexuality in any form must be unnatural, deviant, and—of critical importance—*illegitimate*. Legitimacy is required for authority, moral or otherwise. Legitimacy is required for sanctioned power. Therefore, that which is illegitimate has no proper claim on authority or power, no moral justification, and thus no standing. It exists to whatever extent it is permitted to exist by the sufferance of others. By making heterosexuality natural and non-heterosexuality unnatural, we immediately establish grounds for heterosexism.

Heterosexism—also sometimes called *heterosexual bias*—is the gender equivalent of racism. It is a social institution bearing the characteristics multicultural scholars Derald Wing Sue and David Sue attach to ethnocentric monoculturalism: a belief in the superiority of one's own group; a belief in the inferiority of other groups; the power to impose standards; a manifestation in the program, policies, practices, structures, and institutions of society; and, an invisibility to the person who belongs to the superior group, like a veil that shields the conscious mind from awareness of the cultural self-centeredness.[910] Among the many negative consequences heterosexism yields are a social blindness to non-heterosexuals (e.g., assumption everyone is heterosexual, failure to recognize needs of non-heterosexuals), a segregation of non-heterosexuals away from heterosexuals when they are recognized, and unequal treatment of non-heterosexuals in a multitude of ways, including in matters basic to human existence (e.g., discrimination in housing and employment). Heterosexism is serious.

Accompanying heterosexism is *homophobia*—an irrational fear of homosexuality. It may display itself as discomfort or disgust, as shunning or as aggression, but its essential character is a feeling unsubstantiated by facts.[911] This feeling elicits in many of us—even well-educated college students!—a fear that a loved one might prove to be homosexual, or that society is in moral decline because of the presence of homosexuals.[912] The price of homophobia is most strongly felt by those against whom it is directed, but *all* of us pay a price. As one man wrote, after recounting in detail the effects of homophobia in his life:

> Homophobia, in sum, means that I am afraid of homosexuals because they threaten a part of myself, that I do not know how to know myself, that I cannot admit that I have problems, that I cannot look to share myself with other men, that I treat women extremely unfairly to avoid the truth about myself, and that my sexuality becomes about many things other than sharing erotic expressions of intimacy.[913]

Overcoming heterosexism (and homophobia) requires a multifaceted approach. First, we must acknowledge the beam in our own eye before attacking the splinter in someone else's. The veil must come down as those of us who are heterosexual accept that we hold unearned privilege and wield power in coercive and unfair ways toward those unlike us. We must be willing to share power. Second, our self-awareness must be followed by active efforts to translate insight into application through social action. This requires us to participate in education efforts, to support legislative reforms protecting sexual minorities, to advocate policies that grant equal opportunities in housing, employment, and other matters. Ultimately our goal must be to bring down the institution of heterosexuality that grounds and supports heterosexism. We may not believe we can make a difference, but we surely cannot if we neither see the problem nor make any effort to end it.

Chapter 14

Gender & Dress

Introduction: At various moments in our ongoing dialog we have remarked upon how crossdressing plays an important role in the gender experience and expression of some of us. But all of us rely on *dress*—our appearance in clothes and attendant accessories—to communicate gender. *Gender differentiated dress* is perhaps the most visible marker of gender among human beings.

The connection between dress and gender is a sensible one. The spread of humanity across the globe made coverings suitable for different climates and seasons necessary, but *the need to differentiate genders* made differentiating clothing just as essential. Human bodies, though possessing distinctive secondary sexual characteristics, are not so dramatically different when clothed. So differentiating characteristics are useful in aiding visual identification of gender. But once gender differentiated dress started to happen, these differentiating characteristics could be used to make *social comments* about the genders.

The basic function of dividing the conforming genders creates a *golden rule of dress*—a fundamental precept that establishes a guiding logic in dress. That rule is simply put: 'Males must appear masculine, or at least not feminine.' Above all, the boundary between the dominant genders must be kept clear. The dominance of masculinity must be clear and unchallenged. From this logic flows a history of dress customs and fashions emphasizing not only the divide between men and women, but also the superiority of men.

If this sounds terribly political, it is. The *politics of dress* is about *power*. Men have it, women want it. If gender differentiated dress did not play such a powerful role in maintaining the gender hierarchy, then why would *crossdressing* cause such concern? Early feminists in their push for dress reform correctly grasped that dress is an important instrument that can and is manipulated for political power between the genders.

In light of the stakes involved in a culture where dress is critical to personal and social identity, *gender socialization through dress* begins at birth and is lifelong. We immediately color code infants and teach kids what is appropriate for boys and girls to wear. But childhood is not the only time when gender differentiation in dress is expected. Adults face these expectations too, especially in the workplace. Gender differentiated dress extends right down to our underwear. In our culture it is extensive, nuanced—and constantly challenged.

The Relation of Dress to Gender

Let us start with why we dress at all.[914] We might assume it is because we need *physical protection*, and so we do. But even in environments where such a need is minimal we seem to dress beyond the simple satisfying of this need. One proposal has been that dress originated to serve *sexual purposes*. It not only marks the sexes as different, but sets a modest barrier between them while serving social functions such as signaling sexual availability or unavailability.[915]

However much we may enjoy sexual coupling, though, we spend comparatively little time engaged in it. Gender's functioning in culture is much broader than sexual signaling. Yet we still require aid in *gender identification*, and clothing still provides that help. Sociologist Gregory Stone once remarked that while gender is known silently, to dress in clothes associated with a gender is to make an announcement of one's gender—an announcement rarely questioned.[916] Dress is behavior, and alongside other behavior places each of us in a social matrix. Culturally, gender is a code dictating societal expectations and beliefs about identity, roles, privileges and duties.

Clothing and accessories—the basic elements of dress—serve a variety of *social functions*. Among these are signifying membership in various groups, and status within those groups. We can, for example, mark ourselves as members of a profession by our clothing (e.g., doctors, nurses, clergy, police, firemen), or a social organization (e.g., boy scouts or girl scouts), or even an institution (e.g.; school uniforms). As members, we can still differentiate ourselves as to rank or role. Dress offers ways to mark both inclusion and place in a hierarchy. Sex and gender groups, likewise, are served by clothes differentiated to mark not only membership, but to signal availability, to enhance attractiveness, and to make value statements (e.g., about one's modesty). These explanations for why we wear clothes contribute to the reasons clothes matter to us.

Dress—the Heart of an Experiencing & Expressive System

Collectively, these reasons suggest that clothes and the other elements that contribute to dress occupy a central position in a complex and subtle *expressive and experiencing system*. This system provides a context in which personal experience acquires dimensions impossible apart from wearing clothes. The system also constructs a social context in which experience can be translated into expressions aimed at others. We are able through clothes to express ourselves to ourselves and to others. In so doing we communicate values, feelings, personality characteristics, social affiliations, and other important information.

This system remains largely unconscious to us most of the time and in most of its aspects. Although principally unconscious, this system is also partly conscious. We are aware at times of the role of dress in our personal and social living. We make conscious choices about dress, even if what guides us in those choices is often below consciousness. So, in discussing the social and personal aspects of the system we would do well to remember that both possess conscious and unconscious dimensions. Social and personal duality may be simplistically portrayed like this:

❑ *Social* aspects of the system:

- *social experiencing*—the role of clothing as a conduit for shared experiences; and,
- *social expressiveness*—the role of clothing in displaying social aspects of the self, such as our group affiliations and identities.

❑ *Personal* aspects of the system:

- *personal experiencing*—the sensual experience of wearing various kinds of clothing and the experienced changes in self from so doing; and,
- *personal expressiveness*—the use of clothing to make personal statements regardless of conformity to social rules.

What beguiles us into thinking we understand the experience of clothes and what they express is the truth that the system formed around clothes is a social one and that we are conscious of this to some degree. That means shared rules and features that we can participate in and generalize. For instance, in various cultures specific colors have taken on symbolic meaning, and this meaning is conveyed to clothes, where it becomes another aspect of what the clothing means to the wearer and to others. To the extent we grasp such matters in a culture and embrace them, we can utilize them in our clothing choices both as a means of manipulating our experience (e.g., through choosing colors to boost our mood), or to express ourselves (e.g., through displaying a color to tell others how we feel).

Fashion developed as a social tool important in clothing choices. Fashion helps guide choices about experience and expression, as well as interpretations about both. Yet, as researchers Craig Thompson and Diana Haytko point out, the ways we talk about fashion—'fashion discourses'—afford so many different interpretive positions that an astounding range of juxtapositions are possible, including opposing values and beliefs. Somehow we need to honor both our individual experience and our obligations to society (largely met through our membership in various groups).[917] Accordingly, our notion that there is a shared set of meanings around dress may not be incorrect, but it will lead us astray if we suppose that such a set prevails for all people all the time. Rather, the social system of dress is best seen as an ongoing conversation in which the few general lines of discourse we discern are always set against a backdrop of babble.

Dress and the Construction of Gender

If dress can play such a role in experience and expression, in the personal and social aspects of human existence, then it seems inevitable it would attach to gender, which in our culture is so central to constructing identity and relationships. But dress does more than merely visibly represent gender. *Dress participates in the construction of gender.* Dress not only *symbolizes* what a culture believes about a gender (e.g., delicate fabrics to communicate feminine vulnerability), but also works to *shape* gender (e.g., clothes that restrict movement to make certain kinds of work difficult of impossible).

The notion that we use clothes to construct gender should not surprise us; it is inherently human to use tools to make things, including psychological things. Sociologist Diana Crane reminds us that while clothes are artifacts—produced by human agency—they are also creative agents capable of crafting behavior either by imposing social identities, or by empowering the assertion of latent social identities.[918] Dress creates vehicles into which human shapes are poured and reconstructed. Through dress a society can exercise a measure of control—an exercise most notably demonstrated by the sumptuary laws.

But the instrumentality of dress is a two-edged sword. The manipulated can manipulate. All of us are able to stand convention on its head by making contrary choices in what we wear—and when we do, we alter more than our dress expression; we affect our self-experience to some degree. One way our experience of our self can be altered by what we wear occurs through what we imagine ourselves capable of when we put on certain clothes. Actors accomplish this regularly through costume. So do the rest of us when we choose, for instance, 'power clothing' for a business presentation or otherwise 'dress for success.' We choose clothing to alter our mood. In athletics we select clothes to enhance our performance. We dress to improve our appearance and become more desirable. Members of both conforming genders do this—and so do others. Crossdressers are doing no differently than the rest of us, save that they are crossing gender lines imposed on them by others instead of staying inside them. They manipulate dress to affect both experience and expression.

The Physical Dimension of Gender Differentiated Clothing

The *physical properties of gendered clothing* play one part in constructing gender. Self-experiencing via dress is possible because clothes have an independent reality. The self is formed and develops by boundary constructions, which require the existence of other things and people to form. Of the objects that populate our ordinary world, clothes prove the most significant in boundary formation. This conclusion is driven by the intimacy we have with apparel, which resides so close to us it constitutes a second skin. In putting on dress we construct a body boundary that is part of our self's boundary system.[919]

Apparel does more than block or mediate sensory signals from the environment. Clothes offer something tangible, with traits that embody symbolic meanings. In putting clothes on we create a boundary that extends our body boundary system and protects it, incorporates the sensations provided by the clothing, and simultaneously appropriates any symbolic meanings associated with the apparel for the self-contents within the boundaries of the self. Simply said, clothes become part of the self both by acting as a self-boundary and by lending their physical properties as well as their symbolic meanings. The physical properties of clothes have been shown to have specific effects on human bodies and minds.[920]

Much masculine and feminine clothing looks and feels different along lines meant to convey gender difference. Anyone who has examined a range of masculine and feminine apparel readily recognizes the differences extend beyond style and color. The *feel of clothing* is gender differentiated to some extent. Most noticeable may be things like the use of lace, a dependable gender marker of femininity these days. But we notice a difference too when we handle clothing. Devoid of visual cues, the feel of the fabric used, often remarkably different between masculine and feminine garb, can lead us to distinguish among items and make judgments as to their gender association. Clothing scholar Mary Lou Rosencranz, in the early 1970s, reported studies on gender associations with fibers. On one end of the spectrum, wool was judged the least feminine; on the other end, lace and especially silk were judged the most feminine.[921] Given the properties of these fibers the symbolic connection is unsurprising. Softness, sensuous luster and luxuriousness—all qualities silk has in abundance—are associated with femininity. Nylon and acetate yarns also are more often associated with femininity, as are satin weaves. Even in materials widely used for both genders, like cotton, surprising differences can emerge. For example, among children boy's clothing is far more likely to be 100% cotton than is girl's clothing. The greatest use of synthetic fibers is found in girls' apparel, particularly skirts.[922] By the time boys become young men (ages 25-34) it is little surprise to find they have the strongest preference for natural fibers.[923]

Of course, *vision* remains the sense we most often consciously tie to our judgments of clothing. Studies have demonstrated, for instance, that visual perception of the texture of the textiles used,[924] and sight-based associative aspects like *colors*, which yield psychological import based on symbolic meanings,[925] are both important to us. Long before we can easily differentiate male bodies from female ones, infants are conveniently color-coded to assign them gender and set them on a prescribed course of identity and role-playing. But it isn't merely babies we color code. To some degree we do so with adults as well. In general, darker colors and solid color patterns are more associated with masculinity while lighter colors and mixed color patterns are more associated with femininity.

Gender socialization utilizes color in clothing. Some research indicates children by school age already have established strong color preferences and associations. In a study published in the mid-1990s, groups of children ages 5 and 6½ displayed some general agreement that brighter colors are more likely to produce positive feelings than darker colors, but also showed gender differences, with boys being more likely than girls to have positive responses to darker colors.[926] Another series of studies with children found that they use color to predict someone's sex and to form impressions about persons whose sex is known. In particular, these studies demonstrated the reliance of children on clothing color to assist themselves in sex determination and inferences about the characteristics of others. The use of stereotypes in this regard begins at least by preschool age.[927]

We are accustomed to evaluating clothes by sight, but consider also the role *sound* plays. Studies have demonstrated that the sound a garment makes elicits a psychological response. In one experiment reported in 2005, women, while attached to physiological monitors, were asked to rate various sensations (softness, pleasantness, comfort, noisiness, annoyance, clearness, and highness) associated with the distinctively different rustling sounds of three differently structured polyester warp knitted fabrics. The results support that such rustling sounds not only elicit physical sensations, but that these are variably differentiated as pleasant (e.g., the rustling sound of double denbigh) or unpleasant (e.g., sharkskin).[928]

The physical qualities of clothes, added to their symbolic associations, afford strongly gendered elements of experience. This offers another important reason for crossdressing's appeal to those who do not fit within the conforming genders. A male may never know what a female body feels like, but he can know what feminine clothes feel like. Though the sensations may be somewhat different on his male body, the femininity of the clothes lends itself to his experience in some manner. In fact, it may do so in a felt way to such a degree that 'he' becomes 'she.' A male transvestite may only borrow the feminine gender for a time, and then only very partially. A transsexual male, whose inner sense of gendered self is feminine, experiences the kind of psychological right fit in feminine clothes that is complete and persistent, despite the inadequacy of the body sex. The physical elements of dress cohere with the symbolic associations to facilitate a gendered experience as well as gender presentation.

So, we have established that dress matters, and that it plays a role in our experience of gender and our expression of gender. We have learned this arises in part from the very nature of clothing, as well as the uses to which it is put. Now we must investigate other dynamics, such as how the specific gender differentiations in dress we know today came about. What logic prompted the actual differences? How does this logic play itself out in children and adults? Such questions lead us immediately to a matter of decisive importance.

The Golden Rule of Gendered Dress

Dress is supposed to reliably differentiate males from females and indicate the inclusion of the former into masculinity, the latter into femininity, with nothing properly standing between. Males are to be masculine, females feminine. Yet, given the complexity of how dress functions for us, the only way we can make everything work so that all the various demands placed on it have a chance of being met is to keep the rules governing gender differentiation relatively few and flexible. But one grand exception—a single inflexible standard—serves as lynchpin to the whole. This is the 'Golden Rule' for gender-differentiated dress: 'Males must appear masculine, or at least not feminine.'

With regard to the question, 'What do clothes say about our gender?' the only essential answer pertains to men and it is: 'I am not feminine.' Girls and women can be masculine—'tomboys'—with mild to moderate sanctions even in adulthood, depending on other contexts, such as the nature of a chosen occupation. A woman police officer has more sanction to be tomboyish than does a woman flight attendant. For women the dress spectrum is wide because the gender spectrum is wide. They can be feminine, androgynous, or relatively masculine. Since in a gender hierarchy there is little difference between second place and last place, how one dresses in the lower ranks is interesting, but ultimately inconsequential.

Men are restricted to a narrow dress spectrum to safeguard their perch on the high rung of masculinity. Even then their perch is precarious. A slender, particular kind of appearance of masculine maleness reaps rewards. Other masculine presentations, even those stereotypically 'macho,' face negative repercussions. For instance, the ruggedly masculine association attached to being dressed as a cowboy carries with it far less reward than a man in a business suit. Men dressed androgynously tend to be subject to bemused stares. Men dressed femininely are judged as not men (at least, *real* men) at all.

If this sounds political, it is because dress *is* political.[929]

Dress and the Politics of Gender

Of course, so is gender, as we have discussed often enough in our dialog. In a certain respect, gender is the ultimate arena of politics. Just as there is no form of governance indisputably dictated by nature, there is no natural obligation to construe gender along the lines done in our culture. Even as politics takes varying shapes in cultures around the world and throughout history, so also do genders. Politics manifests itself in the institutions of government, the dictates of policy, the processes of law. Gender manifests itself in appearance, including a broad range of behaviors, but preeminently dress. To put it bluntly, "we concretize the nonexistence of gender in our clothing. . . ."[930]

Famed costume historian and clothes scholar James Laver cuts right to the heart of how dress and gender politics converge. In an interview in 1967, Laver remarked, "In a patriarchal society—one in which the man is dominant—the clothes of men and women are vastly different. But in a matriarchal society the clothes worn by the two sexes become more and more alike."[931] If Laver is right, we may detect the direction our society is moving through the dress of its citizens. Certainly we shall be able to see that dress provides a readily visible ground for expressing underlying social currents about gender.

The politics of gender sometimes erupt in conflict. Dress, by virtue of its omnipresence, becomes a natural and critical weapon in the gender wars. As Joanna Brewis, Mark Hampton, and Stephen Linstead observe, gender-differentiated dress behavior only happens because all of us are under the sway of the power effects flowing from a discourse of gender difference.[932] All parties use it to advance their own causes. In a society like our own, where sex and gender are more neatly paired than reality warrants, clothing constitutes an arena for making a social and political statement that gender issues *can* be clear and *should be.*

For example, research shows that most of us try to align our biological sex, assigned gender and sex stereotypical clothes. Biological sex proves to be a solid predictor of choosing sex stereotypical clothing. Males are more likely to select masculine clothing and females are more likely to select feminine clothing.[933] Of course, this makes sense in a society where a strict pairing between sex and gender prevails and where violations of such a pairing in dress are predictable. Most of us, wittingly or not, are involved in sustaining the divide.

Men in power may be strongly motivated by the advantages of masculine privilege to keep the gender line clear and firm. They are likely to desire distinctly masculine and feminine dress, with men in the former and women in the latter. Women, wanting to equalize the power, may adopt masculine clothing and make it their own. But they, too, want men to remain in masculine clothing,[934] while redefining what constitutes 'feminine' dress.[935] Crossdressers, exploiting the fuzzing of the gender line by such machinations, present gendered dress in such a manner as to accent the relation of clothing and gender. Crossdressing, in an important sense, depends on the politics and conflicts of gender.

Politics involves posturing for position and power—and so does gender. With due apologies to those who use certain terms in ways other than what is said here, in broad strokes clothing can be used to express gender in one or another of at least five ways:

- ❑ *Be gender*—the use of dress to enact a gender; in its most common use this is dressing congruent to one's assigned gender and so mythically stating we *are* a gender rather than that we *do* gender.
- ❑ *Borrow gender*—the use of dress to occupy another gender temporarily.
- ❑ *Blend gender*—the use of androgynous dress or mixed gender elements to minimize or eliminate the gender divide.
- ❑ *Blur gender*—the use of dress to make gender uncertain.
- ❑ *Bend gender*—the use of dress to change or challenge the perception of gender.

No matter how we dress, we likely end up fitting into one of these patterns; gender and dress are inescapably intertwined.

Be Gender

Most of the time we practice and observe the first pattern in its most common use. We dress congruently with our assigned gender and no fuss is raised. Our goal is clear and so is the process: we aim to present a calculated congruence between our assigned gender and apparent, designated body sex. We do so by following as best we can culturally sanctioned rules governing the use of gender-differentiated clothing. We seldom, if ever, consider that the only difference between ourselves and transsexuals is a different starting point—our congruence of sex and gender as contrasted to their incongruence between the two.

In various societies at various times this gender congruence with the paired sex is accompanied by specific and exaggerated attempts to draw attention to sexual anatomy. In this manner the tie between gender and sex is especially emphasized and gender qualities are particularly depicted in sexual language, as in the virile or potent man and the fertile or receptive woman. This plays out in dress, for example, with feminine garments designed to provide maximum exposure of the female breast or to emphasize physical features associated with fertility. In masculine fashion it occurs through garments accenting the phallus, such as the codpiece in England or the ancient Egyptian skirt starched in front to display constant aroused virility.[936]

Borrow Gender

Borrowing gender occurs far more frequently than we might imagine. We all do it imaginatively whenever we try to place ourselves in the situation of someone of a different gender—an advisable strategy in the effort to understand and get along with others no matter how difficult it may be. In terms of dress behavior it also happens more commonly than we might imagine. Non-transgender people sometimes engage in transgender behavior.

Crossdressing as a way of borrowing gender happens in a variety of casual settings. In schools often a day is set aside for students (and sometimes faculty and staff) to crossdress in ways such that their assigned gender remains obvious by their talk or other behavior. Especially for festivities, many people indulge in dress meant to represent a gender other than their own, but in such a way that there is no possibility of passing for that gender. In short, they mean for others to know that what they are wearing does *not* represent or express their gender identity or ordinary gender role. They are only borrowing the gender. Though it may be playful, it is hardly immature play; borrowing a gender at least hypothetically means putting on all the things associated with it—no light or laughing matter.

Blend Gender

Many of us are bothered by the gender divide and gender stratification whether or not we identify as transgendered. We see how a gender hierarchy inherently disadvantages girls and women—and harms everyone. Boys and men also are trapped within their gender status and because of masculine privilege find themselves confined within narrow but weighty expectations. Ways of easing the pressure may be sought through minimizing or eliminating the gender divide.

Once more dress affords rich possibilities. Androgyny, as we have learned, offers a balancing through blending of characteristics associated with both genders. Androgynous dress does the same thing, blending masculine and feminine elements in order to be somewhere between the two genders. This gender choice is often seen among professional women.

Consider, for example, the ethnographic and interview research conducted by Carrie Yang Costello. She studied students in two professional school settings: law and social work. Her interest was in how the appropriation of a new professional identity might be complicated by preexisting personal identity, resulting in dissonance that would show up, for example, in dress behavior. Her work reveals that the entrance into these professional groups carries with it dress expectations that, especially for women and people of color, elicit wardrobe changes that have a gendered quality. "Because," Costello observes, "Western male professional dress style is so well-established, men are able easily to approximate it. But the scenario is quite different for professional women, and I observed a lot more variation in style."[937]

As women's wardrobes changed, consistent with their striving to gain a new professional identity, their gendered self-presentation altered. In a typical scenario, Costello found that when new students determined they were dressed inappropriately they showed identity dissonance. They responded to this sense by shopping for new clothes—putting on a new skin better suited to their new identity. The trend for female students both at the law school and the school of social work was toward androgyny. But they could achieve this androgynous dress appearance by two paths. Some used what Costello terms 'subtractive androgyny': they removed signifiers of gender. Others practiced 'additive androgyny': they combined gender elements dramatically. In Costello's view, the former course was associated more with negative dissonance.[938]

Androgyny sometimes is seen as a 'third gender' (cf. chapter 11). Historically, when children are seen as asexual beings, their dress tends to be either androgynous or, because of their inferior social status, like that of women.[939] In societies with a rigid gender hierarchy androgyny is likely to be judged as closer to femininity. So androgynous dress is acceptable for girls and women but only (barely) tolerated for boys and men.[940] Ironically, today many of the young people who are choosing to blend gender through androgynous dress (and use of makeup) are males. This probably reflects both protest against masculine stereotypes and the lessened distance between the genders. Nevertheless, particularly among other males, androgynous dress among men and boys commonly fetches disparaging comments.

Blur Gender

Others aim to blur gender so that those who observe them are left guessing as to whether they are anatomically male or female. The motivations vary. Some may do so because they object to the artificiality of society constructed along lines drawn based on sex and gender. Others may do so because of a sense of personal uncertainty, confusion, or disturbance about their own gender identity and status. Some may find the confusion it creates to be amusing or offer opportunities they can exploit in one manner or another. All these different motivations are likely to have in common is a use of dress such that the net effect is uncertainty over the person's sex and gender. Whether that uncertainty extends to the person so dressing varies from individual to individual; it is by no means necessary to have a vacillating or ambivalent sense of gender to blur it in practice.

Bend Gender

Finally, dress can be used to bend (or even bash) gender. While all of the ways of expressing gender are political, this avenue is most likely to be seen as such. After all, it is the use of dress to change or challenge the perception of gender. Perhaps it is the intentionality of the manipulation that makes bending gender in dress so likely to be noticed and to startle observers. Most of us, most of the time, think little about matters such as whether gender is natural or artificial, reasonable or irrational, absolute or arbitrary. Dress that bends gender intends observers to know that the sex of the body is different from the gender of the dress, but it is the gender of the dress that is being championed. Most of the time people borrow gender in dress they make sure to also bend it so that all observers are clear they are enacting a gender farce.

Regardless of whether dress is manipulated to be, borrow, blend, blur, or bend gender, it results in a *Gestalt*—a perceptual whole attendant with value meanings. In dress behavior the name for this *Gestalt* is a 'silhouette.'[941] This is an optical illusion of the clothed body generated by the dress. As such it can be manipulated to achieve a desired effect.[942] The silhouette is also a figure cast against the background of personal experience and identity, culture and social identity. No matter how dress is used, for whatever purpose, a silhouette results. While there are a number of what we might think of as 'stock' silhouettes in dress, we can also more generally think of the silhouette as the individual's complete dressed form seen as though it were a shadow on the wall, an artful illustration meant to depict the body in a certain manner.

The Silhouette

Normally in discussions of gender and dress the conversation stays to the kinds of clothes selected and how they are worn. So, when we think of gender-differentiated apparel, we may speak of pants for men and dresses for women. Limiting our conversation to clothing items misses a significant element involved. Dress, including both clothes and costume ornamentation, holistically shapes a silhouette. In short, it drafts an overall form that is perceived by observers. That form likely is associated with a particular gender. Even more potently, it may rely on a cultural expectation of how a gender represents a sexed body, because the silhouette is principally influenced on the one side by the garment (gender-differentiated), and on the other by the physical proportions of the person (the sexed body).[943]

For example, in contemporary Western culture the most feminine females are associated with dress that in its separate elements reflects femininity while collectively shaping a silhouette unambiguously female. Gender and sex converge in the silhouette. The most desired silhouette in our culture constitutes the stereotype of the feminine female: the Barbie doll girl or woman. This silhouette reflects a slender waist, wide hips, and pronounced bust. Despite the fact that the physical reality to match the Barbie doll image is virtually unattainable and undesirable health-wise, it inspires behavior to attain it. Since the easiest way to approximate it is through dress, fashion styles accommodate the goal. Women for whom such an ideal is impossible, or undesired, seek through dress to embody one or another silhouette they regard as portraying an authentic feminine female, such as a matron, Madonna, or working woman.

Silhouettes are not merely created by stylistic elements of dress—they influence those separate elements' contribution to the whole. The silhouette suggests how a masculine male or feminine female is to sit, stand, and walk. Posture and movement are both influenced by dress designed to attain and maintain a silhouette. The silhouette draws attention to some features of the body and away from others. As various body parts are associated with one gender/sex pairing or the other, those receive corresponding fashion emphasis and contribute to the desired silhouette. For example, an item like a corset modifies the silhouette to highlight certain anatomical features that are different from those drawn attention to by another item, such as a bustle.

In sum, different uses of dress to express gender still must contend with the reality of the silhouette. Different paths affect the nature of the silhouette. The effort to be a gender, where gender is conceived as matching sex, will aim at a silhouette unmistakably male or female (e.g., big biceps for males, big busts for females). The goal of blending gender, also influenced by the cultural pairing of sex and gender, will aim at a silhouette neither clearly male nor female. If, as remarked earlier, gender politics involves posturing for position and power, the posture of the silhouette makes a statement whose grammar may be made from the elements of dress, but whose semantics rests in a context of intent and interpretation. The silhouette matters in childhood and adulthood alike. So do other aspects of gender differentiated dress. We must now turn our attention to how dress and gender relate throughout our lifetime.

Clothing and Gender Among Children

Our attention to dress in relation to gender begins immediately in life. We might well wonder why we find it necessary to color code infants. Obviously, a baby in wraps is androgynous in appearance; hence a convention of color-coding is convenient for declaring the child's sex—which is what our culture gives primacy to in starting the long labor of constructing a gender. In our culture we are at birth not merely beings-with-sex, but also beings-with-gender. Since gender assignment is made based on determination of sex, clothes that declare gender are construed in our culture to also declare sex. So *dress is used to express gender assignment*—a public declaration before the child can say anything on its own behalf that masculinity or femininity has been assigned as an identity and as an expectation.

Color Coding Infants & Dress Expectations for Small Children

Our society is so obsessed with this declaration that no opportunity seems too trivial to miss. Nor is there such a thing as starting too early. As Gregory Stone observed in the early 1960s, "The diaper folded in front *invests* the child with masculinity; in back, with femininity."[944] Even more obviously we rely on color cues: masculinity turns out to be blue, while femininity is pink. This situation has reached the point where even disposable diapers are color-coded!

Do we really need such gender labeling? Apparently we do. A study published in 1985 found that strangers could only determine an infant's gender if provided the visual cue of color-coded clothes. In the study, 48 infants were dressed either in gender-stereotyped clothes (pink for girls, blue or red for boys), or gender-neutral clothes. The 90% of infants dressed in gender-coded clothing were readily identified as boys or girls by observers; the same was not true otherwise.[945]

Research indicates that children's early environments typically are gender-differentiated. For example, one study investigated the home environments of 120 girls and boys in three equal groups of 40 children at three different ages: 5, 13, and 25 months (infancy into toddlerhood). The environments for both boys and girls were filled with toys, clothes, and colors endorsed by the culture as appropriate for the gender. Thus, girls were surrounded with dolls and jewelry, and wore multicolored clothes and pink; boys' toys were sports and work related, and their clothes more often red, white or blue.[946] Early acculturation into gender stereotypes seems a social constant that both teaches gender expectations and reinforces them.

Development psychologist Carole Beale summarizes the matter well when she writes:

> Gender supports many inferences about the baby's probable characteristics and behavior. Even though these initial inferences have a very high probability of being wrong, they reassure the viewer who is faced with an unfamiliar small baby. The drawback is that, as we have seen, once the baby is perceived as a boy or girl, the process of social interaction will be altered accordingly.[947]

Instant judgments, typically based on visual cues like dress, produce profoundly different patterned responses. If this process appears troubling for all children, it proves highly problematic for transgender children.

Transgender Children

Immediately in life everyone around an infant—parents, siblings, and others—facilitates the process of acculturation into the assigned gender identity and role. Typically the amount of environmental reinforcement of gender expectations is immense. Yet virtually all children exhibit some gender-crossing behavior. Of course, much of this is exploratory and naïve. Parents typically respond with firm displeasure and the child learns such exhibitions are not approved. With the cognitive development of gender schemas the child ordinarily joins the throng of society, accepting, endorsing, and expressing the expected gender identity and its accompanying roles.

But what happens when a child persists in gender-crossing behavior? What results from a persistent preference for articles of clothing associated with a gender different than that assigned the child at birth? Although it may be tolerated in a toddler, such behavior almost always meets increasing resistance as the child grows older, if not at home, then certainly from peers and authority figures in social institutions such as school. Moreover, in keeping with the gender hierarchy in our culture, different standards apply to boys and girls.

Sociologist Kane, interviewing a diverse group of parents of preschool children (ages 3-5), found a clear double standard. These parents welcomed gender nonconformity among girls. They often dressed them in sports clothes, provided them with masculine toys, applauded their involvement in activities associated with boys, and encouraged their ambitions to someday participate in traditionally male occupations. The term 'tomboy' was used approvingly.[948] The situation with boys proved markedly different. There the openness to nonconforming behavior was conscientiously balanced by attention to eliciting from their sons gender behavior approximating masculine ideals. Heterosexual fathers, in particular, were central to these efforts. There was approval, or at least acceptance, of boys learning to perform domestic skills or show nurturance. On the other hand, when sons engaged in certain dress behavior—wearing pink or frilly clothing, wearing skirts, dresses or tights—the parents responded with negative reactions.[949] Indeed, David Plummer's study of the role homophobia plays in the construction of a Western sense of masculinity provides evidence of how crossdressing is linked to homosexuality; to cross the gender line in dress is correlated with also crossing out of heterosexuality.[950]

As we discovered earlier, if the child is a boy, he is more than six times likelier than a comparable girl to be referred to mental health professionals. They are also more likely to be diagnosed with Gender Identity Disorder. Susan Langer and James Martin—both mental health professionals—point out that, "current criteria maintain a lower diagnostic threshold for boys on preferences for wearing clothes associated with the opposite sex; girls have to insist on wearing such clothes, but boys need only to prefer them."[951] We are returned again to the Golden Rule of Gender-differentiated Dress: "Males must appear masculine, or at least not feminine."

Developmental Process Related to Gender

Even with all the pressure to conformity provided by others and the culture at large, small children require some time to master the language of dress and other gender standards. In the first two years of life children themselves typically do not label gender—although they already have a lifetime experiencing it. Sometime between ages 2-3 most kids acquire a basic sense of gender identity, an awareness of self and others as 'boy' or 'girl.' Now gender labeling becomes a cognitive task in the child's process of socialization. From this time forward throughout childhood dress functions as a primary criterion used by children to differentiate boys from girls.[952]

Awareness of gender distinctions in dress doubtless precedes understanding of these differences. Development of awareness, endorsement, and expressed *preferences along stereotyped expectations for dress* may vary from individual to individual, but research suggests such matters are generally attained before a child starts school. A study reported in 1990 by developmental researchers Carol Lynn Martin and Jane Little found that a quarter of the 61 children (ages 3-5) tested attained a stereotyped knowledge about gendered clothing at age three, that more than half (54.5%) had done so at age four, and about three quarters (73.7%) at age five. As they put it, children need "only a rudimentary understanding of gender for preferences and knowledge to be influenced."[953] Given the pervasiveness of concern over sex and gender in our culture it might be said they are part of the very air children breathe.

Dress Preferences in Childhood

With the strong incentives to master gender, significantly coded and presented in dress, children very early form distinct notions about what they should wear and wish to wear. In 2004, *Textile Consumer* began a report on the children's apparel market by noting that as early as age three children express brand preferences. The report, based on data collected in 2003, shows that as children age from toddlers through childhood and adolescence, apparel offerings steadily increase. The report also documents similarities and differences between adults and children. For example, where adults rely far more heavily on tops (by a 3:1 ratio) to diversify their wardrobes, apparel offerings for children favor bottoms (47%) over tops (45%).[954] This may reflect, at least in part, that immature bodies are visibly sexually different below the waist and, lacking visible cues above the waist, dress accents bottoms. A skirt or dress is more important as a cue in childhood than it is in adulthood.

One thing that stays constant is the imbalance in clothing options by gender: girls at every age have more options than boys, just as women have more than men. Other gender distinctions emerge. While cotton plays a major role both in adult and children's clothing, it plays a relatively greater role for children. Further, a gender difference emerges between boys and girls: nearly three-quarters (73%) of boys' wear is 100% cotton, but this is true of only 56% of girls' apparel. The largest use of synthetic fibers in children's attire is found in girls' clothing like skirts, blouses, and dresses.[955] As we heard earlier, fabric differences produce different physiological sensations, eliciting different psychological perceptions and reactions. It seems plausible to conclude these differences become part and parcel of our perceptions and expectations about gender.

The differences in what boys and girls are permitted to wear may prompt a variety of responses. Children of either gender may experience *dress envy*, the desire to have freedoms perceived granted to others but not to self. Girls raised always to wear unbifurcated garb—skirts and dresses—may envy the freedom of those who wear pants. On the other hand, some boys may envy the latitude most girls have to wear bifurcated or unbifurcated clothing. Moreover, as we have seen, feminine clothing embraces greater diversity of style, color, and feel. Any or all of these qualities may elicit some resentment from a boy.[956] But both boys and girls soon learn that there is too high a price to be paid for acting on such envy, so it is renounced, or at least set aside as much as possible.

A rather common response to gender differentiation is *experimentation.* Younger children, especially, enjoy more liberty to play at dressing in others' clothes. They may play at being grown-up and use items of either parent at different times. Or they may explore gender differences, only slowly being mastered, by crossdressing. Yet the risks in such activity are unequal between the genders; boys are at much more risk for censure and punishment. For example, David Plummer observes among the males he interviewed a careful retrospective distinguishing between their childhood 'dress up' play and 'crossdressing.' The same act of wearing feminine items might be involved, but the motivation—having fun, acting grownup—kept it from being transgressive (i.e., crossdressing) in their minds.[957]

The gender distinctions in dress learned in childhood are frequently relied on in a variety of social contexts throughout life. They often give rise to dress codes, informal or formal. In childhood and adolescence these codes may be expressed in school uniforms that minimize many distinctions clothing might ordinarily provide while preserving the one distinction our culture insists upon—gender. Accordingly, girl's dress is always clearly distinguished from boy's dress in school uniforms. Apart from formal dress codes, informal ones among children also reinforce the gender divide. Children can be quite punitive in efforts to enforce gender conformity among peers.[958]

Gendered Dress & Adolescence

One of the features that may help distinguish adolescence from childhood is a change in orientation to dress. This change has several facets. Social scientists Jason Cox and Helga Dittmar point to one: "Although clothing tends to be gender-marked from birth, gender differences in the *activity* of shopping for clothes and the *use* of clothes in terms of their peer-group relationships clearly emerge in adolescence."[959] They point out that girls begin shopping with their peers for clothes earlier than do boys, and rely more heavily on peers to evaluate clothing choices. They also observe that girls are more likely to swap clothes and, following Alison Lurie, suggest this activity can be interpreted as a mutual sharing of their identities.

While dress in recent decades has seemed to be much more important to adolescent girls than adolescent boys, the distance between the genders in the value placed on clothes and attention given to their selection appears to be narrowing. This perception has some empirical support and may reflect changes that have been taking shape over the last three decades. For example, some research shows a modest decline among girls in the percent using clothes to acquire prestige in high school between cohorts in 1978-1982 (40.6%) and in 1988-1989 (36.9%); these same cohorts for boys show an increase (15.9% to 22.2%).[960] Anecdotal reports suggest this trend has continued to the present.

With adolescent efforts to further separate and individuate—to carve out an independent identity—there often are uses of dress to experiment with gender or challenge gender norms. The contemporary interest many youth show in androgynous clothing, or dress that mixes what are seen as masculine and feminine elements, retains gender expression as central to the identity quest. Other youth cling to rigid separations of the genders, using dress to preserve the perceived status quo even if the manner in which they express gender in their clothing choices is different from their parents or from other adolescent social groups. Gender remains inescapable in clothing choices.

Clothing and Gender Among Adults

Research into the relationship between dress and gender in adults establishes it as important to both men and women. Generally, contemporary women are more involved with clothes and show a greater interest in fashion. Nevertheless, within each gender group a range of interest and involvement exists. Overall, evidence suggests men and women relate differently to their possessions, and it might be expected such differences extend to dress items.[961] Some research indicates men use dress more for self-expression while women use it more for social interrelatedness—though these differences may not be large enough to be significant.[962]

There may be important differences among men and women even when both are fashion conscious. Research reported in 1989 found that fashion conscious women tend to focus more on their public appearance and seem to be more publicly self-conscious than other women. Fashion conscious men, however, appear to be more focused on who they are as gendered beings. As the investigators phrase it, "That fashion conscious men are more gender conscious suggests that these men connect fashion with their self-identity and internalized maleness, their concept of what it means to be a man."[963]

Even where the genders converge in interest and attitude, gender lines still create differences. For example, both genders rank qualities like comfort as very important in making clothing choices. Yet the decision about what constitute comfortable clothes considers only apparel designated appropriate for the gender, despite differences in composition for many garments for men and women. Thus, even in apparently gender free or gender neutral matters, gender lines operate to constrict choices.

Nowhere in the adult world is that more apparent than in work wear. There dress codes—formal or informal—expect conformity to prevailing gender distinctions. Job environments commonly have policies, guidelines, or rules governing dress, even so-called 'casual dress.'[964] As seen elsewhere in discussing uniforms, manner of dress can be very important in identifying professional affiliations.[965] But even apart from uniforms as such, most work settings carry with them associated styles of dress. Moreover, clothing can be used to identify workplace values and characteristics so that workers in that environment dress in such a way as to not only identify their affiliation but also to influence their own self-perception.[966] This includes workers' self-perception of their feelings, sociability, and work competence.[967] The introduction of 'casual Fridays,' with their relaxed dress codes, also affords opportunities to relax the gender hierarchy.[968]

Clothing and Gender Among Women

But the gender hierarchy never disappears. As cultural studies scholar Jennifer Craik succinctly says, "Gender—especially femininity—is worn through clothes."[969] Though important to both sexes, the connection of dress to gender has been studied more with women, for whom clothes are often assumed to play a more important role.[970] Perhaps more accurately, dress may play a *different* role, rather than a more important one. They appear to rely on dress more for public and relational aspects than do men.[971] Evidence also suggests women attribute more symbolic dimensions to clothing than do men. Perhaps because of these things, and other factors such as greater choices in apparel offerings and higher expectations for wardrobe diversity, women are also more likely than men to experience dissatisfaction about their clothes (or lack thereof).[972]

At the end of the 1940s clothing researcher Mary Lou Lerch Rosencranz reported her study with a sizable and diverse group of women aimed at determining factors significant in women's interest in clothing. She found that in addition to various demographic factors (age, occupation, education, etc.), time, effort, money, and personal attention given were relevant in measuring such interest. Also, diversity of wardrobe emerged as a significant indicator of interest—a factor alongside the number and diversity of groups a woman belongs to.[973] All of these factors have been reaffirmed in subsequent studies.

Women may also attend more to dress for cues about others. One study that investigated this matter, reported in 2002, evaluated interview responses garnered from 39 adult women, ages 20-62. The research found that women form impressions about others based on appearance and dress, and believe others do the same about them. While some women acknowledged the influence of situations and specific clothing cues on the accuracy of their impressions, the majority of the women were confident that their impressions—which included assessments about personality, behavior, health, hygiene, biological traits and social roles—were reliable.[974]

Some research suggests that dress is more influential than either physical attractiveness or the kind of job being sought when a woman applies for work.[975] Yet women generally less endorse the notion that manipulating dress enhances occupational attributes.[976] Nevertheless, they often adopt a clothing strategy for other purposes, such as leveling the playing field. In a male-dominated work environment, women often turn to styles like those used by the men in similar positions or desired ones. For example, so-called 'power dressing' by women—black or navy blue suits with large shoulder pads, accompanied by high heels, and a severe hairstyle—creates a silhouette distinctly masculine.[977]

Other research also has indicated that the 'masculinity of clothing' selected by a woman may be related to a perception by others of her managerial characteristics; the more masculine the style, the more favorable the impression.[978] However, because of expectations about clothing also distinguishing the genders, women must be careful to maintain an apparent female version of the male garb or risk censure.[979] Even feminists feel pressure to balance their values and philosophical orientation with workplace factors when choosing dress.[980]

In short, women must conform to the prevailing system in such a manner that they accomplish two ends: they remain reliably identifiable as feminine, but they simultaneously affiliate with and appropriate masculine status. The latter end is acceptable as long as it remains an evident fiction—they are, after all, still female—and as long as the assumed status does not seriously jeopardize male prerogatives. Current women's fashion for the workplace admirably accomplishes all this, thus leaving women the illusion of a shift in status that men grant them because it remains more apparent than real.

Clothing and Gender Among Men

Men also experience cultural expectations and pressures with regard to dress. Preeminently, they must adhere to the rule of appearing masculine, or at least not feminine. Beyond that, is there any other reason for men to care about their clothing? Perhaps not. In 1949, Rosencranz reported earlier research involving 100 Harvard men and 59 Radcliffe women. That study found that men's interest in clothing had no relationship to their personal values.[981] Yet this conclusion may be misleading. While men may not be as accustomed as women to think of clothing reflecting personal ideals, they mostly manage to conform to the Golden Rule of dress for their gender. Moreover, longstanding social values also exert a siren-like call.

Where women are actively encouraged by fashion to shift presentation of their sexualized bodies from one erogenous zone to another,[982] thus needing grand diversity in apparel styles, men require relatively little, and quite modest garments to communicate what is important about them—status. Commensurate with their privileged position in the gender hierarchy, their dress must symbolically display the characteristics most attached to privilege: power and social standing.[983] Since these are variable, men are subject to the pressure of competition to outdo one another in power and social standing—in masculinity as it were—and to show the results in dress.

Others judge personal qualities such as attractiveness, intelligence and popularity based on their apparel styles.[984] Like women, men need to show some concern about how they dress. In fact, it has been argued that male attitudes and concern over dress may be even more complicated than those held by women.[985] Unfortunately, the connection of men to dress as a way of expressing how they feel about their bodies is little studied. What research has been done, though, shows men also use clothing to fit cultural ideals.[986] Perhaps ironically, most of the attention men garner in connection to dress seems to come when they crossdress!

Interestingly, it may be the influence of transgender realities that lies behind today's reawakening of masculine fashion. Although men in the United States typically express a reluctance to shop for clothes or to make fashion statements in what they wear—both activities being viewed as feminine—there are signs that actual behavior tells another story. Perhaps more than at any other time in a century men are showing interest in fashion and taking a more active role in clothes purchases.[987] The so-called 'metrosexual' phenomenon, rooted in transgender reality, has helped loosen some of the restrictiveness of masculine fashion, though not without controversy and challenge. Resistance to metrosexualism focuses on its perceived threat to the Golden Rule by suggesting that it tends unacceptably toward feminine elements.

In the public arena what matters about masculine dress becomes clearest. In the workplace, even as women are granted greater freedom in dress, men sometimes find a strong expectation remains that they 'dress up' rather than 'dress down.' The terminology itself has almost a Freudian tone—men dressing in more casual fashion styles may be perceived as dressing 'down' to the feminine gender. Judith Rasband, writing for the Conselle Institute of Image management, comments:

> This whole trend toward casual dress or dressing down works to expose the male body. By taking off the tie—that longstanding symbol of male corporate power—unbuttoning the shirt, and opening the collar, men expose their neck and throat. Increased exposure more nearly matches feminine rather than masculine stereotypes in our culture.[988]

Clearly, men no less than women confront significant cultural pressures, often expressed in rules either formal or informal.

Underwear and Gender

To this point our discussion of the relation of dress to gender has implicitly assumed a focus on outerwear. After all, if clothing is to be a principal signifier of gender, it needs to be visible to others to be effective. So our attention has been on outerwear. But we must not leave out another important aspect of dress: underwear.

It may not be immediately apparent how underwear is related to gender. Unlike outerwear, underwear typically remains unseen by the general public. In fact, those who appear in public dressed only in their underwear risk arrest; they are generally seen as disrupting public order. This situation would *prima facie* appear to render underwear a very poor signifier of gender.

Gender Differentiation in Underwear

Yet underwear is routinely gender-differentiated: men wear boxers or briefs, women wear panties; women wear bras, men don't. Later we will examine briefly the history of underwear and document some of the relevant changes such clothing has undergone. But here our interest is in understanding why we bother to gender differentiate clothing that will more often than not remain invisible to others. Since the notion we have been relying on is that dress serves as a highly visible public expression of gender, we must solve the riddle of why largely invisible dress nevertheless would become at least as highly gender-differentiated as outerwear. To accomplish this we must revisit some ideas.

Our Intimate Connection with Underwear

Clothing, we noted earlier, acts like a 'second skin.' Underwear especially fits this metaphor because it resides closest to the skin. This 'skin' functions as part of our boundary system even as it retains an independent reality. These two aspects intersect and render possible deeply personal experiences of clothing. It is no exaggeration to regard *underwear as the most personal kind of clothing*; these are the garments we have the most intimate association with.

There is more than one reason for this intimate connection. First, a basic utilitarian function of underwear is to protect our natural skin from our other clothes—and simultaneously protect those clothes from soiling produced by our own bodies. As a 'second skin' the first boundary formed is between ourselves and the other clothes we wear—a reality that creates not only physical distancing, but some psychological distancing as well. No such distance intervenes with underwear; as a popular advertisement proclaimed about its apparel, nothing comes between us and our under garments.

Just as we take care of our natural skin through washing it, applying lotions, and so forth in order to be healthy and comfortable, so we do with our underwear. Over time the emphasis in making and marketing underwear has changed from utilitarian and health reasons to comfort and pleasure. In fact, as comfort increases through the pure sensuousness of fabric and fit, so does the intrinsic potential to eroticize the garment by symbolic substitution for the body regions the apparel resides by. This can lead in extreme cases to fetishism (see chapter 13), but typically only elicits a felt connection between the pleasure of the garment and the pleasure felt from stimulation of the body parts beneath the garment by whatever means.

Our first reason for our intimate connection to underwear thus leads to a second. In a culture where so much of the construction of identity revolves around sex and gender, these garments cover the body's erogenous zones. We forge early in life a learned association between these clothes and our selves as sexual and gendered beings. This learned association is reinforced by the pleasures derived from comfortable, appealing underwear, the fantasy of such garments being part of a sexual encounter, and the sexual stirrings thus aroused.

Precisely because gender has been predicated solely on sex, the clothing most associated with sex must also be the garb most connected to gender.

Culture describes gender in clothing, right down to the names for various apparel items. This is particularly evident in women's lingerie and underwear, where we find items like 'teddies' and 'babydoll' lingerie, and 'boyshort' panties. Such names indirectly highlight two related matters. First, womenswear, including underwear, is derived from masculine fashion. Second, masculine ideals and ideas still shape conceptions of femininity, ranging feminine dress—and women—along an androcentric continuum extending from 'most like men' to 'most unlike men.'

The gendered nature of undergarments proves ideal for crossdressers. It means that underwear associated with a gender different from that assigned to them can be worn secretly while a connection to the desired gender is attained. This so-called 'partial crossdressing' may be for some complete crossdressing if it succeeds in creating the gender experience sought. Of course, all too often it does not fully succeed because the outerwear creates gender dissonance. Thus the normal progression in crossdressing is from underwear only to complete crossdressing.

Unfortunately, another hazard awaits the crossdresser. Because gender is viewed as founded on sex, and sexual anatomy is seen as meant for sexual activity, any crossdressing is construed as sexual in nature. The gender experience of the crossdresser is displaced by the sexual construal of the observer, leading to the generally erroneous judgment that crossdressing is a perversion intending to substitute the pleasure of clothes for the pleasure of another person. While gender trumps sex for the crossdresser, noncrossdressers generally assume that gender has nothing to do with it—all the crossdresser is out for is a guilty sexual pleasure.

That notion indirectly leads us to a third reason for the intimate nature of our connection to underwear. Because of our values with respect to sexuality, these garments also become signifiers of modesty, eroticism, and guilt. They remind us of our stance with respect to such values, or move us toward behaviors suited to our values.[989] By virtue of association with values—things that matter to us and hold meaning for us—clothing, and especially underwear, becomes subject to personal and societal taboos. The emotional stakes are thereby raised. This means we become more conscientious about how these clothes, above all others, will be regarded by others.

This step leads us to a final reason for intimacy with underwear: unlike our outerwear, open to inspection by all we encounter, our underwear is meant to be selectively revealed. Those we show our underwear to are typically those we have the most intimate relationships with.[990] Of course that often means sexual relationships, but we need not be so narrow. Since underwear covers those parts of the body most associated with sex, and sex is central to the construction of identity, nudity becomes the greatest risk of self-disclosure. When we remove our underwear we remove a boundary protecting our self and thus make that self vulnerable. Most of us are more likely to share our deepest feelings before we are to share the sight of our naked body.

We treasure underwear as both the bastion protecting our modesty and the gate to erotic pleasures. We rely on what we wear to protect us; we depend on it to reveal us. Underwear is revelation—it hides and it discloses, and in both it is the self revealed. If we are casual in our choice of the underwear we put on, it is only because we reckon the odds someone else will see it as slender. As soon as we calculate the likelihood of another seeing our underwear, our regard for what we wear rises. If we expect that the most intimate of encounters will occur, we give most special attention to our underwear—or do our best to get it hidden aside as quickly as possible! Either way our action signifies some awareness that these garments truly matter.

Given such factors it would be surprising if we did not feel differently toward our underwear than we do our outerwear.

Gender Trumps Sex

In what we have been discussing the chain linking clothes to gender to sex has been evident. Despite the primacy our culture awards sex over gender, clothing has the power to reverse the hierarchy. Through clothes gender can triumph, at least temporarily, over sex. Our intimate connection with clothing, especially with undergarments, makes possible an experience of gender more immediate and substantial than anything happening in the genitals.

For example, a transgendered male can choose to wear a panty with a gaff to hide his genitals and create a simulation of female sex anatomy. The biology of sex stays the same; only the appearance of bodily sex changes—yet this appearance constitutes a reality all its own. In fact, this reality suffices psychologically for many transgendered males. The superficial appearance of being female trumps the biological reality, perhaps in a manner similar to the way any of us sees what we want to see when we look at the imperfect forms of those we love.

The Eroticism of Underwear

While gender through clothing can trump sex, often enough sexuality coopts gender. Twin factors greatly facilitate the eroticism of undergarments. First, the cultural decision that gender is completely dependent on sex, which defines it, binds gender implicitly to sexuality. Second, gender differentiation in clothing means that symbolization of gender in terms of sexuality becomes possible in dress. Being a woman, for example, means being seen a certain way as a sexual being and her clothing, particularly her undergarments, can be eroticized so that her gendered self is reduced to a sexual self.

Since sexual behavior in Western culture has come to be regarded as hierarchical and heterosexual in character, where masculine men actively pursue passive feminine females, a differentiation in roles elicits a differentiation in dress goals. For males, safeguarding masculine privilege generates the 'Golden Rule' that men must at all costs not appear feminine; if women are viewed as wantonly sexual beings (or objects), then men's own sexuality must be either down-played or depicted in strikingly different ways. The latter course results in mas-culine dress fashions like the codpiece, which emphasize virility through atten-tion to the genitals. Less crudely but no less effectively the modern business suit symbolizes virility by signifying competence, success, and status. The wearer is publicly declared as someone with resources—the very thing available females are likely to desire. At the same time, while demonstrating virility such dress presents a restrained and orderly sexuality. Unlike the wildness of women, men are portrayed as procreative producers for whom all good things must come as an order of course. Men can possess women because they first have possessed their own virile sexuality.

In this scenario, men's underwear bears no more need to be ostentatiously erotic than does masculine outerwear. Yet, in fact, men's underwear has been eroticized. A 2004 article in *The New York Times* observes that the trend in men's underwear that first gained notoriety in the 1980s with provocative Calvin Klein ads had reached a point in the early 21st century where "there are underwear boxes out there that make a man's crotch look as monumental as an Ansel Ad-ams picture of El Capitan."[991] Since the 1930s these garments have undergone transformation in representation from utilitarian items to fashion ones. In style and color range alike men's underwear increasingly finds itself part of an erotic fashion context—masculine lingerie. Ethnologist Bo Lönnqvist is surely right in situating this development in a matrix of changes in consumer culture, gender roles, and body ideals.[992]

Perhaps principal contributors to this development have been the effect of diminished distance in the personality characteristics associated with masculinity and femininity, and the relatively greater gender equality in society. Especially with the greater admission of women into the workforce a change in sexual economy[993] has rendered desirable new strategies for men in seeking mating opportunities. Since women in general no longer need depend principally on men for access to resources, men must increase their value in the sexual econ-omy by other means. One possibility is to mimic the strategy associated with women: accent the desirability of the body.

Western culture, at least in recent centuries, has placed the fashion burden of erotic clothing principally on women. The pairing, dubbed 'fashion and pas-sion' by Feona Attwood, reflects in her view an increasingly sexualized culture where women are more and more targeted as sexual consumers.[994] To females are especially offered the diversity of styles and colors meant to fetch attention and signal sexual interest. Changing feminine fashions over the centuries have mirrored what societies regard at the time as principal erogenous zones. Much more than in masculine clothing, feminine apparel displays variety and is de-signed for erotic appeal. This is even more the case for undergarments than for outerwear.

In women's garments the bra and panty are two basic lingerie items. The former, according to Jane Ferrell-Beck and Colleen Gau, began to be associated with the erotic appeal of movie stars in the 1930s, but became more completely eroticized during the 1950s. They write, "The renewed emphasis on feminine sexuality produced brassiere designs to harmonize with body-revealing décolleté styles: plunging necklines, bare midriffs, halters, backless models, and strapless dresses."[995] The Wonder-bra, invented by Canadian designer Louise Poirier in the mid-1960s, became a cultural icon in the U.S. only in the 1990s. A marvel of technology, the Wonder-bra touted not only its comfort, but its ability to cast the appearance of a perfect breast—at least as socially construed.[996] Millions of women gained new hope for creating the kind of silhouette that passes as the erotic ideal in contemporary times.

The panty, like the bra, underwent a significant change in the 1930s by becoming a part of the cultural mainstream through wider availability and attention by retailers. Panty styles are but a microcosm of the diversity typical for women's clothes—and personalities.[997] There are bikini panties, boyshorts, briefs, culottes, g-strings, hipsters, low rise, tangas, thongs, and more. What this diversity means remains debated.

Once the motivation urged on women to wear panties was health and modesty. This gradually gave way to an emphasis on comfort and style. Now the preoccupation is with erotic appeal, even at the cost of comfort. The end result is a situation in which women are sharply at odds with one another as to whether what is available represents freedom for individuality or enchainment to a cultural one-size-fits-all view of gender as a superficial mask for a sexual body.

Just as bras and panties come in a nearly bewildering range of alternatives, so do other kinds of lingerie. There are camisoles, chemises, corsets, negligees, nighties, peignoirs, slips, and teddies—just to name a few. All these come in a variety of colors, fabrics and sizes. Since the 1970s-1980s the explosion of lingerie has expanded the erotic imagination while exerting pressure on women to present themselves not merely as sexually alluring, but erotically varied as well. Many women ask if lingerie is really made for what women want, or for what men desire—but even those asking often acquiesce if what they want is men.

Much of today's lingerie for women is so calculatedly erotic that it has sometimes been called 'porno chic'—and raises ethical issues about the role of the erotic in modern retailing.[998] When popular figures like Madonna began to wear underwear as outerwear a whole new light was shed on how such apparel can be construed. Contemporary lingerie does more than present an equation of 'feminine = erotic.' It constructs a particular notion of a sexual woman. For example, Nancy Workman argues that the revival of the Victorian corset by Victoria's Secret reinforces traditional roles as construed through the vision of a man rather than any group of women. That vision is of a woman who must be constrained and shaped to be desirable. [999]

Where fashion will head next is anyone's guess. But the eroticism of masculine and feminine underwear today reflects a cultural truth: a preoccupation with sexuality so pronounced that we appear unable to interpret gender as much more than that. We have made our most intimate garments a sexual skin. To an extent—greater for some, less for others—we have succumbed to seeing our gendered selves as principally sexual selves. Regardless of how firmly or loosely we may individually construe the tie between the sex of the body and our experience of gender, this cultural shift to merge them at the focal point of the erotic constitutes for us all a dangerous narrowing of identity, both personal and social. In a society like our own, where sexual aggression and violence run rampant, the trend to reduce the self to a sensual object is as foolhardy as it is unwarranted by the facts.

The Impermanence of Gender Differentiation

We can readily see that fashions change—and gender differentiation in dress remains. But an interesting question arises: are the markers of gender differentiation in clothing constant? Can we point to any reliable markers across time? The most likely candidates are the following:

❑ *Angularity* vs. *curves*—masculine garments accent angles while feminine garments accent curves.

❑ *Verticality* vs. *horizontality*—by and large, masculine garments claim vertical space while feminine garments are more expansive into horizontal space (as exemplified, for instance, by the use of fringes and expanders such as the bustle or dress hoops).

❑ *Free* vs. *restricted motion*: typically masculine clothing has provided a greater range of motion—and thus activity—than feminine clothing.

❑ *Short* vs. *long*: feminine garments have customarily been longer than masculine ones; women's legs have been more likely to be covered.

❑ *Rich colors* vs. *muted colors*—relatively speaking, feminine ornamentation has been more brightly (and lightly) colored, even when masculine clothing is vibrantly (though more darkly) colored. Far more often than not, masculine colors are muted and solid, with black particularly favored.[1000]

❑ *Durable* vs. *soft* fabrics—masculine clothing traditionally has been aimed at the practical necessities of the workplace, while feminine clothing has accented softer, less durable but more sensuous tactile properties.

❑ *Heavy* vs. *light* fabrics—not only the texture but the weight also tends to differentiate gendered clothing, with feminine clothes being lighter.

❑ *Bifurcated* vs. *unbifurcated*—unbifurcated garments embracing both the whole garment (i.e., not divided at the waist), or just the legs (i.e., not divided below the waist), have been almost exclusively feminine. Bifurcated garments were typically regarded as masculine in Western societies until their thorough appropriation by women in the 20th century, but they still retain a mild masculine association.

An important caveat with even such a modest list is the relativity both culturally and historically for all these items. Exceptions may readily spring to mind and may even do so to the degree they cast serious doubt on how valid a claim can be made for them as truly enduring and stable gender differentiators.

But while exceptions come to mind so, too, should recognition of the gender stereotyping communicated. The elements above are calculated to reinforce cultural ideas about each gender's characteristics and proper domains. Women dressed in light, soft, unbifurcated garments are reinforced to appear and act gentle, passive, and demure. Their clothing excludes them from work for which heavier, more durable and bifurcated garments are clearly desirable. Obviously, male crossdressers project gender traits the wider culture discourages in men—a situation far more serious than the upward striving of women through dress in a patriarchal hierarchy.

Probably more important than the separate elements is the holistic effect they aim to contribute towards. Though we may judge articles of clothing as masculine or feminine based on individual features, we are probably more interested in the total effect: is the result more feminine or masculine? When placed in an ensemble of clothing the desired effect is typically the silhouette of a sexed body, male or female.[1001] In our culture, the total effect of dress with regard to gender is to reinforce the pairing of gender with sex. Feminine clothing contributes to the silhouette of the female body; masculine apparel enhances the silhouette of the male body.

However, when we deconstruct the silhouette into separate items of apparel our attention is focused more on gender than on sex. That is one reason why we care about the elements listed above; they help reinforce gender distinctions apart from the silhouette. The fact that there are so few enduring elements is offset both by the abundance of ephemeral elements in any given historical period serving the same end and by the cumulative effect in the silhouette. In sum, whether or not the actual number of enduring and stable elements for gender differentiation is large or small, the net gain is a dependable ability to tell boys from girls, and women from men, by their dress.

Children's Clothing

We can relatively easily demonstrate the *inconstancy* of gender differentiated markers. Consider, for example, children's clothing. Blue is associated in contemporary minds with traits associated with males, while pink is joined to feminine traits.[1002]

This logic has not always prevailed. Once the preference was for the opposite: pink for boys and blue for girls. Clothing historian Jo Paoletti points out that the current fashion in the United States was a French import that began in the mid-19th century but did not come into dominance until about a century later, with the post-World War II baby boom. In fact, at the end of World War I (1918) the 'debate' over what color was most appropriate for which gender had reached such heights that a trade journal, *The Infant's Department*, finally weighed in with an effort to settle the matter:

> There has been a great diversity of opinion on the subject, but the generally accepted rule is pink for the boy and blue for the girl. The reason is that pink, being a more decided and stronger color, is more

suitable for a boy, while blue, which is more delicate and dainty, is prettier for the girl.[1003]

Clearly the associations of traits for these colors were different once than they are now.

If we retreat even a little further in time, we discover that gender distinction in infant dress was nonexistent—another clue that our contemporary way of understanding gender is not all that old. For centuries all infants and young children wore dresses. It was not until the end of the 19th century that young boys were put in trousers and many boys continued to wear dresses well into the 20th century. In fact, the white unisex dress continued to appear in catalogs until at least 1957.[1004] Further, it was not unusual for boys to wear dresses until around age 6 or 7, and these would shock modern American sensibilities:

> Historical clothes for boys will seem remarkable to the modern parent. Even the most fashion conscious mom will marvel at the elegant brocades, lustrous velvets, silks, taffetas, printed, striped and flowered cottons, and laces from which boys' clothes were once made.[1005]

Consistent with other changes we have seen originating in the late 19th century, a new innovation came with the creation of dresses designed especially for boys.[1006] These were often less lacy than designs for girls, but remained unmistakably dresses, with puffy sleeves and pleated skirts. The preferred color for a boy's dress was pink. As a general rule, as the child grew older his dresses became shorter until a 'breeching' ceremony formally transferred him from dresses to pants. This could occur anywhere between ages 3-8. At least until the 1930s, fashion magazines carried pictures of boys clothed in dresses.[1007]

Various reasons have been advanced for why boys wore dresses. One is that prior to the psychological theories of the 20th century children were commonly viewed as genderless.[1008] In that case, unisex garments made sense. Another explanation is that parents feared the tight constriction of pants might hinder a boy's growth.[1009] Perhaps more than one reason came into play, but of the acceptability of such wear for young boys there is no doubt.

As sociologist Daniel Cook documents, as the 19th century gave way to the 20th there developed a growing interest in manufacturing and selling children's clothing. Where before 1890 factories specializing in producing children's wear were virtually nonexistent, by the end of the 1920s sale of children's clothes had led department store chains like Sears to create children's departments. Cook remarks, "Concerns about how transparently clothing indicates the sex of a child have intensified since the 1920s."[1010] Arguably, we may see here the influence both of Freud's ideas and the triumphing medicalization of sex. In the early decades of the 20th century there was an increasing preoccupation with gender that accompanied growing realization of children's sexuality.

After World War I, even as boy's wear was becoming more distinct and unisex garments were passing from the scene, girl's wear was changing too. The flapper style of the Roaring 20s retained the formal characteristic of being a dress, yet was accompanied by elements that signaled a more 'mannish' appearance (slender, small breasted, short hair). In the 1930s and 1940s, girls were occasionally sporting pants and shorts, though dresses and skirts remained the norm. Cries against too masculine an appearance in dress seemed less directed against girls than women. By the 1950s and 1960s, girls were able to move between pants and dresses with relative social ease. By the 1970s, girls in pants were commonplace in school; what had been casual wear was now becoming commonplace in more formal settings. By the end of the 20th century, in some societies dresses were less common than pants or slacks in a wide range of settings.

Today, girls enjoy much wider freedom of expression than boys in clothes choices. It is no longer generally acceptable for boys in Western culture to wear dresses, though sporadic news articles remind us that adolescent boys in various schools continue to push against dress codes by occasionally doing so. Girls can dress in styles ranging from what society identifies as very feminine to styles virtually indistinguishable from what boys are wearing. This freedom offers them experiences preparatory to adulthood and the fashion alternatives open to women. In contemporary Western societies like the United States, it is not until adulthood that males attain enough independence to mount more serious challenges to gender stereotypes in clothes wear. But on that matter, we shall wait a moment longer. We need to summarize the current situation with regard to children and clothing.

These days the role of clothing plays an important part in early sex-role socialization. Children associate dresses with stereotypically feminine activities and pants with traditionally masculine activities.[1011] Color, too, remains important to children. As one team of researchers discovered, "Very young children may identify clothing color as one of several defining attributes of sex even before they are knowledgeable about the biological differences between the sexes."[1012] Both boys and girls meet violations of social gender norms with censure.[1013]

Adult Clothing

As with children, the connection of gender to dress has an interesting history for adults. In some respects, gendered distinctions in appearance have always existed, though in terms of clothing these differences in the West, prior to the 14th century, were not pronounced; that came with the rise of fashion and, especially, its developments. Gender distinctions in dress are a function of more than merely sexual anatomy—they reflect gendered social status, economic power, and so forth, too. For example, Carolyn Balkwell examined 161 preindustrial cultures to see what, if any, effect economic development had on gender distinctions in dress. She found that societies with less advanced economic activities ('folk' societies) were associated either with more ornate male dress or no appreciable difference in garb between genders. Agrarian societies, on the other hand, were more associated with ornate females.[1014] Such modifiers on dress costume constitute a reminder of how robust and wide is the system with clothing at its center, and how integrally tied gender is to other matters.

The clothing used to identify a specific gender proves not to be as constant as we might imagine. Today we take for granted that males wear *bifurcated* (i.e., divided into pant legs) garments, like pants, but do not wear unbifurcated clothes, like skirts or dresses.[1015] Yet, prior to the Renaissance (14th-16th centuries), both men and women wore basic covering garments that were unbifurcated. These were typically simple in shape and similar in appearance. For centuries the *tunic* was a basic garment for many Western peoples. It might be longer or shorter, sleeved or unsleeved, worn as an outer garment or beneath other clothing, but always it was unbifurcated. It was generally gathered at the waist, like a skirt or many dresses are.[1016] The tunic generally served as a single, relatively unisex garment.

It was only with advances in the art of tailoring, beginning in the 14th century, that bifurcated garments began to be seen as masculine garb. However, as French fashion historian and theorist Gilles Lipovetsky points out, the first bloom of fashion in the mid-14th century, replete with gendered distinction in dress, did not produce a fixed and static divide. Apparel and attendant accessories could be—and were—swapped between the genders.[1017] Fashion was predominantly men's fashion—not surprising in a cultural context where gendered distinctions reflected a patriarchal gender order and masculine needs were served first.

If fashion was men's fashion, men's fashion was bifurcated clothing, especially from the waist down. As culture scholar Steven Connor notes, this meant the acknowledgement of the male leg—and in certain cases its glorification as well.[1018] In the 15th century, even as men's tunics shortened and fit more closely, outer leg-wear began to appear, particularly among the upper class. New possibilities were realized late the next century when, in 1589, Reverend William Lee of Nottinghamshire, England invented a machine that would make the production of hose, including silk hose, feasible on a new scale; Lee's production was aimed at the gentlemen of his era.

We should not think that women's fashion was of no consequence, but we should recognize it was relegated to second place for a considerable stretch of history. Men in previous centuries—especially men of the upper classes—typically showed more interest in fashion styles than would be true of men in the 20th century. Lois Banner calls medieval European history a time when both young male bodies and young female bodies were eroticised, but it remained masculine clothing that set the standard for what reflected gender and sexuality—including erotic sexuality. Not until the 16th and 17th centuries did feminine fashion gain prominence.[1019]

Bifurcated clothing remained the basic gender divide in clothing, though the nature of the garb was changing. In the 16th century, men were wearing breeches; by the 19th century trousers were common. This development offered practical advantages to many tasks men pursued—and the association as masculine helped keep women excluded from both the dress and the tasks accompanying it. However, as men's clothing eventually covered the legs with pants, reducing their hosiery to ankle stockings, women's clothing increasingly showed glimpses of her legs and made more desirable hosiery to cover them. The climax of that development was reached in the 20th century with the introduction of nylon stockings.

From the advent of fashion through the next several centuries Western culture's use of dress to convey social information focused on two matters: gender and social class.[1020] The 19th century was pivotal in that industrialization and other factors converged to effect a democratization of dress. Social class distinctions still existed but apparel no longer served as forcefully to show them. That left gender as the sole primary focus—and the century witnessed dramatic attention to gender differentiation through dress.

This development had dramatic repercussions for masculine and feminine fashion. Both genders were confronted with increasing pressure to conform to clothing deemed appropriate for the gender. But for men this meant fewer options, while for women their apparel options expanded. Masculine fashion became—in a word—narrow. The business suit captures the essence of the trend for men: relatively simple, uniform, and dark. In fact, bright and varied colors became almost exclusively the provenance of women. By the mid-19th century a man in brightly colored clothes was taken to show the poor taste of the lower classes, or the ignorance of a foreigner.[1021]

For much of the last half millennium, it has been men who have enjoyed the greater freedom in clothing choices. During the long transition from unbifurcated common wear for men to the predominance of bifurcated garments, the former remained a part of male clothing in items like long gowns and full-skirted coats. Only in the 20th century did such unbifurcated garments finally become excluded from mainstream masculine clothing.[1022] In fact, it took until the latter half of the 20th century that it could truly be argued that women had gained the greater freedom and range in clothing choices. Corresponding to that development was a disproportionate interest in fashion; in the 20th century women far exceeded men in attention to fashion. By century's end an interest in fashion was firmly established as feminine. Real men didn't care.

Feminine Fashion as the Adoption & Adaptation of Masculine Clothing

Nevertheless, in broad perspective across the half millennium of fashion change, masculine fashion generally proved more influential on feminine fashion than the other way around.[1023] Or, as contemporary fashion designer Philippe Ducac bluntly says, "Women have always borrowed from men, whether it be for fashion or women writers at the turn of the 20th century who dressed as men in order to get recognized for their work."[1024] Beginning at the dawn of Western fashion, clothing later associated predominantly with women started as menswear or unisex. So pronounced has been the influence of men's fashion on women's fashion that even the skirt—a supposedly quintessential feminine item—can be argued to have been caught up by it. Thus John Connor contends that bifurcation of the body at the waist, so that there are different garments above and below, long served as a gender divide, with men wearing bifurcated apparel and women wearing dresses—a garment that drapes from the shoulders. Accordingly, the skirt, which bifurcates the body at the waist, can be said to facilitate the masculinization of female dress.[1025]

Consider this brief, eclectic list, all dozen items originally made principally for men, first defined by masculine fashion, but later so appropriated by women as to either make them gender neutral or feminine:

- ❑ *Blouse*—this derivation from the masculine shirt, named by the French in the early 19th century, first referred to a short blue, loose garment made of silk or cotton and worn by workmen; similar terms for similar masculine garments are found in other languages.[1026]

- ❑ *Buttons*—an item with a long history, their prominence in clothing was predominantly among men's styles; the persistent gender distinction in which side buttons appear on does not seem to have been well established before the 19th century, and buttons at the back of a garment is a distinctively feminine feature.[1027]

- ❑ *Corset*—perhaps the item most often seen as thoroughly feminine, its European origin c. 1500 as an iron corset cover was for men, and padded with silk underneath.[1028]

- ❑ *Hosiery*—men's legs got the early attention and even silk hosiery was made first for men.

- ❑ *Lace*—the use of lace as garment fringes has come to be associated with feminine fashion but beginning in medieval Europe it was first and foremost an aspect of masculine fashion.[1029]

- ❑ *Pajamas*—brought to the West from India in the 19th century, these were made for men and replaced the earlier nightshirt—another article of clothing made in masculine fashion.

- ❑ *Pants*—pride of place in the gender divide is commonly awarded to pants, here used generically for the long history of bifurcated garments reserved for men.

- ❑ *Petticoats*—originally made for men, approximating to the waistcoat.[1030]

- ❑ *Pockets*—pockets sewn into garments had replaced pouches for fashionable men by the end of the 17th century; by the 19th century they constituted a significant gender distinction in dress in English society.[1031]

- ❑ *T-shirt*—now a ubiquitous unisex garment, the T-shirt originated in the 20th century as an item for men, adopted from European soldiers who used cotton undershirts in their uniform attire.

- ❑ *Underwear*—the construction of modern bifurcated undergarments focused first on men; 'panties' are derivative from underpants for men.

- ❑ *Zippers*—though invented in the 19th century, the use of zippers in clothing really began with their adoption by the U.S. army in World War I. The next big boost came in the 1920s-1930s when zippers were added to men's trousers.

In addition to items borrowed from men that in time became associated also with women, sometimes as 'feminine' rather than unisex, are items that for most of history were regarded as belonging to both genders. For example, the wig dates back thousands of years and over that long span has been popular with both men and women. While men today may still wear hairpieces, the wig itself, especially with long hair, is regarded as feminine. Similarly, the chemise— a simple shift worn next to the skin—was a unisex garment, and precursor to men's shirts. In fact, by the end of the last century the net effect of fashion trends was to reduce the inventory of masculine apparel while expanding that of feminine apparel, with the latter succeeding in part by appropriation of items previously restricted to men, or making unisex styles distinctively feminine.

Dress Reform for Women

Clearly, fashion has been and remains a prominent vehicle for envisioning and enforcing a gender divide. Women, especially, felt the brunt of its effects in previous generations.[1032] But over a period of time efforts on women's behalf by both men and women aimed at and ultimately accomplished significant dress reform. The demands and opportunities afforded by the modern industrial world facilitated efforts in redefining what is acceptable for women to wear. Inevitably, over the long and arduous period of transition, women crossdressed. Some did so as part of a complete adoption of masculine identity and role, but many more did so in a way that made it perfectly plain they remained women— only their dress had changed.[1033] In time they won an even greater range in what is accepted as gender appropriate clothing than men enjoy.

Resistance to this development came from many quarters.[1034] Religious leaders decried the erosion of morality represented by women sacrificing their femininity by donning pants. Politicians passed laws making women dressed in clothes associated with men a criminal offense, unless they had obtained express permission. Women themselves were divided on the propriety of females in masculine attire. But even as the debates wore on, and eventually wore out, fashion was adapting to the changing reality. Women continued to dress in garb associated with men, but the manner of the clothes was changing so that a dis-tinction could be made that preserved the gender divide. Slacks were feminized, as were shirts. Artificial but telling distinctions were made in details like the side of a shirt on which the buttons appeared. Women had successfully appropriated masculine clothing and feminized it into widespread acceptability among both men and women.

Men in Skirts

As the 20th century waned and the 21st century dawned there were signs of something similar happening for men. Already in the early 1950s, writes home economics professor and clothing scholar Mary Lou Rosencranz, beachwear for men with a wraparound, sarong-type cover-up was being offered to men. By the mid-1960s, European fashion, influenced by the popularity of the Beatles and

Rolling Stones, showed men adopting clothing and hairstyles previously associated with femininity. In 1966, a Munich men's shop displayed men in miniskirts.[1035] For the remainder of the century there would be periodic efforts in fashion to put men in styles regarded widely as feminine.

Entering the new millennium, Western fashion designers are still putting men in skirts (once a term reserved for menswear),[1036] and other clothing with elements that contemporary people typically associate with women, like garters and touches of lingerie.[1037] These bold fashion designers include both women, like Vivienne Westwood and Anna Sui, as well as noted men such as Jean Paul Gaultier, Dries van Noten, and Carlo Pignatelli. At the 2004 Paris show for men's fashion, Dior designer Hedi Slimane presented ordinary young men, rather than professional models, to wear his designs, which included skirts. The choice of wear and model was a calculated one and a pointed statement. Slimane, declaring that androgyny belonged to the late 60s, remarked that, "I wanted the clothes to feel very much like the time we're living in."[1038]

That the times are opening up to men once more wearing unbifurcated garments may be indicated by the public support of highly visible celebrities. Not surprisingly, it is among male rock stars that we find the most public resistance to gender stereotyping in clothes. Nor can these artists' choices be dismissed as mere ploys to gain publicity as they publicly display an attitude of rebellion toward the culture. For that to be true the musicians would have to embrace crossdressing as travesty.

Yet Boy George, who may have attained the most notoriety for his clothing, vigorously defends his apparel as masculine and not the garb of a transvestite. He is far from alone in creative fashion statements intended to stretch the perception of what is masculine dress. David Bowie has bent gender in his garb, most notably in a dress for the cover of his album *The Man Who Sold the World* (1971), which he defended as 'a man's dress.' Other presentations are more ambiguous. A generation after Bowie, Kevin Rowland's cover for his album *My Beauty* much more provocatively depicted a crossdressed man. More notably, Curt Cobain put on a baby doll outfit that was his wife's inspiration. That he was wearing feminine clothing—and didn't care—seemed to be the point. Any number of other examples of musical artists could be put forward with various debates about what their dress intends to convey, if anything.[1039]

But where much of the public expects musicians to be outlandish, they don't expect sports figures to be so. Probably the best known gender-bender in dress has been the soccer player David Beckham (inspiration for the movie, *Bend It Like Beckham*), who in 1998 sported a Jean Paul Gaulthier sarong—and liked it so well he bought several in different colors.[1040] But he isn't the only athlete finding comfort in such wear. The male Balinese Olympic contingent wore sarongs for their uniform at the opening ceremonies of the 1996 games in Atlanta.[1041] Sometimes transgendered athletes use dress as a way to challenge stereotypes about themselves. A team comprised principally of gays, transvestites, and transsexuals—'the Iron Ladies'—won the national volleyball championship in Thailand in 1996.[1042]

Male movie icons also have shown that masculinity is not compromised by putting on an unbifurcated garment, and is not wear only for period pieces. Mel Gibson donned a kilt in *Braveheart*, Samuel L. Jackson did so for his role in *The 51st State*, and the more youthful Ewan McGregor has worn one in public. Brad Pitt was garbed in skirted Greek warrior dress for the epic *Troy*. Pitt was quoted as remarking about the 'man skirts' he wore that "I'm in, I'm all for it." He also played prognosticator: "I predict it's our future."[1043]

If so, the future is the past revisited. Andrew Bolton, associate curator of the Costume Institute at the Metropolitan Museum of Art, has chronicled both the history and the modern phenomena of men-wearing-skirts in his *Bravehearts: Men in Skirts*. His book emphasizes that the men in skirts described are fully secure in their masculine identities.[1044] Indeed, ordinary men in many walks of life have embraced a heritage of skirts as suitable male attire, and some have even championed a new term for such garb, 'MUGS'—male unbifurcated garments— to emphasize that it is not feminine wear. Outside the world of high fashion this new term was being accompanied with advice concerning how to introduce such wear to others.[1045] Men, especially young men, were venturing more often into territory previously associated with young women: fashions that challenge gender stereotypes.

This new movement is not exactly parallel to the women's movement and its association with dress reform. But it is not entirely different either and feminists offended by the suggestion there are similarities are overreacting. Women once used changes in dress behavior to challenge inadequate social conventions; some men are doing so now. Women capitalized on the status men enjoyed by copying their dress and thus borrowing some of the privilege and power associated with the wearers of masculine apparel. Some men are reacting to the success and perceived power of women by utilizing a similar strategy. Some women in appropriating elements of dress considered masculine lived with the charge of crossdressing; others denied it, claiming their dress was appropriate to their gender despite the wider public perception. Today some men—regardless of their motivation for dressing as they do—are living with the charge of crossdressing, while others are vigorously denying it and contending their apparel is appropriately masculine regardless of what many might believe.

If men are borrowing elements of dress from women, it is only fair play, since as we have seen the reverse has long been true. The real difficulty lies in the persistence of a vertical gender order seeking to keep men above women. In such a framework borrowing from women constitutes a tacit acknowledgement of their power and weakens masculine privilege. It matters not that men might do so for comfort, because they like the look or feel of a garment style, find a certain style utilitarian, or simply think men should be accorded the same right women enjoy to wear whatever they want. In order to preserve the gender hierarchy the gender divide must be maintained and that means perpetuating the idea that men in clothing culturally designated as feminine are crossdressing and that such crossdressing reflects mental illness, specifically a profound disturbance of gender identity or sexual perversity—or both!

In such a cultural climate it may be especially surprising to some of us to discover the degree of acceptance such fashion trends are finding. A survey conducted by Mark Clements Research in 2000 in Los Angeles, New York, and Chicago of women ages 21-39 revealed that slightly more than 1-in-5 (20.8%) said they would be willing to date a man dressed in a skirt. Similar levels were found for the percentage of those surveyed who stated they viewed men wearing skirts as "very" or "somewhat" acceptable (24%). Perhaps surprisingly, the survey found a similar degree of support for accepting even a brother or father who engaged in such dress (20.3%). A like percentage even expressed a willingness to share their own skirts with a man (22.3%).[1046]

The question remains as to why this is happening now, and why it is happening at all. Eminent Italian sociologist Francesco Alberoni offers some hypotheses. First, the economic slump of the early 1990s provided designers incentive to be creative in the hope of sparking interest in fashion—adding feminine elements to menswear certainly accomplished that. But since there are other ways to respond to such slumps, this answer is probably not sufficient explanation. A second hypothesis, then, is that the introduction of such elements reflects either a narrowing of the gap between models of masculinity and femininity, or even a cultural dominance by women. Alberoni observes that the success of women—accompanied by their appropriate of masculine style elements—has now won the admiration and attraction of men, who are taking on feminine traits. Perhaps designers are perceiving this "urge for feminization" and responding. At the same time other forces are also at work, leading to two additional hypotheses. Ours is an increasingly multicultural world and many parts of the world are less gender divided than Western European and American societies. As Westerners tune in to other cultures they may relax more into wearing styles already acceptable elsewhere. Finally, as rigid gender lines break down, so also do rigid sexual boundaries. Radical feminists, homosexuals and bisexuals all have helped weaken "the force of heterosexual eroticism." Perhaps male clothing with feminine elements is a response to a wider anti-hetero trend—a provocation. Alberoni believes all four of these hypotheses compatible with one another. Hearkening back to Freud's notion that artistic products express different impulses it is entirely plausible to see in recent men's fashion impulses reflecting the age—and contributing to its change.[1047]

Conclusion

Fortunately, clothing's robust nature preserves hope. The sheer diversity of clothing available, the restless pressure of fashion, and the multiple demands we place on dress all predict that change will occur. The great attention paid these days to transgender also offers hope for a welcome antidote to the poison of too rigid and confining a conception of gender. The promise of crossdressing is that what it offers as alternative ways to see gender, and the relation of dress to gender, may yet free us from the prisons we seem so often bent on building about ourselves.

Chapter 15

Gender & Religion

Introduction: A principal cultural force is religion. By nature conservative, in the sense of *conserving cultural values*, particularly with respect to ethics and morality, religion also can be a dramatically *reconstructive social force*. Typically, religions—especially those dominant in a society—preserve both the society and themselves by supporting the reigning power. In terms of gender, this means religions generally justify, support, and even promote the social status quo. In the West, major religions mostly bolster patriarchy.

Christianity is, arguably, the most powerful religion in the world. It is the dominant religion of the highest social status societies and many of its strongest nations. It serves as the bastion of Western culture's principal ideas and values. With respect to gender, *Christianity is patriarchal*. While not all individual Christians, nor every Christian group, support patriarchy, by and large most do. Not only is cultural patriarchy supported, it is practiced in the religion. Support is claimed for this in biblical tradition. Despite this—or rather, because of it—women have had to resort to creative measures whenever they have sought to equalize the religion's power dynamics. This has ranged from the *crossdressing saints* of past centuries to the *feminists* of our own time.

Many of us look especially to our religious tradition's depiction of deity to frame a sense of how we ought to relate to the divine. The matter of *divine gender*, when examined both across religions and to a surprising extent within them, displays many of the same issues we have been discussing throughout our dialog. Divine gender forces us to reckon with both conforming and nonconforming genders.

The relation between ourselves and the divine proves as complex as that we have with one another. Gender plays a key role. *Sacred gender crossings*—the movement of an individual from one gender to another—occur in a variety of ways. But these often highlight the role of individuals who do not fit within the conforming genders. Such folk seem to occupy a special place in religion.

Finally, one of the saddest continuing realities in most societies, including our own, is how religion is used as a vehicle of *oppression*. In many religions there is a distance between higher ideals of gender acceptance and equality, and the actual practice of gender discrimination and inequality. The potential always resides in religion—and religious people—to challenge this oppression.

Religion as Cultural Conserver

Religion is by nature *a conservative social institution*, in that it conserves values and passes them along as enduring and right. Religion tends to provide a society both stability and a moral compass. On occasion religion also serves a prophetic role calling a society to reform itself in line with values identified as representing the truest and best of its beliefs and practices. Whether as protector of social ideals or reformer of them, religion has a tremendously significant role with regard to gender. Most often it preserves, supports, and passes on cultural notions of gender. Sometimes it responds to culture by challenging those notions and demanding reform.

Most of us are unaccustomed to thinking of gender and religion side-by-side. Yet historian Merry Wiesner-Hanks is correct in observing of religions that, "all of them are gendered, that is, they have created and maintained differences between what it means to be male and female." She offers brief illustrations of such matters in both major world religions and those less well-known. For example, with reference to Confucianism and Taoism, she observes that the Chinese language character for 'wife' shows a woman with a broom—a sign of her desired place as a 'Treasure of the House,' in contradistinction to a man's ideal pursuit as a sage. [1048]

In its conserving role, *religions tend to support the predominant form of other social institutions*. Thus, if a society is polygamous, the dominant religion will tend to justify that practice. If families are structured along extended kinship lines, the dominant religion will support that structure. If gender relations are hierarchical, the dominant religion will find reasons why. In short, dominant religions in a society preserve their own status and influence by supporting the reigning powers. Religions both shape and are shaped by other social iinstitutions.

In Western culture, under the sway of Christianity, Judaism, and Islam, there has been a *general sanction of the gender hierarchy* that prizes masculinity and gives men status, power, and privilege. Western religions have been *patriarchal* in their dominant manifestations. Girls and women, occupying lower status, have been largely banned from occupying pivotal posts and significant leadership roles. However, even cross-cultural research shows a tendency to exclude women or severely constrain their religious roles.[1049]

Christianity & Patriarchy

It seems one of the more interesting ironies of history that the world's most powerful religion depends on women who support patriarchy. Without women actively practicing Christianity, the pews in Christian churches on Sundays would mostly be empty.[1050] Yet despite being the heart, soul, and backbone of the faith, women remain mired in subordinate positions at home and in the institutions of the Church throughout most of Christianity. This situation of inequality in almost every respect continues to support the cultural subordination of women in other social spheres, including education, employment, and politics.

Religion & Christian Patriarchy

Within Christianity, masculine dominion has been substantiated by appeal to the Bible, particularly the New Testament writings attributed to the apostle Paul. In writing to the Church at Corinth, he teaches, "the head of a woman is her husband" (1 Corinthians 11:3), and urges, "As in all the churches of the saints, the women should keep silence in the churches. For they are not permitted to speak, but should be subordinate, as even the law says" (1 Corinthians 14:33b-34). In the so-called Pastoral Epistles, the same ideas are present, that a woman is not permitted to teach or hold authority over men, that she should dress modestly, and attend to duties such as childbearing—all justified on the basis that Adam was created before Eve, and that she was the one deceived and became a transgressor (1 Timothy 2:11-15). But Paul is not alone in speaking thus. In letters attributed to the apostle Peter, Christians are told that women are "the weaker sex" (1 Peter 3:7), who should be obedient wives to their husbands (1 Peter 3:1-6).

The masculine privilege of this gender hierarchy theologically depends on an argument from a particular view of creation. One biblical depiction, the classic account found in Genesis 1, has creation culminating in God's resolve to make 'man' (a generic term) in the divine image, and so creates *both* male *and* female in one act.[1051] This account is followed immediately by a second one, which many Christians read as an elaboration of the first. In it 'man' (*'adam*) is made from the ground (*'adamah*), animated by the breath of life, and set to work in the Garden of Eden. This *'adam* is a male being. From his side is fashioned another being, with the express intent that this new being serve as "a helper fit for him" (Genesis 2:18). This second being is female. The man proclaims upon her creation, "This at last is bone of my bone, and flesh of my flesh. She shall be called 'Woman,' because she was taken out of 'Man'" (Genesis 2:23). The woman's subordination is marked by several potent things: her secondary arrival, her created purpose to serve man, her derivation from man, her being named by man (a signal act of dominion—see Genesis 1:28, 2:19-20), and her name itself. Which creation account is given preeminence clearly matters.

When the disruption of communion with God occurs, resulting in the loss of the Edenic paradise, the contact between man and the deceitful serpent is mediated by the woman (Genesis 3:6). *Woman is the instrument of man's fall from grace.* Key to her punishment is her consignment to sexually desire man, bear his children, and be subject to his rule (Genesis 3:16).

Both by the order of creation and as punishment for her sin, woman is subordinated to man. The Christian New Testament reinforces this 'gender doctrine.' Paul makes explicit appeal to it when writing to the Corinthian Christians (1 Corinthians 11:2-16). He wants them to remember the importance of a clear gender division along hierarchical lines. This division is to be *visible*, as in the woman wearing a veil over her head and her hair worn long. Woman, the apostle declares, is the glory of *man*—a declaration followed by a reminder she was made from man (11:7-8). Although he also proclaims that neither gender is independent from the other, he insists on visible signs of difference in appearance and behavior. Later in the same letter, he specifies this in terms of a woman's subordinate role in church matters (1 Corinthians 14:33b-36).

Early Responses to Christian Patriarchy

This is not to say there are no dissenting strands in the early Christian tradition. Paul himself famously wrote, "There is neither Jew nor Greek, there is neither slave nor free, there is neither male nor female; for you are all one in Christ Jesus" (Galatians 3:28).[1052] However, this seems to have been meant with respect to eligibility for salvation rather than social conduct; he continues to urge that "Everyone should remain in the state in which he was called" (1 Corinthians 7:20)—whether Jew, Greek, slave, free, or gender subordinated.

An early document that did not make the canon—the official standard for belief and practice—is *The Gospel of Thomas*, a collection of sayings of Jesus held in high regard by scholars and possibly containing authentic sayings of Jesus not found in the New Testament. The collection ends with Jesus saying, in reference to Mary: "See, I shall lead her, so that I will make her male, that she too may become a living spirit, resembling you males. For every woman who makes herself male will enter the Kingdom of Heaven."[1053] Various movements in the Church's first few centuries took such ideas in one or another way, including trying to obliterate social distinctions between the sexes (consider the example of the Eustathians), or singling out women who succeeded in performing masculine piety as well as or better than the holiest of men (consider the many crossdressing female saints).[1054]

Women themselves could reason in this manner, as in the following saying preserved from the lips of a woman who was a notable desert recluse, Amma Sara: "I may be a woman in body, but not in spirit."[1055] Ironically enough, the women who best exemplify the spirit of Galations 3:28 are those who by their 'making themselves male' demonstrated the senselessness of gender-based distinctions that preserved a male-dominated gender hierarchy. In short, crossdressing female saints illustrate Paul's Gospel of liberation.

Crossdressing Saints

As a rule, Christian authorities have not looked with favor on women who crossdress because in crossing gender lines they threaten the order that religion preserves. Indeed, both the Bible and early Christian teaching endorse gender differentiated dress, even though dress itself is in general downplayed in importance (see, for example, Jesus' teaching in Matthew 25:36-44). The late Pastoral Epistle of 1 Timothy expounds, "I also want women to dress modestly, with decency and propriety, not with braided hair or gold or pearls or expensive clothes, but with good deeds, appropriate for women who profess to worship

God" (2:9-10), while 1 Peter 3:3 declares, "Your beauty should not come from outward adornment, such as braided hair and the wearing of gold jewelry and fine clothes." Both of these texts are directed at women.

So it may come as a surprise to learn that a number of crossdressing women came to be viewed as especially pious, and many of them gained sainthood. Curiously enough, those women who proved exceptionally adept at passing as men escaped lasting censure despite most seriously violating jealously guarded male prerogatives, such as various venues of Christian ministry and leadership, and habitation among monks. These women chose to live as men because only in so doing could they realize a spiritual vocation they recognized as coming from God. While pursuing their vocation could and did mean different things for various ones of them, often enough it entailed entering a world set apart for men—the religious monastery. As Lynne Dahmen observes, their putting on men's clothing offered them a chance to join in "a realm inherently masculine," a cloistered religious life.[1056] Their drive and complete devotion to the service of their Lord proved far weightier than their crossdressing. Such piety amazed other Christians, eventually winning for these women dispensations of acceptance and respect unexpected in the face of their gender violations. In fact, the tolerance of the Church is notable in the number of crossdressing women who came to be recognized as saints. Valerie Hotchkiss has identified 34 so-called *crossdressing female saints*.[1057]

Often the crossdressing had something to do with *marriage*—a social institution whose obligations on women have long been used to keep them from pursuing other vocations, even religious ones. Some of the women were virgin singles, some married or widowed. Of those who were virgins (e.g., Anastasia the Patrician, Apollonaria, Eugenia, and Euphrosyne), crossdressing was pursued to protect that virginity when marriage looked imminent. Of those who were married, crossdressing was pursued either to escape marriage (e.g., Matrona), or to be close to one's husband while remaining chaste (e.g., Athanasia). A married woman might take up crossdressing as part of penance for adultery (e.g., Theodora). Even a widow might crossdress (e.g., Anna). Of course, not only 'respectable' women might crossdress; the formerly dissolute might do so as well, as they escaped their former life (e.g., Pelagia). Interestingly, these saints' crossdressing proved instrumental in establishing their innocence when accused of impregnating others (e.g., Apollonaria, Eugenia, Mary, and Theodora).

There were other practical purposes served by crossdressing. In some cases it was *modesty* that prompted a naked saint to borrow a man's garment to cover herself (e.g., Mary of Egypt and Theoktiste). Sometimes crossdressing was for *staying safe* from predatory men through disguise, especially when traveling (e.g., Thecla and Hildegund). Only one of the women was openly, ostentatiously crossdressed: Joan of Arc. That behavior was a central concern at her trial. But her reason crossdressing—the beckoning of God—was not unprecedented; Hilaria and Matrona, too, had received instruction that led to their behavior.

Whatever else they communicate, the lives of these crossdressing saints certainly proclaim that anatomical sex is not the basis for Christian piety, nor its boundary. Women who *trans*gress gender order can *trans*cend gender discrimination through *trans*vestism. In putting on male clothes they embraced a perceived masculinity that was all their society permitted as the vehicle for certain forms of spiritual expression. In performing masculine piety these women—because they were women—exposed the falsity of notions of spiritual ascendancy based on sex or gender. Simultaneously they exposed the ludicrousness of the proposition that either sex or gender pose legitimate divisions for establishing a hierarchy of spiritual worth or work in the worshipful service of God.

Modern Responses to Christian Patriarchy

Just as some women in the past addressed in their own way the gender inequities of Christianity, so are some contemporary women. Not all of them would call themselves feminists, but *feminists* have led the way in calling the religion to accountability. Feminist scholar Mary-Paula Walsh, in compiling an annotated bibliography on feminism and the Christian tradition, writes that even a casual perusal of the literature can generate a sizable list of the issues feminists have with Christianity: "They are the equality of women, the destruction of sexism, the eradication of gender bias in research and writing, the full acceptance of women in ordained ministry, the need for inclusive rather than exclusive language, mutuality rather than hierarchy, etc., etc., etc."[1058]

Although all of the issues just mentioned matter—and others besides—we have time in this discussion to only examine a few. We may give pride of place to the *theological challenge to the logic used to support patriarchy*. Roman Catholic writer Mary Kenny wryly observes how, "Women in the feminist movements have bitterly resented what they have termed the 'framing' of Eve, right from the start." She points to the desire of some Christian women to appeal to the text's detail that Eve was made from Adam's *side* (his rib), thus meant to stand at his side as *equal*. Beyond that, as she notes, Jesus himself in the story of Mary and Martha (Luke 10:38-42) commends Mary for choosing theological discussion over housework. Moreover, the alleged stain of Eve did not prevent the Christian church from early on using women in important positions of leadership (Acts 12:12; Romans 16:7).[1059]

The matter of leadership—specifically, *the ordination of women*—has also been a contentious issue. Supporters of patriarchy like to point out that none of Jesus' twelve disciples was a woman, and that the Pastoral Epistles make being a man a prerequisite for being a bishop (1 Timothy 3:1-7) or elder (Titus 1:5-9). On the other hand, as critics observe, the disciples weren't formally ministers with congregations, Jesus' inner circle did include women (who were the first witnesses to his resurrection), there were women who held church offices, and there isn't anything in the Bible that directly forbids ordination of women. Natalie Watson comments that women's struggle for equal rights within the Church has "found its focal point" in debates about the ordination of women. In this matter, Protestant Churches have proved more receptive than Roman Catholicism, which steadfastly refuses to yield on the issue.[1060]

One matter named earlier, *inclusive rather than exclusive language*, extends from translations of scripture to liturgical formulae. In this respect, there has been some responsiveness among some Christian scholars and groups. An instance of this sort of change can be glimpsed in the matter of the creation story we discussed earlier. Instead of retaining the word 'man' the *New Revised Standard Version* (NRSV) uses 'humankind'—a concession not to political correctness, but to scholarly accuracy. When we turn in a moment to depictions of deity in different religions, including Christianity, we will see further the rational grounds for shifting to more inclusive language.

We should ask what has been the result of the feminist challenge. On the one hand, we would be right to pessimistically point out that little has changed in much of the religion, either in its thinking or practice. Christianity remains deeply and thoroughly saturated in patriarchy. On the other hand, we would be wrong to conclude that feminism has made no difference at all. Angela Pears is surely right in commenting that sustained feminist enquiry has "often proved to be deeply challenging and sometimes transformative of Christianity." One tangible result has been the emergence of an identifiable *Feminist Theology*. Pears remarks:

> Some of the most significant aspects of this theological movement and encounter include, the politicizing of issues of gender and Christianity; the explosion of omen's scholarship that refuses to recognize and comply with traditional theological and religious boundaries; the painful passage away from religious and theological institutions; the theological articulation of boundary Christian living; the recovering, naming and reconstruction of women's historical and religious selves; and also, the apparent exclusion and marginalization of women by the very ideas and structures of feminisms that have spoken in such promising terms of justice.[1061]

We would do well to remember that feminism remains a young movement historically. That makes what it has accomplished all the more remarkable. At the same time, there is a creative ferment that foments controversy. To date, feminist challenges to Christianity appear to have done better at provoking the religion rather than substantially reforming it.

Divine Gender

Most of us who have an allegiance to a particular religious tradition at some point desire to focus more on the divine authority and less on human leadership. For most of us, religion or spirituality provides ways for us to explore and connect to transcendent realities. Because most of us believe there are realities both greater than our own limited existence and to some extent removed from us, many of us turn to religion for a bridge to such realities. But bridges reach both ways. Even as we may seek what lies on the other side, whatever is there may be reaching out toward us. Thus religion is a two-way avenue with our portion involving both giving and receiving sacred actions.

On our side, the task is complicated by certain factors such as our relative inability to see or understand realms beyond our own, and by our corresponding need to draw upon things in our realm to comprehend and represent divine realities. One of the basic problems concerns sex and gender. Do deities have bodies? Are they sexed and gendered? What roles do sex and gender play in transactions between mortals and immortals?[1062]

Complicating the situation is cultural variety in conceptions of sex and gender—particularly the latter. While our modern Western culture is only just beginning to reconsider the idea that there are more than two sexes and genders, such openness to a wider range of alternatives for human beings can be found both throughout history (including that of the West), and around the world.

Divine manifestations of gender may be divided generally into three kinds:

- ❑ Deities appearing as *ambiguous* in gender (i.e., neither clearly male nor female, usually because they are absent gender);
- ❑ Deities appearing as *androgynous* (i.e., with both male and female characteristics), such as hermaphroditic deities; and,
- ❑ Deities appearing as an *altered* gender, one different from the one they are traditionally assigned (e.g., a female deity appearing in male guise), and thus engaged from the human standpoint as emasculated, masculinized, or in a gender masquerade.

These are not mutually exclusive. A deity may appear in more than one category, as Artemis does by exhibiting both androgyny and gender altering. Moreover, the kinds themselves may mix as happens when Hermaphroditus, originally male, is altered in gender to become androgynous. Also, strictly speaking, one could argue that only the last kind (gender altering) represents 'gender *crossing.*' And to these we might add curiosities like the crossdressed Heracles, a demigod figure. But these three general types are relevant to our discussion because all three confound in some way the dichotomous scheme most of us find so comforting and in so doing raise gender questions and issues pertinent to a broad examination of religious crossdressing. The following table provides exemplars for each type:

Table 15.1 Examples of Gendered Deities

Gender Ambiguous	Gender Androgynous	Gender Altering
'Unities': *Allah* (Islam) or '*God*' (Christianity, Judaism); *Cghene* (Nigeria/Isoko)	'Assigned gender deities': *Aphrodite, Artemis, Athena, Dionysus* (Classical Greek); *Inanna* (Sumerian); *Jesus* (Christianity); *Shiva* (Hinduism)	'Emasculated gods': *Mahadeva* (Hinduism); *Odin* (Norse); *Quetzalcoatl* (Aztec) *Ra* (Egyptian); *Uranus* (Classical Greek)
'One-as-Many':	'Either gender deities':	'Masquerading deities':

Brahman (Hinduism)	*Agni* (Hinduism); *Asgaya Gigagei* (Cherokee Nation); *Atutahi* (Polynesia); *Atum*? (Egyptian); *Nyame* (Ghana)	*Athena* (Classical Greek); *Vishnu* (Hinduism); Zeus (Classical Greek)
'Spirits': *Kami* (Shintoism)	'Hermaphroditic deities': *Agdistis* (Classical Greek); *Ardhanari* and *Ayyappan* (Hinduism); *Hermaphroditus* (Classical Greek); *Inle* (W. Africa/Yoruba)	'Tricksters': *Hermes* (Classical Greek); *Loki* (Norse)

Some brief remarks and examples drawn from this table for further elaboration should make clearer these different types. They will also serve to demonstrate that both conforming and nonconforming genders matter in religion.

Gender Ambiguous Deities

Many deities, especially the greatest figures, are conceived as possessing no inherent gender—and perhaps no body either. Such beings can, however, assume any gender shape they wish. Even if they do not do so, their followers can use gender language to metaphorically speak about them. Such divine figures are found around the globe, both in major world religions and in smaller indigenous ones. The appropriateness of applying gender descriptors to such deities might be debated, but practical necessity dictates it happening.

Robert Hannaford explains that, "a personal God cannot be spoken of other than in images and language drawn directly from human experience. . . . Gender terms are inevitably a part of the logical grammar of a personal God." According to him, "believers cannot avoid using language which has the effect of evoking a gender identity in God." However, this use of gendered language is circumscribed by particular meanings: connotations of the gendered words used are narrowly circumscribed so that some qualities associated with a human gender are meant, but not others. Thus, for example, God as 'Father' is meant to convey a kind of relational status characterized by some qualities (e.g., love and care), and not by others (e.g., literal paternage).[1063]

The Monotheistic God of the West

In this manner the God of the Western traditions (Judaism, Christianity, Islam) can be spoken of using either masculine or feminine attributes since the deity is beyond any gender—as the Christian New Testament makes explicit when Jesus declares, "God is spirit" (John 4:24, RSV). Though masculine pronouns, attributes, and metaphors abound, feminine ones are not unknown. Thus, for example, the Hebrew Bible has the prophet Isaiah's utterance from God that pictures a woman in childbirth: "Now I will cry out like a woman in travail, I will gasp and pant" (Isaiah 42: 14, RSV). Or the same prophet's message from God wherein the deity compares self with motherhood: "As one whom his mother comforts, so I will comfort you" (Isaiah 66:13, RSV). Gender, to hearken back to Judith Butler's ideas (see chapter 2), is *performed* by God rather than possessed as an aspect of divine being.[1064]

In Islam, Allah is variously referred to as 'He' (*huwa*) or 'She' (*hiya*), though the masculine form of reference predominates as it does in Judaism and Christianity. It is especially in Sufism—Islam's mystical tradition—that the feminine expressions are given voice. In Sufi texts Allah can be depicted as feminine (cf. Jalal al-Din Rumi's *Masnavi*,I.2437), the Beloved One (the *ma'shûq*), and even the Divine Mother (cf. *Masnavi*, V.701).[1065]

The same freedom holds true in Judaism. There, one term especially preserves a sense of the feminine: the 'Divine Presence' (*Shechinah* or *Shekhinah*; the *–ah* ending is a feminine form). Daniel Matt, an expert of Judaism's mystical traditions, has expressed the judgment that "the rabbinic concept of *Shekhinah*, divine immanence, blossoms into the feminine half of God, balancing the patriarchal conception that dominates the Bible and the Talmud."[1066] This counterbalance is especially felt in the mystical tradition of Kabbalism.

In Kabbalah the Eternal and Infinite One (*Ein Sof*), though a transcendent unity, manifests as a personal God through divine emanations (*sefirot*). Some of these are masculine, some feminine. Thus, for instance, 'Malkhut' ('Mouth')—the Oral Torah, which expounds the Written Torah—is feminine.[1067] So, too, is 'Bimhah' ('Understanding'); conversely, 'Hokhmah' ('Wisdom') and 'Tif'eret' ('Beauty') are masculine. The interplay of various sefirot express divine characteristics metaphorically, as the following text makes plain:

> Hokhmah and Binah are called man and woman, father and mother. Just as human sexual union requires the medium of genitalia, so above, these two qualities unite by means of Da'at, which mediates between father and mother. . . .
>
> This manner of union may be found in Tif'eret and Malkhut, who are male and female, groom and bride, lower father and lower mother, son and daughter of the upper couple, king and queen, the Holy One, blessed be He, and *Shekhinah*. All these are metaphors.[1068]

Christianity, too, has had those who have kept alive a sense of the feminine in God. Especially notable are the writings of Mother Julian, a Christian mystic of the early 15th century. She wrote in her *Showings* (chapter 52) that God both enjoyed being Father, and also being Mother. The truth of the Trinity is 'father,' but the wisdom of the Trinity is 'mother' (chapter 54). Even Christ can be depicted as mother, in whom the believer is endlessly born (chapter 57). In fact, the second person of the Trinity is especially singled out for use of metaphors of the feminine (see chapters 58-62).[1069]

Despite the mystics, though, the mainstream in each of the major Western religious traditions almost exclusively relies on male gender terms and the masculine pronoun with reference to God.[1070] This strong reliance on associating deity with masculinity led noted religious scholar Mary Daly to proclaim, "If God is male, then the male is God."[1071] In other words, over-reliance on this gender association serves the patriarchal structure.

African Deities Without Gender

The peoples of Africa—so often looked down upon by Westerners as spiritually ignorant—also know of deities without inherent gender. For example, in southern Nigeria the Isoko religion extols Cghene as Supreme Being. Cghene is "beyond human comprehension, has never been seen, is sexless, and is only known by his actions, which have led men to speak of Cghene as 'him,' because he is thought of as the creator and therefore Father of all the Isokos."[1072] Thus, Cghene, having no gender being, performs gender through acts assigned a gender connection by the faithful. Apparently, the Isoko have little difficulty keeping gender performance separate from gender as a possession of being.

Other tribal religions also separate deity from gender. A traditional Pygmy song about a genderless Supreme Being (Khonvoum) includes this praise:

In the beginning was God,
> Today is God
> Tomorrow will be God.
Who can make an image of God?
He has no body.[1073]

A Supreme Deity is found in many African religions, and whether designated by a masculine or feminine pronoun, a characteristic of such deities is that they are beyond gender. Gender designations are a matter of human convenience.

Eastern Deities Without Gender

Deities ambiguous in gender (or absent gender) are found in the East as well. Hinduism's Brahman is described in an Upanishad as "Soul alone, in the shape of a Person."[1074] Though English translations use the pronoun 'he' for Brahman, Hindus understand the deity as genderless. We should note in passing that the antiquity and breadth of Hinduism makes it a particularly rich religion to study with respect to gender, whether divine or otherwise. We shall regularly encounter divine manifestations in Hindu stories that show the many ways the divine and gender can be associated.

The *kami* of Japan's Shintoism, described by eminent religious scholar Mircea Eliade as "omnipresent manifestations of the sacred,"[1075] may also be called ambiguous deities, though only with qualification (some, for example, are venerated ancestors). The original, heavenly kami are spirit-beings, shapeless in their own domain, but able to take shape in our world. The kami Omononushi-no-kami offers an example of how one of these spirits can utilize either masculine or feminine gender. In the *Nihongi* ('Chronicles of Japan'), the tale is told of how this kami possessed Princess Yamatototohimomoso and spoke to the emperor. Upon learning who the kami was, the emperor offered veneration. That very night, in the emperor's dreams, Omononushi-no-kami appeared to him again, this time as a noble man.[1076]

All of these genderless deities *use* gender rather than *possess* it. Though we have termed them 'ambiguous' with reference to gender, it might do as well to call them 'absent gender.' Any preference for the term 'ambiguous' reflects the practical reality that human beings insist on using gender referents when talking about divine beings they insist are without gender. The gender absence creates an ambiguity that is resolved by using various gender pronouns. In making sacred crossings to interact with their followers these deities can shun any gender presentation or use whatever gender performance suits them. Similarly, human beings attempting to describe them, or have contact with them, can avoid gender terms or employ those they wish to metaphorically express one or another divine trait or action. In many respects, gender ambiguity permits the maximum flexibility for both human and divine.

Androgynous Deities

Another group of divine figures express more than one gender simultaneously—another way of solving the problem posed by the limitations of dichotomous gender. Androgyny in divine figures was explained by Eliade as existing "to express—in biological terms—the coexistence of contraries, of cosmological principles (male and female) within the heart of the divinity."[1077] For those of us raised in Western societies where the ambiguous deity—routinely rendered by masculine pronouns reflective of our patriarchal heritage—is the norm, the idea of an androgynous deity can be challenging. Mark Matousek has aptly observed that, "an appreciation of divine androgyny is difficult to grasp in a hemisphere dominated by a church in which women cannot be ordained as priests."[1078]

Jesus

Nevertheless, even Christianity has not completely resisted the appeal of an androgynous representation of deity. Jesus, revered as the Son of God, is in orthodox Christology viewed as both wholly divine and wholly human (cf. the Definition of Chalcedon, 451 C.E.). Hildegard of Bingen explained the matter thusly: "man signifies the divinity of the Son of God and woman his humanity."[1079] Although Jesus is traditionally and almost universally assigned masculinity and referred to by masculine pronouns, in his Passion he plays the traditionally feminine role of passive victim, the recipient of God's wrath on behalf of his children. Steven Connor argues that this is "status as feminized victim—God would be fatally compromised" should Jesus be portrayed in bifurcated garments like breeches or trousers.[1080] Judaic and gender scholar Lori Hope Lefkovitz believes that Christian culture sought to balance an omnipotent God of patriarchy with a more feminine male son.[1081]

Also against the weight of most contemporary depictions of a masculine Jesus, Christian New Testament and Early Christian History scholar Stephen

Davis reminds us that, "among different early Christian communities, Christ was viewed as an androgynous or gender-ambiguous figure: he was variously identified as the incarnation of the female, divine Wisdom, pictured in eschatological visions as a woman, and depicted in early Christian art in the form of Orpheus, the androgynous figure of Greek myth."[1082]

The visionary appearance of Christ that Davis has in mind is found in the *Panarion* ('the breadbasket,' against heresies) of Epiphanius, 4th century Christian bishop at Salamis, Cyprus. In the relevant text, a Christian woman speaks as follows: "'In the form of a woman,' says she, 'arrayed in shining garments, came Christ to me and set wisdom upon me and revealed to me that this place [= Pepuza] is holy and that Jerusalem will come down hither from heaven.'"[1083] But Epiphanius—and the weight of Christian tradition—judged such utterances 'madness' and their speakers heretics.

Nevertheless, such visions of Jesus have not entirely disappeared and have on occasion even surfaced dramatically. For example, the medieval saint, Mother Julian of Norwich (1342-c. 1417), among the most famous of Christian mystics, depicted Jesus as 'Mother.' To Jesus such attributes as childbearing and nurturance are ascribed. Julian images Christ as a pregnant woman who, after sustaining Christians in his womb, brings them forth safely through the travails of childbirth. The idea of the maternal Jesus is sustained by Julian as she depicts Christ as a mother raising a child.[1084]

Meister Eckhart's disciple Henry Suso, a Dominican friar and 14th century mystic, was famed in his own time for his devotion to the suffering Jesus and his ministry to women. He extolled the figure of Christ/Sophia ('Wisdom'). Barbara Newman comments that in his *Horologium Sapientiae* (*Wisdom's Watch Upon the Hours*), Suso plays with gender—both human and divine—referring to himself at times as a feminine soul longing for Christ the Bridegroom, and at other times imagining himself as a masculine disciple in love with Christ the goddess. As this hints, Jesus is imaged both as male and female, as an excerpt from his autobiographical *Life of the Servant* also makes clear in talking about his beloved Eternal Wisdom: "The minute he thought her to be a beautiful young lady, he immediately found a proud young man before him." In his use of gender Suso offered male believers a way to spiritually embrace a heterosexual marriage to God, with the added benefit of retaining their own masculinity. Newman quotes Suso's depiction in the *Horologium* of coming from the royal wedding where "the supreme King and divine Emperor himself has given me his only beloved daughter, Eternal Wisdom, as a bride." Far from proving scandalous and resulting in Suso's rejection as a heretic, his work was warmly embraced; the *Horologium* was one of the most widely read devotional works of the Medieval period.[1085]

This inclination to re-envision the gender of Jesus persists, showing up sporadically in Christian expressions, especially artistic ones, right down to our current era.[1086] In fact, theologian Eleanor McLaughlin has gone so far as to suggest the notion of a transvestic Jesus—Jesus the crossdresser. She is not arguing for an effeminate Jesus but an appreciation of a Jesus who "is like a 'crossdresser,' one not 'caught' by the categories" but free to express feminine ways of love, sacrifice, and forgiveness. McLaughlin's goal is to weaken the association of Jesus to masculinity that has so often and forcefully been used to support inequality, even oppression, in the Church. She likens Jesus to the Trickster figure, who can open us to new understandings, *if* we are freed from "a merely male Jesus," who she regards as "a violation of the scandal and transgression which is the Gospel."[1087]

Dionysus

The Greeks excelled at the idea of androgyny among divinity. Hans Licht, in his famous *Sexual Life in Ancient Greece*, remarks that "the Greeks possessed a really astonishing notion of the double sexual (hermaphroditic) nature of the human being in the embryonic condition and of the androgynous idea of life generally."[1088] He enumerates a variety of instances in which this idea surfaces through stories and practices. For Licht the 'androgynous idea of life' is rooted in the very subconscious of the ancient Greeks.[1089]

In the Western classical tradition, perhaps the best known example of a divine gender-blender was Dionysus. The god of vibrant fertility, especially associated with wine, Dionysus came by his androgyny quite naturally. Another of his names, Dithyrambos ('double entrances'), tells the story—Dionysus was borne by both his mortal mother and then, after her death, by his immortal father Zeus, who sewed the fetus in his thigh until he was ready to be born.[1090] Greek literature scholar Albert Henrichs once noted of him: "Perceived as both man and animal, male and effeminate, young and old, he is the most versatile and elusive of all Greek Gods."[1091] Among his other associations are those of impersonation and the theater [1092]—both fitting for a crossdressing god.

Just as there are many legends about him, so there are varied depictions. Sometimes he is depicted bearded, other times with a smooth chin. Many statues represent him as "a youth of soft and feminine shape, with a dreamy expression, his long, clustering hair confined by a fillet or crown of vine or ivy, generally naked, or with a fawn or panther skin thrown lightly over him."[1093] Camille Paglia notes other artistic representations of Dionysus: "Archaic vases show him in a woman's tunic, saffron veil, and helmet. His name Bassareus comes from the Thracian *bassara*, a woman's fox-skin mantle."[1094]

Aphrodite

Another well-known deity who expressed both maleness and femaleness was Aphrodite (Venus)—whom we discussed earlier (chapter 6), but who requires a second look. Let's recall the basics: though ostensibly female, and best known as a goddess, Aphrodite was depicted in various places as an androgynous deity. The Roman writer Lucian (2nd century) speaks of "Aphrodite, who had two natures and double beauty."[1095] Macrobius (early 5th century), in his *Saturnalia*, reports concerning Venus that, "there is in Cyprus a bearded statue of the goddess with female clothing but with male attributes, so that it would seem that the deity is both male and female."[1096] The deity in this form was known as *Venus Barbata* ('Bearded Venus'). As *Venus Castina* the goddess defended her temple at Ascalon by transforming the attacking Scythian men into women. By this name she was also the patron deity of men who have feminine souls caught in male bodies.[1097] Yet Venus was not a deity merely for men to adore. Macrobius also observed that, "Philoshorus, too, in his *Atthis* says that Venus is the moon and that men offer sacrifice to the moon dressed as women, and women dressed as men, because the moon is thought to be both male and female."[1098] Another possible representation of the androgynous deity may be the *Venus Calva* ('Bald Venus'), whose images show a woman as bald as any man might be. But while one scholar may see in this analogy with the priests of Isis, another finds in it reference to the lock of hair Roman women dedicated to Venus on their wedding day.[1099]

Interestingly, though imaged in some places as an androgynous deity, for most of Western history Aphrodite—especially in the Roman form of Venus—has been known as the most feminine and sexually alluring member of the Greek and Roman pantheon. As a goddess, she was associated with beauty, love, marriage, and birth. Yet, her connections with androgyny are more than a few isolated representations and a couple odd names. She was also linked with androgynous Dionysus, with whom she had a son—the god Priapus, who was especially associated with Roman sexuality. Another of their reputed offspring was Hymen, a deity both beautiful and bisexual, and celebrated as the god of marriage. Finally, as noted before, our term 'hermaphrodite' conjoins her name with that of Hermes. By him she had a son who while bathing in a pool was joined with the spring's nymph. They became one body with the characteristics of both sexes. Aphrodite is a potent symbol for the differently gendered.

Hermaphroditus

The very notion of a hermaphroditic deity comes from Hermaphroditus, offspring—as the name suggests—of Aphrodite (an androgynous deity) and Hermes (a trickster deity). Hermaphroditus is routinely imaged by ancient artists as possessing female breasts and male genitals. But this was not a mere matter of birth. The story is told that as a youth Hermaphroditus was male, and very comely. He attracted the attention of Salmacis, a nymph, who desired him, and all the more when she glimpsed him naked as he went to swim in her pool. The Roman poet Ovid (32 B.C.E. – 17 C.E.) described what then happened:

'I've won, for he is mine,'
She cried, clothes torn away and naked, as she
Leaped to follow him, her arms about him fast,
Where, though he tried to shake her off, she clung,
Fastening his lips to her, stroking his breast,
Surrounding him with arms, legs, lips, and hands
As though she were a snake caught by an eagle . . . .
The heir of Atlas struggled as he could

Against the pleasure the girl desired,
But she clung to him as though their flesh were one,
'Dear, naughty boy,' she said, 'to torture me;
But you won't get away. O gods in heaven,
Give me this blessing; clip him within my arms
Like this forever.' At which the gods agreed;
They grew one body, one face, one pair of arms
And legs, as one might graft branches upon
A tree, so two became nor boy nor girl,
Neither yet both within a single body.[1100]

The figure of Hermaphroditos, in Licht's estimation, reveals "a being that has its root in the dim consciousness of the androgynous idea of life, artistically perfected by sensually aesthetic longings, who was worshipped as the good spirit of the house and private life, more than as a divinity who was the object of public worship."[1101]

Gender-altered Deities

Deities do not always retain the gender presentation they started with, or are best known by. While gender alteration may happen by gender masquerade, other alterations are possible. A deity might alter dress without also affecting a masquerade, as the Greek river god Acheloös does in donning the feminine *peplos* (a long, loose-fitting tunic worn by women). In dramatic instances a male deity even may emasculate himself. Barbara Walker has cited examples from various parts of the world: Ra in Egypt, Mahadeva in India, Quetzalcoatl in Mexico, Uranus in Greece, and Odin in Northern Europe, among others.[1102]

Deities often take disguises. When the disguise involves appearing as a gender different from the one typically associated with that deity, then a gender masquerade has happened. Athena, for example, in Homer's *Odyssey* disguises herself as Mentor, the male friend of Odysseus.[1103] Though Athena is placed among the androgynous deities, the appearance as Mentor is clearly not meant to represent the divine presence and it does involve a change in gender from that typically associated with 'her'—and so qualifies as an instance of gender masquerade. Other Greek gods also masqueraded. Zeus, first among the gods, disguised himself to appear like Artemis. His aim was one of those familiar to gender-crossings: to gain an access he would have otherwise lacked. In this case, it was to the nymph Callisto.

In the East, Vishnu—that popular deity of Hinduism—is typically viewed as a male god. When he takes form among mortals it can be as he wishes—human or otherwise, male or female. His best known *avatars* are male: Krishna, Rama, Buddha. Yet he took the form of an enchantress named Mohini in order to distract some demons (*asuras*).[1104] The ruse succeeded. On another occasion, Vishnu utilized the same guise to rescue the god Shiva by again distracting a demon. Later, Shiva also was enamored of the masquerading god when he encountered Vishnu-as-Molina in a garden. Shiva and Vishnu engaged in a sexual encounter that left Vishnu-as-Mohini pregnant. Their child was the hermaphroditic deity, Ayyappan (or Harihараputra).[1105]

A common figure in many religions, both ancient and modern, who may employ a gender masquerade is the *trickster*. Such a figure is not always a deity; it may be an animal, as in various Native American religions, or a quasi-divine figure, such as Satan in Christianity. But tricksters can be deities, as Loki (who spent years in female form) is in Norse mythology,[1106] or Hermes in Classical Greek religion. Though the essential nature of the trickster may be characterized as male or female, the trickster has the ability to change shape and gender. This 'gender-bending' being plays a vital role in many mythologies, often involved in creation or reshaping creation, posing temptations or challenges, and being a vehicle for driving home moral lessons in stories.[1107]

Sacred Gender Crossings

Our problem in modern Western societies is that limited notions of gender have particularly hindered our comprehension of all that might be entailed in sacred gender crossings. Indeed, with respect to gender crossings in general, Lisa Penaloza got it exactly right when she remarked, "Gender crossings remain misunderstood if left within a dualist conceptualization of gender."[1108] As she points out, gender crossings as such pose a problem for gender schemes like that embraced in the modern West—their very existence poses a challenge to Western assumptions. At the very least we should be left open to the possibility we have gotten things wrong with our insistence on a two sex/two gender framework, with rigid pairing of masculinity to maleness and femininity to femaleness. *It is in the matter of sacred gender crossings that nonconforming gender individuals most often acquire their special status in society.*

As we mere mortals have wrestled with how such matters apply not merely to ourselves but to divine beings, a number of ideas have emerged. How divine entities have or express sex and gender, and how these things enter into divine-human interactions, has been variously conceived—much like corresponding ideas about human beings. In fact, whether taking a cue from realities seen in this sphere or trying to start from knowledge of a sacred realm, once these things have been figured out about deities, then we can fashion appropriate human responses. On the human side, gender crossings have proven time and again to be instrumental in this process of responding to the divine. Antiquities scholar Margaret Miller writes, "It has been observed that the transformation of gender is often associated with the process of coming closer to divinity by breaking down the categories of ordinary experience."[1109] And that is where crossdressing often enters. Crossdressing frequently has played a role in sacred transactions.

Why? The reasons vary. Sometimes it is a case of *imitation*. The manipulation of dress is the most visible and convenient way for human beings to do what divine beings accomplish by other means, including crossing gender. Sometimes crossdressing is not an imitation of divine behavior, but imitation of divine being. In this sense, crossdressing is imitation through *transformation*, with the result of becoming more like the deity being worshipped. In other circumstances, crossdressing is not imitative at all, but pursued as a way of sacred *transgression*. The transgression often is against artificial boundaries that keep our realm and the divine realm apart. By breaking down these barriers crossdressing itself becomes a bridge between deity and humanity. But because this bridge is constructed by transgressing a boundary set either on our end or the divine end, it stirs some controversy. In any event, all these reasons and others are meant to serve a religious purpose.

We should be wary in light of all this to assume that crossdressing, when it occurred, was deviant religiosity. In our culture, if we are aware of any connection between crossdressing and religion at all, we are likely only to have heard that the Christian Bible condemns it—an oversimplified generalization that has unfortunately colored and complicated our understanding of transgender realities in religious contexts.[1110] Miller reminds us, with reference to practice in the ancient Greek world, that crossdressing was not only condoned, but in certain ritual contexts *required*.[1111]

The advantages presented by religious crossdressing have figured in numerous religions. In fact, religions both modern and ancient have made a place for sacred crossdressing. In the ancient world crossdressing served various functions such as those described above in a range of religions found both East and West. Because crossdressing intends a human response to divine realities, we must spend some time looking at how these divine realities have been viewed. Only by comprehending the broader context of sacred gender crossings by both human *and* divine figures can religious crossdressing make full sense.

Sacred gender crossings reflect violation of normal gender boundaries for sacred reasons or by deities for their own reasons, whatever those may be. The ancient world has numerous instances of which various examples are offered below. In general, sacred gender crossings typically fall into one or the other of the following broad categories:

❑ Divine or other sacred nonhuman beings appearing in unexpected gender manifestations;

❑ Human beings pursuing sacred roles or tasks in a gender performance different from the gender identity and role assigned them at birth; and,

❑ Sacred festivals, where divine and human interact, *and* where an aspect of that interaction involves gender crossing.

These are all explored in what follows.

The key element in sacred gender crossings is not the gender crossing itself. It is that it is *sacred*. The gender crossing is an act set apart from ordinary acts. Things become holy by being removed from mundane occurrence or use, and in sacred gender crossing it is gender thus removed. The individual—whether divine, semi-divine, or human—sets apart (or aside) normal gender presentation for the express purpose of some kind of interaction (e.g., human with divine, or divine with human). Just as food becomes holy and wholly different by being offered to a deity, so gender becomes holy and wholly different in sacred gender crossings.

Divine gender crossings exist in various forms. One form concerns the manifestation of certain divinities. Another resides in characters found within the pantheon of non-human religious figures (e.g., demons and demigods). Though best known in the West through stories coming down from the ancients, divine gender crossings persist in religious traditions kept alive today in various parts of the world.

Human Sacred Gender Crossings

In addition to figuring out the nature of divine figures and how best to relate to them, ancient folk also had to determine the role of sex and gender in their own lives, and how these fit in the religious sphere. Answers differed radically. Some viewed sex and gender as those aspects of human experience most directly relevant to religion, particularly because they involve relationships and the renewal of life. Others thought human sex and gender were those parts of human existence that most interfere with connecting to the divine because they are distracting and deluding powers. In fact, some regarded humanity's division into male and female as a fall from an original androgynous state. Many others took one or another position in-between the extremes, finding a place for sex and gender without making it central or excluding it as evil.

In a great many of these varying responses crossdressing played a part. As indicated earlier, it might be done for a variety of reasons, such as imitation of the divine, for transformation, or as an act of transgression. Ancient expressions of sacred gender crossings in their geographical and religious tradition contexts are a matter for extended discussion; here we only shall explore briefly various ways of utilizing cross-gender religiously, retaining our present focus on crossdressing. Among the more notable avenues for transcending gender—or at least crossing culturally dominant gender conventions—are these:

- ❑ *Shamanism*—perhaps the religious phenomenon most famously associated with gender crossings;
- ❑ *Priests and priestesses*—religious officials serving deities who themselves play with gender crossings often follow suit;
- ❑ *Eunuchs*—transgendered either by nature or by human hand, eunuchs have long had special roles in different social institutions, including religion;
- ❑ *Disciples*—devoted followers who imitate their leaders will defy social conventions of gender if their master has done so; and,
- ❑ *Gender artifice in social relations*—where gender conventions are crossed or transcended in order to serve some particular social relation.

Let us briefly consider each of these.

Shamanism

Shamanism utilizes crossdressing as part of the transformation by which a shaman not only mystically transcends the boundaries of mundane reality, but also the artifice of gender. Shamans thus can be interpreted as masters of deconstruction who transgress social convention in the service of a higher end. "Shamans break down categories; confound boundaries, especially those between worlds; and specialize in ambiguity."[1112] Certainly in this regard crossdressing by a shaman proves a deconstructive act. Like crossdressers in mainstream society, shamans represent those of us who are marginalized by society. Their exhibition of "ambiguous sexuality"[1113] confounds norms while opening up new possibilities.

Shamanism is a phenomenon found around the world, albeit in various forms and under different names. One matter held in common, though, is the religious character of the shaman. Mircea Eliade, using a history of religions approach, noted that shamanism, in its purest sense, is a phenomenon rooted in Siberia and central Asia. Starting with and focusing upon Siberian shamanism, Eliade found connections to shamanism elsewhere in the world, both East and West. The shaman as a religious figure is one who bridges the mundane and sacred spheres. Shamans are also masters of religious ecstasy. But of importance to us, Eliade cited shamans as an example of 'ritual androgyny.' They unite, or 'reconcile,' opposing principles such as masculinity and femininity.[1114]

The androgyny achieved by uniting male and female in one's own person is represented in the clothing the shaman wears. The Siberian shaman, for example, dons a caftan (a unisex garment) adorned with iron disks, bars, and other things that symbolize various aspects of nature, such as the human body, including two orbs for breasts. Anthropologists early in the 20th century observed that among the Siberian Yakut the male shaman, when not in his costume, wore as his ordinary wear a woman's dress fashioned from the skin of a foal.[1115] In Korea, female shamans wear male clothing; "the rare male shaman in Korea (*paksu mudong*) performs *kut* wearing women's clothing, down to the pantaloons that hide beneath his billowing skirt and slip."[1116] In the Philippines, the Spanish conquerors encountered both female shamans and male shamans—the *Bayog* (aka. *Bayoc, Bayoguin*, or *Asog*)—who appeared as women in dress, hairstyle and effeminate behavior.[1117]

Comparable examples come from Africa, and the Americas. In the United States, for example, about two dozen Native American societies have shamans (commonly referred to as 'medicine men' or 'medicine women'), with male shamans predominating in about two-thirds of these. Sabine Lang remarked about these 'women-men':

> Where men were the primary healers or medicine men, the women-men moved partly within the domain of the masculine gender role, both with respect to their status as medicine "men" and also with regard to acquisition of the necessary su-

pernatural powers. Women's clothes and components of the feminine gender role appeared there as the expression of the personal "medicine" of a woman-man. In such cases, women-men were not healers in the framework of the feminine gender role, but—despite their ambivalent gender status—they were males with a special kind of supernatural power.[1118]

Notable in these and other instances that might be mentioned is the lack of sexual fetishism in the crossdressing connected to shamanism. Instead, the crossdressing is an aspect of costuming, ritual in character, and highly symbolic. Through crossdressing a tangible manifestation of a spiritual embracing of male and female together occurs. In this manner it matters little whether we style the shaman as 'man' or 'woman' for doing so misses the point that the shaman's appearance creates a point of integration (or, if you prefer, 'reconciliation').

Priests & Priestesses

Priests and/or priestesses also are often involved in sacred gender crossings and crossdressing. At the dawn of literature, in ancient Sumeria, we find references to crossdressing priests called the *kurĝara*, whom may have been a template for later gender-crossing priests, such as the effeminate male *assinnu* of Ishtar, or the "male shrine prostitutes" referred to in the Jewish and Christian sacred literature (1 Kings 12:24).[1119] We might count among their figurative descendants the 'Galli,' priests of Cybele, famed throughout the classical world. They not only crossdressed, but sometimes castrated themselves. These acts represented their imitation of a revered figure (Attis) and constituted a dramatically transformative action whereby the priests became acceptable to the deity they served.

In northern Europe, crossdressing was also a part of the worship of the Alcis, twin deities whom 1st century Roman historian Tacitus identified as equivalent to the Roman deities Castor and Pollux. According to Tacitus, the presiding priest of the Alcis dressed in women's clothes.[1120] It is worth noting that the Alcis have also been identified with the *Haddingjar*—'they of womanly hair.'[1121] Perhaps, then, the priestly crossdressing indicates something about how the duality of the gods was understood by those who followed them.

Eunuchs

In our earlier look at ancient Western culture (chapter 6), we noted that eunuchs occupied a unique and often privileged place in many ancient societies—both East (e.g., Persia) and West. They often occupied sensitive positions, such as service among the women of a ruler's harem, where they could watch out over the harem without the ruler's fear the eunuchs would impregnate any of the women. Some were eunuchs 'made by nature.' Others were eunuchs 'made by man'—whether voluntarily or not. But it was common to see them as in a border state between sexes—and that made them candidates for more than just secular service.

Dominic Montserrat, as we heard earlier, notes that alongside eunuchs were a number of other 'third gender' members, who like eunuchs were uniquely positioned for more than one useful social function.[1122] The eunuch's position *between* sexes and gender statuses was ideal for religion. Richard Gordon observes that castration also placed an individual 'between worlds' and was parallel to other acts of devotion such as voluntary poverty or homelessness. Some way was needed to mark out such persons and things like face whitening or cross-dressing served such a purpose admirably. Gordon distinguishes two forms of religious eunuchs: senior priests (perhaps even High Priest), or religious attendants who remained outside the priesthood.[1123] We already noted the eunuch priests of Cybele. But eunuchs involved in one or another aspect of religious service were common. They were known in both the East and the West.

Perhaps the most famous eunuchs are those of the Byzantine Empire (5th-15th centuries C.E.). Roberta Gilchrist comments, "The eunuch is now widely regarded by Byzantine scholars as a third gender, neither male nor female, although the precise physical definition of this category is insecure."[1124] Gilchrist notes the reports of such individuals as mixing physical characteristics of male and female. Whatever their physical nature, in terms of gender they were a third gender by virtue of a set of distinct mannerisms and accompanying social perception that combined to create for them a separate gender class. Their high social status carried with it political, religious, and ceremonial duties, which can be generally described as mediating and supervising life boundaries (e.g., that between healthy and ill, alive and dead).

Gilchrist perceptively notes that social—not sexual—concerns were central in the construal of the Byzantine eunuch as a third gender. Whether by nature or by choice, the eunuch comes to occupy a place between genders. In this respect, applying a term like 'crossdressing' may be meaningless—though it has not been uncommon when the genetic sex of the eunuch was male and feminine dress was adopted. What we need to recognize here is that eunuchs cross gender conventions, willingly or not, and once between the gender poles are often called upon to perform religious, or quasi-religious, roles and functions. These range from priestly duties, to those of sacred healers, to social mediators in conflicts between gender (and other) groups.

Disciples

The faithful following of a special figure—in the Judaeo-Christian tradition termed 'discipleship'—entails a keen observation and imitation of the beloved master. Interestingly, some early Christian literature suggests that becoming a follower of Jesus means changes with gender implications. At least, that is a contention made by biblical studies scholar Richard Valantasis with reference to the *Gospel of Thomas*. He writes that the new person envisioned by Jesus in the sayings of this document "has become in essence a third gender"—a person outside the cultural categories of masculinity and femininity. This new individual, Valantasis declares, "makes concrete and defines the new third gender that replaces the former dual-gender paradigm."[1125]

Gender Artifice in Social Relations

Gender artifice within a religious system can arise as a way of constructing a particular social relation. In the religious/philosophical system of China's Confucianism, social relations in general are central and carefully proscribed. Among the most fundamental relations are those of husband to wife and of ruler to ruled. In both instances, the relationship is vertical; the latter is subordinate to the former. Moreover, Confucianism is a rigidly patriarchal system where females occupy a limited and inferior position. The male ruler stands alone, in a special class, and must be treated as such in social discourse. Thus, as we mentioned in an earlier discussion (chapter 6), in the *Analects* of Confucius, we find the wife of the emperor accorded a special ritual etiquette:

> The wife of the ruler of a State is referred to by the ruler as 'That Person.' She refers to herself as Little Boy. The people of the country call her 'That person of the Prince's.' When speaking of her to people of another State the ruler calls her 'This lonely one's little prince.' But people of another State likewise call her 'That person of the Prince's.'[1126]

Arthur Waley, translator of this passage, notes that *Hsiao T'ung* ("Little Boy") refers to a page boy and is exclusively masculine. Waley remarks, "the sovereign's wife may not be referred to (either by himself or anyone else) by any term that is feminine in implication and must in referring to herself use a term that is definitely masculine."[1127] In short, the inflexibility of social relations mandates a flexibility in gender designation in order to protect the social order.

Yet the *yin/yang*, feminine/maculine divide was bridged by at least one Chinese ruler. In the late 7th century, during the T'ang Dynasty, Empress Wu Zetian (624-705) declared herself 'Son of Heaven' and emperor (690 C.E.).[1128] In Confucian China this was not only unparalleled, but unthinkable—*yin* had usurped *yang*! Even prior to her attainment of supreme power, Wu had occupied the role of an advisor to the throne, sporting a beard like 'his' male advisors.[1129] In the hands of a capable, ambitious woman like Wu, the social artifice of Confucian China could be employed to transcend gender rather than transgress it.

Sacred Festivals Involving Gender Crossings

In sacred festivals divine figures interact with human ones. Frequently this interaction is a solicited *meeting* of the parties. Often this is construed as a passive act on the part of the deity, who may merely hear a prayer or accept an offering. But in some instances the deity takes a more active part, typically through a representative human figure who may be a priest (or priestess) in a priestly role, or masquerading as the deity. In meetings between divine and human beings one or the other may engage in gender crossing. The deity may do so for any number of reasons, including putting the worshippers to the test, seducing a person, or utilizing a masquerade for some other purpose, such as mixing among the faithful. A human may also gender cross, because such is suitable for the worship of the divine being, or perhaps because the human is attempting a subterfuge to trick the deity for some reason.

In other instances, the human participation in the festivities may involve actions to *avoid* a divine, semi-divine, or demonic figure. In such cases the person may cross gender as a way to deceive a wrathful deity or a malevolent one. Through successful deception the person escapes harm until the danger is past. Rarely, the divine figure might be portrayed as gender crossing to avoid being met by human pursuers. In such a case the idea is to take a disguise in order not to have to yield some benefit.

While the above ideas are not exclusive to sacred festivals (i.e., they can occur in individual experience outside any religious structure), they take on special meaning in a festival. The occasion of the festival adds regularity and fixes the contextual form and process for the gender crossing. It has a sacred character by virtue of being set apart from ordinary action. The gender crossing is *not* typical of ordinary, mundane experience. Instead, it exists in a special time and place for a concrete and sanctioned reason.

The easiest way to convey a gender crossing is through dress. It is not the only way, however. Dramatic and extreme steps might also be taken, as among eunuch priests who self-castrate and undertake a life of gender crossing that sets them apart from others. Obviously, for the majority of the faithful this is not a course that will be taken. Festivals offer a way to do something similar, though limited in time and extent. In a festival a male can become female, or a female male in order to effect a meeting with a deity or, perhaps, to avoid a meeting with one or with a malevolent spirit.

In ancient religious festivals both male and female crossdressing occurred—though not necessarily in the same festival, nor for the same reasons. Since crossdressing inherently represents a transition, it often was connected to rites of transition such as initiation. "In many initiatory rituals, novices wear opposite sex clothing, signifying a ritual transformation into the other sex, a state of androgyny."[1130] In other cases—such as in what has been term 'ritual transvestism'—it represented a temporary gender role reversal or (more rarely) a permanent gender role change.[1131] No matter the aim, motivations might vary and appraisals by others certainly did.

Finally, humanities scholar Camille Paglia, in a rather striking assertion, contended the following:

> Ritual transvestism, then and now, is a drama of female dominance. There are religious meanings to all female impersonation, in nightclubs or bedroom. A woman putting on man's clothes merely steals social power. But a man putting on women's clothes is searching for God.[1132]

This is putting the matter rather too strongly in light of the evidence (even her own), but it does prompt us to regard crossdressing in a way we might not have done before. To whatever extent crossdressing may or may not reflect connection to an eternal feminine, it certainly had—and can retain—a sacred connection to deep and abiding forces. The ancient festivals understood this reality.

Ancient Eastern Religious Festivals

In southern India, at the festivals of Kuvakkam and Pillaiyarkuppam, a re-enactment of a story from one version of the *Mahabharata* occurs. That story is of Vishnu appearing as Mohini to honor and fulfill the condition of a princely warrior fated to die the following day. The hero, Aravan, did not wish to die without having married. Thus he was wed to Vishnu-as-Mohini. The Tamils know a group of male devotees of Vishnu-as-Mohini, called the 'Ali,' who crossdress and whose principal religious ritual has this story at its center.

A variety of other occasions and manners existed by which to honor Mohini. The Hindu Mohini Attam—the dance of the enchantress—commemorates the story of Vishnu's cross-gender appearance as Mohini in order to distract the demon Bhasmasura and thus save fellow deity, Shiva. Also, on the fifth day of the festival of the Brahmotsavams of Tirumala, 'Mohini Avatarotsavam,' the same story of Vishnu-as-Mohini is honored, with the divine lord dressed as Mohini and taken in a procession.

Ancient Greek Religious Festivals

As we might expect, deities associated with gender bending or gender blending might also have followers who followed their example. This is indeed the case. Devotees of Dionysus crossdressed in connection with different sacred occasions. Dionysian festivals, as Henrichs has observed, frequently featured role reversals such as crossdressing.[1133] In the festival of *Oschophoria*, for example, young, wealthy noblemen dressed as women and led a sacred procession from the Temple of Dionysius to that of Athena.[1134]

Saturnalia

Ritual crossdressing occurred in a number of religious contexts, especially where rituals of reversal were involved. The best known example of these is Saturnalia, a festival rooted in the worship of the Roman deity Ssaturnus, but which persisted long after the religious tones were well-subordinated or even forgotten. The Saturnalia might last from 3-7 days (depending on the era), and was characterized by role reversals such that, for example, slaves dined before their masters did, and leisure wear was donned when formal wear could be expected.[1135] Crossdressing was part of the amusements of the festival, a practice that persisted in later festivals such as Carnival.[1136]

Carnival

'Carnival' (Mardi Gras in the United States) derives its name from the Italian *carnevale* (itself from the Latin *carnelevarium*) and refers to the 'removing of

meat' characteristic of the Lenten period. It was known by this form—
"Carnival"—as early as the 13th century, but centuries earlier as "Carne Levale."
In 1091 C.E., the Synod of Benevento formally established Ash Wednesday at
the conclusion of Carnival, thus joining the festival to Lent. Christian missions
spread the festival everywhere Catholicism prospered so that it became a fixture
in many cultures, from Brazil to Trinidad to the United States. Carnival customs
include feasting, games, parades, costumes—and crossdressing. Role reversal is
a fixture of Carnival practice, including gender reversal through crossdressing.[1137]

In his influential exploration of Carnival, Mikhail Bakhtin elucidates the
idea of this festival season as a clearly defined period in time when normal social
rules and conventions are suspended, when "life is subject only to its own
laws."[1138] The natural liberty of life, freed from social constraints, allows movements and changes otherwise unknown or disapproved. Both physical realities
and social constructions can be given freer reign. Thus the sexed body and gender representations in dress and manner become things open to manipulation.
That these manipulations occur in a festive context gives them the character of
play—and play is a serious matter.[1139]

Typically, when considering Carnival scholars regard the comedic spirit of
gender crossing as something needed to discharge any anxiety over the behavior
involved. While this is plausible enough it depends on the idea that if it is play it
need not, perhaps *cannot* be taken seriously. Play is all too often relegated to
childhood, though by whatever other name (e.g., 'leisure') it is called, play persists throughout life. Festival occasions where gender crossing behavior occur
help remind us that such activities, whatever they may signify, are enjoyable.

Play is pleasurable in itself. Indeed, the nature of gender crossing during
Carnival as *play* may be the very key to best understanding it. Though Freud
viewed play as determined by wishes, Erik Erikson probably offers a richer explanation. He understands play as an activity both of childhood and adulthood.
His comments on its purposes in childhood may be pertinent to comprehending elements of gender crossing play. Erikson proposes play as a way of mastering and remastering experience through "meditating, experimenting, planning,
and sharing."[1140] Few experiences in life are more demanding than gender with
its expectations for identity and role behavior imposed from birth to the grave.
Carnivalesque periods afford uniquely suitable ways of 'meditating, experimenting, planning, and sharing' different explorations and expressions of gender.
Given their sanction in the festival season, and guided by Carnival conventions,
an individual can safely stretch or cross boundaries in public while aware of the
safety net below. Such play enriches gender experience even as it provides release and relief from the rigid work of ordinary gender performance.

Gender Oppression

Gender can be the site of play—or oppression. Throughout the discussions
of our ongoing dialog we have tried to be sensitive to the role played by lan-

guage, with its power to clarify or obscure, to constrain or to liberate. Our gender vocabulary occupies a significant place in both how we converse and what we can say. Sometimes that vocabulary is manipulated to shift the grounds of discussion, to redirect attention either toward or away from specific issues. Religious scholar Pamela Dickey Young observes how the very word 'gender' can be thus manipulated. She remarks, "It can mask what is happening when we pass over the very real differentials of power and position between women and men to some assumed 'gender neutrality.'"[1141]

Therefore, our brief discussion of religion cannot end without our expressing awareness of how *religion can oppress gender*. Young herself points to the apparent disjunction between the evidence of history and the claims of religious bodies. For example, she notes that the Roman Catholic Church maintains that priests always have been men, though ancient Christian documents depict women in leadership roles both liturgical and ecclesiastical. She speculates that this distance between accounts flows from a church history wherein, as Christianity slowly became the 'official' religion of the Roman Empire, women became progressively less appropriate 'actors' in the story told by the religion.[1142]

But no religion succeeds long in simply ignoring all but a single gender. Even the most patriarchal expressions of religion have to do something about women and others. *Gender segregation of religious duties* accomplishes this task. Thus, in Judaism men traditionally lead Shabbat services—but women conduct prayers at home welcoming the Sabbath. In Christianity, most ministers are men, but probably most Sunday School teachers are women. The status is not equal, but women are granted a service role, or liturgical function. As the two instances just named show, these also tend to reinforce the societal gender hierarchy and the gender role stereotypes. The Jewish woman's religious duties are in the home; the Christian woman's teaching is almost invariably of children.

The most noticeable separations of gender, and the greatest apparent gender inequalities, typically arise in the most socially conservative wings of a religion. Religious *fundamentalism* often interprets a 'return to the fundamentals' as a retrenchment to more patriarchal structures. Not infrequently, as a response to criticisms from others, fundamentalist groups adopt a peculiar manipulation of discourse to accompany their oppression of one or another gender (or other minority group). For example, talk might be of the 'glory' or 'honor' in being subservient and humble. Women who serve men might be extolled as paragons of the godly virtue that carries special reward in the after life. Thus, rather than women being oppressed, the religion can speak of them being honored with the 'grace' or 'calling' ('vocation') of a station and service especially revered by the deity. Or, another way of dealing with the apparent inequality is to redefine it as 'equal in different ways'—whatever that means! Often this comes as a variant on the 'separate but equal' idea encountered in race relations; women and men have separate spheres—he the world, she the home—and these 'equal out.' She is supposed to be dominant in the one, he in the other, though curiously her 'leadership' in the home typically extends only to the children. In sum, religious fundamentalists generally deny gender inequality by redefining what they believe equality means.

Yet again we meet here with why our conversation on gender matters. *Words* matter—and we should be careful in the ones we choose. There is much more we could say on this matter; indeed, much more *should* be said. But mindful of the introductory nature of this dialog, perhaps we have said enough for now. We can return to Young for a final sobering thought on the role of religion in responding to gender and especially to gender difference. "There is a basic agreement among feminist adherents of religion that difference needs to be recognized and privileged," she notes. "There is no agreement about how to do this."[1143]

Notes

Chapter 1 Notes

[1] Joan Wallach Scott, *Gender and the Politics of History,* rev. ed. (N. Y.: Columbia Univ. Press, 1999), pp. ix-xi. Cf. Kate Bornstein, *My Gender Workbook: How to Become a Real Man, a Real Woman, the Real You, or Something Else Entirely* (N. Y.: Routledge, 1998), p. 113.

[2] In contradistinction to the history of our word 'gender' consider the lineage for 'sex.' Social constructionist Jeffrey Weeks writes, "The earliest usage of the term 'sex', in the sixteenth century, referred precisely to the division of humanity into the male section and the female section (that is, to differences of gender)." *Sexuality* (N. Y.: Routledge, 1986), p. 13.

[3] Aristotle, *Rhetorica* 1407 [b]7.

[4] For details on these matters, see the *Oxford English Dictionary*, or the one volume *Oxford Universal Dictionary.*, as well as Latin dictionaries such as the *Oxford Latin Dictionary* or *The New College Latin & English Dictionary*.

[5] A. M. MacDonald (Ed.), *Chambers' Etymological English Dictionary* (Paterson: Littlefield, Adams & Co., 1964), p. 257 (emphasis added).

[6] C. T. Onions (Ed.), *The Oxford Universal Dictionary* (Oxford: Clarendon Press, 1955), p. 783 (emphasis added).

[7] 'Devolved' does not seem too harsh a word given that the concept of gender has narrowed over time. This process of simplification does not appear to reflect a growing awareness that only two genders manifest in the world, but rather a cultural decision that only two genders *should* manifest in the world.

[8] The relation between 'sex' and 'gender' will be explored more fully in chapter 3.

[9] *The American Heritage Book of English Usage. A Practical and Authoritative Guide to Contemporary English* (N. Y.: Houghton Mifflin, 1996), p. 176: 5. Gender: Sexist Language and Assumptions, §10 gender/sex. Accessed online at http://www.bartleby.com/64/C005/010.html.

[10] The word 'apparent' is crucial. We make distinctions based on what we perceive, but what we perceive is rarely the naked body with the genitalia on full display. Rather we shape our decision of someone's gender-based-on-sex from dress appearance and manners. See G. G. Bolich, *Crossdressing in Context, vol. 1: The Context of Dress and Gender* (Raleigh: Psyche's Press, 2006).

[11] Political theorist Raia Prokhovnik writes, "The view that the sex/gender distinction means that there is an essential difference between men and women, determined by the reproductive capacities of their bodies, is still so widely held as to be dominant." *Rational Woman: A Feminist Critique of Dualism* (N. Y.: Routledge, 1999), p. 126.

[12] Angela Goddard & Lindsey Mean Patterson, *Language and Gender* (N. Y.: Routledge, 2000), p. 1.

[13] Lisa Maurer, "Transgressing Sex and Gender: Deconstruction Zone Ahead?" *SIECUS Report, 28* (no. 1), 1421 (1999, Oct./Nov.), p. 14.

[14] Chris Beasley, *Gender & Sexuality: Critical Theories, Critical Thinkers* (Thousand Oaks, CA.: Sage, 2005), p. 11. Cf. his remarks (p. 12) on the narrower and broader uses.

[15] Mr. Barb Greve, "Courage from Necessity," in J. Nestle, C. Howell, & R. A. Wilchins (Eds.), *Genderqueer: Voices from Beyond the Sexual Binary*, pp. 247-249 (L.A.: Alyson Publications, 2002), p. 249.

[16] See Goddard & Patterson, 'Making Up Gender,' pp. 27ff.

[17] Goddard & Patterson, p. 34.

[18] Ibid.

[19] The four terms 'boy,' 'girl,' 'man,' 'woman,' combine sex and gender but give predominance to gender. Consider, for example, the word 'woman.' Though it presumes the female sex, it is derived from a gendered role—'a man's wife.' In this work, such terms are typically used to refer to gender rather than sex.

[20] Goddard & Patterson, p. 1.

[21] *The Oxford Universal Dictionary* (p. 795) notes that in the 16th century the word 'girl' was applied to all unmarried females.

[22] Ibid.

[23] Francesca Santoro L'Hoir, *The Rhetoric of Gender Terms: Man, 'Woman', and the Portrayal of Character in Latin Prose* (Leiden: E. J. Brill, 1992), p. 1f.

[24] Niels Davidsen-Nielsen & Carl Bache, *Mastering English: An Advanced Grammar for Non-Native and Native Speakers* (N. Y.: Mouton de Gruyter, 1997), p. 406.

[25] Leslie Feinberg, *Trans Liberation: Beyond Pink or Blue* (Boston: Beacon Press, 1998), p. 70f. Cf. the *Queers and Allies Dictionary* accessed online at http://www.gustavus.edu/oncampus/orgs/queers/main/dictionary_full.html.

[26] Leslie Feinberg, *Transgender Warriors: Making History from Joan of Arc to Dennis Rodman* (Boston: Beacon Press, 1996), p. x.

[27] Feinberg, *Trans Liberation*, p. 71.

[28] Goddard & Patterson, p. 1f.

[29] See Robert W. Connell, *Masculinities* (Berkeley: Univ. of California Press, 1995).

[30] Psychologist Sandra Bem has been the most prominent name in this regard. Her pioneering work in gender studies firmly established androgyny as an important concept. See Sandra L. Bem, "The Measurement of Psychological Androgyny," *Journal of Consulting and Clinical Psychology, 42*, 155-162 (1974).

[31] Sandra Bem, "Gender Schema Theory: A Cognitive Account of Sex Typing," *Psychological Review, 88* (no. 4), 354-364 (1981), p. 363.

[32] The androgynous character of dress for males and females before adulthood exists in many social groups and contexts. For one manifestation in American history, consider the dress of slaves in the antebellum United States; see Shane White & Graham White, "Slave Clothing and African-American Culture in the Eighteenth and Nineteenth Centuries," *Past & Present, 148*, 149-186 (1995).

[33] Androgynous dress by males can be tolerated because it does *not* violate the golden rule that a male must look masculine, or at least not feminine. See Bolich, *Cross-dressing in Context, vol. 1: The Context of Dress and Gender*, p. 77.

[34] Walter O. Bockting, "From Construction to Context: Gender Through the Eyes of the Transgendered," *SIECUS Report, 28* (no. 1), 3-7 (1999, Oct./Nov.), p. 3.

[35] Richard A. Carroll, "Assessment and Treatment of Gender Dysphoria," in S. R. Leiblum & R. C. Rosen (Eds.), *Principles and Practice of Sex Therapy,* 3rd ed., pp. 368-397 (N. Y.: Guilford, 2000), p. 370. This is preferable to the succinct but misleading phrase suggested by activist writer Leslie Feinberg, who writes, "trans*gender* people traverse, bridge, or blur the *sex* they were assigned at birth." I dislike the commingling of the terms sex and gender in this fashion; the 'traversing, bridging, or blurring' is primarily of gender assignment, though it may often also encompass sex assignment. See Leslie Feinberg, *Transgender Warriors: Making History from Joan of Arc to Dennis Rodman* (Boston: Beacon Press, 1996), p. x.

[36] *GenderPAC. First National Survey of TransGender Violence* (GenderPAC, 1997), p. 3. Accessed online at http://hatecrime.transadvocacy.com/documents/TransViolence%20Svey%20Results.pdf.

[37] B. Thom & K. More, "Welcome to the Festival," in *The Second International Transgender Film and Video Festival* (London: Alchemy Festival Productions, 1998), cited in Richard Ekins & Dave King, "Transgendering, Migrating and Love of Oneself as a Woman: A Contribution to a Sociology of Autogynephilia," *The International Journal of Transgenderism, 5* (no. 3) (2001), accessed online at http://www.symposion.com/ijt/ijtvo05no03_01.htm.

[38] My list is similar to that offered by Bockting (p. 3), except that I include the intersexed. The variability of cross-gender identification among transvestites extends across members of the category and often is variable within individual members as well.

[39] Patricia Gagne & Richard Tewksbury, "Conformity Pressures and Gender Resistance Among Transgendered Individuals," *Social Problems, 45* (no. 1), 81-101 (1998), p. 100.

[40] The noted transgender activist Virginia Prince claimed to have coined the terms 'transgenderism' and 'transgenderist' to refer to people who live full time as members of the opposite sex but without intending sexual reassignment. See Virginia Prince, "Seventy Years in the Trenches of the Gender Wars," in B. Bullough, V. L. Bullough, & J. Elias (Eds.), *Gender Blending*, pp. 469-476 (Amherherst, NY: Prometheus Books, 1997), p. 469. Prominent theorist Richard Doctor prefers to confine the term to refer to those who live for periods of time fully in the identity and role of a member of the opposite sex. See Richard F. Doctor, *Transvestites and Transsexuals: Toward a Theory of Cross-Gender Behavior.* (N. Y.: Plenum Press, 1988). Cf. Richard F. Doctor, "Dimensions of Transvestism and Transsexualism," *Journal of Psychology & Human Sexuality, 5* (no. 1), 15-37 (1993). Sexologists Bonnie and Vern Bullough followed this usage in their 1997 report of research with 372 adult male crossdressers, of whom they found 11% met this description. See Bonnie Bullough & Vern Bullough, ""Men Who Cross-Dress: A Survey," in B. Bullough, V. L. Bullough, & J. Elias (Eds.), *Gender Blending*, pp. 174-188 (Amherst, NY: Prometheus Books, 1997), p. 184.

[41] Simone de Beauvoir, *The Second Sex* (N. Y.: Penguin Books, 1972), p. 295.

[42] See Maurer, p. 16.

[43] C. Neil Macrae, Alan B. Milne, & Galen V. Bodenhausen, "Stereotypes as Energy-Saving Devices: A Peek Inside the Cognitive Toolbox," *Journal of Personality & Social Psychology, 66* (no. 1), 37-47 (1994). Gender stereotypes are examined more closely in chapters 4, 7, & 10.

[44] J. Z. Rubin, F. J. Provenzano, & Z. Luria, "The Eye of the Beholder: Parents' Views on Sex of Newborns," *American Journal of Orthopsychiatry, 44* (no. 1), 47-55 (1974).

[45] J. A. Will, P. A. Self, & N. Datan, "Maternal Behavior and Perceived Sex of Infant," *American Journal of Orthopsychiatry, 46* (no. 1), 136-139 (1976). Also see Rex E. Culp, Alicia S. Cook, & Patricia C. Housley, "A Comparison of Observed and Reported Adult-Infant Interactions: Effects of Perceived Sex," *Sex Roles, 9* (no. 4), 475-479(1983).

[46] John Money & Anke A. Ehrhardt, *Man and Woman, Boy and Girl* (Baltimore: John Hopkins Univ. Press, 1972).

[47] Marjorie S. Hardy, "The Development of Gender Roles: Societal Influences," in Louis Diamont & Richard D. McAnulty (Eds.), *The Psychology of Sexual Orientation, Behavior, and Identity. A Handbook*, pp.425-443 (Westport, CT: Greenwood Press, 1995), p. 425.

[48] See G. G. Bolich, *Crossdressing in Context, vol. 2: The Context of Transgender Realities* (Raleigh: Psyche's Press, 2007), Q. 21-22.

[49] My view thus varies from those who, like consultant Lisa Maurer ("Transgressing Sex and Gender," p. 16), conceive of gender expression as necessarily congruent with gender experience.

Chapter 2 Notes

[50] Marjorie S. Hardy, "The Development of Gender Roles: Societal Influences," in Louis Diamont & Richard D. McAnulty (Eds.), *The Psychology of Sexual Orientation, Behavior, and Identity. A Handbook*, pp.425-443 (Westport, CT: Greenwood Press, 1995), p. 425.

[51] Elaboration and further substantiation of this contention may be found in G. G. Bolich, *Crossdressing in Context, vol. 1: The Context of Dress and Gender* (Raleigh: Psyche's Press, 2006).

[52] Jessica Xavier, "Introduction," in M. Boenke (Ed.), *Trans Forming Families: Real Stories About Transgendered Loved Ones*, 2nd ed., pp. xii-xiv (New Castle, DE: Oak Knoll Press, 2003), p. xiii.

[53] Sabrina Petra Ramet (Ed.), *Gender Reversals and Gender Cultures* (London: Routledge, 1996), p. 2.

[54] Claudine Griggs, *S/He: Changing Sex and Changing Clothes.* (Oxford: Berg Publishing Ltd., 1998), p. 1.

[55] Linda B. Gallahan, "Research and Conceptual Approaches to the Understanding of Gender," in M. Biaggio & M. Hersen (Eds.), *Issues in the Psychology of Women*, pp. 33-52

(N. Y.: Kluwer Academic, 2000), p. 47. The idea is that biology guides personality rather than culture.

[56] Daly's first book, *The Church and the Second Sex* (Boston: Beacon Press, 1968) appeared at the beginning of the second wave of feminism. Her critique of sexism within Christianity was furthered in *Beyond God the Father* (Boston: Beacon Press, 1973), which coincided with the full blossoming of second wave feminism in the mid-1970s. Near the end of that decade she published *Gyn/Ecology. The Metaethics of Radical Feminism* (Boston: Beacon Press, 1978), a breakthrough approach which led to perhaps her most important philosophical statement, *Pure Lust. Elemental Feminist Philosophy* (Boston: Beacon Press, 1984). Daly's feminism is more than intellectual exercise; in 1999 she was forcibly 'retired' by Boston College because of how she implemented her philosophy in her teaching practices.

[57] The critical period for this development has been dated at c. 1885-1910. See Robert A Nye (Ed.), *Sexuality* (N. Y.: Oxford Univ. Press, 1999), esp. pp. 115-121, which collects together excerpts from important primary sources.

[58] Michel Foucault locates the transition in Western culture from the 17th century through the Victorian Age (19th century) down into the medicalization of sex in the late 19th-early 20th century. He views the Victorian period as one in which sexuality became more discussed in a particular way, one designed to control it. Science medicalized it and turned certain behaviors into scientifically classified illnesses. See *La Volonté de savoir Vol. 1 of Histoire de la sexualité* (1976). Trans. Robert Hurley as *The History of Sexuality Volume 1: An Introduction* (NY: Pantheon, 1978; also, Vintage Books, 1990). On medicine's pathological approach to sex, see pp. 54-56; on the medicalization of sex, see pp. 117-119. The modern Western emphasis on *whom* we have sex with rather than on *what* we do during sex stands in contrast with previous centuries of sexual values in the West. The pre-modern Western stress on sexual acts rather than sexual objects also may have pertained to the East. Sam Winter of the University of Hong Kong, writing about sex and gender in classical China, has contended that "a Chinese male's sexuality was defined less in terms of whom he had sex with (man or woman) than what he did during sex (acting as inserter or insertee)." See Sam Winter, *'Country Report': Hong Kong: Social and Cultural Issues* (2002). Accessed online at http://web.hku.hk/~sjwinter/Transgender ASIA/country_report_hk_social.htm.

[59] See, for example, John R. Clarke, *Looking at Lovemaking: Constructions of Sexuality in Roman Art, 100 B.C.-A.D. 250* (Berkeley: Univ. of California Press, 1998). Clarke, an art historian, shows how through their artistic depictions the ancients viewed sexual behavior in many ways, with variety of both 'objects' and 'aims' (to use Freud's terms) apparent. They were *not* focused on sexual activity for procreation—though they did not ignore that aspect—and they did not conceive of sex as 'sin.'

[60] Angus McLaren, *Twentieth-Century Sexuality. A History* (Oxford: Blackwell, 1999), p. 90.

[61] Ibid.

[62] Robert A. Nye, "Honor, Impotence, and Male Sexuality in Nineteenth-Century French Medicine," *French Historical Studies, 16* (no. 1), 48-71 (1989), p. 48.

[63] Numerous instances of this desire could be made, but the point is sufficiently illustrated by the persistent desire to explain homosexuality or transsexualism as hormones gone awry, or otherwise due to an 'unnatural' biology.

[64] The dubious heritage of this approach is the American Psychiatric Association's *Diagnostic and Statistical Manual of Mental Disorders*, now in its 4th edition. For an examination of this work, see Herb Kutchins & Stuart A. Kirk, *Making Us Crazy: DSM: The Psychiatric Bible and the Creation of Mental Disorders* (N.Y.: Free Press, 1997); with reference to issues of sex and gender, cf. chs. 3 and 5. Also see Stuart A. Kirk & Herb Kutchins, *The Selling of DSM. The Rhetoric of Science in Psychiatry* (N. Y.: Aldine de Gruyter, 1992). Cf. Paula J. Caplan, *They Say You're Crazy. How the World's Most Powerful Psychiatrists Decide Who's Normal* (N.Y.: Perseus Books, 1995). Also see Rachel Cooper, "What is Wrong with the DSM?" *History of Psychiatry, 15* (no. 1), 15-25 (2004). Finally, cf. Karen Eriksen & Victoria E. Kress, *Beyond the DSM Story. Ethical Quandaries, Challenges, and Best Practices* (Thousand Oaks, CA: Sage, 2005).

[65] Toril Moi, *What Is a Woman? And Other Essays* (N. Y.: Oxford Univ. Press, 1999), p. 21.

[66] Ibid, p. 22.

[67] Ibid, p. 22, fn. 29. Moi cites Money's complaint in 1985 that Robert Stoller's articulation of gender vocabulary not only was contrary to his own, but that Stoller's usage led to highly undesirable consequences: "Its outcome was to restore the metaphysical partitioning of body and mind. Sex was ceded to biology. Gender was ceded to psychology and social science. The ancient regime was restored!"

[68] John Money, "Gender Role, Gender Identity, Core Gender Identity," *The Journal of the American Academy of Psychoanalysis and Dynamic Psychiatry, 1*, 397-402 (1973), p. 397. Cf. John Money, J. G. Hampson, & J. L. Hampson, "An Examination of Some Basic Sexual Concepts: The Evidence of Human Hermaphroditism," *Bulletin of Johns Hopkins Hospital, 97*, 301-319 (1955), p. 302. Also see by the same authors, "Hermaphroditism: Recommendations Concerning Assignment of Sex, Change of Sex, and Psychological Management," *Bulletin of Johns Hopkins Hospital, 97*, 284-300 (1955).

[69] Robert J. Stoller, "A Contribution to the Study of Gender Identity," *International Journal of Psychoanalysis, 45*, 220-226 (1964). Also see Stoller, "A Contribution to the Study of Gender Identity: Follow-Up," *The International Journal of Psycho-Analysis, 60*, 433-441 (1979). Cf. Moi, *What Is a Woman?*, p. 22. Lynne Segal writes, "It was what Robert Stoller saw as the plight of transsexuals—desiring bodily modifications to align their genitals with their sense of self—which had prompted him to promulgate the notion of 'gender' as the core catrgory of identity." *Why Feminism? Gender, Psychology, Politics* (N. Y.: Columbia Univ. Press, 1999), p. 60.

[70] Moi, *What Is a Woman?*, p. 22 fn. 29.

[71] For example, Stoller in the first volume of his *magnum opus* on sex and gender early on declares that gender "has cultural or psychological rather than biological connotations." See Robert J. Stoller, *Sex and Gender. The Development of Masculinity and Femininity*, vol. 1 (N. Y. : Science House, 1968), p. 9. This is the portion of his work Moi cites (p. 22) in *What Is a Woman?*

[72] Robert J. Stoller, *Sex and Gender. The Development of Masculinity and Femininity* (London: Karnac Books, 1984 reprint of N. Y.: Science House, 1968, 1974), p. 72.

[73] Robert J. Stoller, *Presentations of Gender* (New Haven: Yale Univ. Press, 1985), p. 11f.

[74] Ralph V. Exline, "Explorations in the Process of Person Perception: Visual Interaction in Relation to Competition, Sex, and Need for Affiliation," *Journal of Personality, 31* (no. 1), 1-20 (1963).

[75] Kathleen Brehony, Mark Augustine, Dave Barachie, Beth Miller, & William Woodhouse, "Psychological Androgyny and Social Conformity." Paper presented at the 85th annual convention of the American Psychological Association, San Francisco (1977). The subjects had been typed using the Bem Sex Role Inventory and were compared in a social conformity paradigm involving 160 trials.

[76] Rhoda K. Unger, "Toward a Redefinition of Sex and Gender," *American Psychologist, 34* (no. 11), 1085-1094 (1979).

[77] Despite the flow of our story, which depicts the ebb of essentialism as alternative perspectives gained dominance, this traditional perspective has never gone away. It remains dominant in society at large and has new academic champions, especially in evolutionary psychology (see chapter 9).

[78] Varda Burstyn, *Rites of Men* (Toronto: Univ. of Toronto Press, 1999), p. 120. Burstyn was speaking with reference to sports, but her remark aptly addresses the broader scene.

[79] Jane Pilcher & Imelda Whelehan, *50 Key Concepts in Gender Studies* (Thousand Oaks, CA: Sage Publications, 2004), p. 146, date its beginning point to 1968. 'Second wave feminism' is also sometimes referred to as 'modernist feminism.'

[80] See the succinct review of developments vis-à-vis feminism in Nancy Shoemaker, *Clearing a Path: Theorizing the Past in Native American Studies* (N. Y.: Routledge, 2002), p. 77. Shoemaker contends, "This attempt to separate gender and sex first developed in Western feminist writings in the 1960s as a means of escaping the biologism of early-20th-century physiologists who viewed femaleness as an inherent quality of the female body and argued from these biological assumptions concerning proper behaviors and roles of women."

[81] Judith Baxter, *Positioning Gender in Discourse: A Feminist Methodology* (N. Y.: Palgrave Macmillan, 2003), p. 4.

[82] Though Freud cheerfully confessed that neither he nor other men understood women, that did not slow him down from attempting to explain their psychological development. See, for example, his 1925 essay "Some Psychological Consequences of the Anatomical Distinction Between the Sexes," or his 1931 paper "Female Sexuality," both included in Sigmund Freud, *Sexuality and the Psychology of Love*, edited by P. Rieff (N.Y.: Collier Books, 1963). Early women psychodynamic writers who made important contributions on feminine psychology include Clara M. Thompson, *On Women*, edited by M. R. Green (N. Y.: Meridan, 1986 printing of 1964 Mentor ed.)[see chapter 10], and Karen Horney, *Feminine Psychology*, edited by H. Kelman (N. Y.: W. W. Norton, 1967).

[83] Nancy Chodorow says of the late 1960s-early 1970s that, "The dominant feminist stance during this period, beginning with Betty Friedan, and continuing with major statements by Firestone, Millett, Weisstein, and others, was an enormous hostility to and condemnation of Freud. Freudian theory and therapy were taken as major factors in women's oppression." *Feminism and Psychoanalytic Theory* (New Haven, CT: Yale Univ. Press, 1989), p. 165.

[84] See, for example, Jean Strousse (Ed.), *Women & Analysis. Dialogues on Psychoanalytic Views of Femininity* (N. Y.: Grossman Publishers, 1974).

[85] Leslie C. Bell, "Psychoanalytic Theories of Gender," in A. H. Eagly, A. E. Beall, & R. J. Sternberg (Eds.), *Psychology of Gender*, 2nd ed., pp. 145-168 (N. Y.: Guilford, 2004), p. 152.

[86] Ibid, p. 173: "Differing relational capacities and forms of identification prepare women and men to assume the adult gender roles which situate women primarily within the sphere of reproduction in a sexually unequal society."

[87] Chodorow, *Feminism and Psychoanalytic Theory*, p. 168.

[88] Ibid, p. 184. Chodorow (p. 187) maintains that "the object-relations perspective in particular moves radically away from essentialist views of gender toward a view that constructs feminine and masculine personality and male dominance in a contingent, relationally constructed context."

[89] Ibid, pp. 185-187.

[90] Ibid, p. 187.

[91] Ibid, pp. 187-189.

[92] See, for example, Vivian Gornick & Barbara K. Moran (Eds.), *Woman in Sexist Society: Studies in Power and Powerlessness* (N. Y.: Basic Books, 1971). Also see Michelle Zimbalist Rosaldo & Louise Lamphere (Eds.), *Women, Culture and Society* (Stanford: Stanford Univ. Press, 1974).

[93] Sandra L. Bem, *An Unconventional Family* (New Haven, CT: Yale Univ. Press, 1998).

[94] Sandra L. Bem, "The Measurement of Psychological Androgyny," *Journal of Consulting and Clinical Psychology, 42*, 155-162 (1974). Also see her "Probing the Promise of Androgyny," in A. G. Kaplan & J. P. Bean (Eds.), *Beyond Sex-Role Stereotypes: Readings Toward a Psychology of Androgyny* (Boston: Little Brown, 1976). The BSRI is further described in chapter 12.

[95] In 1995, Bem would write, "At the center of all my previous work on gender and sexuality has been the goal of shrinking both the relevance and the reach of the male-female dichotomy by trying, insofar as possible, to make it as minimal a presence in human social and psychological life as, say, eye color or foot size." Sandra L. Bem, "Dismantling Gender Polarization and Compulsory Heterosexuality: Should We Turn the Volume Down or Up?" in R. Heasley & B. Crane, *Sexual Lives: A Reader on the Theories and Realities of Human Sexualities*, pp. 253-261 (N. Y.: McGraw-Hill, 2003), p. 253. (This work was originally published in *Journal of Sex Research, 32* (no. 4), 329-334 (1995).)

[96] The vampirism of essentialism metaphorically captures the idea that masculine privilege in patriarchal systems depends for its life on sucking the life out of other genders.

[97] Ann Oakley, *Sex, Gender and Society* (London: Temple Smith, 1972). Also see *Becoming a Mother* (Oxford: Martin Robertson, 1979).

[98] Gayle Rubin, "The Traffic of Women: Notes on the Political Economy of Sex," in L. Nicholson (Ed.), *The Second Wave: A Reader in Feminist Theory*, pp. 27-62 (N. Y.: Routledge, 1997).

[99] Gayle Rubin interviewed by Judith Butler, "Sexual Traffic," in M. Merck, N. Segal, & E. Wright (Eds.), *Coming Out of Feminism?* pp. 36-73 (Malden, MA: Blackwell, 1998) p. 38f.

[100] The nature, role, and importance of Women's Studies is further examined in chapter 11.

[101] Pilcher & Whelehan, p. ix.

[102] The Men's Movement is elaborated upon in chapter 10.

[103] Chris Beasley, *Gender & Sexuality: Critical Theories, Critical Thinkers* (Thousand Oaks, CA.: Sage, 2005), p. 12.

[104] Ibid, p. 169. Third wave feminism will be discussed more fully in chapter 11.

[105] Carol Sorisio, "A Tale of Two Feminisms: Power and Victimization in Contemporary Feminist Debate," in L. Heywood & J. Drake (Eds.), *Third Wave Agenda: Being Feminist, Doing Feminism*, pp. 134-167 (Minneapolis: Univ. of Minnesota Press, 1997), p. 142. Sorisio, an English literature scholar, hardly ignores gender, though. Her own studies focus on both gender and race.

[106] Sara Mills, *Gender and Politeness* (N. Y.: Cambridge Univ. Press, 2003), p. 239. See her "Post-feminist Text Analysis," in M. J. Toolan (Ed.), *Critical Discourse Analysis: Critical Concepts in Linguistics*, vol. 4, pp. 202-223 (N. Y.: Routledge, 2002), originally published under the same title in *Language and Literature, 7* (no. 3), 235-253 (1998).

[107] "After well over fifteen years of debate on the essentialist/constructionist divide, we can see that the constructionist paradigm has largely carried the day, at least within intellectual circles. It has not, however, become part of 'popular knowledge', that is, of the people at large. . . ." Judith Schufy, "Hidden from History? Homosexuality and the Historical Sciences," in T. Sandfort, J. Schuyf, I. W. Duyvendak, & J. Weeks (Eds.), *Lesbian and Gay Studies: An Introductory, Interdisciplinary Approach*, pp. 61-80 (Thousand Oaks, CA: Sage, 2000), p. 65.

[108] Liam O'Dowd, "Constructionism, Social," in R. L. Miller & J. D. Brewer (eds.), *The A-Z of Social Research: A Dictionary of Key Social Science Research Concepts*, pp. 41-43 (Thousand Oaks, CA: Sage, 2003).

[109] Mary Gergen & Kenneth J. Gergen, "Introduction," in M. Gergen & K. J. Gergen (Eds.), *Social Construction: A Reader*, pp. 2-6 (Thousand Oaks, CA: Sage, 2003), p. 2.

[110] Stevi Jackson & Sue Scott, "Introduction," in S. Jackson & S. Scott (Eds.), *Gender: A Sociological Reader*, pp. 1-26 (N. Y.: Routledge, 2002), p. 1f.

[111] Nikki Sullivan rightly notes the use of the word is varied, and that even when applied to homosexuals it is not always negative. But the strongly censorious nature of the term when used as an epithet is what most of us are most aware about the word. See Nikki Sullivan, *A Critical Introduction to Queer Theory* (N. Y.: New York Univ. Press, 2003), p. v.

[112] Beasley, p. 164. See Teresa de Lauretis, "Queer Theory: Lesbian and Gay Sexualities: An Introduction," *differences: A Journal of Feminist Cultural Studies, 3,* iii-xviii (1991).

[113] Cf. Pilcher & Whelehan, p. 129. The appropriation of a derogatory term by the group against which it is directed has been used successfully in the past, most notably by Christians. The word 'Christian,' meaning 'little messiah,' was meant as a term of derision by the enemies of the early Christians, who mocked their efforts to offer salvation to the world.

[114] GenderPAC is the 'Gender Public Advocacy Coalition.' Their website may be found at http://www.gpac.org/.

[115] Riki Wilchins, *Queer Theory, Gender Theory: An Instant Primer* (L.A.: Alyson Publications, 2004), p. 5.

[116] David M. Halperin, *Saint Foucault: Towards a Gay Hagiography* (N. Y.: Oxford Univ. Press, 1995), p. 62.

[117] Michel Foucault, *The History of Sexuality: An Introduction* (N. Y.: Pantheon Books, 1978). This first volume of three published is the most often referenced. It is also known by the title *The History of Sexuality: The Will to Know.* The subsequent volumes are titled *The History of Sexuality: The Use of Pleasure* and *The History of Sexuality: The Care of the Self.*

[118] Judith Butler, *Gender Trouble: Feminism and the Subversion of Identity* (N. Y.: Routledge, 1990). Note that 'performativity' is not identical to 'performance.' Butler states that the latter presumes a subject while the former disputes even the notion of 'subject.' That which is performative brings into being what it speaks of as it speaks it.

[119] Ibid, pp. 78.

[120] Judith Butler, "Restaging the Universal: Hegemony and the Limits of Formalism," in J. Butler, E. Laclau, & S. Zizek (Eds.), *Contingency, Hegemony, Universality: Contemporary Dialogues on the Left,* pp. 11-43 (N. Y.: Verso, 2000) p. 29.

[121] Judith Butler, "Critically Queer," in S. Phelan (Ed.), *Playing with Fire: Queer Politics, Queer Theories,* pp. 11-30 (N. Y.: Routledge, 1997), p. 17. Cf. Judith Butler, *Bodies That Matter: On the Discursive Limits of Sex* (N. Y.: Routledge, 1993).

Chapter 3 Notes

[122] Gerda Siann, *Gender, Sex and Sexuality: Contemporary Psychological Perspectives* (London: Taylor & Rancis, 1994), p. vi.

[123] Remember when President Clinton said, "I did not have sex with that woman"? Was he telling the truth? If we interpret the word 'sex' to mean any sexual activity at all (e.g., kissing or fondling), then clearly not. But if we interpret the word 'sex' to mean what most Americans mean—sexual intercourse—then our judgment on its veracity may change. This one example can be multiplied many times and helps explain why the

word today is so problematic. We find the difficulty also in scholarly work. When pollsters ask how many partners a person has had sex with, we consistently find men claiming more partners than women do, and to such a degree the numbers just don't add up. Assuming neither group is lying or exaggerating, the explanation may lie in gender differences as to how 'sex' is understood. What constitutes 'sex' or a 'sexual partner' may be different for most women than what those words mean to most men.

[124] Like it or not—and I don't—this is the notion of sex at present. I think a more accurate definition of sex is "the differentiation of human beings along a range of genital presentations where a presumed relation to reproductive function circumscribes the poles." This definition overcomes a rigid binary system while recognizing both that reproduction cannot be entirely severed from defining sex and that the points along the continuum most associated with reproduction are the poles of male and female. However, this definition limits the role of reproduction and identifies it as having an artificial component (the occasionally inaccurate presumption of reproductive capability based on a certain presentation of genitalia). Further, it legitimizes points along the continuum and offers no names for any points, including the poles, thus allowing for either the retention of existing terms (male, female, intersex) or the creation of new ones.

[125] As we saw in the previous chapter, social constructionists contend even sex is a social construction. See, for example, the 1970s essay by sociologist Stevi Jackson, "The Social Construction of Female Sexuality," in S. Jackson & S. Scott (Eds.), *Feminism and Sexuality: A Reader*, pp. 62-73 (N. Y.: Columbia Univ., 1996). Also see Liz Stanley, "Should 'Sex' Really Be 'Gender'—Or 'Gender' Really Be 'Sex'," in S. Jackson & S. Scott (Eds.), *Gender: A Sociological Reader*, pp. 31-41 (N. Y.: Routledge, 2002).

[126] 'Karyotype' is a medical term meaning the total portrait of the chromosomes in an individual's body cell. It includes the number, size, form and arrangement of chromosomes within the nucleus. See *The Mosby Medical Encyclopedia* (N. Y.: New American Library, 1985), p. 408.

[127] Moira Gatens, *Imaginary Bodies: Ethics, Power and Corporeality* (London: Routledge, 1996), p. 9.

[128] A consequence of this view is that sexual orientation becomes a junction for sex and gender; masculine male needs feminine female in heterosexual desire and behavior. Another consequence, then, is that homosexuality becomes not only unnecessary, but illegitimate. Corollary to this outcome, the construction of heterosexual masculinity incorporates homophobia.

[129] Myra J. Hird, "Naturally Queer," *Feminist Theory, 5* (no. 1), 85-89 (2004), p. 85.

[130] Joan Roughgarden, "Evolution and the Embodiment of Gender," *GLQ: A Journal of Lesbian and Gay Studies, 10*, 287-291 (2004), p. 289.

[131] Ibid.

[132] Lisa Maurer, "Transgressing Sex and Gender: Deconstruction Zone Ahead?" *SIECUS Report, 28* (no. 1), 1421 (1999, Oct./Nov.), p. 14.

[133] Anne Fausto-Sterling, *Sexing the Body: Gender Politics and the Construction of Sexuality* (N.Y.: Basic Books, 2000), p. 3. The International Olympic Committee (IOC) adopted chromosomal testing in 1968, which continued through 1998.

[134] Ibid, p. 4.

[135] Alice D. Dreger, (1998). *Hermaphrodites and the Medical Invention of Sex* (Cambridge: Harvard Univ. Press, 1998).

[136] Ibid. See especially p. 190ff. Please note, though, the encouraging signs that things are changing among these professionals. Cf. Anne Fausto-Sterling, "The Five Sexes, Revisited," *The Sciences, 40* (no. 4), 18-23 (2000, July/Aug.).

[137] Susan J. Bradley, Gillian D. Oliver, Avinoam B. Chernick, & Kenneth J. Zucker, "Experiment of Nurture: Ablatio Penis at 2 Months, Sex Reassignment at 7 Months, and a Psychosexual Follow-up in Young Adulthood," *Pediatrics, 102* (no. 1), e. 9 (1998). Accessed online at http://www.pediatrics.org/ cgi/content/full/102/1/e9.

[138] Suzanne J. Kessler, *Lessons from the Intersexed.* (Piscataway, NJ: Rutgers Univ. Press, 1998), p. 12.

[139] Ibid, p. 12f.

[140] Martine Rothblatt, *The Apartheid of Sex: A Manifesto on the Freedom of Gender* (N. Y.: Crown Publishers, 1995).

[141] *Intersex FAQ (Frequently Asked Questions)* (2003-2004). Accessed on-line at http://www.intersexinitiative.org/articles/intersexfaq.html.

[142] Ibid. Cf. the 'Patient-Centered Model' set forth by the Intersex Society of North America, in its FAQ section, 'What does ISNA recommend for children with intersex?' (ISNA, 1993-2005), accessed online at http://www. isna.org/faq/patientcentered.

[143] The idea of 'opposition' will occupy us in chapter 5.

[144] See Robert W. Connell, *Masculinities* (Berkeley: Univ. of California Press, 1995).

[145] While virtually every part of our dialog entails recognition of a gender hierarchy, we shall give it special attention later, especially in terms of gender relations (chapter 5).

[146] If masculinity is all that ultimately matters, it doesn't really matter what you call anything else. So there is little logical pressure to differentiate beyond two genders: masculinity and 'femininity' (i.e., non-masculinity, which can include all transgender and third gender alternatives).

[147] Vern Bullough, *Cross Dressing, Sex, and Gender* (Phila.: Univ. of Pennsylvania Press, 1993), p. 174.

[148] Fausto-Sterling, *Sexing the Body,* p. 3.

[149] Vern L. Bullough & Bonnie Bullough, *Crossdressing, Sex, Gender.* (Phila.: Univ. of Pennsylvania Press, 1993), p. 5.

[150] Sigmund Freud, *New Introductory Lectures on Psychoanalysis,* translated by James Strachey (N. Y.: W. W. Norton, 1965), p. 113. It is worth noting that Freud grasps better than most how problematic our gender notions are. In a 1915 footnote to his seminal work on human sexuality he comments, "It is essential to understand clearly that the concepts of 'masculine' and 'feminine,' whose meaning seems so unambiguous to ordinary people, are among the most confused that occur in science." See Sigmund Freud,

Three Essays on the Theory of Sexuality, translated by James Strachey (N. Y.: Basic Books, 1962), p. 85, n. 1.

[151] The process of gender socialization is the focus of the next chapter.

[152] Thomas Eckes & Hanns M. Trautner, "Developmental Social Psychology of Gender: An Integrative Framework," in T. Eckes (Ed.), *The Developmental Social Psychology of Gender*, pp. 332 (Mahwah, NJ: Lawrence Erlbaum, 2000), p. 9f.

[153] Freud, p. 114. Freud believes that masculinity and femininity are constructs that no one science is adequate to explain. He examines biology, psychology and psycho-analysis, concluding even for the last a limited perception and one still dependent on a relatively straightforward connection of gender to sex.

[154] Ibid.

[155] Indeed, self-designations such as 'tomboy' may even be presented as third gender alternatives by children. Consider, for example, the case of elementary school-aged Jodie, who after remarking that all the girls in her class "act all stupid and girlie," declared this judgment did not apply to her "cos I'm not a girl, I'm a tomboy." However, exactly what Jodie intended is unclear. She succeeded in persuading two male classmates to identify her as a boy. The researcher concluded Jodie appeared to be operating at the boundary line between masculinity and femininity—a justifiable interpretation where no other gender alternatives are allowed recognition. See Diane Reay, "'Spice Girls', 'Nice Girls', 'Girlies', and 'Tomboys': Gender Discourses, Girls' Cultures and Femininities in the Primary Classroom," *Gender and Education, 13* (no. 2), 153-166 (2001), p. 161f.

[156] Thomas Laqueur, *Making Sex. Body and Gender from the Greeks to Freud* (Cambridge: Harvard Univ. Press, 1990). Although not without his critics, Laqueur has been immensely influential in the matter of modern historical changes in our perception. This is considered a truly seminal work in the field.

[157] Helen E. Fisher, *Anatomy of Love. The Natural History of Monogamy, Adultery, and Divorce* (N. Y.: W. W. Norton, 1992), p. 191.

[158] Ibid, pp. 191-194; the quote is from p. 194.

[159] Shawn Meghan Burn, *The Social Psychology of Gender* (N. Y.: McGraw-Hill, 1996), p. 139, with references to several studies.

[160] Patrice L. Engle & Cynthia Breaux, "Fathers' Involvement with Children: Perspectives from Developing Countries," *Social Policy Report, XII* (no. 1), 1-21 (1998), p. 7.

[161] A nice summary on the importance of fathers and their functions within the family, with an excellent bibliography, may be obtained at the Civitas website in the factsheet, *How Do Fathers Fit In?* (Civitas, 2001 (Dec.)), accessed online at http://www.civitas.org.uk/hwu/FatherFactsheet.pdf. Civitas: The Institute for the Study of Civil Society, is based in London, England. For a more complete treatment, see psychiatrist Kyle D. Pruett, *The Nurturing Father* (N. Y.: Warner Books, 1987). Also see his *Fatherneed. Why Father Care Is as Essential as Mother Care for Your Child* (N. Y.: Broadway Books, 2000).

[162] Joel Arnoff & William D. Crano, "A Re-examination of the Cross-Cultural Principles of Task Segregation and Sex Role Differentiation in the Family," *American Socio-*

logical Review, 40, 12-20 (1975). Also see William D. Crano & Joel Arnoff, "A Cross-Cultural Study of Expressive and Instrumental Role Complementarity in the Family," *American Sociological Review, 43*, 463-471 (1978).

[163] George P. Murdock, "Comparative Data on the Division of Labor by Sex," *Social Forces, 15*, 551-553 (1937). Murdock reports that carrying water is usually or always done by women in 126 societies, compared to only 7 where that is true of men. Gathering fuel like firewood is usually or always done by women in 108 societies, compared to just 23 where it is mostly men's work. Carrying loads in general is principally women's work in 77 societies, compared to 18 where it is largely a masculine task.

[164] See Kenneth C. W. Kammeyer, George Ritzer, & Norman R. Yetman, *Sociology. Experiencing Changing Societies*, 5th ed. (Boston: Allyn & Bacon, 1992), p. 338; the reference to the women carrying up to 70% of their body weight they cite from the report by Boyce Rensberger, "African Women Save Energy Using Head for Heavy Loads," *Washington Post* (1986, Feb. 23).

[165] George P. Murdock, *Culture and Society* (Pittsburgh: Univ. of Pittsburgh Press, 1965), p. 451.

[166] Murdock, "Comparative Data on the Division of Labor by Sex."

[167] However, changes in sex-linked divisions of labor in our society, as well as modifications in gender expectations and roles, have been highly selective and continue to serve the essential distinction preserved in our gender order. That is why, for example, women continue to be paid less than men for equal responsibility and work; their sex and gender status alone justify the pay inequity in our gender order.

[168] "Women's responsibility for children in the context of the nuclear family is an important buttress for a male-dominated society." M. Rivka Polatnick, "Why Men Don't Rear Children," in A. Minas, *Gender Basics. Feminist Perspectives on Women and Men*, pp. 500-507 (Belmont, CA: Wadsworth, 1993), p. 504.

[169] This way of sequencing things gives rise to categorizing sexual desire in one of two, or three orientations (heterosexual, homosexual, and perhaps bisexual), with the same hierarchical structure: heterosexuality on top. *If* sex is bipolar, *if* gender is bipolar, *then* sexual desire must be bipolar. *If* male supercedes female, *if* masculinity has priority over femininity, *then* heterosexuality must have precedence over homosexuality. Of course, this logic has so many holes no one can take it seriously. For example, it is perhaps more logical to conclude as the ancient Greeks did that if maleness and masculinity are preeminent, then male homosexuality must be the highest form of desire.

[170] Maurer, p. 14.

Chapter 4 Notes

[171] Sharon Hays, *The Cultural Contradictions of Motherhood* (New Haven: Yale Univ. Press, 1996), p. 222 n.2.

[172] Carole R. Beal, *Boys and Girls: The Development of Gender Roles* (N. Y.: McGraw-Hill, 1994), p. 45.

[173] Marjorie S. Hardy, "The Development of Gender Roles: Societal Influences," in L. Diamont & R. D. McAnulty (Eds.), *The Psychology of Sexual Orientation, Behavior, and Identity. A Handbook*, pp.425-443 (Westport, CT: Greenwood Press, 1995), pp. 427-435.

[174] Ibid, p. 437.

[175] Kenneth C. W. Kemmeyer, George Ritzer, & Norman R. Yetman, *Sociology. Experiencing Changing Societies*, 5th ed. (Boston: Allyn & Bacon, 1992), p. 343.

[176] See Lois W. Hoffman, "Changes in Family Roles, Socialization, and Sex Differences," *American Psychologist, 32*, 644-657 (1977). Also see Susan Grieshaber, "Constructing the Gendered Infant," in N. Yelland (Ed.), *Gender in Early Childhood*, pp. 13-35 (N. Y.: Routledge, 1998), p. 24f. The most notorious instance of this preference may be India, where prenatal testing is not infrequently employed to determine if the fetus is male or female, with female fetuses aborted. However, not all studies have found this preference for boys to be the case. A study of expectant mothers in Jamaica, for example, reported that 78.7% specified a preference for a girl for a first child. See Gwendolyn Sargent & Michael Harris, "Bad Boys and Good Girls: The Implications of Gender Ideology for Child Health in Jamaica," in N. Scheper-Hughes & C. Sargent (Eds.), *Small Wars: The Cultural Politics of Childhood*, pp. 202-227(Berkeley: Univ. of California Press, 1998), p. 205.

[177] As a part of a comprehensive survey conducted in 1970, questions were asked concerning any sign while growing up that either parent would have preferred the respondent to have been born the opposite sex. When it came to the behavior of fathers, four times as many females (1.5%) as males (0.4%) affirmed that such a sign included his preference in how he wanted his child to dress.[177] Yet when it came to the behavior of mothers, more than twice as many males (1.6%) as females (0.7%) affirmed that such a sign included her preference in how she wanted her child to dress.[177] For those answering affirmatively in either scenario, significant percentages of both males and females reported that this continued at least into adolescence. See Albert D. Klassen, Colin J. Williams, & Eugene E. Levitt, *Sex and Morality in the U. S.,* H. J. O'Gorman, Ed. (Middletown, CT: Wesleyan Univ. Press, 1989), p. 382.

[178] See G. G. Bolich, *Crossdressing in Context, vol. 2: The Context of Transgender Realities* (Raleigh, NC: Psyche's Press, 2007), Q. 22.

[179] Sigmund Freud, *Introductory Lectures on Psycho-Analysis*, translated by James Strachey (N. Y.: W. W/ Norton, 1966), pp. 410-420. The remarks in this volume come from Freud's 1915-1917 lectures. Later essays on the same subject include "The Passing of the Oedipus Complex" (1924), and "Some Psychological Consequences of the Anatomical Distinction Between the Sexes" (1926), both included in Sigmund Freud, *Sexuality and the Psychology of Love*, edited by P. Rieff (N. Y.: Collier, 1963).

[180] Lawrence Kohlberg, "A Cognitive-Developmental Analysis of Children's Sex-Role Concepts and Attitudes," in E. E. Maccoby (Ed.), *The Development of Sex Differences*, pp. 82-173 (Stanford, CA: Stanford Univ. Press, 1966). Kohlberg's ideas will be explored in chapter 7.

[181] Kay Bussey & Albert Bandura, "Social Cognitive Theory of Gender Development and Differentiation," *Psychological Review, 106*, 676-713 (1999). Also see Albert Bandura, *Social Foundations of Thought and Action: A Social Cognitive Theory* (Englewood

Cliffs, NJ: Prentice-Hall, 1986). For a multicultural study of this matter, see Hiroko Shimoda & Soili Keskinen, "Ideal Gender Identity Related to Parent Images and Locus of Control: Jungian and Social Learning Perspectives," *Psychological Reports, 94* (no. 3), 1187-1201 (2004). This study looked at Finnish and Japanese cultures.

[182] Michael L. Slaykin, "Gender Schematization in Adolescents: Differences Based on Rearing in Single-Parent and Intact Families," *Journal of Divorce and Remarriage, 34* (nos. 3/4), 137-149 (2001).

[183] Andrée Pomerleau, Daniel Bolduc, Gérard Malcuit, & Louise Cossette, "Pink or Blue: Environmental Gender Stereotypes in the First Two Years of Life," *Sex Roles. A Journal of Research, 22* (nos. 5-6), 359-367 (1990).

[184] Emily W. Kane, "'No Way My Boys Are Going to Be Like That!' Parents' Responses to Children's Gender Nonconformity," *Gender & Society, 20* (no. 2), 149-176 (2006), p. 149f.

[185] Spencer E. Cahill, "Fashioning Males and Females. Appearance management and the Social Reproduction of Gender," *Symbolic Interaction, 12* (no. 2), 281-298 (1989), p. 289.

[186] This ratio was a finding of a study spanning 1978-1995 that examined referrals of children to a clinic treating 'Gender Identity Disorder.' Despite the fact that, if anything, the girls referred actually showed more extreme cross-gender behavior, boys were far likelier to be referred. The ratio was 6.6:1, boys to girls. The authors are surely right in viewing this as evidence of cultural factors weighing in. See Kenneth J. Zucker, Susan J. Bradley, & Mohammed Sanikhani, "Sex Differences in Referral Rates of Children with Gender Identity Disorder: Some Hypotheses," *Journal of Abnormal Child Psychology, 25* (no. 3), 217-227 (1997).

[187] Judith R. Harris, *The Nurture Assumption: Why Children Turn Out the Way They Do. Parents Matter Less Than You Think and Peers Matter More* (N. Y.: Free Press, 1998).

[188] See Shelley Marmion & Paula Lundberg-Love, "Learning Masculinity and Femininity: Gender Socialization from Parents and Peers Across the Life Span," in M. A. Paulid (Ed.), *Praeger Guide to the Psychology of Gender*, pp. 1-26 (Westport, CT: Praeger, 2004).

[189] 'Homosociality' is a term introduced to discuss occupational segregation of women; see Jean Lipman-Blumen, "Toward a Homosocial Theory of Sex Roles: An Explanation of the Sex Segregation of Social Institutions," *Signs, 1* (no. 3), 15-31 (1976). Today it is more often applied to adult and especially masculine groups, but the concept fits any gendered group where the interaction is social and not sexual in nature. Also see Suzanna M. Rose, "Same- and Cross-Sex Friendships and the Psychology of Homosociality," *Sex Roles, 12* (nos. 1-2), 63-74 (1985).

[190] On peer groups accentuating gender stereotypes, see Shirley Weitz, *Sex Roles: Biological, Psychological, and Social Foundations* (N. Y.: Oxford Univ. Press, 1977), p. 87.

[191] Eleanor E. Maccoby, "Gender and Group Processes," *Current Directions in Psychological Science, 11* (no. 2), 54-58 (2002), p. 54. Maccoby persistently uses the term 'sex' where most others would use 'gender.' So she refers to 'same-sex' segregation and

groups, where I have rendered 'same-gender' segregation and groups; my changes are to avoid confusion for the uninitiated by retaining consistent usage of the distinct terms.

[192] Ibid, pp. 54-55.

[193] Shannon Wyss, "'This Was My Hell': The Violence Experienced By Gender Non-conforming Youth in US High Schools," *International Journal of Qualitative Education, 17* (no. 5), 709-730 (2004), p. 710. For more information on the experience of transgender individuals in childhood and adolescence, see Bolich, *Crossdressing in Context, vol. 2*, Q. 49.

[194] Maccoby, p. 57, with reference to A. Nicolopoulou, "Worldmaking and Identity Formation in Children's Narrative Play-Acting," in B. Cox & C. Lightfoot (Eds.), *Sociogenic Perspectives in Internalization*, pp. 157-187 (Hillsdale, NJ: Erlbaum, 1997).

[195] A plethora of studies over time shows this tendency. See, for example, the continuing study of this by Myra Sadker and David Sadker. See M. P Sadker & D. M. Sadker, *Teachers, Schools, and Society*, 7th ed. (N. Y.: McGraw-Hill, 2005). For a shorter review, see their "Sexism in the Schoolroom of the '80s," *Psychology Today*, pp. 54-57 (1985, Mar.).

[196] Lenore J. Weitzman, Deborah Eifler, Elizabeth Hokada, & Catherine Ross, "Sexual Socialization in Picture Books for Preschool Children," *American Journal of Sociology, 77* (no. 6), 1125-1150 (1972).

[197] Gwyneth E. Britton, "Danger: State Adopted Texts May Be Hazardous to Our Future," *The Reading Teacher, 29*, 52-58 (1975, Oct.).

[198] Elizabeth Grauerholz & Bernice A. Pescosolido, "Gender Representation in Children's Literature: 1900-1984," *Gender and Society, 3* (no. 1), 113-125 (1989).

[199] Reported in William Kornblum & Joseph Julian, *Social Prblems, 10th* ed. (Upper Saddle River, NJ: Prentice Hall, 2001), p. 300.

[200] Denise M. DeZolt & Stephen H. Hull, "Classroom and School Climate," in J. Worrel (Ed.), *Encyclopedia of Women and Gender*, pp. 257-264 (San Diego, CA: Academic Press, 2001).

[201] Joseph G. Kosciw, *The GLSEN 2001 National School Climate Survey: The School-Related Experiences of Our Nation's Lesbian, Gay, Bisexual and Transgender Youth* (N. Y.: Gay, Lesbian, and Straight Education Network, 2002), p. 11. For more information, see Bolich, *Crossdressing in Context, vol. 2*, Q. 57.

[202] James W. Fowler, *Stages of Faith* (S. F.: Harper & Row, 1981).

[203] Howard Francis Taylor & Margaret L. Andersen, *Sociology: Understanding a Diverse Society* (Belmont, CA: Wadsworth, 2004), p. 353.

[204] For more on religion in society, see G. G. Bolich, B. R. Care, & G. C. Kenney, *Introduction to Religion* (Dubuque, IA: Kendall/Hunt, 1988), pp. 126-162. On the matter of Christianity's relation to authority, see G. G. Bolich, *Authority and the Church* (Washington, D.C.: Univ. Press of America, 1982).

[205] Cf. Taylor & Andersen, p. 354; also see their chapter 17 (pp. 462-493).

206 A full accounting of this may be found in G. G. Bolich, *Crossdressing in Context, vol. 3: The Context of Religion* (forthcoming).

207 Linda Holtzman, *Media Messages: What Film, Television, and Popular Music Teach Us About Race, Class, Gender and Sexual Orientation* (Armonk, NY: M. E. Sharpe, 2000), p. 72.

208 Donald F. Roberts & Ulla Goette Foehr, with Victoria J. Rideout & Mollyanne Brodie, *Kids and Media in America* (N. Y.: Cambridge Univ. Press, 2004), p. 138.

209 Ibid. The researchers calculated from reports by parents and teens that the younger children use media about 3 ½ hours each day, while the older kids use media about 6 ¼ hours a day.

210 Ibid, p. 110.

211 Ibid, p. 74.

212 For the treatment of transgender in theater, television, and film, see Bolich, *Crossdressing in Context, vol. 2*, Q. 29.

213 Nancy J. Chodorow, *The Reproduction of Mothering: Psychoanalysis and the Sociology of Gender* (Berkeley: Univ. of Calif. Press, 1999 updated edition of 1978 ed.), p. 30.

214 Ibid, p. 32.

215 Chodorow (p. 169) summarizes these differences as meaning that while boys grow up defining themselves as more separate and distinct beings, with more rigid ego boundaries, girls ego boundaries prove more flexible and permeable, their experience of themselves as continuous with others and connected to the world. "Thus," she claims, "relational abilities and preoccupations have been extended in women's development and curtailed in men's."

216 Ibid, pp. 57-170 (Part I: The Psychoanalytic Story) with reference to the summary in this paragraph.

217 Ibid, p. 173: "Differing relational capacities and forms of identification prepare women and men to assume the adult gender roles which situate women primarily within the sphere of reproduction in a sexually unequal society."

218 Chodorow, *Feminism and Psychoanalytic Theory*, p. 168.

219 Bussey & Bandura, p. 676.

220 Ibid, p. 685.

221 Ibid.

222 Ibid, p. 685f.; quote is from p. 685. Modeling is elaborated upon pp. 686-689; enactive experience and direct tuition are discussed further on p. 689.

223 Ibid, pp. 689-691; quote is from p. 689.

224 Ibid, pp. 691-694.

225 Ibid, pp. 694-698.

226 Ibid, pp. 698-702.

227 Ibid, pp. 703-704; quote is from p. 703.

228 The notion of bidirectional influencing goes back at least to the late 1960s; see R. Q. Bell, "A Reinterpretation of the Direction of Effects in Studies of Socialization," *Psychological Review, 75* (no. 1), 81-95 (1968). The idea began influencing theory in the 1970s and by the end of the 1990s was being much researched and adopted.

229 I am not the first to use the word 'reciprocal' for such models. See Martha A. Rueter & Rand D. Conger, "Reciprocal Influences Between Parenting and Adolescent Problem-Solving Behavior," *Developmental Psychology, 34* (no. 6), 1470-1482 (1998).

230 Eva M. Pomerantz, Florrie Fei-Yin Ng, & Qian Wang, "Gender Socialization. A Parent x Model," in A. H. Eagly, A. E. Beall, & R. J. Sternberg (Eds.), *Psychology of Gender*, 2nd ed., pp. 120-144 (N. Y.: Guilford, 2004), p. 121. For an example of how this dynamic interaction is related to a specific feature, see Eva M. Pomerantz, Wendy S. Grolnick, & Carrie E. Price, "The Role of Parents in How Children Approach Achievement: A Dynamic Process Perspective," in A. J. Elliot & C. S. Dweck (Eds.), *Handbook of Competence and Motivation*, pp. 259-278 (N. Y.: Guilford, 2005). Also see Eva M. Pomerantz & M. M. Eaton, "Maternal Intrusive Support in the Academic Context: Transactional Socialization Processes," *Developmental Psychology, 37* (no. 2), 174-186 (2001).

231 Ibid.

232 Terrence P. Thornberry, "Toward an Interactional Theory of Delinquency," *Criminology, 25* (no. 4), 863-891 (1987).

233 Rueter & Conger, p. 1479.

234 Ibid, p. 127.

235 Ibid, p. 132; elaborated pp. 133-136.

236 Ibid, pp. 127-128; cf. p. 134f.

237 Ibid, p. 128f.

238 Alice H. Eagly & V. J. Steffen, "Gender Stereotypes Stem from the Distribution of Women and Men Into Social Roles," *Journal of Personality & Social Psychology, 46*, 735-754 (1984).

239 Margaret Mead, *Sex and Temperament in Three Primitive Societies* (N. Y.: Morrow Quill Paperbacks, 1963 reprint of 1935 ed.), p. 280.

240 Curt Hoffman & Nancy Hurst, "Gender Stereotypes: Perception or Rationalization?" *Journal of Personality & Social Psychology, 58* (no. 2), 197-208 (1990).

241 The conceptualizations of 'masculinity' and 'femininity'—as well as possible other genders—are more closely examined in chapter 10.

242 Jacqueline McGuire, "Gender Stereotypes of Parents with Two Year-olds and Beliefs About Gender Differences in Behavior," *Sex Roles. A Journal of Research, 19* (nos. 3-4), 233-240 (1988).

243 Kay A. Chick, Rose Ann Heilman-Houser, & Maxwell W. Hunter, "The Impact of Child Care on Gender Role Development and Gender Stereotypes," *Early Childhood Education Journal, 29* (no. 3), 149-154 (2002). The researchers noted that while the boys

in their study received more attention from the caregivers than the girls did, the girls were more likely to be reinforced for their dress behavior (p. 151).

[244] Carol Lynn Martin, Carolyn H. Wood, & Jane K. Little, "The Development of Gender Stereotype Components," *Child Development, 61* (no. 6), 18911904 (1990).

[245] Studies focus on how women are disadvantaged by gender stereotypes. This occurs for women regardless of where on the economic ladder they stand. For instance, women in welfare-to-work programs may face gender stereotypes that hardly encourage growth and economic liberation. See Natalie G. Adams & James H. Adams, "'Bad Work Is Better Than No Work': The Gendered Assumptions in Welfare-to-Work Training Programs," *Journal for Critical Education Policy Studies, 4* (no. 1) (2006), accessed online at http:// www.jceps.com/index.php? pageID=article&articleID=61. On a much higher rung, women managers disciplining subordinates are more likely than their male counterparts to be perceived as unfair and ineffective. See Leanne F. Atwater, James A. Carey, & David A. Waldman, "Gender and Discipline in the Workplace: Wait Until Your Father Gets Home," *Journal of Management, 27* (no. 5), 537-561 (2001).

[246] Paul Lester (Ed.), *Images That Injure: Pictorial Stereotypes in the Media* (Westport, CT: Greenwood, 1996). See especially 'Part III. Gender Stereotypes,' pp. 69-106.

[247] Jack Glascock & Catherine Preston-Schreck, "Gender and Racial Stereotypes in Daily Newspaper Comics: A Time Honored Tradition?" *Sex Roles. A Journal of Research, 51* (nos. 7-8), 423-431 (2004).

[248] Macrae, Milne, & Bodenhausen, p. 37.

[249] Leon Festinger, *A Theory of Cognitive Dissonance* (Stanford, CA: Stanford Univ. Press, 1957), p. 3. Also see Leon Festinger, *Conflict, Decision, and Dissonance* (Stanford: Stanford Univ. Press, 1964). Cf. E. Harmon-Jones & J. Mills (Eds.), *Cognitive Dissonance: Progress on a Pivotal Theory in Social Psychology* (Washington, D.C.: American Psychological Association, 1999).

[250] Erving Goffman, *Stigma: Notes on the Management of Spoiled Identity* (N. Y.: Touchstone Books, 1986; original work published 1963), p. 5. Goffman (p. 3) delineates a stigma as "an attribute that is deeply discrediting within a particular social interaction." He distinguishes three types (abominations of the body, blemishes of character, and tribal stigma of race, nation, religion). For more on stereotyping, cognitive dissonance, and stigmatizing in connection to gender nonconformity, see G. G. Bolich, *Crossdressing in Context, vol. 1: The Context of Dress and Gender* (Raleigh, NC: Psyche's Press, 2006), Q. 8.

Chapter 5 Notes

[251] Kate Bornstein, *Gender Outlaw. On Men, Women, and the Rest of Us* (N. Y.: Vintage Books, 1995), p. 127.

[252] The social upheaval of the 1960s, both in regard to race relations and the Women's Movement, brought a creative (and sometimes chaotic) vigor to conversing on all matter of things, including gender in relation to a democratic society.

[253] Chris Beasley, *Gender & Sexuality: Critical Theories, Critical Thinkers* (Thousand Oaks, CA.: Sage, 2005), p. 11.

254 Ibid. He observes this tendency showing itself in such common phrases as 'the opposite sex.'

255 Gayle Rubin, "The Traffic of Women: Notes on the Political Economy of Sex," in L. Nicholson (Ed.), *The Second Wave: A Reader in Feminist Theory*, pp. 27-62 (N. Y.: Routledge, 1997).

256 Ibid, p. 28.

257 Ibid, p. 39.

258 Ibid, p. 58. Later, Rubin amended her position by emphasizing that sex and gender, though related, are not the same and therefore, "they form the basis of two distinct arenas of social practice." See Gayle Rubin, "Thinking Sex: Notes for a Radical Theory of the Politics of Sexuality," in C. S. Vance (Ed.), *Pleasure and Danger: Exploring Female Sexuality*, pp. 267-319 (Boston: Routledge, 1984), p. 308.

259 Albert D. Klassen, Colin J. Williams, & Eugene E. Levitt, *Sex and Morality in the U. S.*, H. J. O'Gorman, Ed. (Middletown, CT: Wesleyan Univ. Press, 1989), p. 272f. Even earlier, anthropologist Margaret Mead also noted how modern cultures are struggling to adapt to the changing economic position of women. See her *Sex and Temperament in Three Primitive Societies* (N. Y.: Morrow Quill Paperbacks, 1963), p. 308. Original work published 1935. These ideas will be explored more fully later in the chapter.

260 On this experiencing and expressing system, and other matters related to dress and gender, see G. G. Bolich, *Crossdressing in Context, vol. 1: The Context of Dress and Gender* (Raleigh, NC: Psyche's Press, 2006).

261 An account of this situation in the United States can be found in G. G. Bolich, *Crossdressing in Context, vol. 2: The Context of Transgender Reality* (Raleigh, NC: Psyche's Press, 2007), Q. 32.

262 The role of dress in relation to gender is explored in chapter 14.

263 Marjorie Garber writes, "For me, therefore, one of the most important aspects of crossdressing is the way in which it offers a challenge to easy notions of binarity, putting into question the categories of 'female' and 'male,' whether they are considered essential or constituted, biological or cultural." *Vested Interests. Cross-Dressing and Cultural Anxiety* (N. Y.: Routledge, 1992), p. 10. Cf. Libby Purves, "Trouser Girls, Boys in Frocks and Sequin Envy," *The Times* (1992, May 6), LT 5.

264 This idea has become a popular explanation for why male crossdressing is not tolerated while female crossdressing is.

265 Feminists are in disagreement what stance, if any, they should take toward the transgender movement. Chris Weedon notes that transgender behavior and transsexuality have been variously regarded by feminists as a form of male envy of females (Janice Raymond), as internalized homophobia (Sheila Jeffreys), or as some other form of betrayal of feminism; only since queer theory have attitudes become more positive, though they remain varied. *Feminism, Theory and the Politics of Difference* (Malden, MA: Blackwell, 1999), p. 74.

266 Sylvia Walby's faculty webpage at Lancaster University, accessed online at http://www.lancs.ac.uk/fss/sociology/staff/walby/walby.htm. Walby coordinates the

Gender Equality Research Network International (GENIe) and is co-organizer of an international network on Gender Globalization and Work Transformation (GLOW).

[267] So-called 'radical feminists' are perhaps best known for their use of the term 'patriarchy,' which they indicted as determining the fundamental division of society into a tiered system with masculine men on top and everyone else in an inferior position. But other theoretical systems also informed second wave feminists. Marxist feminists appealed to the capitalistic base to modern patriarchy, which both mandates and prospers from a gender division that keeps women's primary labor unpaid and in the home. Rather than seeing gender as the fundamental dividing point, Marxist feminists see class, and regard class distinctions and inequalities as determining gender inequalities. Dual systems theory offers yet another alternative. It suggests both patriarchy and capitalism interact interdependently to keep women oppressed. For more, with indications of the relevant literature, see Jane Pilcher & Imelda Whelehan, *50 Key Concepts in Gender Studies* (Thousand Oaks, CA: Sage Publications, 2004), pp. 93-96.

[268] Sylvia Walby, *Patriarchy at Work. Patriarchal and Capitalist Relations in Employment* (Minneapolis: Univ. of Minnesota Press, 1986). The quote is from p. 51.

[269] Sylvia Walby, *Theorizing Patriarchy* (Oxford: Blackwell, 1990). Note the similarity to the list in her 1986 work, though it has undergone modest modification (see p. 20). Cf. her earlier article, "Theorizing Patriarchy," *Sociology, 23* (no. 2), 213-234 (1989). In it she (p. 214) defines patriarchy as "a system of social structures, and practices in which men dominate, oppress and exploit women."

[270] Ibid.

[271] Sylvia Walby, *Gender Transformations* (N. Y.: Routledge, 1997), pp. 22-26; quote is from p. 25.

[272] Sylia Walby, **Gender Equality Research Network International (GENIe)**, accessed online at http://www.lancs.ac.uk/fss/sociology/staff/walby/GENIe.pdf.

[273] Sylvia Walby, "Gender Mainstreaming: Productive Tensions in Theory and Practice," *Social Politics, 12* (no. 3), 321-343 (2005), p. 321.

[274] Ibid, p. 322.

[275] Ibid, pp. 322-325.

[276] Ibid, pp. 325-329.

[277] Ibid, p. 329f. To this list we may add gender identity. For more on gender and the law, see Bolich, *Crossdressing in Context, vol. 2*, Q. 56.

[278] Ibid, pp. 329-331.

[279] Ibid, pp. 331-336.

[280] Alison MacEwen Scott, "Gender Segregation and the SCELI Research," in A. M. Scott (Ed.), *Gender Segregation and Social Change: Men and Women in Changing Labour Markets*, pp. 1-38 (N. Y.: Oxford, 1994), p. 1.

[281] Joyce P. Jacobsen, *The Economics of Gender* (Malden, MA: Blackwell, 1998), pp. 205-207.

[282] Ibid, p. 209.

[283] George P. Murdock, *Culture and Society* (Pittsburgh: Univ. of Pittsburgh Press, 1965), p. 451; the information is nicely tabled in Martin Daly & Margo Wilson, *Sex, Evolution, and Behavior*, 2nd ed. (Boston: PWS Publishers, 1983), pp. 262-263 (Table 101).

[284] Robert M. Blackburn, Bradley Brooks, & Jennifer Jarman, *The Gendering of Work Around the World: Occupational Gender Segregation and Inequality* (Cambridge: Cambridge University, SRG Publications, 2001). This was the authors' Report to the United Nations on International Occupational Gender Segregation, 1999.

[285] The structuring and discussion of this material is loosely based on Robert M. Blackburn, Jude Browne, Bradley Brooks, & Jennifer Jarman, "Explaining Gender Segregation," *British Journal of Sociology, 53* (no. 4), 513-536 (2002).

[286] Heidi Hartmann, "Capitalism, Patriarchy, and Job Segregation By Sex," *Signs, 1*(no. 3), 137-169 (1976), p. 137.

[287] M. Rivka Polatnick, "Why Men Don't Rear Children," in A. Minas, *Gender Basics. Feminist Perspectives on Women and Men*, pp. 500-507 (Belmont, CA: Wadsworth, 1993); quotes are from pp. 501, 504.

[288] Sharon Hays, *The Cultural Contradictions of Motherhood* (New Haven: Yale Univ. Press, 1996), p. 162.

[289] For elaboration and critique of this position, see Blackburn, Browne, Brooks, & Jarman, pp. 515-520 on 'Human Capital and Rational Choice.' Quote is from p. 516.

[290] Catherine Hakim, *Work-Lifestyle Choices in the 21st Century: Preference Theory* (Oxford: Oxford Univ. Press, 2000). Also see her *Occupational Segregation: A Study of the Separation of Men and Women's Work in Britain, the United States, and Other Countries* [Research Paper No. 9] (London: Department of Employment, 1979). Also see her *Key Issues in Women's Work: Female Heterogeneity and the Polarization of Women's Employment* (London: Athlone, 1996).

[291] See the discussion in Blackburn, Browne, Brooks, & Jarman, pp. 523-526.

[292] Hakim, *Work-Lifestyle Choices in the 21st Century*. Cf. Blackburn, Browne, Brooks, & Jarman, esp. p. 523f. For more on Preference Theory, see S. McRae, "Constraints and Choices in Mothers' Employment Careers: A Consideration of Hakim's Preference Theory," *British Journal of Sociology, 54* (no. 3), 339-345 (2003).

[293] Dana Dunn, Elizabeth M. Almquist, & Janet Saltzman Chafetz, "Macrostructural Perspectives on Gender Inequality," in P. S. England (Ed.), *Theory on Gender/Feminism on Theory*, pp. (N. Y.: Walter de Gruyter, 1993), p. 86.

[294] MacEwan Scott, p. 35.

[295] Carolyn Vogler, "Segregation, Sexism, and Labour Supply," in A. M. Scott (Ed.), *Gender Segregation and Social Change: Men and Women in Changing Labour Markets*, pp. 39-79 (N. Y.: Oxford, 1994), p. 39.

[296] Talcott Parsons, *The Social System* (N. Y.: Free Press, 1951), and *Sociological Theory and Modern Society* (N. Y.: Free Press, 1967). Also see Talcott Parsons & Robert F. Bales, *Family, Socialization and Interaction Process* (Glencoe, IL: Free Press, 1955).

[297] Randall Collins, *Conflict Sociology: Toward an Explanatory Science* (N. Y.: Academic Press, 1974). See especially pp. 56ff.

[298] Ibid, p. 234. Also see Randall Collins, *Sociology of Marriage and the Family: Gender, Love, and Property* (Chicago: Nelson-Hall, 1985), pp. 386-406; cf. Scott L. Coltrane & Randall Collins, *Sociology of Marriage and the Family: Gender, Love, and Property*, 5th ed. (Belmont, CA: Wadsworth, 2000).

[299] Randall Collins, "A Conflict Theory of Sexual Stratification," *Social Problems, 19*, 3-21. Cf. his *Conflict Sociology*, pp. 228-259.

[300] Rae Lesser Blumberg, "A General Theory of Gender Stratification," in R. Collins (Ed.), *Sociological Theory 1984*, pp. 23-101 (S. F.: Jossey-Bass, 1984). Cf. R. L. Blumberg (Ed.), *Gender, Family, and Economy: The Triple Overlap* (Newbury Park, CA: Sage, 1991).

[301] Collins, "A Conflict Theory of Sexual Stratification." A test of this idea in 74 societies did not confirm Collin's hypothesis. Instead, kinship and family variables proved to have more predictive power. See G. David Johnson & Lewellyn Hendrix, "A Cross-Cultural Test of Collins's Theory of Sexual Stratification," *Journal of Marriage and the Family, 44* (no. 3), 675-684 (1982).

[302] Collins, *Conflict Sociology*, p. 243.

[303] Ibid.

[304] Ibid, p. 244.

[305] Randall Collins, "Women and the Production of Status Cultures," in M. Lamont & M. Fournier (Eds.), *Cultivating Differences. Symbolic Boundaries and the Making of Inequality*, pp. 213-231 (Chicago: Univ. of Chicago Press, 1992), p. 213.

[306] Collins, *Conflict Sociology*, pp. 94-103 (esp. p. 100f.), 161-168. Also see Jörge Rössell & Randall Collins, "Conflict Theory and Interaction Ritual: The Microfoundations of Conflict Theory," in J. Turner (Ed.), *Handbook of Sociological Theories*, pp. 509-531 (N. Y.: Plenum, 2002).

[307] Ibid, especially p. 73.

[308] Collins, "Women and the Production of Status Cultures," p. 223.

[309] John Scanzoni, "A Personal and Intellectual Journey," in S. K. Steinmetz & G. W. Peterson (Eds.), *Pioneering Paths in the Study of Families: The Lives and Careers of Family Scholars*, pp. 405-425 (N. Y.: Haworth Press, 2002), p. 410.

[310] John Scanzoni, *Sexual Bargaining: Power Politics in the American Marriage* (Englewood-Cliffs, NJ: Prentice-Hall, 1972), p. 2. Cf. Letha Dawson Scanzoni & John H. Scanzoni, *Men, Women, and Change: A Sociology of Marriage and Family* (N. Y.: McGraw-Hill, 1976, 1981, 1988).

[311] Ibid, pp. 32-34.

[312] Ibid, p. 35ff.

[313] Ibid, p. 41.

[314] Ibid, p. 69.

[315] See John Scanzoni, *Sex Roles, Women's Work, and Marital Conflict* (Lexington, MA: Lexington Books, 1978). Scanzoni focuses in several works on the reproductive choices of women (or, how fertility rates are affected by gender role perceptions and preferences). See his *Sex Roles, Life Styles, and Childbearing* (N. Y.: Free Press, 1975). Also see his "Work and Fertility Control Sequences Among Younger Married Women," *Journal of Marriage and the Family, 41*, 739-748 (1979).

[316] John Scanzoni, "A Historical Perspective on Husband-Wife Bargaining Power and Marital Dissolution," in G. Levinger & O. Moles (Eds.), *Divorce and Separation*, pp. 20-36 (N. Y. Basic Books, 1979).

[317] Ibid, pp. 6-19.

[318] Scanzoni, "A Personal and Intellectual Journey," p. 412.

[319] Scanzoni, *Sexual Bargaining*, pp. 62-64; quote is from p. 63.

[320] Ibid, pp. 67ff. Also see "Social Processes and Power in Families," in W. R. Burr, R. Hill, F. I. Nye, & I. L. Reiss (Eds.), *Contemporary Theories About the Family: Research-Based Theories*, vol. 1, pp. 295-316 (N. Y.: The Free Press, 1979). Also see John Scanzoni & Maximiliane Szinovacz, *Family Decision-Making: A Developmental Sex-Role Model* (Beverly Hills, CA: Sage, 1980).

[321] Scanzoni, *Sex Roles, Women's Work, and Marital Conflict*, p. 140.

[322] Ibid, p. 140f. Scanzoni follows the work of H. L. Raush, W. A, Barry, R. K. Hertel, & M. A. Swain, *Communication, Conflict, and Marriage* (S. F.: Jossey-Bass, 1974).

[323] Scanzoni, *Sexual Bargaining*, p. 71. In his *Sex Roles, Women's Work, and Marital Conflict* (pp. 94-96), Scanzoni lists seven categories of conflicts named by wives (listed in order of frequency reported): socioeconomic, peer/kin relations, child-related issues, husband's household-task performance, socio-emotional issues, wife-autonomy, and miscellaneous (personal complaints about husband's shortcomings).

[324] Ibid, p. 75.

[325] Ibid, pp. 86-97. The kinds listed here are grouped into divisions by their varying character. Cf. John P. Spiegel, "The Resolution of Role Conflict Within the Family," in N. W. Bell & E. F. Vogel (Eds.), *A Modern Introduction to the Family*, pp. 391-411 (N. Y.: Free Press, 1968).

[326] Scanzoni, *Sex Roles, Women's Work, and Marital Conflict*, p. 90.

[327] Scanzoni, "A Personal and Intellectual Journey," p. 410.

[328] Scanzoni, *Sexual Bargaining*, p. 163.

Chapter 6 Notes

[329] Roberta Gilchrist, *Gender and Archaeology. Constructing the Past* (N. Y.: Routledge, 1999), p. 13.

[330] Dwight B. Heath, "Sexual Division of Labor and Cross-Cultural Research," *Social Forces, 37* (no. 1), 77-79 (1958), p. 77.

[331] Melville Herskovits, *Economic Anthropology. A Study in Comparative Economics*, 2nd ed. (N. Y.: Knopf, 1952), p. 132.

332 On his sample aimed at representing all regions of the world, including modern and primitive societies, and those both present and past, see George P. Murdock "World Ethnographic Sample," *American Anthropologist, 59*, 664-687 (1957). Also see his *Culture and Society* (Pittsburgh: Univ. of Pittsburgh Press, 1965).

333 George P. Murdock, "Comparative Data on the Division of Labor By Sex," *Social Forces, 15* (no. 4), 551-553. (1937).

334 Scott J. South, "Sex Ratios, Economic Power, and Women's Roles: A Theoretical Extension and Empirical Test," *Journal of Marriage and the Family, 50* (no. 1), 19-31 (1988).

335 Scott J. South & Katherine Trent, "Sex Ratios and Women's Roles: A Cross-National Study," *American Journal of Sociology, 93* (no. 5), 1096-1115 (1988).

336 Gwen Moore & Gene Shackman, "Gender and Authority: A Cross-National Study," *Social Science Quarterly 77*, 273-88 (1996); quote is from p. 273.

337 Ibid, especially pp. 285-287.

338 Judith Ochshorn, "Sumer: Gender, Gender Roles, Gender Role Reversals," in S. P. Ramet (Ed.), *Gender reversals and Gender Cultures*, pp. 52-65 (London: Routledge, 1996).

339 A good place to start, because it points us in so many other directions to follow the conversation, is Maria Wyke (Ed.), *Gender and the Body in the Ancient Mediterranean* (Malden, MA: Blackwell, 1998).

340 Historians today use B.C.E. (Before the Common Era) and C.E. (Common Era) in place of the culturally slanted B.C. (Before Christ) and A.D. (*Anno Domine*, 'Year of Our Lord'). The Common Era is that shared between Christians and other people, so C.E. corresponds to A.D. in dates, and B.C.E. corresponds to B.C.

341 Plato, *Symposium*, in *The Essential Plato*, translated by B. Jowett, with M. J. Knight (N. Y.: Quality Paperback Book Club, 1999), p. 719. Cf. pp. 719-722.

342 Terms like 'sexual orientation' and 'homosexuality' have been placed in quotes to remind us that neither the words nor the modern concepts existed in the ancient world.

343 Plato, *Timaeus* 91. Translations from *Plato. IX. Timaeus. Critias. Cleitophon. Menexenus. Epistles* [Loeb Classical Library], translated by R. G. Bury (Cambridge: Harvard Univ. Press, 1989 reprint of 1929 ed.), pp. 249, 251. Cf. the remark in the Hippocratic medical work 'The Seed and the Nature of the Child': "Another point about women: if they have intercourse with men their health is better than if they do not." See G. E. R. Lloyd (Ed.), *Hippocratic Writings*, translated by J. Chadwick & W. N. Mann (N. Y.: Penguin Books, 1983 reprint of 1978 ed.), p. 320; see pp. 317-323.

344 Aristotle, *The Politcs*, Bk. 3.4.1277b. See *Aristotle. The Politics*, rev. ed., translated by T. A. Sinclair, rev. by T. J. Saunders (N. Y.: Penguin Books, 1992), p. 182 (which see for other comparisons between men and women).

345 Xenophon, *Oeconomicus* 7.22. For a brief summary of women's household duties in the classical world, see Edith Gillian Clark, "Housework," in S. Hornblower & A. Spaworth (Eds.), *The Oxford Classical Dictionary*, 3rd ed. (N. Y.: Oxford Univ. Press, 1996), p. 732.

[346] Helen King, "Women," in S. Hornblower & A. Spaworth (Eds.), *The Oxford Classical Dictionary*, 3rd ed. (N. Y.: Oxford Univ. Press, 1996), pp. 1623-1624.

[347] Gillian Clark, *Women in Late Antiquity. Pagan and Christian Lifestyles* (Oxford: Clarendon Press, 1994), pp. 139-141; quote is from p. 140.

[348] See *Yebamoth* 79b; cf. *Tosefta Yebamoth* 8.4 ("A woman has no right to be married even to a eunuch [sterile but capable of sexual relations]"—translation by Jacob Neusner, *The Tosefta. Nashim* (N. Y.: Ktav, 1979), p. 28).

[349] Dominic Montserrat, "Essay Six: Reading Gender in the Roman World," in J. Huskinson (Ed.), *Experiencing Rome: Culture, Identity, and Power in the Roman Empire*, pp. 153-182 (N. Y.: Routledge, 2000), p. 158.

[350] See, for example, Luc Brisson, *Sexual Ambivalence: Androgyny and Hermaphroditism in Graeco-Roman Antiquity* (Berkeley: Univ. of California Press, 2002). Also see M. Delcourt, *Hermaphroditea: recherches sur l'etre double promoteur de la fertilite dans le monde classique* (Brussels: Latomus, 1966).

[351] Ibid, p. 2.

[352] See the Mishnah at *Bikurim* 4.1-2, which says that an *androginos* is like a man in some ways, like a woman in some ways, and unlike both men and women in other ways. Cf. Mishnah *Yebamoth* 8.6 (*Yebamoth* 81a).

[353] The phrase translates the Greek τὸ ἄνδρας ὄντας μιμεῖσθαι γυναῖκας. A. M. Harmon (Trans.), "The Fly," *Lucian, vol. 1* (pp. 82-95). Loeb Classical Library (Cambridge: Harvard Univ. Press, 1913), p. 95.

[354] Macrobius, *The Saturnalia*, III.viii.2, in P. V. Davies (Trans.), *The Saturnalia* (N. Y.: Columbia Univ. Press, 1969), p. 214.

[355] Clarence J. Bulliet, *Venus Castina. Famous Female Impersonators, Celestial and Human* (N. Y.: Covici, Friede, 1928).

[356] Macrobius, §3, p. 214.

[357] Seneca, *Ad Lucilium Epistulae Morales (Letters to Lucilius)*, vol. II, translated by William Heinemann (Cambridge: Harvard Univ. Press, 1920), Epistle LXVI (p. 35).The Latin context is: "Ut muliercula aut aliquis in mulierculam ex viro versus digitulos meos ducat?"

[358] Maragaret C. Miller, "Reexamining Transvestism in Archaic and Classical Athens: The Zewadski Stamnos," *American Journal of Archaeology, 103* (no. 2), 223-253 (1999). Miller reviews different lines of interpretation for the figures on the objects in question. These include the ideas that the figures are women wearing beards, crossdressed males engaged in religious practices, men crossdressed for some other reason, or men not crossdressed at all though their dress is culturally effeminate.

[359] Eva Cantarella, *Bisexuality in the Ancient World*, translated by C. O. Cuilleanain (New Haven,CT: Yale Univ. Press, 1992), pp.177-179.

[360] An indication of the breadth and vitality of the discussion can be seen in Martha A. Brozyna (Ed.), *Gender and Sexuality in the Middle Ages* (Jefferson, NC: McFarland, 2005).

361 Robert L. A. Clark & Claire Sponsler, "Queer Play: The Cultural Work of Crossdressing in Medieval Drama," *New Literary History, 28* (no. 2), 319-344 (1997), p. 320.

362 Michel Rouche, "The Early Middle Ages in the West," in P. Veyne (Ed.), *A History of Private Life, vol. 1: From Pagan Rome to Byzantium*, pp. 411-549 (Cambridge, MA: Belknap Press, 1987), p. 481.

363 Ibid, p. 483.

364 Kathleen A. Bishop, "The Influence of Plautus and Elegiac Comedy on Chaucer's Fabliaux," *The Chaucer Review, 35* (no. 3), 294-317 (2001), p. 309.

365 Ibid. Bishop herself is citing from Joan Cadden, *Meanings of Sex Difference in the Middle Ages* (N. Y.: Cambridge Univ. Press, 1993), p. 160.

366 Cited in James D. Cain, "Unnatural History: Gender and Genealogy in Gerald of Wales's *Topographia Hibernica*," *Essays in Medieval Studies, 19* (no. 1), 29-43 (2002), pp. 31-32.

367 Cain, p. 32.

368 James M. Blythe, "Women in the Military: Scholastic Arguments and Medieval Images of Female Warriors," *History of Political Thought, XXII* (no. 2), 242-269 (2001). Accessed online at http://www.imprint.co.uk/hpt/179.PDF.

369 Ibid.

370 Cary J. Nederman & Jacqui True, "The Third Sex: The Idea of the Hermaphrodite in Twelfth-Century Europe," *Journal of the History of Sexuality, 6* (no. 4), 497-517 (1996).

371 Peter Cantor, *De Vitio Sodomitico*, translated in John Boswell, *Christianity, Social Tolerance, and Homosexuality* (Chicago: Univ. of Chicago Press, 1980), p. 376.

372 Cited in Nederman & True, p. 512.

373 Joan Cadden, *Meanings of Sex Difference in the Middle Ages: Medicine, Science, and Culture* (N. Y.: Cambridge University Press, 1993). See chapter 4, 'Feminine and Masculine Types,' especially pp. 212-213.

374 Sharon E. Preves, "Sexing the Intersexed: An Analysis of Sociocultural Responses to Intersexuality," *Signs: Journal of Women in Culture and Society, 27* (no. 2), 523-556 (2001). Preves notes, for instance, that in 17th century France an intersexed individual was permitted to marry a member of which male/female sex was 'opposite' the male/female end of the continuum they had chosen to identify with. Thus, a hermaphrodite who elected to live as a woman could legally marry a man. But once such a choice was made, it was deemed irreversible. By the 18th-19th centuries, far less tolerance existed in Western Europe.

375 Kate Chedgzoy, "Impudent Women: Carnival and Gender in Early Modern Culture," *The Glasgow Review, no. 1* (1993). Accessed online at http://www.arts.gla.ac.uk/SESLL/STELLA/COMET/ glasgrev/issue1/chefgz.htm.

376 Philippe Ariès, *Centuries of Childhood: A Social History of Family Life*, translated by R. Baldick (London: Jonathan Cape, 1962), p. 48.

[377] See G. G. Bolich, *Crossdressing in Context, vol. 1: The Context of Dress and Gender* (Raleigh, NC: Psyche's Press, 2006), Q. 9.

[378] Merry E. Wiesner-Hanks, *Gender in History* (Malden, MA: Blackwell, 2001), p. 92.

[379] Devdutt Pattanaik, *The Man Who Was a Woman and Other Queer Tales from Hindu Lore* (Binghamton, NY: Haworth Press, 2002)., p. 4.

[380] For a more complete consideration of this logic, see G. G. Bolich, *Crossdressing in Context, vol. 3: The Context of Religion* (forthcoming), Q. 79.

[381] Pattanaik, p. 10.

[382] Akshay Khanna, *A Language for Love* (2006, Apr. 2). Accessed online at Boloji.com at http://www.boloji.com/wfs5/wfs577.htm.

[383] Erick Laurent, "Sexuality and Human Rights: An Asian Perspective," *Journal of Homosexuality, 48* (nos. 3-4), 163-225 (2005), p. 172. *Zenanas* is a term more commonly heard in Pakistan.

[384] See Sunita Bose & Scott J. South, "Sex Composition of Children and Marital Disruption in India," *Journal of Marriage and Family, 65* (no. 4), 996-1006 (2003).

[385] Denise L. Carmody & John T. Carmody, *Ways to the Center. An Introduction to World Religions*, 4th ed. (Belmont, CA: Wadsworth, 1993), p. 107.

[386] Allerd Stikker, *Closing the Gap: Exploring the History of Gender Relations* (Amsterdam: Amsterdam Univ. Press, 2002), p. 72. On *yin* and *yang*, also see Vern L. Bullough, *Sexual Variance in Society and History* (N. Y.: John Wiley & Sons, 1976), p. 299. Also see Fang Fu Ruan, "Taoism and Sex," in V. L. Bullough & B. Bullough (Eds.), *Human Sexuality: An Encyclopedia*, pp. 575-577 (N. Y.: Garland, 1994). Cf. A. Ishihara & H. S. Levy, *The Tao of Sex* (Yokohama: Shibundo, 1968).

[387] Lao-Tzu, *Tao Te Ching*, translated by Stephen Addiss & Stanley Lombardo (Indianapolis, IN: Hackett, 1993), p. 28.

[388] Livia Kohn, *Monastic Life in Medieval Daoism. A Cross-Cultural Perspective* (Honolulu: Univ. of Hawai'I Press, 2003), p. 81.

[389] Confucius, *Analects* XVI.14, in Arthur Waley (Trans.), *The Analects of Confucius* (N. Y.: Vintage, 1938), p. 208; quote is from p. 251.

[390] *Xunzi* 5/15, quoted in Jane Geaney, "Guarding Moral Boundaries: Shame in Early Confucianism," *Philosophy East and West, 54* (no. 2), 113-142 (2004), p. 124. For the complete context of the passage see John Knoblock (Translator), *Xunzi: A Translation and Study of the Complete Works,* vol. 1: *Books 1-6* (Stanford: Stanford Univ. Press, 1988).

[391] This argument is conducted in more depth in Bolich, *Crossdressing in Context, vol. 3*, Q. 82.

[392] Wiesner-Hanks, p. 15.

[393] Stikker, p. 73.

[394] Mary Pat Fisher, *Living Religions*, 3rd ed. (Upper Saddle River, NJ: Prentice-Hall, 1997), p. 179.

395 See Bolich, *Crossdressing in Context, vol. 2: The Context of Transgender Realities* (Raleigh, NC: Psyche's Press, 2007), Q. 39.

396 Peter A. Jackson, "Performative Genders, Perverse Desires: A Bio-History of Thailand's Same-Sex and Transgender Cultures," *Intersections: Gender, History and Culture in the Asian Context, 9* (2003, August), §§10, 53-54. Accessed online at http://wwwsshe. murdoch.edu.au/intersections/issue9/ jackson.html. Also see Peter A. Jackson, "The Persistence of Gender: From Ancient Indian *Pandakas* to Modern *Thai Gay-Quings*," *Australian Humanities Review, Issue 1* (1996, April-June; original work published in *Meanjin,* 1996). Accessed online at http://www.lib.latrobe.edu.au/AHR/ archive/Issue-April-1996/Jackson.html.

397 Ibid, especially §§1-25, 63-76. Jackson's history covers much more than what I have presented, dealing also with how the nation's authorities responded to criticisms of the Thai people's 'nakedness' and 'sexual excesses' in sanctioning polygamy.

398 Ibid, §§32-37. Just as the women were commonly viewed as too masculine, the men were commonly regarded as too feminine by Westerners.

399 Ibid, §39.

400 Ibid, §49; cf. §62.

401 Ibid, §69.

402 Ibid, §60. Jackson references Lucien M. Hanks & Jane Richardson Hanks, "Thailand: Equality Between the Sexes," in B. E. Ward (Ed.), *Women in the New Asia: The Changing Social Roles of Men and Women in South and Southeast Asia,* pp. 423-459 (Paris: UNESCO, 1963), p. 447, with regard to dress distinctions instituted for children and gendered role differentiation in activities and professions.

403 Ibid, §77.

404 Ibid, §88. Jackson argues that today's *kathoey* prominence in popular media is "thoroughly modern and utterly recent."

405 Rosalind C. Morris, "Educating Desire: Thailand, Transnationalism, and Transgression," *Social Text, 15* (nos. 3/4), 53-79 (1997), p. 62.

406 Kittiwut Jod Taywaditep, Eli Coleman, & Pacharin Dumronggittigule, "Thailand," in R. T. Francoeur (Ed.), *The International Encyclopedia of Sexuality,* Vols. I-III (N. Y.: Continuum, 1997). Accessed online at http://www2.rz.hu-berlin.de/sexology/ GESUND/ARCHIV/IES/THAILAND.HTM#7.%20GENDER%20CONFLICTED %20PERSONS. See §7.

407 See *Islam and the Divine Feminine.* Accessed online at http://www.penkatali.org/ feminine.html.

408 Leila Ahmed, *Women and Gender In Islam: Historical Roots of a Modern Debate* (New Haven, CT: Yale Univ. Press, 1992), pp. 1-8. The book explores and elaborates these various contributors to the gender discourse from early history to the present.

409 Mary Elaine Hegland, "Gender and Religion in the Middle East and South Asia: Women's Voices Rising," in M. L. Meriwether & J. E. Tucker (Eds.), *Social History of*

Women and Gender in the Modern Middle East, pp. 177-212 (Boulder, CO: Westview Press, 1999), pp. 182-186; quote is from p. 186.

[410] W. Qidwai, "Perceptions About Female Sexuality Among Young Pakistani Men Presenting to Family Physicians at a Teaching Hospital in Karachi," *Journal of the Pakistan Medical Association, 50* (no. 2), 74-77 (2000).

[411] Yik Koon Teh, "*Mak Nyahs* (Male Transsexuals) in Malaysia: The Influence of Culture and Religion on Their Identity," *The International Journal of Transgenderism, 5* (no. 3) (2001, July-September). Accessed online at http://www.symposion.com/ijt/ijtvo05no03_04.htm.

[412] Abu-Dawud, *Sunan Abu-Dawud,* Bk. 32, #4095. Accessed online at http://www.usc.edu/dept/MSA/fundamentals/hadithsunnah/abudawud/032.sat.html#032.4095.

[413] Abu-Dawud, *Sunan Abu-Dawud,* Bk. 41, #4910. Accessed online at http://www.usc.edu/dept/MSA/fundamentals/hadithsunnah/abudawud/032.sat.html #041.4910. Cf. the comment of Ibn Qudamah, with the *Qur'an* (*Surah* 24:31) in mind, who says the *mukhannath* feels no desire for women.

[414] This inability to sustain an erection (impotence) was remarked upon by Ibn 'Abbaas, with *Surah* 24:31 in view.

[415] For a more complete treatment of this subject, see Bolich, *Crossdressing in Context, vol. 3*, Q. 78.

[416] See, for example, the hadith of Abu-Dawud in *Sunan Abu-Dawud,* Bk. 32, #4095, which speaks of a *mukhannath*—one "free of physical needs" (i.e., not interested in sex)—in the presence of the Prophet's wives. See the hadith online at http://www.usc.edu/dept/MSA/fundamentals/hadithsunnah/ abudawud/ 032.sat.html#032.4095.

[417] M. Muhsin Kahn (Translator), *Translation of Sahih Bakhari*, Vol. 7, Bk. 72, #773. Accessed online at http://www.usc.edu/dept/MSA/fundamentals/hadithsunnah/bukhari/. A book translation of the *Al-Sahih* is available in English; see Muhammad Ibn Ismail Bukhari, *The English Translation of Sahih al-Bakhari with the Arabic Text*, 9 vols., trans. Muhammad Muhsin Kahn (Alexandria, VA: Al-Saadawi Publications, 1996). The transliterated Arabic for the first text, as rendered by Faris Mailk is: *la'ana rasoolullah salla allahu 'alaihi wa sallama al-mutashabbiheena min ar-rijaali bil-nisaa'i wal-mutashabbihaati min annisaa'i bir-rijaali.* Accessed online at http://www.well.com/user/aquarius/Qurannotes.htm. Cf. Vern L. Bullough, *Sexual Variance in Society and History* (N. Y.: John Wiley & Sons, 1976), p. 141.

[418] Jakob Skovgaard-Petersen, "Sex Change in Cairo: Gender and Islamic Law," *The Journal of the International Institute, 2* (no. 3) (1996, Spring), accessed online at http://www.umich.edu/ ~iinet/journal/ vol2no3/sex_in_cairo.html.

[419] *Coming Out in Dialogue: Policies and Perceptions of Sexual Minority Groups in Asia and Europe* (2005), §2.1.5 (p. 15). Research paper commissioned by the Intellectual Exchange Department of the Asia-Europe Foundation for its "Talks on the Hill" series. Accessed online at http://asef.on2web.com/subSite/ccd/documents/briefingpaper_001.pdf.

420 "Kuwait Sex-Change Upheld," *BBC News World Edition* online (2004, Apr. 25). Accessed online at http://news.bbc.co.uk/2/hi/middle_east/3657727.stm.

421 "A Fatwa for Freedom," *The Guardian* (2005, July 27), maintained on the Guardian Unlimited website, accessed online at http://www.guardian.co.uk./g2/story/0,,1536658,00.html.

422 Ibid. Also see, Frances Harrison, "Iran's Sex-Change Operations," *BBC News* (2005, Jan. 5), accessed online at http://news.bbc.co.uk/2/hi/programmes/newsnight/4115535.stm.

423 Nazila Fathi, "As Repression Lifts, More Iranians Change Their Sex," *New York Times* (2004, Aug. 2). With NYTimes.com membership the article can be accessed online at http://www.nytimes.com/ 2004/08/02/international/middleast/02iran.html?hp=&adxnnl=1&adxnnlx=1091489991-2sBf34Gerj 3nlXAaASXZcQ.

424 See Bolich, *Crossdressing in Context, vol. 2*, Q. 37; also see *Crossdressing in Context, vol. 3*, Q. 78.

425 Julanne McCarthy, "Bahrain," in R. T. Francoeur (Ed.), *The International Encyclopedia of Sexuality*, Vols. I-III (N. Y.: Continuum, 1997). Accessed online at http://www2.rz.hu-berlin.de/sexology/GESUND/ARCHIV/IES/BAHRAIN.HTM#7.%20GENDER%20CONFLICTED%20PERSONS. See §7. Gender Conflicted Persons.

426 Unni Wikan, "Man Becomes Woman: Transsexualism in Oman as a Key to Gender Roles," *Man, 12* (no. 2), 304-319 (1977); originally published in *Tidsskrift for Samfunnsforskning, 17* (1976).

427 *Sydney Star Observer*, no. 421 (1998, Sept. 3), p. 6.

428 Garay Menicucci, "Homosexuality in Egyptian Film," *Middle East Report* (1998, Spring). Accessed online at http://www.merip.org/mer/mer206/egyfilm.htm.

429 Paula E. Drew, "Iran," in R. T. Francoeur (Ed.), *The International Encyclopedia of Sexuality*, Vols. I-III (N. Y.: Continuum, 1997) [hereafter *IES*]. Accessed online at http://www2.rz.hu-berlin.de/sexology/GESUND/ARCHIV/IES/IRAN.HTM#7.%20 GENDER%20CONFLICTED%20PERSONS. See §7. Gender Conflicted Persons. Drew speculated on the possibility that such theater might provide a 'niche for gender-conflicted males.'

430 Türker Özkan & Timo Lajunen, "Masculinity, Femininity, and the Bem Sex Role Inventory in Turkey," *Sex Roles. A Journal of Research, 52* (nos. 1-2), 103-110 (2005).

431 The Associated Press, "Turkey Blocks Cross-Dressing TV Reality Show" (2006, May 4). Also see Nicholas Birch, "Cross-Dressing Show Falls Victim to Disquiet; Conservative Attitudes About Family Also Reveal Skepticism Over EU," *The Washington Times* (2006, May 24), p. A15.

432 Deniz Kandiyoti, "Transsexuals and the Urban Landscape in Istanbul," *Middle East Report 206* (1998, Spring), accessed online at http://www.merip.org/mer/mer206/turksx.htm.

433 Ibid. I have been unable to determine the precise English equivalent to *lubinya*.

[434] A useful introduction to the subject, at manageable length, is offered by Oyeronke Oyewumi, "Conceptualizing Gender: The Eurocentric Foundations of Feminist Concepts and the Challenge of African Epistemologies," *Jenda: A Journal of Culture and African Women Studies, 2* (no. 1) (2002). Accessed online at http://www.jendajournal.com/vol2.1/oyewumi.html. Cf. Oyeronke Oyewumi, *The Invention of Women: Making an African Sense of Western Gender Discourses* (Minneapolis: Univ. of Minnesota Press, 1997). Also see Oyeronke Oyewumi, "Discourse on Gender: Historical Contingency and the Ethics of Intellectual Work," *West Africa Review, 3* (no. 2) (2002). Accessed online at http://www.westafricareview. com/vol3.2/owomoyela.html. Another helpful examination may be found in C. Otutubikey Izugbara, "Patriarchal Ideology and Discourses of Sexuality in Nigeria," *Understanding Human Sexuality Seminar Series 2* (Africa Regional Sexuality Resource Centre, 2004). Accessed online at http://www.arsrc.org/en/resources/documents/izugbara.pdf.

[435] David F.Greenberg, *The Construction of Homosexuality* (Chicago: Univ. of Chicago Press, 1988); see chapter 2 (pp. 25-88), 'Homosexual Relations in Kinship-Structured Societies.' Each of the three categories is covered, as follows: Transgenerational (26-40); Transgenderal (40-65); and Egalitarian (66-73).

[436] A more complete account of these transgender realities in Africa can be found in G. G. Bolich, *Crossdressing in Context, vol. 2*, Q. 39.

[437] Burt H. Hoff, "Gays: Guardians at the Gates. An Interview with Malidoma Somé," *MEN Magazine* (1993, Sept.), accessed online at http://www.menweb.org/somegay.htm.

[438] Brian H. MacDermot, *Cult of the Sacred Spear: The Story of the Nuer Tribe in Ethiopia* (London: Hale, 1972), p. 119. Cf. the belief among the Hua people of New Guinea that gender under certain circumstances can change; older males, through ritual imitation of menstruation and childbirth can assume feminine gender and status as women, while some women can become masculine and gain status as men. See Anna S. Meigs, "Male Pregnancy and the Reduction of Sexual Opposition in a New Guinea Highlands Society," *Ethnology, 15* (no. 4), 393-407 (1976).

[439] Oyewumi, "Conceptualizing Gender."

[440] Ibid.

[441] Cf., too, the discussion on the tribal chief and his—or her—'wife' in Kwesi Yankah, *Speaking for the Chief: Okyeame and the Politics of Akan Royal Oratory* (Indianapolis: Indiana Univ. Press, 1995).

[442] Edward E. Evans-Pritchard, "Sexual Inversion Among the Azande," *American Anthropologist, 72*, 1428-1434 (1970). Also see, E. E. Evans-Pritchard, *The Azande: History and Political Institutions* (Oxford: Clarendon Press, 1971), p. 83. Cf. Adolphe L. Cureau, *Savage Man in Central Africa: A study of Primitive Races in the French Congo*, trans. E. Andrews (London: T. Fisher Unwin, 1915).

[443] The term *gynaegamy* was coined by Victor Chikezie Uchendu in the late 1960s with reference to the Igbo. See V. C. Uchendu, *Ezi Na Ulo—The Extended Family in Igbo Civilization* (1995). Ahiajoku Lecture Series. Accessed online at the IgboNet website at http://ahiajoku.igbonet.com/1995/.

444 On the Nandi see Regina Smith Oboler, "Is the Female Husband a Man? Woman/Woman Marriage Among the Nandi of Kenya," *Ethnology, 19* (no. 1), 69-88 (1980). Also see Myrtle S. Langley, *The Nandi of Kenya: Life Crisis Rituals in a Period of Change* (London: C. Hurst and Co., 1979).

445 On the practice among the Nuer, see Edward E. Evans-Pritchard, *Kinship and Marriage Among the Nuer* (Oxford: Clarendon Press, 1951).

446 Roberta Perkins notes more than two dozen, Denise O'Brien puts the number at more than thirty, and Beth Greene at more than forty; suffice it to say the practice has been well-established and widespread. Cf. Joseph M. Carrier & Stephen O. Murray, "Woman-Woman Marriage in Africa," in S. O. Murray & W. Roscoe (Eds.), *Boy-Wives and Female Husbands: Studies in African Homosexualities*, pp. 255-266 (N. Y.: Palgrave, 1998).

447 Biko Agozino, "Between Divas and Dimpers: A Review of Ifi Amadiume's *Daughters of the Goddess, Daughters of Imperialism: African Women, Culture, Power & Democracy*, London, Zed, 2000," *Jenda: A Journal of Culture and African Women Studies, 1* (no. 1) (2001). Accessed online at http://www.jendajournal.com/vol1.1/ agozino.html.

448 Ifi Amadiume, *Male Daughters, Female Husbands: Gender and Sex in an African Society* (London: Zed Books, 1987).

449 Ibid.

450 See Edwin S. Segal, *Gender Transformation in Cross Cultural Perspective*. Paper prepared for presentation at Women's Worlds 99, the seventh International Interdisciplinary Congress on Women, Program Section II: New Constructions of Gender, session 2, Friday, June 25, Tromsø, Norway, June 20-26, 1999. Accessed online at http://www.skk.uit.no/WW99/papers/Segal_Edwin_S.pdf. On the Mbuti, cf. Colin Turnbull, "Sex and Gender. The Role of Subjectivity in Field Research," in T. Larry & M. E. Conaway (Eds.), *Self, Sex, and Gender in Cross-Cultural Fieldwork*, pp. 17-27 (Urbana, IL: Univ. of Illinois Press, 1987).

451 Mircea Eliade & Ioan P. Couliano, *The Eliade Guide to World Religions* (S. F.: HarperSanFrancisco, 1991), p. 16.

452 James Boyd Christensen, *Double Descent Among the Fanti* (New Haven: Human Relations Area Files [HRAF], 1954).

453 The work of African scholar Oyeronke Oyewumi is only one example among many works chronicling the effects of colonialism. Also see A. Adu Boahen, *African Perspectives on Colonialism* (Baltimore: John Hopkins Univ. Press, 1987).

454 Arlene Masquelier, "The Scorpion's Sting: Youth, Marriage and the Struggle for Social Maturity in Niger," *Journal of the Royal Anthropological Institute, 11* (no. 1), 59-83 (2005).

Chapter 7 Notes

455 Peter Wilson, "Development and Mental Health: The Issue of Difference in Atypical Gender Development," in D. Di Ceglie (Ed.), with D. Freeman, *A Stranger in My Own Body. Atypical Gender Identity Development and Mental Health*, pp. 1-8 (London: Karnac Books, 1998), p. 4. Wilson is perhaps best known for his work as director of

386

Young Minds, London. This organization provides services to parents and professionals regarding the mental health of children and adolescents.

[456] Marjorie S. Hardy, "The Development of Gender Roles: Societal Influences," in L. Diamont & R. D. McAnulty (Eds.), *The Psychology of Sexual Orientation, Behavior, and Identity. A Handbook*, pp.425-443 (Westport, CT: Greenwood Press, 1995), p. 326.

[457] Carol Tavris & Carole Wade, *The Longest War. Sex Differences in Perspective*, 2nd ed. (San Diego, CA: Harcourt Brace Jovanovich, 1984; 1st ed., 1977). See, for example, p. 74f. Significantly, Tavris and Wade (p. 301f.) acknowledge what they call "a fascinating new idea in anthropological research" that gender may be "a human invention" and in some cultures is less important, or flexible, or changeable.

[458] Toni Cavanagh Johnson, "Childhood Sexuality," in E. Gil & T. Cavanagh Johnson (Eds.), *Sexualised Children. Assessment and Treatment of Sexualised Children and Children Who Molest*, pp. 1-20 (Rockville, MD: Launch Press, 1993).

[459] John Bancroft (Ed.), *Sexual Development in Childhood* (Bloomington: Indiana Univ. Press, 2003). On the widespread displacement of sex by gender in scholarly conversation, see David Haig, "The Inexorable Rise of Gender and the Decline of Sex: Social Change in Academic Titles, 1945-2001," *Archives of Sexual Behavior, 33* (no. 2), pp. 87-96 (2004).

[460] Julia T. Wood, *Gendered Lives: Communication, Gender, and Culture* (Belmont, CA: Wadsworth, 2005), p. 44.

[461] Freud's explication of these stages is found in a number of places. A good place to start is his second and third essays in Sigmund Freud, *Three Essays on the Theory of Sexuality*, translated by J. Strachey (N. Y.: Basic Books, 1962; original work published 1905 and revised by Freud often over the years).

[462] Freud, *Three Essays on the Theory of Sexuality*, p. 85f., n. 1.

[463] Sigmund Freud, *New Introductory Lectures on Psychoanalysis*, translated by J. Strachey (N. Y.: W. W. Norton, 1963; original work published 1933), p. 114. Cf. Freud's *Civilization and Its Discontents*, translated by J. Strachey (N. Y.: W. W. Norton, 1961; original work published 1930), p. 52f., n. 3.

[464] Ibid, pp. 114-116; quote is from p. 116.

[465] Ibid, pp. 117-118; quote is from p. 118.

[466] Sigmund Freud, *Introductory Lectures on Psycho-Analysis*, translated by James Strachey (N. Y.: W. W/ Norton, 1966), pp. 410-420. The remarks in this volume come from Freud's 1915-1917 lectures. Later essays on the same subject include "The Passing of the Oedipus Complex" (1924), and "Some Psychological Consequences of the Anatomical Distinction Between the Sexes" (1926), both included in Sigmund Freud, *Sexuality and the Psychology of Love*, edited by P. Rieff (N. Y.: Collier, 1963).

[467] Freud, *New Introductory Lectures on Psychoanalysis*, pp. 118-125.

[468] Ibid, pp. 125-130.

[469] Ibid, pp. 130-132, 134f.

[470] Ibid, pp. 132-134; quote is from p. 134.

[471] See the collection of papers gathered in Karen Horney, *Feminine Psychology* (N. Y.: W. W. Norton, 1967). Cf. Horney's *New Ways in Psychoanalysis* (N. Y.: W. W. Norton, 1939).

[472] Erich Fromm, *Love, Sexuality, and Matriarchy: About Gender* (N. Y.: Fromm International Publishing Corporation, 1997). Quote is from p. 41.

[473] Mischel's basic ideas can be found in the following works: *Personality and Assessment* (N. Y.: Wiley, 1968); "Towards a Cognitive, Social Learning Reconception of Personality," *Psychological Review, 80*, 252-283 (1973). "On the Interface of Cognition and Personality," *American Psychologist, 34*, 740-754 (1979). Mischel highlights the role of what he calls *person variables*, of which he names five types: perceptions, expectations, competencies, values, and self-regulation and plans. In other words, how we perceive our environment, what we expect as the outcome of our actions, our sense of what we actually can do, our ideals and personal goals, and our plans and personal standards all enter into what our actual behavior is in a given situation.

[474] Neal A. Miller & John Dollard, *Social Learning and Imitation* (New Haven, CT: Yale Univ. Press, 1941).

[475] Walter Mischel, "A Social Learning View of Sex Differences in Behavior," in E. E. Maccoby (Ed.), *The Development of Sex Differences*, pp. 56-81 (Stanford, CA: Stanford Univ. Press, 1966). Also see his "Sex-Typing and Socialization," in P. H. Mussen (Ed.), *Carmichael's Manual of Child Psychology*, vol. 2, pp. 3-72 (1970).

[476] Kay Bussey & Albert Bandura, "Social Cognitive Theory of Gender Development and Differentiation," *Psychological Review, 106*, 676-713 (1999).

[477] Lawrence Kohlberg, "A Cognitive-Developmental Analysis of Children's Sex Role Concepts and Attitudes," in E. E. Maccoby (Ed.), *The Development of Sex Differences*, pp. 82-173 (Stanford, CA: Stanford Univ. Press, 1966), p. 82.

[478] See Lawrence Kohlberg, "Stage and Sequence: The Cognitive-Developmental Approach to Socialization," in D. Goslin (Ed.), *Handbook of Socialization Theory and Research*, pp. 347-480 (Chicago, IL: Rand McNally, 1969).

[479] Kohlberg, "A Cognitive-Developmental Analysis," p. 89.

[480] Ibid, p. 95.

[481] Lawrence Kohlberg, *The Philosophy of Moral Judgment* (N. Y.: Harper & Row, 1981); for a shorter, popular explanation, see his "The Child as a Moral Philosopher," *Psychology Today*, 25-30 (1968, Sept.). Also see his "Moral Stages and Moralization: Cognitive Developmental Approach," in T. Lickona (Ed.), *Moral Development and Behavior: Theory, Research, and Social Issues*, pp. 31-53 (N. Y.: Holt, Rinehart & Winston, 1976).

[482] Lawrence Kohlberg & Robert A. Ryncarz, "Beyond Justice Reasoning: Moral Development and a Consideration of a Seventh Stage," in C. N. Alexander & E. J. Langer (Eds.), *Higher Stages of Human Development: Perspectives on Adult Growth*, pp. 191-207 (N. Y.: Oxford Univ. Press, 1990).

[483] See Jean Piaget, *The Child & reality. Problems of Genetic Psychology* (N. Y.: Penguin Books, 1973).

[484] Kohlberg's 'stage 0' can be compared to Freud's idea of the child before the development of the superego, or Piaget's first stage of moral reasoning, which he called *anomy* ('without governance,' or 'without rules'). This first stage, though, is *not* a type of moral reasoning. See Jean Piaget, *The Moral Judgment of the Child* (N. Y.: Free Press, 1965).

[485] In this level there is progression from Piaget's preoperational thinking into concrete operational thinking. Piaget's second stage—and first type of moral reasoning—is pertinent here: *heteronomy*, which he thought typical of children ages 4-7 years old.

[486] By the time we reach Kohlberg's conventional level we have also reached Piaget's third stage—and second form of moral reasoning—*autonomy*, or 'self-rule.' See Piaget, *Moral Development*, p. 197.

[487] Lawrence Kohlberg, "The Claim to Moral Adequacy of a Highest Stage of Moral Judgment," in B. Puka (Ed.), *The Great Justice Debate: Kohlberg Criticism*, pp. 2-18 (N. Y.: Garland, 1994). This is a reprinted article from *Journal of Philosophy, 70*, 630-646 (1973).

[488] James Rest, Elliot Turiel, & Lawrence Kohlberg, "Level of Moral Development as a Determinant of Preference and Comprehension of Moral Judgments Made By Others," *Journal of Personality, 37*, 225-252 (1969).

[489] See Lawrence Kohlberg & R. Kramer, "Continuities and Discontinuities in Childhood and Adult Moral Development," *Human Development, 12*, 93-120 (1969). Recall also Freud's suspicion that femininity is associated with an inferior moral sensibility. Kohlberg's conclusions were consistent with Piaget's. Piaget found in comparing how girls master the rules of a game that their moral reasoning proceeds much the same as in boys, at least until about age 8. Then half of the girls exhibit behavior that is "more tolerant and more easily reconciled to innovations" in a way that struck him as different from boys. Indeed, Piaget wrote, "The most superficial observation is sufficient to show that in the main the legal sense is far less developed in little girls than in boys." See *Moral Development*, pp. 82, 77.

[490] Carol Gilligan, *In a Different Voice. Psychological Theory and Women's Development* (Cambridge, MA: Harvard Univ. Press, 1982), p. 18.

[491] Ibid, p. 19.

[492] Ibid, p. 17.

[493] Ibid, p. 22.

[494] Ibid, p. 23.

[495] Ibid, p. 170.

[496] Ibid, p. 148.

[497] Ibid, p. 173.

[498] Ibid, p. 174.

[499] For a discussion of this matter up to the early 1990s, see Carol Tavris, *The Mismeasure of Woman* (N. Y.: Simon & Schuster, 1992), pp. 79-90, especially pp. 85-86. For a slightly later study, see Cindy J. P. Woods, "Gender Differences in Moral Development and Acquisition: A Review of Kohlberg's and Gilligan's Models of Justice and Care,"

Social Behavior and Personality: An International Journal, 24 (no. 4), 375-383 (1996). Also see Mary M. Brabeck & Erika L. Shore, "Gender Differences in Intellectual and Moral Development? The Evidence That Refutes the Claim," in J. Demick & C. Andreoletti (Eds.), *Handbook of Adult Development,* pp. 351-368 (N. Y.: Plenum, 2003).

[500] Sandra Bem, "Gender Schema Theory and Its Implications for Child Development: Raising Gender Aschematic Children in a Gender Schematic Society," *Signs, 8,* 598-616 (1983), pp. 598-602.

[501] Sandra Bem, "Gender Schema Theory: A Cognitive Account of Sex Typing," *Psychological Review, 88* (no. 4), 354-364 (1981), pp. 354-355; quote is from p. 354.

[502] Ibid, p. 355.

[503] Ibid.

[504] Ibid, pp. 355-356.

[505] Ibid, p. 362.

[506] Ibid, p. 363.

[507] Bem, "Gender Schema Theory and Its Implications for Child Development," p. 608.

[508] Ibid, p. 600.

[509] Ibid, pp. 610-615. Throughout this discussion Bem offers concrete examples drawn from the parenting undertaken by herself and her husband.

[510] Spencer K. Thompson, "Gender Labels and Early Sex Role Development," *Child Development, 46* (no. 2), 339-347 (1975).

[511] The developmental processes at work, their progression, and the role of dress are covered in G. G. Bolich, *Crossdressing in Context, vol 1: The Context of Dress and Gender* (Raleigh, NC: Psyche's Press, 2007), Q. 6.

[512] In fact, these pressures are at the heart of one possible explanation for male crossdressing; see G. G. Bolich, *Crossdressing in Context, vol 2: The Context of Transgender Realities* (Raleigh, NC: Psyche's Press, 2007), Q. 22. In the literature, see Manuel X. Zamarripa, Bruce E. Wampold, & Erik Gregory, "Male Gender Role Conflict, Depression, and Anxiety: Clarification and Generalizability to Women," *Journal of Counseling Psychology, 50* (no. 3), 333-338 (2003), p. 333. Cf. J. M. O'Neil, "Patterns of Gender Role Conflict and Strain: Sexism and Fear of Femininity in Men's Lives," *Personnel and Guidance Journal, 60,* 203-210 (1981).

[513] Elizabeth S. Spelke & Cynthia J. Owsley, "Intermodal Exploration and Knowledge in Infancy," *Infant Behavior and Development, 2,* 13-27 (1979).

[514] Diane Poulin-Dubois, Lisa A. Serbin, Brenda Kenyon, & Alison Derbyshire, "Infants' Intermodal Knowledge About Gender," *Developmental Psychology, 30* (no. 3), 436-442 (1994).

[515] Cynthia L. Miller, Barbara A. Younger, & Philip A. Morse, "Categorization of Male and Female Voices in Infancy," *Infant Behavior and Development, 5,* 143-159 (1982).

[516] Beverly I. Fagot & Mary D. Leinbach, "Gender-Role Development in Young Children: From Discrimination to Labeling," *Developmental Review, 13*, 205-224 (1993).

[517] The constancy and importance of dress as a marker for children has been noted in many studies. At least as far back as 1947 a large study involving 200 boys and girls ages 412 found they relied on dress cues first and foremost in making differentiations among peers. See J. H. Conn & L. Kanner, "Children's Awareness of Sex Differences," *Child Psychiatry, 1*, 357 (1947).

[518] Thompson.

[519] Beverly I. Fagot & Mary D. Leinbach, "The Young Child's Gender Schema: Environmental Input, Internal Organization," *Child Development, 60* (no. 3), 663-672 (1989). Even as small children are learning and applying expectations about dress based on gender, these expectations are being applied to them by adults. For example, a study reported in 1993, involving 100 young women in an introductory early childhood education course found that they held expectations about preschoolers based on the children's sex-typed clothing, their perceived sex (the students were shown photos in which the clothing and child images were manipulated), and the students' own sex-role stereotypes. See K. K. P. Johnson & J. E. Workman, "Effect of Clothing, Sex, and Sex Role Stereotypes on Behavioral Expectations of a Preschool Kid," *Clothing & Textiles Research Journal, 11* (no. 2), 1-6 (1993).

[520] Consider, for example, a developmental study of 95 girls ages 210 using the Measure of Attitudes Toward Clothing for Play (MACP) to assess them. Four different clothing styles were matched with play activities; as the girls grew older they increasingly associated wearing jeans with more aggressive and physically active play, while frilly dress was associated with doll play. A follow-up study, involving 43 of the same subjects, focused on traits, found similar results: jeans were associated with aggression, strength and bravery; frilly clothes were associated with a concern with appearance and popularity. See S. B. Kaiser, "Clothing and the Social Organization of Gender Perception: A Developmental Approach," *Clothing & Textiles Research Journal, 7* (no. 2), 46-54 (1989).

[521] Carol Lynn Martin & Jane K. Little, "The Relation of Gender Understanding to Children's Sex-Typed Preferences and Gender Stereotypes," *Child Development, 61* (no. 5), 1427-1439 (1990); quote is from p. 1436.

Chapter 8 Notes

[522] Daniel R. Miller & Guy E. Swanson, *Inner Conflict and Defense* (N. Y.: Holt, Rinehart and Winston, 1960). Quoted in Lorraine Nadelman, *Research Manual in Child Development* (Mahwah, NJ: Lawrence Erlbaum, 2004), p. 321.

[523] Nathaniel MacConaghy, *Sexual Behavior: Problems and Management* (N. Y.: Plenum, 1993).

[524] Linda J. Nicholson, "Interpreting Gender," in L. Nicholson & S. Seidman (Eds.), *Social Postmodernism: Beyond Identity Politics*, pp. 39-67 (N. Y.: Cambridge Univ. Press, 1995), p. 48.

525 John P. DeCecco & Michael G. Shively, "From Sexual Identity to Sexual Relationships: A Contextual Shift," *Journal of Homosexuality, 9* (nos. 2/3), 1-26 (1983-1984), p. 1f.

526 Michael G. Shively & John P. DeCecco, "Components of Sexual Identity," *Journal of Homosexuality, 3* (no. 1), 41-48 (1977).

527 Ibid. For a consideration of how the use of terms has changed since this use by Shively and DeCecco, see Janis S. Bohan, *Psychology and Sexual Orientation: Coming to Terms* (N. Y.: Routledge, 1996), p. 4.

528 Walter O. Bockting, "From Construction to Context: Gender Through the Eyes of the Transgendered," *SIECUS Report, 28* (no. 1), 37 (1999, Oct./Nov.), p. 3.

529 Walter O. Bockting & Eli Coleman, "A Comprehensive Approach to the Treatment of Gender Dysphoria," in W. O. Bockting & E. Coleman (Eds.), *Gender Dysphoria: Interdisciplinary Approaches in Clinical Management*, pp. 131-153 (Binghamton, NY: Haworth, 1992), p. 137.

530 Andrew J. Weigert, J. Smith Teitge, & Dennis W. Teitge, *Society and Identity: Toward a Sociological Psychology* (N. Y.: Cambridge Univ. Press, 1986), pp. 67-68.

531 Jacquelyn N. Zita, *Body Talk: Philosophical Reflections on Sex and Gender* (N. Y.: Columbia Univ. Press, 1998), p. 95.

532 Ibid, p. 93.

533 Ibid, pp. 93-95.

534 Diane Reay, "'Spice Girls', 'Nice Girls', 'Girlies', and 'Tomboys': Gender Discourses, Girls' Cultures and Femininities in the Primary Classroom," *Gender and Education, 13* (no. 2), 153-166 (2001), p. 161f.

535 George A. Kelly, *The Psychology of Personal Constructs*, 2 vols. (N. Y.: Norton, 1955). Also see his *A Theory of Personality: The Psychology of Personal Constructs* (N. Y.: Norton, 1963).

536 Richard F. Docter, *Transvestites and Transsexuals: Toward a Theory of Cross-Gender Behavior.* (N. Y.: Plenum Press, 1988). See especially chapter 4, pp. 73-91.

537 Docter acknowledges a number of theorists, beginning with William James. Among the most influential are the following: George A. Kelly, *The Psychology of Personal Constructs*, 2 vols. (N. Y.: W. W. Norton, 1955); S. Epstein, "The Self-Concept Revisited: Or a Theory of a Theory," *American Psychologist, 28*, 404-416; Ernest R. Hilgard, *Divided Consciousness Multiple Controls in Human Thoughts and Actions* (N. Y.: Wiley, 1977).

538 Docter, pp. 3, 86-87, 93-102, 112-118, 198-201.

539 Ibid, p. 9.

540 Ibid, pp. 201-215.

541 C. D. Doorn, J. Poortinga, & A. M. Verschoor, "Cross-Gender Identity in Transvestites and Male Transsexuals," *Archives of Sexual Behavior, 23* (no. 2), 185-201 (1994). The authors conclude their research demonstrates that Docter's theory is not completely correct, particularly the idea that the gender identity subsystem is dichoto-

mous, i.e., either masculine or feminine. In their Discussion section they also discuss the "special form" of crossdressing—fetishistic crossdressing—where the theoretically separate identity subsystems are expressed in combination.

[542] Sam Larsson & Maj-Briht Bergström-Walan, "Multi-sexuality, Cross-dressing and the Multiplicity of Mind," *Scandinavian Journal of Sexology, 2* (no. 3), 141-161 (1999).

[543] Richard Ekins & Dave King, "Towards a Sociology of Transgendered Bodies," *The Sociological Review, 47*, 580-602 (1999). Also see Richard Ekins & Dave King, "Tales of the Unexpected: Exploring Transgender Diversity Through Personal Narrative," in F. Haynes and T. McKenna (Eds), *Unseen Genders: Beyond the Binaries* (N. Y.: Peter Lang, 2001).

[544] Richard Ekins & Dave King, "Telling Body Transgendering Stories," in K. Milburn and L. McKie (Eds), *Constructing Gendered Bodies*, (London: Palgrave, 2001).

[545] Ekins & King, "Tales of the Unexpected."

[546] John M. Sloop, *Disciplining Gender: Rhetorics of Sex Identity in Contemporary U.S. Culture* (Amherst: Univ. of Massachusetts Press, 2004), p. 2.

[547] John Money, "Gender Role, Gender Identity, Core Gender Identity," *The Journal of the American Academy of Psychoanalysis and Dynamic Psychiatry, 1*, 397-402 (1973), p. 397. Cf. John Money, J. G. Hampson, & J. L. Hampson, "An Examination of Some Basic Sexual Concepts: The Evidence of Human Hermaphroditism," *Bulletin of Johns Hopkins Hospital, 97*, 301-319 (1955), p. 302. Also see by the same authors, "Hermaphroditism: Recommendations Concerning Assignment of Sex, Change of Sex, and Psychological Management," *Bulletin of Johns Hopkins Hospital, 97*, 284-300 (1955).

[548] Cf. Freud's remarks in *Three Essays on the Theory of Sexuality*, translated J. Strachey (N. Y.: Basic Books, 1962; original ed. 1905). His discussion of sexual aberrations is representative of thinking common then and now. He writes (p. 15) that "the normal sexual aim is regarded as being the union of the genitals in the act known as copulation. . . ." But the mere act of intercourse hardly suffices for most people so that Freud (p. 15) can observe the "rudiments" of sexual perversion (i.e., deviations from the normal sexual aim) in even "the most normal sexual process." He defines *perversions* (p. 16) as sexual activities that either involve regions of the body (e.g., mouth or anus) not designed for sexual union, or that linger in their focus prior to intercourse itself (i.e., the things we collectively call 'foreplay'). Given this state of affairs, Freud concludes (p. 26), "No healthy person, it appears, can fail to make some addition that might be called perverse to the normal sexual aim; and the universality of this showing is in itself enough to show how inappropriate it is to use the word perversion as a term of reproach."

[549] *Bias* is a negative predisposition toward someone or something. *Prejudice* means a prejudgment, typically negative, toward someone or something, generally reflecting bias. *Discrimination* are judgmental acts, whether actively doing something or passively refusing to do something, that carry out the judgment of prejudice.

[550] Patricia Gagne, Richard Tewksbury, & Deanna McGaughey, "Coming Out and Crossing Over: Identity Formation and Proclamation in a Transgender Community," *Gender and Society, 11* (no. 4), 478-508 (1997), p. 504.

[551] Ibid.

[552] Ibid, p. 479.

[553] Holly Devor, "Who Are 'We'? Where Sexual Orientation Meets Gender Identity," *Journal of Lesbian and Gay Psychotherapy, 6* (no. 2), 5-21 (2002).

[554] American Psychiatric Association, *Diagnostic and Statistical Manual of Mental Disorders, 3rd ed.* (Washington, D. C.: American Psychiatric Association, 1980), p. 262. Hereafter cited as DSM-III.

[555] American Psychiatric Association, *Diagnostic and Statistical Manual of Mental Disorders, 4th ed., Text Revision* (Washington, D. C.: American Psychiatric Association, 2000), p. 582. Hereafter cited as DSM-IV-TR. The text revision shows the strong influence of Ray Blanchard, discussed in the main body of the chapter. For his connecting of gender identity and sexual orientation see Ray Blanchard, "The Classification and Labeling of Nonhomosexual Gender Dysphorias," *Archives of Sexual Behavior, 18* (no. 4), 315-334 (1989). Curiously, perhaps reflecting our culture's fascination and unease with the differently gendered, attention to sexual orientation only seems to attach itself to consideration of those labeled gender dysphoric.

[556] DSM-III, pp. 261-266. The three diagnostic possibilities were 'transsexualism,' 'gender identity disorder of childhood,' and 'atypical gender identity disorder.'

[557] American Psychiatric Association, *Diagnostic and Statistical Manual of Mental Disorders, 3rd ed. rev.* (Washington, D. C.: American Psychiatric Association, 1987), pp. 71-78. The four diagnostic possibilities were 'transsexualism,' 'gender identity disorder of childhood,' 'gender identity disorder of adolescence or adulthood, nontranssexual type' (GIDAANT), and 'gender identity order not otherwise specified' (NOS).

[558] American Psychiatric Association, *Diagnostic and Statistical Manual of Mental Disorders, 4th ed.* (Washington, D. C.: American Psychiatric Association, 1994), pp. 532-538. The two diagnostic possibilities are 'gender identity disorder' and 'gender identity disorder NOS.'

[559] DSM-IV-TR, p. 578. For a more complete treatment of the history of transgender conditions in the DSM model, see G. G. Bolich, *Crossdressing in Context, vol. 4: The Context of Mental Health* (forthcoming), Q. 96.

[560] Ibid, p. 581; DSM-IV, p. 537.

[561] Ray Blanchard, "Gender Dysphoria and Gender Reorientation," in Betty W. Steiner (Ed.), *Gender Dysphoria: Development, Research, and Management*, pp. 365-392 (N. Y.: Plenum Press, 1985), p. 365. Cf. Ray Blanchard, Betty W. Steiner, & Leonard H. Clemmensen, "Gender Dysphoria, Gender Reorientation, and the Clinical Management of Transsexualism," *Journal of Consulting & Clinical Psychology, 53*, 295-304 (1985).

[562] Nancy H. Bartlett, Paul L. Vasey, & William M. Bukowski, "Is Gender Identity Disorder in Children a Mental Disorder?" *Sex Roles, 43* (nos. 11-12), 753-785 (2000). See DSM-IV, p. 537f., or DSM-IV-TR, p. 581f. for the criteria; cf. the answer to Q. 96. See especially the authors' discussion of the DSM logic in their section entitled 'Concept of Mental Disorders in DMS-IV' (p. 755).

[563] Bartlett, Vasey, & Bukowski, pp. 755-757.

564 Holly Devor, "Female Gender Dysphoria in Context: Social Problem or Personal Problem?" *Annual Review of Sex Research, 7*, 44-89 (1996).

565 Justin Richardson, "Setting the Limits on Gender Health," *Harvard Review of Psychiatry, 4*, 49-53 (1996). Cf. Justin Richardson, "Response: Finding the Disorder in Gender Identity Disorder," *Harvard Review of Psychiatry, 7*, 43-50 (1999).

566 "Government Policy Concerning Transsexual People," *Department for Constitutional Affairs*. Accessed online at http://www.dca.gov.uk/constitution/transsex/policy. htm. Point #6 in the 'Introduction' declares: "It is *not* a mental illness. It is a condition considered *in itself* to be free of other pathology (though transsexual people can suffer depression or illnesses like anyone else)."

567 See Lawrence Morahan, "Psychiatric Association Debates Reclassifying Pedophilia," *CNSNews.com* (2003, June 11). Accessed online at http://www.cnsnews.com/ViewCulture.asp? Page=%5CCulture%5Carchive%5C200306%5CCUL20030611c.html.

568 Susan J. Langer & James I. Martin, "How Dresses Can Make You Mentally Ill: Examining Gender Identity Disorder in Children," *Child and Adolescent Social Work Journal, 21* (no. 1), 5-23 (2004).

569 Joan Roughgarden, "Evolution and the Embodiment of Gender," *GLQ: A Journal of Lesbian and Gay Studies, 10*, 287-291 (2004), p. 291.

Chapter 9 Notes

570 Carol Lynn Martin, "Gender," in A. S. R. Manstead & M. Hewstone (Eds.), *The Blackwell Encyclopedia of Social Psychology*, pp. 253-258 (Malden, MA: Blackwell, 1995-1996), p. 255.

571 A great deal has been written on this matter. A convenient introduction can be found in G. G. Bolich, *Crossdressing in Context, vol. 2: The Context of Transgender Realities* (Raleigh, NC: Psyche's Press, 2007), Q. 29.

572 Kay Bussey & Albert Bandura, "Social Cognitive Theory of Gender Development and Differentiation," *Psychological Review, 106*, 676-713 (1999), p. 689.

573 Lee Combrinck-Graham & Lawrence Kerns, "Intimacy in Families with Young Children," in D. Kantor & B. F. Okun (Eds.), *Intimate Environments: Sex, Intimacy and Gender in Families and Family Therapy*, pp. 74-92 (N. Y.: Guilford, 1989), p. 86f.

574 Another term occasionally encountered is *sex role identity*. While this term seems inherently confusing, what it typically does is subsume the concept of identity under that of role and treat both in terms of social expectations and socialization (i.e., sex typing). So, identity becomes endorsement of a sex label (male or female) for the self, and this becomes the hub for sex role performance. Unfortunately, as with other terms discussed throughout our dialog, consistency of usage does not exist.

575 Eleanor Emmons Maccoby & Carol Nagy Jacklin, *The Psychology of Sex Differences* (Stanford, CA: Stanford Univ. Press, 1974), p. 2.

576 Eleanor Maccoby, "Gender Identity and Sex Role Adoption," in H. Katchadourian (Ed.), *Human Sexuality*, pp. 194-203 (Berkeley: Univ. of California Press, 1979).

577 Eleanor Maccoby, "Gender as a Social Category," *Developmental Psychology, 24* (no. 6), 755-765 (1988), p. 755.

578 Ibid.

579 Eleanor Maccoby, *The Two Sexes: Growing Up Apart, Coming Together* (Cambridge: Harvard Univ. Press, 1998).

580 Maccoby has been criticized by other scholars who believe her efforts to hedge her assertions by reminding us that many observed social behaviors do not fall clearly into gendered patterns are overshadowed by her basic contention that evolutionary biology, universal in scope, guides and constrains gender roles. For criticism of Maccoby, see, for example, Rosalind C. Barnett & Caryl River, *Same Difference. How Gender Myths Are Hurting Our Relationships, Our Children, and Our Jobs* (N. Y.: Basic Books, 2004), pp. 218ff. On some of the worrisome implications of using this approach to understand gender, see Kira Hall, "Exceptional Speakers: Contested and Problematized Gender Identities," in J. Holmes & M. Meyerhoff (Eds.), *The Handbook of language and Gender*, pp. 353-380 (Malden, MA: Blackwell, 2003), pp. 368-369.

581 Bernadette J. Brooten, *Love Between Women: Early Christian Responses to Female Homoeroticism* (Chicago: Univ. of Chicago Press, 1996), p. 209 n. 51.

582 Paula Nicolson, "Feminist and Evolutionary Psychology: Ideology or Method?" [Editorial], *Psychology, Evolution & Gender, 1* (no. 1), 1-10 (1999), p. 3.

583 Imagine how hard it is to study a sex other than male or female when those are the only choices permitted by a culture. Even when indisputable visual evidence shows a body with the apparent characteristics of both male and female, this evidence must be seen in light of the two allowed alternatives and interpreted in that light. Thus the intersexed must be seen as either *more male* or *more female* and sex-assigned to one or the other. The same problems hold for gender, only they are exacerbated by the tie to sex. The failure to see that sex does *not* determine gender leaves us vulnerable to the power of culture, not biology, because we remain oblivious to the way in which our world is filtered by our culture. We may think we are doing good science when all we are doing is perpetuating cultural propaganda.

584 Linda Gannon, "A Critique of Evolutionary Psychology," *Psychology, Evolution & Gender, 4* (no. 2), 173-218 (2002). Gannon herself has sought common ground between feminism and evolutionary psychology. See her "A Common Ground for Feminism and Evolution," *Psychology, Evolution & Gender, 1* (no. 1), 45-56 (1999). Gannon's contention is that feminists, in opposing sociobiology, ended up throwing the baby out with the bathwater by dismissing evolution and ultimately biology from consideration. She believes the richness of evolutionary theory offers alternatives feminist science can be enriched by. In particular, Gannon favors following Nobel prize winner Gerald Edelman's understanding of evolution, dubbed 'neural Darwinism.' It posits a brain structure that at birth is genetically determined, but largely unspecified. Genetics *constrains* rather than *determines*; the way an individual's brain develops is the result of interactions among biology, development, and experience. In human beings, natural selection and species-specific genetic programming have yielded *language*, the heart of culture. Together, language, social context and culture create the potential for change. In fact, Gannon argues (p. 51), evolution has produced a human species that "is less determined

by genetics and more influenced by experience." Human beings have the potential to effect significant environmental adaptation *within a single lifetime*. What Gannon thinks feminists will find appealing is that this 'neural Darwinism' is not deterministic and views human beings as capable of transcending the dictates of biology. Gannon writes (p. 52), "Although neural Darwinism is, indeed, biological, the biology is continually shaped and created by experience in a social context throughout the individual's lifetime." In terms of our gendered world—a creation of our predecessors—it is neither as unchanging or unchangeable as it might seem. In this theory, subjectivity and objectivity meet. An individual's biological system itself is socially constructed, replete with values and subjectivity. In this respect, as Gannon concludes (p. 55), "The socially constructed self *is* the biologically constructed self."

[585] David Buss, *Evolutionary Psychology. The New Science of the Mind* (Boston: Allyn & Bacon, 1999), pp. 18-22; quote is from p. 20.

[586] Anne Campbell, *A Mind of Her Own: The Evolutionary Psychology of Women* (N. Y.: Oxford Univ. Press, 2002), p. 1.

[587] Anne Campbell, "Gender, Evolution and Psychology: Nine Feminist Concerns Addressed," *Psychology, Evolution & Gender, 1* (no. 1), 57-80 (1999), p. 57. Campbell writes that a 'broad sense' feminist is one who believes that women have been oppressed by men and women's standing should be improved. That she believes evolutionary psychology and feminism do not have to be oppositional is the thrust in her article.

[588] Campbell, *A Mind of Her Own*, p. 3.

[589] Ibid.

[590] Robert L. Trivers, "Parental Investment and Sexual Selection," in B. Campbell (Ed.), *Sexual Selection and the Descent of Man, 1871-1971*, pp. 136-179 (Chicago: Aldine-Atherton, 1972). However, be sure to note as well the challenge posed by the research of primatologist Sarah Blaffer Hrdy, "Sex-Based Parental Investment Among Primates and Other Mammals: A Critical Evaluation of the Trivers-Willard Hypothesis," in R. J. Gelles & J. B. Lancaster (Eds.), *Child Abuse and Neglect: Biosocial Dimensions*, pp. 119-146 (Hawthorne, N Y: Aldine De Gruyter, 1987). Hrdy remarks "It suits the male imagination to think about how the dominant male can get the maximum number of copulations"; see V. Morrell, "Seeing Nature Through the Lens of Gender," *Science, 260*, 428-429 (1993), p. 429.

[591] Buss, pp. 99-130, especially p. 105, Table 4.1.

[592] Ibid, pp. 131-160.

[593] David J. Boller, "Sex, Jealousy & Violence. A Skeptical Look at Evolutionary Psychology," *Skeptic, 12* (no. 1). Accessed online at http://www.skeptic.com/the_magazine/featured_articles/v12n01_sex_jealousy.html.

[594] Valerie J. Grant, "The Maternal Dominance Hypothesis: Questioning Trivers and Willard," *Evolutionary Psychology, 1*, 96-107 (2003), pp. 99-101.

[595] Ibid, p. 100.

596 Tim Megarry, "What Made Us Human? Reflections on Sex and Gender in Human Evolution," *Psychology, Evolution & Gender, 3* (no. 2), 167-187 (2001), p. 169. His argument for why men are hunters and women gatherers is found p. 179f., where he observes that women are "productive, efficient predators" of fish and small animals, no evidence exists of them having status as hunters of large animals. He also points out that this sex-determined division of labor is not usually a source of social conflict.

597 Ibid, p. 170.

598 Edward O. Wilson, *Sociobiology: The New Synthesis* (Cambridge: Harvard Univ. Press, 1975). Also see his Pulitzer prize winning, *On Human Nature* (Cambridge: Harvard Univ. Press, 1978). On the question of culture from an evolutionary perspective, see Stephen C. Levinson & Pierre Jaisson (Eds.), *Evolution and Culture* (Cambridge, MA: MIT Press, 2005).

599 On her professional profile for the Social Psychology Network, Eagly lists as one of her primary projects "developing a critique of evolutionary psychology, which provides an alternative origin theory of sex differences." Accessed online at http://eagly. socialpsychology.org/

600 Wendy Wood & Alice H. Eagly, "A Cross-Cultural Analysis of the Behaviorr of Women and Men: Implications for the Origins of Sex Differences," *Psychological Bulletin, 128* (no. 5), 699-727 (2002), p. 699. *Proximal* and *distal* are terms familiar to anatomy students and refer to 'nearer' (close at hand) and 'further' (distant). A proximal cause is the antecedent of an effect, the closest link in the causal chain. A distal cause is further removed up the causal chain. The quest for distal causes is one for ultimate causes, in this case the 'origin' of sex differences.

601 Alice H. Eagly, *Sex Differences in Social Behavior: A Social-Role Interpretation* (Hillsdale, NJ: Lawrence Erlbaum, 1987), pp. 1-2.

602 Ibid, p. 3.

603 Ibid.

604 Ibid, pp. 4-5.

605 Alice H. Eagly & Wendy Wood, "The Origins of Sex Differences in Human Behavior. Evolved Dispositions Versus Social Roles," *American Psychologist, 54* (no. 6), 408-423 (1999), p. 408.

606 Ibid, p. 409.

607 Ibid, p. 421.

608 Wood & Eagly, "A Cross-Cultural Analysis," p. 701. Also see Alice H. Eagly, Wendy Wood, & Mary C. Johannesen-Schmidt, "Social Role Theory of Sex Differences and Similarities: Implications for the Partner Preferences of Women and Men," in A. H. Eagly, A. E. Beall, & R. J. Sternberg (Eds.), *The Psychology of Gender*, 2nd ed., pp. 269-295 (N. Y.: Guilford, 2004).

609 Ibid, p. 702.

610 Ibid, p. 717.

611 Ibid, p. 701.

612 Ibid, p. 704.

613 Ibid, pp. 710-718; quote is from p. 718.

614 Maccoby & Jacklin, *The Psychology of Sex Differences*, pp. 349-351.

615 Ibid, pp. 351-352.

616 Ibid, pp. 352-354. For a brief critique of Maccoby & Jacklin, see Martin Daly & Margo Wilson, *Sex, Evolution, and Behavior*, 2nd ed. (Boston: PWS Publishers, 1983), pp. 265-266.

617 On this general subject, see Robin Lakoff, *Language and Woman's Place* (n. Y.: Harper & Row, 1975).

618 Deborah Tannen, *That's Not What I Meant!* (N. Y.: Ballantine Books, 1986), p. 125.

619 Ibid.

620 Ibid, pp. 15-20. Tannen (e.g., p. 126) does remind us that regardless of gender we all need both kinds of talk, even if the genders tend to favor one or the other.

621 Deborah Tannen, *You Just Don't Understand. Women and Men in Conversation* (N. Y.: Ballantine Books, 1990), p. 76f.

622 This simplification is not meant in any way to diminish the standing of social role theory or the biosocial model proposed by Wood and Eagly. They have plenty to say in various works on matters like the ones discussed here. For example, they dispute evolutionary psychology in regard to physical dimorphism between the sexes being a major influence on either male aggressiveness or competitive dominance ("A Cross-Cultural Analysis," p. 702). Both because their position takes a mediating position, and because so much of the conversation on differences is set as a contrast between social constructionist and evolutionary psychologists, they are set to one side here. To get a sense of how alleged trait differences are treated by social role theory, see Michele Grossmann & Wendy Wood, "Sex Differences in Intensity of Emotional Experience: A Social Role Interpretation," *Journal of Personality & Social Psychology, 65* (no. 5), 1010-1022 (1993). Also see Alice H. Eagly & Anne M. Koenig, "Social Role Theory of Sex Differences and Similarities: Implications for Prosocial Behavior," in K. Dindia & D. J. Canary (Eds.), *Sex Differences and Similarities in Communication*, 2nd ed., pp. 161-177 (Mahwah, NJ: Lawrence Erlbaum, 2006).

623 Buss, pp. 281-283.

624 See Buss, pp. 285-287.

625 Robert O. Deaner, "More Males Run Relatively Fast in U. S. Road Races: Further Evidence of a Sex Difference in Competitiveness," *Evolutionary Psychology, 4*, 303-314 (2006); quote is from p. 303.

626 John E. Edlund, Jeremy D. Heider, Cory R. Scherer, Maria-Magdalena Farc, & Brad J. Sagarin, "Sex Differences in Jealousy in Response to Actual Infidelity," *Evolutionary Psychology, 4*, 462-470 (2006). Cf. Buss, pp. 325-329.

627 Buss, p. 325. He references two studies not finding such differences. They are G. L. White, "Some Correlates of Romantic Jealousy," *Journal of Personality, 49*, 129-147

(1981), and A. P. Buunk & R. B. Hupka, "Cross-Cultural Differences in the Elicitation of Sexual Jealousy," *Journal of Sex Research, 23* (no. 1), 12-22 (1987). A critique of Buss' position can be found in Boller, "Sex, Jealousy & Violence."

[628] Cf. the discussion in Ivan Illich, *Gender* (N. Y.: Pantheon, 1982), pp. 46-47, notes 31-32.

[629] See Michele Adams & Scott Coltrane, "Boys and Men in Families: The Domestic Production of Gender, Power, and Privilege," in M. S. Kimmel, J. Hearn, & R. W. Connell (Eds.), *Handbook of Studies on Men & Masculinities*, pp. 230-248 (Thousand Oaks, CA: Sage, 2005), p. 240. Cf. Janet Z. Giele, "Gender and Sex Roles," in N. J. Smelser (Ed.), *The Handbook of Sociology*, pp. 291-323 (Newbury Park, CA: Sage, 1988).

[630] Gloria Bird & Keith Melville, *Families and Intimate Relationships* (N. Y.: McGraw-Hill, 1994), pp. 207-208.

[631] M. Rivka Polatnick, "Why Men Don't Rear Children," in A. Minas (Ed.), *Gender Basics. Feminist Perspectives on Women and Men*, pp. 500-507 (Belmont, CA: Wadsworth, 1993), p. 505.

[632] Nicolson, p. 1.

Chapter 10 Notes

[633] Cf. Amanda B. Dickman & Wind Goodfriend, "Rolling with the Changes: A Role Congruity Perspective on Gender Norms," *Psychology of Women Quarterly, 30*, 369-383 (2006), p. 369f. They distinguish descriptive beliefs from prescriptive ones as the former designating the *likelihood* groups will possess certain traits and the latter designating the *value* of those traits.

[634] See Janet T. Spence & Camille E. Buckner, "Instrumental and Expressive Traits, Trait Stereotypes, and Sexist Attitudes. What Do They Signify?" *Psychology of Women Quarterly, 24* (no. 1), 44-62 (2000).

[635] David Bakan, *The Duality of Human Existence. Isolation and Communion in Western Man* (Boston: Beacon Press, 1966), p. 14f.

[636] Ibid, p. 110.

[637] Ibid, p. 15.

[638] Evalyn Jacobson Michaelson & Leigh M. Aaland, "Masculinity, Femininity, and Androgyny," *Ethos, 4* (no. 2), 251-270 (1976). Quote is from p. 169.

[639] Diekman & Wind, especially p. 380.

[640] Stephanie Kasen, Henian Chen, Joel Sneed, Thomas Crawford, & Patricia Cohen, "Social Role and Birth Cohort Influences on Gender-Linked Personality Traits in Women: A 20-Year Longitudinal Analysis," *Journal of Personality and Social Psychology, 91* (no. 5), 944-958. Quote is from p. 944.

[641] Ibid, pp. 951-954; quote is from p. 952.

[642] Lloyd B. Lueptow, Lori Garovich-Szabo, & Margaret B. Lueptow, "Social Change and the Persistence of Sex Typing: 1974-1997," *Social Forces, 80* (no. 1), 1-36 (2001). Quotes are from p. 2 (cf. p. 16) and p. 23 (italics in original). The authors sug-

gest their findings are bad news for social constructionists and good news for evolutionary psychologists.

[643] Lloyd B. Lueptow, *Adolescent Sex Roles and Social Change* (N. Y.: Columbia Univ. Press, 1984); summarized in Lueptow, Garovich-Szabo, & Lueptow, p. 6.

[644] Simone de Beauvoir, *The Second Sex* (N. Y.: Alfred Knopf, 1952), p. xvi.

[645] As may have been inferred by now, research into stereotypes relies much on the use of lists of adjectives. Research participants are asked to associate or rank selected adjectives with reference to gender.

[646] Robert Crooks & Carla Baur, *Our Sexuality*, 7th ed. (Pacific Grove, CA: Brooks/Cole, 1999), pp. 68-71.

[647] Lewis M. Terman & Catherine C. Miles, *Sex and Personality* (N. Y.: McGraw-Hill, 1936).

[648] Peter Hegarty, "'More Feminine Than 999 Men out of 1,000.' Measuring Sex Roles and Gender Nonconformity in Psychology," in T. Lester (Ed.), *Gender Nonconformity, Race, and Sexuality. Charting the Connections*, pp. 63-83 (Madison: Univ. of Wisconsin Press, 2002). Quote is from p. 67. Also see B. G. Rosenberg & B. Sutton-Smith, "The Measurement of Masculinity and Femininity in Children," *Child Development, 30* (no. 3), 373-380 (1959). The authors, a quarter century after the Terman & Miles test appeared, report problems with its applicability to a current generation of children.

[649] Harrison G. Gough & Alfred B. Heilbrun, *The Adjective Check List Manual*, rev. ed. (Palo Alto, CA: Consulting Psychologists Press, 1983; original edition, 1965).

[650] John E. Williams & Deborah L. Best, *Measuring Sex Stereotypes: A Multination Study*, rev. ed. (Beverly Hills, CA: Sage, 1990). Also see their "Sex Stereotypes and Trait Favorability on the Adjective Check List," *Educational and Psychological Measurement, 37*, 101-110 (1977), and *Measuring Sex Stereotypes: A Thirty Nation Study* (Newbury Park, CA: Sage, 1982).

[651] Janet T. Spence & Robert L. Helmreich, *Masculinity and Femininity: Their Psychological Dimensions, Correlates and Antecedents* (Austin: Univ. of Texas Press, 1978). Also see Jan D. Yoder, Robert W. Rice, Jerome Adams, Robert F. Priest, & Howard T. Prince II, "Reliability of the Attitudes Toward Women Scale (AWS) and the Personal Attributes Questionnaire (PAQ)," *Sex Roles, 8* (no. 6), 651-657 (1982).

[652] Brief descriptions of each of these can be found in Donald F. Walker, David M. Tokar, & Ann R. Fischer, "What Are Eight Popular Masculinity-Related Instruments Measuring? Underlying Dimensions and Their Relations to Sociosexuality," *Psychology of Men and Masculinity, 1* (no. 2), 98-108 (2000), pp. 100-102.

[653] See the *Gender Role Conflict Research Program* website maintained by Jim O'Neil at the University of Connecticut, accessed online at http://web.uconn.edu/joneil/Gender Home.html. In the literature, see J. M. O'Neil, B. J. Helms, R. K. Gable, L. David, & L. S. Wrightsman, "Gender-Role Conflict Scale: College Men's Fear of Femininity," *Sex Roles, 14* (nos. 5-6), 335-352 (1986). A thorough listing of the literature is also available at the website.

654 Glenn E. Good, John M. Robertson, Jim M. O'Neil, Louise F. Fitzgerald, Mark Stevens, Kurt A. DeBord, Kim M. Bartels, & David G. Braverman, "Male Gender Role Conflict: Psychometric Issues and Relations to Psychological Distress," *Journal of Counseling Psychology, 42* (no. 1), 3-10 (1995).

655 See Manuel X. Zamarripa, Bruce E. Wampold, & Erik Gregory, "Male Gender Role Conflict, Depression, and Anxiety: Clarification and Generalizability to Women," *Journal of Counseling Psychology, 50* (no. 3), 333-338 (2003), p. 333.

656 John E. Williams, Robert C. Satterwhite, & Deborah L. Best, "Pancultural Gender Stereotypes Revisited: The Five Factor Model," *Sex Roles, 40* (nos. 7-8), 513-525 (1999).

657 Cf. Jane Pilcher & Imelda Whelehan, *50 Key Concepts in Gender Studies* (Thousand Oaks, CA: Sage, 2004), p. 83.

658 Robert W. Connell, *Masculinites* (Cambridge: Polity Press, 1995). Also see his *The Men and the Boys* (Cambridge: Polity Press, 2000).

659 Kevin R. Murphy & Charles O. Davidshofer, *Psychological Testing. Principles and Applications*, 6th ed. (Upper Saddle River, NJ: Prentice-Hall, 2005), p. 163.

660 John Stoltenberg, *Refusing to be a Man* (London: Routledge, 2003 reprint of 2000 rev. ed.; work originally published 1989), p. 182.

661 Williams, Satterwhite, & Best, Table I.

662 Robert W. Connell, "R. W. Connell's 'Masculinities': Reply," *Gender and Society, 12* (no. 4), 474-477 (1998), p. 476.

663 Robert W. Connell, *Masculinities* (Berkeley: Univ. of California Press, 1995), p. 3.

664 Connell, "Reply," p. 475.

665 Tim Corrigan, Bob Connell, & John Lee, "Toward a New Sociology of Masculinity," *Theory and Society, 14* (no. 5), 551-604 (1985), pp. 589-590; quote is from p. 590.

666 Ibid, p. 590.

667 Ibid, pp. 591-592.

668 Ibid, p. 592. Cf. his "The Big Picture: Masculinities in Recent World History," *Theory and Society, 22* (no. 5), 597-623 (1993), p. 610f.

669 Ibid, p. 594. Toby Miller complains, "The thing about hegemony as a concept is that it explains everything and nothing in a circular motion." For his critique, see "Masculinity," in P. Essed, D. T. Goldberg, & A. Kobayashi (Eds.), *A Companion to Gender Studies*, pp. 114-131 (Malden, MA: Blackwell, 2005), p. 117.

670 R. W. Connell, *Gender and Power: Society, the Person and Sexual Politics* (Stanford, CA: Stanford Univ. Press, 1987). With reference to gender relations, see especially pp. 90-118.

671 Robert W. Connell, *The Men and the Boys* (Berkeley, CA: Univ. of California Press, 2001), p. 4f.

672 Ibid, p. 26.

673 See, for example, Demetrakis Z. Demetrious, "Connell's Concept of Hegemonic Masculinity: A Critique," *Theory and Society, 30* (no. 3), 337-361 (2001). Demetrios attempts to modify Connell's theory by eliminating the dualism between hegemonic masculinity and non-hegemonic masculinity. His notion of a "hegemonic masculine bloc" advances the contention (p. 355) that "the form of masculinity that is capable of reproducing patriarchy is in a constant process of negotiation, translation, hybridization, and reconfiguration."

674 Robert W. Connell, "Hegemonic Masculinity. Rethinking the Concept," *Gender and Society, 19* (no. 6), 829-859 (2005), pp. 845-853; quote is from p. 846.

675 Ruth E. Hartley, "Sex-Role Pressures and the Socialization of the Male Child," in J. H. Pleck & J. Sawyer (Eds.), *Men and Masculinity*, pp. 7-13 (Englewood Cliffs, NJ: Prentice-Hall, 1974), p. 7.

676 In fact, these pressures are at the heart of one possible explanation for male crossdressing. In the literature, cf. J. M. O'Neil, "Patterns of Gender Role Conflict and Strain: Sexism and Fear of Femininity in Men's Lives," *Personnel and Guidance Journal, 60,* 203-210 (1981).

677 Hartley, p. 7.

678 M. E. Hamburger, M. Hogben, S. McGowan, & L. J. Dawson, "Assessing Hypergender Ideologies: Development and Initial Validation of a Gender-Neutral Measure of Adherence to Extreme Gender-Role Beliefs," *Journal of Research in Personality, 30,* 157-178 (1996). They developed the Hypergender Ideology Scale (HIS).

679 Lisa Hinkelman & Darcy Haag Granello, "Biological Sex, Adherence to Traditional Gender Roles, and Attitudes Toward Persons with Mental Illness: An Exploratory Investigation," *Journal of Mental Health Counseling, 25* (no. 4), 259-270 (2003).

680 Carole R. Beal, *Boys and Girls: The Development of Gender Roles* (N. Y.: McGraw-Hill, 1994), p. 151.

681 David Plummer, *One of the Boys: Masculinity, Homophobia, and Modern Manhood* (Binghamton, NY: Haworth Press, 1999), p. 137.

682 Ibid, p. 138.

683 Homosexual boys and men, too, may take recourse to blatant homophobia in the effort to protect themselves, including their sense of being a masculine gendered self.

684 David Plummer, *One of the Boys: Masculinity, Homophobia, and Modern Manhood* (Binghamton, NY: Haworth Press, 1999), p. 145.

685 Because of the cultural decision to make gender so dependent on sex, gender challenges inevitably threaten perceptions and values tied to the physical body. If we are made to doubt even that, the unconscious worry goes, what else is left? On the role of homophobia in the construction of Western masculinity, see David Plummer, *One of the Boys: Masculinity, Homophobia, and Modern Manhood* (Binghamton, NY: Haworth Press, 1999).

686 We have known for more than a half century that boys identify more strongly with the gender expectations set for them and simultaneously show a more homoge-

nous conception of those expectations—signs consistent with the need to protect a higher class status. See D. G. Brown, "Masculinity-Femininity Development in Children," *Journal of Consulting Psychology, 21*, 197-202 (1957).

[687] Manuel X. Zamarripa, Bruce E. Wampold, & Erik Gregory, "Male Gender Role Conflict, Depression, and Anxiety: Clarification and Generalizability to Women," *Journal of Counseling Psychology, 50* (no. 3), 333-338 (2003), pp. 336-338. Cf. J. M. O'Neil, "Patterns of Gender Role Conflict and Strain: Sexism and Fear of Femininity in Men's Lives," *Personnel and Guidance Journal, 60*, 203-210 (1981).

[688] Herb Goldberg, "Men Have Changed for the Better," in N. Bernards & T. O'Neill (Eds.), *Male/Female Roles: Opposing Viewpoints*, pp. 115-121 (San Diego, CA: Greenhaven Press, 1989), p. 119.

[689] So Corrigan, Connell, and Lee (p. 575) are hesitant to even grant it status as a 'movement,' especially when compared to the Women's Liberation Movement or Gay Liberation Movement.

[690] "Berkeley Men's Center Manifesto (1973)," in J. H. Pleck & J. Sawyer (Eds.), pp. 173-174 (N. Y.: Simon & Schuster, 1974), p. 173.

[691] Warren Farrell, *The Liberated Man* (N. Y.: Random House, 1974).

[692] See Warren Farrell, *Why Men Are the Way They Are* (N. Y.: McGraw-Hill, 1986). Also see his *The Myth of Male Power: Why Men Are the Disposable Sex* (N. Y.: Simon & Schuster, 1993). For more about Farrell, and for some information about his books, see his website, accessed online at http://www.warrenfarrell.org/.

[693] Chris Beasley, *Gender & Sexuality. Critical Theories, Critical Thinkers* (Thousand Oaks, CA: Sage, 2005), p. 179.

[694] Bruce J. Schulman, *The Seventies: The Great Shift in American Culture, Society, and Politics* (Cambridge, MA: De Capo Press, 2001), p. 183.

[695] See Robert Bly, *Sleepers Joining Hands* (N. Y. : Harper & Row, 1973). Also see his *Talking All Morning: Collected Conversations and Interviews* (Ann Arbor: Univ. of Michigan Press, 1980).

[696] Robert Bly, *Iron John: A Book About Men* (Reading, MA: Addison-Wesley, 1990).

[697] This is the fourth of the seven promises. See *Seven Promises* at the Promise Keepers website, accessed online at http://www.promisekeepers.org/7Promises.aspx.

[698] These and other quotes, including from such well-known evangelical leaders as Bill Bright (Campus Crusade for Christ) and Jerry Falwell (Jerry Falwell Ministries), are posted as part of NOW's 'Promise Keepers Mobilization Project' on their *Promises of the Patriarchy* webpage, accessed online at http://www.now.org/issues/right/promise/quotes.html.

[699] Beasley, p. 181.

[700] The transcript of Minister Farrakhan's speech accessed online at the CNN website, at http://www-cgi.cnn.com/US/9510/megamarch/10-16/transcript/index.html.

[701] Barbara E. Hort, Beverly I. Fagot, & Mary Driver Leinbach, "Are People's Notions of Maleness More Stereotypically Framed Than Their Notions of Femaleness?" *Sex Roles, 23*, 197-212 (1990).

[702] We have known for more than a half century that boys identify more strongly with the gender expectations set for them and simultaneously show a more homogenous conception of those expectations—signs consistent with the need to protect a higher class status. See D. G. Brown, "Masculinity-Femininity Development in Children," *Journal of Consulting Psychology, 21*, 197-202 (1957).

[703] Manuel X. Zamarripa, Bruce E. Wampold, & Erik Gregory, "Male Gender Role Conflict, Depression, and Anxiety: Clarification and General-izability to Women," *Journal of Counseling Psychology, 50* (no. 3), 333-338 (2003), pp. 336-338. Cf. J. M. O'Neil, "Patterns of Gender Role Conflict and Strain: Sexism and Fear of Femininity in Men's Lives," *Personnel and Guidance Journal, 60*, 203-210 (1981).

[704] Craig Thompson, "Interview with Scot Cromer," *Advertising & Society Review, 4* (no. 2) (2003). Electronic journal accessed online through Project Muse.

[705] To trace this development in the United States, and to see it in relation to cross-dressing, see G. G. Bolich, *Crossdressing in Context, vol. 2: The Context of Transgender Realities* (Raleigh, NC: Psyche's Press, 007), Q. 32.

[706] For more details, see G. G. Bolich, *Crossdressing in Context, vol. 1: The Context of Dress and Gender* (Raleigh, NC: Psyche's Press, 2006), especially Q. 9.

[707] Clara M. Thompson, *On Women*, edited by M. R. Green (N. Y.: New American Library, 1964), p. 141.

[708] Joanna Brewis, Mark P. Hampton, & Stephen Linstead, "Unpacking Priscilla: Subjectivity and Identity in the Organization of Gendered Appearance," *Human Relations, 50* (no. 10), 1275-1304 (1997), p. 1281.

[709] Kenneth C. W. Kammeyer, George Ritzer, & Norman R. Yetman, *Sociology. Experiencing Changing Societies*, 5th ed. (Boston: Allyn and Bacon, 1987), p. 340. We might note that 'more moral' here refers to *behavior* rather than the moral *reasoning* talked about in earlier discussions.

[710] Thompson, *On Women*, p. 41.

[711] Ibid, p. 73. Here, as elsewhere, she refers to colleague Karen Horney. See Horney's *New Ways in Psychoanalysis* (N. Y.: W. W. Norton, 1936), chapter 6.

[712] Ibid, pp. 76-77.

[713] Ibid, p. 83. It should be noted that Thompson expends a fair amount of space to considering the difference between hat she terms the 'normal homosexual' life of the American woman (what we today would be more inclined to label 'homosocial'), and homosexual sexual relationships, which she regarded as pathological (see p. 88). (Thompson was, after all, a psychoanalyst of her time, when virtually all of them—and most everyone else—was culturally biased in this regard.)

[714] Ibid, p. 111.

[715] Ibid, pp. 112-113; quotes are from p. 112 and p. 113, respectively.

[716] Ibid, pp. 116-119; quote is from p. 118.

[717] Ibid, pp. 125-128; quote is from p. 128.

[718] Ibid, pp. 130-133.

[719] Ibid, pp. 133-138; quote is from p. 138.

[720] Ibid, pp. 140-161; quote is from p. 155.

[721] Albert D. Klassen, Colin J. Williams, & Eugene E. Levitt, *Sex and Morality in the U. S.*, H. J. O'Gorman, Ed. (Middletown, CT: Wesleyan Univ. Press, 1989), p. 272f. Even earlier, anthropologist Margaret Mead also noted how modern cultures are struggling to adapt to the changing economic position of women. See her *Sex and Temperament in Three Primitive Societies* (N. Y.: Morrow Quill Paperbacks, 1963), p. 308. Original work published 1935.

[722] See Bolich, *Crossdressing in Context, vol. 1*.

[723] Susan A. Gelman, Marianne G. Taylor, & Simone, P. Nguyen, *Mother-Child Conversations About Gender* (Boston: Blackwell, 2004).

[724] Cf. Jane Pilcher & Imelda Whelehan, *50 Key Concepts in Gender Studies* (Thousand Oaks, CA: Sage Publications, 2004), p. 48. They briefly trace the use of the term (derived in the 19th century from the French *féminisme*) from a designation of one particular group and its beliefs, to a broader label for those who took a political stance to change women's social standing, to today's yet broader use.

[725] Colleen Adams, *Women's Suffrage. A Primary Source History of the Women's Rights Movement in America* (N. Y.: Rosen, 2003), pp. 7, 17.

[726] See the National Organization of Women's website at http://www.now.org/. NOW's history is recounted at the site, accessed online at http://www.now.org/history/the_founding.html. The quote is from *The Statement of Purpose*, accessed at http://www.now.org/history/purpos66.html.

[727] Jo Freeman, *The Women's Liberation Movement: Its Origin, Structures and Ideals* (Pittsburgh: Know, Inc., 1971), available as one of the Documents from the Women's Liberation Movement: An Online Archival Collection hosted by the Special Collections Library of Duke University, accessed online at http://womenshistory.about.com/gi/dynamic/offsite.htm?zi=1/XJ/Ya&sdn=womenshistory&cdn=education&tm=48&gps=200_13_1020_626&f=00&tt=14&bt=1&bts=1&zu=http%3A//scriptorium.lib.duke.edu/wlm/womlib/.

[728] Robin Morgan, "Goodbye to All That," in R. Baxandall & L. Gordon (Eds.), *Dear Sisters. Dispatches from the Women's Liberation Movement* (N. Y.: Basic Books, 2000), pp. 53-57; quotes are from pp. 53, 54f.

[729] William Kornblum & Joseph Julian, *Social Problems*, 10th ed. (Upper Saddle River, NJ: Prentice-Hall, 2001), p. 297.

[730] Roger Lancaster & Micaela Di Leonardo (Eds.), *The Gender/Sexuality Reader: Culture, History, Political Economy* (N. Y.: Routledge, 1997), p. 2.

[731] Pilcher & Whelehan, p. 52.

[732] Vicky Randall, *Women and Politics: An International Perspective*, 2nd ed. (Chicago: Univ. of Chicago Press, 1987), p. 208.

[733] The more popular date appears to be the mid-19th century. Chris Beasley offers a general range of late 18th-19th centuries; see *Gender & Sexuality: Critical Theories, Critical Thinkers* (Thousand Oaks, CA.: Sage, 2005), p. 18. For brief elaboration, see Cynthia Eller, *Living in the Lap of the Goddess: The Feminist Spirituality Movement in America* (Boston: Beacon Press, 1993), p. 176. Vicky Randall sees Wollstonecraft's treatise as symbolic of a number of earlier efforts to call attention to women's concerns, but locates the true birth of first wave feminism in the politic movement initiated in the mid-19th century. The 1848 convention was an actual *movement* in that some 300 women and men participated and drafted a platform to carry action forward. See *Women and Politics: An International Perspective*, 2nd ed. (Chicago: Univ. of Chicago Press, 1987), p. 208f. Jane Pilcher and Imelda Whelehan note the importance of Wollstonecraft's book but locate the 'first concerted demand for women's rights' to the French Revolution of 1789. The claim first wave feminism is 'most often dated' to the period between c. 1880s-1920s; see *50 Key Concepts in Gender Studies* (Thousand Oaks, CA: Sage Publications, 2004), p. 52.

[734] Chapter 2 provides more detail on the history and philosophy of feminism.

[735] Charles Sowerwine with Patricia Grimshaw, "Equality and Difference in the Twentieth-Century West: North America, Western Europe, Australia and New Zealand," in M. E. Wiesner-Hanks & T. A. Meade, *A Companion to Gender History*, pp. 586-610 (Malden, MA: Blackwell, 2004), p. 607.

[736] Leslie Heywood & Jennifer Drake, "Introduction," in L. Heywood & J. Drake (Eds.), *Third Wave Agenda: Being Feminist, Doing Feminism*, pp. 1-19 (Minneapolis: Univ. of Minnesota Press, 1997), p. 3.

[737] Julia T. Wood, *Gendered Lives: Communication, Gender, & Culture*, 6th ed. (Belmont, CA: Thomson/Wadsworth, 2005), pp. 78-80.

[738] Deborah G. Felder, *A Century of Women. The Most Influential Events in Tentieth-Century Women's History* (N. Y.: Citadel Press, 1999), p. 261.

[739] Ibid, p. 262.

[740] Pilcher & Whelehan, p. 176.

Chapter 11 Notes

[741] Ana Mariella Bacigalupo, "The Struggle for Mapuche Shamans' Masculinity: Colonial Politics of Gender, Sexuality, and Power in Southern Chile," *Ethnohistory, 51* (no. 3), 489-533 (2004), p. 514. Bacigalupo prefers the term 'co-gendered,' though even that term does not work equally well for the different groups she describes. She credits Barbara Tedlock for her notion of 'co-gendered'; see Barbara Tedlock, "Recognizing and Celebrating the Feminine in Shamanic Heritage," in M. Hoppal (Ed.), *Rediscovery of Shamanic Heritage*, pp. 297-316 (Budapest: Akademiai Kiado).

[742] Sandra L. Bem, "Gender Schema Theory: A Cognitive Account of Sex Typing," *Psychological Review, 88* (no. 4), 354-364 (1981), p. 363.

[743] Sandra L. Bem, "The Measurement of Psychological Androgyny," *Journal of Consulting and Clinical Psychology, 42*, 155-162 (1974). Also see her "Probing the Promise of

Androgyny," in A. G. Kaplan & J. P. Bean (Eds.), *Beyond Sex-Role Stereotypes: Readings Toward a Psychology of Androgyny* (Boston: Little Brown, 1976). A brief description of the BSRI is offered by Bem in "Gender Schema Theory and Its Implications for Child Development: Raising Gender Aschematic Children in a Gender Schematic Society," *Signs, 8*, 598-616 (1983), p. 606 n. 18.

[744] This sorting into four groups results from an adjustment made to the BSRI. For details, see Sandra L. Bem, "Androgyny and Gender Schema Theory: A Conceptual and Empirical Integration," in T. B. Sonderegger (Ed.), *Nebraska Symposium on Motivation, 1984: Psychology and Gender*, pp. 179-226 (Lincoln: Univ. of Nebraska Press, 1985). Bem (p. 195) observes that both androgynous and undifferentiated scorers on the BSRI should be less gender schematic; high scorers in either masculinity or femininity should be highly gender schematic.

[745] See, for example, Patricia A. Oswald, "An Examination of the Current Usefulness of the Bem Sex-Role Inventory," *Psychological Reports, 94* (no. 2), 1331-1336 (2004). The BSRI also has been shown to be a valid instrument for distinguishing between 'gender-schematic' and 'gender-aschematic' individuals; see Bernd H. Schmitt & Robert T. Millard, "Construct Validity of the Bem Sex Role Inventory (BSRI): Does the BSRI Distinguish Between Gender-Schematic and Gender-Aschematic Individuals?" *Sex Roles, 19* (nos. 9-10), 581-588 (1988).

[746] See, for example, the following three articles, each relating to a different society: Yoko Sugihara & Emiko Katsurada, "Gender-Role Personality Traits in Japanese Culture," *Psychology of Women Quarterly, 24* (no. 4), 309-318 (2000). Türker Özkan & Timo Lajunen, "Masculinity, Femininity, and the Bem Sex Role Inventory in Turkey," *Sex Roles. A Journal of Research, 52* (nos. 1-2), 103-110 (2005). D. Wilson, J. McMaster, R. Greenspan, L. Mboyi, T. Ncube, & B. Sibanda, "Cross-Cultural Validation of the Bem Sex Role Inventory in Zimbabwe," *Personality & Individual Differences, 11* (no. 7), 651-656 (1990).

[747] Wendy Doniger O'Faherty, *Women, Androgynes, and Other Mythical Beasts* (Chicago: Univ. of Chicago Press, 1980), p. 283. O'Flaherty observes that the term 'androgynous' in religion in more comprehensive and abstract. God, for example, is sometimes called androgynous, but not in the sense of an androgyne as half-male, half-female.

[748] Ibid, p. 284.

[749] Virginia Prince, "Seventy Years in the Trenches of the Gender Wars," in B. Bullough, V. L. Bullough, & J. Elias (Eds.), *Gender Blending*, pp. 469-476 (Amherherst, NY: Prometheus Books, 1997), p. 469.

[750] Richard F. Docter, *Transvestites and Transsexuals: Toward a Theory of Cross-Gender Behavior* (N. Y.: Plenum Press, 1988).

[751] Richard F. Docter & Virginia Prince, "Transvestism: A Survey of 1032 Cross-Dressers," *Archives of Sexual Behavior, 26* (no. 6), 589-605 (1997), Table I.

[752] Virginia Prince & Peter M. Bentler, "Survey of 504 Cases of Transvestism," *Psychological Reports, 31*, 903-917 (1972), p. 911.

[753] Vern Bullough, Bonnie Bullough, & Richard Smith, "A Comparative Study of Male Transvestites, Male to Female Transsexuals, and Male Homosexuals," *The Journal of*

Sex Research, 19 (no. 3), 238-257 (1983). For a more in-depth examination of this topic, see G. G. Bolich, *Crossdressing in Context, vol. 2: The Context of Transgender Reality* (Raleigh, NC: Psyche's Press, 2007), Q. 22; cf. Q. 46.

[754] Bullough, Bullough, & Smith report 38% of their subjects characterized their childhoods as 'happy,' 39% as 'mixed' (both happy & unhappy), and 23% as 'unhappy.' A later, larger study reported percentages in each category as follows: happy (42%), mixed (46%), unhappy (12%). Compared to nontransgender individuals, these respondents were comparable in reporting unhappiness (23% to nontransgender subjects 19%), but less likely to report happiness (38% to 60%). See Bonnie Bullough & Vern Bullough, ""Men Who Cross-Dress: A Survey," in B. Bullough, V. L. Bullough, & J. Elias (Eds.), *Gender Blending*, pp. 174-188 (Amherst, NY: Prometheus Books, 1997), p. 181, Table 2.

[755] Ibid, p. 180.

[756] Prince & Bentler, p. 906, Table 1. This figure represents a number in excess of the educational attainment of the general male population of the mid-1960s as indicated by census reports.

[757] Docter & Prince, Table I.

[758] Richard F. Docter & James S. Fleming, "Measures of Transgender Behavior," *Archives of Sexual Behavior, 30* (no. 3), 255-271 (2001). The 73% was extrapolated from their report that 90% of the 516 subjects had at least an A.A. degree, and of that number 19% earned an A.A., 44% a B.A. or B.S., 26% a Masters degree, and 11% a doctorate. Thus some 464 subjects had degrees, some 88 of them the A.A., leaving 376 with a bachelors degree or higher. The 516 subjects were all male, with 88% identified as 'transvestite' and 12% as 'transsexual.' The transvestite group was all periodic crossdressers who dressed fully as women; partial crossdressers were not included.

[759] Bullough, Bullough, & Smith, p. 250, Table 7.

[760] Prince & Bentler, p. 907.

[761] Bullough, Bullough, & Smith, pp. 252-254, especially Tables 11-12. Vernon Coleman speculates that one reason crossdressing is so often kept secret is because it is "particularly common" among successful males in business, the services, and professions—occupations where exposure may carry the highest price. See Vernon Coleman, (1996). *Men in Dresses: A Study in Transvestism/Crossdressing*, §2, 'Why Do Men Crossdress?' European Medical Journal. Chilton Designs Publishers. Accessed online at http://www. vernoncoleman.com/downloads/mid.htm.

[762] Docter, 1988, p. 126, which reports above average occupational status for the subjects of his sample, and Docter & Prince, Table I. Similarly, the 1981 report by a team of researcher showed 64% of their subjects in skilled or professional/managerial positions. See Jack L. Croughan, Marcel Saghir, Rose Cohen, & Eli Robins, "A Comparison of Treated and Untreated Male Crossdressers," *Archives of Sexual Behavior, 10* (no. 6), 515-528 (1981), Table I.

[763] Peter M. Bentler, "A Typology of Transsexualism: Gender Identity Theory and Data," *Archives of Sexual Behavior, 5* (no. 6), 567-584 (1976).

764 Peter M. Bentler, R. W. Sherman, & Virginia Prince, "Personality Characteristics of Male Transvestites," *Journal of Clinical Psychology, 26*, 287-291 (1970); quote is from p. 290.

765 Michael Fleming, David Jones, & Jack Simons, "Preliminary Results of Rorschach Protocols of Pre and Post Operative Transsexuals," *Journal of Clinical Psychology, 38* (no. 2), 408-415 (1982); quote is from p. 414.

766 F. S. Morgenstern, J. F. Pearce, & W. L. Rees, "Predicting the Outcomes of Behavior Therapy by Psychological Tests," *Behavior Research and Therapy, 2*, 191-200 (1965).

767 Peter M. Bentler & Virginia Prince, "Personality Characteristics of Male Transvestites, III," *Journal of Abnormal Psychology, 74*, 140-143 (1969). Quote is from p. 141.

768 D. Daniel Hunt, John E. Carr, & John L. Hampson, "Cognitive Correlates of Biologic Sex and Gender Identity in Transsexualism," *Archives of Sexual Behavior, 10* (no. 1), 65-77 (1981). It is worth noting that a Czechoslovakian assessment of 64 transsexuals and 18 homosexuals found above average IQ scores for most subjects. See *Ceskoslovenska Psychiatriae, 71* (nos. 2-3), 131-136 (1975).

769 George R. Brown, Thomas N. Wise, Paul T. Costa, Jr., Jeffrey H. Herbst, Peter J. Fagan, & Chester W. Schmidt, "Personality Characteristics and Sexual Functioning of 188 Cross-Dressing Men," *The Journal of Nervous and Mental Disorders 184*, 265-273 (1996), pp. 265-268.

770 Chris C. Gosselin & Sybil B. Eysenck, "The Transvestite 'Double Image': A Preliminary Report," *Personality and Individual Differences, 1* (no. 2), 172-173 (1980).

771 This finding corresponds both to self-reports of crossdressers and reports from their significant others. See, for example, Neil Buhrich, "Motivation for Cross-Dressing in Heterosexual Transvestism," *Acta Psychiatrica Scandinavica, 57* (no. 2), 145-152 (1978).

772 John T. Talamini, *Boys Will Be Girls: The Hidden World of the Heterosexual Male Transvestite* (Lanham, MD: Univ. Press of America, 1982), chapter 6.

773 Ibid, p. 66.

774 Richard F. Docter & James S. Fleming, "Measures of Transgender Behavior," *Archives of Sexual Behavior, 30* (no. 3), 255-271 (2001). For report of mean differences between groups see Table II.

775 Brown et al., p. 265.

776 D. J. Ziegler, "Transvestism," in R. J. Corsini (Ed.), *Encyclopedia of Psychology*, 2nd ed. (N. Y.: John Wiley & Sons, 1994), p. 551f. This same entry notes, "Interestingly, over three-fourths of transvestites consider themselves to be a different personality when crossdressed, perhaps experiencing in female clothing a significant facet of their psychological makeup that cannot otherwise be expressed. . . ."

777 For more on this subject, see G. G. Bolich, *Crossdressing in Context, vol. 4: The Context of Mental Health* (forthcoming).

778 Gianna E. Israel, "Impact on Children." *Gianna Israel Gender Library* (1997). Accessed online at http://www.firelily.com/gender/gianna/impact.children.html.

779 See Bolich, *Crossdressing in Context, vol. 2*, Q. 48 for a review of nearly two dozen studies from 1951 to the present on when crossdressing begins. They agree that the majority of individuals who crossdress began before age 10, with a significant percentage starting before age 5. One example of a recent large scale study (N = 1,032) found two-thirds (66%) began crossdressing before age 10; 29% between 10-20 years old. See Docter & Prince, Table II.

780 Richard L. Schott, "The Childhood and Family Dynamics of Transvestites," *Archives of Sexual Behavior, 24* (no. 3), 309-327 (1995), p. 324.

781 Neil Buhrich & Trina Beaumont, "Comparison of Transvestism in Australia and America," *Archives of Sexual Behavior, 10* (no. 3), 269-279 (1981), Table 1. 'Characteristics of Feminine Gender Identity.'

782 Shannon Wyss, "'This Was My Hell': The Violence Experienced By Gender Non-conforming Youth in US High Schools," *International Journal of Qualitative Education, 17* (no. 5), 709-730 (2004), p. 710.

783 "Adding Sexual Orientation and Gender Identity to Discrimination and Harassment Policies in Schools," *SIECUS Report, 28* (no. 3), 17-18 (2000, Feb.-Mar.), p. 17.

784 Ibid, p. 18.

785 Joseph G. Kosciw, *The GLSEN 2001 National School Climate Survey: The School-Related Experiences of Our Nation's Lesbian, Gay, Bisexual and Transgender Youth* (N. Y.: Gay, Lesbian, and Straight Education Network, 2002), p. 11.

786 Moulton, p. 442.

787 Hate crimes are motivated by intolerance toward members of one or another group simply because they belong to that group, which the perpetrator objects to. There are other defining characteristics. Hate crimes are meant to send a message; by victimizing one member of the group the entire group is targeted. The fact that one has been targeted by virtue of whom he or she is, plus the awareness that the victimization intends to have a chilling effect on others, may be why such crimes tend to carry more psychological impact. In effect, the perpetrator has managed at one and the same time to say, 'I picked you because of who you are, but who you are doesn't matter to me because I hate the entire group you belong to.' The hate crime is thus highly personal even as it depersonalizes the victim.

788 For more information on GenderPAC, see their website, accessed online at http://www.gpac.org/. GenderPAC's address is 274 W. 11th St, New York, NY 10014.

789 *GenderPAC. First National Survey of TransGender Violence* (GenderPAC, 1997). Survey accessed online at http://hatecrime.transadvocacy.com/documents/TransViolence%20Survey%20Results.pdf. Percentages reported have been rounded. See 'Data Summary' on p. 1. The report also documents variations due to factors such as age and economic conditions, and details aspects such as locations of incidents and relationship of the victim to the perpetrator.

790 Yvonne, "Who We Are," *Yvonne's Place for Crossdressers* (1999). Accessed online at http://www.yvonnesplace.net/index2.html.

[791] Brian Tully, *Accounting for Transsexuality and Transhomosexuality: The Gender Identity Careers of Over 200 Men and Women Who Have Petitioned for Surgical Reassignment* (London: Whiting and Birch, 1992), p. 266. Tully's work discloses the results of a large scale, systematic study of 204 transsexuals that was conducted by the Gender Identity Clinic at Charing Cross Hospital in London.

[792] For a review of legal issues, see Bolich, *Crossdressing in Context, vol. 2*, Q. 56.

[793] Kosciw, p. 32.

[794] These figures are as reported in two accounts: Jennifer J. Smith, "New HRC Survey Changes Trans Politics, Activists Say," *Washingtom Blade* (2002, October 11). Accessed online at http://www.tgcrossroads.org/ news/archive.asp?aid=399, and Mubarak Dahir, "HRC: Transgender Breakthrough," *The Advocate* (2002, Oct. 15). Accessed online at http://www.tgcrossroads.org/news/archive.asp?aid=384.

[795] Duhar, op. cit.

[796] Dahir. The description reads:

> A transgender person is someone who is born as one gender but feels they are the opposite gender. This person may do certain things so that their outward appearance fits who they feel they are on the inside. They might dress as a person of the opposite gender, get medical treatment such as hormone therapy, or have surgery to change their appearance so they look like the gender that they feel they are. This could be a man changing to a woman or a woman changing to a man.

[797] Ibid. Dahir reports the numbers as follows with regard to the query whether the respondent felt 'favorable,' 'neutral,' or 'unfavorable' toward transgendered people:

	Unfavorable	Neutral
Before hearing description	24%	32%
After hearing description	31%	26%

And with reference to believing transgenderism is "morally wrong" and "a choice":

	Morally wrong	Choice
Before hearing description	26%	42%
After hearing description	33%	47%

[798] Ibid.

[799] Akshay Khanna, *A Language for Love* (2006, Apr. 2). Accessed online at Boloji.com at http://www.boloji.com/wfs5/wfs577.htm.

[800] Laurent, p. 172. *Zenanas* is a term more commonly heard in Pakistan.

[801] Naz Foundation International, *Development Manual. Developing Community-Based Organizations Addressing HIV/AIDS, Sexual Health, Welfare and Human Rights Issues for Males-Who-Have-Sex-with-Males, Their Partners, and Families* (London: Naz Foundation International, 2005), p. 7. Accessed online at http://www.nfi.net/NFI%20Publications/Manuals/Book%201%20manual.pdf.

[802] Ibid, p. 12. Also see Naz Foundation International, *Annual Report, 2003-2004. Planning for the Future* (London: Naz Foundation International, 2004), p. 25f. Accessed online at http://www.nfi.net/NFI%20Publications/Annual%20Reports/aAR2003-4.pdf.

[803] Shivananda Khan, "Men Who Have Sex with Men and Disempowerment in South Asia," *Sexual Health Exchange 2005-2* (2005). Accessed online at the Royal Tropical Institute (KIT) website at http://www.kit.nl/frameset.asp?/ils/exchange_content/html/2005-2_men_who_have_sex_with_m.asp&frnr=1&.

[804] National AIDS Control Organization (NACO), *Some Important Chapters of a Training Curriculum on VCT* (NACO, 2004), III/3-4 (p. 110f.), accessed online at http://www.nacoonline.org/ publication/trainingcuricullum.pdf. NSCO operates under India's Ministry of Health & Family Welfare.

[805] Gayatri Reddy, "Crossing 'Lines' of Subjectivity: the Negotiation of Sexual Identity in Hyderabad, India," in S. Srivastava (ed.), *Sexual Sites, Seminal Attitudes: Sexualities, Masculinities, and Culture in South Asia*, pp. 147-164 (Thousand Oaks, CA: Sage Publications, 2004), p. 155.

[806] Ibid. The *Kothi* are discussed separately in this answer.

[807] Laurent, p. 172.

[808] Bahuchara Mata is a 'mother goddess' like Cybele. See Pattanaik, chapter 4 for her story. Cf. Will Roscoe, "Priests of the Goddess: Gender Transgression in Ancient Religion," *History of Religions, 35* (no. 3), 295-330 (1996).

[809] Many *Hijra* in Pakistan, an Islamic nation, are associated with the Sufi tradition of that religion. See the answer to Q. 78.

[810] On their contemporary struggles, see "Eunuchs Want Two Percent of Society," *India Briefly* (2006, May 26), accessed online at the Despardes.com website at http://www.despardes.com/India/newsbriefs/2006/20060530-india-news.html. At the same place is the account by Siddarth Narrain, "Being a Eunuch."

[811] Siddharth Narrain, "In a Twilight World," *Frontline, 20* (no. 21) (2003, Oct. 11-24). Accessed online at http://www.hinduonnet.com/fline/fl2021/stories/20031024002509800.htm. *Frontline* is a national publication in India.

[812] Jayaji Krishna Nath, & Vishwarath R. Nayar, "India," in R. T. Francoeur (Ed.), *The International Encyclopedia of Sexuality*, Vols. I-III (N. Y.: Continuum, 1997). Accessed online at http://www2.rz.hu-berlin.de/sexology/GESUND/ARCHIV/IES/INDIA.HTM#7.%20GENDER %20CONFLICTED%20PERSONS. See §7. Gender Conflicted Persons.

813 See Serena Nanda, "Hijras: An Alternative Sex and Gender Role in India," in Gilbert Herdt (Ed.), *Third Sex, Third Gender: Beyond Sexual Dimorphism in Culture and History*, pp. 373-418 (N. Y.: Zone Books, 1993). For an account of modern *Hijra*, albeit with reference to Pakistan, see Nauman Naqvi & Hasan Mujtaba, "Two Baluchi *Buggas*, a Sindhi *Zenana*, and the Status of *Hijras* in Contemporary Pakistan," in S. O. Murray & W. Roscoe (Eds.), *Islamic Homosexualities: Culture, History, & Literature*, pp. 262-266 (N. Y.: New York Univ. Press, 1997).

814 Michael G. Peletz, "Transgenderism and Gender Pluralism in Southeast Asia Since Early Modern Times," *Current Anthropology, 47* (no. 2), 309-340 (2006), p. 318 n. 15.

815 This matter is explored further in G. G. Bolich, *Crossdressing in Context, vol. 3: The Context of Religion* (forthcoming), Q. 82.

816 Eli Coleman, Philip Colgan, & Louis Gooren, "Male Cross-Gender Behaviour in Myanmar (Burma): A Description of the Acault," *Archives of Sexual Behavior, 21* (no. 3), 313-321 (1992).

817 Ibid, p. 317f.

818 Stephen O. Murray, *Homosexualities* (Chicago: Univ. of Chicago Press, 2000), p. 335. Cf. Coleman, Colgan, & Gooren, p. 317.

819 Ibid. Also see Leonard Andaya, "The Bissu: A Study of a Third Gender in Indonesia," in B. Andaya (Ed.), *Other Pasts: Women, Gender and History in Southeast Asia*, pp. 27-46 (Honolulu: University of Hawaii Press, 2000).

820 Ibid. For an account of such a ceremonial blessing, also see, Sharyn Graham, "Sulawesi's Fifth Gender," *Inside Indonesia*, no. 64 (2001, Apr.-June). Accessed online at http://www.insideindonesia.org/ edit66/ bissu2.htm. Cf. R. Anderson Sutton, *Calling Back the Spirit. Music, Dance, and Cultural Politics in Lowland South Sulawesi* (N. Y.: Oxford Univ. Press, 2002), pp. 74-78.

821 Unni Wikan, "Man Becomes Woman: Transsexualism in Oman as a Key to Gender Roles," *Man, 12* (no. 2), 304-319 (1977); originally published in *Tidsskrift for Samfunnsforskning, 17* (1976).

822 Ibid. See Unni Wikan, "The Omani Xanith—a Third Gender Role?" *Man, 13* (no. 3), 473-476 (1978). Also see Unni Wikan, *Behind the Veil in Arabia: Women in Oman* (Chicago: Univ. of Chicago Press, 1982). See chapter 9, 'The Xanith: a Third Gender Role?' (pp. 168-186).

823 Alan P. Merriam, *An African World: The Basongye Village of Lupupa Ngye* (Bloomington: Indiana Univ. Press, 1974). See Murray & Roscoe, pp. 144-146. Cf. Louis A. Berman, *The Puzzle. Exploring the Evolutionary Puzzle of Male Homosexuality* (Wilmette, IL: Godot Press, 2003), p. 186.

824 Ana Mariella Bacigalupo, "The Struggle for Mapuche Shamans' Masculinity: Colonial Politics of Gender, Sexuality, and Power in Southern Chile," *Ethnohistory, 51* (no. 3), 489-533 (2004), p. 505.

825 Ibid, pp. 505, 524. In the latter place Bacigalupo adds, "The Reche had co-gendered identities in which *machi weye* oscillated between masculine and feminine poles.

They combined women's and men's behavior, dress, and style in varying degrees, and this co-gendered condition could be associated with passive or active sexual acts or with celibacy, the meanings of which varied according to context."

[826] Ibid, p. 505. Bacigalupo argues that *machi weye* primarily became feminine to receive spirits. This ability was instrumental in healing practice, important religiously, and conferred social status and power to the individual.

[827] Bacigalupo (ibid, p. 517) notes that today some such males are labeled *domo-wentru* ('woman-man').

[828]Ibid, p. 504. Bacigalupo observes that this loincloth among the Reche-Mapuche was a garment worn by men in battle or to play a war-like game, but to Spaniard eyes it resembled a woman's skirt. Though the *machi weye* might incorporate feminine items (e.g., rings and necklaces), their gender presentation was more feminine to Spanish eyes than to their own people.

[829] Ibid, pp. 489f., 503. Bacigalupo notes that the Spanish view of sex, sexuality, and gender prompted them to view all crossdressing males as homosexuals who, like women, took a passive, receptive role in sexual activity.

[830] Ana Mariella Bacigalupo, "Rethinking Identity and Feminism: Contributions of Mapuche Women and *Machi* from Southern Chile," *Hypatia, 18* (no. 2), 33-57 (2003), p. 37.

[831] Ana Mariella Bacigalupo, "The Mapuche Man Who Became a Woman Shaman: Selfhood, Gender Transgression, and Competing Cultural Norms," *American Ethnologist, 31* (no. 3), 440-457 (2004). Cf. Ana Mariella Bacigalupo, "The Mapuche Man Who Became a Woman Shaman: Conflict and Conformity in the Life and Spiritual Practice of Machi Marta," in S. Marcos (Ed.), *Gender, Orality, and Indigenous Religions* (Cuernavaca, Mexico: ALER Publications, 2002).

[832] Antonia Young, Women Who Become Men: Albanian Sworn Virgins. (N. Y.: Berg Publishers, 2000). Cf. Rene Grimaux, "Woman Becomes Man in the Balkans," in Gilbert Herdt (Ed.), Third Sex, Third Gender: Beyond Sexual Dimorphism in Culture and History, pp. 241-282 (N. Y.: Zone Books, 1993).

[833] Jeannette Marie Mageo, "Male Transvestism and Cultural Change in Samoa," *American Ethnologist, 19* (no. 3), 443-459 (1992). Cf. Jeannette Marie Mageo, "Samoa, on the Wilde Side: Male Transvestism, Oscar Wilde, and Liminality in Making Gender," *Ethos, 24* (no. 4), 588-627 (1996).

[834] Paul Miles, "Transgender in the Pacific: Fa'afafine, Fakaleiti and Mahu," *ACP-EU Courier Transgender in the Pacific*, No. 183, pp. 45-48 (2000, Oct.). Accessed online at http://europa.eu.int/comm/development/body/publications/courier/courier183/en/en_045_ni.pdf.

[835] Johanna Schmidt, "Redefining Fa'afafine: Western Discourses and the Construction of Transgenderism in Samoa," *Intersections: Gender, History and Culture in the Asian Context, 6* (2001, August), §12. Accessed online at http://wwwsshe.murdoch.edu.au/ intersections/issue6/schmidt.html. Cf. Johanna Schmidt, "Paradise Lost? Social Change and Fa'afafine in Samoa," *Current Sociology, 51* (nos. 3-4), 417-432 (2003).

[836] This context may help explain the observation of late birth order for *fa'afafine*; see Kris Poasa, Ray Blanchard, & Kenneth Zucker, "Birth Order in Transgendered Males from Polynesia: A Quantitative Study of Samoan Fa'afafine," *Journal of Sex and Marital Therapy, 30* (no. 1), 13-23 (2004).

[837] Antonia Young, *Women Who Become Men: Albanian Sworn Virgins*. (N. Y.: Berg Publishers, 2000), p. 114.

[838] Schmidt, "Redefining Fa'afafine," §§13-17. Cf. the notion of Mageo that the increase in numbers of *Fa'afafine* in the 20th century helps meet a cultural need for expression of feminine sexuality—a need partly frustrated by Western missionaries when they curbed indigenous women from traditional sexuality displays. The *Fa'afafine*, for example, now occupy the place in evening entertainments once held by females.

[839] See the *Charting the Pacific* website page on 'people,' accessed online at http://www.abc.net.au/ra/pacific/people/hazy.htm. Also cf. Laura Fraser, "The Islands Where Boys Grow Up to Be Girls," *Marie Claire* (2002, Dec.). Accessed online at http://www.laurafraser.com/fafafine.html.

[840] N. H. Bartlett & P. L. Vasey, *Does Your Mother Know? Parental Reactions to Childhood Cross-Gender Behaviors in Samoan Fa'afafine*. Poster presented at the Annual Meeting of the International Academy of Sex Research (IASR), June 16-19, 2004. Abstract accessed online at http://www.iasr.org/meeting/2004/abstracts2004.pdf (p. 10). Apparently, in Samoa (as elsewhere), transgender behavior is unlikely to be stopped by parental rejection of it, but such opposition may prompt more gender dysphoria.

[841] Ingrid M. Sell, "Third Gender: A Qualitative Study of the Experience of Individuals Who Identify as Being Neither Man Nor Woman," *The Psychotherapy Patient, 13* (nos. 1-2), 131-145 (2004), pp. 139-140.

[842] Ibid, pp. 140-142; quote is from p. 142.

Chapter 12 Notes

[843] The material in this discussion previously appeared in G. G. Bolich, *Crossdressing in Context, vol. 1: The Context of Dress and Gender* (Raleigh, NC: Psyche's Press, 2006), Q. 5.

[844] Per Schioldborg, Address at the Meeting of the Nordic Association for Clinical Sexology (NACS), Oslo, Norway, September 28-30, 1983, cited in Elsa Almas & Esben Esther Pirelli Benestad, "Norway," in R. T. Francoeur (Ed.), *The International Encyclopedia of Sexuality*, Vol. IV, pp. 460-462 (N. Y.: Continuum, 2001), p. 461. Accessed online at http://www.SexQuest.com/IES4. See §7. Gender Conflicted Persons.

[845] A. E. Eyler & K. Wright, "Gender Identification and Sexual Orientation Among Genetic Females with Gender-Blended Self-perception in Childhood and Adolescence," *The International Journal of Transgenderism, 1* (no. 1) (1997). Accessed online at http://www. symposion.com/ijt/ijtc0102.htm.

[846] I often refer to gender 'statuses' or 'states,' without elaborating further. I mean by this usage an openness to interpreting gender labels as distinctly different realities ('states') or as discernibly different gradations ('statuses') within general states, however many of the latter are numbered.

847 Erica Reischer & Kathryn S. Koo, "The Body Beautiful: Symbolism and Agency in the Social World," *Annual Review of Anthropology, 33*, 297317 (2004), p. 298.

848 Ibid, p. 301.

849 The proposal here is intended along the lines of the "utopian fantasy" suggested by Sandra Bem: "I propose that we let a thousand categories of sex/gender/desire begin to bloom in any and all fluid and permeable configurations and, through that very proliferation, that we thereby undo (or, if you prefer, that we de-privilege or de-center or destabilize) the privileged status of two-and-only-two that are currently treated as normal and natural." Sandra L. Bem, "Dismantling Gender Polarization and Compulsory Heterosexuality: Should We Turn the Volume Down or Up?" in R. Heasley & B. Crane (Eds.), *Sexual Lives. A Reader on the Theories and Realities of Human Sexualities*, pp. 253-261 (Boston: McGraw-Hill, 2003), p. 255.

850 There are signs of an emerging vocabulary to accompany and accommodate a paradigm shift in the way we perceive and discuss gender. The transgender community has proliferated numerous self-descriptors to move away from those associated with psychological pathology. Author and activist Leslie Feinberg has proposed we adopt new, non-gendered pronouns like 's/he,' or 'sie' (pronounced like 'see'), or 'ze' (to replace she/he) and 'hir' (pronounced like 'here,' to replace him/her). See Leslie Feinberg, *Trans Liberation: Beyond Pink or Blue* (Boston: Beacon Press, 1998). Cf. the *Queers and Allies Dictionary* accessed online at http://www.gustavus.edu/oncampus/orgs/ queers/ main/dictionary_full.html. (This matter was discussed briefly in chapter 1, pp. 16-17.)

Chapter 13 Notes

851 Alfred C. Kinsey, Wardell B. Pomeroy, & Clyde E. Martin, *Sexual Behavior in the Human Male* (Phila.: W. B. Saunders, 1948). Also see Alfred C. Kinsey, Wardell B. Pomeroy, Clyde E. Martin, & Paul H. Gerhard, *Sexual Behavior in the Human Female* (Phila.: W. B. Saudners, 1953).

852 Morton Hunt, *Sexual Behavior in the 1970s* (Chicago: Playboy Press, 1974).

853 M. Michele Burnette, "Gender, Gender Identity, and Sexuality," in R. D. McAnulty & M. M. Burnette (eds.), *Sex and Sexuality, vol. 1. Sexuality Today: Trends and Controversies*, pp. 185-201 (Westport, CT: Praeger, 2006), p. 185. Note, however, that some research has found *statistically* significant differences in many attitudes. For example, one study in the 1980s found significant differences on 73 of 102 items on the Sexual Attitude Scale. See Judith A. Howard, "Gender Differences in Sexual Attitudes: Conservatism or Powerlessness?" *Gender and Society, 2* (no. 1), 103-114 (1988), pp. 106-108. Cf. Susan Hendrick, Clyde Hendrick, Michelle J. Slapion-Foote, & Franklin H. Foote, "Gender Differences in Sexual Attitudes," *Journal of Personality and Social Psychology, 48*, 1630-1642 (1985).

854 Albert D. Klassen, Colin J. Williams, & Eugene E. Levitt, *Sex and Morality in the U.S. An Empirical Enquiry Under the Auspices of the Kinsey Institute*, edited by H. J. O'Gorman (Middletown, CT: Wesleyan Univ. Press, 1989), pp. 25-28, 137-164. The qualifier 'without love' matters because the numbers change when 'with love' is used instead. In that case, only 30.5% of men still felt premarital sex is always wrong (-15%), and the percentage among women dropped to 44.4% (-17.1%). The focus was on sexual intercourse.

855 Howard, p. 197, Table 1.

856 Samuel S. Janus & Cynthia L. Janus, *The Janus Report on Sexual Behavior* (N. Y.: John Wiley & Sons, 1993), p. 68.

857 Despite the attitudes people hold on premarital sex, actual practice seems another matter. Michael and associates note wryly that, "58 percent of our respondents who said premarital sex is always wrong also told us that they themselves had had sex before they were married." See Robert T. Michael, John H. Gagnon, Edward O'Laumann, & Gina Kolata, *Sex in America. A Definitive Survey* (Boston: Little, Brown & Co., 1994), p. 239.

858 Klassen, Williams, & Levitt, p. 29.

859 Janus & Janus, p. 393.

860 Michael, et al., *Sex in America*, pp. 234-236.

861 Tom W. Smith, "Sexual Behavior in the United States," in R. D. McAnulty & M. M. Burnette (eds.), *Sex and Sexuality, vol. 1. Sexuality Today: Trends and Controversies*, pp. 103-132 (Westport, CT: Praeger, 2006), p. 108. He argues that despite many contentions of high incidences of marital infidelity, the most methodologically sound research reports estimates of about 3-4% of presently married people having a sexual partner other than their spouse in any given year.

862 Ibid, pp. 102 (number of sex partners), 140 (anal & oral sex), 158 (masturbation). With reference to masturbation, exact percentages are not provided in the text.

863 Edward O. Laumann, John H. Gagnon, Robert T. Michael, & Stuart Michaels, *The Social Organization of Sexuality: Sexual Practices in the United States* (Chicago: Univ. of Chicago Press, 1994).

864 Mark Clements, "Sex in America Today," *Parade Magazine* (1994, Aug. 7), pp. 4-6. This report was based on a representative sample of 1049 men and women ages 18-65. The respondents represented nine geographic divisions and were further differentiated by age, household income, and household size. The collected information was weighted according to U.S. census data on the demographic variables.

865 Michael et al., *Sex in America*, pp. 140-141.

866 Burnette, p. 197. She does point to one difference: men are most aroused by same-sex behavior between women, while women are most aroused by heterosexual activities.

867 Emily W. Kane & Mimi Schippers, "Men's and Women's Beliefs About Gender and Sexuality," *Gender and Society, 10* (no. 5), 650-665 (1996), pp. 650-65.

868 Ibid, pp. 655-656; percentages from Table 1.

869 Ibid. On differences in sexual power, see Howard, p. 105f. She notes an earlier study of more than 6,000 heterosexual couples that found the partner with the greater power was the one more likely to engage in sexual activity outside the relationship. See Philip Blumstein & Pepper Schwartz, *American Couples: Money, Work, and Sex* (N. Y.: William Morrow, 1983).

870 Ibid, pp. 655-657; percentages from Table 1.

871 Ibid, pp. 662-663; quote is from p. 663.

872 June Crawford, Susan Kippax, & Catherine Waldby, "Women's Sex Talk and Men's Sex Talk: Different Worlds," in K. Lebacqz with D. Sinacore-Guinn (Eds.), *Sexuality. A Reader*, pp. 161-178 (Cleveland: Pilgrim Press, 1999), pp. 166-170.

873 Ibid, pp. 170-178; quote is from p. 174.

874 Put more formally, "sexual difference becomes codified into the presence or absence of a single feature—the male sexual organ." See Elizabeth Grosz, *Jacque Lacan: A Feminist Introduction* (Sydney, Australia: Allen & Unwin, 1990) p. 188.

875 Gary R. Brooks, "Challenging Dominant Discourses of Male (Hetero)Sexuality: The Clinical Implications of New Voices About Male Sexuality," in P. J. Kleinplatz (Ed.), *New Directions in Sex Therapy. Innovations and Alternatives*, pp. 50-68 (Phila.: Taylor & Francis, 2001), p. 54.

876 Bernie Zilbergeld, *Male Sexuality: A Guide to Sexual Fulfilment* (N. Y.: Bantam Books, 1978, 1981). The sexual scripts/myths Zilbergeld explores in detail have been paraphrased and slightly reworked here.

877 Bernie Zilbergeld, *The New Male Sexuality* (N. Y.: Bantam Books, 1992). Quote is from p. 4.

878 Gayle Rubin, "Thinking Sex: Notes for a Radical Theory of the Politics of Sexuality," in C. S. Vance (Ed.), *Pleasure and Danger: Exploring Female Sexuality*, pp. 267-319 (Boston: Routledge, 1984), p. 308.

879 Lonnie Barbach, *For Yourself: The Fulfilment of Female Sexuality*, rev. ed. (N. Y.: Signet, 2000 revision of 1976 ed.), p. 2.

880 Lonnie Barbach, *For Each Other: Sharing Sexual Intimacy* (Garden City, NY: Doubleday, 1982), pp. 12-40. The wording for this presentation has been reworked to heighten the dualism between masculine and feminine sexuality, with the sense that femininity is the antithesis of masculinity (discussed in chapter 10).

881 Sharon Horne & Melanie J. Zimmer-Gembeck, "The Female Sexual Subjectivity Inventory: Development and Validation of a Multidimensional Inventory for Late Adolescents and Emerging Adults," *Psychology of Women Quarterly, 30*, 125-138 (2006).

882 Ibid, p. 136.

883 Ibid.

884 For a very thorough investigation of crossdressing see G. G. Bolich, *Crossdressing in Context, 4 vols.* (Raleigh, NC: Psyche's Press, 2006-2008).

885 Freud, however, observed that everyday experience shows that the things we call perversions are "rarely absent" even in "healthy" people, and he urged that the term 'perversion' should therefore not be a term of reproach. See, Sigmund Freud, *Three Essays on the Theory of Sexuality*, Tr. J. Strachey (N. Y.: Basic Books, 1975; original work published 1905), p. 26. For greater elaboration on Freud's ideas about fetishism, see G. G. Bolich, *Crossdressing in Context, vol. 4: The Context of Mental Health* (forthcoming), Q. 88.

886 Ibid, p. 19.

887 Donovan Miyasaki, "The Evasion of Gender in Freudian Fetishism," *Journal for the Psychoanalysis of Culture & Society, 8* (no. 2), 289-298 (2003), esp. pp. 289-292.

888 Ibid, p. 293.

889 Ibid.

890 American Psychiatric Association, *Diagnostic and Statistical Manual of Mental Disorders, 4th ed.* (Washington, D. C.: American Psychiatric Association, 1994), p. 531. Hereafter referred to as DSM-IV.

891 See Bolich, *Crossdressing in Context, vol. 4*, Q. 99.

892 DSM-IV, pp. 529-530.

893 Virginia Prince & P. M. Bentler, "Survey of 504 Cases of Transvestism," *Psychological Reports, 31*, 903-917 (1972), p. 915.

894 Betty W. Steiner, R. Michael Sanders, & Ron Langevin, "Crossdressing, Erotic Preferences, and Aggression; a Comparison of Male Transvestites and Transsexuals," in R. Langevin (Ed.), *Erotic Preference, Gender Identity, and Aggression in Men. New Research Studies*, pp. 261-276 (Hillsdale, NJ: Lawrence Erlbaum Associates, 1985), p. 271f.

895 Chris Gosselin & Glen D. Wilson, *Sexual Variations: Fetishism, Sadomasochism and Transvestism* (N. Y.: Simon & Schuster, 1980).

896 Yvonne, "Who We Are," *Yvonne's Place for Crossdressers* (1999). Available online at http://www.yvonnesplace.net/index2.html.

897 For more detailed analysis, see Bolich, *Crossdressing in Context, vol. 4*, Q. 89.

898 George R. Brown, Thomas N. Wise, Paul T. Costa, Jr., Jeffrey H. Herbst, Peter J. Fagan, & Chester W. Schmidt, "Personality Characteristics and Sexual Functioning of 188 Cross-Dressing Men," *The Journal of Nervous and Mental Disorders 184*, 265-273 (1996), p. 267f.

899 Thomas N. Wise, Peter J. Fagan, Chester W. Schmidt, Yula Ponticas, & Paul T. Costa, "Personality and Sexual Functioning of Transvestitic Fetishists and Other Paraphilics," *Journal of Nervous and Mental Disease, 179* (no. 11), 694-698 (1991).

900 Ira B. Pauly & Thomas W. Lindgren, "Body Image and Gender Identity," *Journal of Homosexuality, 2* (no. 2), 133-142 (1977). Cf. Ira B. Pauly, "A Body Image Scale for Evaluating Transsexuals," *Archives of Sexual Behavior, 4* (no. 6), 639-656 (1975). The BI-I considers 30 body features assessed along a 5 point scale.

901 D. J. Ziegler, "Transvestism," in R. J. Corsini (Ed.), *Encyclopedia of Psychology*, 2nd ed. (N. Y.: John Wiley & Sons, 1994), p. 551.

902 Smith, "Sexual Behavior in the United States," p. 109f. See his text for references to the literature.

903 Karin A. Martin, "Gender and Sexuality: Medical Opinion on Homosexuality, 1900-1950," *Gender and Society, 7* (no. 2), 246-260 (1993), p. 255.

904 Christine Overall, "Heterosexuality and Feminist Theory," in K. Lebacqz with D. Sinacore-Guinn (Eds.), *Sexuality. A Reader*, pp. 295-311 (Cleveland: Pilgrim Press, 1999), p. 295f.

905 Ibid, pp. 296-297.

906 Ibid, pp. 297-298.

907 Ibid, pp. 298-301.

908 Ibid, p. 301f.

909 Ibid, pp. 302-309.

910 Derald Wing Sue & David Sue, *Counseling the Culturally Diverse. Theory and Practice*, 4th ed. (N. Y.: John Wiley & Sons, 2003), pp. 68-72.

911 While feelings are a source of information, too many of us privilege this one source above all others. This tendency predictably proves problematic because feelings are so variable and transient. Reason and evidence are more dependable. Morally, it is indefensible to justify attitudes and behaviors on just feelings—as we all recognize when we contemplate someone else treating us poorly based on a 'feeling' rather than on any knowledge of us as an individual.

912 See, for example, Lawrence A. Kurdek, "Correlates of Negative Attitudes Toward Homosexuals in Heterosexual College Students," *Sex Roles, 18*, 727-738 (1988).

913 Benjamin B. Harold, "The *Straight*jacket of My Homophobia," in R. Heasley & B. Crane (Eds.), *Sexual Lives. A Reader on the Theories and Realities of Human Sexualities*, pp. 407-412 (Boston: McGraw-Hill, 2003), p. 412.

Chapter 14 Notes

914 The material in this chapter reproduces content drawn from different parts of G. G. Bolich, *Crossdressing in Context, vol. 1: The Context of Dress and Gender* (Raleigh, NC: Psyche's Press, 2006).

915 Numerous studies investigate this notion, frequently in terms of the perceived link between a girl or woman's attire and sexual assault. Since that has been discussed elsewhere in this work, here we will examine the broader context. In general, feminine apparel that exposes or draws attention to female erogenous zones is seen as sexually inviting. Two studies may be illustrative. One examines men's appraisal in bars of a woman's sexual availability noted that while men show an awareness that their judgment on this matter based on her dress appearance may be inaccurate, they make it nonetheless. See Kathleen A. Parks & Douglas M. Scheidt, "Male Bar Drinkers' Perspective on Female Bar Drinkers," *Sex Roles. A Journal of Research, 43* (nos. 11-12), 927-941 (2000). Another study, on mate poaching, found that participants identified as one strategy for women suggesting easy sexual access to themselves is to wear seductive clothing. Tactics involving disguise of mate poaching enticement also involved men manipulating clothing, including dressing conservatively, changing clothes often, and hiding new clothes from his current partner. See David P. Schmidt & Todd K. Shackelford, "Nifty Ways to Leave Your Lover: The Tactics People Use to Entice and Disguise the Process of Human Mate Poaching," *Personality & Social Psychology Bulletin, 29* (no. 8), 1018-1035 (2003), p. 1020, 1027.

916 Gregory P. Stone, "Appearance and the Self," in M. E. Roach & J. B. Eicher (Eds.), *Dress, Adornment, and the Social Order,* pp. 216-245 (N. Y.: John Wiley & Sons, 1965), p. 236.

917 Craig J. Thompson & Diana L. Haytko, "Speaking of Fashion: Consumers' Uses of Fashion Discourses and the Appropriation of Countervailing Cultural Meanings," *Journal of Consumer Research, 24*, 15-42 (1997).

918 Diana Crane, *Fashion and Its Social Agendas: Class, Gender, and identity in Clothing* (Chicago: Univ. of Chicago Pr., 2000), p. 2.

919 For our purposes, we will imagine the self as comprised of complex, internalized self-contents (such as personality and character attributes), protected and delineated by a complex system of boundaries, both physical and psychological. See G. G. Bolich, *Serving Human Experience: The Boundary Metaphor* (Ann Arbor, MI: Doctoral dissertation for the Union Institute, 1993).

920 Polish researchers Malgorzata Zimniewska and Ryszard Kozlowski reported in 2004 a variety of studies conducted on physiological changes attributable to fibers used in clothing. Their experiments revealed that subjects using linen or cotton bedding slept deeper, with a lower body temperature and a higher immunoglobulin A (IgA) content, all indications of a more restful and healthier sleep. They compared these results with research done by others that found cotton pajamas, compared to polyester pajamas, significantly changed sebaceous gland activity in the skin. These changes were associated with less stressful sleep and, with enhanced sebaceous gland activity, better skin defense against bacteria and other environmental contaminants. In another study reported by Zimniewska and Kozlowski, male volunteers were tested to see what physiological differences occurred in various trials (resting, mild exercise, and post-exercise recovery), where the subjects wore either linen garments or ones made of polyester. They found total antioxidant status (TAS), part of our natural defense system, lower for those who wore polyester across the trials compared to those wearing linen. Other studies find similar results favoring the health properties of linen over polyester. For example, muscle fatigue appears greater in individuals who wear polyester over several hours. Natural fibers like linen and hemp offer protection against ultraviolet rays of the sun. Such materials are, in fact, the best protection for the skin when outdoors. In sum, natural fibers, by producing physiological changes conducive to health, prompt psychological changes such as feelings of being more rested, comfortable, vigorous, and so forth. These kinds of studies provide a physiological foundation that contributes to our better understanding the psychological effects of clothing. See Malgorzata Zimniewska & Ryszard Kozlowski, "Natural and ManMade Fibers and Their Role in Creation of Physiological State of Human Body," *Molecular Crystals and Liquid Crystals, 418*, 113-130 (2004).

921 Mary Lou Rosencranz, *Clothing Concepts. A Social-Psychological Approach* (N. Y.: Macmillan, 1972), p. 180. The low rating for wool is not surprising given its physical properties, which affect comfort in wear. When wool is compared to other fibers like cotton, silk, polyester, or blends, for use in apparel worn next to the skin it fares more poorly in perceived comfort. See G. Wang, W. Zhang, R. Postle, & D. Phillips, "Evaluating Wool Shirt Comfort with Wear Trials and the Forearm Test," *Textile Research Journal, 73* (no. 2), 113-119 (2003).

922 "Insight into the Children's Apparel Market," *Textile Consumer, 32* (2004, Spring). Accessed online at the Cotton Incorporated website at http://www.cottoninc.com/TextileConsumer/TextileConsumerVolume32/.

[923] "Checking the Pulse: Toplines on Consumer Attitudes and Preferences," [Womenswear articles], *Lifestyle Monitor* (1999, Mar. 11). Accessed online at the Cotton Incorporated website at http://www.cottoninc.com/ lsmarticles/?articleID=263.

[924] Wonjoung Lee & Masako Sato, "Visual Perception of Texture of Textiles," *Color Research & Application, 26* (no. 6), 469-477 (2001).

[925] Numerous works, both scholarly and popular, consider this aspect, though typically not specifically with reference to clothing. See, for example, Hilaire Hiler, "Some Associative Aspects of Color," *Journal of Aesthetics and Art Criticism, 4* (no. 4), 203-217 (1946). For a more comprehensive examination, see F. Birren, *Color and Human Response* (N. Y.: Van Nostrand Reinhold, 1978).

[926] Chris J. Boyatzis & Reenu Varghese, "Children's Emotional Associations with Color," *Journal of Genetic Psychology, 155* (no. 1), 79-86 (1994).

[927] Martha Picariello, Danna Greenberg, & David Pillemer, "Children's Sex-Related Stereotyping of Colors," *Child Development, 61* (no. 5), 1453-1460.

[928] Jayoung Cho, Chunjeong Kim, & Jiyoung Ha, "Physiological and Subjective Evaluation of the Rustling Sounds of Polyester Warp Knitted Fabrics," *Textile Research Journal, 75* (no. 4), 312-318 (2005).

[929] Foucault's remark about the body seems no less suited to the *clothed* body: "The body is directly involved in a political field; power relations have an intimate hold upon it: they invest it, train it, and torture it, force it to carry out its tasks, to perform ceremonies, to emit signs." See Michel Foucault, *Discipline and Punish: The Birth of the Prison*, translated by A. Sheridan (N. Y.: Vintage, 1979), p. 25f.

[930] Joanna Brewis, Mark P. Hampton, & Stephen Linstead, "Unpacking Priscilla: Subjectivity and Identity in the Organization of Gendered Appearance," *Human Relations, 50* (no. 10), 1275-1304 (1997), p. 1285.

[931] Quoted in Mary Lou Rosencranz, *Clothing Concepts. A Social-Psychological Approach* (N. Y.: Macmillan, 1972), p. 176.

[932] Brewis, Hampton, & Linstead, p. 1285.

[933] L. L. Davis, "Sex, Gender Identity, and Behavior Concerning Sex-Related Clothing," *Clothing & Textiles Research Journal, 3* (no. 2), 20-24 (1985). The 174 male and female subjects completed both the Bem Sex Role Inventory (BSRI) and a Sex-related Clothing Inventory.

[934] One way women participate in the construction and maintenance of masculinity is through the purchase of clothing for the boys and men in their lives.

[935] The mutual desire of men and women to have men dress in masculine attire reinforces the Golden Rule, while the acceptability of women dressing more like men broadens the available choices for women. Both forces thus converge to limit masculine dress alternatives relate to feminine ones.

[936] See Michael Hayworth, "Fashion, Clothing, and Sex," in V. L. Bullough & B. Bullough (Eds.), *Human Sexuality: An Encyclopedia* (N. Y.: Garland Reference Library of Social Science, 1994), at the Magnus Hirschfeld Archive for Sexology maintained by the

HumboldtUniversität zu Berlin, accessed online at http://www2.hu-berlin.de/sexology/GESUND/ARCHIV/SEN/CH10. HTM.

[937] Carrie Yang Costello, "Changing Clothes: Gender Inequality and Professional Socialization," *NWSA Journal,16* (no. 2), 138-155 (2004), p. 144. This finding is consistent with what we have seen in answering previous questions: men have only to obey a single Golden Rule; women have much greater dress freedom.

[938] Ibid, especially pp. 138f., 152.

[939] The androgynous character of dress for males and females before adulthood exists in many social groups and contexts, including among American slaves in the antebellum United States; see Shane White & Graham White, "Slave Clothing and African-American Culture in the Eighteenth and Nineteenth Centuries," *Past & Present, 148*, 149-186 (1995).

[940] Androgynous dress by males can be tolerated because it does *not* violate the golden rule that a male must look masculine, or at least not feminine.

[941] "In clothing design the term, silhouette, is used to express the effect the costume creates as a whole as it appears from a distance, when details of construction and even of color are not noticeable, and the only things observed are the boundary line of the silhouette and its general proportions." Helen Goodrich Buttrick, *Principles of Clothing Selection* (N. Y.: Macmillan, 1923), p. 53f.

[942] Sarah J. Doyle, "Clothing Can Create an Optical Illusion—Good or Bad!" *Wisdom from the Professionals: A Collection of Articles* (2003), accessed online at the Fabrics.net website at http://www.fabrics. net/SarahIllusion.asp.

[943] Cf. Buttrick, p. 54.

[944] Stone, p. 234.

[945] Madeline Shakin, Debra Shakin, & Sarah Hall Sternglanz, "Infant Clothing: Sex Labeling for Strangers," *Sex Roles. A Journal for Research, 12* (nos. 9-10), 955-964 (1985).

[946] Andrée Pomerleau, Daniel Bolduc, Gérard Malcuit, & Louise Cossette, "Pink or Blue: Environmental Gender Stereotypes in the First Two Years of Life," *Sex Roles. A Journal of Research, 22* (nos. 5-6), 359-367 (1990).

[947] Carole R. Beal, *Boys and Girls: The Development of Gender Roles* (N. Y.: McGraw-Hill, 1994), p. 45.

[948] Emily W. Kane, "'No Way My Boys Are Going to Be Like That!' Parents' Responses to Children's Gender Nonconformity," *Gender & Society, 20* (no. 2), 149-176 (2006), p. 156f.

[949] Ibid, pp. 158-160. Interestingly, Kane (pp. 162-164) notes that only with sons was gender nonconformity connect with a concern about sexual orientation. Feminine behavior was viewed as a warning sign of possible homosexuality.

[950] David Plummer, *One of the Boys: Masculinity, Homophobia, and Modern Manhood* (Binghamton, NY: Haworth Press, 1999), p. 145.

951 Susan J. Langer & James I. Martin, "How Dresses Can Make You Mentally Ill: Examining Gender Identity Disorder in Children," *Child and Adolescent Social Work Journal, 21* (no. 1), 523 (2004), p. 8.

952 The constancy and importance of dress as a marker for children has been noted in many studies. At least as far back as 1947 a large study involving 200 boys and girls ages 412 found they relied on dress cues first and foremost in making differentiations among peers. See J. H. Conn & L. Kanner, "Children's Awareness of Sex Differences," *Child Psychiatry, 1*, 357 (1947).

953 Carol Lynn Martin & Jane K. Little, "The Relation of Gender Understanding to Children's Sex-Typed Preferences and Gender Stereotypes," *Child Development, 61* (no. 5), 1427-1439 (1990); quote is from p. 1436.

954 "Insight into the Children's Apparel Market," *Textile Consumer, 32* (2004, Spring). Accessed online at the Cotton Incorporated website at http://www.cottoninc.com/TextileConsumer/TextileConsumer Volume32/.

955 Ibid. A Table shows, for example, that 26% of girls' skirts are made 100% from synthetic fibers.

956 Plummer, p. 144.

957 Ibid, p. 143f.

958 See Carol Lynn Martin, "Stereotypes About Children with Traditional and Non-traditional Gender Roles," *Sex Roles. A Journal of Research, 33* (nos. 11-12), 721-757 (1995).

959 Jason Cox & Helga Dittmar, "The Functions of Clothes and Clothing (Dis)satisfaction: A Gender Analysis Among British Students," *Journal of Consumer Policy, 18* (nos. 2-3), 237-265 (1995), p. 243.

960 J. Jill Suitor & Rebel Reavis, "Football, Fast Cars, and Cheerleading: Adolescent Gender Norms, 1978-1989," *Adolescence, 30* (no. 2), 265-272 (1995), Table I.

961 Cox & Dittmar, p. 240f. The authors conclude that these differences may be construed as reflecting, broadly, differences in masculine and feminine gender identities, with the former more self-oriented and activity centered, where the latter is more other-oriented and relationship-centered.

962 Ibid, p. 251.

963 Stephen J. Gould & Barbara B. Stern, "Gender Schema and Fashion Consciousness," *Psychology & Marketing, 6* (no. 2), 129-145 (1989), p. 142.

964 Timothy M. Franz & Steven D. Norton, "Investigating Business Causal Dress Policies: Questionnaire Development and Exploratory Research," *Applied H.R.M. Research, 6* (nos. 1-2), 79-94 (2000).

965 See, for example, Michael G. Pratt & Anat Rafaeli, "Organizational Dress as a Symbol of Multilayered Social Identities," *Academy of Management Journal, 40* (no. 4), 862-898 (1997). This article explores at some length the function of dress in relation to identity in the professional setting of a rehabilitation unit in a large hospital.

[966] Yoon-Hee Kwon, "The Influence of Appropriateness of Dress and Gender in the Self perception of Occupational Attributes," *Clothing & Textiles Research Journal, 12* (no. 3), 33-39 (1994). Also see Sherry E. Sullivan, "Do Clothes Really Make the Woman? The Use of Attire to Enhance Work Performance," *The Academy of Management Executives, 11* (no. 4), 90ff. (1997).

[967] Yoon-Hee Kwon, "Feeling Toward One's Clothing and Self-perception of Emotion, Sociability, and Work Competency," *Journal of Social Behavior and Personality, 9* (no. 1), 129-139 (1994).

[968] Feminist Carole Turbin suggests that casual wear in such contexts can temporarily modify the gender hierarchy, signaling less formality in authority relationships and permitting more display of sexual interest. See Carole Turbin, "Refashioning the Concept of Public/Private. Lessons from Dress Studies," *Journal of Women's Studies, 15* (no. 1), 43-51 (2003), p. 46f.

[969] Jennifer Craik, *The Face of Fashion: Cultural Studies in Fashion* (N. Y.: Routledge, 1994), p. 56.

[970] A sizeable number of studies have been done on the role of dress in the lives of girls and women. One such is by Alison Guy & Maura Banim, "Personal Collections: Women's Clothing Use and Identity," *Journal of Gender Studies, 9* (no. 3), 313-327 (2000). In this article they cluster the 'dynamic relationship' women have with their clothes around three distinct but coexisting views of the self: 'the woman I want to be,' 'the woman I fear I could be,' and 'the woman I am most of the time.' For a more extended treatment see Ali Guy, Eileen Green, & Maura Banim, *Through the Wardrobe: Women's Relationships with Their Clothes* (N. Y.: Berg, 2001).

[971] Gould & Stern, p. 142.

[972] Cox & Dittmar, pp. 254-257. They conclude (p. 256) that social psychological functions of clothes are, for women, much greater predictors of clothing satisfaction.

[973] Mary Lou Lerch Rosencranz, "A Study of Women's Interest in Clothing," *Journal of Home Economics, 41* (no. 8), 460-462 (1949), p. 462.

[974] Kim P. Johnson, Nancy A. Schofield, and Jennifer Yurchisin, "Appearance and Dress as a Source of Information. A Qualitative Approach to Data Collection," *Clothing & Textiles Research Journal, 20* (no. 3), 125-137 (2002).

[975] Kim K. P. Johnson & Mary Ellen Roach-Higgins, "Dress and Physical Attractiveness of Women in Job Interviews," *Clothing & Textiles Research Journal, 5* (no. 3), 18 (1987).

[976] Yoon-Hee Kwon, "The Influence of Appropriateness of Dress and Gender on the Self-perception of Occupational Attributes," *Clothing & Textiles Research Journal, 12* (no. 3), 33-39 (1994).

[977] Brewis, Hampton, & Linstead, p. 1287. See their discussion on power dressing, pp. 1287-1288, 1292-1293.

[978] S. M. Forsythe, "Effect of Clothing Masculinity on Perceptions of Managerial Traits: Does Gender of the Perceiver Make a Difference?" *Clothing & Textiles Research Journal, 6* (no. 2), 10-16 (1988). The answer to the title's question was that there is not a

significant difference between males and females, although the latter tended to see the women subjects being examined as more forceful and self-reliant.

[979] Kim P. Johnson, C. Crutsinger, & Jane E. Workman, "Can Professional Women Appear Too Masculine? The Case of the Necktie," *Clothing and Textiles Research Journal, 12* (no. 2), 27-31 (1994). At least as late as 1977, women were still having to go to court for the right to wear pants at work; see the United Kingdom case of Schmidt vs. Austicks Bookshops Ltd.

[980] K. E. Koch & L. E. Dickey, "The Feminist in the Workplace: Applications to a Contextual Study of Dress," *Clothing & Textiles Research Journal, 7* (no. 1), 46-54 (1988).

[981] Rosencranz, "A Study of Women's Interest in Clothing," p. 460.

[982] Cf. James Laver, *Modesty in Dress. An Inquiry into the Fundamentals of Fashion* (Boston: Houghton Mifflin, 1969).

[983] Cf. Susan Kaiser, "Minding Appearances: Style, Truth, and Subjectivity," in J. Entwhistle & E. Wilson (Eds.), *Body Dressing*, pp. 79-102 (Oxford: Berg, 2001).

[984] E. L. Bell, "Adult's Perception of Male Garment Styles," *Clothing & Textiles Research Journal, 10* (no. 1), 8-12 (1991).

[985] Kate Soper, "Dress Needs: Reflections on the Clothed Body, Selfhood and Consumption," in Joanne Entwistle & Elizabeth Wilson (Eds.), *Body Dressing. Dress, Body, Culture* (N. Y.: Berg, 2001), pp. 13-32.

[986] Hannah Frith & Kate Gleeson, "Clothing and Embodiment: Men Managing Body Image and Appearance," *Psychology of Men & Masculinity, 5* (no. 1), 40-48. Frith and Glesson identify four themes in men's use of dress: practicality, unconcern about appearance, dressing to conceal or reveal the body, and using clothes to fit cultural ideals.

[987] In the U.S. the market for men's clothing has been volatile in the early 21st century with a decline in 20002003, but followed by an upswing in 2004-2005. In the United Kingdom men's designer wear expenditures in 1997 constituted 39% of the market; in 2001 they were 43% (Priest, p. 258).

[988] Judith Rasband, *Real Men Don't Wear Tees!* (Conselle L. C., 2000). Accessed online at Conselle.com at http://www.conselle.com/Business_Programs/real_men. html. Rasband argues that, taken together, the woman who wears business casual attire (i.e., pants), which assumes a traditionally masculine appearance, and the man who dresses casually, thus becoming less covered and appearing more feminine, both appear to reflect changing gender roles. Resistance to men wearing casual attire, she thinks, indicates a fear of the feminization of the workplace.

[989] For example, we might be motivated by modesty to adhere to our mother's advice to always wear clean and plain underwear that might in an emergency be seen by strangers—who we would not wish to form an impression of us as loose or wanton! Similarly, we may choose to wear underwear we view as erotic to cultivate inside ourselves a feeling of being sexy—and perhaps with the hope of a sexual encounter, in which the sight of our apparel will boost our partner's libido.

[990] When couples feel less intimate with one another they are likely to change there dress habits so that they no longer dress or undress in front of one another; their underwear, like their inmost self, becomes invisible.

[991] Guy Trebay, "When Did Skivvies Get Rated NC17?" [Cultural Studies] *The New York Times* (2004, Aug. 1). Accessed online at *The New York Times'* 'Fashion & Style' webpage, at http://www.nytimes.com/2004/08/01/fashion/01SKIV.html?ei=5090& en=f0088a3b25fa1e4b&ex=1249185600&partner=rssuserland&pagewanted=all&positi on=. Trebay traces this development to the influence of a portion of the gay community.

[992] Bo Lönnqvist, "Fashion and Eroticism: Men's Underwear in the Context of Eroticism," *Ethnologia Europaea, 31* (no. 1), 75-82 (2001).

[993] The idea of a sexual economy depicts sexual exchanges as economic ones: a female grants access to her body in exchange for the male granting access to his resources. Thus men will desire sexually attractive, fertile women while women will desire successful, virile men.

[994] Feona Attwood, "Fashion and Passion: Marketing Sex to Women," *Sexualities, 8* (no. 4), 392-406 (2005).

[995] Jane FerrellBeck & Colleen Gau, *Uplift: The Bra in America* (Phila.: Univ. of Pennsylvania Press, 2002), p. 116; cf. p. 56.

[996] For an interesting perspective, see Garry S. Brody, "The Perfect Breast: Is It Attainable? Does It Exist?" *Plastic & Reconstructive Surgery, 113* (no. 5), 1500-1503 (2004).

[997] For a look at the history of panties and panty fashion, as well as speculations about what various panty styles suggest about their wearers, see Sarah Tomczak & Rachel Pask, *Panties: A Brief History* (London: Dorling Kindersley, 2004).

[998] Tony Kent, "Ethical Perspectives on the Erotic in Retailing," *Qualitative Market Research: An International Journal, 8* (no. 4), 430-439 (2005).

[999] Nancy V. Workman, "From Victorian to Victoria's Secret: The Foundations of Modern Erotic Wear," *Journal of Popular Culture, 30* (no. 2), 61-73 (1996); see especially pp. 68-70.

[1000] "What remains undeniably striking as one observes the evolution of men's clothing fashions is how one unchanging feature persists over time and space: the fondness for black. Black forms a constant in menswear, despite the not inconsiderable changes in the cut of male clothes between the sixteenth and the twentieth centuries." Marco Belfanti & Fabio Giusberti, "Global Dress: Clothing as a Means of Integration (17th – 20th Centuries)," p. 11. Paper presented at the XIII Economic History Congress, Buenos Aires, July 22-26, 2002. Accessed online at http://www.eh.net/XIIICongress /cd/papers/64Belfanti Giusbertil70.pdf.

[1001] The silhouette is discussed more at pp. 299-300.

[1002] Of course, the resurgence of interest in pink as a color for men qualifies this generalization. On the early 21st century use of pink in masculine clothing, see Kelly Grannan, "Pink Moves Into the Masculine Mainstream," *The Daily Texan* (2004, Oct. 4), accessed online at http://www.dailytexan online.com/media/paper410/news/2004/

10/04/Entertainment/PinkMoves.Into.The.Masculine.Mainstream740552.shtml. Also see "Real Men Wear Pink," *The Early Show* (CBS) (2005, Apr. 27), accessed online at http:// www.cbsnews.com/stories/2005/04/27/earlyshow/living/beauty/main691184 .shtml.

[1003] Jo Paoletti, *Dressing for Sexes* (n.d.). Accessed online at http:// www.gentlebirth.org/archives/pinkblue.html. Also see Jo Paoletti, "The Gendering of Infants' and Toddlers' Clothing in America," in Katharine Martinez and Kenneth Ames (Eds.), *The Material Culture of Gender/ The Gender of Material Culture* (The Henry Francis du Pont Winterthur Museum, 1997); "Clothes Make the Boy 1860-1910," *Dress, 8* (1983); "Clothing and Gender in American Children's Fashions 18901920," *Signs, 13* (no. 1), 136-143 (1987, Autumn); "Comment: Children's Clothes and Gender," *Threads, 19*, 98 (1988, Oct./Nov.). Paoletti holds a Ph.D. in textiles and teaches American Studies at the University of Maryland College Park. Cf. the short comment in Marjorie Gerber, *Vested Interests. CrossDressing and Cultural Anxiety* (N. Y.: Routledge, 1992), p. 1.

[1004] Ibid. Interestingly, the first appearance in the Sears Catalog of gender specific infant wear did not occur until 1962. See K. Huun & S. B. Kaiser, "The Emergence of Modern Infantwear, 1896-1962," *Clothing & Textiles Research Journal, 19* (no. 3), 103-119 (2001). The authors view the changes in young children's clothing between 1896-1962 as an aspect of male "flight from femininity" as society constructed its modern binary system of gender.

[1005] *Boys' Historical Clothing: Introduction* (Christopher Wagner's Historical Boys Clothing website). Accessed online, with numerous photographic examples, at http://histclo.hispeed.com/intro. html.

[1006] Ibid.

[1007] Jane Ellen, "Historic Costuming Series: Why Boys Wore Dresses," *What's New at Jane Ellen's, 3* (no. 1) (2000, February). Accessed online at http://www. dressmaker.com/ezine0200.shtml. Cf. Kristina Harris, *The Child in Fashion 1750 to 1920* (Atglen, PA: 1999). Some evidence exists that boys on occasion wore dresses until nearly puberty. The implicit notion was that all children and women were more alike to one another than any of these groups were like men.

[1008] "Why Did Mothers Outfit Boys in Dresses?" *Boys' Historical Clothing*. Accessed online at http://histclo.hispeed.com/style/skirted/dress/dresswhy. html.

[1009] Jane Ellen.

[1010] Daniel Thomas Cook, *The Commodification of Childhood: The Children's Clothing Industry and the Rise of the Child Consumer* (Durham, NC: Duke Univ. Press, 2004); quote is from p. 101.

[1011] Susan B. Kaiser, Margaret Rudy, & Pamela Byfield, "The Role of Clothing in Sex-Role Socialization: Person Perceptions Versus Overt behavior," *Child Study Journal, 15* (no. 2), 83-97 (1985).

[1012] Martha L. Picariello, Danna N. Greenberg, & David B. Pillemer, "Children's Sex-related Stereotyping of Colors," *Child Development, 61*, 1453-1460 (1990). Quote is from p. 1459.

[1013] Judith E. Owen Blakemore, "Children's Beliefs About Violating Gender Norms: Boys Shouldn't Look Like Girls and Girls Shouldn't Act Like Boys," *Sex Roles: A Journal of Research, 43,* 411-419 (2003). As might be expected, perceptions and reactions among children are inconsistent and vary with age. However, of relevance to us, this research found that children ages 3-11 are more tolerant of girls with clothing and hairstyles like that of boys than of boys whose clothing and hairstyle is more feminine.

[1014] Carolyn Balkwell, "On Peacocks and Peahens: A Cross-Cultural Investigation of the Effects of Economic Development on Sex Differences in Dress," *Clothing & Textiles Research Journal, 4* (no. 2), 30-36 (1986).

[1015] My use of 'bifurcated' here is limited to clothing that divides below the waist, though Steven Connor makes the valid point that bifurcated can also refer to the division that occurs at the waist, so that there is a vertical bifurcation as well as a horizontal, bilateral one. See Steven Connor, "Men in Skirts," *Women: A Cultural Review, 13* (no. 3), 257-271 (2002), p. 258.

[1016] Thomas, p. 69, contends that emphasis of the waist line became the dominant idea in women's fashion.

[1017] Gilles Lipovetsky, *The Empire of Fashion. Dressing Modern Democracy,* translated by C. Porter (Princeton: Princeton Univ. Press, 1994; original work published 1987).

[1018] Connor, p. 259.

[1019] Lois Banner, "The Fashionable Sex, 1100-1600," *History Today, 42* (no. 4), 37-44. Cf. Thomas, p. 70, who views the transition of fashion focus from male to female as reflective of men moving their focus and energy to the realm of business, where wealth is attractive enough without ornament and the importance of appearance is transferred from their persons to their goods.

[1020] Diana Crane, *Fashion and Its Social Agendas. Class, Gender and Identity in Clothing* (Chicago: Univ. of Chicago Press, 2000), p. 3. Cf. her remarks on the 19th century, pp. 3-6.

[1021] Sara Melissa Pullum-Piñon. *Conspicuous Display and Social Mobility: a Comparison of 1850s Boston and Charleston Elites* [Ph.D. dissertation] (Austin: The University of Texas, 2002), p. 147f. Pullum-Piñon (p. 148) also notes that too excise display in this respect among women was also frowned upon as it came to be associated with women of low repute such as prostitutes, entertainers, or working women.

[1022] Cf. the "Men in Skirts" exhibit at the Victoria & Albert Museum website accessed at http://www.vam.ac.uk/exploring/collections/fashion/short_stories/men_in _skirts/?view=Mainframe. Interestingly, the current revival of male interest in—and appropriation of—unbifurcated garments is raising considerable attention and controversy.

[1023] Cf. Fred Davis, *Fashion, Culture, and Identity* (Chicago: Univ. of Chicago Press, 1992), pp. 34-37.

[1024] Dubuc quoted in Siobhan O'Connor, "Philippe Dubuc Pushes the Limits of Masculine Fashion," *Montreal Mirror* (2001, Mar. 29), accessed online at http://www.montrealmirror.com/ARCHIVES/2001/032901/fashion3.html.   John Connor (p. 268) regards this statement as mostly true only from the mid19th century on.

[1025] Connor, p. 263.

[1026] The German *Blusen* has applied to masculine clothing. The Luftwaffe uniform, for instance, included a 'field blouse.' The English 'blouse' early on referred to a garment either a male or female might wear; boys in the 19th century typically wore blouses where men wore shirts.

[1027] The positioning of buttons on the left side, which makes for ease for right-handed people—the majority of the population—was allocated to masculine fashion. Award winning artist and writer David Lance Goines remarks in history of the button that as an article of clothing the button *per se* was "an inviolate masculine preserve for three hundred years and more." See David Lance Goies, *Button, Button* (1999), accessed online at http://www.goines.net/Writing/button _button.html.

[1028] Substantiating claims for the corset at an earlier date is difficult, though it is common to see the corset attributed to Cretan and Greek women of antiquity. The term's connection to men in armor is evident in its original meaning as a 'breastplate.' Men have worn corsets throughout history; President John F. Kennedy used one to help with back pain. For more information see *History of Corsets—An Overview Through the Centuries*, a webpage on the European Corset Society's website, accessed online at http://www.eucosy.org/uk/corset/ history/.

If one wishes to be ingenious, even the brassiere—an irrefutably feminine article of clothing—can be regarded as derived from male clothing if its origin is seen as an off-shoot from the corset and the latter is accorded its start in men's armor.

[1029] Male clergy in particular used lace. On the early history and use of lace in Europe, see Wim J. Lauriks, "Birthplace of Lace," *LACE Magazine International,* Issue 49, pp. 33-35 (1999, Spring). Cf. Wim J. Lauriks, "Growth of Lace," *LACE Magazine International,* Issue 50 (1999, Summer).

[1030] Connor, p. 260. He writes (p. 260): "The phrase 'petticoat breeches' could actually be used of two slightly different things: either long underdrawers with deep flounces of lace that fell out over the knee from underneath breeches; or a skirt or petticoat worn short enough to show the fringes of the bloomertype breeches worn underneath."

[1031] Barbara Burman, "Pocketing the Difference: Gender and Pockets in Nineteenth-Century Britain," *Gender and History, 14* (no. 3), 447-469 (2002). With reference to the gendered body, see the discussion on pp. 460-464. Cf. Connor, p. 267.

[1032] Thomas, pp. 71-72, sees the development of women's fashion—so fully incorporated within the business of man—as having an "altogether bad" effect on the character of women by reinforcing negative stereotypes such as their helplessness. In effect, he says, it makes her a thing rather than a person, an object for male manipulation. Yet already in 1908 he could see that change would come as women asserted independence.

[1033] Numerous works exist documenting this struggle. See, for example, P. C. Warner, "Feminism and Costume History: Synthesis and Reintegration," *Clothing & Textiles Research Journal, 18* (no. 3), 185-189 (2000).

[1034] Cf. Thomas, p. 71, who quotes the remark of Sir Henry Maine that the greatest calamity that might befall our modern society would not be war, pestilence or famine, but a revolution in fashion where women would dress as men—in one material of one color.

[1035] Mary Lou Rosencranz, *Clothing Concepts. A Social-Psychological Approach* (N. Y.: Macmillan, 1972), pp. 172, 175.

[1036] Although the early 21st century witnessed a fair amount of publicity for this trend in both Europe and the United States, it was at least as far back as the Fall of 1984 that fashion shows in London and Paris had men wearing skirts. An American designer, Stephen Sprouse, had earlier placed a male model in a black denim miniskirt over black denim jeans in an April, 1983 show. See John Duka, "Skirts for Men? Yes and No," *New York Times* (1984, October 27th). For examples of the recent trend, visit any of a number of websites. While this volume was being prepared I sampled various places online, such as a German fashion site accessed at https://ssl.kundenserver.de/menintime.de/start_en.php3?VID=pwYIqgr5sRhjtLvF&PID=no. Also see the German fashion site Persus de accessed at http://www.persus. de/index2.htm. Cf. the British site for Midas Clothing in Manchester, England, accessed at http:// www.persus.de/index2.htm. For a U.S. example, see the site for Macabi Skirt, Salt Lake City, Utah, accessed at http://www.macabiskirt.com/.

[1037] Cathy Horyn, "Face Off," *Men's Fashions of the Times. The New York Times Magazine, Part 2*, pp. 48-52 (2004, Spring).

[1038] Ibid, p. 52.

[1039] Bowie also sings of erotic crossdressing, as in "Cactus" when he solicits a lover to send her sweat-soaked dress for him to wear. Pictures of Bowie's and Rowland's album covers can be found on the internet. I accessed them online at rateyourmusic.com site *Album Cover Art: Homoeroticism* at http://rateyourmusic.com/lists/list_view/list_id_is_5842. A picture of Cobain in a dress, with comments from fans, can be found at NirvanaPhotos.com, accessed online at http:// www.nirvanaphotos.com/photos.php?Cat=8&Idx=6. A dress worn by Kobain was also featured as part of an exhibit at the New York Metropolitan Museum. Cf. "Men in Skirts."

[1040] David Beckham, *David Beckham: My World* (London: Hodder & Stoughton General, 2000).

[1041] Laurel Wellman, "Skirting an Issue," *SF Weekly* (1996, Sept. 4). Accessed online at http://www.sfweekly.com/issues/19960904/news.html.

[1042] Jean Lowerison, "The Reel Story: 'The Iron Ladies.' Volleyball-Playing Drag Queens," *San Diego Metropolitan Uptown Examiner and Daily Business Report* (2004, June; original article printed 2001). Accessed online at http:// metro.sandiegometro.com/reel/index.php?reelID=300.

[1043] Alex Feld, "Style Sheet: Grecian Formula," *Entertainment Weekly* #767 (2004, May 28), 28. Cf. Erik Kirschbaum, "Pitt Says Men May Start Wearing Skirts After 'Troy,'" *Reuters* (2004, May 9). Accessed online at http://www.reuters.com/ newsArticle.jhtml?type=entertainmentNews&storyID =5082571. Pitt, it should be noted, proved a lousy prophet for the immediate future, and refrained from any post-*Troy* displays of skirt wearing, suggesting his remarks were generated for publicity.

[1044] Andrew Bolton, *Bravehearts: Men in Skirts* (London: Victoria & Albert Museum, 2003). Cf. the museum exhibit which the book accompanies, accessed online at http://www.vam.ac.uk/resources/press/press09?section=index&page= press09.

[1045] Phillip D. Johnson, "Men in skirts: A bridge too far?" *Lucire* (2003). Accessed online at http://www.lucire.com/2003a/1103ll0.shtml.

[1046] Judith Thurman, "Would You Be Caught Dead with This Guy?" *Mademoiselle* (2000). Accessed online at http://users.pandora.be/tripticdesign/ skirt10.html.

[1047] Francesco Alberoni, "A Freudian Skirt," *Mono Uomo, 79*, 44-45 (1994, March).

Chapter 15 Notes

[1048] Merry E. Wiesner-Hanks, *Gender in History* (Malden, MA: Blackwell, 2001), pp. 114-144; quote is from p. 114.

[1049] In a study comparing 93 societies, resource theory best predicted the likelihood of women being permitted to occupy a shamanistic position; they are most likely to be shamans in societies where they meet two conditions: they hold great influence in kin networks but they hold little control of property. See Michael R. Welch, "Female Exclusion from Religious Roles: A Cross-Cultural Test of Competing Explanations," *Social Forces, 61* (no. 1), 79-98 (1982).

[1050] Cf. Natalie K. Watson, *Feminist Theology* (Grand Rapids, MI: Wm. B. Eerdmans, 2003), p. 44.

[1051] The New Revised Standard Version wisely translates Genesis 1:26-27 using the word "humankind" rather than "man."

[1052] The terms for 'male' (αρσεν) and 'female' (θηλυ) are both neuter; an interesting choice since a masculine form is available for 'male' and a feminine one for 'female.'

[1053] A. Guillaumont, et al. (Trans.), *The Gospel According to Thomas* (Leiden: E. J. Brill, 1959), Logia 114, p. 57. See also, Elizabeth Castelli, "'I Will Make Mary Male': Pieties of the Body and Gender: Transformation of Christian Women in Late Antiquity," in Julia Epstein & Kristina Straub (Eds.), *Body Guards: The Cultural politics of Gender Ambiguity* (N. Y.: Routledge, 1991), pp. 29-49. Cf. Wayne A. Meeks, "The Image of the Androgyne: Some Uses of Symbol in Earliest Christianity," *History of Religions, 13,* 165-208 (1973-1974).

[1054] For much of Church history the sentiment expressed in the Gospel of Thomas appears to have triumphed. Thus, for example, we have the words of Gregory of Nyssa (4th century) about his sister, St. Macrina:

> As often happens at such times, the [960 B] talk flowed on until we came to discuss the life of some famous person. In this case it was a woman who provided us with our subject ; if indeed she should be styled 'woman' for I do not know whether it is fitting to designate her by her sex, who so surpassed her sex.

Gregory of Nyssa: *The Life of Macrina*, trans. by W.K. Lowther Clarke, (London: SPCK, 1916). Available online at http://www.fordham.edu/halsall/basis/macrina. html. St. Macrina the Younger lived c. 330-379 C.E.

[1055] *Sayings of the Fathers* V.x.73 (available online at http://www.vitae-patrum.org.uk/ page53.html), in the *Vitae Patrum* (available online at http://www.vitae-patrum. org.uk/index.html). Likewise we might place here St. Uncumber, whose story belongs somewhere between the 7th and 11th centuries. Also known in various other lands by the names Liberata, Liberdade, Liverade, Kümmernis, Ontkommena, or Wilge-fortis, this legend puts into play the notion above, with a twist. Uncumber was the beautiful daughter of a king who intended to marry her to another ruler for political purposes. But Uncumber, a pious girl, had taken a vow of chastity in order to serve God as the bride of Christ alone. In this unequal contest of power, Uncumber seemed to have lost when her father put her in a cell until she should give in. But she fasted and prayed, petitioning God that might take away her beauty so that she would not be the desire of men's affection. Her prayer was granted. When they came to take her from her cell they discovered Uncumber had grown a beard and body hair. She had, in fact, become like a man—a bearded saint. Her father, outraged, put her to death by crucifixion that she might die like the Lord she preferred over other men. For a very interesting article, which might make St. Uncumber the patron saint of those with eating disorders, see J. Hubert Lacey, "Anorexia Nervosa and a Bearded Female Saint," *British Medical Journal, 285,* 18-25 (1982, Dec.), pp. 1816-1817. Available online at http://www.philipresheph. com/ a424/study/lacey.doc. Also, see Paul Halsall, "A Legend of the Austrian Tyrol: St. Kümmernis," Modern History Sourcebook (1998). Available online at http://www.fordham.edu/halsall/mod/kummernis.html.

[1056] Lynne Dahmen, "Sacred Romance: Silence and the Hagiographical Tradition," Arthuriana, 12 (no. 1), pp. 113-122. Quote is from p. 116. Cf. a similar comment by J. Herrin, "In Search of Byzantine Women: Three Avenues of Approach," in A. Cameron & A. Kuhrt (Eds.), *Images of Women in Antiquity* (Detroit: Wayne State Univ. Press, 1983), p. 179: "The monastic disguises adopted by women enabled them to simulate a holiness reserved by male ecclesiastical authorities to men only."

[1057] Valerie R. Hotchkiss, *Clothes Make the Man: Female Cross-Dressing in Medieval Europe* (N. Y.: Garland Publishing, Inc., 1996). Please note that one immediate complication about such accounts is that the antiquity of the stories, coupled with doubt in some cases about the facts set forth, may cause some to dismiss them. But whether the events actually happened as told seems inconsequential for our study since the record—which tells of these women dressing as men—has been preserved as part of the story. I think it obvious that if fiction, the storytellers or later Church censors surely could have expunged the crossdressing aspect had it offended them.

[1058] Mary-Paula Walsh, *Feminism and Christian Tradition: An Annotated Bibliography and Critical Introduction to the Literature* (Westport, CT: Greenwood Press, 1999), p. xv.

[1059] Mary Kenny, "Reflections of Feminism and Christianity," in J. Tolhurst (Ed.), *Man, Woman and Priesthood*, pp. 121-141 (Bloomington: Gracewing, 1989), pp. 121-124. Quote is from p. 121.

[1060] Watson, p. 44; also see p. 22f.

[1061] Angela Pears, *Feminist Christian Encounters: The Methods and Strategies of Feminist Informed Christian Theologies* (Burlington, VT: Ashgate, 2004), p. 1.

[1062] Many scholars over the years have remarked on the role that sex and/or gender play in religions of the world. See, for example, Geoffrey Parrinder, *Sex in the World's Religions* (N. Y.: Oxford Univ. Press, 1980). Also see Joseph Runzo & Nancy M. Martin (Eds.), *Love, Sex and Gender in the World Religions* (Oxford: Oneworld Publications, 2000). In the latter volume, Christian readers may be especially interested in Karen Jo Torjesen, "Gendered Imagery in Early Christian Theologies" (pp. 203-222).

[1063] Robert Hannaford, "Gender and the Person God Is," in R. Hannaford & J. Jobling (Eds.), *Theology and the Body: Gender, Text and Ideology*, pp. 30-46 (Herefordshire: Gracewing, 1999), p. 36.

[1064] The Hebrew God—YHWH—eventually triumphed as the 'One God,' but for much of Israel's biblical history there was competition. Popular religion permitted worship of other gods. Asherah, for example, may at various times been viewed as the consort of YHWH, and as Gale Yee observes, "Veneration of the goddess Asherah was a major feature of Israelite religious pluralism . . . ." See Gale Gale A. Yee, "'She Is Not My Wife and I Am Not Her Husband': A Materialist Analysis of Hosea 1-2," *Biblical Interpretation, 9* (no. 4), 345-383 (2001), p. 366; cf. p. 352. Cf. Cf. J. A. Emerton, "'Yahweh and His Asherah': The Goddess or Her Symbol?" *Vetus Testamentum, 49* (no. 3), 315-37 (1999). For an interesting account putting the discussion into a contemporary context, see Ann Arlosoroff Vise Nunes, "The Historical Tradition of Sacral Sex and Contemporary Media Manifestations of Carnal Sex," *Studies in Media and Information Literacy Education, 4* (no. 3), article #51 (2004). Accessed online at http://www. utpjournals.com/jour.ihtml?lp=simile/issue15/nunes1.html.

[1065] For more on Islamic conceptions about Allah, see G. G. Bolich, *Crossdressing in Context, vol. 3: The Context of Religion* (forthcoming), Q. 78.

[1066] Daniel C. Matt, *The Essential Kabbalah* (Edison, NJ: Castle Books, 1995), p. 1.

[1067] *Tiqqunei ha-Zohar*, 17a. Quoted in Matt, p. 50.

[1068] Moses Cordovero, *Or Ne'erav*, 6:1-6 (42a-55b). Quoted in Matt, p. 45f.

[1069] See Julian of Norwich, *Showings*, translated by Edmund Colledge & James Walsh (N. Y.: Paulist Press, 1978); see especially chapters 57-62. Also see Caroline Walker Bynum, *Jesus as Mother: Studies in the Spirituality of the High Middle Ages* (Berkeley: Univ. of California Press, 1982).

[1070] The problem posed by this situation is addressed by Rabbi Zalman Schacter-Shalomi, "God, Our Mother," *Havurah Shir Hadash* website, accessed online at http://www.havurahshirhadash.org/rebzalmanarticle1.html; for the Christian aspect of this issue, see Christian scholar Elaine Pagels, "What Became of God the Mother? Conflicting Images of God in Early Christianity," *Signs. The Journal of Women in Culture and Society, 2* (no. 2) (1976); reprinted in C. P. Christ & J. Plaskow (Eds.), *Womanspirit Rising*, pp. 107-119 (N. Y.: Harper & Row, 1979); reprinted online at *Body, Sex and Gender in the Church*, accessed at http://www.womenpriests.org/body/pagels. htm.

[1071] Mary Daly, *Beyond God the Father: Toward a Philosophy of Women's Liberation* (Boston: Beacon Press, 1973), p. 19.

[1072] James W. Telch, "The Isoko Tribe," *Africa, VII*, 160-173 (1934), excerpted in Mircea Eliade, *Essential Sacred Writings from Around the World* (S. F.: HarperSanFrancisco, 1967), p. 6f.

[1073] Ninian Smart & Richard D. Hecht (Eds.), *Sacred Texts of the World. A Universal Anthology* (N. Y.: Crossroad, 1992), p. 348.

[1074] *Brihad-Aranyaka Upanishad*, I.4.1, in Robert E. Van Voorst, *An Anthology of World Scriptures* (Belmont, CA: Wadsworth, 1994), p. 32.

[1075] Mircea Eliade & Ioan P. Couliano, with Hillary S. Wiesner, *The Eliade Guide to World Religions* (S. F.: Harper & Row, 1991), p. 220.

[1076] *Nihongi*, Bk. 5, 7th year, in Joseph M. Kitagawa, "Religions of Japan," in W. Chan, I. R. al Faruqi, J. M. Kitagawa, & P. T. Raju (compilers), *The Great Asian Religions. An Anthology*, pp. 231-305 (N. Y.: Macmillan, 1969), p. 240.

[1077] Mircea Eliade, *Patterns in Comparative Religion*, translated by R. Sheed (London: Sheed and Ward, 1958), p. 420.

[1078] Mark Matousek, "The Feminine Face of God," *Common Boundary*, pp. 32-37 (1992, May/June), p. 33.

[1079] Hildegard of Bingen, *Liber divinorum operum* I.4.100, edited by A. Derolez & P. Dronke, CCCM 92 (Turnhout: Brepols, 1996), p. 243.

[1080] Steven Connor, "Men in Skirts," *Women: A Cultural Review, 13* (no. 3), 257-271 (2002), p. 261f.

[1081] Lori Hope Lefkovitz, "Passing as a Man: Narratives of Jewish Gender Performance," *Narrative, 10* (no. 1), 91-103 (2002), p. 97.

[1082] Stephen J. Davis, "Crossed Texts, Crossed Sex: Intertextuality and Gender in Early Christian Legends of Holy Women Disguised as Men," *Journal of Early Christian Studies, 10* (no. 1), 1-36 (2002), p. 35.

[1083] Translation from Arland J. Hultgren & Steven A. Haggmark (Eds.), *The Earliest Christian Heretics* (Minneapolis, MN: Fortress Press, 1996), p.129. Also see Frank Williams (Translator), "The Panarion of Epiphanius of Salamis," in *Nag Hammadi and Manichean Studies*, vol.35 (Leiden: E. J. Brill, 1994).

[1084] Mother Julian's mystical writings have been translated; see Julian of Norwich, *Showings*, trans. Edmund Colledge & James Walsh (N. Y.: Paulist Press, 1978). Also see Thomas L. Long, "Julian of Norwich's 'Christ as Mother' and Medieval Constructions of Gender." (Paper presented at the Madison Conference on English Studies, Madison University, March 18, 1995). Accessed online at http://users.visi.net/~longt/julian.htm.

[1085] Barbara Newman, "Henry Suso and the Medieval Devotion to Christ the Goddess," *Spiritus: A Journal of Christian Spirituality, 2* (no. 1), 1-14 (2002). Quotes from Suso are found in Newman, pp. 9, 4. Note the artwork described and presented in this article. Cf. Barbara Newman, *God and the Goddesses: Vision, Poetry, and Belief in the Middle Ages* (Phila.: Univ. of Pennsylvania Press, 2002).

¹⁰⁸⁶ Davis, p. 33, n. 109; also see Arnfríður Guðmundsdóttir, "Female Christ-Figures in Films: A Feminist Critical Analysis of *Breaking the Waves* and *Dead Man Walking*," *Studia Theologica, 56* (no. 1), 27-43 (2002).

¹⁰⁸⁷ Eleanor McLaughlin, "Feminist Christologies: Re-Dressing the Tradition," in M. Stevens (Ed.), *Reconstructing the Christ Symbol. Essays in Feminist Christology*, pp. 118-149 (N. Y.: Paulist Press, 1993). Quotes are from pp. 141-142. Cf. the remark by Eisler, "[I]t is not surprising that Jesus should have been aware that the 'masculine' values of dominance, inequality, and conquest he could see all around him debasing and distorting human life must be replaced by a softer, more 'feminine' set of values based on compassion, responsibility, and love." See Riane Eisler, *The Chalice and the Blade* (N.Y.: HarperCollins, 1988), p. 124.

¹⁰⁸⁸ Hans Licht, *Sexual Life in Ancient Greece* (London: Abbey Library, 1971 printing of 1932 ed.), p. 124.

¹⁰⁸⁹ Ibid, p. 128f.

¹⁰⁹⁰ The *dithyramb* is a choral song sung to Dionysus; the meaning of 'Dithyrambus' has long been debated and remains unsettled. My use is vis-à-vis Camille Paglia, *Sexual Personae* (N. Y.: Vintage Books, 1991), p. 89.

¹⁰⁹¹ Albert Henrichs, "Dionysus," in S. Hornblower & A. Spawforth (Eds.), *The Oxford Classical Dictionary*, 3rd ed., pp. 479-482 (N. Y.: Oxford Univ. Press, 1996), p. 479.

¹⁰⁹² Ibid.

¹⁰⁹³ Oskar Seyffert, *The Dictionary of Classical Mythology, Religion, Literature, and Art* (N. Y.: Portland House, 1995 [based on Seyffert's 1882 ed.; edited and revised by H. Nettleship & J. E. Sandys]), p. 193.

¹⁰⁹⁴ Paglia, p. 89. Henrichs (p. 481) noted that the older representations (pre-430 B.C.E.) showed Dionysus as bearded and older, while after he was more regularly depicted as youthful, beardless, and effeminate.

¹⁰⁹⁵ The phrase translates the Greek τὸ ἄνδρας ὄντας μιμεισθαι γυναικας. A. M. Harmon (Trans.), "The Fly," *Lucian, vol. 1* (pp. 82-95). Loeb Classical Library (Cambridge: Harvard Univ. Press, 1913), p. 95.

¹⁰⁹⁶ Macrobius, *The Saturnalia*, III.viii.2, in P. V. Davies (Trans.), *The Saturnalia* (N. Y.: Columbia Univ. Press, 1969), p. 214.

¹⁰⁹⁷ Clarence J. Bulliet, *Venus Castina. Famous Female Impersonators, Celestial and Human* (N. Y.: Covici, Friede, 1928).

¹⁰⁹⁸ Macrobius, §3, p. 214.

¹⁰⁹⁹ As an example of the former interpretation, see Paglia, p. 87. As an example of the latter interpretation, see Robert E. Bell, *Women of Classical Mythology* (N. Y.: Oxford Univ. Press, 1991), p. 430.

¹¹⁰⁰ Excerpts from Ovid, *Metamorphoses*, IV.287-388, in Horace Gregory (Trans.), *Ovid. The Metamorphoses* (N. Y.: Mentor Books, 1960), p. 122. A translation of the *Metamorphoses* by A. S. Kline (2000) can be accessed online at http://etext.virginia.edu/latin/ovid/trans/Ovhome.htm.

[1101] Licht, p. 126.

[1102] Barbara G. Walker, "Castration," *The Women's Encyclopedia of Myths and Secrets* (N. Y.: Harper & Row, 1983).

[1103] Homer, *The Odyssey*, II.268, 401; XXII.206; XXIV.446, 548.

[1104] *Srimad-Bhagavatam*, 8.9. Accessed online at http://www.srimadbhagavatam.org/canto8/chapter9.html.

[1105] For more on Vishnu-as-Mohini, see Devdutt Pattanaik, *The Man Who Was a Woman and Other Queer Tales from Hindu Lore* (Binghamton, NY: Haworth Press, 2002), pp. 66-76. Cf. *Bhagavata Purana Bhoothanaathopaakhyaanam*.

[1106] The eminent European scholar Viktor Rydberg observed a likeness between Loki, a male, and Gullveig-Heid, a female; both used disguises and were often at the center of trouble. More interestingly, despite their gender assignment, each bent toward the 'opposite gender.' Rydberg remarked: "The interference of both is interrupted at the close of the mythic age, when Loki is chained, and Gullveig, in the guise of Angurboða, is an exile in the Ironwood. Before this they have for a time been blended, so to speak, into a single being, in which the feminine assuming masculineness, and the masculine effeminated, bear to the world an offspring of foes to the gods and to creation." See Viktor Rydberg, *Our Fathers' Godsaga*, translated by William P. Reaves (N. Y.: iUniverse, 2003 translation of 1911 ed.; original work published 1887). Accessed online at the Northvegr Foundation website at http://www.northvegr.org/lore/rydberg/035. php.

[1107] Eliade, Couliano & Wiesner, p. 95f.

[1108] Lisa Penaloza, "Crossing Boundaries/Drawing Lines: A Look at the Nature of Gender Boundaries and Their Impact on Marketing Research," *International Journal of Research in Marketing, 11* (no. 4), 359-379 (1994), p. 375.

[1109] Maragaret C. Miller, "Reexamining Transvestism in Archaic and Classical Athens: The Zewadski Stamnos," *American Journal of Archaeology, 103* (no. 2), 223-253 (1999), p. 243.

[1110] While it is accurate to maintain that Deuteronomy 22:5 ("A woman must not wear men's clothing, nor a man wear women's clothing, for the LORD your God detests anyone who does this.") condemns crossdressing, it is just as accurate to say that the text is widely misunderstood. In the opening phrase—"A woman shall not wear . . . *keli*"—the Hebrew *keli* can be translated by different words *and* be variously interpreted. Thus, one can use the generic "clothing" and still interpret it as referring to specific clothing, as in the male clothing associated with warfare (armor and weapons). Or, one can opt to both translate and interpret the word along such lines by rendering something like, "A woman shall not wear the martial dress of a man," or simply, "the armor of a man." *Keil* is a very versatile term, capable of being translated as "accessory," "armor," "bag," "clothing," "jewelry," "weapons" and various other words. *Simlah*—the Hebrew word in the second clause—has a more limited range, but can be translated as "cloak," "clothes," or "garment." The variation in terms contributes to the different ways this deceptively simple text has been rendered. The clause beginning "A woman shall not wear . . ." is balanced by the clause "neither shall a man wear . . ."; they are clearly intended to stand in juxtaposition. One might suppose the term *keli* to be understood, then, as a synonym for *simlah*. In this case, the interpretation is straightforward:

neither sex should wear the garb of the other. However, since the writer could have used the same word in both places and chose not to do so, the suggestion that the difference was intentional and is meaningful has some weight. Thus, *keli* and *simlah* are to be understood—and translated—differently. If this is the case, then the ordinary usage of *keli* in biblical Hebrew becomes important. Such usage suggests that "implements" (e.g., the implements of war: armor and weapons) would be a more apt choice than "clothing." If we opt to see *simlah* as some kind of counterpoint to *keli*, and different in meaning, we might arrive at: as women are not to wear the military garb of men, so men are not to wear . . . what? What is the distinctive garb of women? Especially in a time and culture where men and women wore what today we might call a 'unisex' garment the question is hard to answer. Interestingly, the rabbinical tradition in Judaism concluded that what Deuteronomy says cannot be simply understood as a general prohibition of men wearing women's clothes or vice versa, because the Torah is talking about something that is an "abomination" and such behavior does not qualify. Whatever position one takes on the meaning of this text, in light of the ambiguities and uncertainties involved, should best be held lightly. Authoritative pronouncements based on it are unwarranted.

[1111] Ibid, p. 246.

[1112] Stanley Krippner, "Conflicting Perspectives on Shamans and Shamanism: Points and Counterpoints," *American Psychologist, 57* (no. 11), 962-977 (2002, November), p. 968. For a general introduction to shamanism, see Graham Harvey (Ed.), *Shamanism: A Reader* (N. Y.: Routledge, 2003).

[1113] Ibid, p. 970.

[1114] Mircea Eliade, *Shamanism: Archaic Techniques of Ecstasy*, translated by W. R. Trask (Princeton: Princeton Univ. Press, 1972 printing of 1951 ed.); see especially chapter 5. Cf. Mircea Eliade, *The Two and the One*, translated by J. M. Cohen (Chicago: Univ. of Chicago Press, 1965).

[1115] M. A. Czaplicka, *Aboriginal Siberia. A Study in Social Anthropology* (Oxford: Clarendon Press, 1914). See Part III, 'Religion' (chapters VII-XIV). Accessed online at http://www.shamana.co.uk/Shamanism_in_Siberia/index5.htm.

[1116] Laurel Kendall, *Shamans, Housewives, and Other Restless Spirits. Women in Korean Ritual Life* (Honolulu: Univ. of Hawaii Press, 1985), p. 27. On Korean shamanism see Tongshik Ryu, "Shamanism: The Dominant Folk Religion in Korea," *Inter-Religio, 5*, 8-15 (1984). Accessed online at http://www.riccibase.com/inter-religio/PDF/ir05.pdf.

[1117] Carolyn Brewer, "*Baylan, Asog,* Transvestism and Sodomy: Gender, Sexuality and the Sacred in Early Colonial Philippines," *Intersections: Gender, History and Culture in the Asian Context, 2* (1999, May).

[1118] Sabine Lang, *Men as Women, Women as Men: Changing Gender in Native American Cultures* (Austin, TX: Univ. of Texas Press, 1998), p. 167.

[1119] Cf. John Barclay Burns, "Devotee or Deviate. The 'Dog' *(keleb)* in Ancient Israel as a Symbol of Male Passivity and Perversion," *Journal of Religion & Society, 2* (2000), accessed online at http://moses.creighton.edu/JRS/2000/2000-6.html.

1120 Tacitus, *Germania*, §43, in A. R. Birley (Trans.), *Tacitus. Agricola and Germany* (N. Y.: Oxford Univ. Press, 1999), p. 59.

1121 See Robert L. Reid, "Frey," *The Wain, 6* (1998). Accessed online at http://homepages.nildram.co.uk/~fealcen/wain6.htm. *The Wain* is "a journal dedicated to the Vanir."

1122 Dominic Montserrat, "Essay Six: Reading Gender in the Roman World," in J. Huskinson (Ed.), *Experiencing Rome: Culture, Identity, and Power in the Roman Empire*, pp. 153-182 (N. Y.: Routledge, 2000), p. 158.

1123 Richard L. Gordon, "Eunuchs," in S. Hornblower & A. Spawforth (Eds.), *The Oxford Classical Dictionary*, 3rd ed. (N. Y.: Oxford Univ. Press, 1996), p. 569.

1124 Roberta Gilchrist, *Gender and Archaeology: Contesting the Past* (N. Y.: Routledge, 1999), p. 60.

1125 Richard Valantasis, *The Gospel of Thomas* (N. Y.: Routledge, 1997), p. 11.

1126 Confucius, *Analects* XVI.14, in Arthur Waley (Trans.), *The Analects of Confucius* (N. Y.: Vintage, 1938), p. 208.

1127 Ibid, p. 251.

1128 For more on the life of Wu, see Cheng-An Jiang (illustrated by De Yuan Xu), *Empress of China Wu Ze Tian* (Monterey, CA: Victory Press, 1998).

1129 Herbert A. Giles, *The Civilization of China* (London, 1911), ch. 4. Accessed online at http://www.romanization.com/books/giles/civilization/chap04.html.

1130 Maggie Macary, "The Symbols and Structures of Initiation," *Myth and Culture* website. Accessed online at http://www.mythandculture.com/publications/initiation.html.

1131 Fritz Graf, "Transvestism, Ritual," in S. Hornblower & A. Spawforth (Eds.), *The Oxford Classical Dictionary*, 3rd ed. (N. Y.: Oxford Univ. Press, 1996), p. 1547.

1132 Paglia, p. 90.

1133 Henrichs, p. 481.

1134 Robert Christopher Towneley Parker, "Oschoporia," in S. Hornblower & A. Spawforth (Eds.), *The Oxford Classical Dictionary*, 3rd ed. (N. Y.: Oxford Univ. Press, 1996), p. 1081.

1135 John Schied, "Saturnus, Saturnalia," in S. Hornblower & A. Spawforth (Eds.), *The Oxford Classical Dictionary*, 3rd ed. (N. Y.: Oxford Univ. Press, 1996), p. 1360f.

1136 See Bolich, *Crossdressing in Context, vol. 3*, Q. 71.

1137 For more on the history of Carnival, see Chris Humphrey, *The Politics of Carnival: Festive Misrule in Medieval England* (Manchester: Manchester Univ. Press, 2001). There is also some interesting material in Philip J. Deloria, *Playing Indian* (New Haven: Yale Univ. Press, 1998).

1138 Mikhail Bahktin, *Rabelais and His World*, translated by H. Iswolsky (Bloomington: Indiana Univ. Press, 1984), p. 7.

[1139] Cf. Freud's remark about how seriously children take play; there is no reason—or evidence—to suggest are any less intense or serious. See Sigmund Freud, "The Relation of the Poet to Daydreaming," in S. Freud, *On Creativity and the Unconscious*, translated by J. Riviere (N. Y.: Harper & Row, 1958).

[1140] Erik Erikson, *Identity and the Life Cycle* (N. Y.: W. W.Norton & Co., 1980; original work 1959), p. 90; cf. p. 91 on the remastering of experience.

[1141] Pamela Dickey Young, "Religion," in P. Essed, D. T. Goldberg, & A. Kobayashi (Eds.), *A Companion to Gender Studies*, pp. 509-518 (Malden, MA: Blackwell, 2005), p. 510.

[1142] Ibid, p. 513.

[1143] Young, p. 516.

Index

H

I

www.ingramcontent.com/pod-product-compliance
Lightning Source LLC
Chambersburg PA
CBHW022345280326
41935CB00007B/77